Château Gaillard 26

Couverture : Kalø, nord-ouest d'Aarhus, Danemark. Photo J. Klerk.

Construit au début du XIVe siècle, Kalø était le plus puissant château du roi Éric VI Menved.
Établi sur sa petite île, à l'extrémité d'un chemin menant au rivage, il est aujourd'hui en ruines mais demeure impressionnant.

Château Gaillard

Fondateur : Michel DE BOÜARD

Responsable de la publication : Luc BOURGEOIS

Comité permanent / comité de lecture des colloques Château Gaillard

Présidents honoraires : Johannes HERTZ, Michel COLARDELLE, Tom MCNEILL, Hans L. JANSSEN

Président : Peter ETTEL

Vice-président : Niels-Knud LIEBGOTT

Secrétaire : Reinhard FRIEDRICH

Allemagne : Peter ETTEL, Reinhard FRIEDRICH ; Belgique : Marie Christine LALEMAN, Philippe MIGNOT ; Danemark : Niels-Knud LIEBGOTT, Rikke Agnete OLSEN ; France : François BLARY, Anne-Marie FLAMBARD HÉRICHER ; Irlande : Conleth MANNING, Kieran O'CONOR ; Grande-Bretagne : Penelope DRANSART, Pamela MARSHALL ; Luxembourg : John ZIMMER ; Pays-Bas : Bas AARTS, Hans L. JANSSEN ; Suisse : Maria-Letizia BOSCARDIN, Werner MEYER ; autres États européens et Orient latin : Lukas CLEMENS

Cet ouvrage a bénéficié du soutien du Museum Sønderjylland, du Dronning Margrethe II's Arkæologiske Fond (Danemark) et du ministère de la Culture et de la Communication (France).

Tous droits de traduction, d'adaptation et de reproduction, sous quelque forme que ce soit, réservés pour tous pays.

ISBN : 978-2-84133-502-2

© Presses universitaires de Caen, 2014

Château Gaillard 26

Études de castellologie médiévale

Château et frontière

Actes du colloque international d'Aabenraa (Danemark, 24-31 août 2012),
réunis par Peter ETTEL, Anne-Marie FLAMBARD HÉRICHER et Kieran O'CONOR

2014

PUBLICATIONS DU CRAHAM | CHÂTEAU GAILLARD

Presses universitaires de Caen

Introduction

◆

Niels-Knud Liebgott

The 26th Colloque Château Gaillard was the fourth that has been held in Denmark. The first took place in Hindsgavl on the island of Funen in 1976, the second was in Karrebæksminde in Southern Sealand in 1982, the third in Gilleleje in Northern Sealand in 1996, and this fourth conference was held at Højskolen Østersøen (People's College) in Aabenraa in North Schleswig, a few kilometres from the border between Denmark and Germany. Warm thanks are due to the College Principal, Peter Burhmann, and his staff, for arranging for us to use the College's accommodation and facilities, and for the excellent food provided for us during our stay.

The theme of the Conference was "Castles of the Borderland", and this lay behind the idea of choosing North Schleswig as the venue. This opened up good opportunities for excursions to castles and fortifications both to the north and to the south of the present Danish-German border, thereby throwing light on the particular situation prevailing in the Middle Ages with regard to relations between the Kingdom of Denmark and the Duchy of Schleswig-Holstein.

The Conference had 80 participants, including a number of Ph.D. students, from 16 European countries and from Russia and the USA. As is apparent from the contents of this publication, there were many lectures, out of the 28 in all given at the Conference, that focused on the main theme, but there were also presentations of new research results and papers with a more theoretical orientation. As has been the traditional practice, the Conference programme alternated presentation of papers with excursions to castles, castle-ruins and earthworks in the region. One of the whole-day excursions north of the border included a visit to the royal castle of Riberhus. In Ribe curator Morten Søvsø showed us the ongoing excavation of the 9th-century Christian Viking-Age burial ground next to the cathedral. This was followed by visits to the earthworks of Solvig and Nørrevolde, excavated respectively by a former president of Château Gaillard's Comité Permanent, Johannes Hertz, and by one of the founding fathers of Colloque Château Gaillard, Hans Stiesdal. On other occasions there were opportunities to visit Sønderborg, the strongest of the Danish royal castles in North Schleswig, with curator Inge Adriansen as guide, and to see Gram Castle, where the owner, Svend Brodersen, generously provided hospitality.

The other whole-day excursion took the participants south of the border to the old border fortification of Danewerk (Danevirke). This earthen rampart, more than 30 kilometres long, was originally constructed as protection against the Saxons in around 500; the structure was continuously reinforced in the following centuries, and in the 12th century a stretch of some 3 kilometres of it was strengthened with a massive brick wall. The Conference excursion continued from there to visit the largest Viking-Age trading centre in the Nordic region, Haithabu, where the Director of Stiftung Schleswig-Holsteinische Landesmuseen, Professor Dr Claus von Carnap-Bornheim, kindly gave us an introduction to the site and to the museum. This was followed by an instructive visit to Schloss Gottorp in Schleswig, which has been the main residence of the Dukes of Schleswig since the Middle Ages.

The optional post-conference excursion went northwards to central and northern parts of the Jutland Peninsula. There a visit was made to the royal castle of Koldinghus, knowledgeably guided by curator Vivi Jensen; Koldinghus was built on the historic border between the Kingdom of Denmark and the Duchy of Schleswig. Visits to the earthworks of Kærsgaard, Hønborg and Bygholm and to the castles of Bjørnkjær and Aakjær were included to illustrate the political position of royal power in Denmark in the late Middle Ages. The final excursion-day comprised visits to the fortified churchyard in Malling and the round church in Thorsager, and concluded with the spectacular royal castle of Kalø on the island in Kalø Bay.

The organisation of the 26th Colloque was carried out by a small team. The overall practical planning was the responsibility of Niels-Knud Liebgott and museum assistant Kirsten Christiansen, both from Rosenborg Castle in Copenhagen, while Rikke Agnete Olsen and chief curator Lennart S. Madsen, from Museum Sønderjylland in Haderslev, were in charge of the excursions and many of the local arrangements. The organizers wish to express warm thanks to all who helped to make this a successful conference and to all who extended to us such generous hospitality in Aabenraa. Particular thanks go to Aabenraa's Mayor, Tove Larsen, for hosting a splendid reception in the Town Hall of the city.

We would also like to express our gratitude to all who supported us financially: Alving-Fonden, c/o Grænseforeningen, Michael Jebsens Fond and Abena supported the costs of bus transport and other arrangements during the excursions; Dronning Margrethe II's Arkæologiske Fond, Museum Sønderjyllands Publikationsfond and Museum Sønderjylland-Arkæologi Haderslev provided the Danish contribution to the publication of this volume; for the skilled editing of its contents we owe a large debt of gratitude especially to Anne-Marie Flambard Héricher (General and French-language editor) but also to Peter Ettel (German-language editor) and Kieran O'Conor (English-language editor).

Many thanks to you all!

Nachruf Tomáš Durdík

◆

Josef Hložek

Am 20. September 2012 starb ganz plötzlich der tschechische Mittelalter-Archäologe und Burgenforscher Prof. PhDr. Tomáš Durdík, DrSc. im Alter von 61 Jahren. Die Forschung hat mit ihm einen über die Grenzen Tschechiens hinaus anerkannten Wissenschaftler verloren, der mit Überzeugungskraft und Arbeitseifer unzählige Projekte und Arbeiten verwirklichte. Sein Enthusiasmus für die Burgenforschung war beispielhaft, seine Entscheidungen waren immer von großer Sachkenntnis geprägt. Er widmete sich – trotz gesundheitlicher Probleme – mit Hingabe seinem Beruf und verstand es wie nur wenige, Baudenkmäler zu begreifen.

Die Arbeiten von Tomáš Durdík wurden zu einem Grundstein der böhmischen Burgenforschung. Zugleich setzte er auch im europäischen Rahmen wichtige Eckpfeiler. Zahlreich sind seine Veröffentlichungen, mit denen er am Mittelalter Interessierte und Fachleute gleichermaßen beeindruckte. Hervorzuheben ist zudem sein Engagement für den Schutz des Europäischen Kulturerbes, wo er sich vehement für die Rettung bedrohter Denkmäler einsetzte.

Tomáš Durdík absolvierte 1974 ein Studium der Urgeschichte und Geschichte an der Philosophischen Fakultät der Karls-Universität Prag. Seine Lehrtätigkeit begann er am Institut für Archäologie der Akademie der Wissenschaften in Prag, wo er zeitlebens arbeitete. Seit 1991 wirkte Tomáš Durdík am Institut für Kunstgeschichte, seit 2006 auch am Lehrstuhl für Kulturologie der Philosophischen Fakultät der Karls-Universität. 1998 wechselte er zum Lehrstuhl für Archäologie der Westböhmischen Universität in Pilsen, wo er im Juni 2012 Direktor wurde.

Im Rahmen seiner Forschungen beschäftigte er sich vor allem mit Burgen und Befestigungsanlagen, mit der Archäologie und der materiellen Kultur des Mittelalters. Er war Autor von mehr als 500 Fachstudien, die in Tschechien und im Ausland publiziert wurden. Wegen seiner wissenschaftlichen Kompetenz, seiner manchmal kompromisslosen Ansichten, seiner enormen Gelehrsamkeit und seines außergewöhnlichen Arbeitseinsatzes hat man ihn in viele wissenschaftliche Beiräte und Forschungseinrichtungen berufen.

1989 wurde er Mitglied des wissenschaftlichen Beirats EUROPA NOSTRA, 1990 Mitglied des wissenschaftlichen Beirats der *Deutschen Burgenvereinigung e. V.* und im selben Jahr Experte von ICOMOS/UNESCO. Seit 1989 wirkte er als Mitglied im Comité Permanent von *Castrum Bene*, seit 1993 als Mitglied des Comités *Castella Maris Baltici*. Regelmäßig nahm er an den Tagungen der Vereinigung *Château Gaillard* teil und steuerte zahlreiche Vorträge bei. Er war zudem Mitglied der Jury für die Verleihung des EU-AWARD zum Schutz des europäischen Kulturerbes und Mitglied des *Zentrums für mediävistische Forschungen* in Prag.

Seit 2011 war er Vorsitzender des Wissenschaftlichen Beirats der Generaldirektorin des nationalen Denkmalinstituts in Prag. Weiter war er Mitglied im Hauptausschuss der Archäologischen Gesellschaft und Vorsitzender der Ständigen Kommission des Kulturministeriums für die Bewertung von Kulturdenkmälern.

Lange Jahre redigierte er als Hauptredakteur und Vorsitzender des Redaktionsrats die Zeitschrift der *Gesellschaft der Freunde der Altertümer*, weiter war er Mitglied im Redaktionsrat der Zeitschrift *Nachrichten der Denkmalpflege* und Hauptredakteur der periodisch erscheinenden Publikation *Castellologica bohemica*. 2011 erfuhr Tomáš Durdík eine besondere Ehrung auf europäischer Ebene: Er erhielt den EUROPA NOSTRA AWARD für seine Fachtätigkeit und den außergewöhnlichen gesellschaftlichen Beitrag für das Verständnis und den Schutz des europäischen Kulturerbes.

Der frühe Tod von Tomáš Durdík ist ein schwerer Verlust für seine Familie, Freunde, Forscher und Kollegen. Mit ihm hat die europäische Burgenforschung, hat Château Gaillard einen überaus engagierten und kenntnisreichen Wissenschaftler verloren.

Château Gaillard trauert um Hans-Wilhelm Heine, verstorben am 2. August 2012

◆

Reinhard Friedrich

Nach schwerer Krankheit verstarb am 2. August 2012 viel zu früh unser geschätzter Kollege Dr. Hans-Wilhelm Heine. Er stand im 65. Lebensjahr kurz vor Vollendung seiner beruflichen Laufbahn, die in hohem Maße der Burgenforschung gewidmet war.

Nach dem Studium der Archäologie und Geschichte promovierte er 1976 bei Wolfgang Hübener über das Thema „Studien zu Wehranlagen zwischen junger Donau und westlichem Bodensee". Ab 1977 arbeitete er in der niedersächsischen Denkmalpflege, ab 1981 dort auch an mittelalterlichen Burgen. Dabei nutzte er zunehmend naturwissenschaftliche Methoden für die Burgenforschung, womit er nicht nur in Niedersachsen Maßstäbe setzte. Seine Forschungen zur Landesgeschichte führten 1984 zur Berufung in die Historische Kommission für Niedersachsen.

Hans-Wilhelm Heine engagierte sich aber auch in zahlreichen anderen Gremien. So nahm er regelmäßig an den Tagungen von Château Gaillard teil.

Wann immer möglich, steuerte er auch mit eigenen Vorträgen aus seinem Forschungsgebiet zum Gelingen einer Tagung bei. Dabei zeichneten sich seine Vorträge immer durch eine hohe, zielgerichtete Qualität aus. Schmückendes Beiwerk und jeglicher Anschein von Selbstdarstellung waren ihm fremd, ebenso die abwertende Beurteilung von Kollegen. In wissenschaftlichen Diskussionen war er von einem tiefen Drang nach Beweisen und Erkenntnissen geprägt.

Die Verbundenheit mit der Burgenforschung zeigte sich auch durch seine zahlreichen außerberuflichen Engagements und Ehrenämter. So war er seit 1978 Mitglied der Deutschen Burgenvereinigung, gehörte sowohl zum Vorstand der Landesgruppe Niedersachsen als auch zum Vorstand des Wissenschaftlichen Beirates.

Seine hohe wissenschaftliche Qualifikation und sein großes Engagement für die Burgenforschung sind durch die lange Liste seiner Publikationen für immer dokumentiert. Dabei gehörten die frühen Burgen sowie die Mottenforschung allgemein zu seinen wichtigsten Forschungsschwerpunkten. In den letzten Jahren widmete er sich zudem wieder verstärkt der Landschafts- bzw. Siedlungsarchäologie, nunmehr unter Anwendung modernster Forschungsmethoden, wie Airborne Laserscaning und naturwissenschaftlichen Landschaftsanalysen, zum Beispiel im Aller-Leine-Tal.

Mit Hans-Wilhelm Heine hat die Burgenforschung nicht nur einen begeisterten und begeisternden Wissenschaftler verloren, sondern auch einen geschätzten Kollegen. Die Lücke, die sein viel zu früher Tod hinterlässt, wird noch lange spürbar sein.

Charles McKean (1946-2013)

◆

Richard Oram

The death of Professor Charles McKean on 29 September 2013 has deprived architectural history in Scotland of one of its leading academic proponents. As Professor of Scottish Architectural History at the University of Dundee from 1997, he embedded the study of architecture and the material culture of elite living at the heart of undergraduate and postgraduate study in a traditional "History" department. As the title of his personal chair at Dundee suggests, Charles's research interests within the field were wide-ranging, an impression confirmed by the diversity of his published research. With publications on a wide range of issues, he would never have described himself as *just* a castles or even a Renaissance architecture specialist, but it is as such that he would have been known to most members of Château Gaillard.

After graduating with a BA from Bristol University in 1968, Charles joined the Royal Institute of British Architects (RIBA) based in London, swiftly rising to become first the London Regional Secretary of the organisation (1968-1971), then expanding his remit as Eastern Regional Secretary (1971-1979), and Projects Officer for Community Architecture and Industrial Regeneration (1977-1979). One of his most important roles was the gathering and presenting of evidence for RIBA to the enquiry stage of the Greater London Development Plan. During this period he was establishing his profile as an influential architectural commentator, a position enhanced by his editorship of the *London Architect* (1970-1975) and from 1977 to 1983 he was the architecture correspondent for *The Times*. His prominence was rooted in his organisational ability and his network-building activities, most notably the London Environment Group which drew together leading architects of the day who were deeply concerned about the development pressures and socio-economic trends already evident in the reshaping of city's identity. Such networks were not simply talking-shops but were agitprop in action, leading to an output of provocative and confrontational texts which established his reputation as an agenda-setter and public communicator.

Charles's interest in Scottish high-status residences was awakened following his return to Scotland in 1979 as Secretary of the Royal Incorporation of Architects in Scotland (RIAS), an institution which he set about turning into a dynamic, forward-looking body which could inspire and drive forward research into Scottish architectural history, as well as provide professional leadership for Scotland's architectural practitioners. It was while he was RIAS Secretary that he published the essay that first signalled his iconoclastic approach to Scottish castle studies, "The House of Pitsligo" (*Proceedings of the Society of Antiquaries of Scotland*, 121, 1991, 369-390). The essay was the result of work undertaken initially to provide background for the construction of a model of the "castle or House of Pitsligo" commissioned for the 1990 RIAS/Edinburgh International Festival exhibition, entitled *The Architecture of the Scottish Renaissance*, and stimulated by a number of puzzles which Charles had encountered during the preparation of the North-East Scottish volumes for the RIAS Scottish regional

Illustrated Architectural Guide series. During work on the *District of Moray* (1987) and *Banff and Buchan* (1990), he had become increasingly aware of a disjunction between traditional views of the supposed cultural retardation of Scottish noble society in the 16th century – in particular, to notions of their attachment to a military architectural tradition arising supposedly from the chronic political instability and endemic violence of the kingdom – and the architectural sophistication of the residences of that same nobility. "The House of Pitsligo" was used by Charles to mount a broadside against the myth of Scottish 16th- and 17th-century cultural primitivism and against the wider "Whiggish" notion that it was only after the Union of 1707 that Scotland's social elite began to embrace English and Continental styles.

Having launched his manifesto in 1990/1991, Charles's appointment first as Head of the School of Architecture at Duncan of Jordanstone College in Dundee in 1995, and then in 1997 as Chair of Scottish Architectural History at the University of Dundee, provided the academic platforms on which to push ahead with his research agenda. A key step in this process was his next major essay, "Craignethan: Castle of the Bastard of Arran" (*Proceedings of the Society of Antiquaries of Scotland*, 125, 1995, 1069-1090), which explored the architectural career of Sir James Hamilton of Finnart, the man whom Charles had come to regard as pivotal in the development of Scottish high-status residential design as King's Master of Works Principal in the 1530s. Charles demonstrated the extent of Finnart's international connections and familiarity with the latest Continental thinking and also the extent of innovation and experimentation in design that was being pushed by Scots at this time.

One element of both these studies that elicited great hostility amongst the Scottish architectural history establishment was his refusal to call the buildings he was analysing either "castles" or "tower houses", the conventional labels applied to the homes of the 16th- and 17th-century Scottish nobility. As he said in 1991, "to call such structures 'castles' is to perpetuate the inaccurate myth of a primitive, savage, backward and largely uncultured country beyond the Central Belt". A sea-change in his thinking had occurred in the course of his research on Pitsligo, where he first began to use the label "châteaux" to describe the Scottish buildings of that period, while Craignethan in 1995 was labelled a "fortified villa", and "castle-wise houses" was used as a generic for Renaissance Scotland's country seats. The result was a barrage of scorn and incredulity focussed mainly on the alternative labels and Charles's enthusiastic promotion of Finnart's status as THE transformative figure, but wholly missing the point that he was making in what he was rapidly beginning to see as a very Scottish problem with the "idea of the castle".

A decade of research on this theme came to fruition in 2001 with the publication of the provocatively-titled *The Scottish Château. The Country House of Renaissance Scotland*. "Cat among the pigeons" would be an understatement for the impact of this book, although, to shamelessly mix metaphors, it was very much a cat with a slow-burning fuse. At first eliciting much the same response from the architectural history establishment as had greeted his earlier work, many of whom had little appreciation of the politically and culturally deterministic historiography that had created the "myth of a primitive, savage, backward and largely uncultured country", by the end of the decade its transformative influence was evident in most writing on Scotland's elite culture in the Renaissance period. Indeed, his questioning of the introspective and culturally retarded character of Scotland's ruling classes in the 16th and 17th centuries also stimulated a reappraisal of cultural connectivity in the Medieval period, including in the work of the present writer. Charles himself contributed directly to that discussion in January 2008 through a weekend conference at Rewley House, University of Oxford, entitled *The Medieval Great House*, which was intended in part as a celebration of Anthony Emery's *Greater Medieval Houses of England and Wales* series, published in 2011. His "A Suggested Chronology for the Scottish Medieval Country Seat" (in *The Medieval Great House*, M. Airs & P. S. Barnwell [eds.], Donington, Shaun Tyas, 2011), however, marked a new turn, for in it he tackled not just traditional Scottish exceptionalism based on a claim to unique possession of "the tower house" but, also, the English historiographical tendency to equate the English experience with a general British architectural experience. His conclusion – that the Renaissance tradition in Scotland that he had explored in detail since the 1990s had late medieval roots – might seem unexpected, but his argument for a divergent trend in the conceptualising of the courtyard house is one with which architectural historians are still coming to terms.

Not content with shaking up the Scottish architectural history establishment, Charles was also launching a personal crusade to secure recognition of Scotland's distinct contribution to British and wider Western European architecture. His tireless promotion of Scotland's cultural contribution was articulated mainly through his membership of the architecture- and material culture-oriented Renaissance Studies network, but publications such as "A Scottish Problem with Castles" (*Historical Research*, 79, 2006, 166-198) shifted the emphasis from architecture and design firmly into the realms of historiographical tradition, historical methodology and, importantly, sociology and psychology. In 2008, he had the opportunity to present his ideas at the Château Gaillard colloquium in Stirling, where his paper "The Emergence of a 'Château de Rêves' in 16th Century Scotland" (in *Château Gaillard 24. Château et représentations*, P. Ettel, A.-M. Flambard Héricher & T. E. McNeill [eds.], Caen, Publications du CRAHM, 2010, 173-183) brought his ideas of a revolutionary transition in Scottish lordly architecture before an international audience of castellologists.

Research papers are all very well as a medium for transmitting ideas and bringing about change, but Charles believed very much in direct action to push at the barriers of tradition. Through innovative degree programmes at Dundee which attracted students into an interdisciplinary approach to Scottish architectural and cultural history, he built a forum within which to test his ideas. The success of those programmes can be seen in the succession of doctoral students that emerged from them, who together have brought specific dimensions of Charles's theories under forensic scrutiny and given them added strength in their outcomes. Alongside this, he was a tireless developer of networks and research groups, most recent of which was his partnership with the present writer in the establishment of what is now known as *Turris*, a European network focussed on research into the tower phenomenon in high-status architecture. Ill-health prevented him from joining the fourth gathering of that group at Amersfoort in the Netherlands in August 2013, but the first volume of *Turris*'s work which will appear in 2014 will contain his "Taxonomy of Towers", an essay that will continue his hall-mark characteristic of shaking the tree and asking "so what…" of established conventions.

It is important, also, to highlight Charles's tireless commitment to advancing knowledge of Scotland's architectural and wider cultural heritage, reflected in his active membership or leadership of the councils and boards that had real influence in shaping Scottish cultural policy over the last three decades. Soon after his return to Scotland in 1979, he became a member of the Exhibitions Panel of the Scottish Arts Council (1980-1983), and then a member of the Advisory Council for the Arts in Scotland (1985-1988) and member of the Council of the Architectural Heritage Society of Scotland (1987-1996). His commitment to preservation and promotion of the built heritage of the nation was reflected in his role as convenor of the Buildings Committee of the National Trust for Scotland (1995-2003), and council membership of the Historic Environment Advisory Council for Scotland (2003-2007), the organisation that gave advice to Scottish Government ministers on the historic environment and cultural heritage of the nation. From 2006 until his retirement in 2012, Charles was chairman of the Edinburgh World Heritage Trust, the charitable body charged with overseeing the conserving, enhancement and promotion of the city's UNESCO World Heritage Site status.

To conclude, however, it is important to highlight another aspect of his work that was central to his beliefs throughout his working life. A passionate believer in public engagement and in reconnecting communities with their architectural heritage, he will be remembered especially in Dundee as a tireless advocate for the preservation of the city's buildings and streetscapes. From his arrival in the city in 1995 until his ill-health intervened in 2012, he organised and led hundreds of walking tours which transformed ordinary Dundonians' understanding of their historic environment. This work was recognised in 2012 when the University of Dundee presented him with an Honorary Stephen Fry Award for his lifetime achievements in engaging the public with his research in Scottish architectural history. For many who knew Charles, it was the energy and enthusiasm which he poured into his eagerness to open the public's eyes to the richness of the built environment around them, his ability as a communicator at all levels, and his willingness to share his knowledge, experience and time freely, that represent his greatest contributions towards the widening, enriching and enlivening of the architectural history debate in Scotland that his many students, colleagues and friends will now carry forward.

Castle Building along the Border of Brabant and Holland (c. 1290-c. 1400)

◆

Bas Aarts*, Taco Hermans**

1. The historical background

1.1. Border zones or linear frontiers

A charter from 1325 states that in recent years men of the Lord of Breda (in the Duchy of Brabant) did cut down a gallows tree and dragged it (with the bodies of the hanged still attached) to the outskirts of the town of Geertruidenberg (in the County of Holland), where it belonged, according to them. But the gallows tree was restored to its former location and for another two times the cutting-and-dragging procedure took place. Undoubtedly we have here some sort of a border dispute taking place[1].

There are two schools of thought about the idea of medieval frontiers in the Low Countries (fig. 1). On the one hand, there is the thesis that there were no real boundary lines, just border zones where the authority of the princes was fluid and sometimes even shared. And physical borders were first to appear during the Burgundian era in the 15th century. On the other hand, there is the opinion that, already during the late 13th century, at least between Brabant and Holland, there existed strict linear frontiers, which had their known marking points and in-between they ran right through farms, churches and even castles, if necessary[2].

With the combined results of more detailed studies, it now is possible to modify both opinions and to demonstrate that there already was a clear notion of an official border between Brabant and Holland around 1200. But, as this "official" line often ran "invisibly" through open waste ground and moorlands, it was the later confrontation of this "official" limit with other and more practical boundary lines, e.g. of existing common fields or concessions to cut peat, that blurred the actual situation on the ground and caused difficulties during the 14th century[3].

It is interesting to see how castle building along the border between Holland and Brabant played its roll during this episode, sometimes just by the building location itself, sometimes as part of the political ambitions of its owner. The examples given will be the castles of Strijen (Oosterhout), Loon op Zand and Onsenoort (Nieuwkuijk) (fig. 2).

1.2. The border

The border between the County of Holland and the Duchy of Brabant was first established by the end of the 12th century. The then Duke of Brabant, Henry I, brought the vast Lordship of Breda under his control. He also stopped the expansion of Holland to the south. Henry even forced Holland to accept, as a Brabantine fief, its own immediate border region between

---

* Historian (www.basaarts.nl), Netherlands.
** Castle expert, Dutch Cultural Heritage Agency (*Rijksdienst voor het Cultureel Erfgoed*), Netherlands.
1. Cerutti 1956, no. 124; Buiks 1987, 972.
2. Genicot 1970; Avonds 1982, 128-132; Avonds 1991, 15-29; Hoppenbrouwers 1993, 45-48; Van Asseldonk 2003, 220-223. In general, see Irsigler 1991.
3. See Verschuren 1985, 146-151; Leenders 1988, 66-74; Leenders 1996, 362; Toorians 2009, 130-131.

Fig. 1 – Map of the Netherlands with the main principalities (c. 1300). The border area of Brabant and Holland is indicated. Drawing Bureau voor Bouwhistorie, Archeologie, Architectuurgeschiedenis en Cultuurhistorie, 's-Hertogenbosch, Netherlands.

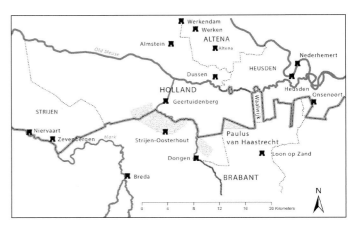

Fig. 2 – Map of the border area of Brabant and Holland (c. 1400). Indicated are the boundaries of Brabant and Holland and those between the main lordships. The disputed borderlands and the main castles in the region are also depicted. The Lordships of Strijen, Altena and Heusden were incorporated into the County of Holland by then. Drawing K. A. H. W. Leenders.

"Strijen" and "Waalwijk" "*ad terram ducis*", "up to the duke's land", as the treaty says in 1200[4]. That may be somewhat vague to us, but it meant an official common boundary line between the two principalities, starting from the still allodial Lordship of Strijen in the west up to the allodial Lordship of Waalwijk[5] (most probably including the territories of Loon op Zand and Dongen[6]) in the east and just along the north-eastern part of the Land of Breda.

In this (enfeoffed) border region, the Count of Holland granted municipal rights to the settlement of Geertruidenberg in 1213[7], to compete with 's-Hertogenbosch, which was founded by the Duke of Brabany at the end of the 12th century[8].

Things changed somewhat when Brabant took over the Lordship of Waalwijk *cum annexis* in 1232. In the meantime, Holland succeeded in forcing the Lord of Altena to present his castle as a fief to the count. This development strengthened the interest of both parties in the riverine border region, with its growing economic importance. Moreover, the Count of Holland especially took responsibility to safeguard Holland from flooding, and therefore he was eager to control water management and to supervise the construction of river dykes and dams in the area[9].

At a local level, land reclamation did not always respect formal frontiers. As the reclamation was stimulated by grants from the lords and princes themselves, they had to intervene. A series of testimonies from 1325 onwards determined the exact course of the border and the location of its marking points, which could be natural phenomena such as pools, hilltops and waterways or manmade landmarks such as stakes with barrels on top and piles of stones. However, there was disagreement about some stretches. The most remarkable of which was about the boundary that was supposed to run right through the castle of Strijen[10]. This problem shall be dealt with below.

After Holland was released from its vassalage for the border region, mentioned above, in 1283, the tensions with Brabant did not end at once. They disagreed, for instance, about the still relatively independent Lordship of Heusden upon the Meuse. In the end, Heusden became temporarily part of Brabant (in 1319), but it went to Holland permanently in 1357[11]. Altogether, the testimonies, discussions and agreements about the exact boundary between Holland and Brabant in the 14th century do illustrate not only the actual changes on the land itself and their juridical consequences, but also the growing idea of "nation building" in the greater principalities[12].

4. AARTS 1992, 22-25; HOPPENBROUWERS 1993, 10-11.
5. LEENDERS 1996, 362.
6. LEENDERS 1988, 66-69; STEURS 1993, 307; TOORIANS 2001a, 41; VAN ASSELDONK 2006, 251-259.
7. ZIJLMANS 1988.
8. CAMPS 1995; JANSSEN 2007.
9. BROKKEN 1982, 123-125.
10. AVONDS 1982, 129-130; AVONDS 1991, 22-24.
11. See AARTS 2006, 4.
12. See AVONDS 1982, 130-131.

To fit the previously mentioned castles into this process, we will start with Strijen.

1.3. The castle of Strijen

In 1288, a large flood drove the Lord of Strijen out of his castle and demesne. As a consequence, this lord, Willem van Strijen, settled himself in the village of Oosterhout, outside his lordship and within the territory of Breda. There he built his new allodial castle "of Strijen" on two parcels of land he bought from some local inhabitants. It is said he built his "tower" on the one lot that was part of the enclosed fields of Oosterhout (in Brabant) and a bailey with a chapel inside on a parcel previously owned by an inhabitant of Geertruidenberg and considered to be a former part of the common grounds of that town (in Holland). This original situation gave birth to the idea that the castle of Strijen was built, around 1290, "in two countries"[13]. An idea (and a long-held historical opinion as well) that was emphasised by the sworn testimonies from the Holland side, during the disputes about the frontier in 1326[14].

More detailed investigation, however, made it clear that it was all a matter of "juridical perception". From the Geertruidenberg – Holland side, it was claimed that the practical use of the common grounds and the town's market rights to the south, justified their view of where the border should be located. That view included half the castle site. From the Oosterhout – Brabant side, it was emphasised that the actual parish boundaries and the exercise of the high justice to the north of the castle proved that the disputed area belonged to them[15].

The solution came by way of early capitalism. Willem van Duvenvoorde, of noble birth, although illegitimate, and a courtier of the Count of Holland, was the richest man of his time. This he had achieved by means of risky but profitable investments. As a bailiff of Geertruidenberg, Willem was ordered by the count to build a castle there, with his own money, and within two years. This he managed in 1323-1325. Excavations revealed remains in brick of what is presumed to have been a square castle situated just outside the town of Geertruidenberg[16]. Although the castle was built against Brabant, it did not stop Van Duvenvoorde from taking the opposing castle of Strijen in Oosterhout on long lease. He greatly modernised this noble house, obtained more lands in the neighbourhood and a part of the lordly rights in Oosterhout as well. He even became Lord of Breda in 1339. With his possessions – and influence – on both sides of the Holland – Brabant border, he was exactly the man to bring the on-going frontier quarrel to an end. Willem van Duvenvoorde made a deal with the town of Geertruidenberg and by an exchange of lands elsewhere, the Brabant claim to the disputed area around the castle of Strijen was accepted (for most of the time)[17].

1.4. The castle of Loon op Zand

In 1383, at the ducal court in Brussels, Paulus van Haastrecht, a minor nobleman in Southern Holland, became invested with the Lordship of Loon op Zand, which he had bought from his distant relative Zweder van Abcoude. Although this was an ideal opportunity – and a prerequisite in those days – to start a governmental career in the Duchy of Brabant, Van Haastrecht made a first and remarkable move in presenting his plans for the castle "to be built"[18] in Loon op Zand as a fief of the Count of Holland. Maybe it was a trick to use the border for an interesting double play? This, however, was not accepted by the old Duchess Johanna in Brussels. When Van Haastrecht's tower house was completed in 1387, he had to accept this fortification to become a fief of Brabant as well.

However, this did not prevent Paulus van Haastrecht starting an astonishing career on both sides of the border. He became Bailiff of South Holland and, at the same time, High Sheriff of 's-Hertogenbosch in Brabant[19]. In his Lordship of Loon op Zand, Paulus built a new church and ordered the construction of a waterway to transport peat from his demesne. This exploitation of peat was very profitable in those days and this was also so for the Lord of Loon op Zand. But the actual cutting campaign in the field brought him across the official border line into Holland. Being on good terms with the Count of Holland, however, this "trespassing" was tolerated and Van Haastrecht was even enfeoffed with these lands by Holland. It even led to a small correction of the official boundary along this section[20].

Nevertheless, high politics were not always that profitable. Paulus got caught up in the internal turmoil in Holland during the 1390s and was even imprisoned at the castle of Loevestein, from which he managed to escape. On the Brabantine side, he got involved in the succession troubles around the old Duchess Johanna. This led to a short siege of the castle of Loon op Zand in 1400. In the same year Paulus seems to have died[21].

1.5. The castle of Onsenoort

The last border castle to address is the tower house of Onsenoort at Nieuwkuijk to the south of Heusden. It was built most probably by Jan van den Plasche, an illegitimate son of Duke Jan III of Brabant, circa 1350. The transfer of the important Lordship of Heusden from Brabant to Holland in 1357, as

---

13. Cerutti 1956, no. 129.
14. See Buiks 1987; Leenders 1988, 69-71; Avonds 1991, 22-23; Leenders 1996, 363-367; Leenders et al. 2009, 84-87; Toorians 2009, 129-131.
15. Leenders 1988, 69-71; Toorians 2009, 130-131.
16. Zijlmans 2009.
17. Toorians 2009, 131, 133-139.
18. Hollandse Leenkamer, no. 50, fol. 205. See Dek 1966, 340; Aarts 1984, 24.
19. Aarts 1984; Hoppenbrouwers 1993, 28-29; Toorians 2001a, 33-36; Toorians 2001b, 76-82.
20. Dek 1966, 352; Verschuren 1985.
21. Aarts 1984, 28-31.

mentioned before, caused some trouble in the region as opinions differed as to exactly which villages belonged to the transfer. The whereabouts of the castle site of Onsenoort reflect these complications.

In 1369, Laurens van den Putte sold the castle of Onsenoort and the surrounding lands to Rutger van Ouden, who presented the purchase as a fief to Holland. In the meantime, Laurens's brother, Henry van den Putte, was registered as holding Onsenoort for Brabant in Brussels. So Holland and Brabant both claimed Onsenoort and by consequence the site was burnt down by forces from Holland in 1370 or 1372[22]. By the territorial agreement made between Holland and Brabant in 1374, Onsenoort was considered to be situated in Holland. For four years, the new owner of the site, Jan Kuist van Wijk, was paid by the count to rebuild "the house and tower" of Onsenoort[23]. And so it happened, despite the on-going opposition of the town of 's-Hertogenbosch (angry about the loss of subordinate countryside), which stated later that "fiefs cannot change the country's borders"[24]. That 15th-century statement mentioned here illustrates even better the growing idea of a "nation", rather than the historical reality how these borders were actually formed in the past[25].

2. The castles

Three castles have been mentioned in the preceding part of this paper. These buildings will be presented here.

2.1. The castle of Strijen[26]

The castle of Strijen was first built around 1290. Its original appearance is unknown to us. With the results of some limited-scale excavations and an engraving from 1656, we have some clues as to what the rebuilt castle of the 14th century looked like before its demolition in the 18th century. It was a square complex of about 40 m x 40 m (fig. 3), with the north-west corner dominated by a great rectangular tower. This tower measured 12.5 m x 10.6 m at its base with walls up to 1.5 m-2 m thick. The tower consists of a basement and a ground floor and five additional floors (figs. 4 & 5). The tower may have been built in two successive periods. The remaining parts of two of its walls are constructed in brick (29 cm x 13.5 cm x 6.5 cm) with sandstone blocks at the corners. The ground plan of the castle is one that is rarely seen in the Netherlands. In fact, it only compares with that of nearby Breda Castle in its second-building period, which also boasted a great tower at one of its corners. This great tower of Breda castle was built by Jan II van Polanen between 1350 and 1362. Van Polanen was probably influenced by the castle of Strijen with its great tower built by his uncle Willem van Duvenvoorde. This successful entrepreneur has to be considered as the builder or rebuilder of Strijen Castle sometime between 1321 and 1325.

There was a bailey situated on the western side of the main complex of which the plan is also unknown. The 14th-century castle was surrounded by three moats with ramparts between them. The sides of these embankments had a revetment in brick to prevent them from collapsing. In the north-east corner of the site there was, if the engraving is correct, an outer gate. According to foundations found at the west side, a water-gate could have been situated there.

The castle of Strijen was destroyed in 1573 and left in ruins. These ruins were used as a quarry for bricks until 1714, when it was officially allowed to demolish what was left of it, except for the great tower which had to remain "for thousand years" as a memorial for the ancestors of the Princes of Orange (as heirs to Van Duvenvoorde)[27]. Part of the great tower collapsed in 1750 and it was then allowed to pull down another part "to make the rest a better memorial and to reuse the bricks", in that order[28]. Eventually more than half the tower was demolished. The remaining part, up to the original height of 27.5 m, still shows some interesting details of a vault, fireplaces, chimneys and loopholes. It also throws light on the ambition of its builder, the illegitimate Willem van Duvenvoorde, who was only able in 1329 to buy off this blot on this name from the Emperor himself[29].

2.2. Tower houses

At the end of the 14th century, two tower houses were built on the border between the County of Holland and the Duchy of Brabant. In the Netherlands, recent research on tower houses has shown that the wall thickness of this type of castle decreased from more than 2 m in the early 13th century to hardly 1 m in the late 14th century for most of these towers[30]. However, the two tower houses mentioned here – Loon op Zand and Onsenoort – have a wall thickness of more than 2 m.

2.3. The castle of Loon op Zand[31]

The castle of Loon op Zand (fig. 6) was built by Paulus van Haastrecht between 1383 and 1387, as is stated by documents. The first phase consists of a rectangular tower house of approx-

---

22. Hoppenbrouwers 1992, 582-583. The literature in general dates the assault to 1372 and blames Brabant for the destruction of the castle (Renaud 1950, 66-67; Kasteel 1964, 11-13).
23. Renaud 1950, 67; Kasteel 1964, 11; Hermans & Orsel 2005, 95.
24. Gemeentearchief 's-Hertogenbosch, inv. nr. A445, p. 138, art. 31. See Avonds 1982, 130-132; Hoppenbrouwers 1993, 27.
25. Avonds 1982, 130-132; Hoppenbrouwers 1993, 27.
26. Hermans & Kamphuis 1990.
27. Regionaal Archief Tilburg, Oud Archief Oosterhout, inv. nr. 37 (resolutieboek 1706-1717), fol. 264 v.
28. Nationaal Archief, Hingman, inv. nr. 4555, fol. 322.
29. Toorians 2009, 136.
30. Hermans 2013.
31. Hermans & Orsel 2009.

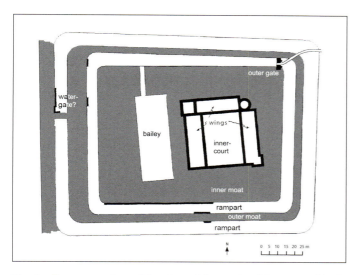

Fig. 3 – Reconstruction of the plan of the castle of Strijen. In black: masonry found during the excavations and reconstruction based on an engraving. Drawing T. Hermans.

Fig. 4 – Ruins of the castle of Strijen in 1656 from the north-east. Engraving A. Santvoort (private collection).

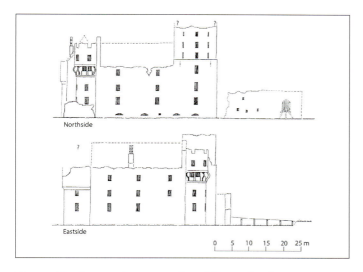

Fig. 5 – Northern and eastern sides of the castle of Strijen in 1656. Reconstruction based on the engraving by A. Santvoort. Drawing T. Hermans.

Fig. 6 – Castle of Loon op Zand from the north. The right side of the building – including the entrance – is the former tower house. Photo T. Hermans.

imately 12.7 m x 11.4 m with a maximum wall thickness of 2.1 m (fig. 7). What the tower looked like is uncertain, apart from the ground-plan and the fact that it had a basement and was three storeys high. Traces in the west wall indicate the former presence of mural stairs and a privy. Probably shortly after the siege of 1400, the tower was expanded on its east side. This expansion is in the north-south direction founded on a base approximately 25 cm less wide than the original foundations on both sides. There is no sound explanation for this phenomenon or it must have been that the tower features had to be recognizable from all sides. The strength of the original tower house can best be explained by the whereabouts of its builder and his remarkable career – not without personal risks – on both sides of the Holland – Brabant border.

The castle had a bailey on the east side. When this bailey was built is unknown. Judging from the engraving from 1692 by Henri Causé, the west and south side of the bailey contained several buildings with some Renaissance features (fig. 8). The access to this bailey was from the south by means of a twin-towered gatehouse. The castle complex was accessible by two bridges. In-between the two bridges stood a solitary outer gatehouse on a kind of second bailey.

The tower was greatly destroyed in 1587 during the Dutch Revolt. In 1663, it was restored on behalf of Thomas van Immerseel. The "corridor" on bridges between the tower and the bailey was rebuilt as well. The tower was raised by one floor and every floor was transformed into a modern apartment with a parlour, a bedroom and a bathroom.

In 1776-1777, the castle was radically changed: the tower was lowered with one floor, the windows were replaced and resized, the facades got a more regular layout and the entrance was moved to the north side. Also, on the inside, the walls were partially cut away to create more inner space. During this renovation, the bailey (east side) was completely dismantled, while a new forecourt appeared on the north side of the castle, flanked with small outbuildings. In this new complex, the original tower house is no longer recognizable.

2.4. The castle of Onsenoort[32]

The first castle of Onsenoort at Nieuwkuijk was built in the middle of the 14th century. In 1370 or 1372, it was destroyed during a dispute about the border and its feudal implications and not rebuilt until 1388. There is no information of what the original castle looked like. Research shows that the rebuilding dates from 1388. This new castle was a tower house on a rectangular ground plan with a size of approximately 13.5 m x 10.5 m (fig. 9). The walls of the basement are 2.5 m thick and 2.2 m at ground floor level. The new 1388 building included a basement, a ground floor and an attic, which probably once had a covered wall walk (fig. 10). This wall walk was situated at what is now the first floor. Apart from one loophole, there are no traces of it left. The basement walls have one loophole each, suitable for arquebuses. It is remarkable that there are no traces of an original access to this basement. It is possible that there was a hatch in the wooden floor with a ladder to descend to it. Later on a staircase in brick was added to give access to the first floor. There are no traces of mural stairs in the tower. It is assumed that there was a spiral staircase in the west corner of the building and these stairs may even be added later. The tower also contains no traces of an original fireplace or privy. Possibly the tower was originally not primarily intended for habitation purposes. Nevertheless, its strength can be explained by its origins in the dispute about the border: a real landmark the Count of Holland was willing to pay for.

The tower was radically transformed in the second half of the 15th century. It was given a fully-fledged first floor and a new attic. The transition between old and new is clearly visible in the masonry at the level of the transom of the windows of the first floor. During the rebuilding, the floor joists above the basement were removed and replaced by vaults between arches.

A new manor house was built at the rear of the tower (as seen from the original entrance side!) during the first half of the 16th century. Whether the access to the castle had already been relocated from the east to the west or whether this was done during the construction of the new house is unknown. In any case, access to the castle was now from the west.

In 1904, the castle had to be adapted to the needs of the new residents, who belonged to a religious order. Between the tower and the main building, a chapel was built and the tower itself was raised again with one floor. Finally in 1934-1935, a major renovation took place. The main building was demolished, except for the basement and replaced by a new building, largely standing on the former cellars. At the rear

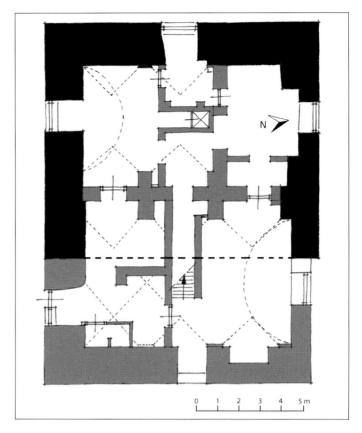

Fig. 7 – Plan of the basement of the castle of Loon op Zand. In black: the original tower house. Drawing T. Hermans.

of the complex, it is still possible to get a good view upon the (now much altered) tower house.

3. Conclusions

The strong tower houses of Loon op Zand and Onsenoort reflect the turbulent times of this border region by the end of the 14th century. A clear argument for this is – for brick castles – the remarkable thickness of their walls. These walls were constructed in anticipation of possible raids and are clearly in contrast with the general tendency to reduce the wall thickness of newly built tower houses to less than 1m seen elsewhere in the Low Countries during this period.

Acknowledgements

The authors wish to thank Messrs T. J. Hoekstra and L. Smals for their kind help in preparing this paper.

---

32. Hermans & Orsel 2005.

Fig. 8 – Castle of Loon op Zand in 1692 from the south. To the left is the tower house after it was extended to the east shortly after 1400 and elevated by one floor in 1663. Engraving H. Causé, after a drawing by J. van Croes (private collection).

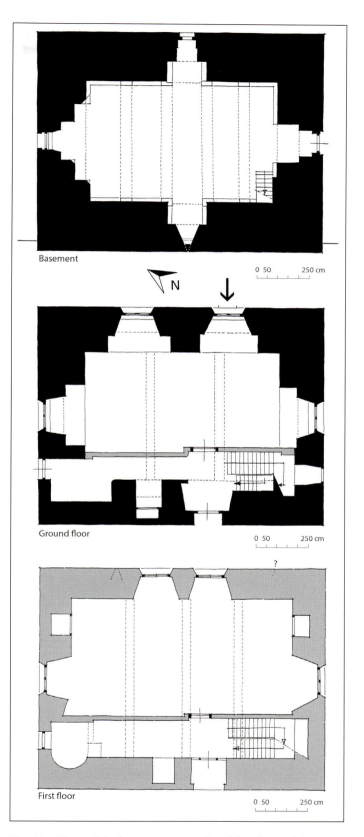

Fig. 9 – Castle of Onsenoort from the north-west. Photo T. Hermans.

Fig. 10 – Plans of the basement, ground and first floor of the castle of Onsenoort. In black: the original tower house. The arrow indicates the original entrance to the tower at the east side. Drawing T. Hermans.

Bibliography

AARTS B. (1984), "Loon op Zand, een terugblik", *Het Brabants Kasteel*, 7, 17-34.

– (1992), "Texandrië, van omstreden gouwbegrip naar integratie in het hertogdom. Hoofdlijn en vraagtekens", in *Geworteld in Taxandria. Historische aspecten van de relatie Tilburg – Turnhout*, H. VAN DOREMALEN et al. (eds.), Tilburg/Turnhout, Stichting tot Behoud van Tilburgs Cultuurgoed/Koninklijke Geschied- en Oudheidkundige Kring der Antwerpse Kempen "Taxandria" (Taxandria, nieuwe reeks; 64; Tilburgse historische reeks; 1), 8-42.

– (2006), "The Castle of Heusden (NL): its Relocation and its Successive Octagonal Towers", in *Château Gaillard 22. Château et peuplement*, P. ETTEL, A.-M. FLAMBARD HÉRICHER & T. E. MCNEILL (eds.), Caen, Publications du CRAHM, 1-12.

AVONDS P. (1982), "De Brabants-Hollandse grens tijdens de late middeleeuwen. Bijdrage aan een controverse", *Holland, regionaal-historisch tijdschrift*, 14, 128-132.

– (1991), *Brabant tijdens de regering van Hertog Jan III (1312-1356). Land en instellingen*, Brussels, AWLSK (Verhandelingen van de Koninklijke Academie voor Wetenschappen, Letteren en Schone Kunsten van België. Klasse der Letteren 53; 136).

BROKKEN H. M. (1982), "De voormalige Hollandse gebieden in de provincie Noord-Brabant", *Holland, regionaal-historisch tijdschrift*, 14, 121-127.

BUIKS J. (1987), "De Haecxhoeve op Den Hout en de grens tussen Holland en Brabant. Gegevens over Den Hout en omgeving in de 14ᵉ eeuw", *Mededelingenblad van de Heemkundekring "De Heerlijkheid Oosterhout"*, 11, 966-1057.

CAMPS H. P. H. (1995), *Het stadsrecht van Den Bosch van het begin (1184) tot het Privilegium Trinitatis (1330). Een exposé met enkele nabeschouwingen*, Hilversum, Verloren (Middeleeuwse studies en bronnen; 46).

CERUTTI F. F. X. (ed.) (1956), *Middeleeuwse rechtsbronnen van stad en heerlijkheid Breda*, vol. 1, Utrecht, Kemink.

DEK A. W. E. (1966), "Bijdrage tot de genealogie van het geslacht Van Arkel, II", *De Nederlandsche Leeuw*, 83, 340-360.

GENICOT L. (1970), "Ligne et zone: la frontière des principautés médiévales", *Bulletin de l'Académie royale de Belgique, Classe des Lettres*, 5th series, 56, 29-42.

HERMANS D. B. M. (2013), *Middeleeuwse woontorens in Nederland. De bouwhistorische benadering van een kasteelvorm*, Dissertation, Leiden University.

HERMANS D. B. M. & KAMPHUIS J. (1990), *Bouwhistorische documentatie en waardebepaling: Ruïne van Strijen te Oosterhout*, Den Haag, Rijksgebouwendienst.

HERMANS T. & ORSEL E. (2005), "Het kasteel Onsenoort", *Bulletin Koninklijke Nederlandse Oudheidkundige Bond*, 104, 94-103.

– (2009), "Het kasteel van Loon op Zand. De verbouwing van een 14e-eeuwse woontoren tot appartementencomplex in 1663", in *Middeleeuwse Kastelen in veelvoud. Nieuwe studies over oud erfgoed*, H. L. JANSSEN & W. LANDEWÉ (eds.), Wijk bij Duurstede, Nederlandse Kastelenstichting (Academic Studies Series; 2), 215-251.

HOPPENBROUWERS P. C. M. (1992), *Een middeleeuwse samenleving. Het Land van Heusden (ca. 1360-ca. 1515)*, Wageningen, Afdeling Agrarische Geschiedenis, Landbouwuniversiteit.

– (1993), "Territorialiteit en landsheerlijkheid. Aspecten van de wisselwerking tussen uitbreiding van bewoning en staatsvorming in het bovenland van Heusden en de westelijke Langstraat in de veertiende eeuw", *Noordbrabants Historisch Jaarboek*, 10, 8-59.

IRSIGLER F. (1991), "Der Einfluß politischer Grenzen auf die Siedlungs- und Kulturlandschaftsentwicklung. Eine Einführung in die Tagungsthematik", *Siedlungsforschung. Archäologie – Geschichte – Geographie*, 9, 9-23.

JANSSEN H. L. (2007), "'s-Hertogenbosch, een *novum oppidum* in de Meierij ca. 1200-1350", *Jaarboek voor Middeleeuwse Geschiedenis*, 10, 95-140.

KASTEEL J. (1964), "De heerlijkheid Onsenoort en de geschiedenis der Nederlanden", *Met Gansen Trou*, 14, 8-26.

LEENDERS K. A. H. W. (1988), "Verkenningen langs de Hollands-Brabantse grens in de omgeving van Geertruidenberg, 1200-1600", in *In de Hollantsche Tuyn II. Historische wetenswaardigheden van Geertruidenberg en naaste omgeving*, T. VAN DE HULSBEEK et al. (eds.), Geertruidenberg, Oudheidkundige Kring "Geertruydenberghe", 66-74.

– (1996), *Van Turnhoutervoorde tot Strienemonde. Ontginnings- en nederzettingsgeschiedenis van het noordwesten van het Maas-Schelde-Demergebied (400-1350). Een poging tot synthese*, Zutphen, Walburg Pers.

LEENDERS K. A. W. H. et al. (2009), "Landschap, ontginning en bewoning, c. 500-1568", in *Oosterhout, niet van gisteren. De geschiedenis van een vitale en veerkrachtige stad van de oude steentijd tot 2009*, C. GORISSE (ed.), Oosterhout, Significant, 53-89.

Renaud J. G. N. (1950), "Kastelen in Noord-Brabant", in *Brabants Jaarboek. Nieuwe Reeks der Handelingen van het Provinciaal Genootschap van Kunsten en Wetenschappen in Noord-Brabant*, 's-Hertogenbosch, Provinciaal Genootschap, 59-77.

Steurs W. (1993), *Naissance d'une région. Aux origines de la mairie de Bois-le-Duc. Recherches sur le Brabant septentrional aux XIIe et XIIIe siècles*, Brussels, Académie royale de Belgique (Mémoires de la Classe des Lettres; 3).

Toorians L. (2001a), "Hoe Paulus van Haastrecht in Loon op Zand kwam: de koop van Loon en wat vooraf ging", *Jaarboek Straet & Vaert*, 33-45.

– (2001b), "Heren en heerlijkheid. Landsheerlijk gezag en lokale autonomie tot 1473", in *Tilburg, stad met een levend verleden. De geschiedenis van Tilburg vanaf de steentijd tot en met de twintigste eeuw*, C. Gorisse et al. (eds.), Tilburg, Regionaal Historisch Centrum Tilburg, 61-82.

– (2009), "Heren en heerlijkheid, *c.* 1200-1566", in Gorisse 2009 (ed.), 125-153.

Van Asseldonk M. (2003), *De Meierij ontrafeld. Plaatselijk bestuur, dorpsgrenzen en bestuurlijke indeling in de Meierij van 's-Hertogenbosch, circa 1200-1832*, Tilburg, Stichting Zuidelijk Historisch Contact Tilburg.

– (2006), "De Tol van Venloon en het gezag in de regio Drunen-Dongen omstreeks 1230", *Noordbrabants Historisch Jaarboek*, 22-23 (2005-2006), 235-288.

Verschuren G. (1985), "De grens Holland-Brabant onder de heerlijkheid Venloon", *Brabants Heem*, 37, 146-151.

Zijlmans B. (1988), "Het stadsrecht van Geertruidenberg", in Van de Hulsbeek et al. 1988 (eds.), 11-25.

– (2009), "Het grafelijke kasteel van Geertruidenberg (1323-1547). Historisch en archeologisch onderzoek", in Janssen & Landewé 2009 (eds.), 61-99.

Die Burg Brauneck und ihr so genannter Kapellenbau

Baugeschichtliche, archäologische und geophysikalische Untersuchungen auf einer Staufischen Burg bei Creglingen in Baden-Württemberg

Susanne Arnold*

Topographie

Auf der westlich in das Steinachthal steil und felsig vortretenden Bergzunge, die gegen Süden und Westen vom Steinachthal, im Norden von einer jähen in dasselbe ziehenden Schlucht schützend umfangen wird, thronte die Burg, die an der allein zugänglichen Ostseite durch eine ebenfalls viereckige mit Wall und Graben umgebene Vorburg, jetzt ganz kahl mit drei einsamen Linden, geschirmt wurde. Wall und Graben sind von dieser noch sichtbar…

So wird in der 1800 erschienenen Oberamtsbeschreibung die Burg Brauneck vorgestellt (Abb. 1)[1].

Die etwa 50 mal 90 m längsrechteckige, von einer Ringmauer umgebene Anlage verjüngt sich zum Sporn in Richtung Westen und weist an der schmalsten Stelle einen hufeisenförmigen Turm, den so genannte Eulenturm, auf (Abb. 2).

Die Ringmauer führt an der Ostseite in eine massive, etwa 2,80 m breite Schildmauer mit flankierenden Ecktürmen und der Toranlage. Allein im ummauerten Geviert, etwa mittig der Schildmauer und ca. 8 m von ihr entfernt steht der aus Buckelquadern errichtete Bergfried. Der zur Frühzeit der Burganlage gehörende *Palas* erstreckte sich im Nordosten im Zwickel von Ring- und Schildmauer; bauhistorische Befunde sind beredte Zeugen dieses Herrschaftsbaus.

Die übrigen Gebäude innerhalb des Burgbereichs reihen sich entlang der Umfassungsmauer. Eine mit Schießscharten versehene Mauer verbindet die nordöstliche Ecke des Bergfrieds mit der Schildmauer.

Über einen Graben gelangte man zur ehemaligen Vorburg, einer plateauartigen Fläche, auf der etwa vor 10 Jahren eine Maschinenhalle errichtet wurde, leider ohne eine archäologische Untersuchung zu ermöglichen. Die Vorburg war durch einen weiteren Graben gegen die Angriffsseite geschützt. An dessen Südseite kann man die Reste eines Steinbruchs erkennen, der wohl ehemals ortsnah Baumaterial (anstehenden Muschelkalk[2]) lieferte.

Geschichtlicher Überblick

Die erste urkundliche Erwähnung der Burg Brauneck um 1230 weist Conrad von Hohenlohe als Besitzer aus[3]. Er und sein Bruder Gottfried von Hohenlohe waren Gefolgsleute von Friedrich II., der sie reich entlohnte. So hatten sie auch bis ins 14. Jahrhundert um das Taubertal das Geleitrecht an den dortigen Straßen.

1365 verlieh Gottfried von Brauneck, der sicher noch als Mitglied der Hohenlohischen Familie angesehen werden kann, das Erbburglehen an seinen Diener Lutz Bachrat,

---

* Regierungspräsidium Stuttgart, Referat 86 – Denkmalpflege, Archäologie des Mittelalters und der Neuzeit, Deutschland.
1. Beschreibung des Oberamtes Mergentheim Doppelband I/II, herausgegeben von dem königlichen statistisch-topographischen Bureau Stuttgart 1880, 695.
2. Pfefferkorn 2008, 2.
3. Hohenlohisches Urkundenbuch (Hoh.UB), Bd. I, 60,Z.9.

Abb. 1 – Luftbild 6526-024-01 Baden-Württemberg, Flugdatum 24.3.1979. Foto O. Braasch.

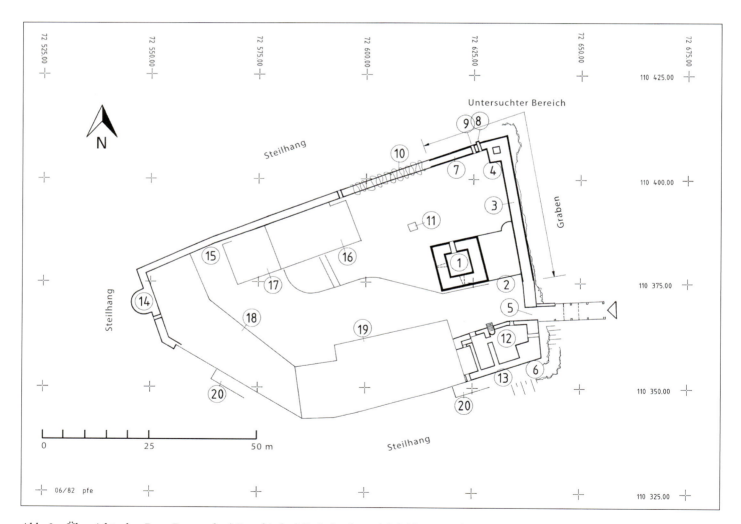

Abb. 2 – Übersichtsplan Burg Brauneck: 1) Bergfried; 2) Zwischenbau; 3) Schildmauer; 4) Nordostturm; 5) Burgtor; 6) Südostturm; 7) Nordmauer; 8) Aborterker; 9) Spezialerker; 10) verdeckter Erker; 11) neuzeitlicher Brunnen; 12) sog. Kapellenbau; 13) Südmauer; 14) Westturm (Eulenturm); 15) restliche Ringmauer; 16) neuzeitliches Wohnhaus; 17) Garagen; 18) moderne Scheune; 19) Stallgebäude; 20) moderne Rampen. Plan Pfefferkorn, Archiv LAD Esslingen.

was darauf hinweist, dass dieser wohl Burgmannendienst zu leisten hatte.

Im Jahr 1448 gelangte die Burg schließlich in den Besitz Albrechts von Brandenburg-Ansbach, der sie wiederum an die Herren von Ehenheim zu Lehen gab.

Einen großen Einschnitt in die Geschichte der Burg stellen die Bauernkriege dar. Die Aufständischen belagerten und brandschatzten Brauneck am 10. Mai 1525. Die dadurch entstandenen Schäden waren enorm und sind zum Teil noch heute an einigen Gebäudeteilen ablesbar. Auch durch die im Nachgang erstellten Schadenslisten von verlorenem Hausrat und landwirtschaftlichen Erzeugnissen wie Wein und Getreide kann der Umfang der Verluste belegt werden[4]. Ein Wiederaufbau durch die Herren von Ehenheim ist ebenfalls mittels Urkunden bezeugt, sowohl die gewährte, durch den Schaden entstandene Summe[5] als auch anhand eines Berichts von 1530, in dem die Anlage als fertig instand gesetzt gilt[6].

1615 ging die Burg lehensweise an die Herren von Gundelsheim[7], die auch dort saßen.

1699 verkauften schließlich die Eigentümer, die Herren von Brandenburg-Ansbach-Onolzbach, die Burg an zwei Bauernfamilien, die in der Folge das Anwesen ausschließlich landwirtschaftlich nutzten und auch umfangreiche Umbauten in Angriff nahmen. Die Nachfahren einer dieser Familien bewirtschaften die Burganlage noch heute.

Das Vorhandensein einer Kapelle wird in den schriftlichen Zeugnissen ebenfalls dokumentiert: 1424 wird ein „Peter Erbeter, Caplan zu Brauneck" genannt[8], 1464 eine „Capella in Brawneck"[9].

Bauliche Entwicklung der Burg

Als ältester Bauteil kann die Ringmauer benannt werden. Sie und die Schildmauer mit den im Norden und Süden flankierenden Türmen sowie der einstige *Palas* in der Nordostecke werden in der Literatur in die Zeit um 1200 datiert. Bauhistorische Befunde stützen diesen zeitlichen Ansatz (siehe unten) (Abb. 2).

Aus der Zeit der ersten urkundlichen Erwähnung um 1230 stammt der mächtige, aus Buckelquadern errichtete Bergfried mit seinen zahlreichen Steinmetzzeichen und einem mächtigen Fundamentsockel[10].

Gegen Ende des 13. Jahrhunderts ist der so genannte Kapellenbau entstanden. Diese Bezeichnung taucht für das Gebäude in der Südostecke der Burganlage ab dem 19. Jahrhundert wohl aufgrund der aufwändig gestalteten Nordfassade auf[11].

Der Eulenturm, der sich an der westlichen Schmalseite der Umfassungsmauer erhebt, wird ins 14. Jahrhundert datiert[12]. Eine baugeschichtliche Untersuchung dieses Turms ist bisher nicht erfolgt.

Damit ist die noch erhaltene mittelalterliche Bausubstanz der Burg beschrieben. Im Zuge der Bauernkriege wurden fortifikatorische Maßnahmen notwendig, die sich in der Mauer zwischen Bergfried und Ringmauer widerspiegeln.

Nach dem Verkauf an zwei Landwirtfamilien 1699 entstanden nach und nach Ökonomiegebäude und ein Wohnhaus, im Wesentlichen entlang der Ringmauer im westlichen Bereich des Burggeviert. Die Bausubstanz, die heute – außer der Beschriebenen aus dem Mittelalter und der frühen Neuzeit – im Burghof zu sehen ist, stammt aus dem 19. und 20. Jahrhundert. Leider wurden im Zuge der Errichtung dieser Gebäude viele archäologische und bauhistorische Befunde unbeobachtet zerstört.

Restauratorische und bauhistorische Aktivitäten

Bereits in den Jahren 1979 bis 1983 waren verschiedene Sicherungsmaßnahmen im Burgbereich notwendig: Am nördlichen Bereich der Schildmauer mit zugehörigem Eckturm, an der daran anschließenden Nordseite der Umfassungsmauer mit Befunden zum hier ehemals stehenden *Palas* und am Bergfried[13]. Vor allem mussten in diesen Bereichen die Mauerkronen gesichert und Fehlstellen im Mauerwerk ausgebessert werden. Für den Bergfried entschied man sich für einen Abschluss mittels eines Ziegeldaches – eine optisch nicht befriedigende Lösung.

Abbildungen aus der damaligen Zeit belegen, dass auch der so genannte Kapellenbau bereits in Ruinen stand. Durch jahrzehntelang eindringendes Wasser war die Bausubstanz in einem derart schlechten und vor allem baufälligen Zustand, dass dringender Handlungsbedarf zur Sicherung des Gebäudes bestand. Im Zuge dieser Arbeiten konnten bauhistorische und bauarchäologische Untersuchungen durchgeführt

---

4. Staatsarchiv Nürnberg (StAN): Fürstentum Brandenburg-Ansbach, Bauernkriegsakten, rep. 107I: Nr. 60 und StAN: Fürstentum Brandenburg-Ansbach, Oberamt Creglingen, Urkunden, rep. 146, S. 78, No. 139a. Jetzt: Fürstentum Brandenburg-Ansbach, Ansbacher Oberamtsakten, teil I, rep. 165a, Nr. 453, pag. 4 und 5.
5. StAN: Fürstentum Brandenburg-Ansbach, Bauernkriegsakten, rep. 107 I: Tomus VIII, Nr. 64.
6. StAN: Fürstentum Brandenburg-Ansbach, Ansbacher Oberamtsakten, Teil I, rep. 165a, Nr. 453, pag. 45.
7. StAN: Fürstentum Brandenburg-Ansbach, Oberamt Creglingen, Urkunden, rep. 146, S. 94, No. 159.
8. StAN: Fürstentum Brandenburg-Ansbach, Oberamt Creglingen, Urkunden, rep. 146, S. 43, No. 79.
9. BENDEL 1934, 22. Das Original ist 1945 verbrannt.
10. ANTONOW 1977, 31; ANTONOW 1993, 281 und Abb. 109; LEISTIKOW 2001, 149, Abb. 7. Eingehende Beschreibung des Bergfrieds einschließlich Aufmaß, Plänen und Sicherungsmaßnahmen bei PFEFFERKORN 2008, 2-4.
11. Früheste bekannte Nennung als Kapellenbau: Staatsarchiv Ludwigsburg (StAL): bestand F 98, Bd. CLX.
12. ANTONOW 1977, 129, 130; LEISTIKOW 2001, 150.
13. Eingehende Beschreibung der Maßnahmen an den Umfassungsmauern bei PFEFFERKORN 2008, 6-10.

werden. Zudem stellte sich die Frage nach der ursprünglichen Nutzung und somit nach Belegen für eine eventuelle sakrale Verwendung.

Auch der Umgebungsbereich wie die Toranlage und der so genannte Zwischenbau aus der Zeit der Bauernkriege konnten in die Untersuchungen einbezogen werden, zudem wurde das Wohnhaus auf ältere Befundsituationen hin untersucht.

Geophysikalische Messungen wurden in zwei Bereichen durchgeführt in der Hoffnung, Hinweise auf einstige Bebauung zu erbringen: im Burghof und der ehemaligen Vorburg.

Im Folgenden werden der Vollständigkeit halber alle Bauteile der mittelalterlichen Burg beschrieben, wobei das besondere Augenmerk auf den in den letzten drei Jahren durchgeführten Untersuchungen an Burgtor, Kapellenbau und dem so genannten Zwischenbau liegt.

Ringmauer, Schildmauer und Burgtor

Die Ringmauer misst etwa 1,8 m in der Breite, die grob zugehauenen Bruchsteine sind in etwa lagig verlegt. Sie ist an vielen Stellen schadhaft und zeigt Ausbesserungen. Leider wird auch dem schnell sich verbreitendem Bewuchs nicht Einhalt geboten und so sind etliche Baubefunde, die noch in den 1980er Jahren erkennbar waren, wieder verdeckt (Nordostecke).

Eine weitgehende Erneuerung ist im Südosten der Mauer fotografisch für die 50er Jahre des 20. Jahrhundert überliefert. Offensichtlich stürzte ein großer Teil der Außenschale ab[14] und wurde 1957 wiedererrichtet. Aus diesem Grund fiel eine wichtige Quelle für bauhistorische Aussagen zum so genannten Kapellenbau weg.

Die Schildmauer misst 2,8 m in der Breite, Steinmaterial und -verlegung sind vergleichbar der Umfassungsmauer. Sie wird von zwei quadratischen Türmen im Norden und Süden flankiert, die jeweils eine Seitenlänge von 5,5 m aufweisen. W. Pfefferkorn konnte im Zuge der Arbeiten der 1980er Jahre Reste eines Wehrgangs sowohl an der Schildmauer als auch an dessen Übergang zur Nordmauer dokumentieren[15].

Das Burgtor, dessen Lage in der Schildmauer aus fortifikatorischer Sicht nicht ideal erscheint, ist seit Anbeginn der Zugang der Burg[16]. In späterer Zeit erhöht, war es ursprünglich als niedrigeres spitzbogiges Tor aus Radialquadern errichtet (Abb. 3), die bei der Erhöhung der Durchfahrt abgearbeitet wurden.

Ein Sperrbalkenloch, das im nördlichen Gewände bis zu einer Tiefe von 2,75 m als exakt gemauerter Schacht (15 x 15 cm) in die Schildwand hineinreicht, belegt, dass das Tor an dieser Stelle bauzeitlich sein muss, denn nur im Zuge der Errichtung der Schildmauer kann diese Verriegelungsvorrichtung entstanden sein.

Abb. 3 – Detail des Tores mit zwei Radialquadern, die die Form des frühen Tores belegen. Foto M. Hermann, Archiv LAD Esslingen.

Nur punktuell an sehr wenigen Stellen haben sich im Torbereich und an der Feldseite der Schildmauer auch Reste einer auffälligen Verfugung des Mauerwerks erhalten. Der so genannte *pietra rasa*-Fugenstrich ist ein typisches Merkmal hochmittelalterlicher Baukunst (Abb. 4). Somit dürfte die Datierung der Umfriedung der Burg in die Zeit um 1200 als gesichert gelten.

Ein Ausfalltor, das durch seinen dreieckigen unverzierten Türsturz in romanische Zeit datiert werden kann, war, ursprünglich im Westen angelegt[17]. Dieses wurde in jüngerer Zeit durch den Eigentümer erweitert, um die hofeigenen Pferde auf die hangseitigen Wiesen treiben zu können. Im Zuge dieser Umgestaltung wurden der Sturz und die Gewändesteine vergraben.

---

14. Aufnahme wohl aus dem Jahr 1955, Bildindex Marburg, Weitere Aufnahme nach Reparatur 1957, LAD Esslingen.
15. Pfefferkorn 2008, 9, Abb. 21-22.
16. So nimmt z.B. Antonow an, dass erst im Zuge der landwirtschaftlichen Nutzung der Burg das Tor an dieser Stelle eingebracht wurde (Antonow 1977, 129).
17. Aufnahme von 1955, Bildindex Marburg.

Abb. 4 – Detail der Mörtelverfugung in *Pietra rasa*. Foto M. Hermann, Archiv LAD Esslingen.

Abb. 5 – Gusserker am östlichen Teil der Nordmauer. Foto LAD Esslingen.

Der ehemalige *Palas*

Im Zug der Sicherungsmaßnahmen um die 1980er Jahre wurde ein Teil der östlichen Nordmauer (Umfassungsmauer) freigelegt. Einige Befunde deuteten auf die Lage des ehemaligen herrschaftlichen Wohngebäudes an dieser Stelle hin. Einige Balkenlöcher und zwei Gussscharten sind Zeugen der Lokalisierung dieses Gebäudes (Abb. 5). Leider bestand zu dieser Zeit keine Möglichkeit, eine Bauaufnahme zu erstellen, was besonders bedauernswert ist, da die meisten dieser Befunde nun wieder durch Pflanzenwuchs verdeckt und erneut gefährdet sind. Hier sei nur kurz auf die zwei auffälligsten Einbauten hingewiesen: Zum einen auf einen Aborterker, dessen Zugang vom ehemaligen *Palas* zu sehen ist und der sich an der Ringmauer außen deutlich manifestiert. Schräg oberhalb dieses Erkers ist zum anderen eine weitere, wesentlich kleinere Öffnung einer Gussscharte zu erkennen, die eine auffällige Spolie (romanischer Zickzack-Wulst) zeigt. Pfefferkorn interpretiert diesen „Ausguss" in einer Publikation als Pissoir-Erker, ohne jedoch weitere Belege derartiger Funktion benennen zu können[18].

Weitere Aufschlüsse zum ehemaligen herrschaftlichen Wohngebäude oder dessen Ausmaßen sind leider nicht bekannt oder nicht erkennbar, was eine große Lücke in der Erforschung des ehemaligen Aussehens der Herrschaftsburg darstellt.

Der Bergfried

Im Zuge der Restaurierungsarbeiten Anfang der 70er Jahre des 20. Jahrhunderts stand neben der Sicherung der Umfassungs-/Schildmauer auch die des Bergfrieds im Mittelpunkt. Seine Lage im Burghof mittig vor der Schildmauer ist prägend für das Ensemble und hat sicher zur Bauzeit im 13. Jahrhundert zusammen mit der zinnenbekrönten Schildmauer mit den flankierenden Türmen ein imposantes Bild bei der Annäherung von Osten ergeben[19] (Abb. 6).

Seine Seitenlänge misst 11,5 m bei einer Mauerstärke von etwa 3,3 m. Die heute noch erhaltene Höhe beläuft sich auf etwa 18 m über Hofniveau. Leider wurde im Zuge der Sanierung dem mächtigen Turm ein Zeltdach mit Ziegeln aufgesetzt, was seine Wirkung schmälert.

Der einstige Zugang erfolgte im ersten Stock über eine rundbogige Öffnung in circa 10 m Höhe. Unter dem Zugangsgeschoss befindet sich ein rechteckiger Raum. Nach oben hat sich wohl mittels einer Holzkonstruktion ein weiteres Geschoss befunden, da die beiden Schlitzfenster sicher nicht der Beleuchtung gedient haben können.

Eine Öffnung an der Südseite des Bergfrieds wurde in jüngerer Zeit eingebracht, um Steine der Innenschale als Baustoff für neue Gebäude auf kürzestem Weg in den Hof transportieren zu können.

---

18. Pfefferkorn 2008, 6, Abb. 2; 13, 18, Nr. 8-9.

19. Leistikow 2001, Abb. 8.

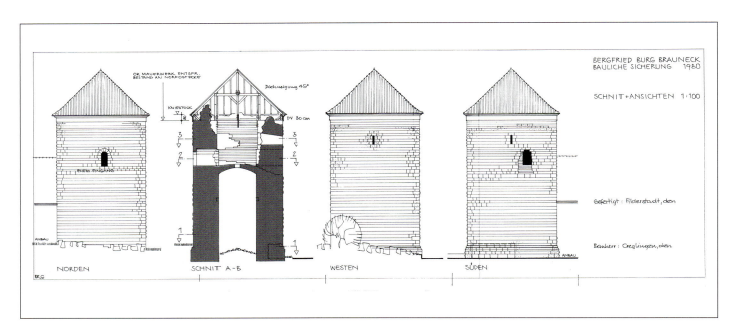

Abb. 6 – Schnittansichten des Bergfrieds. Zeichnung Pfefferkorn, Archiv LAD Esslingen.

Abb. 7 – Fassadenansicht sog. Kapellenbau, Nordseite. Foto LAD Esslingen.

Der Turm weist als Baumaterial ausschließlich qualitätvolle Buckelquader auf, deren Abmessungen in der Höhe von 0,22 bis 0,52 m und in der Länge von 0,3 bis 1,24 m reichen. Innerhalb des etwa 3 cm breiten Randschlags springen die grob gehauenen Buckel zwischen 2 und 20 cm vor. Erkennbar sind zahlreiche Steinmetzzeichen, daneben auch Zangenlöcher[20]. Der in seiner Ausführung qualitätvolle Sockelbereich mit Wulst- und Kehlsteinen[21] ist leider durch den Einbau von Schweineställen im Zuge der landwirtschaftlichen Nutzung arg gestört.

Der so genannte Kapellenbau[22]

Das Gebäude liegt in der Südwestecke der Anlage und bezieht den südlichen Teil der Schildmauer mit dessen Eckturm und den östlichen der Umfassungsmauer mit ein.

Die Vermutung, dass es sich bei dem Gebäude, das sich linkerhand an das Burgtor anschließt, um einen sakralen Bau handeln könnte, fußt wohl auf der relativ aufwändig gestalteten Fassade (Abb. 7). Nach den Bauformen in das späte 13. Jahrhundert datierend, ist der dreipassförmige Zugang aus Radialquadern in das etwas erhöht liegende Erdgeschoss kennzeichnend. Links davon öffnete sich ehemals ein spitzbogiges Biforienfenster, das aber stilistisch in die 1. Hälfte des 14. Jahrhunderts einzuordnen ist und einen nachträglichen Einbau darstellt. Eine weitere wohl vergleichbare, aber später entfernte und vermauerte Lichtöffnung, von der Breite her einbahnig zu rekonstruieren, kann westlich der Eingangstüre ergänzt werden.

Ein monolithisches Doppelfenster, das eher um die Mitte des 14. Jahrhunderts datieren dürfte, wurde ebenfalls nachträglich eingebaut. Auffällig ist der Sitz der Lichtöffnung an einer Stelle, an der das Gebäude leicht nach Süden in Richtung Tor abknickt.

An der Westseite des Kapellenbaus, heute durch eine Scheune verdeckt, sind noch die Reste eines monolithischen Dreipassfensters zu sehen. Dieses ist sicher bauzeitlich und steht eng im Zusammenhang zu dem ebenfalls kleeblattförmigen Zugang des Erdgeschosses.

Eine zweite Toröffnung wurde in späterer Zeit in die Fassade eingebracht: Das mehrfach profilierte rundbogige Gewände, das aufgrund der Bauform und der überlieferten Bautätigkeiten im unmittelbaren Umfeld (Bau eines inzwischen abgegangenen, Bauernhaus genannten, Baus 1691 in den Urkunden verzeichnet, 1875 abgebrochen, westlich des untersuchten Gebäudes) ins 17. Jahrhundert datiert werden kann, führt in den östlich gelegenen Kellerraum des Gebäudes.

Das Erdgeschoss zeigt sich in seinem Grundriss heute als ein großer tonnengewölbter Raum im Osten, der das Geviert des südlichen Eckturmes der Schildmauer mit einschließt, einem schmalen Querraum, in den der Zugang erfolgt, und im Westen ein weiterer tonnengewölbter Raum, der über einen kleinen Stichflur zugänglich ist (Abb. 8).

Der Keller ist ebenfalls tonnengewölbt und durch eine Quermauer in zwei Bereiche unterteilt. In den östlichen Teil führt der Abgang durch die rundbogige Türöffnung, in den westlichen durch eine Treppe aus dem heutigen Schweinestall. Diese ersetzt einen älteren Zugang, der vom Hof (außerhalb des Baukörpers) in einen Flur mit Tonne führte; durch eine Quermauer gelangt man in einen weiteren Raum (Abb. 9).

Auffallend ist, dass der östliche Gebäudeabschnitt nicht unterkellert ist. Im Äußeren dokumentiert sich dieser Bereich durch einen Knick der Nordmauer nach Süden, die dann an das Burgtor anschließt. Da sich eine Baufuge weder im Aufgehenden noch archäologisch aufzeigen ließ, ist diese asymmetrische Grundrissform sicher bauzeitlich und der bereits vorhandenen Toranlage geschuldet. Spuren älterer Bebauung konnten im Boden nicht entdeckt werden.

Das Erdgeschoss war ursprünglich ein einziger, mit einer Balkendecke flach gedeckter Raum. In der Mitte des 14. Jahrhunderts wurde der westliche Teil der Südwand des Gebäudes neu errichtet und eine Wendebohlentür eingebaut, die wohl zu einem Mauerabort gehörte. Auch der Einbau des Biforienfensters ist dieser Baumaßnahme zuzurechnen. Ein Kamingewände, das vielleicht ebenfalls als Hinweis für eine sakrale Nutzung gedeutet werden konnte, wurde erst nach 1350 in die Südwand in Zweitverwendung eingebaut.

Ein weiteres Indiz dafür, dass das Gebäude nicht als Kapelle gedient haben konnte, ist der große, mit einer Balkendecke versehene bauzeitliche Keller, der den gesamten Grundriss einnahm. Abgeschlagene Konsolsteine, die in den Gewölbezwickeln freigelegt wurden, sind hierfür eindeutiges Indiz[23]. Der Zugang erfolgte ursprünglich vom Burghof aus als Abgang in den westlichen Gebäudeteil (wie oben beschrieben). Eine erste räumliche Unterteilung des Untergeschosses erfolgte ebenfalls um 1350. Die endgültige Aufteilung in zwei voneinander abgetrennte, etwa gleich große Kellerräume mit jeweils eigenem Zugang geht sicher auf die Bewirtschaftung durch die zwei Bauernfamilien ab dem Ende des 17. Jahrhunderts zurück.

Im Obergeschoss sind, bis auf die Nordmauer, keine bauzeitlichen Befunde mehr erhalten.

Durch einen dendrochronologischen Befund lässt sich belegen, dass um die Mitte des 14. Jahrhunderts etliche Baumaßnahmen am Gebäude vorgenommen wurden: Die neu

---

20. Pfefferkorn 2008, 2.
21. Leistikow 2001, 149, Abb. 7.
22. Hermann 2008, Burg Brauneck, sog. „Kapellenbau" (13. Jh./1525ff.) 97993 Creglingen-Brauneck. Bauhistorische Untersuchung und Archivrecherche (Archiv LAD Esslingen).
23. Arnold 2009, 280, Abb. 160.

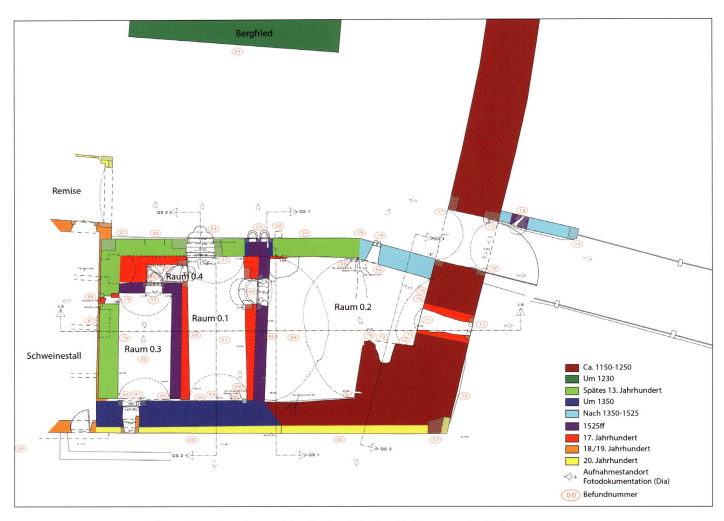

Abb. 8 – Baualtersplan sog. Kapellenbau EG. Plan M. Hermann, Archiv LAD Esslingen.

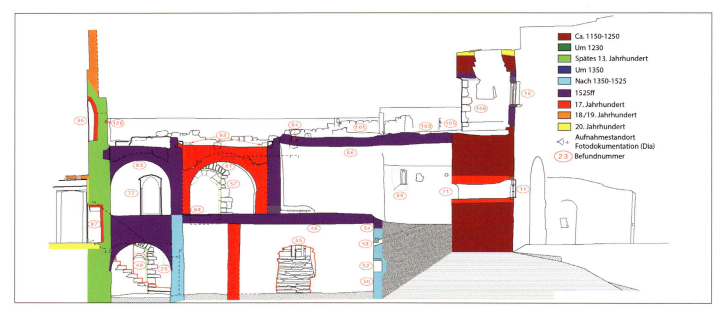

Abb. 9 – Baualtersplan sog. Kapellenbau Längsschnitt. Plan M. Hermann, Archiv LAD Esslingen.

errichtete Südwand wies in einer Nut eine Mauerlatte (Unterzug zur Unterstützung der Balkenlage des Erdgeschosses?) auf, die auf die Zeit zwischen 1349 und 1360 datiert werden konnte.

Es konnte kein einziger Befund beobachtet werden, der den Steinbau, der sich im Südosten der Anlage auf Brauneck erhalten hat, mit Sicherheit als ehemaligen Sakralraum ausweist. Die Position des Gebäudes an der Schildmauer neben dem Eingangstor zur Burg macht eine Nutzung als Burgmannenhaus sehr wahrscheinlich. Dies wird auch durch die überlieferten Urkunden bestärkt: 1365 erhält Lutz Bachrath, wie bereits erwähnt, das Erbburglehen verliehen, sicherlich verbunden mit der Auflage, Burgmannendienst zu leisten.

In diesem Zusammenhang scheint es wohl zu den genannten Umbauten gekommen zu sein. Das Aussehen des Ursprungsbaus, vor allem die Fragen nach der Belichtung und ob bereits damals eine Wohnnutzung bestand, kann nur interpoliert, nicht aber mit letzter Sicherheit behauptet werden. Befunde an der Südwand des Burgmannenhauses aus der Bauzeit fehlen nach dem Wiederaufbau um 1950 völlig.

Das einschneidendste Ereignis für das Aussehen des Gebäudes und die Geschichte der Burg stellt die Erstürmung derselben im Bauernkrieg 1525 dar. Von den Feuereinwirkungen zeugen heute noch angeglühte Mauersteine (wohl durch herabstürzende brennende Balken und sich daraus ergebende Glutnester verursacht) und ein ehemals hölzerner Türsturz im Untergeschoss des Burgmannenhauses, der in der westlichen Zwischenwand nur noch als Negativabdruck erhalten ist.

Umfangreiche Baumaßnahmen nicht nur in diesem Gebäude waren, wie bereits berichtet, die Folge. So wird das Erdgeschoss in drei Räume aufgeteilt und wie das Untergeschoss mit Tonnengewölben versehen. Im Erdgeschoss behielt lediglich der Zugangsraum eine Balkendecke, über die wohl das erste Obergeschoss erschlossen wurde. Über die Raumdisposition des 1. oder gar 2. Obergeschosses sind keine Aussagen möglich. Eventuell kann man aufgrund der Überlieferung von 1691[24], die besagt, dass eine Stube, zwei Kammern und eine Küche vorhanden seien, Rückschlüsse auf die Nutzung nach 1525 ziehen. Küchennutzung für das 17. und 18. Jahrhundert ist an der Westwand nachweisbar und sowohl historische Aufnahmen, die eine neu eingebaute Fensternische zeigen, als auch die aufgefundenen Reste eines offenen Kamins lassen die Lage der Stube im nordöstlichen Bereich als gesichert gelten.

Der Zwischenbau

Fortifikatorische Zwänge, die im Zusammenhang mit den Bauernkriegen und der Erstürmung der Burg zu sehen sind, waren auch ausschlaggebend für weitere Bauaktivitäten. Zwischen Schildmauer und Bergfried erhebt sich der so genannte „Zwischenbau", eine etwa zweigeschossige Wehrmauer, die als Bruchsteinmauer errichtet wurde. Sie schließt mit deutlicher Baunaht an die Nordwand des Bergfrieds an und verläuft in östlicher Richtung zur Schildmauer, an die sie stumpf stößt[25]. An dieser Stelle bildet sie eine etwa viertelkreisförmige Eckbastion. Diese und das gerade verlaufende Mauerstück zeigen je zwei rechteckige Schießscharten, welche alle Ausnehmungen für das Einlegen eines Balkens besitzen, an welchem wiederum die Hakenbüchsen aufgelegt werden konnten (Abb. 10).

Da das gesamte Burgareal wohl nicht mehr verteidigt werden konnte, wurde es wahrscheinlich vorübergehend verkleinert und die Kernburg in den südöstlichen Bereich verlagert. Es umfasste noch Burgtor, Burgmannenhaus und Bergfried. Auch der ursprüngliche Brunnen, der sich im Süden des Burghofes befand und mehr als 40 m tief gewesen sein soll[26], wäre damit in der „neuen" Kernburg als wichtiger Wasserversorger gelegen. Er soll im 18. Jahrhundert zugeschüttet worden sein, ein Brunnen des 19. Jahrhunderts befindet sich im heutigen Gartenbereich nordwestlich des Bergfrieds.

Das Wohnhaus

Eine bauhistorische Untersuchung des Wohnhauses zeigte lediglich, dass das einzige Bauteil, der eventuell in mittelalterliche Zeit datiert, im Keller zu sehen ist. Es handelt sich um einen großen, tonnengewölbten Raum, der etwa die Hälfte des darüber stehenden Gebäudes einnimmt[27].

Geophysikalische Messungen im Burghof und im Bereich der Vorburg

Der Befund der so genannten Zwischenmauer zwischen Schildmauer und Bergfried spricht dafür, dass die Kernburg im 16. Jahrhundert in den südlichen Bereich des Burghofes gelegt wurde. Daher ist eine Verlängerung der Mauer jenseits des Bergfrieds in Richtung Südwest zu vermuten.

In der Vorburg konnten leider im Vorfeld der Errichtung der Maschinenhalle keine archäologischen Grabungen durchgeführt werden. Da die verbliebene Fläche in ihrer Oberflächenstruktur leicht uneben erscheint, war die Hoffnung groß, Bebauungsstrukturen durch Geophysik nachweisen zu können.

Um diese Annahme zu verifizieren, wurde eine geophysikalische Messung in Auftrag gegeben[28].

---

24. StAN: Fürstentum Brandenburg-Ansbach, Salbücher und Partikulare Stuttgarter Abgabe, rep. 112/1, Bd. CXXV.
25. Numberger 2012, Creglingen-Reinsbronn, Burg Brauneck – Wehrmauer – Befunddokumentation. (Archiv LAD Esslingen).
26. Leistikow 2001, 150.
27. Numberger 2009, Creglingen-Reinsbronn, Burg Brauneck – Wohnhaus – Bauhistorische Untersuchung (Archiv LAD Esslingen).
28. Archäologisch-geophysikalische Prospektion auf der Burg Brauneck bei Creglingen-Reinsbronn, Main-Tauber-Kreis. Bodenradarprospektion am 3. und 4.12.2012 sowie am 10.1.2013 durch Posselt und Zickgraf Prospektionen GbR, Marburg (Archiv LAD Esslingen).

Abb. 10 – Ansicht der Zwischenmauer mit Eckbastion und Schießscharten. Foto LAD Esslingen.

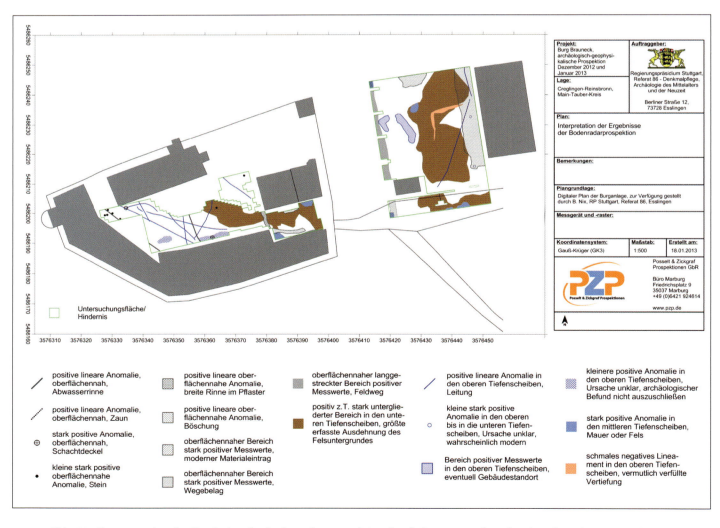

Abb. 11 – Interpretation der Ergebnisse der Bodenradarprospektion durch die Fa. Posselt und Zickgraf. Archiv LAD Esslingen.

Im Burghof ließen sich in den verschieden Tiefenscheiben leider keine archäologischen Befunde erkennen, die einen Hinweis auf die zu erwartende (Burg-)Mauer oder den auch hier vermuteten Brunnen geben konnten. Eindeutig sind lediglich moderne Bodeneingriffe wie ein Drainagesystem und Leitungstrassen. Anomalien, die unter Umständen als Mauer interpretiert werden könnten, sind für eine eindeutige Ansprache nicht ausgeprägt genug (Abb. 11).

Ähnlich unbefriedigend sind die Ergebnisse im Bereich der Vorburg: Hier sind ebenfalls nur neuzeitliche Eingriffe wie die Verfüllung der Baugrube zur Maschinenhalle und ein Feldweg (rechts im Bild) zu erkennen. Die zwei, zum Teil winkelförmigen Strukturen könnten als Hinweis auf ein Gebäude interpretiert werden. Die Ansprache ist jedoch im Hinblick auf ihre Ausrichtung, die sich nicht am Grabenverlauf orientiert, nicht sehr belastbar. Als markante geologische Formation ist allein der anstehende Kalksteinfels anzusprechen. Er könnte Grund dafür sein, dass sich weniger massive archäologische Strukturen nicht abzeichnen[29].

Denkmalpflegerisches Konzept für das Burgmannenhaus

Für das einsturzgefährdete Gebäude des Burgmannenhauses musste ein denkmalpflegerisches Konzept gefunden werden, das sich in die Ansicht des Burgensembles einfügt. Eine Rekonstruktion kam nicht in Frage. Auch das Aufbringen eines Daches über der in der Höhe willkürlich erhaltenen Gebäuderuine analog zum Dachabschluss des Bergfrieds schien nicht erstrebenswert. So wurde beschlossen, den Ruinencharakter zu erhalten und eine Betondecke einzuziehen. Diese dient der statischen Sicherung der historischen Gewölbe, der Erhaltung der Baubefunde und der Abdichtung des Gebäudes gegen Niederschläge. Eine Begrünung wird im Lauf der Jahre den Ruinencharakter wieder stärker betonen.

29. Siehe Anm. 27, 7-8.

Literatur

ANTONOW A. (1977), *Burgen des südwestdeutschen Raums im 13. und 14. Jahrhundert unter besonderer Berücksichtigung der Schildmauer*, Bühl/Baden, Konkordia (Veröffentlichung des Alemannischen Instituts; 40).

– (1993), *Planung und Bau von Burgen im süddeutschen Raum*, Frankfurt am Main, Antonow Verlag (Bibliotheksreihe europäische Baukunst; 1).

ARNOLD S. (2009), „Bauarchäologische und Bauhistorische Untersuchungen auf Burg Brauneck", *Archäologische Ausgrabungen in Baden-Württemberg*, 279-281.

BENDEL F. (1934), „Die Würzburger Diözesanmatrikel aus der Mitte des 15. Jh.", *Würzburger Diözesangeschichtsblätter*, Bd. II, Heft II, No. 959 [das Original ist 1945 verbrannt].

LEISTIKOW D. (2001), „Brauneck und Frauental. Gründungen der Hohenlohe im Zeitalter Kaiser Friedrichs II.", in *Burg und Kirche zur Stauferzeit. Akten der 1. Landauer Staufertagung*, V. HERZNER & J. KRÜGER (hrsg.), Regensburg, Schnell und Steiner, 144-157.

PFEFFERKORN W. (2008), „Burg Brauneck in Württembergisch Franken", *Burgen und Schlösser*, 49, 2-13.

Burg Steuerwald nördlich von Hildesheim

Historie, Bauforschung und Archäologie

◆

Markus C. Blaich, Tillman Kohnert*

1. Geographische und topographische Lage

Burg Steuerwald liegt etwa 1,5 km nordwestlich der Stadtmitte von Hildesheim in der feuchten und sumpfigen Niederung der Innerste. Nur wenige hundert Meter östlich verläuft die wichtige Verkehrsverbindung von Hildesheim nordwärts nach Hannover.

2. Stand der Forschung

Die zwischen 1310 und 1331 unter den Bischöfen Heinrich II. und Otto II. errichtete Burg Steuerwald fand schon recht früh das Interesse der Forschung[1]. So wurde ihre geographisch-politisch bemerkenswerte Lage an der Grenze zwischen bischöflichen und städtischen Ländereien diskutiert, desgleichen die bau- und architekturgeschichtlich interessante Stellung am Übergang vom „klassischen" Burgenbau des Hochmittelalters zu den befestigten Adelssitzen des späten Mittelalters[2]. Mehrfach wurde die außerordentliche Größe der Gesamtanlage hervorgehoben[3].

Burg Steuerwald ist durch spätere Umbauten oder Zerstörungen im äußeren Erscheinungsbild kaum beeinträchtigt[4]. Allerdings stützen sich die bisherigen Untersuchungen vor allem auf die vergleichsweise dichte historische Überlieferung. Eine detailliertere Bauaufnahme liegt allein für das Haupthaus, den so genannten *Palas*, vor[5]. Eine denkmalpflegerische Darstellung des Gesamtbestandes wurde 1997 vorgelegt, die jüngste und umfassende Beschreibung stammt aus dem Jahr 2002[6]. Pläne, die Gebäude zu veräußern und einer neuen Nutzung zuzuführen, weckten das Interesse an einer eingehenderen Untersuchung. Diese wurde in enger Abstimmung mit den derzeitigen Pächtern durch das Institut für Baudenkmalpflege der HAWK Hildesheim 2011 und 2012 geleistet[7], mit einem Schwerpunkt auf dem *Palas* (Abb. 1) und der so genannten „Großen Scheune"[8].

---

* Hochschule HAWK Hildesheim/Holzminden/Göttingen, Fakultät Bauen und Erhalten/Institut für Denkmalpflege Hohnsen 2, Deutschland.

1. Die älteste Gesamtdarstellung stammt immerhin von 1832: Koken & Lüntzel 1832.
2. Albrecht 1999, 126; Meckseper 1999, 133.
3. Schulze 1981, 227; Heine 2006, 154.
4. Ein Großteil der ursprünglichen Innenausstattung ging wohl mit der landwirtschaftlichen Nutzung Ende des 18. Jahrhunderts verloren. Mit der Verpachtung der Anlage an das Frauenwohnheim Himmelsthür im Jahr 1948 wurden durch den Einzug von Betondecken und einer Anpassung des Grundrisses an damals moderne Anforderungen tiefgreifende Veränderungen vorgenommen. Der repräsentative bauzeitliche Charakter des *Palas* ist im Inneren weitgehend zerstört.
5. Wangerin 1978, 85-95. Bei diesem Gebäude handelt es sich um einen Saalgeschossbau. Da sich in der Literatur die Bezeichnung *Palas* durchgesetzt hat, wird auch in diesem Aufsatz entsprechend verfahren.
6. Twachtmann-Schlichter 2007, 276-280; Albrecht 2002.
7. Folgende Studierende waren an diesen Arbeiten beteiligt: G. Albrecht, K. Duraj, K. Fischer, A. Heße, S. Leithäußer, A. Malkovski, C. Müller, M. Prieß, D. Sebening, M. Strack, K. Uschkurat und T. Wiltraut.
8. Die „Große Scheune" wurde von G. Albrecht im Rahmen einer Master-Arbeit ausführlicher untersucht (HAWK Hildesheim, Fakultät Bauen und Erhalten, WS 2012/2013).

Abb. 1 – Burg Steuerwald, Ansicht des *Palas* von Südosten. Foto T. Kohnert, 2012.

3. Historischer Hintergrund

1310 wurde der aus dem Hildesheimer Sprengel stammende und einer zwischen Oker und Leine einflussreichen Familie angehörende Graf Heinrich IV. von Wohldenburg als Heinrich II. zum Bischof von Hildesheim gewählt[9]. Die Wahl selbst verlief ohne Komplikationen, allerdings verweigerte die Stadt Hildesheim dem neuen Bischof die Huldigung und dem Domkapitel die Beschwörung der Freiheit und weitere Vorrechte. Es wurden damit die Rechte des Bischofs sowohl als geistlicher als auch als weltlicher Herrscher angegriffen[10].

Der neu gewählte Bischof versuchte zunächst, einen Konflikt zu vermeiden. Nach weiteren Provokationen seitens der Stadt sah er sich aber gezwungen, seinen bischöflichen Hof beim Dom aufzugeben und seinen Sitz auf (s)ein Gebiet außerhalb der Stadt zu verlegen[11].

Um seinen Machtanspruch gegenüber der Stadt unter Beweis zu stellen, beschloss der Bischof, eine Burg vor den Toren der Stadt zu errichten. Hierzu wurde das Areal beim Dorf Essem gewählt. Dieses liegt in der sumpfigen Niederung der Innerste, bot aber den Vorteil, dass die fraglichen Ländereien bereits zum größten Teil im Besitz des Domkapitels waren und daher die rechtlichen Voraussetzungen für den Bau einer Burg bestanden[12]. Die weiteren Besitzungen in der Dorfmark Essem, die beispielsweise dem Kloster St. Michaelis zustanden, wurden in den folgenden Jahrzehnten schrittweise dem Bischof übertragen, die Ansiedlung fiel wüst und es entstand eine größere, unbebaute Freifläche um die Burganlage[13].

---

9. Koken & Lüntzel 1832, 29-33; Wangerin 1978, 85; Kruppa & Wilke 2006, 303-308; Twachtmann-Schlichter 2007, 276-278.
10. Vgl. die überregionale Darstellung von H. Patze mit dem bezeichnenden Titel „Erosion bischöflicher Herrschaft" (Patze 1997, 674-682, zu Hildesheim besonders 675-679).
11. Koken & Lüntzel 1832, 29-33; Wangerin 1978, 85; Kruppa & Wilke 2006, 323-324.
12. Koken & Lüntzel 1832, 23-29.
13. *Ibid.*, 41-49. Dieser Vorgang muss deutlich vor 1478 abgeschlossen worden sein, wie die Zusammenstellung entsprechender Belege bei K. Koken und H. Lüntzel zeigt (*ibid.*, 96-101).

Ein weiterer Vorteil des Platzes war, dass von hier aus einer der wichtigeren nördlichen Zuwege zur Stadt kontrolliert wurde, d.h. der Bischof konnte die Stadt in ihrem Handlungsspielraum vergleichsweise leicht einschränken. Burg Steuerwald war damit von Anbeginn eine „Grenzburg" und „Rückzugsburg" zur Sicherung der bischöflichen Herrschaft[14].

Wohl noch im Herbst 1310 wurde mit dem Bau der Burg begonnen; gleichzeitig gelang es dem Bischof, in einer bewaffneten Auseinandersetzung mit der Stadt seine Ansprüche durchzusetzen[15]. Der Bau von Burg Steuerwald wurde jedoch nicht aufgegeben. Aus der Tatsache, dass Bischof Heinrich II. bereits 1313 auf Steuerwald urkundete, ist mittelbar zu erschließen, dass er die Burg zumindest gelegentlich für bedeutsamere Anlässe nutzte[16].

Größere Umbauten sind für den Nachfolger von Bischof Heinrich II., Bischof Otto II. (1319-1331) bezeugt. Auch er entstammte dem regionalen Adel, sein Vetter war als Bischof Heinrich II. sein Amtsvorgänger[17]. Otto II. hielt auf Steuerwald offensichtlich häufig Hof und ließ die Anlage dementsprechend aus- und umbauen[18].

In den Auseinandersetzungen um die Nachfolge Bischof Ottos II. spielte Steuerwald insofern eine Rolle, als im Juni 1345 in nächster Nähe die Entscheidungsschlacht zwischen den beiden Kontrahenten – Erich Graf von Homburg und Herzog Heinrich von Braunschweig[19] – stattfand[20]. Steuerwald entwickelte sich in den weiteren Jahrzehnten bis 1405 zu einer der wichtigsten Burgen der Hildesheimer Bischöfe[21]. Die pfandfreie, also jeglichem Zugriff von außen entzogene und allein dem Bischof gehörende Burg war beständiger Sitz eines Vogtes und wurde wiederholt zur Hofhaltung des Bischofs genutzt. Die Bedeutung Steuerwalds für die Hildesheimer Bischöfe lässt sich auch daran erkennen, dass die Burg von nun an mehrfach verpfändet wird: so wird sie nach der für den Bischof ruinösen Niederlage bei Grohnde von Bischof Johannes III. für die außerordentlich große Summe von 14 000 Goldgulden verpfändet (14.1.1424), aber nach knapp zwei Jahren wieder eingelöst (26.12.1425)[22]. Auch die Regelung, dass Bischof und Domherren neben den Burgen Winzenburg und Peine auch Steuerwald schuldenfrei zu halten hatten, weist in diese Richtung: Die Besitzung zählte offensichtlich zum „Tafelsilber" der Bischöfe, dessen (kurzfristige) Verpfändung vor allem in politisch schwierigen Lagen genutzt wurde[23].

1471/1472 kam es erneut zu bewaffneten Auseinandersetzungen zwischen der Stadt Hildesheim, den Braunschweiger Herzögen, dem Gegenbischof Hermann von Hessen auf der einen Seite und dem neugewählten Bischof Henning und Teilen des Domkapitels auf der anderen Seite[24]. Steuerwald erwies sich hierbei wieder als militärstrategisch günstig gelegener Ort: Die Zuwege zur Stadt wurden abgeschnitten, Steuerwald diente Bischof Henning als Truppenlager. Daher begannen die Bürger von Hildesheim die Belagerung der Burg Steuerwald, errichteten schließlich sogar eine kleine Belagerungsschanze und beschossen von dort aus den Turm von Steuerwald. Erst im Juli 1473 ergaben sich die Belagerten. Das weitere Verhalten der Stadt Hildesheim ist sehr aufschlussreich: Die Burg wurde der Verwahrung des städtischen Rates anvertraut, blieb also in bischöflicher Verwaltung, aber nicht mehr als dessen Eigentum[25].

Während der Hildesheimer Stiftsfehde (1519-1523) wurde Steuerwald häufiger umkämpft und war mehrfach das Ziel militärischer Vorstöße[26]. 1528 wurde die Burg nach Verhandlungen zwischen Stadt und Bischof wieder dem Bischof zugesprochen. Nach 1537 gelangte Steuerwald widerrechtlich in adligen Besitz, erst 1564 vermochte der Bischof seinen Besitzanspruch erneut durchzusetzen[27]. Steuerwald entwickelte sich in den folgenden Jahrzehnten zu einem größeren Wirtschaftsgut der Hildesheimer Bischöfe, zugleich war es eines von nur noch dreien, die dem Bistum verblieben waren[28].

Im Dreißigjährigen Krieg spielte Steuerwald wieder als militärische Anlage eine Rolle; 1622 wurden die Verteidigungswerke ausgebaut, jedoch 1626 nach kurzer Belagerung eingenommen. Eine weitere dreimonatige Belagerung ist für 1632 belegt; nach Einnahme der Burg ließen die Truppen der Protestantischen Union die Anlage durch die Hildesheimer Bürger schleifen. Im Oktober 1632 gelang es der Katholischen Liga zwar Steuerwald zurückzuerobern, die Befestigungen wurden jedoch nicht mehr erneuert[29].

---

14. Patze 1997, 602-603.
15. Kruppa & Wilke 2006, 325-327.
16. *Ibid.*, 315.
17. *Ibid.*, 338-343.
18. Koken & Lüntzel 1832, 33-34; 36-37; Wangerin 1978, 85; Kruppa & Wilke 2006, 359.
19. Patze 1997, 696-699; Kruppa & Wilke 2006, 385-397.
20. Koken & Lüntzel 1832, 38-40; Wangerin 1978, 86; Kruppa & Wilke 2006, 406-407.
21. Diese über 20 Jahre währenden Auseinandersetzungen zwischen den beiden Gegenbischöfen und der Stadt führten letztlich den finanziellen Niedergang des Hochstifts herbei (vgl. Patze 1997, 698).
22. Koken & Lüntzel 1832, 40-41. Dies ist die erste Verpfändung Steuerwalds überhaupt; bis dahin hatten die Bischöfe Heinrich III. (bis 1363) und Gerhard von Berge (1365-1398) Verpfändungen von Steuerwald ausdrücklich vermieden (Kruppa & Wilke 2006, 447-448; 543). Zur Bedeutung des Vorgangs als Ausdruck des Machtverfalls: Patze 1997, 645.
23. Koken & Lüntzel 1832, 72-79; Wangerin 1978, 86. Zur politischen Bedeutung des Vorgangs: Patze 1997, 673. Zum Hintergrund derartiger Pfandgeschäfte: Kruppa & Wilke 2006, 323-324.
24. Koken & Lüntzel 1832, 57-59; Patze 1997, 823.
25. Koken & Lüntzel 1832, 61-62; Wangerin 1978, 86.
26. Koken & Lüntzel 1832, 62-65; Nach dieser Fehde war der Niedergang der bischöflichen Gewalt (als weltlicher Herrscher) endgültig besiegelt.
27. Koken & Lüntzel 1832, 65-70; Van den Heuvel & Boetticher 1998, 35-39; 113.
28. Koken & Lüntzel 1832, 78-82; Wangerin 1978, 86-88; Van den Heuvel & Boetticher 1998, 38.
29. Koken & Lüntzel 1832, 88-89. Die Angaben bei G. Wangerin (Wangerin 1978, 88) sind widersprüchlich. Einerseits ist von den „Wehranlagen" die Rede, andererseits von „den Wällen". Es bleibt also offen, ob die heute noch stehenden Steingebäude von den Kriegsereignissen betroffen waren.

Steuerwald wurde im 17. Jahrhundert gelegentlich von den Hildesheimer Bischöfen als repräsentativer Ort genutzt[30]. 1689 wurde eine Brauerei eingerichtet, 1789 erfolgte die Verpachtung des Gutes als Domäne[31]. Mit der Säkularisation kam Steuerwald zunächst an Preußen (1802), dann an das neu gegründete Königreich Hannover (1813/1814). In den ersten Jahren diente der ehemalige *Palas* dem Pächter als Wohnung, nach dem Bau eines neuen Pächterhauses wurde hier eine Brauerei eingerichtet (1819)[32]. Die Domäne Steuerwald gelangte 1912 in den Besitz der Stadt Hildesheim. 1905 fiel die Mühle von Gut Steuerwald einem Brand zum Opfer[33], die Anlage des Hildesheimer Hafens (1924) führte zu einer wesentlichen Veränderung des Geländes. Nach 1945 folgte der schrittweisen Nutzungsänderung[34] der zu Steuerwald gehörenden Ländereien ein endgültiger Bedeutungsverlust[35].

4. Gebäudebestand und Struktur der Gesamtanlage

Die zwischen 1310 und 1313 errichtete Anlage wurde bereits zwischen 1319 und 1331 wesentlich umgestaltet und erweitert. Zahlreiche Umbauten sind für das 16. bis 19. Jahrhundert bezeugt. Die Gesamtstruktur der Anlage kann anhand alter Karten gut nachvollzogen werden. Demnach ist mit einer vergleichsweise kleinen, rechteckigen Kernburg und einer größeren Vorburg zu rechnen. Diese beiden Burgen waren durch Umfassungsmauern und zwei breite, von der Innerste gespeiste Wassergräben umgeben. Die Gesamtausdehnung der rechteckigen Anlage dürfte etwa 120 x 92 m betragen (Abb. 2)[36]. Der Bergfried wird der zweiten Bauphase zugeschrieben; eventuell wurde er 1325 errichtet[37]. Zum Gebäudebestand zählen ferner eine kleine, Anfang des 16. Jahrhunderts erbaute Kapelle und mehrere Wirtschaftsgebäude, von denen die wohl 1324 errichtete sogenannte „Große Scheune" allein aufgrund ihrer Ausmaße besondere Beachtung verdient[38].

5. Der *Palas*

Der heute aus zwei rechtwinklig mit einander verbundenen Gebäudeflügeln[39] bestehende *Palas* zählt zu den ältesten, unter Bischof Heinrich II. (1310-1318) errichteten Gebäuden (vgl. Abb. 1). Mit seiner Traufhöhe von 15 m und einer Firsthöhe von 23,15 m bestimmt dieser Saalgeschossbau mit seinen vier Vollgeschossen das Bild der Burg Steuerwald[40].

Der Hauptflügel im Westen mit den Außenmaßen von 28,3 m Länge und 12,4 m Breite wird der ersten Bauphase (1310-1313) zugewiesen. Dementsprechend wären die Mauern im Erdgeschoss zugleich die Außenmauern der Befestigung, d.h. westliche Längswand und beide Giebelwände wären identisch mit den Außenseiten der rechteckigen Gesamtanlage[41]. Für die Rekonstruktion von Burg Steuerwald ergeben sich damit zwei Möglichkeiten: Die erste Rekonstruktion geht davon aus, dass sich an den *Palas* eine dreiseitig ummauerte Hofanlage anschloss, die erst in der zweiten Bauphase unter Bischof Otto II. (1319-1331) zu einer Vierflügelanlage erweitert wurde. Diese quadratische Anlage verfügte über Außenmaße von etwa 28,3 x 29,1 m. Die zweite Möglichkeit ist, dass von Anbeginn an die Anlage als vierflügeliger Gebäudetrakt konzipiert worden war. Bei der aus den Gebäudemaßen zu erschließenden Gesamtgröße (etwa 28,3 x 29,1 m) würde dies bedeuten, dass der Innenhof allenfalls eine Fläche von etwa 5 x etwa 9 m hatte[42].

Mit den oben genannten Außenmaßen der beiden Gebäudeflügel wird auch die besondere Position von Burg Steuerwald deutlich: Der Hauptflügel erreicht in seinen Maßen die Dimensionen der repräsentativen Saalgeschossbauten in den ottonischen Pfalzen, selbst der kürzere Seitenflügel ist größer als manche der bürgerlichen Kemenaten in Braunschweig (12./13. Jahrhundert)[43]. Etwas größere, jedoch besser ausgestattete Profanbauten sind – jedenfalls bei kursorischer Durchsicht der Literatur – allenfalls noch aus den staufischen Pfalzen und Vogteien des 13. Jahrhunderts bekannt[44]. Für den *Palas* von Steuerwald liegt damit einer der besten Vergleiche mit dem „Hohen Haus" der südlich von Hildesheim gelegenen Domäne Marienburg (errichtet unter Bischof Heinrich III., um 1349/1350) vor[45].

Die an beiden Gebäudeflügeln (West- und Nordflügel)[46] zu beobachtenden Umbauten können einerseits mit den beiden Erbauungsphasen verknüpft werden, vor allem aber mit der Umgestaltung im 17. und 18. Jahrhundert. Zudem ist mit starken Zerstörungen während des Dreißigjährigen Krieges zu rechnen.

Dendrochronologisch ist für die Jahre 1651/1652 der Einbau des heutigen Dachwerks und der Holzbalkendecke

---

30. KOKEN & LÜNTZEL 1832, 89; WANGERIN 1978, 87.
31. KOKEN & LÜNTZEL 1832, 91.
32. *Ibid.*, 91-92; 95-96.
33. WANGERIN 1978, 94.
34. Heute befindet sich hier ein von mittelständischen Unternehmen genutztes Gewerbegebiet.
35. WANGERIN 1978, 88-89.
36. *Ibid.*, 89-90; 86, Abb. 2-3 (Lagepläne von 1769 und 1976).
37. *Ibid.*, 90; TWACHTMANN-SCHLICHTER 2007, 280, Abb. S. 278; KOHNERT 2013.
38. WANGERIN 1978, 93-94; TWACHTMANN-SCHLICHTER 2007, 280, Abb. S. 279; ALBRECHT 2002, 3-14; KOHNERT 2013.
39. WANGERIN 1978, 91-93; 88, Abb. 5 (Grundriss); TWACHTMANN-SCHLICHTER 2007, 278 mit Abbildung; KOHNERT 2013.
40. Zur Terminologie: ALBRECHT 1995, 22-25; ALBRECHT 1999, 126.
41. WANGERIN 1978, 91.
42. Allerdings scheinen derartig kleine Innenhöfe bei Burgen des 14. Jahrhunderts nicht ungewöhnlich zu sein, wie H. W. Böhme (BÖHME 2011, 50) aufzeigte.
43. ALBRECHT 1995, 7-22; besonders 8-13; 56-61; LUDOWICI 2006; RÖTTING 1995, 7-14.
44. BINDING 1996, 257, Abb. 76 (Kaiserslautern); 270, Abb. 79 (Gelnhausen); 354, Abb. 158 (Wimpfen).
45. TWACHTMANN-SCHLICHTER 2007, 255-260; besonders 257-258 mit Abb.
46. Zum Westflügel: WANGERIN 1978, 91-92.

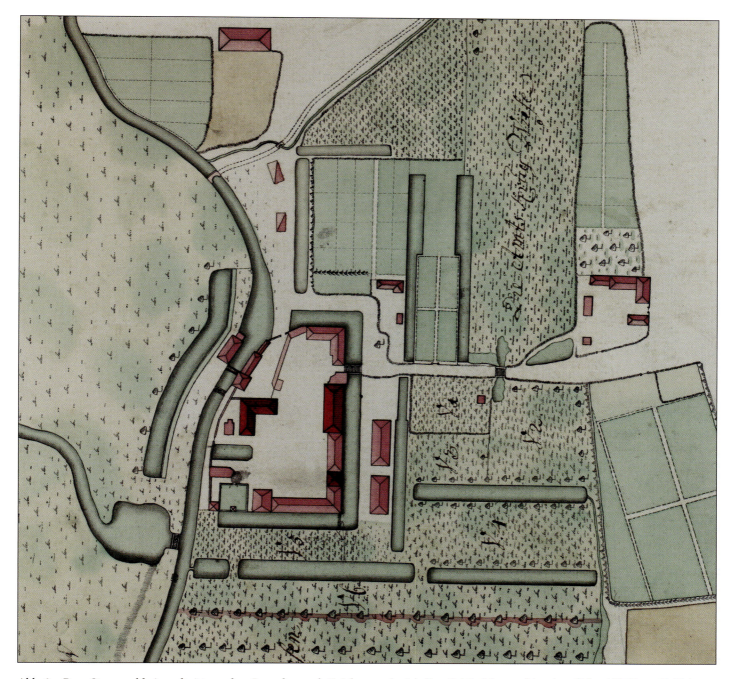

Abb. 2 – Burg Steuerwald, Ausschnitt aus dem Lageplan nach Deichmann (1769). Der Gebäudebestand ist eingefärbt. Abbildung T. Kohnert (nach Kohnert 2013, Abb. 18).

im zweiten Obergeschoss belegt. Allerdings scheint hier ein Widerspruch zur Darstellung bei Matthäus Merian d.Ä. (1653) vorzuliegen, zeigt diese doch eine andere Giebelform[47].

Die Existenz eines Kellers bzw. etwaiger Anbauten an den Nordflügel konnten bei einer Sondage (1960) nicht eindeutig geklärt werden[48]. Betrachtet man den publizierten Grundriss (Abb. 3)[49], so fällt auf, dass die vermutete Innenwand des Ostflügels mindestens ein Fenster im Erdgeschoss des Nordflügels verschließen würde[50]. Dies spricht für die Interpretation der freigelegten Mauerreste als Reste eines

---

47. Twachtmann-Schlichter 2007, 278; Albrecht 2002, 15-19.
48. Wangerin 1978, 92-93; 93, Abb. 11.
49. Der Grundriss ist nicht genordet!
50. Wangerin 1978, 88, Abb. 5.

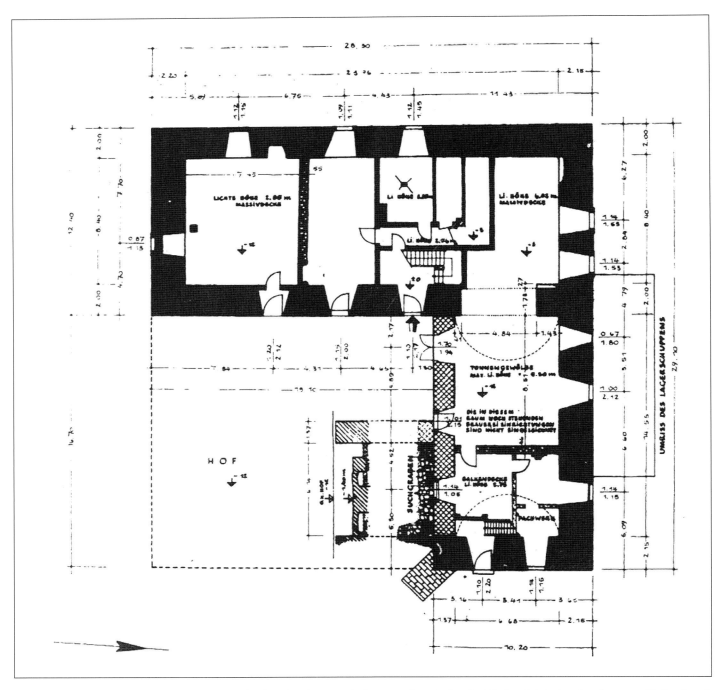

Abb. 3 – Burg Steuerwald, Grundriss des *Palas* (Erdgeschoss). Bauaufnahme aus dem Archiv des Niedersächsischen Landesamtes für Denkmalpflege (etwa 1960). Vgl. WANGERIN 1978, 88, Abb. 5.

Kellergewölbes (Entlastungsbogen; Abb. 4). Die Funktion des südwärts verlaufenden, heute vom Hofpflaster überdeckten Mauerfundamentes bleibt damit aber ungeklärt.

Für Burg Steuerwald möchte Gerda Wangerin sechs entscheidende Bauabschnitte festhalten[51]: Zunächst die Erbauung durch Bischof Heinrich II. (1310-1313), dann den unmittelbar anschließenden Aus- und Umbau unter Bischof Otto II. (1319-1331). Beide Abschnitte betreffen die innere Burganlage und damit auch den *Palas*.

Zwischen 1503 und 1527 wurde Steuerwald als ständiger Sitz von Bischof Johann IV. genutzt, unter Bischof Ferdinand erfolgten zwischen 1613 und 1650 eine weitere Modernisierung sowie kleinere Umbauten (bis 1689). Aus der letztgenannten Phase sind eventuell noch einige Fenster erhalten. 1632 wurde

51. WANGERIN 1978, 94.

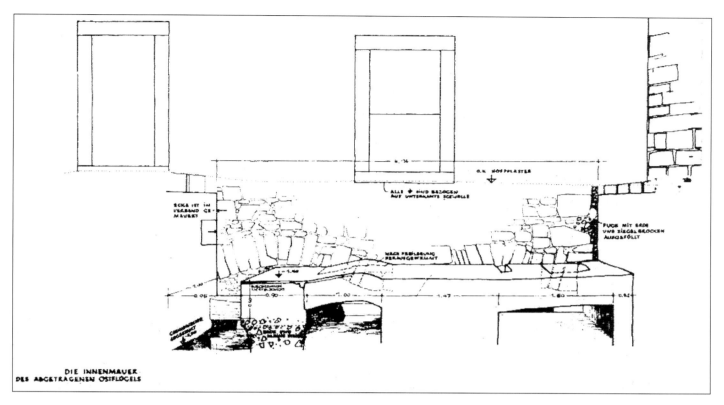

Abb. 4 – Burg Steuerwald, *Palas*. Schnitt durch den Profilgraben an der Südfassade des Nordflügels. Bauaufnahme aus dem Archiv des Niedersächsischen Landesamtes für Denkmalpflege (etwa 1960). Vgl. WANGERIN 1978, 93, Abb. 11.

Steuerwald eingenommen und in Teilen geschleift, 1689 wird erstmals eine Brauerei eingerichtet.

Als fünfter Bauabschnitt sind die großzügigen Renovierungsarbeiten unter Bischof Clemens August (1724-1761) zu erwähnen; 1728 werden die Fenster im Nordflügel erneuert, wie eine Bauinschrift belegt[52]. Der Abbruch des Süd- und Ostflügels erfolgte wohl kurz davor[53].

In Folge der Säkularisation sind weitere Umbauten zu verzeichnen; diese betrafen aber vor allem die Wirtschaftsgebäude und nicht mehr den *Palas* selbst[54].

Die folgenden Fassadenbeschreibungen stellen nur die wesentlichsten für die Baugeschichte bedeutsamen Befunde vor[55].

Zunächst ist die hofseitige Fassade des Westflügels zu diskutieren (Fassade Ost 2; Abb. 5 a). Dieses Gebäude wird anhand der Archivalien der ersten Bauphase zwischen 1310 und 1313 zugeschrieben[56].

Gewichtigstes Argument für den Anbau des heutigen Nordflügels an den Westbau ist die fehlende Verzahnung des Mauerwerks an der inneren Ecke der beiden Flügelbauten (O2-05). Dem steht gegenüber, dass an der südöstlichen Gebäudeecke die Quadereckverzahnung von der Mauerkrone bis zum Terrain fehlt (O2-01). Dies ist ein möglicher Hinweis auf den Ansatzpunkt eines mittlerweile geschleiften Gebäudeflügels. Für einen ehemaligen Südflügel des Gebäudes spricht auch der Gewändestreifen aus sorgfältig gehauenen Quadern, der nach einer durchaus realistischen Außenmauerstärke mit einer nach innen gerichteten glatten Mauerfuge abschließt. In einem Abstand von 5,75 m wiederholen sich diese Gewändequader (O2-02). Die Vermutung liegt nahe, dass sich an dieser Stelle einst ein Durchgang vom Westflügel zum möglichen Südflügel befunden hat.

Die Befundlage an der anderen Hoffassade (Süd 1) ist eindeutiger (vgl. Abb. 5 b). Hier sind klar Ansatzpunkte von zwei Außenmauern zu erkennen. Burg Steuerwald muss also spätestens in der zweiten Bauphase zu einer vierflügeligen Anlage umgestaltet worden sein. Der sich ergebende Innenhof hätte lediglich die Abmessung von maximal 5 x 9 m besessen und wäre durch die enorme Gebäudehöhe nur gering belichtet gewesen[57]. Da sich in West- und Nordflügel keine Toröffnung befindet, muss sich der Zugang auf der östlichen

---

52. TWACHTMANN-SCHLICHTER 2007, 279.
53. Da auf einem Stich von M. Merian (1653) der Ostflügel des Palas noch zu sehen ist, wird er wohl zu dieser Zeit noch bestanden haben (WANGERIN 1978, 85, Abb. 1).
54. TWACHTMANN-SCHLICHTER 2007, 280.
55. Die ausführliche Dokumentation kann im Institut für Denkmalpflege der HAWK Hildesheim sowie im Bauarchiv der Stadt Hildesheim eingesehen werden. Vgl. auch ALBRECHT 2002, 1-26 (Erfassung der Bauschäden).
56. WANGERIN 1978, 89; 91-92.
57. Vgl. hierzu Fußnote 42.

Abb. 5 a – Burg Steuerwald, *Palas*. Hofseitige Fassade des Westflügels (Fassade Ost 2; 2012). Graphik M. C. Blaich.

Abb. 5 b – Burg Steuerwald, *Palas*. Hofseitige Fassade des Nordflügels (Fassade Süd 1; 2012). Graphik M. C. Blaich.

oder der südlichen Seite befunden haben. Über die Gestalt dieses Zugangs zum Innenhof sind keine Aussagen möglich.

Unterhalb und seitlich des Balkons zeigt sich eine massive Störung des Mauerwerks (O2-20). Hier wurden großflächige Ausbesserungsmaßnahmen vorgenommen. Neben Bruchsteinen und Backsteinen sind beispielsweise Fragmente von Dachziegeln in eine dicke Mörtelschicht eingedrückt worden. Die Ausbesserung muss eine Folge der vorangegangenen Schleifung des südlichen Anbaus sein[58].

Die Ausmauerung der großen Gebäudeöffnung im dritten Obergeschoss ist vermutlich zur gleichen Zeit ausgeführt worden (O2-03)[59]. Auf gleicher Höhe sind an der nördlichen Fassadenseite zwei große Entlastungsbögen zu erkennen (O2-07). Sie sind wohl den Fenstergewänden O2-06 und O2-21 zugehörig und stammen aus der ersten Bauphase des Gebäudes. Diese Gewände unterscheiden sich in Form, Anordnung und Bearbeitungstechnik von allen übrigen Fenster- und Türgewänden.

Die Befunde O2-19 zeigen Störungen im homogenen, lagigen Mauergefüge, die für einen nachträglichen Einbau der Fensteröffnung in das Mauerwerk sprechen. Im Sturz der nördlichen Tür befindet sich eine Inschrift mit einer Datierung (O2-09). Die eingemeißelten Kapitalen auf dem scharrierten und auf der Innenseite abgefasten Sandstein zeigen wohl die Initialen bzw. Abkürzungen der am Bau der Anlage beteiligten Bischöfe: „CAC ZCH BZH BVM RENNOVIRT ANNO 1728"[60]. In Verbindung mit der historischen Überlieferung zu den Renovierungsarbeiten unter Bischof Clemens August im Jahr 1728 ist anzunehmen, dass alle Fenster- und Türgewände dieser Art auf das gleiche Jahr zu datieren bzw. der gleichen Umbauphase zuzurechnen sind. Das erste Obergeschoss zeichnet sich durch einen auffälligen Balkon aus, dessen Austritt von drei relativ mächtigen Konsolen getragen wird. Die Gewändesteine sind der Umbauphase im 18. Jahrhundert zuzuordnen.

Im Folgenden soll noch der Nordflügel des *Palas* betrachtet werden (Fassade Süd 1; Abb. 5 b). Dieser Trakt ist mit Außenmaßen von 10,2 x 16,7 m deutlich kleiner als der Westflügel. Gerda Wangerin zufolge ist dieses Gebäude unter Bischof Otto II. (1319-1331) entstanden. Beleg hierfür sind die an der Nordfassade (Außenmauer) im dritten Obergeschoss noch sichtbaren, hochrechteckigen und gekuppelten Fenstergewände[61] und ein auf der Giebelseite im Inneren zwischen Nord- und Westflügel vortretendes Mauerstück, das als Bestandteil der ehemaligen äußeren Ostwand zu deuten ist.

Es sind wohl die beiden inneren Laibungen S1-01 und S1-02, der Entlastungsbogen S1-03, die zwei Fensterlaibungen S1-05 und S1-06 sowie die Türlaibung S1-07 bauzeitlich, d.h. der Zeit von Bischof Otto II. (1319-1331) zuzuordnen. Die beiden Laibungen S1-01 und S1-02 stellen – wie die Fensterlaibung S1-06 – auch ein gewichtiges Argument für die ehemalige Existenz eines Ostflügels dar: Diese Öffnung könnte beispielsweise zu einem offenen Durchgang oder gar einer Galerie geführt haben, die das Obergeschoss des heute nicht mehr bestehenden Gebäudes einnahm[62].

Der Abbruch des Ostflügels muss auch den Verschluss der Öffnung zwischen den beiden Laibungen S1-01 und S1-02 mit dem Bruchsteinmauerwerk S1-43 bedingt haben. Relativchronologisch zeigen S1-09 (Entlastungsbogen) und S1-13 (Fensteröffnung), dass dies vor deren Einbringen geschehen sein muss, denn die beiden Befunde sind in das Mauerwerk eingesetzt. Beachtung verdient aber die Tatsache, dass bei diesem Fenster – anders als bei den anderen Öffnungen – kein ausgebrochenes Mauerwerk zu beobachten ist. Vielmehr scheint es so zu sein, dass das Fenster in das Bruchsteinmauerwerk eingesetzt wurde. Dies würde die Datierung der Umbaumaßnahmen bzw. des Abbruchs (Ostflügel) in das Jahr 1728 zusätzlich stützen.

Während unklar bleibt, ob sich die Umbauten des Jahres 1617 an der Außenwand überhaupt erkennen lassen, so ist für das Jahr 1728 der Einbau neuer Fenster mit Sandsteingewänden überliefert[63]. Zu diesen Fenstern gehören auch die heute noch sichtbaren Entlastungsbögen[64], d.h. der Einbau dieser Fenster setzt das Vermauern älterer Öffnungen voraus. Mit S1-17 und S1-18 sind die für den Einbau der neuen Fenster in das ältere Mauerwerk gebrochenen Öffnungen besonders gut erhalten.

Die Entlastungsbögen S1-19 bis S1-21 sowie die zugehörigen Türöffnungen S1-22 bis S1-24 sind ebenfalls diesen Renovierungsarbeiten zuzuordnen. Auch bei diesen Türen sind die Ausbruchöffnungen sowie Mörtelreste (S1-25) noch zu erkennen.

Die vier Fenster- oder Türöffnungen S1-26 bis S1-29 sind, der Bauweise und dem Material nach zu urteilen, bauzeitlich (1319-1331). Sie müssen allerdings spätestens im Jahr 1728 verschlossen worden sein. Allein das Fenster S1-26 könnte erst in jüngerer Zeit (19./20. Jahrhundert) zugemauert worden sein, wie die Verwendung von sehr akkurat zugehauenen Blöcken (S1-41) zeigt.

Mit den Umbauten des Jahres 1728 wird auch der Abbruch des Ostflügels verbunden. Das Fehlen einer Eckquaderung und die großflächigen Ausbesserungsarbeiten im Obergeschoss (S1-08) rühren sicherlich daher.

Wo die für das Jahr 1689 überlieferte Brauereistube ihren Platz gefunden hatte, ist unbekannt. Für das Jahr 1819 hingegen

---

58. Dies soll G. Wangerin zufolge (WANGERIN 1978, 94) vor den großzügigen Renovierungsarbeiten unter Bischof Clemens August geschehen sein.
59. Oberhalb der Ausmauerung wurde das Mauerwerk großflächig ausgebessert. Diese Veränderung steht im Zusammenhang mit den jüngsten Sanierungsarbeiten am Dach und dem Einbau der Stehgaube.
60. Die Inschrift ist aufzulösen wie folgt: „C(lemens) A(ugust), C(urfürst) z(u) C(öln), H(erzog) i(n) B(ayern), B(ischof) z(u) H(ildesheim), B(ischof) z(u) M(ünster), rennovirt Anno 1728": TWACHTMANN-SCHLICHTER 2007, 279.
61. WANGERIN 1978, 92, Abb. 10.
62. Allerdings wäre auch die Existenz eines Holzerkers möglich, was wiederum ein Argument gegen einen Ostflügel darstellt. Vgl. hierzu KLEIN 2004.
63. Bef. S1-13 bis S1-16.
64. Bef. S1-09 bis S1-12.

sind umfangreiche Umbauten und der Anbau einer Brauereistube belegt. Sehr wahrscheinlich sind die Innenwandung eines Schornsteins (S1-34) und der Ansatz für ein Dach (S1-35) in diesem Jahr entstanden.

Derartige Malzdarren waren vielfach doppelstöckig angelegt: unter einem Schütttrichter für das Malz befand sich die Pfanne für das zu darrende Grünmalz; unter der Pfanne sorgte ein Ofen mit Feuerraum für die erforderliche Hitze, durch seitliche Schlitze rutsche das gedarrte Malz in bereitstehende Behälter[65]. Eine derartige, drei übereinander liegende Bereiche umfassende Anlage könnte in dem fraglichen Bereich zwischen Erdboden und Schornsteinansatz durchaus ihren Platz gefunden haben, stehen doch immerhin Erdgeschoss und erstes Obergeschoss zur Verfügung (Gesamthöhe etwa 5 m).

Möglicherweise wurde seinerzeit auch die Tür S1-36 vergrößert, wie die aus verschiedenen Materialien gefertigte Türlaibung andeutet. Die Türen S1-24 und S1-25 wurden zugemauert[66], nach Abriss des Brauhauses wurde in die Tür S1-24 wieder ein Fenster eingebaut[67].

Der an der Südostecke des Flügels angesetzte Strebepfeiler (S1-39)[68] stammt aus dem Jahr 1933; er ist möglicherweise eine Reaktion auf die an der Fassade zu beobachtenden Setzungsrisse[69]. Stellenweise ist noch der anpassende Mörtel (S1-40) erhalten.

Bei den an der Fassade zu erkennenden Strukturen ist die Verknüpfung mit den oben genannten historischen Daten offensichtlich. Es ergibt sich hieraus für einige der Befunde eine absolute Datierung, die als Gerüst für eine relative Abfolge der anderen Befunde dienen konnte[70].

Die oben erörterte chronologische Abfolge beruht nicht zuletzt auf den Beobachtungen zum verwendeten Baumaterial. So fällt auf, dass die an anderen Fassaden vorhandenen Eckquader aus dem gleichen Gestein gearbeitet sind wie die Laibungen verschiedener Öffnungen. Es handelt sich um große und abgearbeitete, aber nicht regelmäßig quaderförmige Werksteine. Diese sind mit einem hellgrauen Kalkmörtel verbunden. Diese Übereinstimmung legt auch für die Öffnungen S1-09 eine Datierung in die Jahre von 1319 bis 1331 nahe.

Für die 1728 eingebauten Fenster wurden als Gewände große, lange Quader aus Sandstein verwendet; ihre Innenseiten sind abgefast. Die zugehörigen Entlastungsbögen sind aus mittelgroßen Bruchsteinen gesetzt; kleinteilige, unregelmäßig geformte Bruchsteine verschiedener Herkunft in hellgrau-weißlichem Kalkmörtel wurden zum Verschließen der Ausbruchstellen verwendet.

Ziegelsteine verschiedener Formate und kleinere Bruchsteine wurden für den Schornstein der 1819 errichteten Brauereistube sowie die damit verbundenen Umbaumaßnahmen verwendet.

Die durch den Abbruch des Ostflügels entstandene Ausbruchstelle im Obergeschoss wurde mit kleinteiligem Material verschlossen.

Für den 1933 errichteten Stützpfeiler wurden mittelgroße, zugerichtete Werksteine und ein hellgrau-weißlicher Kalkmörtel verarbeitet; dieses Material unterscheidet sich durch seine Zurichtung gut von den nachweislich älteren Befunden.

Der Hauptflügel im Westen stammt aus der Entstehungszeit der Burganlage unter Bischof Heinrich II. (1310-1313). Der längsrechteckige Grundriss des *Palas* (Außenmaße: 28,3 m Länge und 12,4 m Breite) lässt aufgrund der Quaderverzahnung seiner nördlichen Giebelwand mit der westlichen Längswand des Nordflügels auf deren Funktion als Außenmauer der inneren Burganlage schließen (vgl. Abb. 3)[71]. Das Mauerwerk besteht vorwiegend aus unbehauenem Buntsandstein in regelmäßiger Lagerung[72].

Die Längswände des Hauptflügels haben beide eine Mauerstärke von 2 m, die südliche Giebelwand ist 2,2 m stark und die nördliche 2,15 m. Die Verzahnung an der Nordwest- und an der Südwestecke erfolgte mit Sandsteinquadern. Die fehlende Eckverquaderung an der Südostecke deutet auf einen Anschluss des Hauptflügels an die ehemalige Umfassungsmauer als Fortsetzung der südlichen Querwand hin.

Erdgeschoss und erstes Obergeschoss des Westflügels sind durch spätere Um- und Einbauten stark verändert. Der Umbau der Fenster (1728) wurde bereits erwähnt. In die ursprünglich 3,4 m hohen Räume im Erdgeschoss wurde aus unbekannten Gründen ein erstes Obergeschoss als Zwischengeschoss mit einer lichten Höhe von 2,84 m eingezogen. Da die gesamten Fenster an der Ostfassade von 1728 stammen, ist auch der Einzug des Zwischengeschosses in diese Umbauphase einzuordnen.

Im dritten Obergeschoss ist die ehemalige Funktion des Gebäudes jedoch noch gut zu erschließen. Der ehemalige sogenannte „Rittersaal" oder „Festsaal" (Abb. 6) stammt aus der ersten Bauphase. Er stellt den repräsentativsten Raum dar und nimmt die gesamte Geschossfläche ein. Die Erschließung erfolgt heute durch eine Holzwangentreppe in der Mitte des Saals auf der Ostseite und ist mit einer Klappe verschließbar. Die Holzbalkendecke stammt von 1651-1653 (d)[73].

Die Verbindung zum Nordflügel erfolgt im nördlichen Abschnitt der Ostwand über einen breiten Durchgang. Davon

---

65. Heyen 1998, 229-230.
66. Bef. S1-37 und S1-38.
67. Denkbar wäre auch eine andere Interpretation: Demnach wäre die Tür S1-36 Bestandteil der Darrstube (Zugang vom Inneren des Gebäudes) gewesen und wurde erst nach deren Abriss verschlossen bzw. zu einem Fenster umgebaut.
68. Wangerin 1978, 91, Abb. 9.
69. Diese Risse verlaufen vom Trauf aus zum Boden hin, d.h. von links oben nach rechts unten. Sie könnten entstanden sein, weil das Gebäude auf dem sandigen Baugrund ungleich absackte.
70. In den Darstellungen wurden nicht alle Steine und Mörtelflächen nachgezeichnet; die Auswahl beschränkt sich auf eindeutige und gut nachzuvollziehende Strukturen.
71. Vgl. Wangerin 1978, 91.
72. Ruchniewitz 2007, 24.
73. Albrecht 2002, 16.

Abb. 6 – Burg Steuerwald, *Palas*. Grundriss des zweiten Obergeschosses (sogenannter „Rittersaal"). Graphik T. Kohnert und M. C. Blaich.

zeugt ein hervortretendes Mauerstück an der nördlichen Anschlussstelle zum Nordflügel, das vermutlich ursprünglich Teil der östlichen Außenwand des Hauptflügels war. Heute zeugt davon nur noch die Eckquaderung „mit einer gefasten Ecke und einem Rautenmotiv in der Fase des Anfangssteins"[74], die noch bis zum Bogenansatz erhalten ist. Letzte Spuren ehemaliger Durchgänge finden sich auch an der südlichen Hälfte der Ostwand des Westflügels und an der Südwand des Nordflügels. Das folgende Fenster an der Ostwand zeigt über dem Entlastungsbogen noch Spuren eines Entlastungsbogens, der zu einem älteren Fenster gehörte. Weiter in der Mitte der Wand finden sich Spuren einer zugemauerten, vermutlichen Kapellennische. An der Südhälfte der Wand findet sich der schon erwähnte zweite ehemalige Durchgang, welcher durch einen Segmentbogen gekennzeichnet ist (Abb. 7). Um 1728 wurde hier eine Ladeöffnung eingesetzt, die mit einer hölzernen Tür geschlossen werden kann. Im Zuge der landwirtschaftlichen Nutzung des Geschosses diente diese Öffnung zum Einbringen von Lasten[75].

Der zwischen 1319 und 1331 errichtete nördliche Flügel hat eine Länge von 16,7 m und ist 10,2 m breit (vgl. Abb. 3). Die an den Westflügel angrenzende Umfassungsmauer weist die

---

74. Ruchniewitz 2007, 34.

75. *Ibid.*, 34-35.

Abb. 7 – Burg Steuerwald, *Palas*. Zugemauerter Durchgang im zweiten Obergeschoss (Westflügel). Foto T. Kohnert, 2012.

gleiche Mauerstärke wie die des Nordgiebels auf und wurde vermutlich für die nördliche und östliche Außenwand des neuen Flügels verwendet. Die südliche Außenmauer des Nordflügels weist mit einer Mauerstärke von 1,37 m eine geringere Stärke als die übrigen Außenwände auf. Dies deutet darauf hin, dass die hofseitige Außenmauer keinerlei Abwehrfunktion zu übernehmen hatte. Der Ostgiebel hat eine Stärke von 3,18 m. Die Fenster der ersten vier Geschosse stammen alle aus der Umbauphase von 1728. Nur die Öffnungen in den beiden Dachgeschossen sind nachweislich aus der Entstehungszeit. Reste von älteren Entlastungsbögen finden sich oberhalb der Fenster im Erdgeschoss sowie in den folgenden Obergeschossen.

Das Erdgeschoss des Nordflügels (vgl. Abb. 3) ist direkt mit dem Hauptflügel im Westen verbunden[76]. Anfang des 17. Jahrhunderts wurde ein Tonnengewölbe mit einer Höhe von 5,3 m eingezogen. Der Sturz der Eingangstür und Konsolsteine im Inneren sind mit bärtigen Männermasken geschmückt, die mit ihrer Inschrift „1617" auf das Jahr der Renovierung unter Bischof Ferdinand (1613-1650) hinweisen. 1819 wurde in dem Raum eine Brennerei eingerichtet, Mitte des 19. Jahrhunderts eine Brauerei.

Während das erste Obergeschoss durch starke Umbaumaßnahmen überprägt ist, ähnelt der große, saalähnliche Raum im zweiten Obergeschoss dem sogenannten „Rittersaal" im Westflügel. In der östlichen Hälfte der Südwand finden sich Reste eines Segmentbogens, der auf einen möglichen Durchgang zu einem weiteren Gebäudeflügel hinweist. Beide Flügel tragen ein Satteldach mit einheitlicher Firsthöhe. Der noch intakte Dachstuhl stammt von 1652/1653[77].

6. Zu den historischen Bildquellen

Dem historischen Kartenmaterial ist zur Baugestalt von Burg Steuerwald wenig zu entnehmen. Der Bergfried ist jedes Mal

---

76. Ist das Fehlen einer Baufuge ein Hinweis darauf, dass die Burg von Anbeginn als vierflüglige Anlage geplant war?

77. ALBRECHT 2002, 16; TWACHTMANN-SCHLICHTER 2007, 278; vgl. RUCHNIEWITZ 2007, 31.

klar zu erkennen, die Baugestalt des *Palas* jedoch ist stark vereinfacht. Offensichtlich dient die Burganlage als Bezugspunkt in der Landschaft, die kartographische Darstellung verfolgt jedoch andere Ziele.

Allerdings sind auf den historischen Karten die ehemals die Burg umgebenden Wassergräben deutlich zu erkennen. Der Zugang zum Burghof erfolgte über eine Brücke aus östlicher Richtung und über zwei kleinere Brücken von Nordwesten. Erst auf einer Karte von 1685 sind *Palas* und Burganlage in heutiger Gestalt abgebildet[78]. In der Plandarstellung von 1769 (vgl. Abb. 2) ist die Darstellung aller Gebäude mit Walmdächern auffällig, was die Vermutung nahe legt, dass es sich hierbei um eine abstrahierte und vereinheitlichte Darstellung der Gebäude handelt[79]. Jedoch ist das Ausmaß der Burganlage zuverlässig dargestellt und auch die Größenverhältnisse der Gebäude untereinander sind realitätsnah[80].

Bei einer der meist verwendeten Abbildungen von Steuerwald handelt es sich um den Kupferstich von Matthäus Merian d.Ä. aus dem Jahr 1653 (Abb. 8)[81]. Der Stich zeigt auch die im Dreißigjährigen Krieg (1618-1648) entstandenen Schäden. Im Bereich des *Palas* sind zwei freistehende Giebel (mit Schornstein?) zu erkennen. Die Dächer dahinter und auch das Dach des Bergfrieds fehlen jedoch.

Diese Abbildung lässt sich auf zwei, einander durchaus widersprechende Arten deuten: Die erste Möglichkeit geht davon aus, dass es sich um die parallel stehenden Nord- und Südgiebel des Westflügels handelt. Demnach wäre der Westflügel des *Palas* noch nicht wieder gedeckt, denn zwischen 1651 und 1653 wurden der noch heute stehende Dachstuhl und die Decke des zweiten Obergeschosses in Nord- und Westflügel neu errichtet. Die zweite Möglichkeit sieht in den beiden Giebeln die Südgiebel des westlichen und des östlichen Gebäudetraktes. Die nebeneinander stehenden Giebel stammten demnach von zwei unterschiedlichen Gebäuden und gäben damit einen Hinweis auf die ehemalige Baugestalt des *Palas* als Vierflügel-Anlage mit Innenhof[82].

Leider hilft bei dieser Diskussion der ebenfalls 1653 in der Werkstatt von Matthäus Merian d.Ä. entstandene Stich zur Stadt Hildesheim nicht weiter[83]. Hildesheim ist hier aus südöstlicher Richtung dargestellt, Burg Steuerwald liegt im Hintergrund. Hier sind vom *Palas* zwei Satteldächer zu erkennen, und zwar jeweils mit ihrer östlichen Giebelscheibe – doch diese Situation ist weder mit oben diskutiertem Kupferstich noch mit dem heute noch vorhandenen Baubefund vereinbar.

Um das Jahr 1770 entstanden durch den braunschweigischen Landschaftsmaler Pascha Johann Weitsch (1723-1803)[84] zahlreiche Bilder und Skizzen vom alten Hochstift Hildesheim. Zu Burg Steuerwald liegen ein Aquarell und eine Federzeichnung vor (Abb. 9). Die Zeichnung zeigt Steuerwald aus nordöstlicher Richtung, das Aquarell aus südöstlicher Richtung[85]. Diese Darstellungen sind insofern von großem Wert, als sie vor den tiefgreifenden Umbaumaßnahmen im Jahr 1819 entstanden. Allerdings bestehen zwischen der Federzeichnung und dem Aquarell zahlreiche Unterschiede, die offensichtlich der späteren Überarbeitung im Atelier geschuldet sind. Dies betrifft die Proportionen der Nebengebäude und der Magdalenen-Kapelle, vor allem aber auch den Zustand des *Palas*. „Schließlich ist der bemerkenswerte Erker oder Zugang am Giebel auf dem Gemälde nicht so gut zu erkennen wie auf der Skizze. Sie ist die bessere historische Quelle für den Zustand des Amtes um 1770"[86].

Von großem Wert sind schließlich einige historische Photographien, die in den Jahren um 1933 entstanden sind. Die ältere der beiden Aufnahmen zeigt noch den Zustand vor den Sanierungs- und Sicherungsmaßnahmen, während auf der jüngeren der an der Südostecke des Nordflügels angesetzte Strebepfeiler zu erkennen ist (Abb. 10). Leider sind beide Photographien aus so großem Abstand aufgenommen worden, dass nur wenige Aussagen zum Mauerwerk entnommen werden können. Sie belegen aber, dass sich die äußere Gestalt des Gebäudes zwischen 1770 und 1933 fast nicht verändert hat[87] und geben Hinweise auf die ehemalige Nutzung als Wohngebäude. Auffällig ist die tiefgreifende Veränderung des Umfeldes: Die ehemaligen Stellflächen landwirtschaftlicher Geräte sind heute zu einer Grünanlage umgestaltet, ein Geräteschuppen wurde mittlerweile abgerissen.

7. Exkurs: Burg Steuerwald als Residenz der Hildesheimer Bischöfe?

Burg Steuerwald wird gelegentlich als „Residenz der Hildesheimer Bischöfe" bezeichnet. Damit soll offensichtlich der besonderen Bedeutung dieser Anlage für die Stadtgeschichte Hildesheims Rechnung getragen werden:

> Vor allem die 1310 errichtete Wasserburg Steuerwald war die wichtigste Stütze bischöflicher Macht und das Zentrum der Hofversorgung. Es heißt, dass derjenige Herr des Hochstifts sei, der Steuerwald besaß. Bis zum Ende des 16. Jh. blieb die Burg der beliebteste Wohnsitz der Bischöfe[88].

---

78. Der Plan wird im Stadtarchiv der Stadt Hildesheim unter der Inventar-Nummer StadtA Hi best. 950-00355-18 aufbewahrt.
79. Ein vergleichbarer Plan liegt auch aus dem Jahr 1766 vor („Grund-Riß des Fürstlichen Amtes Steuerwalt"). Hier sind die ehemaligen Zugänge über die Wassergräben und die Gestaltung des Kapellengartens deutlich zu erkennen. Der Plan wird im Stadtarchiv der Stadt Hildesheim unter der Inventar-Nummer StadtA Hi best. 950-0354 aufbewahrt.
80. Albrecht 2002, 23-24.
81. Wangerin 1978, 85, Abb. 1; Albrecht 2002, 21; 29-32.
82. Ruchniewitz 2007, 21.
83. Burg Steuerwald ist wegen der besseren Erkennbarkeit farbig unterlegt.
84. Müller-Hofstede 1973.
85. Albrecht 2002, 25-26.
86. Achilles 1977, 68.
87. Man beachte beispielsweise die Schleppgauben. Die beiden aussagekräftigsten Photos werden im Stadtarchiv der Stadt Hildesheim unter den Inventar-Nummern StadtA HI best. 951, Nr. 03598, und StadtA HI best. 951, Nr. 01343-16 aufbewahrt.
88. Aschoff 2000, 14.

Abb. 8 – Matthäus Merian d.Ä.: „Churfürstliches Ambsthaus im Stift Hildesheim" (1653). Abbildung: Verändert nach einer Reproduktion der im Stadtarchiv der Stadt Hildesheim unter der Inventar-Nummer StadtA HI best. 951-0805 aufbewahrten Vorlage.

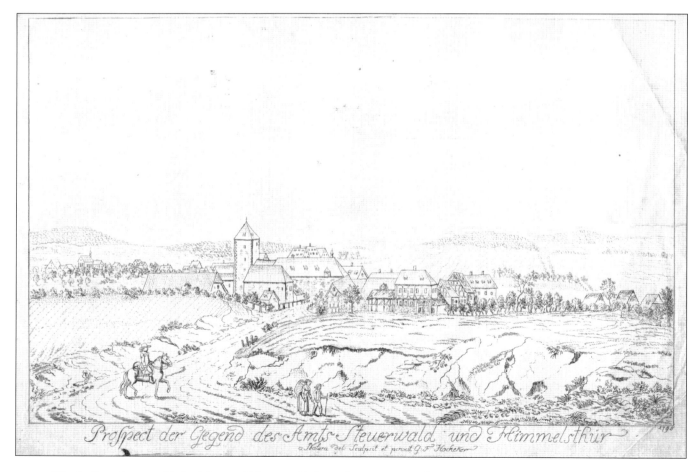

Abb. 9 – Burg Steuerwald, Ansicht von Südwesten. Federzeichnung von Pascha Weitsch (um 1770). Vgl. ACHILLES 1977, 70.

Abb. 10 – Burg Steuerwald, Ansicht von Südosten. Der Stützpfeiler an der Ecke des Nordflügels ist noch nicht vorhanden (um 1930). Foto StadtA HI best. 951, Nr. 03598.

Diese Aussage beruht letztlich auf der Einschätzung durch Gerda Wangerin[89]. Betrachtet man aber die vorliegenden Berichte und Urkunden genauer[90], so wird deutlich, dass Steuerwald unter Bischof Otto II. (1319-1331) häufiger als Wohnsitz diente, und dann noch einmal von den Bischöfen Ernst I. (1458-1460), Henning (1473-1481) und Johann IV. zwischen 1503 und 1527 ständig bewohnt wurde[91]. Nach der Reformation hielt sich Bischof Burchhard mit kurzen Unterbrechungen überwiegend in Steuerwald auf (1564-1573). Ansonsten wurde die Anlage von einem nachgeordneten Bediensteten, einem Drosten oder einem Vogt verwaltet[92]. Steuerwald und seine zugehörigen Ländereien waren offensichtlich, verglichen mit den anderen Gütern der Hildesheimer Bischöfe, überdurchschnittlich große Besitzkomplexe.

Gerade für die hier besonders interessierende Frühzeit von Burg Steuerwald liegen jedoch keine zuverlässigen Angaben vor, und die edierten Ausgaben des bischöflichen Urkundenbuchs erlauben – wie beinahe zu erwarten – nicht einmal die Rekonstruktion in einer Art bischöflichen Itinerars. Auch die kursorische Durchsicht der jüngeren Rechnungsbücher bestätigt diese Einschätzung; es gelingt nicht einmal, den mit der Verwaltung von Steuerwald betrauten Personenkreis vollständig zu erschließen[93]. Steuerwald wird also aller Wahrscheinlichkeit nach eben nicht als dauernder Wohn- und Herrschaftssitz des Bischofs gedient haben[94], dieser ist vielmehr im Bereich des Domareals zu suchen[95].

8. Zusammenfassung

Im Bistum Hildesheim entstehen im 14. Jahrhundert neben Steuerwald (1310-1313) noch zwei weitere Wasserburgen, die

---

89. Wangerin 1978, 86.
90. Eine vollständige Zusammenstellung bietet Albrecht 2002, 33-41.
91. Koken & Lüntzel 1832, 37-38; 46; 62.
92. *Ibid.*, 52-55; 89-90; Wangerin 1978, 85; 94. Demnach ist der erste Vogt für das Jahr 1395 bezeugt, ein Amtsschreiber ab 1434; vgl. auch die Zusammenstellung bei Albrecht 2002, 33-41.
93. Koken & Lüntzel 1832, 52-54.
94. Vgl. Neitmann 1989; Moraw 1991.
95. Hierfür spricht auch, dass nach der Bischofswahl der neue Amtsinhaber in einer Art Umritt von Steuerwald aus das Bistum in Besitz nahm und schließlich in Hildesheim einzog.

sich in Bautyp und Funktion ähneln. Marienburg (1346-1349), knapp 10 km entfernt, und Steinbrück im Fuhsetal (1370-1380), 20 km nordöstlich von Hildesheim, wurden nach einer nahezu identischen Bauart errichtet. Zwischen den auf annähernd rechtwinkligem Grundriss konzipierten Wasserburgen bestand zudem „durch den Abschluss mehrerer Landfriedensverträge und durch das Auftreten der Bischöfe als Vermittler in den Auseinandersetzungen zwischen den Hildesheimer Bischöfen, deren Stiftsadel, den Städten und den Welfen"[96] enger Kontakt. Das Prinzip der Rechtwinkelanlagen fand auch in den, an das Bistum Hildesheim, angrenzenden Gebieten Anwendung und entwickelte sich zu einer bestimmenden Bauform des 14. und 15. Jahrhunderts im Bereich des heutigen Niedersachsens bzw. Norddeutschlands. Diese drei Burgen stehen an dem für Norddeutschland baugeschichtlich bedeutsamen Übergang vom befestigten „festen Haus" zum repräsentativen, adligen Wohnsitz des 15./16. Jahrhunderts. Neben ihrem frühen Baudatum – das auf eine Art Vorreiterrolle schließen lässt – verdient vor allem die verglichen mit anderen Anlagen gute Erhaltung Beachtung[97].

Bei allen drei Burganlagen bildet der mit vier oder gar fünf Geschossen auf rechteckigem Grundriss ausgebildete „Palas" den dominierenden Baukörper. Alle Bauten bestehen aus größeren mit Mörtel gebundenen Bruchsteinen, sie weisen starke Außenmauern und ein zum Teil fensterloses Erdgeschoss auf, das als Bestandteil einer inneren Burganlage diente und von der ursprünglichen Funktion als Wehranlage zeugt. Schmale, gekuppelte spitzbogige Fenster an West- und Nordfassade des dritten Obergeschosses betonen in Steuerwald den repräsentativen Charakter des ehemaligen Saalgeschosses (Abb. 11). Gleiche Gestaltungselemente finden sich auch an der rhythmisch gegliederten Fassade des „Palas" der Marienburg, wo gekuppelte spitzbogige Fenster im ersten Geschoss, im Wohngeschoss sowie dem darüber liegenden Saalgeschoss zu finden sind[98]. Ähnlich wie bei Steuerwald und Marienburg weist auch die Fassade des „Palas" in Steinbrück Spuren gekuppelter und mit Maßwerk versehener Fenster für die repräsentativen Räume des Gebäudes auf[99].

Burg Steuerwald ist, wie die Darstellung des historischen Hintergrundes zeigt, offensichtlich ein „Herzstück der bischöflichen Macht"[100] im Hildesheimer Hochstift. Trotz

Abb. 11 – Burg Steuerwald, Nordgiebel des *Palas*: Doppelfenster des Saalgeschosses. Foto T. Kohnert, 2012.

aller Unwägbarkeiten vermag man diese Bedeutung auch im Baubestand des „Palas" noch abzulesen: es handelt sich um ein für seine Zeit ausgesprochen großes und mächtiges Gebäude, das seinesgleichen bemerkenswerter Weise nur noch in den anderen bischöflichen Burgen im Umland von Hildesheim findet[101]. Besonders faszinierend ist aber, dass die Fassaden zwar alle Spuren der sich beständig ändernden Nutzung zeigen, gleichwohl aber in ihrem Grundbestand seit der Errichtung vor beinahe 700 Jahren vollständig erhalten sind[102].

---

96. Wangerin 1981, 90-91.
97. Wangerin 1977, 83; Albrecht 1999, 174-189.
98. Wangerin 1977, 78.
99. Wangerin 1981, 87.
100. Patze 1997, 645.

101. Die Saalgeschossbauten der bischöflichen Burgen übertreffen hinsichtlich ihrer Höhe und Ausmaße die anderen, zeitgleichen Steinwerke deutlich: Meckseper 1999, 133.
102. Von den bischöflichen Burgen in Osnabrück und Bremen haben sich keinerlei Reste erhalten, die meisten der Burgen wichtiger Grafengeschlechter sind entweder zerstört oder durch Umbauten des 19. Jahrhunderts weitgehend überprägt: *ibid.*, 132.

Literatur

Achilles W. (1977), *Bilder aus dem alten Hochstift Hildesheim. Gemälde von Pascha Weitsch (1723-1803)*, Bd. I: *Hildesheim und der Nordteil*, Hildesheim, Gerstenberg.

Albrecht B. (2002), *Gut Steuerwald: Bauhistorische Untersuchung, Schadensaufnahme und Machbarkeitsstudie. Untersuchung im Auftrag der Steuerwald-Stiftung Hildesheim*, Unpubliziert, Hildesheim/Bad Salzdetfurth.

Albrecht U. (1995), *Der Adelssitz im Mittelalter. Studien zum Verhältnis von Architektur und Lebensform in Nord- und Westeuropa*, München/Berlin, Deutscher Kunstverlag.

– (1999), „Der spätmittelalterliche Burgenbau – Norddeutschland", in *Burgen in Mitteleuropa. Ein Handbuch*, Bd. I: *Bauformen und Entwicklung*, H. W. Böhme (hrsg.), Stuttgart, Theiss, 126-135.

Aschoff H.-G. (2000), *Das Bistum Hildesheim von seiner Gründung bis zur Säkularisation. Ein Überblick*, in *Ego Sum Hildesemensis – Bischof, Domkapitel und Dom in Hildesheim, 815 bis 1810*, U. Knapp (hrsg.), Petersberg, Imhof (Katalog des Dom-Museums Hildesheim; 3), 11-24.

Binding G. (1996), *Deutsche Königspfalzen. Von Karl dem Großen bis Friedrich II. (765-1240)*, Darmstadt, Primus-Verlag.

Böhme H. W. (2011), „Burgenbaukunst und Herrschaftsstreben am Mittelrhein und im Taunus während des Spätmittelalters", in *Befestigungen und Burgen am Rhein*, F. J. Felten (hrsg.), Stuttgart, Steiner (Mainzer Vorträge; 15), 47-74.

Heine H.-W. (2006), „Niederungsburgen des 14. Jh. in Niedersachsen archäologisch gesehen", *Die Kunde*, 57, 135-158.

Heyen H.-P. (1998), „Brautechnik im Wandel", in *Gerstensaft und Hirsebier – 5000 Jahre Biergenuß. Ausstellungskatalog Oldenburg 1998*, F. Both (hrsg.), Oldenburg, Isensee (Archäologische Mitteilungen aus Nordwestdeutschland, Beiheft; 20), 229-245.

Klein U. (2004), „Holz im Burgenbau – ein Überblick", in *Holz in der Burgenarchitektur*, B. Schock-Werner (hrsg.), Braubach, Deutschen Burgenvereinigung (Veröffentlichungen der Deutsche Burgenvereinigung, Reihe B; 9), 65-88.

Kohnert T. (2013), „Burgenforschung – Historische Bauforschung an Hildesheimer Burgen, mit einem kurzen Rückblick auf die Geschichte der Forschungsdisziplin", in *Die Domäne Marienburg bei Hildesheim – Von der Bischofsburg zum Kulturcampus*, T. Borsche et al. (hrsg.), Hildesheim, Gerstenberg, 91-108.

Koken K. L. & Lüntzel H. A. (1832), „Geschichte des Schlosses Steuerwald", *Mittheilungen geschichtlichen und gemeinnützigen Inhalts, für das Fürstentum Hildesheim und die Stadt Goslar* 1, 23-104.

Kruppa N. & Wilke J. (2006), *Das Bistum Hildesheim 4. Die Hildesheimer Bischöfe von 1221 bis 1398*, Berlin, De Gruyter (Germania Sacra; 46).

Kunstdenkmälerinventare Niedersachsens, *Neudruck des gesamten Werkes 1889-1976*, Herausgegeben in Zusammenarbeit mit dem Niedersächsischen Landesverwaltungsamt – Institut für Denkmalpflege – Hannover, Bd. XXX, Hannover, 203-212.

Ludowici B. (2006), „,Die Halle des Königs'. Repräsentative Profanarchitektur der ottonischen Pfalzen im Harzraum", in *Die Ottonen. Kunst, Architektur, Geschichte*, K. G. Beuckers, J. Cramer & M. Imhof (hrsg.), Petersberg, Imhof, 259-263.

Meckseper C. (1999), „Niedersachsen – Späte Burgen", in *Burgen in Mitteleuropa. Ein Handbuch*, Bd. II: *Geschichte und Burgenlandschaften*, H. W. Böhme (hrsg.), Stuttgart, Theiss, 131-134.

Moraw P. (1991), „Was war eine Residenz im späten Mittelalter?", *Zeitschrift für historische Forschung*, 18, 461-468.

Müller-Hofstede A. (1973), *Der Landschaftsmaler Pascha Johann Friedrich Weitsch (1723-1803)*, Braunschweig, Waisenhaus-Buchdruckerei und Verlag (Braunschweiger Werkstücke; 48).

Neitmann K. (1989), „Was ist eine Residenz? Methodische Überlegungen zur Erforschung der spätmittelalterlichen Residenzbildung", *Niedersächsisches Jahrbuch für Landesgeschichte*, 61, 1-38.

Patze H. (1997), *Geschichte Niedersachsens*, Bd. II, Teil I: *Politik, Verfassung, Wirtschaft vom 9. bis zum ausgehenden 15. Jahrhundert*, Hannover, Hahn (Veröffentlichungen der Historischen Kommission für Niedersachsen und Bremen; 36/2).

Reden-Dohna A. (von) (1995), *Die Rittersitze des vormaligen Fürstentums Hildesheim*, Göttingen, Barton.

Rötting H. (1995), *Das Modell Quartier St. Jakobi-Turnierstraße. Braunschweig-Altstadt um 1230*, Braunschweig, Herzog-Anton-Ulrich-Museum.

Ruchniewitz S. (2007), *Zur Geschichte der Burg Steuerwald unter besonderer Berücksichtigung des Saalgeschosses im zweiten Obergeschoss des Palas*, Unpublizierte Facharbeit zum Diplom im Fach Kunstwissenschaftliche Grundlagen der Restaurierung an der Hochschule für angewandte Wissenschaften und Kunst Hildesheim, Hildesheim.

Ruchniewitz S. & Sieroczek J. (2003), *Burg Steuerwald in Hildesheim: Restauratorische Befundsicherung der Architekturoberfläche im westlichen Trakt des 2. Obergeschosses des Palas mit besonderer Berücksichtigung historischer Daten*, Unpublizierte Facharbeit zum Diplom im Fach Konservierung und Restaurierung der Studienrichtung Wandmalerei/Architekturoberfläche, Fachbereich Konservierung und Restaurierung an der Hochschule für angewandte Wissenschaften und Kunst Hildesheim, Hildesheim.

Schulze M. (1981), „Wasserburg Steuerwald", in *Führer zu vor- und frühgeschichtlichen Denkmälern*, Bd. XLIX: *Hannover, Nienburg, Hildesheim, Alfeld*, Teil II: *Exkursionen*, Mainz, Von Zabern.

Twachtmann-Schlichter A. (2007), *Stadt Hildesheim. Denkmaltopographie Bundesrepublik Deutschland. Baudenkmale in Niedersachsen*, Bd. XIV.1, Hameln, Niemeyer.

Van den Heuvel Chr. & Boetticher M. (von) (hrsg.) (1998), *Geschichte Niedersachsens*, Bd. III, Teil I: *Politik, Wirtschaft und Gesellschaft von der Reformation bis zum Beginn des 19. Jahrhunderts*, Hannover, Hahn (Veröffentlichungen der Historischen Kommission für Niedersachsen und Bremen; 36/3).

Wangerin G. (1977), „Die Wasserburg ‚Castrum Mariae' im ehemaligen Bistum Hildesheim", *Burgen und Schlösser*, 18, 73-85.

– (1978), „Die Wasserburg Steuerwald nördlich von Hildesheim", *Burgen und Schlösser*, 19, 85-95.

– (1981), „Steinbrück im Fuhsetal, eine Wasserburg der Hildesheimer Bischöfe", *Burgen und Schlösser*, 22, 79-91.

Châteaux et frontière occidentale du comté de Champagne (XIIe-XIVe siècle)

François Blary*

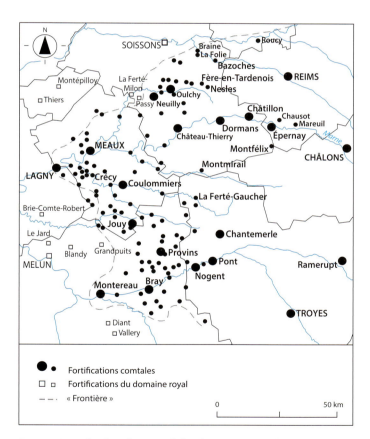

Fig. 1 – Carte des fortifications de la « frontière » occidentale du comté de Champagne et de Brie au XIIIe siècle. Carte F. Blary.

En 1285, la Champagne fut réunie aux domaines de la couronne par l'accession au trône de Philippe IV le Bel, comte palatin de Champagne depuis son mariage avec Jeanne de Navarre. La frontière qui séparait jusqu'à cette date le domaine royal des possessions des comtes a fait l'objet de quelques études historiques. Après les travaux érudits initiaux d'Henri d'Arbois de Jubainville[1] et d'Auguste Longnon[2], cette question a suscité les études pertinentes conduites par Jean Hubert[3] puis Michel Bur[4]. Les châteaux domaniaux ont déjà été abordés par Michel Bur[5] et surtout par Jean Mesqui[6]. Nous proposons ici de revenir sur ce thème et de compléter ce premier examen à partir des études archéologiques récentes conduites sur trois places fortes situées à la frontière occidentale du comté de Champagne : Château-Thierry[7], Fère-en-Tardenois[8] et Nesle-en-Dôle[9] (fig. 1). La première a fait l'objet de fouilles et les deux autres d'études du bâti. Il nous a paru intéressant de nous pencher sur la question du château et de la frontière en observant les effets sur la structure architecturale de sites contenus dans un espace clairement délimité dont le contexte historique est bien documenté. Pour ces résidences seigneuriales fortifiées, la confrontation des données écrites – ou nouvellement acquises par les fouilles ou l'examen attentif du bâti partiellement préservé – permet essentiellement d'apporter des précisions sur l'évolution d'un de ses aspects principaux : la fortification.

---

* Maître de conférences en histoire et archéologie médiévales, université de Picardie – Jules-Verne, TRAME (EA 4284), France.
1. Arbois de Jubainville 1859-1866, t. I et III.
2. Longnon 1901, t. I.
3. Hubert 1955, 14-30.
4. Bur 1976, 237-254.
5. Bur 1977 ; Bur 1982, 237-254.
6. Mesqui 1979, 7-86.
7. Blary 2013, 186-253.
8. Lefèvre-Pontalis 1911 ; Mesqui 1988 ; complété par Blary, observations de terrain réalisées en 2010-2011.
9. Héliot 1974 ; Mesqui 1988 ; complété par Blary, observations de terrain réalisées en 2010.

Le passage d'une entité comtale à une autre insérée dans le domaine royal permet d'isoler des caractéristiques architecturales identitaires. Le prisme de l'appartenance permet ainsi de nuancer les conclusions fondées sur la seule notion d'évolution poliorcétique que l'on développe généralement en archéologie pour les XIIIe et XIVe siècles.

L'étude menée sur le château de Château-Thierry montre que sous l'égide de Thibaud II de Champagne, le site castral défini à l'époque carolingienne fait l'objet d'une refonte importante. Le démantèlement de la ligne de fortification antérieure s'achève en 1130. Les tours de flanquement mises en place dès la fin du Xe siècle ou au début du XIe siècle sont réalisées en pierre, la ligne d'enceinte, seule, étant de bois. Pourquoi ne s'est-on pas limité à remplacer les courtines tout en conservant les tours préexistantes ? L'explication se trouve sans doute en considérant l'encombrement de la cour par les organes défensifs du XIe siècle. Le plan de la nouvelle enceinte montre clairement que la tour de flanquement ne forme plus de saillie vers l'intérieur de la cour mais se fond dans la ligne défensive. Cette nouvelle configuration, tout en conservant les limites antérieures, permet de disposer d'un espace d'activité protégé plus important. Il s'agit donc bien plus d'une amélioration de la défense préexistante en conservant les proportions de l'enceinte que d'un changement radical de l'art militaire : c'est « le changement dans la continuité ». L'organisation fonctionnelle du site ne varie pas : à l'ouest la basse cour, partie économique du site, à l'est, formant la barre de l'éperon, la tour maîtresse résidentielle et vraisemblablement administrative, protégeant l'église en limite des deux espaces.

La rupture avec le modèle du château à tour maîtresse-résidentielle s'effectue au début du XIIIe siècle. Comme nous le verrons plus loin, la fortification du XIIIe siècle consistait à augmenter l'espace initial défini au XIIe en le fortifiant progressivement. L'essentiel de l'enveloppe conservée date de cette période. Dans son état actuel, l'enceinte castrale comporte 18 tours, plus ou moins arasées ou ruinées.

Nous nous sommes livré à un examen approfondi de l'ensemble des tours de flanquement encore accessibles. Les flanquements présentent des caractéristiques qui permettent de distinguer plusieurs groupes. Jean Mesqui inventorie de manière générale les tours à l'aide de trois critères : le plan, le mode de couvrement intérieur et le type d'ouverture de tir ménagé pour chacune d'elles. Aussi, il nous a paru pertinent d'adjoindre à ces premiers éléments discriminants « classiques » de nouveaux critères qui permettent d'affiner notre examen : l'analyse de la composition des parements des revêtements de maçonnerie extérieurs et intérieurs, les modes d'accès, les éléments de confort prévus dès le début de la construction et le nombre de niveaux de circulation présents pour chaque tour.

Depuis la réunion de la principauté champenoise entre les mains de Thibaud II, les comtes champenois figurent parmi les plus grands féodaux du royaume. Après le règne du puissant Henri Ier le Libéral (1152-1181) commence une longue période de fragilité pour le pouvoir, marquée par des règnes courts et des régences se succédant jusqu'en 1222. Le château, de même que les autres places fortes du comté, n'a connu aucun programme particulier de fortification durant cette période. Il en va tout autrement sous le règne de Thibaud IV de 1222 à 1253[10] dont les *opera magna* ont déjà été largement soulignés et étudiés de manière pertinente[11]. Toutefois, l'analyse de l'enceinte castrale de Château-Thierry, forte de nouvelles données archéologiques, montre des aspects particuliers dans sa conception et précise la mise en œuvre du programme de fortification réalisé sous l'autorité comtale.

L'analyse architecturale fournit des indications intéressantes sur les schémas généraux de construction – étapes et organisation de la construction de l'enceinte, standardisation des dimensions et des dispositions des tours. En l'absence de marques lapidaires, l'observation minutieuse de l'agencement des parements et de la nature des matériaux employés permet de concevoir l'organisation de l'approvisionnement en pierre et, de ce fait, le processus d'édification de l'enceinte (fig. 2 et 3). La présence de blocs de calcaire et de grès montre l'exploitation simultanée d'au moins deux carrières. La standardisation des dimensions et du plan des tours, où sont présents des matériaux de construction différents, suggère la mise en place de plusieurs équipes opérant de concert. L'approvisionnement en pierre est une question importante pour la compréhension de l'ouvrage. L'analyse de l'agencement des parements intérieurs des tours 12 et 13 (fig. 3 et 4) montre clairement deux modes de construction, l'un privilégiant l'emploi du calcaire tendre oolithique, l'autre des matériaux mixtes, grès et calcaire grossier, n'utilisant le calcaire que dans les parties délicates à réaliser : angles de maçonnerie, piédroits et coussinets supportant le couvrement des archères. *In situ*, on note l'existence de nombreuses galeries souterraines, anciennement carrières d'extraction de matériaux de construction : pierres de calcaire grossier coquillier, de sables lutétiens et surtout cuisiens pour les liants. Le calcaire utilisé dans la construction des parements intérieurs de la tour 13 ne correspond pas à ce premier approvisionnement. Ce calcaire tendre provient d'une carrière éloignée de quelques kilomètres du site[12]. Toutefois, nous ne pouvons pas écarter l'idée d'une reprise légèrement plus tardive des parements intérieurs de la tour 13. Le grès, majoritairement utilisé pour l'élaboration des parements extérieurs, au XIIIe siècle, provient de carrières

---

10. En 1234, après la mort de Sanche VII le Fort son oncle, frère de sa mère Blanche de Navarre, Thibaud IV de Champagne reçoit la couronne de Navarre. Il est donc connu également sous le titre Thibaud Ier de Navarre.
11. Mesqui 1981, 203-229.
12. Ils sont issus d'une carrière souterraine située au nord-ouest de Château-Thierry, au lieu-dit de *Vincelles*, actuellement transformée en cave à champagne, dont la tradition locale se fait l'écho. Pour l'analyse géologique précise des différentes natures de calcaires utilisés dans les constructions du château et des carrières correspondantes, voir Blary *et al.* 2004, 50-51 et 60-75.

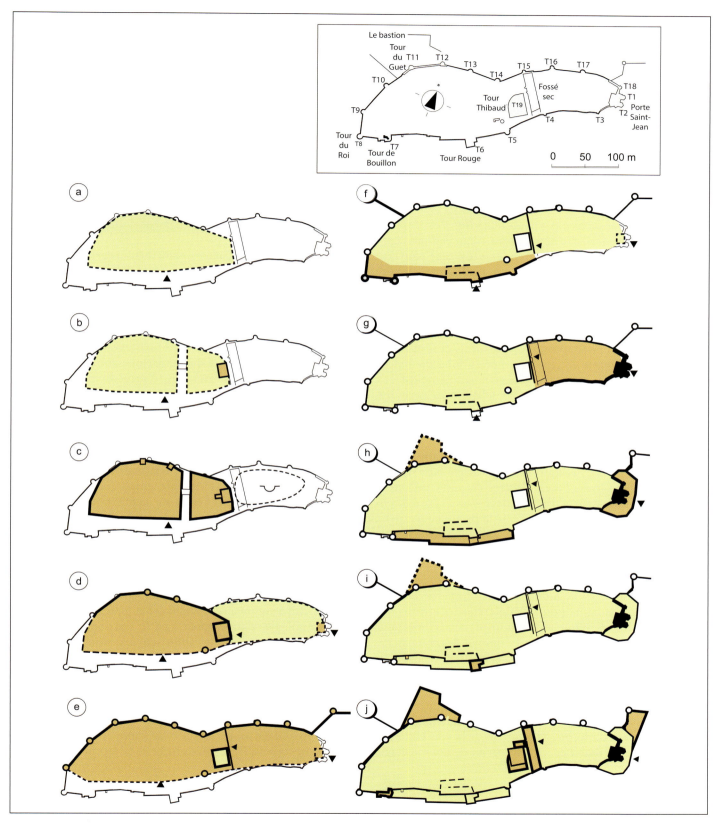

Fig. 2 – Château de Château-Thierry au XIIIe siècle replacé dans les grandes phases d'aménagements des fortifications du site. A) seconde moitié du IXe siècle ; B) première moitié du Xe siècle ; C) seconde moitié du Xe siècle ou début du XIe siècle ; D) campagne de 1120-1130 ; E) campagne de 1222-1236 ; F) campagne de 1230-1270 ; G) campagne de 1285-1316 ; H) campagne de 1386-1402 ; I) campagne de 1402-1407 ; J) campagne de 1478-1504. Dessin F. Blary.

proches, situées aux ruptures des plateaux ceinturant la vallée de la Marne. L'emploi quasi général du grès, dans plus de 80 % de la maçonnerie réalisée, peut se comprendre de plusieurs manières : soit du fait d'une relative pénurie de calcaire au regard de la facilité d'extraction et d'approvisionnement en grès qu'offre la région, soit en raison des considérations – fondées ou non – des bâtisseurs sur la plus grande résistance des matériaux de grès face au calcaire dans un usage militaire.

Les tours de flanquement : une stricte fonction défensive au nord

Les tours 12 et 13 observées lors des fouilles (fig. 3 et 4) appartiennent au groupe I, c'est-à-dire disposant d'un plan circulaire en fer à cheval pourvu de parement en grès, salle couverte par une coupole avec un accès sur cour, disposant d'archère simple étroite à ébrasement triangulaire.

La tour 12 remplace une tour préexistante, moins saillante par rapport à la ligne d'enceinte et probablement « passive », dépourvue d'archères dans les niveaux inférieurs. L'ensemble des tours de ce groupe adopte un plan en forme de fer à cheval dont le diamètre varie entre 6 et 7 mètres. Elles possèdent trois archères à ébrasement triangulaire et fente simple. Deux battent le flanc de l'enceinte, la troisième, disposée au centre, contrôle la pente du glacis. D'une hauteur de 1,20 mètre, leur largeur varie en fonction de leur position par rapport à l'enceinte entre 0,80 et 1,20 mètre. Elles sont couvertes par des dalles de grès reposant sur des coussinets de calcaire.

Le premier niveau des tours est voûté en coupole réalisée en pierre de taille calcaire, l'accès d'entrée, couvert d'un linteau sur coussinets, donne sur la cour. Toutes ces tours possédaient deux niveaux. Nous proposons, pour la partie haute, deux hypothèses de restitution qui purent très bien coexister de manière complémentaire en fonction de la disposition et du besoin propre à la défense de ces tours[13]. Dans la première, une simple terrasse protégée de créneaux permet de combiner l'usage d'engins de jet et la défense des remparts. Dans la seconde, une salle haute pourvue de créneaux et couverte d'une toiture prend appui sur un mur pignon à l'intérieur du site. Deux portes donnent sur le sommet des courtines.

La communication entre les niveaux inférieur et supérieur n'existe pas dans ces tours, à l'exception de la tour 10[14] qui se distingue au sein du groupe I par un système de communication intérieure complexe. La porte sur cour donne sur une petite galerie intermédiaire couverte de linteaux jointifs qui permet d'accéder, d'un côté, à l'intérieur de la salle basse par un escalier à cinq marches, de l'autre, au deuxième étage,

Fig. 3 – Fouille de l'enceinte nord du château de Château-Thierry, secteur 2 de la zone D1 et secteur 1 de la zone C1 en cours de fouille avec la courtine 11/12, la tour 12 et la courtine 12/13 en arrière-plan. Photo F. Blary.

par un escalier en enroulement sur la voûte en coupole du premier niveau et, ainsi, de rejoindre les circulations hautes des courtines. Dans le cas des autres tours, un escalier en bois pouvait être adossé à l'extérieur, au droit du mur d'enceinte, comme dans le cas de la tour 12 où ce type de structure a pu être distingué. La fonction de la tour du groupe I n'était pas, d'une manière générale, d'abriter la communication inter-niveaux, limitée au seul usage défensif.

À l'extérieur, ces tours, saillantes aux deux tiers, sont talutées à la base. Le glacis nord est vraisemblablement aménagé et revêtu de pierre, dans le même temps, comme au château de Fère-en-Tardenois (Aisne) sur lequel nous reviendrons plus loin. Au pied de la butte castrale et ceinturant l'enceinte urbaine se trouvent des douves alimentées en eau par captation des nombreuses sources provenant du plateau des Chesneaux au nord.

À ce stade, seule l'architecture des tours permet de dater cette phase de construction. Le plan en fer à cheval, le type d'archères à embrasure triangulaire et fente simple ainsi que la chronologie relative établie à partir des données stratigraphiques issues des fouilles autorisent à la situer dans la première moitié du XIIIe siècle. Bien que les sources historiques fassent totalement défaut, il paraît possible d'affiner la datation de cet ensemble. L'emploi systématique des voûtes en coupole fait l'objet d'une véritable mode dans le nord-ouest de la Champagne à partir de 1213[15]. Ce type de couvrement est présent dans toutes les tours de flanquement connues de l'enceinte urbaine[16]. Les ouvertures de tir étroites ménagées à

---

13. Cette proposition s'appuie sur l'observation des parties hautes de la tour 11 dite du Guet et les schémas offerts par les tours de l'enceinte urbaine mieux conservées avec notamment la porte Saint-Pierre datant de la même période (voir Mesqui 1981, 53 et suiv.).
14. Cette tour a disparu en avril 1988. Nous avions heureusement pu réaliser l'année précédente un dossier photographique complet et des relevés précis de l'ouvrage avant son affaissement.
15. Mesqui 1981, 66-68.
16. Seules sept tours de flanquement de l'enceinte du XIIIe siècle peuvent encore être observées ; cinq ont conservé leur voûte en coupole.

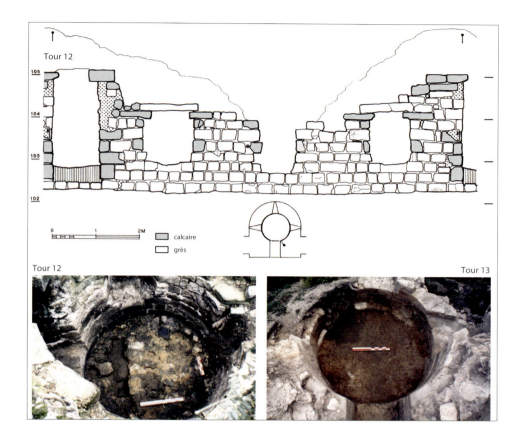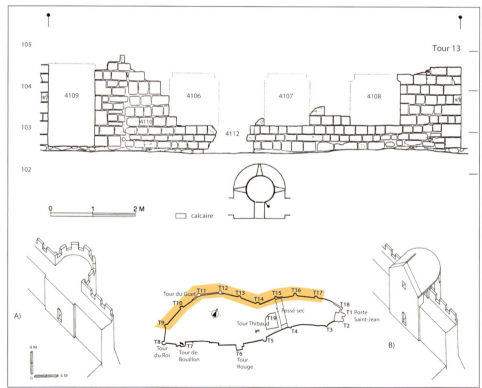

Fig. 4 – Analyse archéologique du bâti, relevés pierre à pierre en déroulé des parements intérieurs des tours 12 et 13 et vues aériennes de celles-ci. Proposition de restitution du volume des tours de flanquement à coupole. A) sans espace couvert au second niveau ; B) couverte avec mur de pignon côté cour. Photos et dessins F. Blary.

l'intérieur de ces ouvrages sont identiques au flanquement du groupe I du château. Celles-ci, selon Jean Mesqui, semblent exclusivement présentes en Champagne aux environs des années 30 du XIIIe siècle. Des quatre accès carrossables à la ville *intra muros* conservés, seule la porte, appelée Saint-Pierre ou de la Barre (fig. 5 a et b), constituée par deux tours encadrant le passage d'entrée, fournit des parallèles intéressants. Les salles basses de ces tours, voûtées d'ogives retombant sur des culs-de-lampe, sont dotées chacune de quatre archères en tous points identiques à celles observées sur le château. De plus, lors des travaux de restauration de cet ouvrage en 1987, une investigation archéologique sur les sols de ces deux tours a révélé l'existence d'une porte antérieure datée du XIIe siècle, constituée d'une tour en pierre au droit du passage d'entrée protégé par un fossé[17]. L'enceinte urbaine semble évoluer selon un schéma identique à celui constaté pour le château. Jean Mesqui, dans son analyse du contexte historique de l'ouest du comté de Champagne au XIIIe siècle, fait ressortir les phases principales pour l'activité de fortification entre 1201 et 1285. À l'instar de ce chercheur, nous pensons que l'étape de construction ne peut avoir débuté qu'après la régence de Blanche de Navarre, à la majorité de Thibaud IV, période marquée par son émancipation face au pouvoir royal entre 1222 et 1226. Toutefois, il paraît raisonnable de penser que l'essentiel de la campagne de fortification considérée fut lancé par Thibaud IV entre 1226 et 1236, lors des troubles guerriers. De nombreuses enceintes urbaines comme Provins ou Meaux furent élevées en grande hâte pendant cette période. Nous retiendrons donc, comme cadre chronologique de cette campagne, une période de quatorze ans comprise entre 1222 et 1236.

Extension sud

La chronologie des ouvrages mis en œuvre au sud est difficile à cerner. Les similitudes architecturales – emploi de la voûte à coupole pleine (tour 7) et forme des archères (tours 7 et 8) – plaideraient pour une contemporanéité de l'ensemble. Toutefois, les variantes – tours hautes à 3 ou 4 niveaux, salles à oculus (tours 5 et 8), salle planchéiée (tour 7), usage de la voûte à ogives quadripartites (tour 8) – forcent à reconsidérer cette proposition. La coexistence de la coupole et de la voûte sur ogives, à une même période, se rencontre également à Dourdan (Essonne). Il semble que le choix entre ces deux modes de couvrement n'était pas tranché. Leur emploi s'observe durant la première moitié du XIIIe siècle. La tour 7 planchéiée nous offre un premier élément de réponse. Les cas de Coucy (Aisne) et de Provins (Seine-et-Marne) observés par Jean Mesqui montrent que l'usage de planchers en remplacement de la voûte n'est pas antérieur à 1230[18].

La logique de l'aménagement qui consiste à augmenter les surfaces d'occupation au sud renforce notre sentiment. La constitution de cette portion d'enceinte ne s'appuie pas sur un tracé préexistant. L'irrégularité du plan des courtines souligne que cette extension a été réalisée par à-coups et non de manière linéaire et uniforme. Comment ne pas évoquer une rupture chronologique au regard de la régularité de la campagne précédente ? L'aménagement de tours mixtes résidentielles et défensives semble se justifier par rapport à l'occupation de la cour qu'elles protègent. La réalisation de l'enveloppe urbaine et castrale entre 1222 et 1230-1236 se conçoit dans un contexte politico-militaire comtal troublé. Cette phase s'attache, en revanche, à une refonte des espaces intérieurs, privilégiant la résidence seigneuriale.

L'imbrication des structures artisanales du IXe jusqu'au XIIe siècle, connues par les fouilles des zones D1-S2 et C1-S1, montre un réel manque d'espace. Au début du XIIIe siècle, ce secteur économique est transféré à l'est, dans une zone protégée par l'enceinte neuve de 1222-1230. L'espace ainsi libéré et élargi au sud permet la création d'une haute cour résidentielle digne de ce nom. Nous pourrions donc situer la mise en forme de ce programme dès la fin des époques guerrières qui déchirent le comté, soit à partir de 1230-1236. La relative disparité des aménagements de ces tours, l'irrégularité des plans et des dimensions des courtines, font penser à une réalisation lente et échelonnée, s'étirant sur une longue période et comportant peut-être plusieurs maîtres d'œuvre.

Le règne de Thibaud IV s'achève en 1253. Nous pourrions considérer que la conception des tours de flanquement observées se situe entre 1230-1236 et 1253. Toutefois, les caractéristiques architecturales de la porte charretière couverte d'un grand arc segmentaire chanfreiné suggèrent une datation plus large. Le portail monumental date du XIIIe siècle, peut-être de sa seconde moitié.

Les textes ne renseignent guère. Après 1253, sur un plan comptable, il n'apparaît plus de grande phase de fortifications. Les comptes royaux, à partir de 1285[19], renforcent l'idée d'une relative négligence dans l'entretien des châteaux des années précédentes à l'exception des lieux de séjours préférés des princes, comme Troyes et Provins. Succédant au Chansonnier, Thibaud V dit le Jeune (1253-1271) résida, presque toute l'année de 1259, au château[20]. Il est possible de lui attribuer l'initiative de quelques travaux ponctuels plus motivés par l'aspect résidentiel que défensif mais les sources écrites ne l'attestent pas cependant. La création de cette large communication sur le flanc sud permettait une circulation directe du château résidentiel vers la ville en évitant la basse cour nouvelle.

Nous retiendrons donc deux périodes, la première de 1230-1236 à 1253 pour l'agrandissement de l'enceinte au sud

---

17. BLARY 2013, 264-271 et 330-332.
18. MESQUI 1981, 58.
19. LONGNON 1901-1904, t. III ; MESQUI 1979, 203-229.
20. BNF, collection Picardie, t. CLXVIII, fol. 32 v., citant plusieurs chartes de l'abbaye de Chézy-sur-Marne (Aisne).

perpétuant l'usage de tours à vocation défensive (tour 7), puis, progressivement, à double vocation défensive et résidentielle (tour 8) allant jusqu'à la spécification des niveaux (tour 5), et, ponctuellement, dans un second temps entre 1253 et 1270, l'aménagement d'une commodité de résidence, une porte monumentale donnant sur la ville.

Le mariage de Jeanne de Navarre, fille de Blanche d'Artois, héritière du puissant comté de Champagne et de Navarre, avec le roi de France Philippe IV le Bel en 1285, est une étape importante pour l'histoire des fortifications du château et marque une rupture nette dans la forme des fortifications commencées quelque soixante ans plus tôt par Thibaud IV. L'entrée du comté de Champagne dans les possessions du domaine royal entraîne, pour les forteresses placées sous l'autorité du roi, une brusque reprise en main, soulignée par de nombreuses réfections de tours, par des réparations de murs et la remise en état de toitures dont les mentions jalonnent les comptes de l'administration royale entre 1285 et 1288, compensant probablement l'absence d'entretien régulier de ces places. Château-Thierry ne fait pas exception, au contraire. Plus encore, les architectes royaux ne se limitent pas, ici, à de simples réfections ou reprises ponctuelles de maçonneries, ils achèvent la liaison de l'enveloppe défensive de la basse cour avec celle de la haute cour en usant de tous les perfectionnements du temps. Cette étape cruciale est marquée par la symbolique du traitement de la monumentale porte Saint-Jean (fig. 6). Celle-ci peut être considérée comme « une véritable petite forteresse autonome », elle constitue un jalon extraordinaire pour l'histoire de la fortification castrale. Elle se compose de deux corps rectangulaires oblongs (tours 1 et 2) formant galeries, terminés à l'ouest, côté extérieur, par des éperons en angle droit. Ces deux organes défensifs encadrent le passage d'entrée formant une sorte d'espace découvert. Le parement extérieur est réalisé en moyen appareil, de calcaire coquillier, avec alternance d'assises lisses et d'assises en bossages rustiques conférant à l'ensemble de l'ouvrage un caractère fort et massif. Le plan du rez-de-chaussée montre deux corps distincts encadrant le passage. Chaque corps possède un escalier menant au premier étage et un couloir d'accès de facture différente du reste de l'édifice percé sur le côté ouest débouchant en chicane sur l'axe du cheminement. Le corps sud se distingue par la présence d'un petit couloir détourné donnant sur une porte extérieure actuellement obturée par un mur en moellons irréguliers. Le corps possède une petite porte dissimulée donnant accès sur l'extérieur. Ces deux galeries voûtées d'arêtes, renforcées régulièrement d'arcs en tiers-point, sont dotées d'archères à ébrasement triangulaire très ouvert, sans plongée, couvertes de voussures en berceau. Une des archères bordant la voie située à l'avant de l'éperon de chaque galerie a été transformée en porte donnant accès aux terrasses d'artillerie ménagées autour de l'édifice. Ces percements sont actuellement murés.

La configuration du premier étage est très différente de la précédente. Le plan est organisé autour d'un espace quadrangulaire ouvert au-dessus de la chaussée par six baies rectangulaires. Quatre galeries couvertes de linteaux le desservaient. Actuellement, deux cloisons de béton interdisent leur bon usage. Encadrant ce dispositif, les deux corps sont reliés par la galerie est. Chaque corps comporte, au revers, un escalier menant au niveau inférieur et sur les courtines, ainsi que des latrines. À l'avant, dans le corps nord, se trouve une salle dont la voûte a disparu, et au sud, deux salles voûtées d'arête, renforcées par des arcs en tiers-point. La plus grande est dotée d'une cheminée dont le tablier a été refait grossièrement. Les archères de ce niveau présentent des différences notables avec celles du rez-de-chaussée. Disposées au ras du sol, sans plongée, à ébrasement triangulaire, elles sont couvertes par de larges linteaux.

L'arase du corps nord, au-dessus du second niveau, conserve encore deux gargouilles à simple gorge et deux lignes de corbeaux en encorbellement au droit de la porte dérobée, actuellement murée. Cette porte est caractérisée par l'utilisation, pour les parements, de l'alternance d'assises lisses et d'assises en bossages rustiques. Elle est pourvue, entre les deux corps défensifs, d'un passage d'entrée avec « sas découvert ». La disposition défensive du sas d'entrée associe plusieurs éléments contribuant à l'originalité de l'ouvrage. La combinaison peut se résumer ainsi : une première herse, un sas assommoir, une seconde herse, et pour finir une porte à deux vantaux. Les deux herses délimitent une zone située sous le tir d'archères placées dans les corps latéraux, et sous la surveillance des niveaux supérieurs, dotés d'une coursière continue entourant ce sas, avec vue directe sur lui par de grandes baies rectangulaires. Le rez-de-chaussée est accessible uniquement par le second niveau, au revers.

Les ruptures d'appareillage et les différences de facture des archères des deux niveaux, constatées à l'intérieur de l'édifice, montrent l'existence d'une porte primitive « reformulée » pour devenir le modèle de « sas découvert » défini par Jean Mesqui[21]. Les latrines et les deux corps du rez-de-chaussée sont conservés et intégrés dans la nouvelle configuration de la porte. Des membres de l'ancienne association « Les Amis du vieux château » nous ont signalé la découverte, dans les années 1970, d'un trésor monétaire à l'intérieur des latrines de la galerie sud[22]. Près d'un kilo de monnaies champenoises, dites au peigne, auraient ainsi été retrouvées, enserrées dans une masse compacte de corrosion, au contact avec le fond de la structure. Seuls sept deniers (!) de cet important trésor monétaire ont été récupérés : ils ont tous été émis à Troyes durant le règne de Thibaud II (1102-1152).

---

21. Mesqui 1979 et 1981.

22. Ces fouilles anciennes n'ont donné lieu ni à autorisation préalable, ni à la rédaction d'un rapport.

Fig. 5 a – Château-Thierry, porte Saint-Pierre, étude du bâti : phase 1 : années 1220-1230 ; phase 2 : seconde moitié du XIVe siècle ; phase 3 : fin du XVe siècle ; phase 4 : seconde moitié du XIXe siècle ; phase 5 : seconde moitié du XXe siècle. Dessin F. Blary.

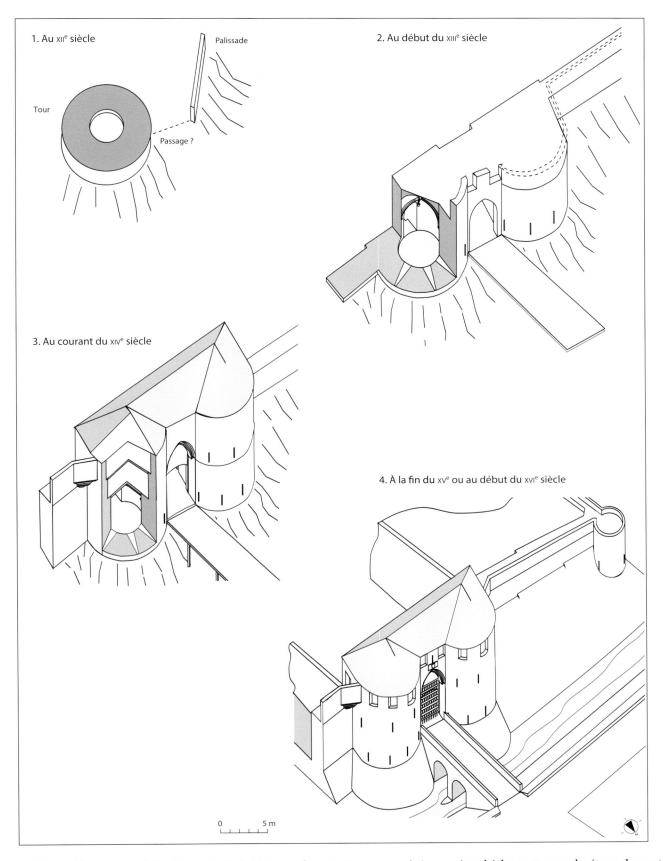

Fig. 5 b – Château-Thierry, porte Saint-Pierre, étude du bâti, essai de restitution axonométrique en écorché des quatre grandes étapes de construction de la porte. Dessin F. Blary.

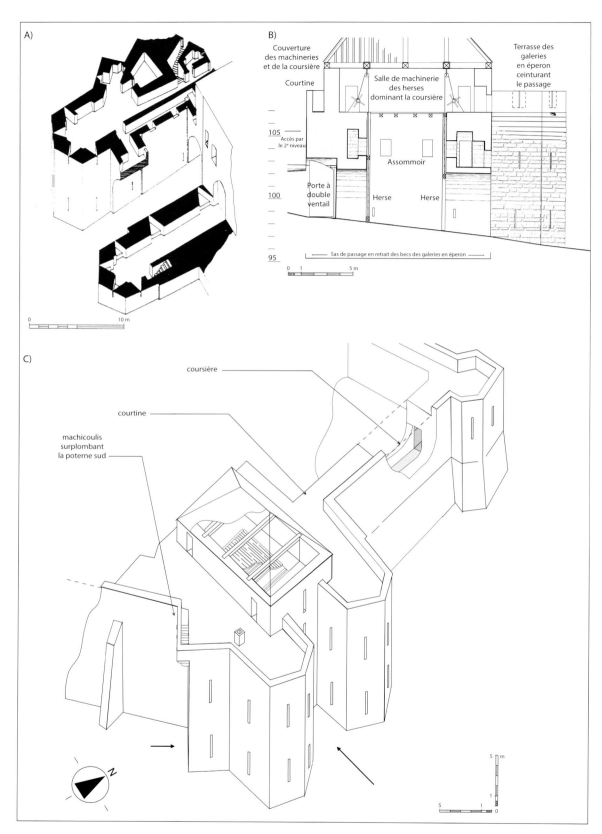

Fig. 6 – Enceinte castrale et porte Saint-Jean au XIVe siècle. A) axonométrie en écorché de la porte (dessin Mesqui 1988, 125); B) coupe longitudinale est-ouest avec proposition de restitution d'une salle de machinerie des herses dominant la coursière et le sas ouvert (dessin F. Blary); C) restitution axonométrique du fonctionnement de l'ensemble du complexe défensif de la porte Saint-Jean et des tours polygonales reliées par des galeries intérieures des courtines (dessin F. Blary).

Fig. 7 – Château de Fère-en-Tardenois, plan des phases XIIIe siècle et XVIe siècle (dessin F. Blary, d'après Mesqui 1988, 198) et vue de la porte en éperon du XIIIe siècle (photo F. Blary).

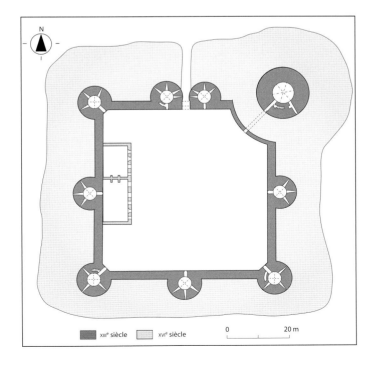

Fig. 8 – Nesle-en-Dôle, plan et vue du château fondé en 1226 (dessin F. Blary, d'après Mesqui 1988, 256 ; photo F. Blary).

La présence d'éperons triangulaires, l'appareil à bossages, le dispositif rarissime du sas découvert, montrent que cette porte est l'aboutissement des recherches menées par les ingénieurs royaux à la fin du XIIIe siècle. La porte Saint-Jean se place dans la lignée des portes d'Aigues-Mortes et de Carcassonne dont elle reprend – en les améliorant – les caractères. Un autre exemple, tout aussi sophistiqué, se trouve dans l'enceinte haute de Provins dans une porte également appelée Saint-Jean. Toutes deux sont postérieures à la prise de possession de la Champagne par le roi Philippe IV le Bel, soit entre 1285 et 1316.

Dans le même temps, les bâtisseurs royaux opèrent le raccordement de part et d'autre de cette porte avec l'enceinte nord et les défenses sud de la haute cour, définissant ainsi, dans un même corps défensif, deux zones, l'une résidentielle noble, l'autre, économique, située 5 à 6 mètres plus bas. Il est probable que l'ensemble de cette campagne remplace une ligne défensive préexistante mise en place dès le début des transformations opérées sous Thibaud IV. Malheureusement, aucun indice sérieux ne renseigne sur la forme que revêtait cette ancienne défense. Ce n'était peut-être qu'une simple palissade ou une fortification grossière dans l'attente d'un aménagement plus efficace. Seules des fouilles archéologiques pourraient lever cette incertitude en l'absence d'autres sources.

Les observations faites sur le château de Château-Thierry se retrouvent de la même manière sur le château de Fère-en-Tardenois (fig. 7, p. 67). Comme pour la place forte de Château-Thierry, le site de Fère-en-Tardenois est issu d'une forteresse carolingienne remodelée essentiellement au début du XIIIe siècle. L'aspect des fortifications champenoises est ici parfaitement décliné. Les tours à coupoles aux archères à ébrasement triangulaire étroit s'y retrouvent nettement développées. Le château de Nesles-en-Dôle créé en 1226 (fig. 8, p. 67) est établi avec un plan philippien parfait reprenant le plan à l'identique de celui développé à Dourdan. Cette forme architecturale marque très nettement l'appartenance de Robert III de Dreux et sa fidélité au roi face au comte de Champagne, donnant à sa maison forte l'allure d'un château royal en terre de Champagne. Ce site ne subit d'ailleurs aucune campagne supplémentaire contrairement aux anciennes places de l'héritage de Champagne.

L'architecture des châteaux de Champagne permet donc bien par leur code architectural de définir une frontière lisible. Le soin apporté lors du rattachement au domaine royal s'attache au contraire à estomper cette appartenance en développant un programme essentiellement consacré aux ouvrages d'entrée des grandes places fortes développées dans le cadre strictement champenois.

Bibliographie

ARBOIS DE JUBAINVILLE H. (d') (1859-1866), *Histoire des ducs et des comtes de Champagne, depuis le VIe siècle jusqu'à la fin du XIe*, Paris/Troyes, A. Durand, 6 vol.

BLARY F. (2013), *Revue archéologique de Picardie*, n° spécial 29 : *Origines et développements d'une cité médiévale – Château-Thierry*.

BLARY F. et al. (2004), *La pierre à Château-Thierry. De la carrière à la ville*, Château-Thierry, Patrimoine vivant.

BUR M. (1976), « La frontière entre la Champagne et la Lorraine du milieu du Xe à la fin du XIIe siècle », *Francia*, vol. IV, 237-254.

– (1977), *La formation du comté de Champagne : v. 950-v. 1150*, Nancy, Université Nancy II (Annales de l'Est. Mémoires ; 54).

– (1982), « Rôle et place de la Champagne dans le royaume de France au temps de Philippe Auguste », in *La France de Philippe Auguste : le temps des mutations* (Actes du colloque international du CNRS, Paris, 29 septembre-4 octobre 1980), R.-H. BAUTIER (dir.), Paris, Éditions du CNRS (Colloques internationaux du Centre national de la recherche scientifique ; 602), 237-254.

HÉLIOT P. (1974), « Le château de Nesles-en-Dôle et la fortification du XIIIe siècle », *Mémoires de la Société d'agriculture, commerce, sciences et arts du département de la Marne*, t. LXXXIX, 107-123.

HUBERT J. (1955), « La frontière occidentale du comté de Champagne du XIe au XIIIe siècle », in *Recueil de travaux offert à M. Clovis Brunel*, t. II, Paris, Société de l'École des chartes (Mémoires et documents publiés par l'École des chartes ; 12), 14-30.

HUBERT M.-C. (1953), *Étude sur les frontières septentrionale et orientale du comté de Champagne (936-1284)*, thèse, École des chartes, 43-49.

LEFÈVRE-PONTALIS E. (1911), « Le château de Fère », *Congrès archéologique de France*, 263-267.

LONGNON A. (1901), *Documents relatifs au comté de Champagne et de Brie (1172-1361)*, t. I : *Les fiefs*, Paris, Imprimerie nationale (Collection de documents inédits sur l'histoire de France).

MESQUI J. (1979), « Les enceintes de Crécy-en-Brie et la fortification dans l'ouest du comté de Champagne et de Brie au XIIIe siècle », *Mémoires de la Fédération des Sociétés historiques et archéologiques de Paris et de l'Île-de-France*, t. XXX, 7-86.

– (1981), « La fortification des portes avant la guerre de Cent Ans. Essai de typologie des défenses des ouvrages d'entrée avant 1350 », *Archéologie médiévale*, t. XI, 203-229.

– (1988), *Île-de-France gothique*, t. II : *Les demeures seigneuriales*, Paris, Picard (Les monuments de la France gothique).

„Tor und Schlüssel zu Italien"

Die Grenzfestung Bellinzona

◆

Maria-Letizia Boscardin*, Werner Meyer**

In den Schweizer Alpen üben die hohen Gebirgskämme mit Gipfeln zwischen 3,000 und 4,500 m sowie Passübergängen mit 1,500 bis 2,500 m Meereshöhe seit Urzeiten eine grenzbildende Wirkung aus. Die tief eingeschnittenen, seit prähistorischen Zeiten unterschiedlich dicht bevölkerten Täler entwässern sich in vier Hauptrichtungen: Nach Norden durch Aare und Rhein in die Nordsee, nach Osten durch den Inn ins Schwarze Meer, nach Süden durch die Rhône ins westliche Mittelmeer und durch den Ticino in die Adria.

Allerdings spielten die durch Bergkämme und Wasserscheiden gebildeten „natürlichen Grenzen", in unwirtlichen, siedlungsfeindlichen Höhen verlaufend, bei der Bildung und Festlegung politischer Grenzen bis weit in die Neuzeit hinein eine untergeordnete Rolle. Genaue Grenzlinien sind zum Teil erst im Zusammenhang mit dem Bau von Autostraßen – wegen der Kostenfolgen – eingemessen und vermarcht worden und stehen in Einzelfällen noch heute nicht genau fest. Im Mittelalter ging der Anstoß zur Grenzbildung in den höheren Lagen des Alpenraumes häufig zunächst von der Anciennität der Nutzung von Alpweiden für die Sömmerung von Viehherden – namentlich von Schafen und Ziegen – aus. Entscheidend für die Erstokkupation war der Bevölkerungsdruck, der über die Passübergänge – auch vergletscherte – in die oberen Stufen der jenseitigen Nachbartäler drängte. Hinter der Besetzung von unbesiedeltem, also „herrenlosem" Land zu Siedlungs- und Nutzungszwecken standen grund- und landesherrliche Machthaber, für welche solche Vorstöße, die auf dem mittelalterlichen Prinzip von „Schutz und Schirm" beruhten, eine Erweiterung ihres herrschaftlichen Einflussbereiches bedeuteten. Im Spätmittelalter traten manchenorts an die Stelle herrschaftlicher Machthaber kommunale und genossenschaftliche Interessengruppen[1]. Burgen, bekanntlich an ein Umfeld mit landwirtschaftlicher Produktion gebunden, sind folgerichtig nicht auf den unwirtlichen Passhöhen, sondern in den Hochtälern im Bereich der ganzjährig bewohnten Dauersiedlungen errichtet worden, wo Siedlungsdruck und Herrschaftsinteressen in feindseliger Konkurrenz aufeinander trafen. Solche Burganlagen, auch wenn es sich bloß um einfache Turmbauten handelte, konnten so die Rolle wehrhafter, herrschaftlicher Grenzmarken übernehmen[2]. Als zu Beginn des 15. Jahrhunderts, um nur ein Beispiel zu nennen, ein Konflikt zwischen den Innerschweizern und Mailand ausbrach (vgl. unten), ging in Uri das Gerücht um, der Herzog *wölti den zoll ze Göschinen jn nehmen und uf der Stiebenden Brüg ein türn machen*, d.h. seinen Machtbereich über den Gotthard hinaus ins Urner Reusstal ausdehnen[3].

Modellhaft zeigt sich die Verbindung von Siedlungsexpansion, Herrschaftsbildung und Burgenbau über die Alpenübergänge hinweg auch am Beispiel von Splügen im Hinterrheintal (Kt. Graubünden): Die Freiherren von

---

* Lehrbeauftragte für Geschichte des Mittelalters/SLA, Departement Geschichte der Universität Basel, Schweiz.
** Professor emeritus, Departement Geschichte, Universität Basel, Schweiz.
1. Einstiegsliteratur zur Problematik der Siedlungsgeschichte, der Herrschaftsbildung und der Entstehung von Grenzen im schweizerischen Alpenraum: Meyer 1911; Brändli 1986; Bundi 1982; Glauser 1988; Meyer et al. 1998; Oehlmann 1879.
2. Poeschel 1930, 66-67: „Das Bild der Burgenbesiedlung im Flussbereich des Hinterrheins trägt die Züge des organischen Lebens. Wie die Vegetation dürftiger wird, je höher wir steigen, so nimmt die Dichtigkeit der Burgenbesetzung hier von Talstufe zu Talstufe gesetzmässig ab". Beispiele für Burgen am Rande der ganzjährigen Dauersiedlungen, errichtet längs einer Passroute: Casaccia GR, Puntraschigna/Spaniola GR, Hospental UR, Bourg-St. Pierre VS, Pontaningen GR. Zu den Standorten der im vorliegenden Aufsatz genannten Burgen vgl. Burgenkarte 2007.
3. Weisses Buch 1947, 37.

Abb. 1 – „Zur Burg" in Splügen. Südfront des Hauptbaues.

Sax-Misox, Herren über das südlich des San Bernardino-Passes gelegene Tal der Mesolcina, versuchten im Laufe des 13. Jahrhunderts, ihren Machtbereich in das obere Rheinwald, d.h. in den höchsten Abschnitt des Hinterrheintales auf der Nordseite des Passes vorzuschieben[4]. 1274 siedelten sie gemäß einem auf ihrer Stammburg Mesocco ausgestellten Schirmbrief deutschsprachige Walser in dem Tal an[5]. Deren Wohnraum – und damit auch ihren eigenen Herrschaftsbereich – grenzten sie bei Splügen talabwärts mit einer wehrhaften Sperrmauer, einer *Letzi* oder *Fraccia*, ab. Dieses Vorgehen stieß auf den Widerstand der Freiherren von Vaz, die im 13. Jahrhundert das Hinterrheintal von Norden her, d.h. talaufwärts, herrschaftlich zu durchdringen versuchten. 1277 unterstellten sie die Leute im Rheinwald ihrer eigenen Schirmgewalt und errichteten um diese Zeit als Zeichen ihres Herrschaftsanspruchs am Standort der Letzi, also auf der alten Grenzlinie, eine Burganlage (Abb. 1). Mit der Festigung der Vazer Herrschaft im Rheinwald verloren Burg und Letzi ihre Funktion. Schon zu Beginn des 14. Jahrhunderts scheint nur noch der zur Burg gehörige Wirtschaftshof in Betrieb gewesen zu sein[6].

Grenzbildung und Burgenbau standen im Alpenraum in engem Zusammenhang mit der Betreuung bzw. Beherrschung von Passrouten sowie der Erhebung von Straßenzöllen. Im Hochmittelalter bildete die Kontrolle der Alpenpässe, namentlich solcher mit gut begehbaren und erschlossenen Wegen, seit den Ottonen einen wichtigen Faktor in der Italienpolitik der römisch-deutschen Herrscher[7]. Wie eng die Aspekte „Grenzbildung", „Burgenbau" und „kaiserliche Passpolitik" miteinander verflochten sein konnten, zeigt das Beispiel von Castelmur im Bergell (Kt. Graubünden; Abb. 2): Oberhalb von Promontogno (Gde. Bondo) liegt die weitläufige Burgruine auf einem unwegsamen Felsriegel. Sichtbar sind Mauerreste aus dem Hoch- und Spätmittelalter. Castelmur kann nach

Abb. 2 – Castelmur im Bergell. Im Vordergrund die Sperrmauer, durch welche die Talstraße führt. Im Hintergrund oben Hauptturm der Adelsburg.

Bellinzona als bedeutendstes Beispiel für eine mittelalterliche Talsperre und Grenzburg im Schweizer Alpenraum gelten. Auf dem höchsten Felskopf in der linken Talflanke erhob sich ein isolierter, viereckiger Wehrturm, über dessen Alter und Nutzung (Wohn- oder Wehrbau?) ohne Grabungen keine sicheren Aussagen möglich sind. In einer tiefer gelegenen Senke liegt die alte Talkirche Nossa Donna. Weiter nördlich finden sich auf einer markanten Felsrippe die Ruinen einer ausgedehnten Adelsburg mit Hauptturm (um 1200), Umfassungsmauer und Nebenbauten. Unzusammenhängende Reste von Sperrmauern ziehen sich in nördlicher Richtung hinunter bis zu einer Felsterrasse hoch über dem Fluss Maira. Diese bildete mit ihren Wehrmauern den nördlichen, am tiefsten gelegenen Abschluss der Talbefestigung. Das Plateau war von einer mit Brustwehr und Scharten ausgestatteten Ringmauer umgeben, welche sowohl talaufwärts als auch talabwärts verteidigt werden konnte.

Über dieses Plateau führte die alte, bis in römische Zeit zurückreichende Talstraße. Grabungen förderten die Reste einer Straßensiedlung aus dem 1. bis 4. Jahrhundert zutage, die wohl mit der im *Itinerarium Antonini*, einem Straßenverzeichnis aus der Zeit um 300, genannten Ort *Murus* zu identifizieren ist[8]. Ob die Bezeichnung *Murus* auf den natürlichen Felsriegel,

---

4. Zu den Freiherren von Sax-Misox vgl. HOFER-WILD 1949.
5. MEYER 1952, 201-204.
6. CLAVADETSCHER & MEYER 1984, 161-162.
7. Zu Passpolitik der Römisch-deutschen Kaiser vgl. MEYER 1911; OEHLMANN 1879.
8. HOWALD & MEYER 1940, 114; ARCHÄOLOGIE GR (o.J.), 155-161.

der sich quer durch das Tal legt, oder auf eine künstliche Sperrmauer zurückgeht, bleibt offen. Die erhaltenen bzw. sichtbaren Mauerreste entstammen erst dem Mittelalter.

Schriftliche Nachrichten über die Befestigungsanlage setzen in karolingischer Zeit ein. Castelmur wird im rätischen Reichsgutsurbar von 842 als *castellum* und *porta Bergalliae* genannt und mit einer Zollstätte in Verbindung gebracht[9]. Zur Grenzburg wurde Castelmur im Jahre 960 mit der Übertragung von Burg und Zoll durch Kaiser Otto I. an den Bischof von Chur, wodurch der wichtige Septimerpass unter die Kontrolle reichstreuer Machthaber geriet[10]. Die Wehranlage markierte fortan im Bergell die Grenze zwischen dem Bistum und dem Stadtgebiet von Chiavenna und stand wiederholt im Brennpunkt bewaffneter Konflikte. 1121/1122 entrissen die Chiavennasker dem Bischof vorübergehend die Feste[11]. Die Adelsburg mit dem mächtigen Hauptturm nahe der Talkirche Nossa Donna bildete den Wohnsitz eines Churer Ministerialengeschlechtes, das sich nach Castelmur nannte und 1190 urkundlich erstmals mit *Albertus de Castello Muro* bezeugt ist[12].

Im 15. Jahrhundert verlor die Burg ihre Bedeutung als Wehranlage. Baumaßnahmen beschränkten sich auf Reparaturarbeiten. Im 16. Jahrhundert wurde die Burg verlassen und war um 1600 Ruine.

Wechselhafter und vielschichtiger bieten sich die Verhältnisse in der Sperrfeste von Bellinzona (Kt. Tessin) dar, welcher das Hauptaugenmerk dieses Beitrages gilt. Mit Domodossola, Chiavenna, Bozen und anderen befestigten Orten am südlichen Alpenrand hat Bellinzona das Zusammentreffen mehrerer Passrouten gemeinsam. Belitione (590), Berinzona (1004), Belinzona (1055) liegt in einem natürlichen Engnis, das durch einen Felsriegel gebildet wird, der sich von Osten her quer in die Talsohle schiebt. Aus deren Mitte ragt das mächtige Massiv des Castel Grande empor, das nach dem Ausweis archäologischer Funde und Befunde – wie der ganze Talabschnitt – seit dem Neolithikum besiedelt war (Abb. 3)[13].

In Bellinzona treffen die Routen über fünf Pässe zusammen, von denen im Mittelalter der Lukmanier, der San Bernardino und – seit dem 13./14. Jahrhundert – der Gotthard die wichtigsten waren. Zudem führt durch das Engnis eine der wenigen inneralpinen West-Ostachsen. Sie verbindet Domodossola über das Centovalli und den Passo S. Jorio mit dem Veltlin. Bis ins Spätmittelalter hinein wurde die verkehrspolitische Bedeutung des Ortes durch die Tatsache unterstrichen, dass sich der Lago Maggiore bis nach Bellinzona erstreckte, wo sich vor den Toren der Stadt eine eigene Hafenanlage befand. Im Hochmittelalter bildete Bellinzona einen Umschlagplatz für den Wechsel vom Land- auf den Wasserweg und *vice versa*. Der eigene Hafen brachte dem festen Platz den Vorteil, dass er auf dem vergleichsweise sicheren und leistungsfähigen Wasserweg direkt mit Baumaterial, Vorräten und Kriegsgerät versorgt werden konnte. Überdies teilten sich in Bellinzona die Landrouten, die gegen Süden in die Lombardei führten. Die Reisenden empfanden Bellinzona unabhängig von den politischen Zuständen als Grenzort zwischen den Alpen mit ihren engen, kargen Tälern und der fruchtbaren, offenen Landschaft Oberitaliens mit seinen reichen Städten[14].

Die Anfänge von Befestigungsanlagen in Bellinzona verlieren sich im Dunkel der Vorgeschichte. Einzelfunde aus dem Neolithikum, der Bronze- und Eisenzeit lassen ahnen, dass der Felshügel des Castel Grande schon in prähistorischer Zeit eine befestigte Siedlung getragen hat[15]. Eine archäologisch durch Funde und stratifizierte Mauerreste gesicherte Wehranlage ist aber erst für die frühe römische Kaiserzeit unter Augustus und Tiberius nachgewiesen. Sie ist offenbar um 15 v. Chr. als Garnisonsfestung im Zusammenhang mit der Eroberung des rätischen Alpenraumes errichtet worden und diente als Operationsbasis gegen die inneren, von den Lepontiern bewohnten Alpentäler. Nach der Befriedung der Region verlor das Kastell seine Bedeutung und wurde verlassen, wie das Auslaufen der Keramikreihe im 1. Jahrhundert n. Chr. zeigt. Als Grenzfestung bildete Bellinzona demnach ursprünglich keine Sperre gegen fremde Einfälle aus dem Norden, sondern im Gegenteil einen Sammelpunkt für Offensivtruppen, die gegen den inneren Alpenraum eingesetzt werden sollten.

Im vorgerückten 4. Jahrhundert erfolgte eine Neubefestigung des Platzes. Archäologisch nachgewiesen ist eine 1,5 m starke Umfassungsmauer, die wohl das gesamte Felsplateau des Castel Grande umgeben und damit eine Fläche von ca. 1,5 Hektar umschlossen hat (Abb. 4). Dieses Kastell gehörte zu den *Clausurae Alpium*, also zu jener Kette von Befestigungsanlagen, die im Laufe des 4. Jahrhunderts an den südlichen Alpenausgängen errichtet worden waren, um Italien vor Einfällen germanischer, namentlich alamannischer Scharen zu schützen, die den immer schwieriger zu verteidigenden Rhein-Donau-Limes durchbrochen hatten. Tatsächlich gelang es 457 der römischen Garnison – schätzungsweise in Stärke einer Kohorte –, einen Alamannenverband auf den *Campi Canini*, d.h. vor Bellinzonas Mauern, zurückzuschlagen[16].

Dieses Ereignis belegt, dass Bellinzona nunmehr die Funktion einer Sperrfestung übernommen hatte. Diese bildete fortan einen nördlichen Eckpfeiler der oberitalienischen Provinz *Liguria* und unterstand – seit wann, ist nicht genau feststellbar – dem *municipium* Mailand. Diese Zugehörigkeit sollte die Auflösung des Weströmischen Reiches am Ausgang des 5. Jahrhunderts überdauern. Nach der Machtübernahme

---

9. BUB 1, 1955, Nr. 142.
10. *Ibid.*, Nr. 148, 156; CLAVADETSCHER & MEYER 1984, 225-229.
11. BUB 1, 1955, Nr. 273, 274.
12. *Ibid.*, Nr. 472.
13. CHIESI 1978, 23-37; MEYER 1976, 12-13; RAHN 1893, 404.
14. CHIESI 1991; MEYER 1994, 4-5.
15. MEYER 1976, 130-132; WIELICH 1970, 7-37. Nur unvollständig publiziert sind die prähistorischen, bis ins Neolithikum zurückreichenden Funde und Befunde, die im Zuge der umfassenden Restaurierung des Castel Grande um 1990 zum Vorschein gekommen sind.
16. *Ibid.*, 92; MEYER 1976, 132-134.

Abb. 3 – Bellinzona, Castel Grande. Gesamtansicht von Süden.

Abb. 4 – Bellinzona, Castel Grande. Römische und frühmittelalterliche Mauerreste unter den Fundamenten spätmittelalterlicher Bauten.

der Langobarden in Oberitalien um 570 unterhielten diese in Bellinzona eine Garnison, die fränkische Einfälle abzuwehren hatte. Wie Gregor von Tours und Paulus Diaconus berichten, wurde 590 im Zuge des Feldzuges König Childeberts II. von Austrasien ein fränkischer Herzog vor Bellinzona durch einen Wurfspeer getötet[17]. In der Folgezeit verblieb Bellinzona mit dem Castel Grande in der Hand des langobardischen Königtums. Die alte römische Ringmauer aus dem 4. Jahrhundert blieb bis ins 10. Jahrhundert bestehen, wurde aber mehrmals abgeändert. Mit der Eingliederung Oberitaliens in das Karolingerreich um 800 und – bei dessen Auflösung mit der Bildung eines Königreiches Italien – spielte Bellinzona als Stützpunkt der jeweiligen Herrscher eine wichtige Rolle. Bautätigkeiten auf dem Castel Grande sind für das 9. und 10. Jahrhundert archäologisch nachgewiesen[18].

Eine nennenswerte Bedeutung als Grenzfestung kam Bellinzona aber für längere Zeit nicht mehr zu, denn von Norden her, über die einzelnen Alpenpässe, drohte wegen des hochmittelalterlichen Machtvakuums im Deutschschweizer Raum keine Gefahr. Umso mehr stritten sich um den festen Platz vom 10. bis ins 14. Jahrhundert all jene in *Guelfen* und *Ghibellinen* gespaltenen Gruppen, die eine Vormachtstellung in Oberitalien anstrebten. Hinter den lokalen und regionalen Machthabern standen die großen Kontrahenten der Reichspolitik, Kaiser und Papst, Como und Mailand. Um 1000 ging Bellinzona – aus dem Versorgungsraum des spätrömischen Kastells war mittlerweile eine kleine Grafschaft (*comitatus*) geworden – an den Bischof von Como über, der als kaisertreu galt. Die oberen Täler unterstanden dagegen dem päpstlich gesinnten Domkapitel von Mailand[19].

Die zwischen dem 11. und frühen 14. Jahrhundert auf dem Castel Grande errichteten Bauten passen nicht ins Bild einer Sperrfestung. Auf dem Burgfelsen übten der Bischof von Como und comaskische Adlige ein freies Baurecht aus, indem sie Wohntürme und Palazzi errichteten. Von diesen Bauten hat sich nur noch ein Restbestand erhalten, etwa die Torre Nera und die Torre Bianca sowie Teile des Südflügels[20]. Das mächtige Comasker Geschlecht der Rusca gründete gegen 1300 auf einem Bergvorsprung der östlichen Talflanke die kleine Burg Montebello, und im Engnis am Fuße des Castel Grande entstand im 13. Jahrhundert – wohl als Folge des zunehmenden Verkehrs über die Alpenpässe – ein kleines Städtchen[21].

In den Machtkämpfen zwischen den Guelfen und Ghibellinen galt das Castel Grande, wiederholt angegriffen und belagert, als schwer einnehmbar. Als es 1242 den Guelfen nach harter Belagerung endlich gelang, die Burg den ghibellinischen Parteigängern Kaiser Friedrichs II. zu entreißen, schrieb der mailändische *Podestà* triumphierend an den päpstlichen Legaten, die Burg von Bellinzona sei bis anhin das Herz im Leibe der Comasken gewesen, sei jetzt aber das in ihrer Brust steckende, todbringende Schwert[22]. In dieser blumigen Formulierung ist die große taktische Bedeutung zu verspüren, die damals dem festen Platz Bellinzona im Dauerkonflikt zwischen Como und Mailand, zwischen Guelfen und Ghibellinen und zwischen lokalen Machthabern zukam.

---

17. WIELICH 1970, 156; MEYER 1976, 134-135.
18. *Ibid.*, 107-108; 136-137.
19. CHIESI 1991, 29-35; WIELICH 1970, 275, Anm. 389.
20. MEYER 1976, 137-138.
21. CHIESI 1978, 184-188. Im Zuge der Stadtgründung im 13. Jahrhundert erfolgte die Verlegung der Tal- und Pfarrkirche S. Pietro vom Castel Grande in das Stadtareal (MEYER 1976, 124-125; BRENTANI 1934, 8-11; CHIESI 1978, 61-110).
22. MEYER 1976, 138, Anm. 23; WINKELMANN 1880, 537, Nr. 678.

Auch in der zweiten Hälfte des 13. Jahrhunderts blieb Bellinzona umkämpft. Das Castel Grande wechselte wiederholt, aber nie auf Dauer den Besitzer. Erst im 14. Jahrhundert kehrte nach und nach Ruhe ein. Nachdem die Visconti um 1300 die Herrschaft über Mailand errungen hatten, gelang es ihnen, auch Como und dessen Hoheitsgebiet zu unterwerfen. 1340 nahmen sie auch Bellinzona ein[23]. Der Ausbau des mailändischen Territorialstaates – um 1395 wurde den Visconti der erbliche Herzogstitel verliehen – ermöglichte den Aufschwung des Handelsverkehrs über den Gotthardpass und erhöhte die Bedeutung Bellinzonas als Zollstation und Umschlagplatz.

Aber um die Wende vom 14. zum 15. Jahrhundert erlangte Bellinzona die alte Funktion als Grenzfestung zurück. Denn im Laufe des 14. Jahrhunderts hatte sich nördlich des Alpenkammes die schweizerische Eidgenossenschaft zu einer aggressiv expandierenden Territorialmacht entwickelt[24]. Die Innerschweizer Orte – heute würde man von Kantonen sprechen – strebten unter der Führung Uris über den Gotthard nach Süden und brachten mit ihren chaotischen Unternehmungen das administrative Gefüge Mailands in den Alpentälern ins Wanken. Auf die ereignisgeschichtlichen Vorgänge des 15. Jahrhunderts braucht hier im Einzelnen nicht eingegangen zu werden. Kriegszüge mit fehlgeschlagenen Angriffen auf Bellinzona, Raubzüge, Verhandlungen und Vertragsabschlüsse wechselten einander ab. Die Mailänder Herzöge, zunächst die Visconti, ab 1450 die Sforza, waren an einem Krieg mit den Eidgenossen nicht interessiert und versuchten, die ungemütlichen Nachbarn mit diplomatischen Mitteln ruhig zu halten, mit Bestechungsgeldern, mit Zoll- und Soldverträgen oder mit Wirtschaftsprivilegien[25].

Die inneren Alpentäler südlich des Gotthardpasses, dessen war man sich in Mailand bewusst, waren militärisch auf die Dauer nicht zu behaupten. Sie besaßen mit ihrer wirtschaftlichen Armut für das Herzogtum auch keinen Wert. Umso größere Bedeutung erlangte nun Bellinzona, wo sich das natürliche, seit langem befestigte Engnis für die Errichtung einer Talsperre bestens eignete (Abb. 5). In der Antike, im Früh- und Hochmittelalter waren die Befestigungsanlagen auf den Felshügel des Castel Grande konzentriert, dessen Besatzung ein gewaltsames Durchqueren der beiden Passagen durch Ausfälle zu verhindern hatte. Im frühen 15. Jahrhundert entschlossen sich die Visconti, das Engnis von Bellinzona mit einer durchgehenden Wehrmauer, der *Murata*, zu schließen. Deren erstmalige Erwähnung im Jahre 1457 betont ihren schlechten Erhaltungszustand und nennt die Zahl von insgesamt 297 Zinnen[26].

Die Eidgenossen hielten Bellinzona mit seinen erweiterten und verstärkten Befestigungen für uneinnehmbar, während sich die Mailänder Ingenieure und Kommandanten beständig über schadhafte Mauern oder über zu wenig Mannschaften und ungenügende Ausrüstung beklagten und immer wieder den Ausbau der Festungsanlagen einforderten. Tatsächlich bildete Bellinzona während des ganzen 15. Jahrhunderts einen einzigen, dauernden Bauplatz, auf dem bald mehr, bald weniger gearbeitet wurde. Um 1475 hob der mailändische Kommissar Maffeo di Como die Bedeutung Bellinzonas und die Notwendigkeit baulicher Verbesserungen mit dem Argument hervor, „questa terra è pur una giave e porta de Italia" (dieser Boden bildet den Schlüssel und das Tor zu Italien). Bellinzona sollte allerdings nicht nur als defensive Sperr- und Grenzfeste dienen, sondern auch als Standort für Mobiltruppen, welche im offenen Vorfeld gegnerische Verbände zu bekämpfen hatten[27].

Auch wenn die zahlreichen Nachrichten des 15. Jahrhunderts über geforderte, angeordnete und tatsächlich ausgeführte Baumaßnahmen nur teilweise genau lokalisiert werden können und gründliche Bauanalysen nur auf dem Castel Grande durchgeführt worden sind, kann die befestigungstechnische Entwicklung der Talsperre wenigstens in groben Zügen nachgezeichnet werden. Allerdings hat die Bausubstanz seit dem 16. Jahrhundert bedauerliche Verluste erlitten, weshalb die Untersuchung verschiedener, wichtiger Baukörper nicht mehr möglich ist. 1515 zerstörte die *Buzza*, eine fürchterliche Schlammlawine, einen großen Abschnitt der *Murata*, der Sperrmauer[28]. Im fortschrittsgläubigen 19. Jahrhundert sind Teile der Stadtbefestigung, namentlich deren drei Tore, abgebrochen worden, desgleichen der *Portone*, der große Torturm in der *Murata*, und die *Torretta*, der mächtige Turm, der die Sperrbefestigung auf dem westlichen, rechten Ufer des Ticino abschloss[29]. Störende Eingriffe hatten auch diverse Sanierungsmaßnahmen mit ihren verfälschenden Rekonstruktionen in der ersten Hälfte des 20. Jahrhunderts zur Folge.

Außer der laufenden Ausbesserung von Schäden, die Unwetter und Kampfhandlungen angerichtet hatten, umfasste die Bautätigkeit des 15. Jahrhunderts die Errichtung des hoch gelegenen, isolierten Castello di Sasso Corbaro, den Bau einer neuen, turmbewehrten Ringmauer auf der Burg Montebello und zweier Schenkelmauern, welche diese mit der Stadtbefestigung in der Talniederung verbanden, vor allem aber einer Sperrmauer (*Murata*), die vom Castel Grande über den Ticino bis zur rechten Talflanke reichte (Abb. 6, 7 & 8)[30].

Nach der Niederlage der Mailänder in der Schlacht von Giornico 1478[31] verstärkte sich der Druck der Eidgenossen auf

---

23. MEYER 1976, 139-143, Anm. 14; WIELICH 1970, 385.
24. MEYER 1915, 42-50.
25. *Ibid.*, 65-71; GAGLIARDI 1, 1919, 47-76.
26. RAHN 1893, 405. Eine Vorgängeranlage unbekannten Ausmaßes wird bereits 1398 erwähnt (MEYER 1915, 38).
27. RAHN 1893, 406. Zu den Kämpfen im offenen Vorfeld (u.a Schlachten von Arbedo und Giornico) vgl. MEYER 1915, 55-56; 70-74.
28. RAHN 1893, 407.
29. *Ibid.*, 412-415; 418.
30. *Ibid.*, 407-412.
31. MEYER 1915, 71-75.

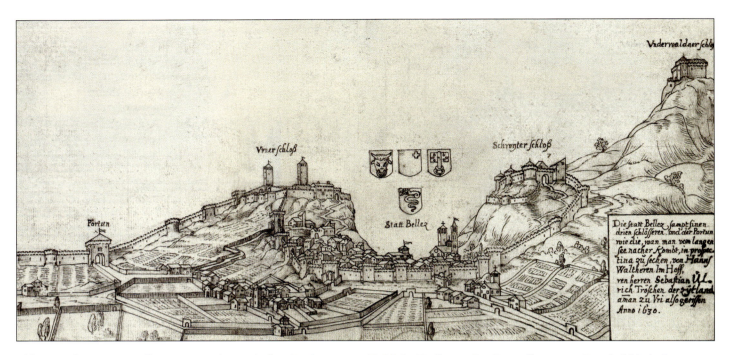

Abb. 5 – Talsperre von Bellinzona, Ansicht von Süden. Zeichnung von H. W. Im Hoff, 1630. Die Darstellung ist in Details fehlerhaft. Nach GILARDONI 1955.

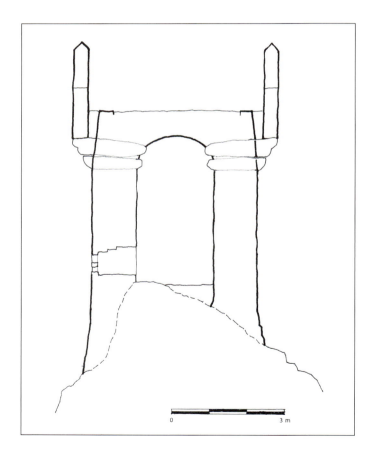

Abb. 6 – Bellinzona, Schnitt durch die *Murata* aus dem späten 15. Jahrhundert. Zeichnung W. Meyer, 1993.

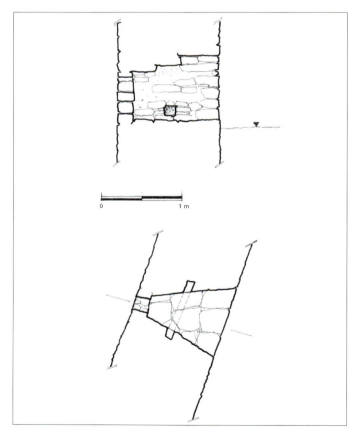

Abb. 7 – Bellinzona, *Murata*. Standardisierte Scharte für leichtkalibriges Geschütz, Planum und Längsschnitt. Zeichnung W. Meyer, 1993.

Abb. 8 – Bellinzona, Castel Grande. Schwalbenschwanzzinne aus dem 13. Jahrhundert in der nachträglich erhöhten südlichen Ringmauer.

Mailand, was eine merkliche Intensivierung und Beschleunigung der Baumaßnahmen in Bellinzona zur Folge hatte[32]. Eigentliche Neubauten sind in der zweiten Hälfte des 15. Jahrhunderts nur ausnahmsweise errichtet worden. Das trifft – wie erwähnt – namentlich auf die dritte, am höchsten gelegene Burg von Bellinzona zu, auf Sasso Corbaro[33]. An der Stelle eines isolierten, wohl zerfallenen Turmes, von dem heute keine Spuren mehr sichtbar sind, ist die Anlage um 1480 auf dringende Empfehlungen der Mailänder Festungsingenieure erbaut worden.

Insgesamt aber blieben die fortifikatorischen Baumaßnahmen des 15. Jahrhunderts auf Reparaturen, Erweiterungen und Verstärkungen der bestehenden Wehranlagen beschränkt. Wegen großer Schadhaftigkeit mussten manche Bauten niedergelegt und ersetzt werden, so etwa die *Murata*, die um 1487-1489 erneuert wurde[34]. Außer dieser Modernisierung der *Murata* und der Errichtung der Feste Sasso Corbaro zählen die Verstärkungen an den Stadtbefestigungen und die Ummauerung der Burg Montebello mit einem erweiterten, turmbewehrten Bering zu den wichtigsten Baumaßnahmen des vorgerückten 15. Jahrhunderts[35]. Zu den auffallendsten Neuerungen gehört die Ausstattung weiter Teile der Stadtbefestigung und der Burgen Montebello und Sasso Corbaro mit durchgehenden Maschikulireihen, die eine effiziente Vertikalverteidigung aus der Deckung heraus ermöglichen.

Die erhaltenen Wehreinrichtungen legen ein beredtes Zeugnis von der oberitalienischen Festungsbaukunst im 15. Jahrhundert ab. Die Tore der Stadt und der Burgen sind mit vorgeschobenen, teilweise mehrfach unterteilten Zwingeranlagen, Zugbrücken und Fallgattern ausgestattet. Die Scharten verraten den geplanten Einsatz von Hakenbüchsen, Armbrüsten und leichtkalibrigen Geschützen. In den Mauerfluchten zielen sie auf frontal angreifenden Gegner, während die halbrund, meist aber viereckig vorspringenden Schalentürme für flankierenden Beschuss eingerichtet sind. Die Vertikalverteidigung erfolgte von den Maschikulireihen aus, deren Zinnen – teils Rechteck-, teils Schwalbenschwanzzinnen – alternierend mit Beobachtungs- und Schießscharten ausgerüstet sind. Die in der *Murata* sitzenden Rundtürme und die Schalentürme der verschiedenen Umfassungsmauern sind gegen oben mit zinnenbewehrten, auf Gewölben ruhenden Plattformen abgeschlossen, die sich für die Postierung schwererer Geschütze eignen (Abb. 9).

Es fällt indessen auf, dass die bis zum Ausgang des 15. Jahrhunderts ausgeführten Wehreinrichtungen ganz auf die Nahverteidigung angelegt worden sind und mit ihren Mauerstärken von 1-1,5 Metern einem Beschuss mit schwerer Belagerungsartillerie kaum hätten standhalten können[36]. Umgekehrt sind die Verteidigungsanlagen nicht nur einseitig gegen einen Frontalangriff von der Landesgrenze her ausgerichtet, sondern gegen einen Ansturm von allen Seiten. Dieses verteidigungstechnische Konzept nimmt Bezug auf die spezifische Kampfweise der potentiellen Gegner, der Eidgenossen, die wegen ihrer Umgehungsmanöver in schwierigem Gelände und ihrer Nahkampfstärke gefürchtet waren, aber keine schweren, mauerbrechenden Belagerungsgeschütze über die Alpenpässe zu transportieren vermochten[37].

Ein Schwachpunkt in der Verteidigung ist freilich hervorzuheben. Die Topographie von Bellinzona und die engen Gassen, Treppen und Wehrgänge machten es schwierig, Truppenteile schnell zu verschieben, während ein Gegner die Stelle für einen Sturmangriff jederzeit frei wechseln konnte. Für eine erfolgreiche Verteidigung bedurfte es deshalb auf der ganzen Länge der Talsperre einer sehr starken Besatzung, wie sie von den Befehlshabern in Zeiten erhöhter Gefahr immer wieder angefordert wurde (Abb. 10).

Ein umfassendes Inventar der in Bellinzona eingelagerten Bewaffnung und Ausrüstung, datiert von 1475, lässt nicht unbedingt auf erhöhte Kriegsbereitschaft schließen[38]. Wie die Erwähnung von Bombarden (von schweren Belagerungsgeschützen) verrät, war mindestens ein Teil der aufbewahrten Waffen nicht für den Einsatz auf den Festungswerken bestimmt, sondern nur zeughausmäßig magaziniert. Das Inventar zählt überdies leichte Geschütze, Hakenbüchsen und Armbrüste nebst Zubehör, ferner veraltete Wurfmaschinen und ansehnliche

---

32. Rahn 1893, 404-407; Meyer 1976, 108-110.
33. Rahn 1893, 446-448.
34. *Ibid.*, 406.
35. Meyer 1976, 140-141 (Bauphasenplan).
36. Die schwachen Mauern von Bellinzona stehen in auffallendem Gegensatz zu den mächtigen Festungswerken des Castello di Mesocco in der nahen Mesolcina, die ebenfalls im späten 15. Jahrhundert angelegt worden sind (Clavadetscher & Meyer 1984, 248-255).
37. Meyer 1976, 149-150.
38. Rahn 1893, 406; BSSI 4, 1882, 70-75.

Abb. 9 – Bellinzona, Teilstück der südwestlichen Stadtmauer mit Maschikuli und Schwalbenschwanzzinnen (spätes 15. Jahrhundert).

Mengen Pulver, Blei und Geräte zur Herstellung von Geschützkugeln auf. An Lebensmitteln sind Wein, Essig, Käse, eingesalzenes Fleisch, Öl und Salz „in ausreichender Menge" vorhanden. Für wie lange die ganzen Waffen- Munitions- und Lebensmittelvorräte im Falle einer Belagerung ausgereicht hätten, ist schwer abzuschätzen. Doch bleibt zu berücksichtigen, dass über den Lago Maggiore, der im 15. Jahrhundert noch bis nach Bellinzona reichte, auf dem Wasserweg Versorgungsgüter jederzeit hätten antransportiert werden können.

Da die fieberhafte Bautätigkeit in Bellinzona bis 1499 anhielt, kann man sich fragen, ob die Sperrbefestigung im Jahre 1500, als diese den Mailändern verloren ging, überhaupt fertiggestellt gewesen sei. Zweifel sind angebracht. Die Möglichkeit, dass in einer letzten, projektierten Ausbauphase die östliche Talflanke von Montebello bis hinauf zum Castello di Sasso Corbaro durch eine weitere Sperrmauer hätte befestigt werden sollen, ist nicht völlig auszuschließen. So aber bildet die Silhouette der Sperrfestung, wie sie sich heute darbie-

Abb. 10 – Bellinzona, Gesamtansicht der Talsperre von Nordosten. Gemälde von G. Lory/J. Hürlimann, 1830. Foto Capri, Bellinzona.

tet – abgesehen von den älteren, hochragenden Türmen des Castel Grande – zur Hauptsache ein Werk des ausgehenden 15. Jahrhunderts.

Nachdem sich die Eidgenossen ein Jahrhundert lang vergeblich bemüht hatten, Bellinzona gewaltsam einzunehmen, fiel ihnen im Jahre 1500 die Festung überraschend kampflos in die Hände[39]. Den Hintergrund bildeten die Wirren im Herzogtum Mailand. Der König von Frankreich erhob auf dieses Erbansprüche, rückte mit einer Armee in die Lombardei ein und besetzte auch Bellinzona. Dessen Bewohner erhoben sich gegen die französische Garnison, fürchteten aber später wegen deren Vertreibung das Strafgericht des Königs. Um diesem zu entgehen, stellten sie sich unter den Schutz und Schirm der Eidgenossen, was diese allerdings in Verlegenheit stürzte, denn die meisten Orte, vorab Bern, trugen Bedenken wegen Schwierigkeiten mit dem befreundeten König von Frankreich. Die Innerschweizer aber wollten die Festung unter keinen Umständen wieder herausgeben und verblieben – der König hatte 1503 im Vertrag von Arona nachgegeben – im Besitz der Grafschaft Bellinzona mit den drei Burgen[40].

Als Grenzfestung hatte Bellinzona nun ausgedient, gelang es doch den Eidgenossen, im Zuge der sogenannten „Mailänder Feldzüge" zu Beginn des 16. Jahrhunderts, ihr Hoheitsgebiet bis auf die Linie der heutigen Landesgrenze am Lago di Lugano vorzuschieben[41]. Bellinzona galt zwar noch immer als „Schloss und Schlüssel nach Italien" und diente bis um 1530 wiederholt als Sammel- und Garnisonsplatz der Eidgenossen für deren kriegerische Unternehmungen in der Lombardei[42]. Der Ort lag aber weit außerhalb der

---

39. Meyer 1976, 150-151, Anm. 63; Chiesi 1991, 359-365; Gagliardi 1, 1919, 495-500.
40. *Ibid.*, 520-549 ; Chiesi 1978, 123-152.
41. Gagliardi 1, 1919, 567-569.
42. Rahn 1893, 407.

Kampfgebiete, die Festungswerke erfuhren keine baulichen Veränderungen mehr. (Zu solchen hätten den Innerschweizern ohnehin die finanziellen Mittel gefehlt.) Uri, Schwyz und Nidwalden, die sich in den Besitz Bellinzonas teilten, gaben den drei Burgen, die ihnen als weithin sichtbare Herrschaftssymbole galten, ihre Namen. Das Castel Grande wurde zum Schloss Uri, Montebello zum Schloss Schwyz, und Sasso Corbaro hieß Schloss Unterwalden[43]. Die Befestigungsanlagen, militärisch nutzlos geworden, begannen zu zerfallen. Erst im 20. Jahrhundert erfolgten umfassende Sanierungsarbeiten[44].

Als Zeuge für die oberitalienische Festungsbaukunst des Spätmittelalters figuriert Bellinzona auf der UNESCO-Liste des Weltkulturerbes.

---

43. Bauliche Ausbesserungen sind noch für 1507 bezeugt (Abschiede 3/2, 1869, 400). Die Umbenennung der drei Schlösser erfolgte nach 1506, als von der Tagsatzung der Beschluss gefasst wurde, je eine Burg den drei Orten Uri, Schwyz und Unterwalden zur Bewachung zuzuweisen. Auf dem Castel Grande sollten acht, auf den beiden anderen Burgen je fünf Mann stationiert werden (Abschiede 3/2, 1869, 352).

44. Zusammenstellung der bis um 1950 ausgeführten Arbeiten auf dem Castel Grande bei BLOK 1967.

Literatur

ARCHÄOLOGIE GR (o.J.), *Archäologie in Graubünden. Funde und Befunde. Festschrift zum 25jährigen Bestehen des Archäologischen Dienstes Graubünden*, Chur o.J.

BLOK H. (1967), *Cronistoria degli interventi di restauro in Castel Grande*, Bellinzona, Archivio storico ticinese.

BRÄNDLI P. J. (1986), *Mittelalterliche Grenzstreitigkeiten im Alpenraum. Mitteilungen des Historischen Vereins des Kantons Schwyz*, Bd. LXXVIII, Einsiedeln, Staatsarchiv des Kantons Schwyz.

BRENTANI L. (1928), *L'antica chiesa matrice di S. Pietro in Bellinzona*, Bd. I, Como, Arti grafiche Bari (Monografie artistiche ticinesi; 2).

– (1934), *L'antica chiesa matrice di S. Pietro in Bellinzona*, Bd. II, Como, Arti grafiche Bari (Monografie artistiche ticinesi; 2).

BSSI, Bollettino Storico della Svizzera Italiana, 1ff., 1879ff.

BUB 1. (1955), *Bündner Urkundenbuch*, bearb. von E. MEYER-MARTHALER & F. PERRET, Bd. I, Chur, Bischofberger, 1955ff.; Bd. II, Chur, Bischofberger, 1973.

BUNDI M. (1982), *Zur Besiedlungs- und Wirtschaftsgeschichte Graubündens im Mittelalter*, Chur, Calven-Verlag.

BURGENKARTE (2007), *Burgenkarte der Schweiz, 2 Blätter West-Ost, 1: 200 000*, Bern, Geogr. Bern.

CHIESI G. (hrsg.) (1978), *Pagine bellinzonesi. Cenni storici, studi e recerche in occasione del centenario de Bellinzona capitale stabile del Cantone Ticino (1878-1978)*, Bellinzona, Stato del Cantone Ticino.

– (1991), *Il Medioevo nelle carte. Documenti di storia ticinese e svizzera dalle origini al secolo 16*, Bellinzona, Stato del Cantone Ticino.

CLAVADETSCHER O. P. & MEYER W. (1984), *Das Burgenbuch von Graubünden*, Zürich, Orell Füssli.

GAGLIARDI E. (1919), *Der Anteil der Schweizer an den italienischen Kriegen, 1494-1516*, Zürich, Schulthess & Co.

GILARDONI V. (1955), *Inventario delle cose d'arte e dell'antichità*, Bd. II: *Distretto di Bellinzona*, Bellinzona, Edizioni dello Stato.

GLAUSER F. (1988), „Von alpiner Landwirtschaft beidseits des St. Gotthards (1000-1350). Aspekte der mittelalterlichen Groß- und Kleinviehhaltung sowie des Ackerbaus der Alpenregionen Innerschweiz, Glarus, Blenio und Leventina", *Der Geschichtsfreund*, 141, 5-173.

HOFER-WILD G. (1949), *Herrschaft und Hoheitsrechte der Sax im Misox*, Poschiavo, Menghini.

HOWALD E. & MEYER E. (1940), *Die römische Schweiz. Texte und Inschriften mit Übersetzung*, Zürich, M. Niehans.

MEYER K. (1911), *Blenio und Leventina von Barbarossa bis Heinrich VII.*, Dissertation Zürich 1911, Zürich.

– (1915), *Ennetbirgische Politik und Feldzüge der Innerschweizer bis zum Siege von Giornico. Schweizer Kriegsgeschichte 3*, Bern, Oberkriegskommissariat.

– (1952), *Die Walserkolonie Rheinwald und die Freiherren von Sax-Misox. Aufsätze und Reden*, Zürich, Rohr in Komm. (Mitteilungen der Antiquarischen Gesellschaft in Zürich; 37).

MEYER W. (1976), *Das Castel Grande in Bellinzona. Bericht über die Ausgrabungen und Bauuntersuchungen von 1967*, Olten/Freiburg im Breisgau, Walter (Schweizer Beiträge zur Kulturgeschichte und Archäologie des Mittelalters; 3).

– (1994), *Die Burgen von Bellinzona*, Bern, Gesellschaft für Schweizerische Kunstgeschichte (Schweizerische Kunstführer. Serie 56; 551/552).

MEYER W. *et al.* (1998), *„Heidenhüttli", 25 Jahre archäologische Wüstungsforschung im schweizerischen Alpenraum*, Basel, Schweizerischer Burgenverein (Schweizer Beiträge zur Kulturgeschichte und Archäologie des Mittelalters; 23/24).

OEHLMANN E. (1879), „Die Alpenpässe im Mittelalter", *Zeitschrift für schweizerische Geschichte*, 163ff.

POESCHEL E. (1930), *Das Burgenbuch von Graubünden*, Zürich, Orell Füssli.

RAHN J. R. (1893), *Die mittelalterlichen Kunstdenkmäler des Cantons Tessin*, Zürich, Antiquarische Gesellschaft Zürich.

WEISSES BUCH (1947), *Das Weisse Buch von Sarnen, bearbeitet von Hans Georg Wirz. Quellenwerk zur Entstehung der Schweizerischen Eidgenossenschaft*, Abt. III: *Chroniken*, Bd. I, Aarau, Sauerländer.

WIELICH G. (1970), *Das Locarnese im Altertum und Mittelalter. Ein Beitrag zur Geschichte des Kantons Tessin*, Bern, Francke.

WINKELMANN E. (1880), *Acta imperii inedita*, Innsbruck, Wagner.

Drawing upon the Line? The Use of Landscape along Shire Borders in Scottish Noble Architecture

◆

Katherine Buchanan*

When considered as key features of spatial interaction, borders present an interesting challenge. Although, by nature, borders can contain characteristics of the limitations and constrictions of marginality[1], they also contain elements of organised movement and permeability[2]. The interaction between castellated structures along borders and the surrounding landscape must be considered with an understanding that the relationship between sites will exhibit elements that both regulate and encourage mobility at these particular points. Each site presents a unique relationship with its surroundings depending on its position within the parameters set by the desired endpoints. Hillier and Hansen developed the concept of access being defined through a point in which all interactions must pass[3]; access with the landscape is also dictated by this stem. The relationships between a castellated site and the features within its "catchment" can be divided into two categories: adjacent and detached. This present project discusses how the landscape setting can orientate a site towards encouraging interaction. This is evident in a study of castellated architecture within the internal border context of Scottish nobles and shire boundaries, particularly Baikie Castle and the Lindsay family in Strathmore (on the Perthshire and Forfarshire border).

Although Baikie Castle does not survive as an upstanding structure, Timothy Pont's maps (1586) and other record sources provide information regarding the placement and function of this site on the boundary between Perthshire and Forfarshire. When depicted by Pont, the castle occupied an island in Baikie Loch, linked to the mainland by a causeway. The two maps on which it is illustrated, Pont 26 and Pont 29, describe the structure differently. As discussed by Shelley[4], Pont 26 displays a single tower with four windowed storeys, a surrounding crenelated wall, and a tree (fig. 1). Pont 29 indicates a more elaborate structure with three towers: one with four storeys and two on either side with two storeys[5] (fig. 2). Both descriptions showed settlement on the shores of the loch, though Pont 29 was more detailed. Pont 29 is clearer about the status of this structure but both depictions suggest a social position that fits into what Charles McKean designated as Category 2 on his scale of significance of the high-status buildings portrayed by Pont[6]. Documentary evidence confirms the presence of a manor-house and a chapel in 1439 and adds a fortification and tenements by 1488[7]. By 1527, a monopoly over local mill rights was added to the list of features attached to the barony of Baikie, further underscoring the substantial level of status attributed to this tower house[8]. Baikie Castle's position within a loch made it a physically distinct feature in the district and further defined its adjacent and detached relationships.

The interactions between Baikie and its adjacent surroundings were defined by its situation within a waterscape; these interactions were mediated by the proximity of the connected settlement. Baikie and its Loch were situated on Baikie Burn, which Pont indicated as a sizeable watercourse flowing south-west to join with the River Isla (which forms the border between Perthshire and Forfarshire at this point).

---

* University of Stirling, United Kingdom.
1. Higham 2004, 17.
2. Backhaus & Murungi 2006, 31.
3. Hillier & Hanson 1984, 2; see also Faulkner 1963, 150.
4. Shelley 2009, 106.
5. Pont, T. 26 & T. 29.
6. McKean 2001, 118: "Category 2 buildings are of scomparable scale – four storeys or more – but lacking the heraldic skyline or perhaps the park. They are much plainer, with only the mere indication of a roof…"
7. RMS, II, 52, 373.

Fig. 1 – Baikie Castle, Pont 26 (reproduced by permission of the National Library of Scotland).

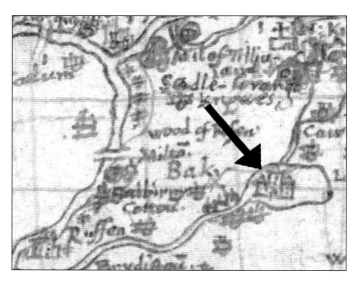

Fig. 2 – Baikie Castle, Pont 29 (reproduced by permission of the National Library of Scotland).

Date	Person receiving property	Property being received	Shire
14 October 1458[9]	Elizabeth Lindsey	C[o]llace Little Butt[er]gask Drumbla[d]e	Pertshire Pertshire Aberdeenshire
14 October 1458[10]	David Lindsey	Balm[o]re	Aberdeenshire
20 July 1459[11]	David Stewart	Ard[12]; Strathglass Balm[o]re; Co[c]klaw C[o]okstown; Buthlaw Drumbla[de]; Colli[e] C[o]llace; Butt[er]gask Strathifentoune[13]	Inverness Aberdeenshire Aberdeenshire Aberdeenshire Pertshire Pertshire

Table 1 – Distribution of lands connected to Baikie Castle.

Although nearby Ruthven Castle stood closer to the confluence of Baikie Burn and the River Isla, Pont 29 indicated that both castles were roughly equidistant from the bridge over the River Isla which he noted and Pont 26 placed more emphasis on Baikie than Ruthven. However, the placement of the 'Wood of Rufven' in Pont 26 (between the bridge and Baikie) and the breadth of the Baikie Burn suggest that a route following the course of Baikie Burn was the primary access way to and from the castle. With a clearly identified route along the waters, Baikie Castle was very well positioned for the nearby developing market town of Coupar Angus (Perthshire), with subsequent direct road links from there to the ports of Perth and Dundee. Within 15 kilometres north and east, there are also two burghs, Kirriemuir (a baronial burgh) and Forfar (a royal burgh). They also provided Baikie Castle with immediate access to the main routes that continued north over the Grampian Mountains, increasing its importance as a central point within key access routes beyond the immediate divisions along the Perthshire and Forfarshire border in Strathmore.

The importance of Baikie Castle as a property of border connection grew as the Lindsays' territorial interest spread beyond the immediate locality. When the lands were quartered and given away in October 1458 to conjoin with lands in other sheriffdoms, this broadened Baikie Castle's relationship with lands beyond its borders. The lands of Baikie were quartered by Margaret Fentoune of Baikie and partially given to David and Elizabeth Lindsay, her children by David Lindsay of Lethnot[14]. These grants and subsequent acquisitions established a

8. RMS, III, 117.
9. RMS, II, 140.
10. *Ibid.*
11. RMS, II, 154.
12. Place not yet identified.
13. Exact location not known, tentatively labelled as near Strathy in Strathearn (possibly Strathy – fermtoune), labelled as Strathy and Strathyplain on the 1856 Ordnance Survey Map.
14. RMS, II, 140.

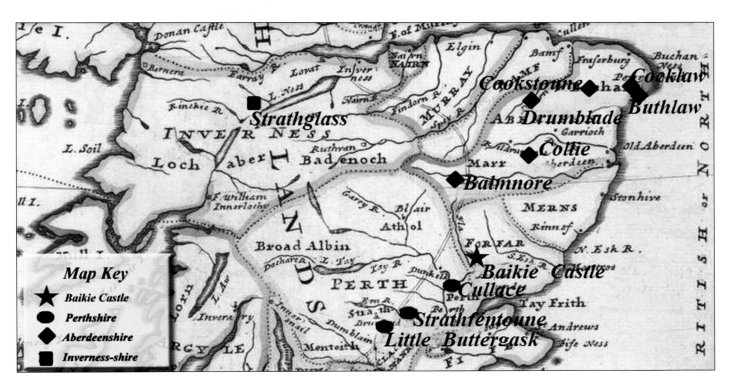

Fig. 3 – Distribution of lands connected to Baikie Castle on H. Moll's 1745 map of the Shires (original version of the map found at the National Library of Scotland).

direct linkage, founded on common ownership, between the Lindsays' Baikie lands and their other properties in Perthshire, Aberdeenshire and Inverness (table 1 & fig. 3). The distribution of these sites placed Baikie within a broader spectrum of border relations. Given Baikie Castle's proximity to local access routes, its central position in the Lindsay lordship remained unaffected when the principal desired destinations of travel from it moved far beyond the immediate borders of their original landholding.

This assessment of Baikie's position demonstrates that the location of a site within specific landscape contexts can drive its relationship with surrounding features, focusing it on access and movement. Baikie's geographically central but, in terms of political-administrative units, marginal location drove the focus of its site towards the exchange of information and goods across nearby borders, opening them up rather than limiting them. Baikie Castle's easy accessibility from and interconnection with important national routeways made it a key location for transit and communication. Demand for a central site to continue social interchange across great distances increases the need for accessibility. The surrounding landscape and Baikie Castle's spatial interaction across internal administrative borders within the context of Scottish noble society suggests a tendency to promote interaction that overcomes social and environmental constraints. It is possible that Baikie's key position within the landscape made it more of a focal point within these cross-boundary relationships than other neighbouring castellated structures, like Ruthven. However, a broader study of interaction between sites across shire borders needs to be undertaken to fully understand individual family policies toward promoting or hindering access.

Bibliography

Backhaus G. & Murungi J. (2006), *Ecoscapes: Geographical Patternings of Relations*, Lanham/Oxford, Lexington Books.

Faulkner P. A. (1963), "Castle Planning in the Fourteenth Century", *Archaeological Journal*, 120, 215-235.

Higham N. J. (2004), *A Frontier Landscape: the North West in the Middle Ages*, Bollington, Windgather.

Hillier B. & Hanson J. (1984), *The Social Logic of Space*, Cambridge, Cambridge University Press.

McKean C. (2001), "Pont's Building Drawings", in *The Nation Survey'd: Essays on Late Sixteenth-Century Scotland as Depicted by Timothy Pont*, I. C. Cunningham (ed.), Edinburgh, Tuckwell, 111-124.

Ordnance Survey Map (1856): *One-inch to the mile maps of Scotland*, 1st ed.

Pont, T. 26: *Lower Angus and Perthshire East of the Tay.*

Pont, T. 29: *Middle Strathmore.*

Registrum magni sigilli regum Scotorum 1306-1668 (RMS), vols. 2-3, Edinburgh, Her Majesty's General Register House [1882].

Shelley M. (2009), *Freshwater Scottish Loch Settlements of the Late Medieval and Early Modern Periods: with Particular Reference to Northern Stirlingshire, Central and Northern Perthshire, Northern Angus, Loch Awe and Loch Lomond*, Unpublished Ph.D. Thesis, University of Edinburgh.

Burgenarchäologie in einer Grenzregion

Ein Beitrag zum Burgenbau im Diemelraum

◆

Andrea Bulla, Hans-Werner Peine*

Der Diemelraum im südöstlichen Westfalen ist für die LWL-Archäologie für Westfalen ein zentraler Forschungs- und Grabungsschwerpunkt. Diese Landschaft, bereits Grenzstreifen zwischen den Sachsen und Franken, trennte auch im Spätmittelalter politische Herrschaftsgebiete, die sich an den naturräumlichen Gegebenheiten orientierten. So markierte die Diemel auf weiten Strecken bis 1803 die Grenze zwischen dem Bistum Paderborn, der Grafschaft Waldeck und der Landgrafschaft Hessen. Moderne archäologische Forschungen geben heute Einblick u.a. in die Geschichte der mittelalterlichen Burgenlandschaft[1].

In Westfalen finden die frühmittelalterlichen Burgen erste schriftliche Erwähnung zur Zeit der Sachsenkriege Karls des Großen. So werden in der zeitgenössischen Überlieferung die Syburg bei Dortmund und die Eresburg bei Obermarsberg erwähnt, die im Grenzland von Franken und Sachsen heftig umkämpft waren. Zu diesen frühen Burgen zählt im Diemeltal neben der Eresburg die Befestigung auf dem Gaulskopf bei Warburg (Abb. 1, Plan)[2]. Die Geschichte der 4,5 ha großen Anlage reicht bis in die mittlere Steinzeit zurück, auf eine intensive Besiedlung während der Jungsteinzeit weist umfangreiches Fundgut hin. Im 7./8. Jahrhundert wurden die heute noch sichtbaren Wälle und Gräben der Anlage errichtet. Sie umgeben ein 370 m hoch gelegenes Bergplateau mit steil abfallenden Hängen, das von Osten her erschlossen wurde. Westlich und östlich der Burg finden sich weitere Wallreste. Der Ringwall stellt die Überreste einer Holz-Erde-Konstruktion mit einer vorgeblendeten Trockenmauer dar. Seine Zweiphasigkeit konnte im Verlaufe der Grabungen belegt werden. So zeigt sich z.B. auf der Krone des Westwalls eine jüngere 1,65 m breite Mauer. Vor dem Hauptwall befanden sich eine 1 m breite Berme und ein 1,5 m tiefer Sohlgraben. Noch heute beträgt der Höhenunterschied zwischen Wallkrone und Sohlgraben 3,3 m. Ausgrabungen der Jahre 1967 und 1990 bis 1995 erbrachten im Osten der Anlage zwei repräsentative Toranlagen. Sie gehören einer jüngeren Bau- und Nutzungsphase der Burg an. Ob die beiden steinernen Kammertore gleichzeitig bestanden, konnte nicht sicher ermittelt werden. Zumindest das nördliche Tor ersetzte einen hölzernen Vorgänger, der vermutlich in die 2. Hälfte des 8. Jahrhunderts datiert. Die Grabungsschnitte der 90er Jahre erbrachten für die Burg auch den Nachweis einer zumindest zweiphasigen Innenbebauung im Zentrum der Anlage. Dort konnten Pfosten- und Schwellbalkenhäuser sowie ein Grubenhaus (Keller?) freigelegt werden. Drei beigabenlose West-Ost ausgerichtete Körpergräber, geschnitten von Haus 4, stehen vielleicht in Bezug zu Haus 3 (Länge 11,2 x 4,5 m), das vom Ausgräber mit einer sakralen Nutzung in Verbindung gebracht wird.

Gegenstände des täglichen Lebens und aus dem Bereich des Handwerks machen deutlich, dass die Burg spätestens im 9./10. Jahrhundert als Wohnsitz diente. Trachtbestandteile wie zwei goldene Fibeln, Waffen- und Waffenteile (Schwergutbeschläge, Pfeilspitzen) sowie Reitzubehör (Sporen) belegen die militärische Nutzung und geben Auskunft über die hohe soziale Stellung des Burgherrn und seiner Gefolgsleute. So findet 1024 ein Graf Ekkika von Asseln Erwähnung. Die frühmittelalterlichen Eliten lebten zuvor auf Herrenhöfen zwischen der ländlichen Bevölkerung: das Geschlecht von Asseln vermutlich

---

* LWL-Archäologie für Westfalen, Mittelalter- und Neuzeitarchäologie, Deutschland.
1. Bulla & Peine 2012a, 64-65; Kneppe & Peine 2005, 169-179.
2. Best 2009, 116-121; Best et al. 1999a, 299-307; Best et al. 1999b; Best 1997; Doms 1986a; Doms 1986b, 81f.

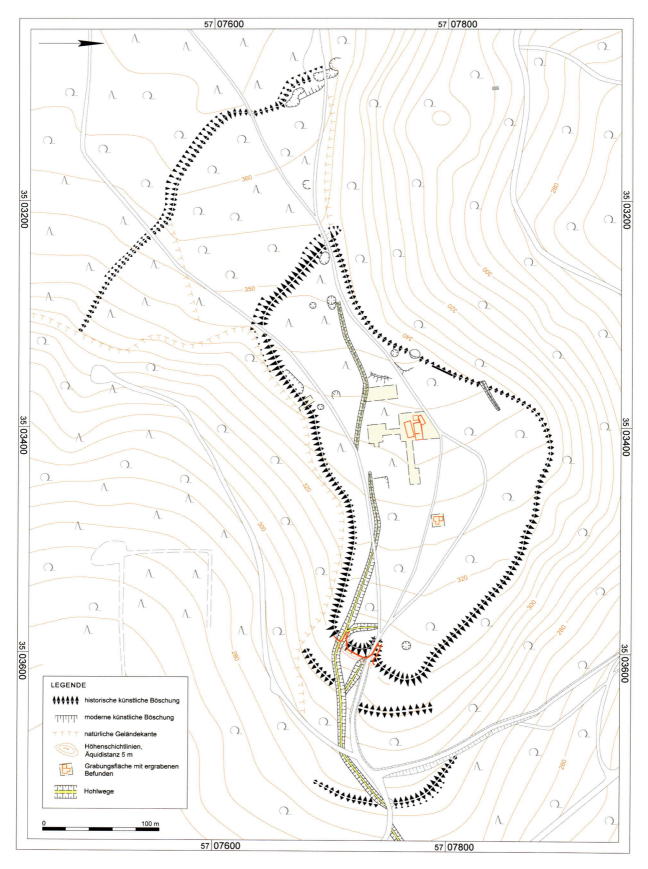

Abb. 1 – Die früh- bis hochmittelalterliche Wallburg auf dem Gaulskopf. Plan LWL-Archäologie für Westfalen.

im wüst gefallenen Ort Asseln unterhalb des Gaulskopfes. Die Grabungsergebnisse belegen, dass die Burg zur Zeit der Sachsenkriege bereits existierte und im Zuge der Auseinandersetzungen aufgrund ihrer Lage im fränkisch-sächsischen Grenzgebiet eine sicherlich nicht unerhebliche Rolle spielte.

In ihrer jüngeren Nutzungsphase diente die Burg dann als repräsentativer Herren- und Verwaltungssitz der Grafen von Asseln.

Mit der Burg Wartberg fassen wir einen weiteren Grafensitz im Diemelraum[3]. Sie bildete das Zentrum einer adligen Grundherrschaft. Die Burg wurde spätestens um 1000 n. Chr. auf dem Wartberg hoch über dem Diemeltal erbaut. So kontrollierten die Burgherren die „Holländische Straße", einen wichtigen Fernverkehrsweg, der die Niederlande mit Hessen verband und bei Warburg die Diemel überschritt[4]. Das Adelsgeschlecht war zuvor wohl auf einem westlich davon gelegenen und in fränkischer Zeit gegründeten Haupthof auf der „Hüffert" ansässig[5]. In der schriftlichen Überlieferung fassen wir auf dem Burgberg im frühen 11. Jahrhundert den Grafen Dodiko, der mütterlicherseits der sächsischen Adelsfamilie der Haholde, väterlicherseits der Asic-Sippe entstammt. Als Parteigänger des ottonisch-sächsischen Königshauses finden wir Dodiko in besonderer Nähe zu König Heinrich II. (1002-1024), so wird er zwischen 1013 und 1020 mehrfach in Königsurkunden als Zeuge benannt. Er war Inhaber von Grafenrechten im Itter-, Hessen- und Nethegau. Am 29. August 1020 verstarb Graf Dodiko. Die Burg auf dem Wartberg, sein Grundbesitz und die Grafenrechte gelangten unter Bischof Meinwerk (1009-1036) an das Bistum Paderborn[6]. Die Burg wurde der wichtigste Rückhalt der Paderborner Bischöfe in den Auseinandersetzungen um die Landesherrschaft im westfälisch-hessischen Grenzraum[7]. Schon bald entwickelte sich im Schutz der Burg eine Siedlung, die bereits 1036 als *villa* Erwähnung findet[8].

Über den Gebäudebestand der Burg erfahren wir aus den Viten der hl. Haimeradus und Meinwerkus, dass eine *capella*, dem hl. Andreas geweiht und von einem Kleriker betreut, ein *solarim* und ein *geniceum* vorhanden waren. Der Nachfolgebau der Kapelle, eine große Basilika mit Krypta des frühen 12. Jahrhunderts, konnte 1963 ergraben werden, des Weiteren stieß man östlich davon auf die 2,45 m starke Wehrmauer der Burg[9]. Der Bau der Großbasilika erscheint für eine einfache Burgkirche zu aufwendig, erklären ließe er sich duch eine vom Bischof von Paderborn in Erwägung gezogene Angliederung einer geistlichen Gemeinschaft auf dem Burgberg, ein Vorhaben, das zum Beispiel auf der durch Bischof Benno I. von Osnabrück (1052-1068) gegründeten Iburg durch dessen Nachfolger Benno II. (1068-1088) umgesetzt wurde. Die Absicht ein Kloster auf dem Warburger Burgberg zu errichten, wird bereits Bischof Meinwerk zugeschrieben, der die ihm 1018 von Heinrich II. übertragene Reichsabtei Helmarshausen in die neuerworbene Burg verlegen und hier mit einer eigenen Klosterstiftung zusammenschließen wollte[10]. Vermutlich erfolgte im frühen 12. Jahrhundert im Zusammenhang mit dem Bau der Großbasilika ein umfangreicher Ausbau der Warburger Bischofsburg. Seit dem 13. Jahrhundert sind auf der bischöflichen Burg Burgmannen bezeugt. Im 15. Jahrhundert verliert die Anlage an Bedeutung, ihr Verfall setzte im 16. Jahrhundert ein. Frühneuzeitliche Bildquellen zeigen den ruinösen Gebäudebestand der Burg bis in das frühe 19. Jahrhundert. Reste der Burggebäude werden im späten 18. Jahrhundert und 1830 abgebrochen. 1831 wird die Burg der Stadt Warburg zur Anlage eines Friedhofs überlassen. Die in den letzten beiden Jahrhunderten vorgenommen Bestattungen auf dem dicht belegten Friedhof stören weite Teile des Burgareals tiefgründig und lassen dort für zukünftige archäologische Untersuchungen kaum Erkenntniszuwachs zur Baugeschichte der Burg erwarten.

Nur wenige Kilometer östlich von ihr erhebt sich auf einem imposanten Bergkegel die Burg Desenberg über die Warburger Börde (Abb. 2)[11]. Diese steht als Beispiel für einen neuartigen Burgenbau, der in der 2. Hälfte des 11. Jahrhunderts in Westfalen Einzug hält[12]. Wie der Salier Heinrich IV. stützte auch der sächsische Hochadel seine Herrschaft auf neu errichtete Gipfelburgen, die mittels kleiner Besatzungen zu halten waren. In unzugänglichem Gelände und weit entfernt von Siedlungen angelegt, stellen diese Burgen den Prototyp der „klassischen Adelsburg" dar.

Als Stützpunkt Ottos von Northeim, einem der führenden Köpfe der sächsischen Adelsopposition, wurde der Desenberg wie die Burg Hanstein im Eichsfeld (Thüringen) durch König Heinrich IV. belagert. Lampert von Hersfeld berichtet hierzu folgendes:

> Vor eine andere Burg, Desenberg mit Namen, hatte er Truppen gelegt. Obgleich sie ihrer Lage wegen uneinnehmbar und mit allen zur Kriegsführung notwendigen Mitteln hinlänglich versorgt war, zogen es die Insassen doch vor, sich freiwillig zu ergeben, als das zweifelhafte Kriegsglück zu versuchen[13].

Nach dem Aussterben der Grafen von Northeim gelangte die Burg spätestens 1152 in den Besitz Herzog Heinrichs des Löwen, der damit Graf Widukind von Schwalenberg belehnte. Der Schwalenberger schloss sich einem Aufstand gegen Heinrich

---

3. Dubbi 2006; Peine 2006; Peine 1997; Decker 1989; Doms 1986b; Schoppmeyer 1986; Irsigler 1976-1977.
4. Kneppe & Peine 1995, 5-68 mit weiterführender Literatur.
5. Kneppe & Peine 1997.
6. Zu Dodiko und Meinwerk siehe zuletzt Balzer 2009; Becher 2009; Kamp 2009; Schieffer 2009.
7. Vgl. Anm. 3; Stiegemann & Kroker 2009; Kneppe & Peine 1995.
8. Vgl. Anm. 4.
9. Engemann 1972; Honselmann 1972; Tümmler 1972.
10. Streich 1984, 503ff.
11. Peine 2006, 235-242; Dubbi & Bialas 2004; Kneppe & Peine 2000; Peine 1997, 172-175.
12. Peine 2006, 238.
13. Hersfeld 1985, 129.

Abb. 2 – Die hoch- bis spätmittelalterliche Gipfelburg auf dem Desenberg bei Warburg. Foto LWL-Archäologie für Westfalen.

Abb. 3 – Die hochmittelalterliche Holsterburg – eine Niederungsburg im Schatten des Desenberges. Foto LWL-Archäologie für Westfalen.

den Löwen an und wurde von diesem erfolgreich auf dem Desenberg belagert, indem Heinrich den Verteidigern das Wasser des Burgbrunnens durch Bergleute vom Rammelsberg abgraben ließ und sie so zur Übergabe der Burg zwang. Vorübergehend im Besitz der Staufer und des Bistums Paderborn, gelangte sie wieder in welfischen Besitz und wurde 1203 im Erbteilungsvertrag der drei Söhne Heinrichs des Löwen zusammen mit der Burg Altenfels Pfalzgraf Heinrich zugesprochen. 1205/1206 wird die Burg durch Abt Widukind von Corvey und Bischof Bernhard III. von Paderborn erobert und teilzerstört. Im 13. Jahrhundert im Kölnischen Besitz fassen wir ab 1256 die Familie „Spiegel zum Desenberg", die im Grenzgebiet zwischen Paderborn und Hessen im Spätmittelalter eine eigene kleine Territorialherrschaft aufbaute. Um die Mitte des 16. Jahrhunderts verlegte die Familie „von Spiegel" ihre Wohnsitze vom Desenberg in die Warburger Börde. Das Ende der funktionslosen Burg war damit besiegelt. Inwieweit Teile des heutigen Baubestandes der Burgruine in die Frühzeit der Anlage zurückgehen, konnten auch archäologische Untersuchungen der Jahre 1962/1963, 1987 und 1999/2000 nicht klären. Ringmauer und Gebäude erfuhren aber im späten Mittelalter durch Umbaumaßnahmen erhebliche Veränderungen[14].

Im ausgehenden Hochmittelalter versuchten neben den großen Landesherren auch kleinere Herrschaften ihre Macht und ihre Territorien auszubauen und zu festigen. Im späten 12. Jahrhundert zählten zu diesen Burgherren in der Region auch die Edelherren von Holthausen, genannt Berkule. Um 1170 wird der Edelherr Wolnandus erstmals in den Archivalien im Zusammenhang mit dem Dorf Holthusen erwähnt. Seine Nachfolger, die Brüder Hermann und Bernhard Berkule, sind im Gefolge der den Staufern nahe stehenden Grafen von Everstein zu finden. Ihr Besitz (Dorf und Burg) wird erstmals im Verzeichnis der käuflichen Erwerbungen des Kölner Erzbischofs Philipp I. von Heinsberg (1167-1191) erwähnt. Beides wird später von beiden Erzbistümern als Lehen vergeben[15]. Ihre Burg kontrollierte die wichtige Wegeführung zwischen der Warburger Altstadt, die zwischen 1168 und 1187 entstand, und Kassel[16]. Im Gegensatz zum landschaftsprägenden Desenberg mit seiner Gipfelburg, die aufgrund ihrer militärischen und politischen Bedeutung im hohen Mittelalter im Fokus der Reichspolitik stand, handelt es sich bei der Holsterburg um eine nahezu unbekannte Niederungsburg über die nur wenige historische und bislang auch archäologische Informationen vorlagen[17].

Immerwährende Konflikte zwischen der Familie Berkule und der Stadt Warburg besiegelten letztendlich den Untergang von Dorf und Burg. 1294 eroberten Warburger Bürger und deren Bündnispartner Marsberg, Höxter, Fritzlar, Hofgeismar, Wolfhagen und Naumburg unter Rückendeckung des Paderborner Bischofs die Burg und zerstörten diese. Nachfolgend wurde der entmachtete Burgherr mit einem Burglehen auf der Burg Warburg in die Dienstmannschaft des Paderborner Bischofs einbezogen, einige der in Gefangenschaft geratenen Ritter wurden hingerichtet[18]. Die

---

14. Kneppe & Peine 2000; Kneppe & Peine 1991; Engemann & Stephan 1979.
15. Decker 1989; Bulla & Kneppe 2011, 145-149; Lagers 2011.
16. Vgl. Anm. 4; Kneppe & Peine 1997, 229-248.
17. Decker 1989; Doms 1986b, 35-87.
18. Bulla & Peine 2012b; Bulla & Kneppe 2011; Decker 1989; Gottlob 1936.

Burg Calenberg in Sichtweite der Holsterburg von einem Familienzweig der Berkules errichtet, übernahm nach der Zerstörung der Holsterburg deren strategische Stellung im Grenzraum südlich der Stadt Warburg[19].

Die Überreste der zerstörten Holsterburg waren bis 2009 unter einem bewachsenen Hügel verborgen. Im Jahr 2010 führte an der als Motte/Turmhügelburg eingeordneten Erhebung die LWL-Archäologie für Westfalen, Mittelalter- und Neuzeitarchäologie, Vermessungsarbeiten und erste kleinere Sondagen durch. Dabei zeigte sich am Rande des Hügels ein großformatiger Kalksteinquader. Der qualitätvoll gearbeitete Glattquader wies an seiner Außenseite einen flachen Winkel auf. Damit ließ dieser Eckquader auf eine ungewöhnliche Bauform schließen und führte zu weiteren archäologischen Sondagen vor Ort, um eine gesicherte Interpretation des offenliegenden Baubefundes zu erzielen. Relativ schnell bestätigte sich in den Suchschnitten der Verdacht auf eine polygonale Ringmauer in Form eines Oktogons. 2010 konzentrierten sich die Arbeiten auf das Freilegen dieser Ringmauer, weitere archäologische Untersuchungen fanden 2011 und 2012 innerhalb der achteckigen Ringmauer statt (Abb. 3)[20].

Das Oktogon besteht aus einer zweischaligen, imposanten Mauer von knapp 1,8 m Stärke und ist in seinem Umfang vollständig erhalten. Das handwerklich hochwertige Quadermauerwerk, bestehend aus großformatigen Glattquadern, bildet einen achteckigen Grundriss und umfasst eine Innenfläche von 431 m². Die acht Segmente des Oktogons weisen dabei Längen zwischen 10,01 m und 11,65 m auf, so dass sich eine Gesamtlänge von 86,83 m ergibt. Die Außenfassade besticht durch bis zu 1,4 m lange und 0,4 m hohe Kalksteinquader. Diese Großquader betonen insbesondere die Ecken des Oktogons. Zwischen ihnen bestehen die Mauerabschnitte aus in regelmäßigen Lagen gesetzten Glattquadern von bis zu 0,94 m Länge und 0,2 m bis 0,3 m Höhe. Die Abbruchoberkante wurde, wie der Innenraum, von einer bis zu 1,3 m mächtigen Schuttschicht aus dem späten 13. Jahrhundert überzogen, die den Zerstörungshorizont von 1294 markiert. Für die Innenschale wurden kleinformatigere Quader gewählt. Das lagenhafte Füllmauerwerk besteht dagegen aus in grobem Mörtel gesetzten Kalksteinplatten. Die Fugen der waagerecht durchlaufenden, gleichhohen Lagen des Großsteinquadermauerwerks der Außenschale wurden durch Kellenfugenstrich zusätzlich betont. Das Zusammenspiel von Bauform, Baumaterial und Verarbeitung erzeugte eine wehrhafte, architektonisch monumental gestaltete, repräsentative Schaufassade. Diese setzte sich bis zum dreifach abgetreppten Fundamentsockel von insgesamt 0,8 m Höhe fort, der in einem Sondageschnitt freigelegt werden konnte. Die oberste Sockelstufe lag im sichtbaren Bereich und überraschte mit einer beschädigten Eckzier direkt oberhalb der Sockelzone. Mit einer erhaltenen Höhe von über 6 m, einer zu ermittelnden Höhe der Ringmauer von bis zu 12 m und einer Gesamtfläche von 568 m² gehört die Holsterburg mit ihrer beeindruckenden Architektur in jenen Kreis von oktogonalen Burgen, die im hochmittelalterlichen Europa an nur wenigen Orten ihre Entsprechung finden. Genannt seien die Burgen von Egisheim, Gebweiler und Wangen im Elsass, von Tübingen-Kilchberg in Baden-Württemberg und vom Torre di Federico in Enna auf Sizilien[21].

Die bislang bekannten Bauten dieser Gruppe belegen, dass die ungewöhnliche Bauform und die qualitätvolle Bauausführung unabhängig vom ständischen Rang ihrer Bauherren (Dienstmann, Edelherr, Bischof, Kaiser) waren. Der ständische Rang spiegelt sich jedoch in den Dimensionen der Burganlagen wider. Er lässt auf die ökonomischen Möglichkeiten der Bauherren schließen und darüber hinaus die sozialen Unterschiede erahnen. Die Holsterburg zeugt in ihrer vollendeten Architektur als weithin sichtbares Statussymbol von der Selbstdarstellung der Edelherren von Holthusen und hebt ihren Wohnsitz als beeindruckendes Architekturzeugnis aus der westfälischen Burgenlandschaft hervor (Abb. 4 a-b).

Fragen zur Innenbebauung der Holsterburg stehen seit 2012 im Focus der archäologischen Untersuchungen, die in den nächsten Jahren fortgeführt werden sollen. Deshalb können zur Innenbebauung derzeit nur begrenzte Aussagen getroffen werden.

Im Nordwesten der Burg lässt sich trotz der stark reduzierten Bausubstanz in der Anlage, bedingt durch deren Zerstörung und den anschließenden Steinraub, bereits eine dreiphasige Innenbebauung nachweisen: In der ersten Bauphase entstand um 1170/1180 ein kleiner, rechteckiger Turm (Ausmaße 2,56 x 2 m), dessen Unterbau als Brunnen gedient haben könnte. In einer zweiten Bauphase fügte sich in nur geringem Abstand westlich zu diesem kleinen Turm ein trapezförmiges Wohngebäude, Haus 1, mit einer Grundfläche von knapp 51 m² an die Ringmauer an. Auf dem 1,8 m starken Fundament gründet ein lagenhaft gesetztes Handquadermauerwerk (Stärke 1,3 m) aus Kalksandsteinblöcken, die in ihren Ausmaßen deutlich unterhalb von denen der Ringmauer liegen. Der Gebäudezugang in der noch 1,3 m hoch erhaltenen Ostwand wurde in einer Umbauphase mit Bruchsteinmauerwerk zugesetzt. In der Südwand des Gebäudes finden sich zwei

---

19. Lagers 2011, besonders 269ff.
20. Bulla & Peine im Druck; Bulla & Peine 2012b, 199-208; Bulla & Kneppe 2011, 145-149.
21. Vgl. zu den Burgen im Elsas Biller 2010, 399-422; Biller & Metz 1995; Biller & Metz 2007; vgl. zu Tübingen-Kilchberg Merkelbach 1965; vgl. zu Enna Beckmann 2007, 469-471; Liessem 2001, 209-220; Krönig 1986a; Krönig 1986b; vgl. ferner zu steinernen Wehrtürmen mit polygonalem Grundriss u. a. Aarts 2006; Heine 2008; Hensch 2005; Schmitt 2007; Schmitt 1999; Schmitt 2004a; Schmitt 2004b; Schmitt et al. 2006. Ein achteckiger Wehrturm wurde auch 2012 bei Ausgrabungen auf der Iburg bei Osnabrück angeschnitten. Für diesen Hinweis und die Einladung auf die Grabung danken wir M. Jansen. Vgl. zu polygonalen hölzernen Türmen Grote 2003; Heine 2006; Heine 2007; Peine 2012. Für Hinweise auf die oktogonalen Burgen von Skeingeborg in Schweden und Ugod in Ungarn danken wir I. Feld (Budapest) sowie F. Biermann (Göttingen) und B. Aarts (Tilburg, NL). Zur Skeingeborg siehe Ödman 2005. Zum allseits bekannten Castel del Monte in Apulien siehe zuletzt Leistikow 2001; Leistikow 2007; Schirmer 2001.

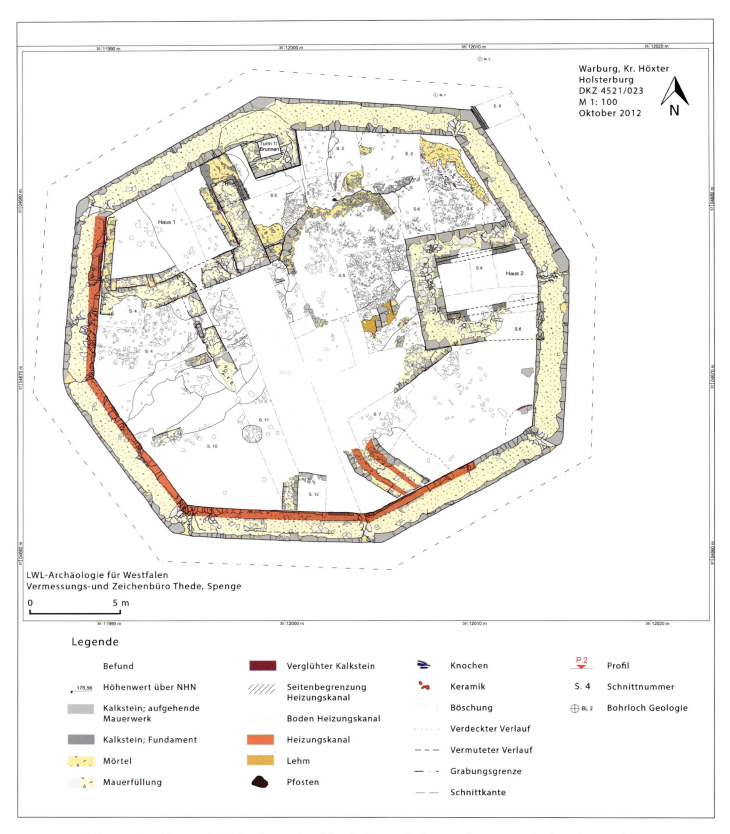

Abb. 4 a – Das Oktogon der Holsterburg – Stand der Grabungen Ende 2012. Plan LWL-Archäologie für Westfalen.

Abb. 4 b – Das Oktogon der Holsterburg – Stand der Grabungen Ende 2012. Plan und Foto LWL-Archäologie für Westfalen.

Abb. 5 – Blick auf die Nordwestecke des Oktogons mit Haus 1 und zugehörigem Heizkanal. Stand der Grabung Sommer 2012. Foto LWL-Archäologie für Westfalen.

konische Fensteröffnung. Später wurde den Gebäudemauern im Inneren eine 0,54 m starke Mauer vorgeblendet. In dieser Mauer sind im Süden zwei rechteckige Vertiefungen angelegt, die als Balkenlager einer Decke zu interpretieren sind und ein weiteres, abgängiges Geschoss belegen (Abb. 5).

Bei einer nahezu quadratischen Grundfläche von etwa 41 m² besteht Haus 2, im Osten der Anlage, aus massivem, 1,8 m starkem Mauerwerk. Es ist bis in das zweifach abgetreppte, 2,2 m starke Fundament nachhaltig gestört und lässt zumindest auf eine Zweigeschossigkeit schließen. Das Gebäude (Wohnturm) wurde in einer der beiden jüngeren Bauphasen der Burg errichtet, denn seine Nord- und Südwand wurden nachträglich in den Mauerverband der äußeren Wehrmauer eingebunden.

Westlich dieses Gebäudes konnte im Abbruchhorizont der Burg ein mächtiger Versturz des Bergfriedes dokumentiert werden. Er weist einen lichten Durchmesser von 2,2 m auf. Seine Lage deutet auf einen zentralen, abgängigen Bergfried hin. Über die exakte Stärke des Mauerwerks kann zurzeit keine Aussage getätigt werden.

Zwei mächtige, flachwinklige Großquaderblöcke am Rand seiner vermutlichen Ausbruchgrube könnten auf eine mehreckige Außenschale des Bergfriedes hindeuten. Den genauen Standort, seine Grundfläche und die Form des Turmes werden die Grabungen der nächsten Jahre erbringen. Befunde zur weiteren Innenbebauung deuten sich in Form von angeschnittenen Fundament- und Mauerzügen an.

Zur außergewöhnlichen Ausstattung der Wohngebäude auf der Süd- und Westseite der Holsterburg zählt eine Warmluftheizung[22]. Freigelegt wurde unter anderem ein 36 m langer, waagerecht verlaufender Heizkanal mit rechteckigem Querschnitt (Breite 0,33 m, Höhe 0,19 m), der in die Ringmauer der Burg integriert ist und hier bündig mit der Innenschale der Ringmauer über vier Seiten des Oktogons verläuft. Diese technisch aufwendige und luxuriöse Form der Beheizung lässt sich fast ausschließlich in repräsentativen Gebäuden des Adels (Pfalzen, Burgen), des Klerus (Pfalzen, Klöster) und der Bürgerschaft (öffentliche und halböffentliche Bauten wie Rathäuser, Spitäler, Bauten der Oberschicht) nachweisen.

Neben der Warmluftheizung, die die Gebäude im Westen und Süden der Burg erwärmte, gibt es Belege für eine weitere äußerst repräsentative Wärmequelle auf der 1294 zerstörten Burg. Scherbenfunde belegen für Gebäude 2 einen repräsentativen Kachelofen aus Halbzylinderkacheln, der zu seiner Zeit in der Raumausstattung als Luxusgut angesehen werden muss. Für die Ausstattung der Gebäude auf der Holsterburg stellt der Kachelofen hier im Vergleich zur Warmluftheizung eine nahezu adäquate Wärmequelle dar. Die oxidierend gebrannten gelben Kachelfragmente sind auf ihrer Schauseite mit einer grünen Bleiglasur versehen, ihre rückwärtigen, unglasierten Wandungen sind stark verrußt, ein eindeutiger Hinweis auf ihren Einbau in einen befeuerten Kachelofen[23].

Wie bei anderen Burggrabungen stellen auch auf der Holsterburg Tierknochen und Keramiken den Großteil des

---

22. Zu Warmluftheizung allgemein siehe u. a. BINGENHEIMER 1998; BINGENHEIMER 2007, 235-245; MEYER 1989. Zu entsprechenden Anlagen im westfälischen Raum siehe PEINE 2001, 43-63; MEYER 1989.

23. Vgl. dazu ausführlicher BULLA & PEINE 2012b, 205f. mit weiterführender Literatur.

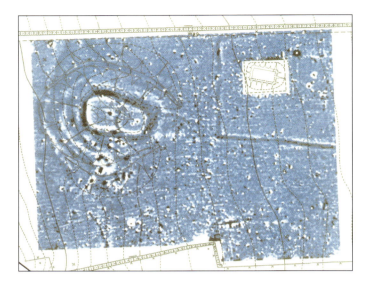

Abb. 6 a-b – Die früh- bis spätmittelalterliche Dorfwüstung Asseln bei Warburg-Ossendorf. Im Luftbild und im geomagnetischen Messbild zeichnen sich insbesondere die beiden Burgstellen des 12. bis 15. Jahrhunderts deutlich ab. Abbildung nach Kneppe & Peine 2005/ Eastern atlas, Berlin.

Fundgutes. Bei den Keramiken dominieren reduzierend gebrannte Irdenwaren, daneben finden sich wenige Scherben uneinheitlich gebrannter Irdenware, oxidierend gebrannter Irdenware Pingsdorfer Art, sowie glasierte Irdenwaren von Fettfängern und Miniaturgefäßen. Das Haushaltsgeschirr entstammt lokaler/regionaler Produktion und datiert in die zweite Hälfte des 12. Jahrhunderts und in das 13. Jahrhundert[24]. Oxidierend und reduzierend gebrannte Spinnwirtel verweisen auf Textilhauswerk innerhalb der Burgmauern. Als Handwerk ist bislang lediglich Knochen-, Horn- und Metallverarbeitung belegt. Eisen und Buntmetallfunde liegen nur in geringer Zahl vor und werden derzeit in den Werkstätten der LWL-Archäologie in Westfalen restauriert. Spielzeug lässt sich in Form einer Murmel, eines Steckpferdchens und eines verzierten Brettspielsteins nachweisen.

Etwa zeitgleich mit der Holsterburg wurde der Ministerialensitz der Familie de Aslen im Diemeltal unterhalb des Gaulskopfes auf dem Areal der Siedlung „Asseln" errichtet. Die ab 1255 häufig bezeugte Ministerialenfamilie „de Aslen" steht nicht im familiären Zusammenhang mit dem im Jahr 1024 erwähnten hochadligen *Ekkika comes des Aslan*, der seinen Sitz auf dem Gaulskopf hatte (s.o.). Der wohl bedeutendste Vertreter des Ministerialengeschlechtes „Elias de Aslen" (verstorben 1298) gehörte dem Ritterstand an. Er zeugte bei wichtigen Friedensverträgen: zum einen 1256 zwischen dem Erzbischof von Köln und dem Bischof von Paderborn, zum anderen 1265 zwischen dem Bischof von Paderborn und dem Landgrafen von Hessen. Die grund- und lehensrechtlichen Rechte am Dorf und den dortigen Burgen sind mehrfach Gegenstand von Verkäufen und Belehnungen. Das vom Haupthof Hardehausen abhängige Vorwerk „Asseln" verschenkte der Paderborner Bischof Meinwerk 1036 an das von ihm gegründete Stift Busdorf in Paderborn. Im Verlauf des Mittelalters erlangte unter anderem das Kloster Hardehausen durch Tausch und Kauf Besitz in „Asseln", genannt seien ferner die Ritter „Raveno de Papenhem" und „Goiswin de Wethen" sowie der Ritter „Rave van dem Kalenberge". Im ausgehenden Mittelalter gehen Siedlung und Burg in den Besitz der Stadt Warburg über. Noch 1557 setzen die Warburger ein Tor der Asseler Burg in Stand[25].

Die früh- bis spätmittelalterliche Siedlung Asseln, die hochmittelalterliche Motte und die Ruine der nachfolgenden spätmittelalterlichen Burganlage waren 2003 Gegenstand einer archäologischen Untersuchung. In einem 150 m langen und 5 m breiten Prospektionsschnitt sollte zum einen geklärt werden, inwieweit die archäologischen Befunde durch Tiefpflügen von Zerstörung bedroht sind. Zum anderen waren die in den Jahren zuvor durchgeführten Prospektionsmaßnahmen (Luftbildarchäologie, Begehung, Vermessung des Oberflächenreliefs, Geophysik) auf die Präzision ihrer Aussagen zu überprüfen (Abb. 6 a-b). Zum Dritten sollten durch den Grabungsschnitt die zeitlichen Verhältnisse von Siedlung, Motte und Ruine untereinander und zur benachbarten Wallburg Gaulskopf geklärt werden. 2004 standen die Bereiche von Motte und Burgruine im Mittelpunkt der Untersuchungen (Abb. 7)[26].

---

24. Zur Keramik in Ostwestwestfalen und Nordhessen siehe u. a. Lobbedey & Sanke 1997; Peine 1988; Röber 1990; Stephan 1982; Stephan 1986.
25. Bergmann 1993, 54ff.; Bulla & Peine 2012b; Kneppe & Peine 2005.
26. Westfälisches Museum für Archäologie, Landesmuseum und Amt für Bodendenkmalpflege 2004, 109-110; Westfälisches Museum für Archäologie, Landesmuseum und Amt für Bodendenkmalpflege 2005, 103-105.

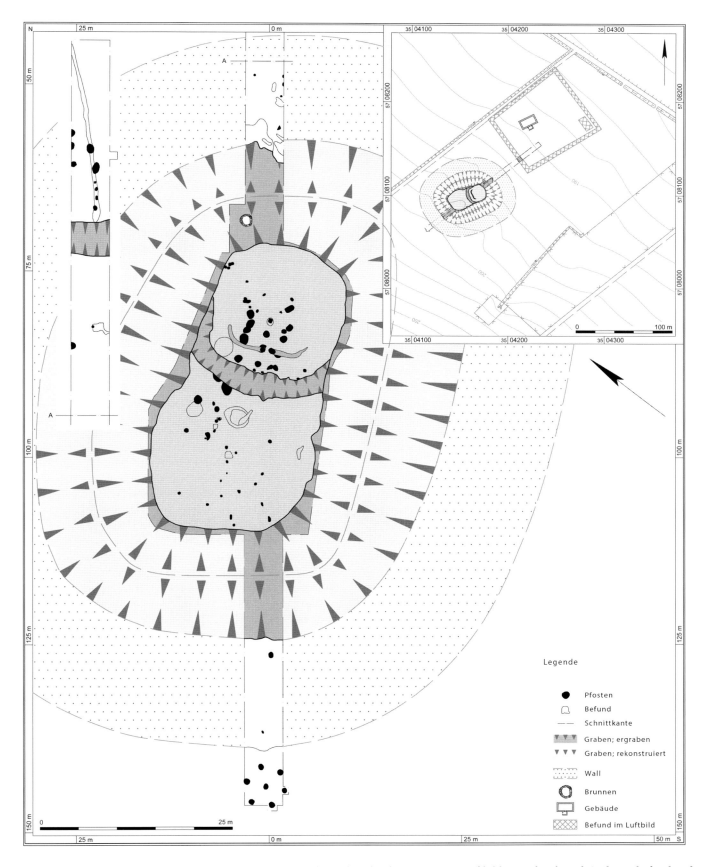

Abb. 7 – Plan von Siedlung, Motte und steinernem Haus Asseln nach Geländevermessung, Luftbild, Geophysik und Grabungsbefunden der Jahre 2003/2004. Plan LWL-Archäologie für Westfalen.

Die ländliche Siedlung setzt nach Lese- und Grabungsfunden bereits im frühen Mittelalter ein. In den Grabungsflächen konnten zahlreiche Abfall- und Pfostengruben dokumentiert werden. Vollständig erfasst wurde im Grabungsschnitt 2003 der Grundriss eines sechseckigen Speicherbaus mit Mittelpfosten. Die zugehörigen sieben Pfostengruben wiesen Durchmesser von 0,6 m bis 0,8 m auf und belegen einen Polygonalspeicher von 6 m Durchmesser. Entsprechende Speicherbauten mit und ohne Dach dienten nicht nur in Westfalen zur Lagerung von Erntevorräten auf einem erhöhten Holzrost[27]. Neben einer Quelle wurde die Wasserversorgung der Siedlung durch einen Brunnen (lichte Weite 1,2 m) aus Bruchstein gesichert. Mächtige Pfostengruben von 1 m Durchmesser, angeordnet in drei parallel verlaufenden Reihen, weisen auf ein massives, zweischiffiges Holzgebäude hin, das sich in seiner Längsausrichtung hangabwärts erstreckte (Abb. 8). Erfasst wurde von ihm auf 6 m Breite und 7 m Länge lediglich der hangaufwärts liegende Gebäudeteil. Die dort vorhandenen mächtigen Pfostengruben verlieren hangabwärts aufgrund von Geländeerosion an Tiefe. Weitere hangabwärts liegende Pfostenreihen fielen höchstwahrscheinlich der Erosion zum Opfer. Eine weitere Pfostenreihe (Giebelwand) hangaufwärts könnte durch den nachfolgenden Mottenbau zerstört worden sein. Gab es zu diesen Pfostenreihen weniger tief gegründete Traufwände, die bedingt durch die Geländesituation nicht mehr erfasst werden konnten? Über die ursprüngliche Länge und Breite des Gebäudes können somit heute keine sicheren Aussagen getroffen werden. Vergleichbare Befunde ließen sich in Nordwestdeutschland z.B. in der Grabung Warendorf-Velsen „Schulze-Althoff" und in der Wüstung Dalem bei Cuxhaven nachweisen[28]. Angelika Speckmann klassifiziert ihre Hausbefunde als Nebengebäude, Wolf Haio Zimmermann deutet seine Befunde als Spuren großer Pfahlrostspeicher. Auch auf der kurz vor 1000 aufgeworfenen und 1016 zerstörten Motte Montferland am Niederrhein (NL), dem Wohnsitz Adelas, der Mutter des Paderborner Bischofs Meinwerks und ihres zweiten Gatten Balderich, konnte ein entsprechender Pfostenbau von 14 x 5,5 m nachgewiesen werden[29].

Im späten 12. Jahrhundert wurden Teile der Siedlung, vielleicht das oben genannte Vorwerk, durch eine Motte von etwa 6.517 m² überbaut. Die langovale Anlage wurde durch einen heute noch 3 m breiten und noch 0,9 m tiefen Binnengraben zweigeteilt. Dabei umfasst die Hauptburg 255 m² und die Vorburg 376 m². Die Längsausdehnung von Vor- und Hauptburg beträgt 39 m. Die Burg umgab ein bis zu 17 m breiter Graben, dessen Sohle noch heute 3 m unter dem Geländeniveau liegt. Bis heute sichtbar ist ein um den Graben geführter mächtiger Außenwall von 17 m Breite, dagegen wurde der aufgeworfene Hügel der Motte im letzten Jahrhundert eingeebnet. Aus diesem Grunde finden sich innerhalb des vom Graben umzogenen Areals fast ausschließlich Spuren der älteren Siedlung. Als Bebauungsspuren der Motte, die bis in die Tiefe der Flachsiedlung herab reichen, lassen sich lediglich zwei je 0,6 m breite, noch 0,3 m tiefe und 6 m lange Gräben nachweisen, die im Abstand zwischen 2,5 m und 3 m parallel zum Binnengraben verlaufen (Abb. 8). Zwischen den aufeinanderstoßenden Kopfenden der Gräben besteht eine Lücke von 0,5 m. Die Kopfenden selbst weisen zwei 0,6 m bzw. 0,9 m starke Pfostengruben auf. Dieser tiefreichende und zentral gelegene Baubefund aus der Zeit um 1200, der das mächtige Pfostengebäude (s.o.) schneidet, darf als Überrest einer Wehrlinie interpretiert werden (Palisadengraben?). Weitere Befestigungs- und Bebauungsspuren ließen sich innerhalb des Außengrabens nicht nachweisen, da die Erdmassen des ursprünglich vorhandenen Burghügels bereits im frühen 14. Jahrhundert zur Auffüllung des Außengrabens verwendet worden waren. So fand sich dort der Abbruchschutt von hölzernen und steinernen Gebäuden, die durch Brand zerstört wurden. Zahlreiche Armbrustbolzen im Brandschutt deuten auf eine kriegerische Auseinandersetzung hin. Hangabwärts wurden im Prospektionsschnitt des Jahres 2003 Pfostenspuren und das Wandgräbchen eines Wohnstallgebäudes vom Typ Gasselte B¹ auf 24 m Länge erfasst[30]. Nach Ausweis des Fundmaterials wurde das Gebäude zeitgleich mit der Motte aufgegeben.

Wahrscheinlich in direkter Nachfolge dieser Bebauung wurde nördlich der Motte eine neue Burg errichtet, deren Mittelpunkt ein großes „steinernes Haus" bildete (Abb. 6 a-b). In einer Buschgruppe haben sich bis heute die bis zu 7 m hohen und 1,4 m starken Mauern des ruinösen Steingebäudes von 17,4 x 10 m Grundfläche erhalten. Im Zuge der Grabungen 2004 konnten seine nördliche Stirnwand und die östliche Längswand freigelegt werden (Abb. 9). In der Nordwand fanden sich zwei Lichtnischen. Der Zugang zum Erdgeschoss erfolgte von Osten einerseits durch eine 1,2 m breite Tür direkt an der Südecke des Gebäudes, andererseits durch einen der Ostwand mittig vorgelagerten 5,2 x 3,6 m großen Anbau. Dieser war über eine 1,5 m breite Tür in seiner südlichen Stirnwand zu betreten. Anbau und Erdgeschoss des „steinernen Hauses" hatten Böden aus Bruchsteinplatten und standen über eine 1,2 m breite Tür miteinander in Verbindung. Auf dem Plattenboden fanden sich unter anderem eine Viehglocke und zwei Rädchensporen.

Das als Saalgeschossbau oder Wohnturm anzusprechende Gebäude bildet das Zentrum eines 5.528 m² annähernd rechteckigen Areals, das von einem bis zu 4,8 m breiten und 1,4 m tiefen Graben umschlossen wird. Dieser konnte zwischen

---

27. Vgl. zuletzt für Westfalen Ruhmann 2012 mit weiterführender Literatur.
28. Speckmann 2010, 296-298; Zimmermann 1991, 37ff.
29. Vgl. zur Motte Montferland und zu den westfälischen Beziehungen zuletzt Aarts 2012a, 3-16; Aarts 2012b, 37-53 mit weiterführender Literatur; ausführlich zu Bischof Meinwerk siehe Beiträge in Stiegemann & Kroker 2009.
30. Vgl. zum Hausbau u. a. Speckmann 2010; Donat 1995; Huijts 1992; Waterbolk 1991.

Abb. 8 – Blick in den Prospektionsschnitt 2003 auf die mächtigen Pfostengruben der Siedlung, die von Gräben der nachfolgenden Mottenbebauung geschnitten werden. Foto LWL-Archäologie für Westfalen.

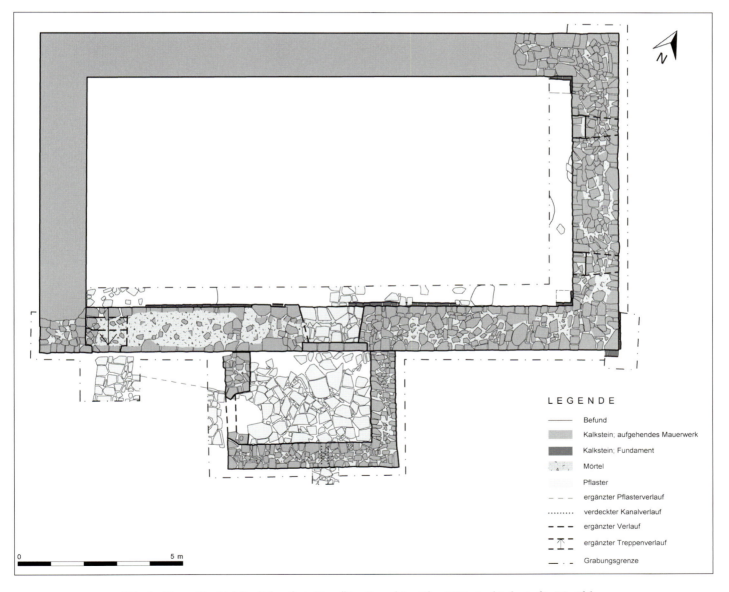

LEGENDE

- Befund
- Kalkstein; aufgehendes Mauerwerk
- Kalkstein; Fundament
- Mörtel
- Pflaster
- ergänzter Pflasterverlauf
- verdeckter Kanalverlauf
- ergänzter Verlauf
- ergänzter Treppenverlauf
- Grabungsgrenze

Abb. 9 – Das spätmittelalterliche „feste Haus" im Grundriss. Plan LWL-Archäologie für Westfalen.

Abb. 10 – Spätmittelalterliches Fundgut der Burgstellen Asseln. Foto LWL-Archäologie für Westfalen.

Motte und Steingebäude 2003 im Prospektionsschnitt erfasst werden. Grabenfüllung und Steingebäude datieren nach Ausweis der Funde (Abb. 10) in das 14. und in die erste Hälfte des 15. Jahrhunderts. Die archäologische Untersuchung eines sich in der Nordostecke der Anlage im Luftbild abzeichnenden Gebäudes, vermutlich ein Torhaus, wird in den nächsten Jahren angestrebt. Im Rahmen diese Beitrages kann auf weitere archäologische Untersuchungen, u. a. durchgeführt auf der Burg Leuchteberg, der „Bonenburg" und der Burg N.N. bei Borlinghausen nicht näher eingegangen werden[31].

31. Neujahrsgruss 2000, 108; Neujahrsgruss 2005, 119; Neujahrsgruss 2006, 124, 127; Neujahrsgruss 2008, 119.

Literatur

Aarts B. (2006), „The Castle of Heusden (NL): its Relocation and its Successive Octagonal Towers", in *Château Gaillard 22. Château et peuplement*, P. Ettel, A.-M. Flambard Héricher & T. E. McNeill (hrsg.), Caen, Publications du CRAHM, 1-12.

– (2012a), „The Origin of Castle in the Eastern Part of the Delta Region (NL/D) and the Rise of the Principalities of Guelders and Cleves", in *Château Gaillard 25. L'origine du château médiéval*, P. Ettel, A.-M. Flambard Héricher & K. O'Conor (hrsg.), Caen, Publications du CRAHM, 3-16.

– (2012b), „De vroege burchten in het oostelijk deel van het rivierengebied (NL/D). Hoofdlijn met opmerkingen in de marge", in B. Aarts et al., *Ambitie in steen. Bijdragen tot de kastelenkunde in Nederland*, Wijk bij Duurstede, Nederlandse Kastelenstichting (Academic Studies Series; 3), 37-54.

Balzer M. (2009), „Vornehm-reich-klug. Herkunft, Königsdienst und Güterpolitik Bischof Meinwerks", in *Für Königtum und Himmelreich. 1000 Jahre Bischof Meinwerk von Paderborn*, C. Stiegemann & M. Kroker (hrsg.), Regensburg, Schnell & Steiner, 88-99.

Becher M. (2009), „Meinwerk von Paderborn. Bischof zwischen König und Adel", in Stiegemann & Kroker 2009 (hrsg.), 108-115.

Beckmann L. (2007), „Die Torre di Federico in Enna", in *Kaiser Friedrich II. (1194-1250). Welt und Kultur des Mittelmeerraums. Begleitband zur Sonderausstellung im Landesmuseum für Natur und Mensch, Oldenburg*, M. Fansa & K. Ermete (hrsg.), Mainz, Von Zabern (Schriftenreihe des Landesmuseums für Natur und Mensch; 55), 469-471.

Bergmann R. (1993), *Zwischen Pflug und Fessel. Mittelalterliches Landleben im Spiegel der Wüstungsforschung*, Münster (Westf.), Westfälisches Museum für Archäologie.

Best W. (1997), „Die Ausgrabungen in der frühmittelalterlichen Wallburg Gaulskopf bei Warburg-Ossendorf, Kreis Höxter. Vorbericht", *Germania*, 75, 159-192.

– (2009), „Von der Wallburg zum Adelssitz. Westfälische Burgen des 11. Jahrhunderts", in Stiegemann & Kroker 2009 (hrsg.), 116-121.

Best W. et al. (1999a), „Frühmittelalterliche Siedlungszentren im Warburger Raum", in *799 – Kunst und Kultur der Karolingerzeit. Karl der Große und Papst Leo III. in Paderborn. Beiträge zum Katalog der Ausstellung Paderborn 1999*, C. Stiegemann & M. Wemhoff (hrsg.), Mainz, Von Zabern, 299-307.

– (1999b), „Burgenbau in einer Grenzregion", in Stiegemann & Wemhoff 1999 (hrsg.), 328-345.

Biller T. (2010), „Burgen zwischen praktischer Funktion und Symbolik", in *Verwandlungen des Stauferreichs. Drei Innovationsregionen im mittelalterlichen Europa*, B. Schneidmüller, S. Weinfurter & A. Wieczorek (hrsg.), Darmstadt/Stuttgart, WBG/Theiss, 399-422.

Biller T. & Metz B. (1995), *Die Burgen des Elsass*, Bd. III: *1250-1300. Der frühe gotische Burgenbau im Elsass (1250-1300)*, München/Berlin, Deutscher Kunstverlag.

– (2007), *Die Burgen des Elsass*, Bd. II: *1200-1250. Der spätromanische Burgenbau im Elsass (1200-1250)*, München/Berlin, Deutscher Kunstverlag.

Bingenheimer K. (1998), *Die Luftheizungen des Mittelalters. Zur Typologie und Entwicklung eines technikgeschichtlichen Phänomens*, Hamburg, Kovac (Schriftenreihe Antiquitates. Archäologische Forschungsergebnisse; 17).

– (2007), „Typologie und Wirkungsweise historischer Heizungen. Burgen und Schlösser", *Zeitschrift für Burgenforschung und Denkmalpflege*, 4, 235-245.

Bulla A. & Kneppe C. (2011), „Die Holsterburg – eine oktogonale stauferzeitliche Burganlage bei Warburg", *Archäologie in Westfalen-Lippe*, 2010, 145-149.

Bulla A. & Peine H.-W. (2012a), „Wallburg – Motte – Oktogon. Burgenarchäologie in einer Grenzregion", *Archäologie in Deutschland*, 2012/2, 64-65.

– (2012b), „Oktogonale Wehrarchitektur aus der Stauferzeit: die Holsterburg bei Warburg", *Burgen und Schlösser*, 2012/4, 199-208.

– (im Druck), „Architektur von europäischem Rang – die Holsterburg bei Warburg", *Archäologie in Westfalen-Lippe*, 4.

Decker R. (1989), *Die Geschichte der Burgen im Raum Warburg/Zierenberg*, Hofgeismar/Zierenberg, Verein für Hessische Geschichte und Landeskunde/Buchh. Die Eule (Die Geschichte unserer Heimat; 4).

Doms A. (1986a), *Der Gaulskopf bei Warburg-Ossendorf, Kreis Höxter*, Münster, Altertumskomm. Für Westfalen im Provinzialinst. für Westfäl. Landes- u. Volksforschung (Frühe Burgen in Westfalen; 7).

– (1986b), „Jäger, Bauern, Bürger. Von der Vorgeschichte zum Hochmittelalter im Stadtgebiet Warburg", in *Die Stadt Warburg 1036-1986. Beiträge zur Geschichte einer Stadt*, Bd. I, F. Mürmann (hrsg.), Warburg, Hermes Verlag, 35-87, 81f.

Donat P. (1995), „Neuere archäologische und bauhistorische Forschungsergebnisse zum ländlichen Hausbau des 11.-13. Jahrhunderts in Mittel- und Süddeutschland", *Germania*, 73, 421-439.

Dubbi F.-J. (2006), *Der Warburger Burgberg. Grafensitz – Landesburg – Schloß – Wallfahrtsort – Friedhof*, Marsberg, Hg. Museumsverein Warburg.

Dubbi F.-J. & Bialas R. (2004), *Der Desenberg. Geschichte – Geschichten – Bilder*, Marsberg, Hg. Museumsverein Warburg.

Engemann H. (1972), „Die Ausgrabung der Andreaskirche auf dem Burgberg zu Warburg", *Westfalen*, 50, 269-290.

Engemann H. & Stephan H.-G. (1979), „Desenberg. Untersuchung zur Klärung der Burgsituation", in *Beiträge zur archäologischen Burgenforschung und zur Keramik des Mittelalters in Westfalen*, Teil I, W. Bauer, H. Engemann & H.-W. Heine (hrsg.), Bonn, Habelt (Denkmalpflege und Forschung in Westfalen; 2), 131-142.

Gottlob A. (1936), *Geschichte der Stadt Warburg*, Münster, Regensberg.

Grote K. (2003), *Bernshausen. Archäologie und Geschichte eines mittelalterlichen Zentralortes am Seeburger See*, Bonn, Habelt (Zeitschrift für Archäologie des Mittelalters. Beiheft; 16).

Heine H.-W. (2006), „Frühe Burgen in Niedersachsen (10.-12. Jahrhundert)", in *Neue Forschungen zum frühen Burgenbau*, H.-H. Häffner (hrsg.), München/Berlin, Deutscher Kunstverlag (Forschungen zu Burgen und Schlössern; 9), 49-66.

– (2007), „Burgen vom Typ Motte und Turmburgen in Niedersachsen und angrenzenden Landschaften", in *Motte – Turmhügelburg – Hausberg. Zum europäischen Forschungsstand eines mittelalterlichen Burgentypus*, P. Csendes, A. Eibner & S. Felgenhauer-Schmiedt (hrsg.), Wien, Österreichische Gesellschaft für Mittelalterarchäologie (Beiträge zur Mittelalterarchäologie in Österreich; 23), 61-84.

– (2008), „Mittelalterliche Burgen in Niedersachsen und seinen Nachbarregionen. Rückblick auf 25 Jahre archäologische Forschung", in *Château Gaillard 23. Bilan des recherches en castellologie*, P. Ettel, A.-M. Flambard Héricher & T. E. McNeill (hrsg.), Caen, Publications du CRAHM, 211-224.

Hensch M. (2005), *Burg Sulzbach in der Oberpfalz. Archäologisch-historische Forschungen zur Entwicklung eines Herrschaftszentrums des 8. bis 14. Jahrhunderts in Nordbayern*, Büchenbach, Faustus (Materialien zur Archäologie in der Oberpfalz; 3).

Hersfeld L. (von) (1985), *Annalen*, 3 Aufl., A. Schmidt (übers.), Darmstadt, Wissenschaftliche Buchgesellschaft.

Honselmann K. (1972), „Zur Geschichte der Andreaskirche auf der Burg zu Warburg", *Westfalen*, 50, 258-268.

Huijts C. S. T. J. (1992), *De voor-historische boerderijbouw in Drenthe. Reconstructiemodellen van 1300 vóór tot 1300 na Chr.*, Arnheim, Stichting Historisch Boerderij-onderzoek.

Irsigler F. (1976-1977), „Bischof Meinwerk, Graf Dodiko und Warburg. Herrschaft, Wirtschaft und Gesellschaft des hohen Mittelalters im östlichen Westfalen", *Westfälische Zeitschrift*, 126/127, 181-200.

Kamp H. (2009), „‚...von edler Herkunft und Lebensart'. Adligsein im 10. und 11. Jahrhundert", in Stiegemann & Kroker 2009 (hrsg.), 100-106.

Kneppe C. & Peine H.-W. (1991), „Der Desenberg bei Warburg, Kreis Höxter. Ein Beitrag zur Geschichte und Archäologie des Stammsitzes der Familie Spiegel", *Ausgrabungen und Funde in Westfalen-Lippe*, 6B, 239-247.

– (1995), „Die Klockenstraße im Siedlungsgefüge der Altstadt", in *Mittelalterliches Leben an der Klockenstraße. Eine Dokumentation des Westfälischen Museums für Archäologie zu den Ausgrabungen 1991 in der Warburger Altstadt*, B. Trier (hrsg.), Warburg, Hermes, 5-58.

– (1997), „Die Hüffert: Fränkisch/Karolingische Keimzelle der Stadt Warburg. Weiterführende Ergebnisse zur Grabung Petrikirche. Mit einem Anhang zur romanischen Kirche von Otfried Ellger", in *Archäologische Beiträge zur Geschichte Westfalens. Festschrift für Klaus Günther*, D. Bérenger (hrsg.), Rahden, Leidorf (Internationale Archäologie. Studia honoraria; 2), 229-248.

– (2000), *Der Desenberg bei Warburg, Kreis Höxter*, Münster, Altertumskommission für Westfalen (Frühe Burgen in Westfalen; 16).

– (2005), „Der Diemelraum: ein regionaler Forschungsschwerpunkt der westfälischen Mittelalter- und Neuzeitarchäologie", in *Von Anfang an. Archäologie in Nordrhein-Westfalen*, H. G. Horn (hrsg.), Mainz, Von Zabern (Schriften zur Bodendenkmalpflege in Nordrhein-Westfalen; 8), 169-179.

Krönig W. (1986a), „Enna – Kastell", in *Kunstdenkmäler in Italien. Ein Bildhandbuch, Sizilien*, Darmstadt, Wissenschaftliche Buchgesellschaft.

– (1986b), *Kunstdenkmäler in Italien. Ein Bildhandbuch, Sizilien*, Darmstadt, Wissenschaftliche Buchgesellschaft.

Lagers M. (2011), *Der Paderborner Stiftsadel zur Mitte des 15. Jahrhunderts. Untersuchungen zum Auf- und Ausbau niederadliger Machtstrukturen im Kontext spätmittelalterlicher Territorialisierungsprozesse*, Unpublizierte Dissertation Universität Bielefeld, 2011.

Leistikow D. (2001), „Zu einer neuen Datierung des Baubeginns von Castel del Monte", *Burgen und Schlösser. Zeitschrift für Burgenforschung und Denkmalpflege*, 2001/4, 209-220.

– (2007), „Castel del Monte im Lichte der Forschung", in Fansa & Ermete 2007 (hrsg.), 142-157.

Liessem U. (2001), „Notizen und Gedanken zur Torre di Federico – eine Burganlage Friedrichs II. in Enna (Sizilien)", *Burgen und Schlösser*, 42, 254-259.

Lobbedey U. & Sanke M. (1997), „Ein Töpferofen des 12. Jahrhunderts in Neuenheerse (Bad Driburg, Kr. Höxter)", in Bérenger 1997 (hrsg.), 271-295.

Merkelbach L. (1965), *Burg und Schloss Kilchberg. Baugeschichte – Ursprung – Kunsthistorische Einordnung*, Stuttgart, Silberburg-Verlag.

Meyer D. (1989), „Warmluftheizungen des Mittelalters. Befunde aus Lübeck im europäischen Vergleich", *Lübecker Schriften zur Archäologie und Kulturgeschichte*, 16, 209-232.

Neujahrsgruss (2000), *Jahresbericht für 1999. Westfälisches Museum für Archäologie. Amt für Bodendenkmalpflege Münster und Altertumskommission für Westfalen*, Münster, Landschaftsverband Westfalen-Lippe.

– (2005), *Jahresbericht für 2004. Westfälisches Museum für Archäologie, Landesmuseum und Amt für Bodendenkmalpflege, Altertumskommission für Westfalen*, Münster, Landschaftsverband Westfalen-Lippe.

– (2006), *Jahresbericht für 2005. Westfälisches Museum für Archäologie, Landesmuseum und Amt für Bodendenkmalpflege, Altertumskommission für Westfalen*, Münster, Landschaftsverband Westfalen-Lippe.

– (2008), *Jahresbericht für 2007 der LWL-Archäologie für Westfalen und der Altertumskommission für Westfalen*, Münster, Landschaftsverband Westfalen-Lippe.

Ödman A. (2005), *Skeingeborg: borgen som Saxo glömde: raport över arkeologiska undersökningar på fastigheterna Björkeberga 1:17, Skeingeborg (Raä nr. 4) och Björkeberga 1:38 (vägbank), Verums socken i Hässleholms kommun, Skåne*, Lund, Institutionen för arkeologi och antikens historia, Lunds universitet (Norra Skånes medeltid; 4/Report Series, University of Lund, Institute of Archaeology; 90).

Peine H.-W. (1988), *Untersuchungen zur mittelalterlichen Keramik Mindens*, Bonn, Habelt (Denkmalpflege und Forschung in Westfalen; 17).

– (1997), „Dodiko, Rütger von der Horst und Simon zur Lippe: Adelige Herren des Mittelalters und der frühen Neuzeit auf Burg, Schloß und Festung", in *Hinter Schloss und Riegel. Burgen und Befestigungen in Westfalen*, H. Polenz (hrsg.), Münster, Westfälisches Museum für Archäologie, Amt für Bodendenkmalpflege, besonders 171-174; 160-223.

– (2001), „Von qualmenden Herdfeuern und Wandkaminen zu rauchfreien. Räumlichkeiten mittels Warmluftheizungen und Kachelöfen. Ein Beitrag zur Ofenkeramik des 12. bis 17. Jahrhunderts in Westfalen", in *Von der Feuerstelle zum Kachelofen – Heizanlagen und Ofenkeramik vom Mittelalter bis zur Neuzeit – Beiträge des 3. Wissenschaftlichen Kolloquiums Stralsund 9.-11. Dezember 1999*, M. Schneider (hrsg.), Stralsund, Kulturhistorisches Museum der Hansestadt (Stralsunder Beiträge zur Archäologie, Geschichte und Volkskunde in Vorpommern; 3), 43-63.

– (2006), „Burgen als Zentren von Macht und Herrschaft – Aspekte der Bautätigkeit des westfälischen Adels im Hochmittelalter", in *Canossa 1077. Erschütterung der Welt. Geschichte, Kunst und Kultur am Aufgang der Romanik*, Bd. I: *Essays*, C. Stiegemann & M. Wemhoff (hrsg.), München, Hirmer, 235-242.

– (2012), „Schloss Horst – Kleinod im Ruhrgebiet. Ein Beitrag zur Geschichte des Hauses Horst im Emscherbruch", in *Château Gaillard 25. L'origine du château médiéval*, P. Ettel, A.-M. Flambard Héricher & K. O'Conor (hrsg.), Caen, Publications du CRAHM, 287-297.

Röber R. (1990), *Hoch- und spätmittelalterliche Keramik aus der Klosteranlage tom Roden*, Bonn, Habelt (Denkmalpflege und Forschung in Westfalen; 21).

Ruhmann C. (2012), „Eine Hofstelle des 10. Jahrhunderts bei Beckum, Bauerschaft Geißler", *Ausgrabungen und Funde in Westfalen-Lippe*, 11, 457-472.

Schieffer R. (2009), „Meinwerk und seine Mitbischöfe", in Stiegemann & Kroker 2009 (hrsg.), 74-87.

Schirmer W. (2001), „Castel del Monte – Einige Ergebnisse der Bauforschung aus den Jahren 1991 bis 1996", *Burgen und Schlösser. Zeitschrift für Burgenforschung und Denkmalpflege*, 2001/4, 202-208.

Schmitt R. (1999), „Zu den achteckigen Türmen im Schloss Neuenburg bei Freyburg an der Unstrut", in *Architektur, Struktur, Symbol. Streifzüge durch die Architekturgeschichte von der Antike bis zur Gegenwart. Festschrift für Cord Meckseper zum 65. Geburtstag*, M. Kozok (hrsg.), Petersberg, Imhof, 247-268.

– (2004a), „Zur Baugeschichte der Neuenburg I.", in *Burg und Herrschaft. Die Neuenburg und die Landgrafschaft Thüringen im hohen Mittelalter. Beiträge zur Ausstellung*, S. Ansorg (hrsg.), Freyburg/Unstrut, Museum Schloss Neuenburg, 30-89.

– (2004b), „Zur Baugeschichte der Neuenburg II.", in Ansorg 2004 (hrsg.), 122-147.

– (2007), „Schloss Neuenburg bei Freyburg/Unstrut. Zur Baugeschichte vom späten 11. bis zum mittleren 13. Jahrhundert nach Untersuchungen der Jahre 1986-2007", *Burgen und Schlösser in Sachsen-Anhalt*, 16, 6-138.

SCHMITT R. *et al.* (2006), „Burgenbau in der 2. Hälfte des 11. Jahrhunderts und im frühen 12. Jahrhundert in ausgewählten Landschaften des Reiches", in STIEGEMANN & WEMHOFF 2006 (hrsg.), Bd. I: *Essays*, 219-234.

SCHOPPMEYER H. (1986), „Warburg in Mittelalter und Neuzeit. Herrschaftssitz – Doppelstadt – territorialer Vorort", in MÜRMANN 1986 (hrsg.), Bd. I, 199-296.

SPECKMANN A. (2010), *Ländlicher Hausbau in Westfalen vom 6./7. Jahrhundert bis zum 12./13. Jahrhundert*, Mainz, Von Zabern (Bodenaltertümer Westfalens; 49).

STEPHAN H.-G. (1982), „Die mittelalterlichen Töpfereien im Reinhardswald", in *Töpferei des Reinhardswaldes vom 12. bis zum 20. Jahrhundert*, U. LEINWEBER (hrsg.), Kassel, Hess. Museumsverb., 57-127.

– (1986), „Mittelalterliche Keramiken in Niederhessen", *Führer zu vor- und frühgeschichtlichen Denkmälern*, 50, Teil I, 209-229.

STIEGEMANN C. & KROKER M. (hrsg.) (2009), *Für Königtum und Himmelreich. 1000 Jahre Bischof Meinwerk von Paderborn*, Regensburg, Schnell & Steiner.

STREICH G. (1984), *Burg und Kirche während des deutschen Mittelalters. Untersuchungen zur Sakraltopographie von Pfalzen, Burgen und Herrensitzen*, Bd. I/2, Teil II, Sigmaringen, Thorbecke (Vorträge und Forschungen, Sonderband; 29).

TÜMMLER H. (1972), „Zur Datierung der Andreaskirche in Warburg", *Westfalen*, 50, 291-294.

WATERBOLK H. T. (1991), „Das mittelalterliche Siedlungswesen in Drenthe. Versuch einer Synthese aus archäologischer Sicht", in *Siedlung und Landesausbau zur Salierzeit*, Teil I: *In den nördlichen Landschaften des Reiches*, H.-W. BÖHME (hrsg.), Sigmaringen, Thorbecke, 47-108.

WESTFÄLISCHES MUSEUM FÜR ARCHÄOLOGIE, LANDESMUSEUM UND AMT FÜR BODENDENKMALPFLEGE (hrsg.) (2004), NEUJAHRSGRUSS, *Jahresbericht für 2003*, 109-110.

– (2005), NEUJAHRSGRUSS, *Jahresbericht für 2004*, 103-105.

ZIMMERMANN W.-H. (1991), „Die früh- bis hochmittelalterliche Wüstung Dalem, Gem. Langen-Neuenwalde, Kr. Cuxhaven. Archäologische Untersuchungen in einem Dorf des 7.-14. Jahrhunderts", in BÖHME 1991 (hrsg.), Teil I, 37-46.

Le rôle des châteaux dans le contrôle de la vallée de la Meuse aux confins de la Lotharingie et du diocèse de Liège (IXe-XIe siècle)

Frédéric Chantinne, Philippe Mignot*

Pour la période abordée, associer château et frontière constitue un anachronisme. Il y a presque 20 ans, Johnny De Meulemeester avait traité de cette question lors du colloque d'Abergavenny consacré au même thème dans un article intitulé « Châteaux et frontière : quelques réflexions sur les principautés territoriales des anciens Pays-Bas méridionaux ». Se focalisant sur les Flandres, et en particulier sur la frontière franco-lotharingienne de l'Escaut, il reprenait les termes de Léopold Genicot dans un article qui a fait date[1] et concluait que pour cette époque « "la frontière n'est jamais linéaire que par abstraction ; c'est une zone". […] Le système défensif dans les "régions flamandes", qu'il soit du IXe, du Xe ou du XIe siècle, reflète ce système de zone de frontière »[2]. Il y voyait « des centres militaires, à l'intérieur de zones assez étendues, et des points de base de la défense du comté »[3]. Partant de ce postulat, nous avons souhaité observer ce qu'il en était plus au sud-est, le long de cette frontière franco-lotharingienne, axée cette fois le long d'une autre vallée fluviale : la Meuse.

Nous tenterons dès lors de répondre à une question : quel rôle tenait le château dans le contrôle territorial de cette vallée mosane aux confins de la Lotharingie aux IXe-XIe siècles ?

Il paraît aujourd'hui indéniable que le statut des premiers édificateurs ou détenteurs de châteaux relève de la haute aristocratie[4]. De nouvelles réflexions ont permis de faire évoluer, ces dernières années, la perception tronquée de cette élite à l'époque qui nous occupe[5]. En effet, elle a joué un rôle prépondérant dans la nouvelle organisation du territoire et des rapports sociaux, perceptibles à travers l'émergence du phénomène castral[6]. Le château, trop longtemps envisagé sous le seul angle militaire[7], fut aussi, sinon avant tout, un outil de gestion, un centre d'exploitation domaniale et le point nodal d'un ensemble complexe de droits et de fonctions d'une autorité légitime, ou reconnue comme telle, sur un espace déterminé[8]. Pour ces élites, le château, en tant que résidence principale, a constitué le moyen emblématique de se distinguer et par conséquent de « dominer » l'espace qu'elles devaient contrôler. Il ne fait dès lors aucun doute que leur autorité était légitime et reconnue tant par le pouvoir central que la population locale. Ceux qui détenaient ces châteaux étaient, dans le territoire qu'ils dominaient, les représentants de fait ou de droit de l'autorité royale, certains diront régalienne[9].

Ces évidences nous mènent aux notions de *comitatus* et de *pagus* difficiles à appréhender pour cette époque[10]. L'espace de pouvoir devait malgré tout être défini, autant que les circonscriptions religieuses. Compte tenu de l'imbrication entre Église et État à cette époque, n'y aurait-il pas dès lors une relation

---

* Archéologues, Direction de l'archéologie du Service public de Wallonie, Belgique.
1. Genicot 1970.
2. De Meulemeester 1997, 58.
3. *Ibid.*
4. Morsel 2004, 105.
5. *Ibid.*, 104-115 ; Margue 2013, 240-241. Nous remercions chaleureusement M. Margue de nous avoir communiqué ce texte avant sa parution. Il y insiste sur le « rôle souvent méconnu, parce que peu documenté, des comtes et autres grands laïcs, face à celui des évêques, très étudié et bien illustré par les sources ».
6. Morsel 2004, 96 ; West 2011, 144-145.
7. De Meulemeester & Mignot 2007.
8. Ettel 2010 ; Debord 1996.
9. West 2011, 140.
10. Nonn 1983.

directe entre circonscriptions civiles et religieuses, comme c'était déjà le cas à la fin de l'Antiquité ? À bien y regarder, le pouvoir comtal, ou *comitatus*, s'exerçait alors sur des *pagi* correspondant peu ou prou aux doyennés[11]. Est-ce dès lors un hasard si ces circonscriptions religieuses apparurent à la même époque ? En pays mosan, comme ailleurs, les centres de doyennés correspondent souvent à des sites castraux attestés au Xe siècle, comme Florennes[12], Chimay[13], Mézières[14], Mouzon[15] et, plus en amont, Dun ou encore Yvois.

La Meuse, un fleuve, une frontière ?

Le premier point à résoudre est de savoir si la vallée de la Meuse a pu constituer une frontière. Le fleuve, situé aux confins des provinces de Belgique Première, Seconde et de Germanie Seconde, Austrasie et Neustrie, puis de la Lotharingie et de la Francie occidentale, a bien servi de repère pour délimiter l'espace depuis la fin de l'Antiquité. Cependant, et au contraire du Rhin ou de l'Escaut, il ne fut jamais une frontière au sens linéaire du terme[16]. Ceci est clair au IXe siècle à travers les traités de Verdun et de Meersen qui seront déterminants pour les futures principautés territoriales de nos régions[17]. La Meuse et la Moselle se présentent comme les axes de la part de Charles le Chauve. Les frontières nous paraissent avoir été établies dans des zones peu peuplées, couvertes de forêts, plutôt que sur les rivières. Cette constatation est encore observable de nos jours, par exemple entre Calestienne et Thiérache où la frontière franco-belge actuelle, toujours identique à celle du traité de Verdun de 843, est matérialisée par l'extrémité de la forêt d'Ardenne. C'est aussi le cas pour la frontière qui se situait à l'ouest de la Meuse, entre Verdun et Stenay, où la forêt d'Argonne formait une zone de frontière naturelle.

Du « palais » au « château », les lieux de la gestion des pouvoirs publics (fig. 1)

L'exercice de l'autorité publique comprend plusieurs pouvoirs qui sont, à l'époque mérovingienne puis carolingienne, des prérogatives royales[18]. Ces pouvoirs s'exercent au sein de « palais », au sens large du terme, qui abritent les trois pôles essentiels à ces fonctions : *aula-camera-capella*[19].

Depuis la fin de l'Antiquité, l'autorité publique, le pouvoir royal, disposait du système administratif et militaire qui, dans une certaine mesure, s'était maintenu. Les centres administratifs établis dans les *vici* les plus importants étaient toujours en activité le long de la Meuse, à Maastricht, Huy, Namur, Dinant, Mouzon, Stenay[20]. Témoins d'activités économiques, les ateliers monétaires y sont attestés aux VIe et VIIe siècles[21]. À l'époque mérovingienne, le pouvoir royal s'appuie aussi sur un réseau de *villae* dites publiques ou fiscales[22]. Elles pouvaient servir, à l'occasion, de résidences royales en fonction des déplacements de la cour. Ces *villae* se retrouvent sur les deux rives de la Meuse. La plupart se présentaient comme des sites de plaine[23].

Le pouvoir public pouvait aussi lever des armées et contrôlait des sites fortifiés[24]. La réorganisation militaire du IVe siècle avait complété la défense linéaire du *limes* par des postes de garnison établis sur les routes et ensuite d'un réseau de sites défensifs de hauteur en retrait des voies de circulation[25]. Quelques fortifications sur la Meuse sont connues : Samson, Namur, Vireux-Molhain. D'autres se trouvaient plus à l'intérieur des terres. Ces fortifications de hauteur continuèrent à être utilisées et d'autres apparurent encore jusqu'à l'époque carolingienne. Sur celles qui ont été fouillées, les recherches archéologiques ont montré que souvent les traces d'occupation, entre le VIe et le IXe siècle, sont ténues voire inexistantes, alors que ces fortifications ont été parfois occupées antérieurement et par la suite, comme pour Faing, Namur, Samson, Vireux, Furfooz, Dourbes[26]… Les traces réapparaissent, à partir de la seconde moitié du IXe siècle, elles prennent la forme de résidences fortifiées pour des membres de la haute aristocratie. On peut dès lors les qualifier de « châteaux »[27].

Il reste à évoquer une prérogative du pouvoir régalien souvent oubliée. Suivant la tradition romaine et jusqu'à la Réforme grégorienne, le roi ou l'empereur avait des droits ecclésiastiques. En fait, il encadrait la gestion du culte et nommait les principaux représentants de l'Église, tant évêques qu'abbés, fonctionnaires bénéficiaires issus de la haute aristocratie[28]. Ceci permet de mieux comprendre pourquoi, à partir du VIIe siècle, les abbayes complètent progressivement les infrastructures encadrant la vie économique et politique,

---

11. Nonn 1983 ; Van Rey 1971.
12. Ruffini-Ronzani 2012.
13. Chantinne 2011.
14. Périn 1979, 15-16.
15. Congar 1972.
16. Parisse 1990b, 49-55 ; Suttor 2010.
17. Parisse 1990a.
18. Devroey 2006, 47-82 ; Magnou-Nortier 2012.
19. « Palais » peut avoir plusieurs synonymes à cette époque, comme « *castellum* » et « *castrum* » : Renoux 2001, 12-14.
20. Mourot 2001, 528-532.

21. Pol 1995 ; Bruand 2011.
22. Devroey 2003, 245-253.
23. Renoux 1994.
24. Magnou-Nortier 2012, 175-191, 457-477 et 538-555.
25. Brulet 2008.
26. *Ibid.*
27. Au sens où nous l'entendons aujourd'hui en tant que résidences fortifiées d'un aristocrate et de sa famille là où les sources contemporaines parlent de « *castellum* », de « *castrum* », de « *palatium* », voire même simplement de « *domus* ». Renoux 2001, 12.
28. Felten 1980 ; Helvétius 1998.

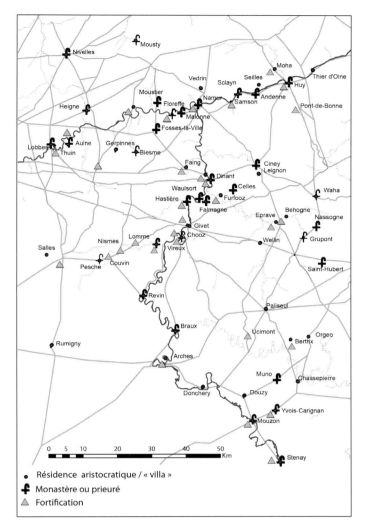
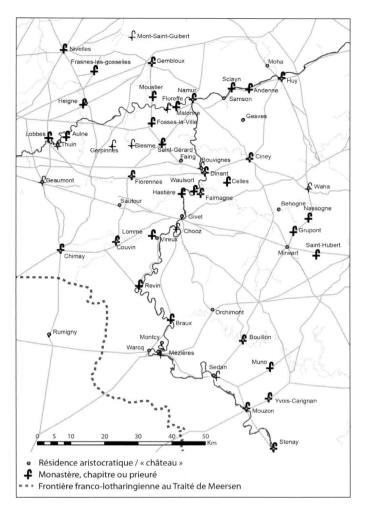

Fig. 1 – Carte des résidences aristocratiques, des fortifications et des établissements religieux, de part et d'autre de la Meuse, avec une esquisse du réseau routier autour des VIIe-IXe siècles. Infographie J.-N. Anslijn.

Fig. 2 – Carte des « châteaux » et des établissements religieux, de part et d'autre de la Meuse, avec une esquisse du réseau routier autour du Xe-XIe siècle. Infographie J.-N. Anslijn.

à tel point que les fondations pippinides deviennent royales à l'avènement des Carolingiens[29].

Au moment du partage du royaume de Lothaire II entre ses oncles, le traité de Meerssen en 870 souligne le rôle politique et institutionnel primordial des abbayes royales en commençant l'énumération de chaque fraction par celles-ci, avant même les *pagi* et comtés. On y retrouve les abbayes royales situées sur la Meuse : Dinant, Andenne, Maastricht (Saint-Servais) et Aldeneik[30]. Outre la fonction religieuse,

ces abbayes étaient d'importants centres du pouvoir public, générant une économie florissante[31].

Ce phénomène va se poursuivre jusqu'à la fin du XIe siècle avec l'implantation de prieurés ou de chapitres au sein des « châteaux », comme à Chimay, Falmagne, Florennes, Walcourt, Namur, Couvin, Chiny[32]…

Ces nouveaux « palais », lieux de pouvoir et résidences fortifiés, semblent avant tout venir compléter le réseau existant des centres qui servaient à contrôler le territoire (fig. 2).

---

29. *Ibid.*, 287.
30. Grat, Viellard & Clémencet 1964, 172-174 ; Gaillard 2003.
31. Bruand 2002, 162.
32. Chantinne & Mignot 2012 ; pour la Lorraine, Kraemer 2012.

Conclusion

Dans l'espace étudié, le château des IXe et XIe siècles a, dans bien des cas, pour origine une fortification militaire du Bas-Empire. Par conséquent, on ne s'étonnera pas que ces sites exploitant au mieux pour leur défense la topographie se soient inscrits dans une logique militaire planifiée dans le but de sécuriser les voies de circulation ; et cela même si le dispositif complet nous échappe, peut-être tout simplement parce que les circonstances l'ont laissé inachevé. Mais ce système cherchait à associer la défense située le long de ces voies et celle qui était en retrait, sur des hauteurs. C'est sans doute ce qui crée l'illusion de frontière dans le sens linéaire du terme. Il n'empêche que les successeurs ne pouvaient ignorer la grande valeur stratégique de ces fortifications de hauteur préexistantes. En effet, entre le IXe et le XIe siècle, il ne s'agissait plus de se contenter de surveiller les routes sur de longues distances mais de valoriser des terroirs et de développer un nouveau maillage de l'espace à contrôler. Dès le VIIe siècle, de nouvelles structures s'étaient mises en place à première vue très distinctes dans leur fonction, comme les villas fiscales, les monastères ou les fortifications. Or, à y regarder de plus près, ces instruments indispensables à l'exercice du pouvoir finirent par se confondre, en tout cas à s'imbriquer, pour former ce que nous appelons « château ». Ces fonctions de centralité correspondent par essence à une organisation spatiale, territoriale et non pas linéaire. Ce n'est que bien plus tard, à partir du XVe siècle, que les châteaux sur la Meuse endossèrent un rôle de défense intercalaire entre les villes défendues par une enceinte.

Bibliographie

Bruand O. (2002), *Voyageurs et marchandises aux temps carolingiens. Les réseaux de communication entre Loire et Meuse aux VIIIe et IXe siècles*, Bruxelles, De Boeck (Bibliothèque du Moyen Âge ; 20).

– (2011), « Les centres économiques locaux dans l'espace lotharingien », in *De la mer du Nord à la Méditerranée. Francia Media, une région au cœur de l'Europe (c. 840-c. 1050)* (Actes du colloque international, Metz, Luxembourg, Trèves, 8-11 février 2006), M. Gaillard et al. (éd.), Luxembourg, CLUDEM (Publications du CLUDEM ; 25), 83-109.

Brulet R. (2008), « Fortifications de hauteur et habitat perché de l'Antiquité tardive au début du haut Moyen Âge, entre Fagne et Eifel », in *Höhensiedlungen zwischen Antike und Mittelalter von den Ardennen bis zur Adria*, H. Steuer et V. Birbrauer (éd.), Berlin, De Gruyter (Reallexikon der germanischen Altertumskunde. Ergänzungsbände ; 58), 13-70.

Chantinne F. (2011), « Aux origines de la "châtellenie de Chimay" : des organes du pouvoir à l'espace du pouvoir à l'espace d'influence d'une famille de rang comtal (IXe-XIIIe siècle) », *Revue belge de philologie et d'histoire*, t. LXXXIX, 191-204.

Chantinne F. et Mignot P. (2012), « L'émergence du phénomène castral dans le sud du diocèse de Liège », in *Château Gaillard 25. L'origine du château médiéval* (Actes du colloque international tenu à Rindern, 23 août-3 septembre 2010), P. Ettel, A.-M. Flambard Héricher et K. O'Conor (éd.), Caen, Publications du CRAHM, 75-88.

Congar P. (1972), « Mouzon gallo-romain et son antique *pagus* », *Revue historique ardennaise*, n° 7, 1-10.

Debord A. (1996), « Le château et le ban : mainmise sur l'espace et les hommes dans le royaume de France (Xe-XIIIe siècle) », in *Châteaux et pouvoir (X[e]-XIXe siècle)*, Bordeaux, CROCEMC/LHAMANS, 4-17.

De Meulemeester J. (1997), « Châteaux et frontière : quelques réflexions sur les principautés territoriales des anciens Pays-Bas méridionaux », in *Château Gaillard 17* (Actes du colloque international tenu à Abergavenny, 29 août-3 septembre 1994), Caen, Centre de recherches archéologiques médiévales, 53-59.

De Meulemeester J. et Mignot P. (2007), « Châteaux et guerres au Moyen Âge : quelques exemples issus des fouilles », in *Le patrimoine militaire de Wallonie*, V. Dejardin et J. Maquet (dir.), Namur, Institut du patrimoine wallon, 33-38.

Devroey J.-P. (2003), *Économie rurale et société dans l'Europe franque (VIe-IXe siècle)*, Paris, Belin (Belin sup. Histoire).

– (2006), *Puissants et misérables. Système social et monde paysan dans l'Europe des Francs (VIe-IXe siècle)*, Bruxelles, Académie royale de Belgique (Mémoires de la Classe des Lettres ; 40).

Ettel P. (2010), « Burgenbau unter den Franken, Karolingern und Ottonen », in *Die Burg. Wissenschaftlicher Begleitband zu den Austellung « Burg und Herrschaft » und « Mythos Burg »*, G. U. Grossmann et H. Ottomeyer (éd.), Dresden, Sandstein, 34-49.

Felten F. J. (1980), *Äbte und Laienäbte im Frankenreich. Studie zum Verhältnis von Staat und Kirche im früheren Mittelalter*, Stuttgart, Hiersemann (Monographien zur Geschichte des Mittelalters ; 20).

Fray J.-L. (2006), *Villes et bourgs de Lorraine. Réseaux urbains et centralité au Moyen Âge*, Clermont-Ferrand, Presses universitaires Blaise-Pascal (Histoires croisées).

Gaillard M. (2003), « La place des abbayes dans la politique territoriale des souverains francs et germaniques en Lotharingie, de 869 à 925 », *Revue du Nord*, t. LXXXV, n° 351, 655-666.

Genicot L. (1970), « Ligne et zone : la frontière des principautés médiévales », *Bulletin de la Classe des lettres et des sciences morales et politiques*, 5ᵉ série, n° 86, 29-42.

Grat F., Viellard J. et Clémencet S. (éd.) (1964), *Annales de Saint-Bertin publiées pour la Société de l'Histoire de France (série antérieure à 1789)*, Paris, Klincksieck.

Helvétius A.-M. (1998), « L'abbatiat laïque comme relais du pouvoir aux frontières du royaume. Le cas du nord de la Neustrie au IXᵉ siècle », in *La royauté et les élites dans l'Europe carolingienne (début IXᵉ siècle aux environs de 920)*, R. Le Jan (dir.), Villeneuve-d'Ascq, Centre d'histoire de l'Europe du Nord-Ouest (Histoire et littérature régionales ; 17), 285-299.

Kraemer C. (2012), « Châteaux et prieurés de Lorraine (Xᵉ-XIIIᵉ siècle) ; essai de topographie historique », in *Châteaux et prieurés* (Actes du Iᵉʳ Colloque de Bellecroix, Chagny, 15-16 octobre 2011), H. Mouillebouche (dir.), Chagny, Centre de castellologie de Bourgogne, 33-64.

Magnou-Nortier É. (2012), *Aux origines de la fiscalité moderne. Le système fiscal et sa gestion dans le royaume des Francs à l'épreuve des sources (Vᵉ-XIᵉ siècle)*, Genève, Droz.

Margue M. (2006), « Mort et pouvoir : le choix du lieu de sépulture (espace Meuse-Moselle, XIᵉ-XIIᵉ siècles) », in *Sépulture, mort et représentation du pouvoir au Moyen Âge* (Actes des XIᵉ Journées lotharingiennes, Centre universitaire de Luxembourg, 26-29 septembre 2000), M. Margue (éd.), Luxembourg, CLUDEM (Publications de la Section historique de l'Institut grand-ducal de Luxembourg ; 118), 293-301.

– (2013), « Face à l'évêque, le comte. Politique ottonienne et pouvoir comtal en Lotharingie à l'époque de Notger », in *Évêque et prince. Notger et la Basse-Lotharingie aux alentours de l'an Mil*, A. Wilkin et J.-L. Kupper (éd.), Liège, Presses universitaires de Liège, 237-270.

Morsel J. (2004), *L'aristocratie médiévale. La domination sociale en Occident (Vᵉ-XVᵉ siècle)*, Paris, Armand Colin (U. Histoire).

Mourot F. (2001), *La Meuse*, Paris, Académie des inscriptions et belles-lettres (Carte archéologique de la Gaule ; 55).

Nonn U. (1983), *Pagus und Comitatus in Niederlothringen. Untersuchungen zur politischen Raumgliederung im früheren Mittelalter*, Bonn, L. Röhrscheid (Bonner historische Forschungen, 49).

Parisse M. (1990a), *Encyclopédie illustrée de la Lorraine. 2 : Histoire de la Lorraine. Austrasie, Lotharingie, Lorraine*, Metz/Nancy, Éd. Serpenoise/Presses universitaires de Nancy.

– (1990b), « La frontière de la Meuse au Xᵉ siècle », in *Haut Moyen Âge. Culture, éducation et société : études offertes à Pierre Riché*, M. Sot (coord.), Nanterre/La Garenne-Colombes, Éd. Publidix/Éd. européennes Érasme, 427-437.

Périn P. (1979), « Le site de Charleville à l'époque mérovingienne : quelques témoins archéologiques », *Revue historique ardennaise*, n° 14, 1-29.

Pol A. (1995), « Les monétaires à Huy et à Maastricht. Production et distribution des monnaies mérovingiennes mosanes », *Bulletin de l'Institut archéologique liégeois*, n° 107, 185-200.

Renoux A. (dir.) (1994), *Palais médiévaux (France-Belgique). 25 ans d'archéologie*, Le Mans, Publications de l'université du Maine.

– (dir.) (2001), *« Aux marches du palais » : qu'est-ce qu'un palais médiéval ? Données historiques et archéologiques* (Actes du VIIᵉ Congrès international d'archéologie médiévale, 9-11 septembre 1999, Le Mans, Mayenne), Le Mans, Publications du LHAM, 9-20.

Ruffini-Ronzani N. (2012), « Enjeux de pouvoir et compétition aristocratique en Entre-Sambre-et-Meuse (fin Xᵉ-milieu XIᵉ siècle) », *Revue bénédictine*, vol. CXXII, n° 2, 294-330.

Suttor M. (2010), « Le rôle d'un fleuve comme limite ou frontière au Moyen Âge. La Meuse, de Sedan à Maastricht », *Le Moyen Âge*, t. CXVI, n° 2, 335-366.

Van Rey M. (1971), « Les divisions politiques et ecclésiastiques de l'ancien diocèse de Liège au haut Moyen Âge », *Le Moyen Âge*, t. LXXXVII, 165-206.

– (1977), *Die Lütticher Gaue Condroz und Ardennen im Frühmittelalter. Untersuchungen zur Pfarrorganisation*, Bonn, L. Röhrscheid (Rheinisches Archiv ; 102), 1977.

West C. (2011), « Principautés et territoires : comtes et comtés », in *De la mer du Nord à la Méditerranée. Francia Media, une région au cœur de l'Europe (c. 840-c. 1050)* (Actes du colloque international, Metz, Luxembourg, Trèves, 8-11 février 2006), M. Gaillard et al. (éd.), Luxembourg, CLUDEM (Publications du CLUDEM ; 25), 131-150.

The Influence of Anglo-Norman Lordship upon the Landscape of Monmouthshire

◆

Owain James Connors*

1. Introduction

Since David Austin's call for castellologists to look beyond the architecture and military function of castles in order to analyse both their effects on the landscape and the landscape's effects upon them[1], there has been a distinct swing towards a more holistic viewpoint of medieval fortifications, studying castles as social and political phenomena, rather than simply as mere fortresses designed for warfare[2]. These "revisionist castellologists" have noted that castles were only very occasionally actively caught up in warfare, but were constantly at the centre of the ordinary lives of all classes of medieval society[3] and aim to overcome the massive imbalance in contemporary academia and popular castle publications between the emphasis on the military design of castles and the space given within (and without) to social, aesthetic and cultural aspects of life. This project investigates the extent to which patterns of political power and social identity in post-Conquest medieval Wales (c. 1066-1300 AD), specifically in the border county of Monmouthshire, are visible within the historic landscape. The historic county of Monmouthshire was one of the new counties created out of the Welsh Marcher lordships in the "Laws in Wales Acts 1535 and 1542" and was comprised of land formerly constituting part of the Marcher lordships of Monmouth and Three Castles, Ewyas, Abergavenny, Usk, Newport, Caerleon, Caldicot and Chepstow, which prior to the Conquest had formed the bulk of the Welsh kingdom of Gwent (fig. 1). As a border county, Monmouthshire has a fairly mixed Anglo-Welsh identity with parts of the region being viewed as more English than Welsh in culture, as exemplified by the county's motto *Utrique Fidelis* ("Faithful to Both").

Meeting this objective, of course, involves determining whether the Anglo-Norman conquest of Wales, and the subsequent establishment of Anglo-Norman lordships upon Welsh territory, affected the character of the landscape at the time, as well as defining to what degree this process manifests itself in the buried, relict and historic landscapes that are still evident today. Studies into the medieval landscapes of Ireland, Scotland and Wales, and the impact of Anglo-Norman lordships in these areas, have often highlighted the "alien" nature of the methods of manorial structure, settlement and farming brought in by the newcomers[4]. Parallel to this, there are a number of related issues that are investigated, the most important of these being determining which was more important in defining the nature of the landscape: the power of the local lordship or the social identity of the local populace. Furthermore, this project examines the extent to which the imposition of Anglo-Norman power, most notably through castles and towns, differed from lordship to lordship, and what factors contributed to any differences discovered. Obviously, this work also finds an academic niche within the discipline of landscape archaeology and builds on previous landscape studies in Wales, most of which tend to be focused on fairly discrete areas[5] or upon a single facet of the landscape[6]. Another theoretical idea this piece of research

---

* Ph.D. research student, University of Exeter, United Kingdom.
1. Austin 1984.
2. E.g. Coulson 1996; Coulson 2003; Creighton 2002; Liddiard 2005.
3. Coulson 2003, 1-2.
4. Edwards 1997, 6; McNeill 1992, 84; Yeoman 1995, 89-95; Kissock 1997, 124-126; Barry 2000, 194; Creighton 2002, 176.
5. E.g. Rippon 2008; Bezant 2009.
6. E.g. Roberts 2006.

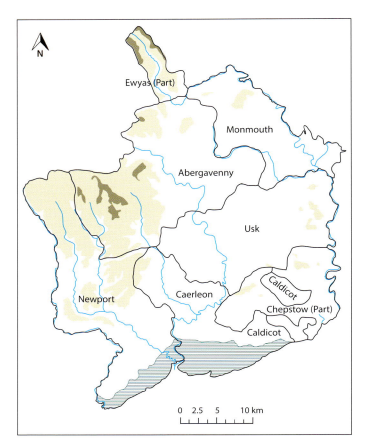

Fig. 1 – The Anglo-Norman lordships within the boundaries of the historic county of Monmouthshire (*c.* 1170) (after CONNORS 2014, fig. 2.8).

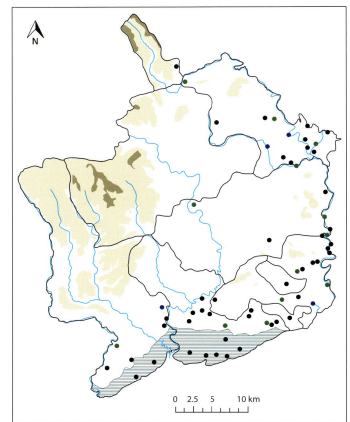

Fig. 2 – Place-names of Anglo-Norman (English or French) origin within Monmouthshire recorded prior to 1300. Black dots: place-names of English origin; blue dots: place-names of French origin; green dots: place-names of mixed origin. After CONNORS 2014, fig. 3.26.

draws upon is Fernand Braudel's ideas of "annaliste history"[7], a theory that has previously been applied to other landscape archaeology studies[8]. It is necessary to determine whether the Anglo-Norman conquest of Wales falls into Fernand Braudel's category of short-term *événements*, medium-term *conjonctures* or the long-term *longue durée*.

Finally, this project investigates whether the theoretical ideas of social identity, popular amongst Roman archaeologists, apply to the medieval world, and, if so how does the "identity stress" caused by the Anglo-Norman conquest affect the Welsh and how does this manifest itself in the archaeological record and the landscape of a "liminal" area such as the Welsh March? This topic has been touched upon at a micro level, such as resistant identities in peasant material culture[9] and power and identity conflict in the village landscape[10]. These theories can also be applied to the landscape as it has long been identified as an archaeological artefact and the "richest historical record we possess"[11]. In today's multicultural society we hear many stories of the struggles caused by differing cultures being forced to coexist. In medieval Wales we have evidence of a clash of two cultures and this research will allow examination of issues of "continuity versus change" and the extent to which there was resistance on the part of the native Welsh to the incoming Anglo-Norman ways of managing the landscape. The aim is to provide an original contribution to all these fields by presenting original data (GIS surveys and landscape characterisation work), as well as in depth analysis of the aforementioned data.

2. Methods

There are two main strands to this project; a county-wide survey followed more detailed case-studies focussed on indi-

---

7. BRAUDEL 1972.
8. E.g. BARKER 1995.
9. SMITH 2009.
10. DYER 1985.
11. HOSKINS 1955.

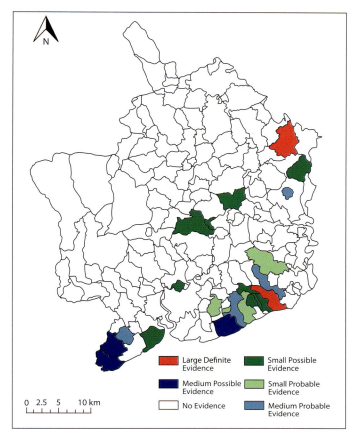

Fig. 3 – Evidence for former open-field in Monmouthshire present in 19th-century mapping (after CONNORS 2014, fig. 3.24).

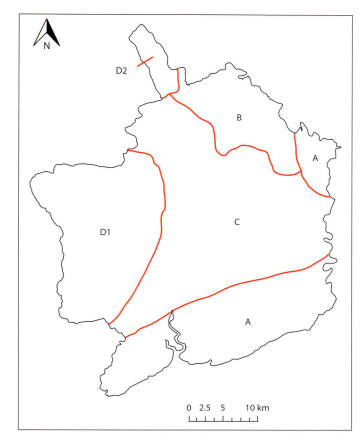

Fig. 4 – Regions of differing influence of Anglo-Norman lordship upon the landscape of the historic county of Monmouthshire. Red lines: boundaries between the different regions. After CONNORS 2014, fig. 3.27.

vidual lordships. The county-wide study examines evidence for the impact of Anglo-Norman lordship upon the landscape of Monmouthshire as a whole (most obviously typified by the construction of castles at the centre of manors and as lordship *capita* – such as Chepstow, Monmouth and Abergavenny, etc.), taking into account factors such as monastic foundations, church typology, place-name evidence, settlement pattern (dispersed or nucleated), evidence for former open-fields and evidence for a seigneurial "designed" landscape (i.e. deer parks, dovecotes, fishponds, rabbit warrens, etc.). This data was collected from a variety of sources, including Historic Environment Records, historical sources (such as *Domesday*, *inquisitions post mortem* and estate records) and accurate 19th-century mapping before being collated and analysed using a GIS program and related to the patterns of Anglo-Norman lordship, exemplified by the construction of lordship centres, such as castles. The use of GIS is integral to this project due to the ability of the software to handle large amounts of geo-spatial data quickly and accurately. Furthermore GIS allows the layering of data on top of other elements (and other data sets) in order to provide comparison and analysis of how various facets of the historic landscape are changed and moulded by the influence of other features. This being a short paper, it is impossible to show all the results of the county-wide survey, but two of the most clear findings are presented in figures 2 and 3. These show that both evidence for former open-field and pre-1300 place-names of English origin were largely limited to southern and eastern borders of the county (figs. 2 & 3).

All of the results of the county-wide survey were then used to produce a model of the "regions" of Anglo-Norman influence in Monmouthshire (fig. 4) where the landscape was broken up into categories A through to D1 and D2 representing the degree to which Anglo-Norman lordship impacted upon the landscape. Category A represents those low-lying regions of Monmouthshire where Anglo-Norman influence was most keenly felt – centred on the lordships of Monmouth, Newport, Chepstow and Caldicot. Here we have multiple lordship centres, a high density of place-names of English origin, the presence of boroughs and monasteries, examples of seigneurial "designed" landscapes and plenty of evidence for rural settlement nucleation and former open-field systems. Category B comprises the Monnow Valley, where Anglo-Norman influence is still strong, but not as intense as it is around Monmouth and on the Gwent Levels. Category C makes up the majority of the county, including the wide and fertile Usk valley. Here we have "islands" of minor Anglo-Norman influence surrounding important lordship centres (e.g. Usk, Abergavenny, etc.), whilst the majority of the landscape seems to be largely "Welsh" in character and the Anglo-Norman conquest appears to have had little impact. Finally category D (both 1 and 2) represents the upland areas of the county where Anglo-Norman influence is minimal.

3. Conclusions

The first stage of this project, the county-wide study, has shown that large-scale Anglo-Norman landscape influence was largely limited to the coastal and border regions of Monmouthshire, where there were stronger logistical ties with England. Outside of this zone we see "islands" of Anglo-Norman influence in the vicinity of major lordship centres (most significantly castles and associated towns) surrounded by a landscape largely Welsh in character. Importantly, in the regions where there were no major Anglo-Norman lordship centres, we see very little evidence for landscape change. This suggests a "top-down" elite driven model of landscape change, with lordship sites as the main engines of change, which was not particularly successful, because in the majority of the county the native populace seem to have maintained control of their surrounding landscape and we see largely "Welsh" methods of landscape management. The findings of this county-wide study will be built upon by more detailed case-studies of individual lordships (fig. 1) on a parish by parish basis, looking for reasons for variations in the patterns of landscape change between lordships (topography, politics, regional differences, personal influence, etc.). This phase of the project, currently being undertaken, involves detailed analysis of the landscape of the lordship centres for each lordship, as well as the minor seigneurial centres and some of the parishes which show no evidence of Anglo-Norman lordship centres. If present, parishes which show evidence of previous Welsh lordship will also be examined to provide a comparison. In the absence of accurate contemporary medieval maps, detailed examinations of 19th-century tithe maps, as well as earlier estate maps, are being employed allowing an in-depth investigation of important landscape features such as the patterns of settlement, field morphology, land tenure, field names and land use, as well the relationship of all these elements to Anglo-Norman lordship centres.

Bibliography

Austin D. (1984), "The Castle and the Landscape. Annual Lecture to the Society for Landscape Studies, May 1984", *Landscape History*, 6, 69-81.

Barker G. (1995), "Approaches to Mediterranean Landscape History", in *A Mediterranean Valley. Landscape Archaeology and "Annales" History in the Biferno Valley*, G. Barker (ed.), London, Leicester University Press, 1-16.

Barry T. (2000), "The Chronology and Development of Medieval Rural Settlement in Munster", *Journal of the Cork Historical and Archaeological Society*, 105, 191-198.

Bezant J. (2009), *Medieval Welsh Settlement and Territory. Archaeological Evidence from a Teifi Valley Landscape*, Oxford, Archaeopress (BAR. British Series; 487).

Braudel F. (1972), *The Mediterranean and the Mediterranean World in the Age of Philip II*, London, Collins.

Connors O. J. (2014), *The Effects of Anglo-Norman Lordship upon the Landscape of Post-Conquest Monmouthshire*, Unpublished Ph.D. thesis, University of Exeter.

Coulson C. L. H. (1996), "The State of Research. Cultural Realities and Reappraisals in English Castle-Study", *Journal of Medieval History*, 22/2, 171-208.

– (2003), *Castles in Medieval Society. Fortresses in England, France and Ireland in the Central Middle Ages*, Oxford, Oxford University Press.

Creighton O. H. (2002), *Castles and Landscape. Power, Community and Fortification in Medieval England*, London, Equinox.

Dyer C. C. (1985), "Power and Conflict in the Medieval Village", in *Medieval Villages. A Review of Current Work*, D. Hooke (ed.), Oxford, Oxford University Committee for Archaeology (Oxford University Committee for Archaeology Monograph; 5), 27-32.

Edwards N. (1997), "Landscape and Settlement in Medieval Wales. An Introduction", in *Landscape and Settlement in Medieval Wales*, N. Edwards (ed.), Oxford, Oxbow Books (Oxbow Monograph; 81), 1-12.

Hoskins W. G. (1955), *The Making of the English Landscape*, London, Hodder and Stoughton.

Kissock J. (1997), "'God Made Nature and Men Made Towns': Post-Conquest and Pre-Conquest Villages in Pembrokeshire", in Edwards 1997 (ed.), 123-138.

Liddiard R. (2005), *Castles in Context. Power, Symbolism and Landscape (1066-1500)*, Macclesfield, Windgather Press.

McNeill T. E. (1992), *English Heritage Book of Castles*, London, Batsford/English Heritage.

Rippon S. (2008), *Beyond the Medieval Village. The Diversification of Landscape Character in Southern Britain*, Oxford, Oxford University Press (Medieval History and Archaeology).

Roberts K. (ed.) (2006), *Lost Farmsteads. Deserted Rural Settlements in Wales*, York, Council for British Archaeology.

Smith S. V. (2009), "Materializing Resistant Identities among the Medieval Peasantry: an Examination of Dress Accessories from English Rural Settlement Sites", *Journal of Material Culture*, 14/3, 309-332.

Yeoman P. (1995), *Medieval Scotland: an Archaeological Perspective*, London, Batsford (Historic Scotland).

Castle, *Burh* and Borough: Unravelling an Urban Landscape of Power at Wallingford, Oxfordshire

◆

Oliver Creighton*

1. *Burh* to Borough: the Wallingford Research Project

Wallingford, Oxfordshire, is a modestly sized market town located by the River Thames approximately mid-way between Oxford and Reading (fig. 1). The medieval town plan, framed by the rectangular embanked and ditched defences of an Anglo-Saxon *burh*, testifies to an unusual urban story. Large swathes of space within the former *burh* are open ground, indicating a contracted urban settlement or else that streets and housing did not ever fully occupy the entire intra-mural area. The unusual circumstances of Wallingford's decline present rich potential for archaeological investigation that the *Wallingford Burh to Borough Research Project* has sought to capitalise upon in order to produce a major case study of urban transformation across the medieval period[1].

Between 2001 and 2010, the Project conducted a programme of archaeological fieldwork within the town and its immediate hinterland with the aim of unravelling Wallingford's total urban story. The programme combined non-intrusive fieldwork (geophysical and topographical survey and standing building analysis) with archaeological excavations targeted to answer specific questions, alongside garden archaeology ("test pits", mainly within private gardens), documentary and cartographic analysis, and the re-interpretation of past archaeological interventions within the town, both developer-funded and research-led[2]. Conceived as a collaborative venture between academic researchers and local stakeholders, this was also a project characterised by public participation; the archaeological site in question here is a living and thriving entity to be studied in partnership with its community.

Within the context of this wider urban study, Wallingford's medieval castle was a particularly important focus for investigation. Its excellent conditions of earthwork preservation, combined with the untapped potential of documentary sources and an archive of largely unpublished excavations from the 1960s and 1970s presented rich opportunities for unravelling the castle's place in the urban sequence and the agency of authority in the transformation of this remarkably intact medieval townscape. The following account first summarises how the *Burh to Borough Research Project* has contributed to our understanding of the castle and its setting and then goes on to reflect on the complex, multi-layered and evolving interrelationship between fortress, town and community.

2. Introducing castle and town

In the first published history of Wallingford in the late 19th century, John Kirby Hedges thought that the town had Roman origins and could be equated with the documented *Calleva Atrebatum*[3]. He was mistaken: it is now well established that Wallingford was founded in the late 9th century AD as

---

* Professor of Archaeology, University of Exeter, United Kingdom.
1. Christie & Creighton 2013.
2. For interim reports, see Speed *et al.* 2009 and Christie *et al.* 2010a on the town, and Christie *et al.* 2010b on the castle.
3. Hedges 1881.

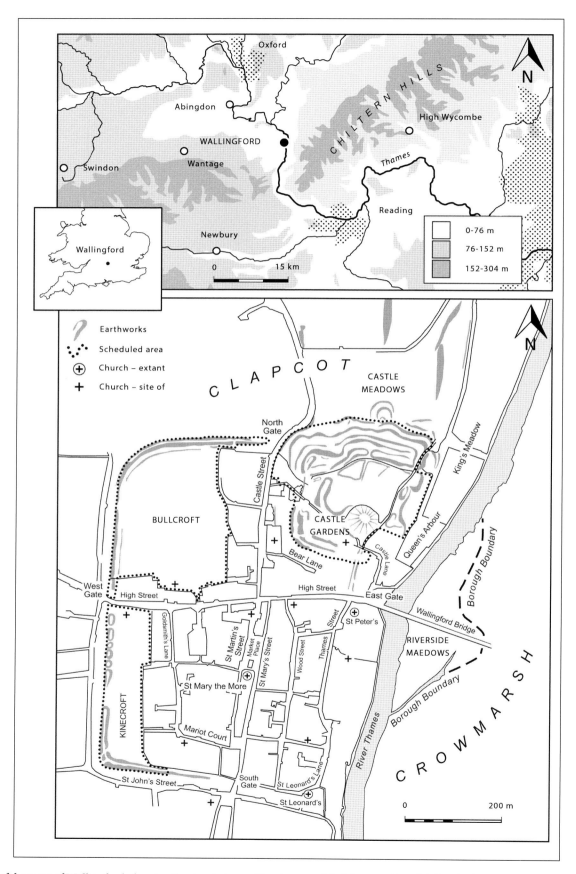

Fig. 1 – Map of the town of Wallingford, showing the street plan and key topographical features. Doc. *Wallingford Burh to Borough Research Project*.

Fig. 2 – View of the earthworks of Wallingford Castle, showing a rebuilt fragment of the inner bailey curtain wall. Photo *Wallingford Burh to Borough Research Project*.

an Anglo-Saxon *burh*, or fortified place – not necessarily a town – on the frontier of the Kingdom of Wessex[4]. As such, Wallingford has attained something of the status of a "classic" site in British medieval archaeology and is often invoked as a quintessential Wessex *burh*: with 2,400 hides attached to it in the early 10th-century document known as the Burghal Hidage, Wallingford was equal to Winchester, the capital of Wessex[5]. The massive embanked and ditched *burh* defences, forming a rectangular perimeter against the river, are arguably the finest anywhere in England[6].

Less well known is the site of Wallingford's important royal castle, which was superimposed into the north-east corner of the *burh* shortly after the Norman Conquest and later enlarged into a concentric fortress whose precincts took up the town's entire north-east quarter (fig. 1). Wallingford Castle does not feature prominently in the narrative of English castle development, however, largely due to the paucity of its upstanding masonry remains (fig. 2). In addition to some fragments of curtain walling, the principal masonry vestige of the castle comprises part of the College of St Nicholas, a foundation of the late 11th century later embraced within the defences[7]. Wallingford Castle survives primarily an earthwork site, although the present-day field remains are the product of several episodes of adaptation, including the re-fortification of the (then derelict) castle in the mid-17th-century English Civil War and the post-medieval adaptation of its grounds into a designed landscape. Although this was a major urban castle its setting and appearance are now essentially rural in character.

Established in the then shire capital of Berkshire shortly after 1066, Wallingford Castle was a major administrative centre at the heart of a wealthy and extensive honour,[8] and hosted a well documented royal prison[9]. Variously in the hands of the king or other prominent members of the royal family it was an occasional stopping point on royal itineraries but was on a day-to-day basis staffed by a busy and complex community of constables, under porters, chaplains and gate-keepers[10]. The castle's principal role in military affairs was during "the Anarchy" of the mid-12th century, when it was besieged on three occasions[11], while its peacetime heyday was in the middle years of the 13th century, when it was in the hands of Richard, Earl of Cornwall – Crusader, brother of Henry III and "King of the Romans"[12]. It is also from the late 13th century onwards that the castle's role as a pleasure palace grew; it was the venue for lavish tournaments and was accompanied by hunting grounds in Clapcot to the north, and gardens, meadows, mills, ponds and swanneries along the Thames to the east. By 1540 the castle was derelict, as described by the antiquarian John Leland, who commented on the castle's three water-filled ditches, its ruinous walls, and that the only remaining buildings lay within the inner bailey[13].

3. Investigating Wallingford Castle

The *Burh to Borough Research Project* conducted resistivity and magnetometry surveys of accessible areas across the castle site as part of the project's wider aim of generating sub-surface geophysical plots of available open spaces within and around the town. These surveys covered a large swathe of the castle's inner and outer baileys, plus the areas to the north ("Castle Meadows") and to the east ("Queen's Arbour" and "King's Meadow"). The geophysical plots informed the choice of location for the Project's excavation trenches across the site, as detailed below, but also formed an immensely valuable source of information on the castle's below-ground archaeology in their own right. In conjunction with a detailed topographic survey, the geophysical results provide an entirely new perspective not only on the castle and its development, but also its wider landscape setting.

The resistivity plot (fig. 3) proved especially informative. Particularly striking is the high level of sub-surface stonework survival despite the castle's apparently thorough slighting after the mid-17th-century Civil War siege. Clear traces survive of three concentric curtain walls on the north flank of the site, the outermost of which had at least two artillery bastions built against it in the mid-17th century. Traces of medieval buildings within the castle's precincts are more ephemeral, although the inner bailey contains a complex array of geophysical traces suggestive of some of the domestic structures recorded in

---

4. On the origins of Wallingford, see KEATS-ROHAN & ROFFE 2009.
5. HILL & RUMBLE 1996.
6. CREIGHTON & HIGHAM 2005, 223.
7. DURHAM 1987.
8. KEATS-ROHAN 1989; KEATS-ROHAN 2009.
9. PUGH 1955.
10. RICKARD 2002, 90-93.
11. SPURRELL 1995; SPEIGHT 2000, 272-273.
12. DENHOLM-YOUNG 1947.
13. TOULMIN SMITH 1907, 119.

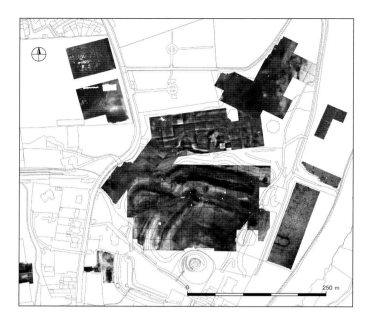
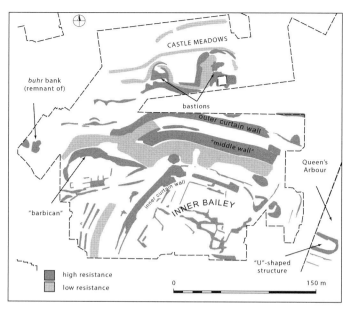

Fig. 3 – Resistivity survey of Wallingford Castle (left), with an interpretation of results identifying key features (right). Doc. *Wallingford Burh to Borough Research Project*.

the site's many campaigns of refurbishment and repair, as revealed by documentary sources, which are most informative for the 14th century but require more detailed study[14]. A major challenge is, however, to disentangle geophysical signatures of medieval structures from the evidence of post-medieval landscaping and gardening across the site. On the east flank of the castle, meanwhile, a U-shaped structure projecting into the floodplain was revealed and later excavated (see below). The project also used GPR (ground-penetrating radar) in a more limited but targeted way. This work recorded sections through the northern defences of the site in an attempt to pinpoint the underlying *burh* bank (also visible on the resistivity plot: see fig. 3), and within the inner bailey to clarify the plans and survival of domestic buildings.

4. Excavating Wallingford Castle

Wallingford Castle's below-ground archaeology has been sampled on at least ten different occasions (fig. 4). While quite large-scale interventions have been conducted in pursuit of academic research, a number of other smaller-scale evaluations took place in advance of projected building development on the site and its surroundings, while 19th-century searches for subterranean passageways are another part of the site's complex archaeological biography[15]. Given the vast scale of the castle, these multiple interventions – widely spaced and employing different methods of excavation and recording – are little more than tiny windows into an exceptionally complex and deeply stratified archaeological record. As is the case for many other urban castles in Britain and Europe the most appropriate archaeological research strategies for advancing our understanding of these challenging sites – revealing not only their plans and development but also ideally something of their everyday social and economic lives – involve synthesis of such existing information alongside any new investigations that will usually combine non-intrusive survey with carefully targeted excavation.

The northern approaches to the castle

Large-scale excavations on the north-west corner of the castle site led by Nicholas P. Brooks in 1965, 1966 and 1968 were intended chiefly to investigate the defences and planning of the Anglo-Saxon *burh* rather than to explore the later medieval castle (fig. 5)[16]. In 1965 Brooks was able to pinpoint the location of the "lost" North Gate of the *burh*, which had been rebuilt in a new location further west when the castle's defences were replanned. The excavated road running up to this gate preserved a Saxo-Norman street frontage lined with properties and industrial features, all sealed beneath the castle's outer bank, which formed the third line of its defences. The pottery assemblage from the destruction layers dated the burial of the old road and gate broadly to the 13th century and, on balance, the tenure of Richard, Earl of Cornwall, who held the fortress from 1231 until his death in 1272, is the most likely context for the fortress's transformation into what was a visually imposing concentric show-castle (see below for further discussion).

14. Colvin 1963, 850-852; see also Keats-Rohan forthcoming.
15. Christie & Creighton 2013, 145-218.
16. Brooks 1965.

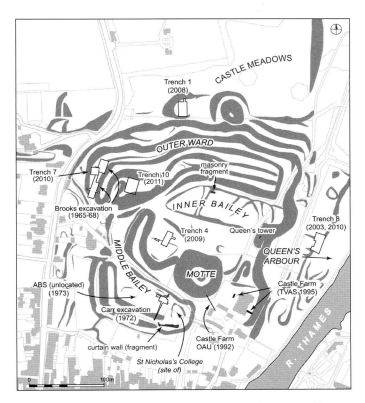

Fig. 4 – Plan of Wallingford Castle, showing the locations of known archaeological interventions on the site and other key features. Trenches 1, 4, 7, 8 and 10 were excavated by the *Wallingford Burh to Borough Research Project*. Doc. *Wallingford Burh to Borough Research Project*.

Further insight into the impact of the castle on the town's changing road system was provided by a *Burh to Borough Research Project* trench in the School Playing Fields north of the castle in 2010. This confirmed that the northern route in and out of the town immediately west of the castle underwent a series of changes – meandering almost like a river as it was replanned in response first to the planning of the *burh* and then the castle – until around *c*. 1300, when it stabilised, but on a circuitous route that skirted the castle's defences (hence the curving line of Castle Street, west of the castle: see fig. 1). By this stage much of the northern half of the town comprised an elite zone. A medieval traveller entering Wallingford from this direction would have been confronted with the symbols not only of state (in the form of the castle), but also church (in the form of the Benedictine priory planted shortly after the Norman Conquest in the north-west quarter of the town, in the area now known as the Bullcroft).

Other *Burh to Borough Research Project* trenches in 2008 (Trench 1) and 2011 (Trench 10) proved especially informative about the site's refortification by a royalist garrison in 1643

Fig. 5 – Excavations on the site of Wallingford's North Gate by N. P. Brooks in the late 1960s. Photo N. P. Brooks.

during the English Civil War. On the northern side of the site Trench 1 revealed a bastion, which microfossil analysis has shown was built in the autumn from imported Glauconitic Marl[17]. Commercial evaluations and watching briefs elsewhere on the site provided further evidence for the scale of the castle's reactivation in this period[18]. On the north-west side of the site Trench 10 revealed a substantial reworking of a presumed medieval barbican space at a point overlooking the town's north gate.

The middle bailey

The only large-scale excavation within the castle's middle bailey took place in 1972, directed by Robert D. Carr and carried out in advance of projected building development[19]. The trench sampled an area south of the motte and west of the standing structure related to St Nicholas's College, with an extension cutting across the southern defences of the middle bailey rampart (see fig. 4 for location). The most remarkable finding was a pair of cob-built (i.e. constructed of mud) medieval buildings (fig. 6). The walls of the main building rose to a height of 1.80 m and evidence for doorways, internal hearths and "fixed" furniture such as work benches was identified. The complex can confidently be identified as the new medieval kitchen constructed in October 1229, during works for Henry III[20]. The excellent preservation of these structures was due to the fact that the kitchens had been buried during a massive operation of earth movement related to the refortification and extension of the castle in the mid- to late 13th century that dumped material excavated from the new outer ditch into the middle bailey. Medieval kitchens on any type of site are notoriously ephemeral structures, making this archaeological evidence from Wallingford Castle especially

---

17. Wilkinson *et al*. 2010.
18. Saunders 1995; Oxford Archaeological Unit 1992; Mundin 2008; Hull & Pine 2001; Ford 1995.
19. Anon. 1972; Carr 1973; Webster & Cherry 1973.
20. Calendar of the Liberate Rolls, 1226-1240, vol. 1, 149.

Fig. 6 – Excavations in the middle bailey by R. D. Carr in 1972. The cob-built structure is part of a 13th-century complex of castle kitchens. Photo R. D. Carr.

Fig. 7 – Excavations in the inner bailey by the *Burh to Borough Research Project* in 2009, showing the walls of a service building. Photo *Wallingford Burh to Borough Research Project*.

significant. The use of cob may well have been standard for functional buildings such as stables, servants' quarters and stores as well as kitchens, and may be one reason why the geophysical plots for the inner and middle baileys are not packed with easily identifiable stone structures.

The inner bailey

The opening of an 8 x 20 m trench in the inner bailey by the *Burh to Borough Research Project* in the summer of 2009 represented the first time the innermost core of the castle complex had been sampled archaeologically (see fig. 4 for location). Positioned to sample a large rectangular feature detected through geophysical survey and thought to be a medieval building platform, the trench also examined part of the area between this putative building and the curtain wall of the inner bailey (fig. 7). Logistical factors prevented full excavation of the lower stratigraphical layers, although sufficient was revealed to confirm a sequence of occupation extending back to the first phase of the Norman castle. The earliest archaeological feature was an oval oven or dryer that went out of use in the 12th century. Above this, and beneath a much later spread of demolition rubble relating to the castle's slighting in the aftermath of the mid-17th-century Civil War, a complex suite of archaeological features including pits, gullies, and walls was cut into a series of imported silty marl layers that formed the level ground surface of the bailey interior. This evidence could be rationalised as part of an undercroft attached to a larger service building – perhaps a storage area or wine cellar first built in the late 12th or 13th century. The presence of intact stretches of (levelled) medieval walling alongside robber trenches demonstrates some structural survival despite the apparently thorough post-medieval slighting and later landscaping.

The environs

The area known as the Queen's Arbour, located between the east curtain wall of the inner bailey and the River Thames, was the focus of the *Burh to Borough Research Project*'s excavations in the summer of 2010 (Trench 8). Here, a U-shaped masonry structure 16.6 m across stretching across the flood plain from the curtain wall (fig. 8) proved to be the earliest feature on the site, underlain by a thick layer of alluvial clay. The small assemblage of pottery dated the structure to the late 12th or 13th century, although it was cut by a post-medieval mill leat and musket balls recovered from overlying layers clearly date to the mid-17th-century siege. Seemingly undocumented, this cannot be easily categorised or labelled, although earthwork survey shows that it was embedded within a complex of water management features including ponds, channels, mills and a swannery documented by the late 13th century[21]. Lying beneath the documented "Queen's Tower", within which one can still observe the base mould of a large 14th-century window, the entire area was at the very least an elite and very private enclave and may have had garden-like qualities (the area is first documented as the *Quenesherber* in 1376)[22]. Alternative interpretations might see the U-shaped feature, projecting towards the river, as a quay, although it probably did not extend into the water and no clear trace of a water channel from the river to the wall was evident in the geophysical or topographic surveys.

---

21. MIDGLEY 1942, 84-91.

22. GELLING 1974, vol. 2, 587.

Fig. 8 – Excavations in the Queen's Arbour by the *Burh to Borough Research Project* in 2010, showing the outline of a U-shaped masonry structure beneath the castle walls. Photo *Wallingford Burh to Borough Research Project*.

Another important aspect of Wallingford Castle's setting is the evidence for multiple siegeworks built against it during the three sieges of the Anarchy in the mid-12th century, when the town's bridge and the area on the opposite (east) bank of the Thames were a particular focus for conflict. Here *Burh to Borough Research Project* surveys have revealed geophysical traces of siegeworks while a developer-funded excavation in 2011 on the Wilder Yard site revealed traces of the "lost" ringwork of Crowmarsh Castle, built by King Stephen as a "counter-castle" and violently contested and eventually slighted during the Anarchy[23].

5. Phasing the castle: a summary

Wallingford Castle's structural development can be rationalised into the sequence illustrated in figure 9 (fig. 9). It is important to bear in mind, however, that such a chronology is artificially neat and does not reflect the complex reality of almost constant building and rebuilding campaigns within the fortress's many zones.

1. Wallingford Castle was first planned *c*. 1066-1070 as a large motte attached to a single sub-rectangular bailey that took up only the extreme north-east corner of the *burh*, thus reusing the defences of the massive Anglo-Saxon rampart. In common with other very early mottes there appears to have been no ditch between it and the bailey.[24] The defences were initially of earth and timber but renewed in stone, with rectangular mural towers, by the early to mid-12th century. Various strands of circumstantial evidence strongly suggest that the Norman castle perpetuated the site of an Anglo-Saxon royal hall or compound in this part of the *burh*, although this cannot be verified archaeologically. The College of St Nicholas was founded shortly after the castle, again perhaps on the site of an earlier Anglo-Saxon institution, but lay outside the first castle's defences, although perhaps within a demarcated castle quarter.

2. The castle's "middle bailey", enclosing the area west of the initial motte and bailey, is an addition of the mid-12th century, most probably reflecting an Anarchy-period upgrade of the 1140s or 1150s. Embracing the College of St Nicholas, its defences comprised a box rampart fronted with a stone wall, as revealed by Robert D. Carr's excavations of 1972.

3. Construction of the castle's outer (third) wall and moat was carried out during the lordship of Richard, Earl of Cornwall in the middle years of the 13th century, perhaps from the 1240s onwards, although no building accounts of this period survive. The concentric outer defences were built on the north side of the castle only, beyond the perimeter of the middle bailey; they comprised a curtain wall studded with rounded towers, with a rampart piled in front of it and a moat beyond. This phase was closely associated with a reorientation of the townscape involving the removal of the north gate and its resiting to the west and probably the settlement of a Jewish community near the castle[25]. By this phase the castle also possessed drawbridges and a barbican-like feature flanking access to its main gatehouse to the west. A major area of uncertainty is the motte-top structure, which is very poorly documented but seems most likely to have been a circular shell keep; given the castle's importance it might have been rebuilt by Richard, Earl of Cornwall, for example in the showy style of his triple-tiered donjon at Launceston, Cornwall[26]. The water supply system to the castle's multiple moats, mills, ponds and swanneries in this fully developed phase was complex, with the Queen's Arbour and King's Meadow areas developed from this period onwards as dedicated managed and leisure spaces.

The circumstances of Wallingford Castle's transformation into a concentric castle are worth reflecting upon briefly. The building campaign pre-dates both Edward I's famous castle-building campaigns in north Wales and his addition of concentric defences to the Tower of London in the 1270s, although these works at London most likely reactivated an initiative of Henry III in 1238 or 1239 to add an outer moat and wall to the royal castle[27]. Richard's castle-building campaign at Wallingford may thus have rivalled that of his brother, Henry III. A more specific source of inspiration or influence behind Wallingford Castle's unusual plan might have been his experience of fortifications in the Holy Land. Richard was closely involved in and personally financed an elaborate

---

23. LABAN 2011.
24. On this phenomenon generally, see AARTS 2007.
25. Berkhamsted's Jews were moved to Wallingford in the 1240s: DENHOLM-YOUNG 1947, 69.
26. SAUNDERS 2006.
27. GOODALL 2011, 191, 200-227.

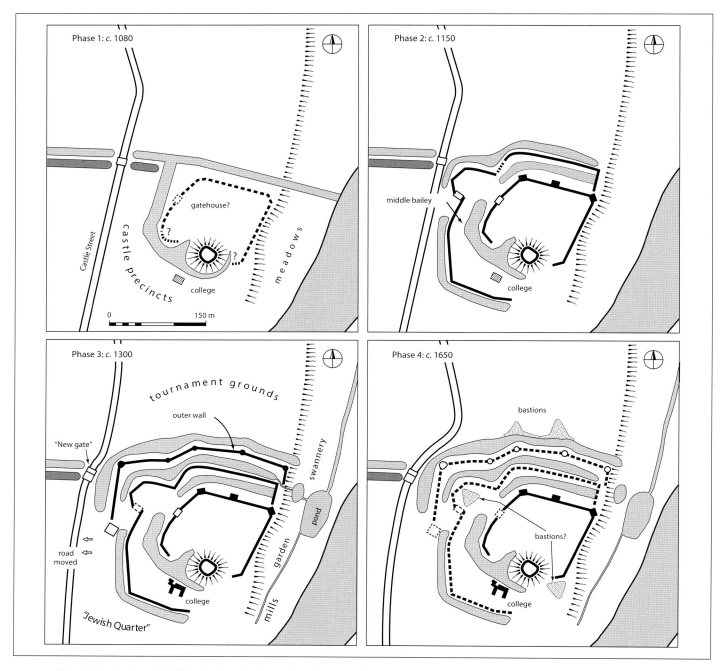

Fig. 9 – Evolution of Wallingford Castle from the 11th to the 17th century. Doc. *Wallingford Burh to Borough Research Project*.

refortification of Ascalon (now on Israel's Mediterranean Coast), which was already underway when he arrived in October 1240 and completed by the end of April 1241[28]. A letter written by Richard and recounted by Matthew Paris specifies that the castle – as distinct from the ancient town defences – was completed with "a double wall enclosing it"[29]. Although little survives of the castle today, it was clearly a concentric fortress. While the notion of the Crusades as an important axis of influence in the diffusion of military architecture is today rather tarnished, this closely datable episode, and the intimacy of Richard's involvement with it, present a clear argument that the refortification of Wallingford under Richard's tenure could well have drawn on this experience as a model.

4. The 14th and 15th centuries saw the castle continue to be used as a centre of luxurious living, albeit sporadically, although no major changes were made to its plan and by the

---

28. Denholm-Young 1947, 42-43; Pringle 1984, 143-146.

29. *Ibid.*, 143.

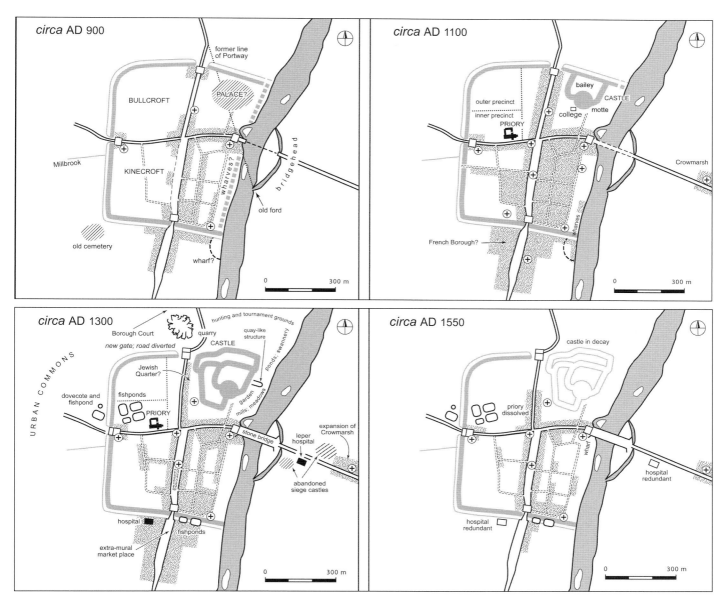

Fig. 10 – Evolution of Wallingford's urban topography from the late Anglo-Saxon to the post-medieval period. Doc. *Wallingford Burh to Borough Research Project*.

mid-16th century the defences and buildings were dilapidated, as recorded in a sketch-plan and survey of the period[30]. The castle witnessed a final short, sharp burst of activity during the mid-17th-century Civil War, after which it was slighted. These refurbishments modified the defences only, with the internal buildings remaining ruinous. The royalist garrison added artillery bastions on the northern side of the castle's outer ditch, two of which survive as earthworks, while archaeological evidence shows that the stone wall of the middle bailey at least was crudely rebuilt and that in places the decaying ramparts were heightened.

6. Castle, *Burh* and Borough: connections and disconnections

The interrelationship between castle and borough at Wallingford was complex, multi-facetted and evolving (fig. 10). In some senses the two institutions were symbiotically linked, with the castle's administrative importance and high-status presence boosting the urban economy, but in other ways the precincts of the castle constituted a separate sphere that was both legally distinct and aloof from the townscape beneath it.

The physical relationship between castle and borough was fluid rather than fixed. The sequence of Wallingford Castle's development highlights how the zone physically enclosed by the castle expanded – and then perhaps contracted – until the only buildings lay within the inner bailey by the mid-16th century.

30. COLVIN 1963, 852.

It is also clear from documentary sources that during periods of tension, for military purposes the castle's defences in effect extended as far as the bridge across the Thames, as in the mid-12th-century sieges and again in the English Civil War when a drawbridge was installed on the town bridge. The castle also controlled a complex arrangement sluices at the town's west gate that regulated the flow of water into the fortress's multiple moats. As Abigail Wheatley has shown, medieval literary sources often show a considerable degree of overlap in understanding between the "private" institution of the castle and the "communal" defences of towns and cities, so that the distinction between the two was not at all clear-cut to contemporaries on the ground[31]. Indeed, it is questionable whether a medieval traveller passing through Wallingford's north gate in the 14th century would have had the experience of entering a town, a castle or both.

While the castle was the most obvious physical manifestation of secular power in Wallingford, it is very clear that the wider townscape also bears the imprint of authority to an unusual level that made this place's urban story quite exceptional. The debate about medieval "landscapes of lordship" intended to display status and authority has mainly focused on rural sites[32]. Could the same be true of urban settings? Wallingford was no small castle borough, but a shire centre. Urban castles are readily characterised as destructive influences in the townscape[33], but here the physical relationship between castle and town was nuanced and fluctuating. As has been demonstrated, the Norman castle and monastery were effectively twinned and formed a visibly elite zone, although this in all probability perpetuated a royal intra-mural compound of the late Anglo-Saxon period. It is quite possible that visual experiences of entering the town were structured to showcase the place's status. This was especially the case from the north (it was only on this side that the castle was provided with its imposing triple line of defence), while the eastern and southern approaches to the town were flanked by hospitals founded by the monarchy and fishponds flanked the south and west gates and a dovecote also lay outside the west gate. More private zones attached to the castle were carefully secluded for the use of the household and guests, most obviously on the east flanks of the castle where there were gardens and meadows. The open space north of the castle was kept free of development; here were grounds for hunting, hawking and tournaments, with Wallingford's sporting facilities gaining international fame in the popular Arthurian romance *Cligés*[34].

Also crucial here is the often underestimated role of water and its management in the creation of Wallingford's identity and in defining the relationship between castle and community. Water was integral to the structuring of an elite landscape attached to the castle that included a string of fishponds, a swannery and water mills, representing symbols of privilege, display and control as well as the working apparatus of estate management. The Thames was integral to the town's defences, identity and its economic role, but it was also an arena for contestation – not just in the martial sense, as in the Anarchy, but between different interest groups within the town. The great bridge over the Thames, meanwhile, was renewed in stone during the time of Richard Earl of Cornwall's tenure of the castle in the mid-13th century and it is difficult not to see this too, as an ostentatious statement of favour and privilege as well as an amenity. These watery landscapes – and the means of negotiating them – were far more than parts of the settings of sites, but active elements of material culture that deserve detailed consideration.

It is also due to the presence of the castle and its high-status household, plus the human concourse that went back and forth to a busy fortress at the heart of an extensive honour, that the town grew niche elements to its economy. The borough court rolls show that the place had vintners, goldsmiths and huntsmen, for example[35]. Medieval Wallingford was also more ethnically diverse than was typical for a town of its size. A French borough was established shortly after the Norman Conquest[36], while a small but wealthy Jewish population was deliberately settled here, presumably close to the castle, during the tenure of Richard, Earl of Cornwall[37].

Did the periodic presence of a large and wealthy household create commercial opportunities, or is there any sense in which Wallingford's elite somehow held back the development of the town as an economically flourishing unit? Wallingford's decline was not only severe, but it was early and it is tempting to link this the unusually high-status presence. The movement of the earldom to Berkhamsted shortly after 1272 might have been a "tipping point" in Wallingford's fortunes, as the town's population was in sharp decline before the crises of the mid-14th century – from around 2,000 in 1100 to around 1,250 in 1300, meaning that Wallingford dropped from being in England's top 20 towns to a position outside the top 100[38]. Might a town under the shadow of authority have been especially vulnerable to dislocations? We only have to look as far afield at nearby Windsor to find a royal borough where the "urban" community was constricted (in this case by the royal parks), remained small and never possessed its own defences, despite its location beneath a prominent and busy royal fortress[39]. From this perspective, is it possible to characterise Wallingford – a town originating as a royal *burh*, always bearing the imprint of authority but never developing a sustainable economy of its own – as always somehow subservient to the wishes of the very highest ranks of the social elite?

---

31. WHEATLEY 2004, 19-43.
32. CREIGHTON 2009.
33. DRAGE 1987.
34. BULLOCK-DAVIES 1981, 28-29; TASKER GRIMBERT & CHASE 2011, 1-3.
35. HERBERT 1971.
36. ROFFE 2009.
37. SCOTT 1950.
38. CHRISTIE & CREIGHTON 2013, 294.
39. ASTILL 2002.

Bibliography

Aarts B. (2007), "Motte-and-Bailey Castles of Europe: some Aspects Concerning their Origin and Evolution", *Virtus: Jaarboek voor Adelsgeschiedenis*, 14, 37-56.

Anon. (1972), "A Medieval 'Cob' Building", *Current Archaeology*, 35, 318.

Astill G. (2002), "Windsor in the Context of Medieval Berkshire", in *Windsor: Medieval Archaeology, Art and Architecture of the Thames Valley*, L. Keen & E. Scarff (eds.), Leeds, British Archaeological Association (The British Archaeological Association Conference Transactions; 25), 1-14.

Brooks N. P. (1965), "Excavations at Wallingford Castle, 1965: an Interim Report", *Berkshire Archaeological Journal*, 62, 17-21.

Bullock-Davies C. (1981), "Chrétien de Troyes and England", in *Arthurian Literature I*, R. Barber (ed.), Woodbridge, Brewer, 1-61.

Calendar of the Liberate Rolls (1916-1964), London, His Majesty's Stationery Office, 6 vols.

Carr R. D. (1973), "Wallingford Castle", *Council for British Archaeology*, Group 9, Newsletter 3, 18.

Christie N. & Creighton O. H., with Edgeworth M. & Hamerow H. (2013), *Transforming Townscapes. From* Burh *to Borough. The Archaeology of Wallingford, AD 800-1400*, London, The Society for Medieval Archaeology (Society for Medieval Archaeology Monograph; 35).

Christie N. *et al.* (2010a), "'Have you Found Anything Interesting?' Exploring Late-Saxon and Medieval Urbanism at Wallingford: Sources, Results and Questions", *Oxoniensia*, 75, 35-47.

– (2010b), "Mapping Wallingford Castle", *Medieval Archaeology*, 54, 416-420.

Colvin H. M. (ed.) (1963), *The History of the King's Works*, vols. 1 & 2, London, Her Majesty's Stationery Office.

Creighton O. H. (2009), *Designs upon the Land: Elite Landscapes of the Middle Ages*, Woodbridge, Boydell Press (Garden and Landscape History).

Creighton O. H. & Higham R. A. (2005), *Medieval Town Walls: an Archaeology and Social History of Urban Defence*, Stroud, Tempus.

Creighton O. H. *et al.* (2009), "New Directions in Tracing the Origins and Development of Wallingford: Targets and Results of the Wallingford Burh to Borough Research Project", in Keats-Rohan & Roffe 2009 (eds.), 68-76.

Denholm-Young N. (1947), *Richard of Cornwall*, Oxford, Blackwell.

Drage C. (1987), "Urban Castles", in *Urban Archaeology in Britain*, J. Schofield & R. Leech (eds.), London, Council for British Archaeology (Research Report; 61), 117-132.

Durham B. G. (1987), "Wallingford: Castle, South Curtain Wall and St Nicholas' College", *South Midlands Archaeology*, 17, 99.

Ford S. (1995), *Castle Farm, Wallingford. An Archaeological Evaluation*, Unpublished Report for Thames Valley Archaeological Services, Reading.

Gelling M. (1973-1976), *The Place-Names of Berkshire*, Cambridge, University Press (English Place-Name Society; 49), 2 vols.

Goodall J. (2011), *The English Castle, 1066-1650*, New Haven, Yale University Press.

Hedges J. K. (1881), *The History of Wallingford, in the County of Berks, from the Invasion of Julius Cæsar to the Present Time*, London, Clowes.

Herbert N. M. (1971), *The Borough of Wallingford 1155-1400*, Unpublished Ph.D. thesis, University of Reading.

Hill D. & Rumble A. R. (eds.) (1996), *The Defence of Wessex. The Burghal Hidage and Anglo-Saxon Fortifications*, Manchester/New York, Manchester University Press.

Hull G. & Pine J. (2001), *The Lamb Garage Site, Castle Street, Wallingford, Oxfordshire*, Unpublished Report for Thames Valley Archaeological Services, Reading.

Keats-Rohan K. S. B. (1989), "The Devolution of the Honour of Wallingford, 1066-1148", *Oxoniensia*, 54, 311-318.

– (2009), "The Genesis of the Honour of Wallingford", in Keats-Rohan & Roffe 2009 (eds.), 52-67.

– (forthcoming), "Propping up the Walls, or Setting the Record Straight(er): Accounts of Wallingford Castle 1071-1411", in *Wallingford Castle and Town in Context*, N. Christie, K. S. B. Keats-Rohan & D. R. Roffe (eds.), Oxford, Archaeopress.

Keats-Rohan K. S. B. & Roffe D. R. (eds.) (2009), *The Origins of the Borough of Wallingford: Archaeological and Historical Perspectives*, Oxford, Archaeopress (BAR. British Series; 494).

Laban G. (2011), *Land at the Street, Lister Wilder Site, Wallingford, Crowmarsh OX10 8EB*, Unpublished Report for Museum of London Archaeology, London.

Midgley L. M. (1942), *Ministers' Accounts of the Earldom of Cornwall, 1296-1297*, vol. 1, London, Offices of the Royal Historical Society (Camden Third Series; 66).

Mundin A. (2008), *Former Lamb Garage Site, Castle Street, Wallingford, Oxfordshire. An Archaeological Watching Brief for Greyswood Limited*, Unpublished Report for Thames Valley Archaeological Services, Reading.

Oxford Archaeological Unit (1992), *Castle Farm, Wallingford. Archaeological Watching Brief/Excavation*, Unpublished Report by Oxford Archaeology, Oxford.

Pringle D. (1984), "King Richard I and the Walls of Ascalon", *Palestine Exploration Quarterly*, 116, 133-147.

Pugh R. B. (1955), "The King's Prisons before 1250", *Transactions of the Royal Historical Society*, 5, 1-22.

Rickard J. (2002), *The Castle Community. The Personnel of English and Welsh Castles, 1272-1422*, Woodbridge, Boydell Press.

Roffe D. R. (2009), "Wallingford in Domesday Book and Beyond", in Keats-Rohan & Roffe 2009 (eds.), 27-51.

Saunders A. (2006), *Excavations at Launceston Castle, Cornwall*, Leeds, Society for Medieval Archaeology (Society for Medieval Archaeology Monograph; 24).

Saunders M. J. (1995), *Castle Farm, Wallingford, Oxfordshire. An Archaeological Watching Brief*, Unpublished Report for Thames Valley Archaeological Services, Reading.

Scott K. (1950), "The Jewish Arcae", *Cambridge Law Journal*, 10, 446-455.

Speed G. *et al.* (2009), "Charting Saxon and Medieval Urban Growth and Decay at Wallingford", *Medieval Archaeology*, 53, 355-363.

Speight S. (2000), "Castle Warfare in the *Gesta Stephani*", in *Château Gaillard 19*, Caen, CRAM, 269-274.

Spurrell M. (1995), "Containing Wallingford Castle, 1146-1153", *Oxoniensia*, 60, 257-270.

Tasker Grimbert J. & Chase C. J. (trans.) (2011), *Chrétien de Troyes in Prose: the Burgundian Erec and Cligés*, Cambridge, Brewer (Arthurian Studies; 78).

Toulmin Smith L. (1907), *The Itinerary of John Leland in or about the Years 1535-1543*, London, Bell.

Webster L. E. & Cherry J. (1973), "Medieval Britain in 1972", *Medieval Archaeology*, 17, 138-188.

Wheatley A. (2004), *The Idea of the Castle in Medieval England*, Woodbridge, Boydell Press.

Wilkinson I. P. *et al.* (2010), "Micropalaeontology Reveals the Source of Building Materials for a Defensive Earthwork (English Civil War?) at Wallingford Castle, Oxfordshire", *Journal of Micropalaeontology*, 29, 87-92.

A Previously Unknown Late 14th-Century Brick Castle Excavated at Aalter (Flanders, Belgium)

A Burgundian Stronghold that Lay between the Rebellious Flemish Towns of Ghent and Bruges

◆

Koen De Groote*

1. Introduction

In 2010 a large-scale excavation took place at Aalter, at a locality called "Woestijne". The site, which is situated between Bruges and Ghent, revealed the foundations of a brick castle that dates from the late 14th century. The castle was probably built by the noble family of Flanders, lords of Woestijne, who were related to the count of Flanders. Almost no written sources are known to refer to this castle. The study presented here is preliminary, as neither the archaeological evidence, nor the building characteristics of the castle remains, nor the historical sources, are fully studied yet.

Because of the development of a large industrial zone of 33 hectares, an archaeological research programme was set up at Woestijne. A field survey of the complete area was carried out between September 2009 and January 2010. Based on the results of this survey, a full 20 hectares were subjected to a large-scale, open-area excavation that lasted 22 months from March 2010 until December 2011. The excavation was carried out by the former Flemish Heritage Institute (now Flanders Heritage Agency): in the field two teams of four archaeologists were active, who were advised and supported by period specialists from Flanders Heritage and Ghent University. The results were spectacular. A multi-period site was recovered, with finds and traces from the Neolithic, the Bronze Age, the Iron Age, the Roman Period and the Middle Ages.

One result of the field survey of 2009 was the initial registration of a circular moated structure in the alluvial zone of a small brook, opposite the known post-medieval moated site called Woestijnegoed ("estate of Woestijne"). This structure was already recognised by an aerial survey and air photograph research project carried out by Ghent University. But the open-area excavation of 2011 did not reveal the remains of a late, maybe 13th-century, motte castle, as was expected based on the information of the survey. Instead, the remains of an unknown late medieval, square brick castle were found (fig. 1).

2. The archaeological evidence

2.1. The structures[1]

Most of the castle structures have been searched, only a small part of the northern moat section was lying outside the excavation area. The castle had a 20 m-wide, circular moat with a central residential island, which had a diameter of about 40 m (fig. 1). The moat was preserved to a maximum depth of 0.92 m in the excavation trenches. Its original depth would have been between 1.5 m and 1.7 m. After the demolition of the buildings, the central zone had been completely levelled onto the C horizon, the plain natural soil, causing a devastating

---

* Flanders Heritage Agency, Belgium.

1. Schynkel et al. 2012, 15-22.

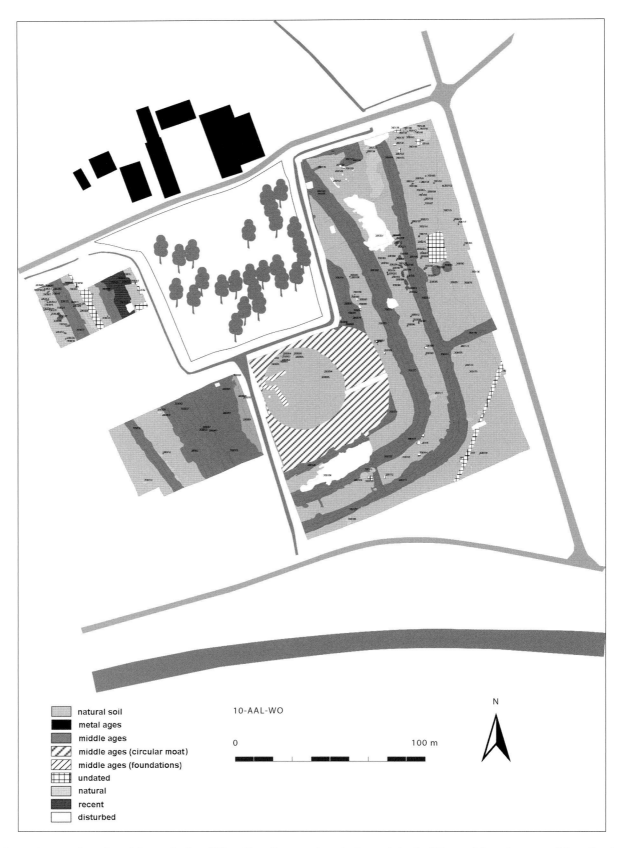

Fig. 1 – General excavation plan of the castle site of Woestijne. Orange: the actual remaining buildings of the 19th-century Woestijne farmstead; light grey: the circular moat of the brick castle; dark grey: earlier and later ditches; red: the remaining brick foundations of the castle. Doc. Flanders Heritage Agency.

Fig. 2 – Plan of the remaining brick foundations of the castle. Doc. Flanders Heritage Agency.

Fig. 3 – View from the north of the foundations of the western tower of the castle of Woestijne. Photo Flanders Heritage Agency.

Fig. 4 – General view from the south of the castle site of Woestijne. The circular residential island is situated in the middle (light coloured sand). The small semi-circular black strip left of it represents the organic refuse layer. Photo Flanders Heritage Agency.

effect on the conservation of the residential traces. Only on the north-western side, a part (about one fifth) of the foundations was preserved, showing a corner tower following a U-shaped plan and, on both sides of it, the connecting parts of the northern and western walls (fig. 2). The foundations were built in brick of different sizes, the smallest measuring 24 cm x 12 cm x 5.5 cm, the largest ones showing a length of 28 cm-29 cm. Remarkably, many of the bricks used for the foundations were reused ones, originating from an older, 14th-century building in the vicinity (fig. 3). Even complete blocks of masonry were recycled. These remains show that a square brick castle was once built here, measuring about 28 m per side.

2.2. The finds

At the south-western side, the filling of the moat contained a shallow but extended refuse layer with some building debris but also with a lot of pottery and organic material in it, including animal bone (fig. 4). The ceramic assemblage recovered from this refuse layer consists of more than 7,500 sherds, representing at least 842 vessels. Redware is by far the main pottery group, with a great dominance of two-handled cooking pots (41 %) and large so-called milk bowls[2] with a typical high-collared rim (31 %). Stoneware is present with 7 %, mainly salt-glazed jugs and bottles from the production centres of Raeren, Aachen or Langerwehe. Unglazed stoneware from Siegburg has only a minor presence of 1.7 % of the assemblage. Based mainly on the stoneware vessels, the pottery assemblage can be dated to the last quarter of the 15th century or the first quarter of the 16th century. The assemblage is very consistent and hardly contains older, residual sherds. Remarkable is the presence of two vessels of

2. In Dutch: *teil*; in French: *tèle à lait*.

Fig. 5 – Bowl of Classic Valencian tin-glazed ware, dating from the first half of the 15th century. Photo Flanders Heritage Agency.

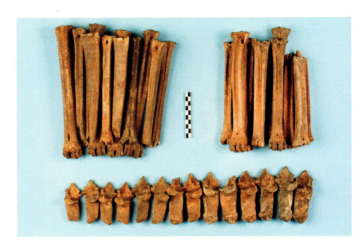

Fig. 6 – Red deer bones. Photo Flanders Heritage Agency.

Classic Valencian tin-glazed ware. One of these was a bowl that has a cobalt blue decoration with a flower motive, maybe once combined with goldluster, which is not visible anymore (fig. 5)[3]. A base fragment from a typical albarello in Classic Valencian lusterware was also found. Seven coins were found in the ditch, four of them from the 15th century[4]. The latest or youngest one dates from the reign of the Burgundian Duke Philip IV the Fair, more precisely from 1490. The earliest or oldest coin found dates from the 14th century and is coined for the Flemish Count Louis II of Male between 1368 and 1370. Two coins could not be identified.

Due to the organic composition of the waste layer, animal bone was well preserved, despite the acidic sandy soil. The animal bone collection contains more than 10,000 bones, both hand collected as well as recovered from sieved soil samples[5]. A first assessment revealed that more than 80 % of the identified bones of consumed animals are from cattle. The second group is sheep, with only 8 %. Two species are represented at around 5 %: pig and red deer. The presence of hundreds of bones of red deer from a late 15th- to early 16th-century context is very exceptional for Flanders (fig. 6). For that period, it is the largest archaeological collection of hunted animals in Flanders, and the finds must clearly be related to the high status of the castle's inhabitants. Other animal remains represented in the hand-collected assemblage, but by less than 1 %, are hare, rabbit, dog and cat. The scarce amount of bird remains contains skeletal elements of chicken, duck and goose. Finally, molluscs and fish are present. The former group comprises mussels, oysters and cockles while the rather scarce fish remains, which mainly came from the sieved samples, have not yet been studied.

3. The historical evidence

The written sources are rather silent about the late medieval castle of Aalter Woestijne[6]. In the second book of his chronicles, dated before 1388, Jean Froissart mentions the "house" of Woestijne amongst other castles in Flanders, such as the ones at Gavere and Schendelbeke[7]. In this context, the term "house" seems to refer to a fortified place, but it remains uncertain if the brick castle is meant or one of its residential predecessors, so it is difficult to use this reference as proof for the existence of that castle at that time. Only two known, written sources definitely mention this castle. A text from 1491 talks about the presence of *gens de guerres … sur les chastelletz de la Woestine et Praet*, while a source of 1530 mentions the motte (*mote*) with the debris of the castle, its bailey and the brewery outside the gate[8]. At this moment, the latter is the only known clear reference to a castle at this place, of which the text says that only some bricks (*brycken*) remained. At that time, the lords of Woestijne had already transferred their residence to the *huus van Praet* in the centre of the large village of Aalter nearby.

In 1376 Count Louis II of Flanders, known as Louis of Male, donated the fiefdom of Woestijne to his bastard son, Louis the Frisian, together with the villages of Aalter and Knesselare, and in 1379 the fiefdom of Praet. Woestijne becomes the family estate of the family of Flanders, lords of Woestijne and Praet.

The *Woestijnegoed* (Woestijne estate) is probably the location of the original central estate of the fiefdom of Woestijne. The first lord of the Land of Woestijne, in 1203 named as *dominus de Wastina*, was William, son of Zeger of Zomergem. He received this fief from the count of Flanders, probably

---

3. Guttiérrez 2000, 28-39, 147, fig. 5.9: 4.
4. Schynkel *et al.* 2012, 19.
5. *Ibid.*, 43-45.
6. Buntinx 1957; Verhoustraete 1966; Stockman 1979; Stockman 1980.
7. De Groote *et al.* 2013.
8. Stockman 1989.

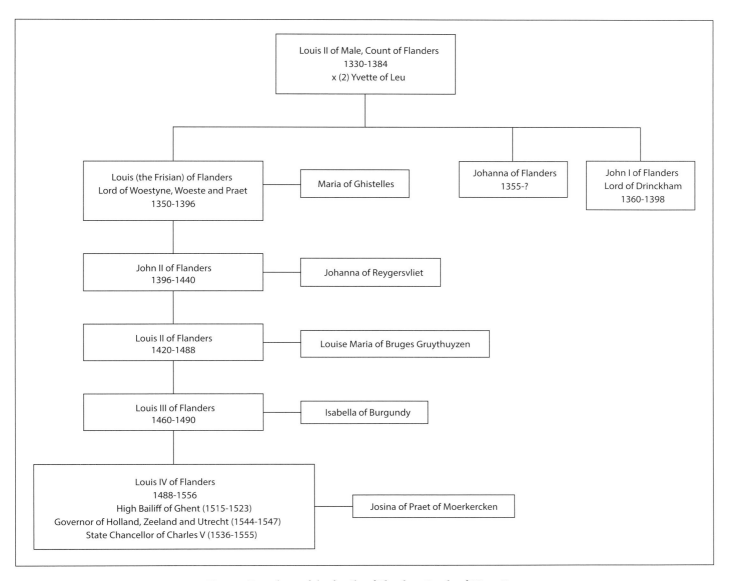

Fig. 7 – Genealogy of the family of Flanders, Lords of Woestijne.

sometime in the last quarter of the 12th century. The oldest known reference to the exploitation *ex Wastina de Haltra* dates from 1187, in the administration of the so-called *Spijker* of Ghent. The Land of Woestijne was stretched out over the municipalities of Aalter, Knesselare, Ruiselede, Tielt, Ursel, Zomergem, Bellem and Waarschoot. It was a dependent of the *Wetachtige Kamer* of Flanders, the feudal court of the main fiefs of the county. Probably by sale, the fief returned temporarily back under the direct administration of the Flemish count, Louis II of Male, who donated it to his bastard son Louis of Flanders, known as the Frisian, as noted. His offspring remained lords of Woestijne, Praet and Woeste until 1555, when Louis IV of Flanders died without children (fig. 7). This noble family of Flanders was always very loyal to the Flemish count and later the Burgundian dukes, supporting them in several wars at the end of the 14th and during the 15th century. Members of the family were active at the Burgundian Court, and the duke did not only regularly call upon them for military campaigns but also for meetings of the Council of Flanders. The last descendent of this family, Louis IV of Flanders, was an important person at the court of Emperor Charles the Fifth, being his ambassador to England and France, and governor of Holland, Zeeland and Utrecht. At the peak of his career, he was state chancellor/chamberlain from 1536 until 1555, and head of the Council of Finance from 1540.

4. Interpretations and discussion

4.1. Castle type

The combined archaeological and historical evidence suggests that the construction of the castle took place between 1376 and 1388. The square brick castle of Aalter Woestijne is of a generally known type widespread across the late medieval

Low Countries[9]. Good contemporary parallels, both in design and in size, can be found in the Netherlands and in Belgium. A good example of this type of castle is the famous castle of Muiderslot in the Netherlands, probably built between 1370 and 1386, and measuring 32 m by 35 m. The destroyed brick castle of Schendelbeke, located in the valley of the Dender about 60 km away from Woestijne, was founded in the late 13th or first half of the 14th century[10]. The exact location of this castle was only rediscovered some years ago by an archaeological field survey project. The survey revealed a brick castle of 25 m by 26 m with at least two corner towers. The castle was destroyed by the duke of Burgundy during the 1449-1453 war with the rebel city of Ghent[11].

This type of castle served very well to combine a military function with a use as residence[12]. The important political position of the lords of Woestijne and the militarily strategic position of their estate were main conditions to gain the authorization from the Flemish count to build such a castle. It is not sure whether the family was wealthy enough to finance this construction completely from their own resources, if not, a substantial support by the count would have been likely, because of the direct family relationship and as part of the comital political and military strategy (cf. *infra*).

No specific historical information exists as to the reasons for its erection or later demolition. For its history, some hypotheses can be formulated to answer these questions, however, which are based on what is known about the lords of Woestijne and the general political developments in Flanders at that time, in combination with the scarce archaeological information.

4.2. *The foundation of the castle*

The transfer of the Woestijne estate from the central comital administration to the family of Flanders took place in a turbulent period during which the Flemish count not only fought a number of wars in the nearby Duchy of Brabant, but also lived in discord with the large Flemish towns[13]. The uprising of Ghent, under the leadership of Philips of Artevelde, started in 1379. Soon, his troops succeeded to control large parts of the county, and also managed to conquer Bruges. Philips of Artevelde fell in the battle of Oostrozebeke in 1382, but Ghent only definitively surrendered three years later.

Possibly it was the intention to establish at Aalter-Woestijne a comital support, a stronghold, in the hands of a trustworthy and loyal family, at a strategically important place. In fact, the site is located on the border between the castellanies of Ghent and Bruges, in the vicinity of the crossing of a small river called the Durme (also known as Hoge Kale during the Middle Ages), and near the main road connecting those two dominant and rebellious cities of Ghent and Bruges (fig. 8).

It is not clear whether the foundation of the castle took place before or after the Ghent uprising, but a causal relationship with the political situation at that time seems plausible. Since the years 1370 the Flemish count already started to support, strengthen and actively restore all his important military strongholds[14]. This active policy was continued by the first Burgundian duke, Philip the Bold, who became count of Flanders in 1384, after his marriage to Margaretha van Male, only daughter and heir of the last count. It included the erection or extension of strongholds in places along the main rivers to the large cities. In particular, the river Scheldt, flowing through Ghent, the largest and most powerful town in the county, and in particular after its rebellion from 1379 to 1385, received special attention, both in the south as in the north.

The historical study of Kevin Poschet on the Burgundian castles in Flanders shows that the dukes had a very active defence policy, for which existing castles were renovated and restored, and new ones built. To support this, they gave grants to local lords who were commissioned to execute this infrastructural work. As already said, the main purpose was to control what were the main supply routes to the large towns, especially the rivers. Four defensive quarters are identified by Kevin Poschet: the quarter of Bruges and the Liberty of Bruges, being the defence of the Zwin; the quarter of Ypres and the surrounding castellany; the French-Flemish border defence in the castellanies of Lille, Douai and Orchis; lastly, the quarter of Ghent, on the rivers Scheldt and Lys. Philip the Bold was looking for a means to cut Ghent, the most powerful and most rebellious city, from its supply routes, if necessary. These were mainly the rivers Lys and Scheldt upstream and the Scheldt downstream. South of Ghent, the castles of Courtrai on the Lys and Oudenaarde on the Scheldt controlled the routes from the south, through which, in particular, grain from Picardy and Artesia was imported. North of Ghent supporting points and strongholds along the Scheldt were activated at Rupelmonde, Beveren and Saaftinghe. From the castles of Beveren and Saaftinghe, many accounts are kept documenting the late 14th-century renovations at these places.

In the east, along the border with Brabant, the duke started to give tax favours to the small towns of Geraardsbergen, Aalst and Dendermonde, all along the river Dender, in order to restore and strengthen their defences and city walls. Kevin Poschet's study does not mention any military support or stronghold west of Ghent. But as already shown, the castle of Woestijne lies on the borderline between the castellanies of Ghent and Bruges, on the small river Durme, not far from the road between Ghent and Bruges, and near the crossing with the southern route towards Deinze, Courtrai and Oudenaarde.

Combining the historical and the archaeological evidence in relation to the castle of Woestijne and its inhabitants, and

---

9. JANSSEN 1996, 58-74; JANSSEN 1990, 238-244.
10. VAN KEMPEN & VAN DEN HOVE 2012; VAN KEMPEN & KEIJERS 2009.
11. VAN TRIMPONT *et al.* 2009.
12. JANSSEN 1996, 62.
13. BLOCKMANS 1980.
14. POSCHET 2007.

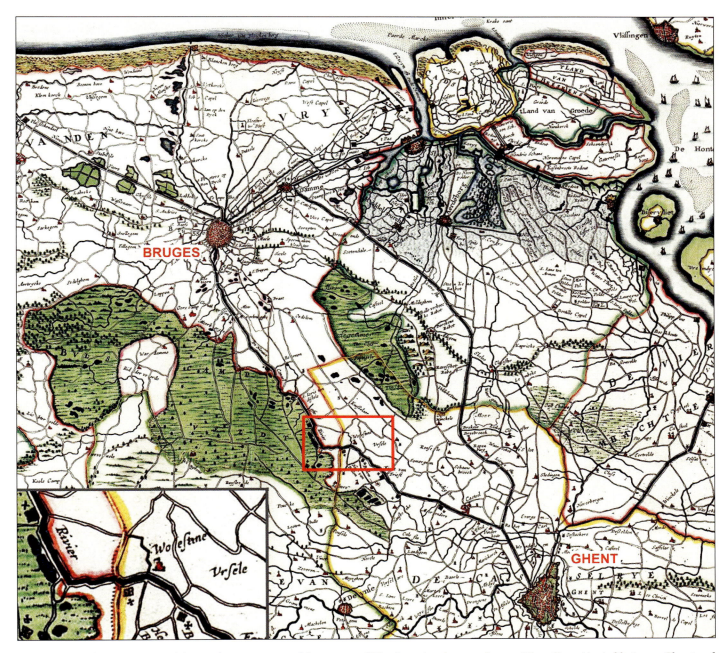

Fig. 8 – Late 17th-century map of the north-eastern part of the county of Flanders. A red square locates Woestijne, situated between Ghent and Bruges. Map Koninklijke Bibliotheek, Den Haag, Netherlands. Doc. Flanders Heritage Agency.

taking into account its strategic position, it seems very plausible to suppose that this castle was erected as part of the Burgundian defence policy in Flanders during the very late 14th century. Focused historical research in the future hopefully can yield new evidence to support this hypothesis.

4.3. Abandonment and demolition of the castle

Based on the archaeological evidence, the abandonment and demolition of the castle of Woestijne has to be situated at the end of the 15th or the beginning of the 16th century. Possibly, its downfall can be linked to the decade-long war that started after the death of Mary of Burgundy in 1482[15]. It was the start of a new power struggle between the Holy Roman Emperor Maximilian of Austria, her husband and unrecognized guardian of their son Philip the Fair, then a minor, and the Flemish towns under leadership of Ghent and Bruges. For some time, the towns were on the winning side. In 1488 Maximilian was even imprisoned for some months at Bruges. Possibly, the castle of Woestijne was destroyed by the troops of one of

15. Van Uytven 1980.

the Flemish cities during the ten years of this uprising. The rebellion ended in 1492 with the execution by decapitation of the Ghent leader, Van Coppenolle, on the Vrijdagsmarkt, one of the main marketplaces of that city.

When strategically needed, the destruction and demolition of castles were a policy that was rather common at that time, on both sides. A good example is the castle of Schendelbeke, already mentioned as a castle very similar architecturally to Woestijne, lying at the river Dender, south-east of Ghent. This castle also formed part of the comital defence organisation. It was originally in possession of the Flemish counts, being restored and strengthened in 1373 by Count Louis II, and in 1381 already conquered and burnt down for the first time by the rebels from Ghent. It is one of the many castles that were repaired by Duke Philip the Bold in 1389[16]. But at the end of another uprising of Ghent during the period 1449-1453, Duke Philip the Good conquered the castle in 1453 and broke it completely down to the ground[17]. The castle of Schendelbeke was never rebuilt again.

5. Conclusion

The square brick castle of Woestijne was probably built in the last quarter of the 14th century by the noble family of Flanders, related to the counts of Flanders, and lords of Woestijne since 1376. It was their residence until the late 15th century or maybe a bit later. The archaeozoological remains found in the castral moat, representing a specific, high nobility diet, which included much venison from hunted red deer, prove that the site was indeed a high status one.
The remains of the castle of Aalter Woestijne are probably silent witnesses to the difficult relationship between the last Flemish Count, his successors, the Burgundian Dukes, and the large and powerful Flemish towns, in their constant struggle for power and dominance. Its history sits in well with the comital and Burgundian policy of controlling the main towns by founding or rebuilding castles at strategic points on the border of the county and inland on the large supply routes to these towns, mainly the rivers.

Acknowledgments

I wish to thank all colleagues and former colleagues of the Flanders Heritage Agency who were or still are working on the Woestijne project:
– the project team: Evelyn Schynkel, Mieke Van de Vijver, Stefanie Sadones, Jeroen Vanhercke, Sibrecht Reniere, Jonathan Jacops, Kristof Keppens, Hans Vandendriessche and Jana Van Nuffel;
– the archaeozoologists An Lentacker and Anton Ervynck;
– and the restoration team: Marc Saeys (ceramics) and Frans De Buyser (coin determination).

I also owe words of gratitude to Prof Dr Frederik Buylaert (Free University of Brussels) and Prof Dr Wim De Clercq (Ghent University) for the general historical information and feedback, and to Dr Jaume Coll Conesa (Museo Nacional de Cerámica, Valencia) and Dr Alejandra Guttiérrez (Durham University) for their help with the identification of the Valencian tin-glazed pottery. Finally, many thanks to Jan Moens and Mieke Van de Vijver (Flanders Heritage Agency) for realising the maps and figures. The photography of figure 4 is from Kris Vandevorst and of figures 5 and 6 from Hans Denis (Flanders Heritage Agency).

---

16. Poschet 2007.

17. Van Trimpont et al. 2009.

Bibliography

Blockmans W. P. (1980), "Vlaanderen 1384-1482", *Algemene Geschiedenis der Nederlanden*, 4, 201-223.

Buntinx J. (1957), *Rijksarchief te Gent. Inventarissen: Land van de Woestijne en Heerlijkheid Woeste*, Brussels, Rijksarchief te Gent, 1957.

De Groote K. et al. (2013), "Het laat-middeleeuwse kasteel van Aalter-Woestijne (O.-Vl.)", *Archaeologia Mediaevalis*, 36.

Gutiérrez A. (2000), *Mediterranean Pottery in Wessex Households (13th to 17th Centuries)*, Oxford, J. and E. Hedges (BAR. British Series; 306).

Janssen H. L. (1990), "The Archaeology of Medieval Castle in the Netherlands. Results and Prospects for Future Research", in *Medieval Archaeology in the Netherlands*, J. C. Besteman et al. (eds.), Assen/Maastricht, Van Gorcum (Studies in pre- en protohistorie; 4), 219-264.

– (1996), "Tussen woning en versterking. Het kasteel in de middeleeuwen", in *1000 jaar kastelen in Nederland. Functie en vorm door de eeuwen heen*, H. L. Janssen et al. (eds.), Utrecht, Matrijs, 15-111.

Poschet K. (2007), "De kastelen Singelberg (Beveren) en Saaftinge rond 1400: voorbeelden van de Bourgondische defensiepolitiek in Vlaanderen (1)", *Het Land van Beveren*, 50/2, 114-224.

Schynkel E. *et al.* (2012), Interimrapport van het archeologisch onderzoek te Aalter-Woestijne, Zone 2 (prov. Oost-Vlaanderen), Intern Rapport Onroerend Erfgoed 1, Brussels.

Stockman L. (1979), "Het domein van de heer van de Woestijne in de 14de eeuw", *Appeltjes van het Meetjesland*, 30, 147-156.

– (1980), *Geschiedenis van Aalter*, Aalter, Gemeentebestuur.

– (1989), "Het domein van de heer van de Woestijne in de eerste helft van de 16de eeuw", *Appeltjes van het Meetjesland*, 40, 167-171.

Van Kempen P. & Keijers D. (2009), Archeologische evaluatie en waardering van een kasteelsite te Schendelbeke, gemeente Geraardsbergen, provincie Oost-Vlaanderen, RAAP rapport 1995, Weesp.

Van Kempen P. & Van den Hove P. (2012), "Archeologisch onderzoek naar het kasteel van Schendelbeke", *M&L*, 31/3, 6-31.

Van Trimpont M. *et al.* (2009), "Kasteel van Schendelbeke, veroverd en weggevaagd in 1453", *Gerardimontium*, 226, 3-8.

Van Uytven R. (1980), "Crisis als cesuur 1482-1494", *Algemene Geschiedenis der Nederlanden*, 5, 420-435.

Verhoustraete A. (1966), "Leenroerig overzicht van Aalter II", *Appeltjes van het Meetjesland*, 17, 69-99.

Reflections of a Divided Country?
The Role of Tower Houses in Late-Medieval Ireland

Gillian Eadie*

1. Introduction

It is estimated that at least 3,000 small castles known as tower houses were built in Ireland between 1400 and 1650[1]. They were versatile buildings that appealed to great overlords, minor gentry and wealthy merchants alike and they appear in rural, urban and coastal environments. Tower houses were also the first stone castles to be built in great numbers by the native Gaelic Irish, as well as families of Anglo-Norman descent, and as such they offer the opportunity to compare the priorities of several different groups within late-medieval Irish society. This paper examines evidence of social differences across Ireland as expressed in the architecture of the tower house.

2. Regionalism: cultural or chronological?

Tower houses are intensely regional in character, however, it is now generally accepted that there is a marked contrast between the style of towers found in the east of the island and those found in the west[2]. Figure 1 shows Kilclief Castle (County Down) as a typical eastern example and Clara Castle (County Kilkenny) as a typical western example (fig. 1). The towers of the east are generally of small size, between 3 and 4 storeys in height with simple internal spaces consisting of a single chamber on each floor. In contrast, the towers of the west tend to rise to between 5 and 6 storeys and are more complex internally having a major and minor chamber on each floor. Another key difference is the location of the principal chamber, usually referred to as a hall, which in both cases generally sits above a vault, but in the east this is usually at first-floor level, whereas in the west it is at the uppermost level. David Sweetman has suggested that these differences in the level of sophistication between the towers of the east and west may be a consequence of the chronological development of these buildings whereby the tower houses of the east were introduced or developed by the Anglo-Norman settlers and the idea spread westwards with the towers becoming bigger and implicitly better as time passes and as the tower is adopted by the Gaelic Irish[3]. This argument at first seems logical, especially looking at figure 1 and considering the construction dates of the buildings shown. Kilclief Castle, the eastern example, is documented as in use by 1441[4], whereas Clara Castle, the typical western example, has recently returned dendrochronological dates ranging from 1523-1540 for surviving oak timbers[5]; almost 100 years later than Kilclief.

In contrast to this model, however, new evidence in the west of Ireland shows that the east to west theory is an oversimplification of a much more nuanced picture. Rory Sherlock's recent dating of wickerwork centring at the De Burgh tower house of Claregalway, in County Galway on the western coast of Ireland, complicates this simple model. The two samples submitted returned dates of 1407-1446 cal AD and 1408-1449 cal AD[6], placing Claregalway relatively early

---

*   Archaeological Research Services Ltd, United Kingdom.
1. Sweetman 2004, 272-273.
2. See Sweetman 1999, 174; O'Keeffe 2004, 10-11; Eadie 2009, 381; Sherlock 2011.
3. Sweetman 1999, 174.
4. Jope 1966, 233.
5. Manning 2009, 27.
6. R. Sherlock, pers. comm.

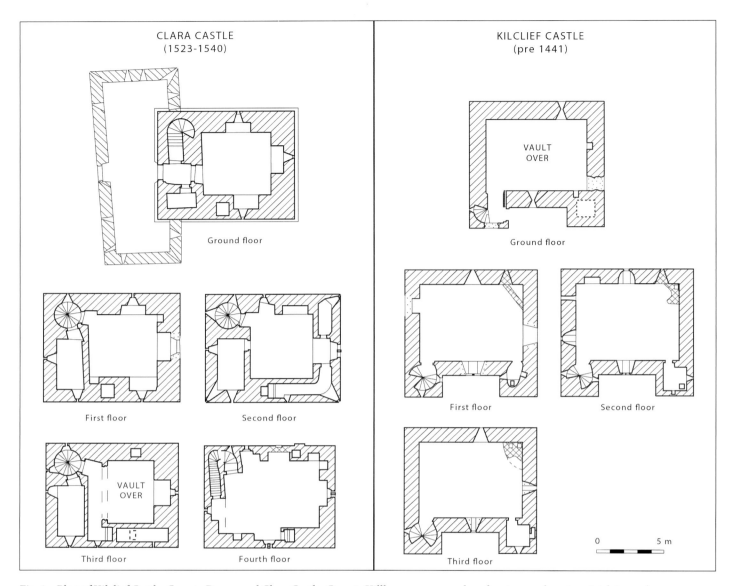

Fig. 1 – Plan of Kilclief Castle, County Down, and Clara Castle, County Killkenny, as examples of eastern and western Irish tower houses respectively. Doc. G. Eadie.

in the time span of Irish tower house construction and in the same general period as Kilclief Castle in the east. That these two buildings were constructed at around the same time shows that there must be factors other than chronology that influence tower house design, and suggests that there may have been several concurrent strands of tower house development across the country. Sherlock has produced a typology of Irish tower houses which shows the regional distribution of different forms, based upon the location of their principal chambers and private apartments[7]. He sees these different types of tower house as a product of chronology and development in tower house architecture, and whilst this may be the case, this paper argues that the differences seen in the architectural record also reflect local building practices and the social status and personal preferences of their builders. The notion that we can tease out the priorities behind tower house construction by the detailed examination of the built remains leads us to question whether there are other "typologies of purpose" that we can produce to represent the tower houses of Ireland, and if so what do these mean?

The key questions of this paper, therefore, are twofold. Firstly, can we see differences in purpose across the tower houses of Ireland? Secondly, can these differences in purpose be linked to Ireland's status as a divided nation or a land of borders?

3. Political background

The history of Anglo-Norman involvement in Ireland is a tale of only partial success and as such Ireland remained largely

7. Sherlock 2011.

marginal to the affairs of the English administration[8]. The Anglo-Norman invasion began in County Wexford, on the south-east coast, in 1169 and through a process of conquest and colonisation, the lordship expanded throughout the late 12th and 13th centuries, reaching its largest extent by around 1300[9]. The 14th century marked a period of retraction in the Anglo-Norman lordship, in a process known as the Gaelic Resurgence[10] and by the late 14th century, the colony had contracted to the eastern coast of Ireland, losing territories in South Munster and Connacht, but retaining much of Leinster as before. This period is marked by several problems for the English administration, including the Bruce Invasion, famine and the Black Death, all putting pressure on the colony which was already depleted of numbers due to absentee landlords[11].

At the same time, confidence returned to the Gaelic Irish as they embarked on a cultural revival, championing their traditions and emphasising a continuity with the pre-invasion past[12]. Several Anglo-Norman lords at this time adopted the traits of the Gaelic Irish after long periods of close contact and intermarriage. This process is known as Gaelicisation, but as Kenneth W. Nicholls states, Gaelisication did not make the English Irish, nor did necessarily mean that they were rejecting the English crown[13]. The Anglo-Irish were simply neither English to English observers, nor Irish to Irish observers. Whilst the history of this period stresses Gaelicisation, it would be naive to think that Gaelic culture survived 150 years of colonisation entirely unchanged[14] and the period should therefore be viewed as one of both Anglicisation and Gaelicisation.

The political situation by the close of the 15th century, at the height of the period of tower house construction in Ireland, is a tale of a much depleted lordship, hugging the eastern coast, with a boundary of direct English control limited to the area of the Pale around Dublin[15]. The surrounding lordship was overseen by the earldoms of Desmond, Ormond and Kildare, and whilst these were loyal to the English, they had a great deal of autonomy within their respective regions and had taken on many Gaelic customs[16].

4. Tower house construction

It has been argued that the first tower houses in Ireland were constructed in the late 14th century[17] when the colony was in retreat and the Gaelic regions were experiencing a cultural renaissance. Documented sites that may have been tower houses are known in the urban areas of the Pale[18] as well as in Counties Kilkenny[19] and Limerick[20], however standing remains of these structures are scarce, and can either not be reliably dated to the 14th century, or cannot be positively identified as tower houses. In any case the tower house was developed, or introduced, within a complex political situation with a history of simultaneous integration and segregation of cultures. The impact of the Anglo-Norman colonisation is summarised in figure 2 which shows all of the area affected by direct Anglo-Norman involvement by the 15th century (fig. 2)[21]. It demonstrates the multitude of fluid borders that must have existed across Ireland at this time, whilst also demonstrating how this dilutes any idea of two separate and distinct nations within the island in the 15th century.

When Caoimhín Ó Danachair's[22] distribution of tower houses is plotted against this political backdrop (fig. 3), this highlights some interesting points for discussion, particularly regarding tower house construction within areas that largely escaped strong Anglo-Norman influence. In the Central West coast, for instance, County Clare is almost as densely packed with towers as the neighbouring county of Limerick, loyal to the English administration. Whilst in North Connacht and West Ulster there are scarcely any tower houses, and those that do exist are generally late in the sequence[23]. Rory Sherlock's typology of Irish tower houses did not note any significant differences between the construction style of towers in County Clare in comparison with the surrounding counties of Galway and Limerick[24]. This suggests that there was a high level of social interaction and integration in this area that can be seen, perhaps, as a form of cultural assimilation.

Meanwhile in Ulster it has been suggested that the dearth of tower houses is due a lack of cultural assimilation in an area where older forms of settlement, such as crannogs, continued in use or were re-used in the late-medieval period[25]. Certainly when the distribution of crannogs is superimposed with that of tower houses (fig. 4), it does appear to fill the gaps. However, it must be stressed that only a proportion of these sites would have seen continued use into the late-medieval period and it therefore could not have provided the same density of settlement seen in the tower houses of the south-west.

A further consideration is the possibility that timber tower houses were constructed in Ulster as Colm Donnelly draws attention to what appear to be timber towers on mapping

---

8. GLASSCOCK 1987, 225-226.
9. SMITH 2000, 36.
10. MALLORY & MCNEILL 1991, 283.
11. SMITH 2000, 42.
12. O'CONOR 1998, 103; FRAME 1998, 131-132.
13. NICHOLLS 1999, 24.
14. NICHOLLS 2003, 16.
15. *Ibid.*, 219.
16. DUFFY 1997, 168.

17. See CAIRNS 1984; DAVIN 1983; BARRY 1987; MCAULIFFE 1992.
18. See DAVIN 1983.
19. BRADLEY & MURTAGH 2003.
20. HODKINSON 2005.
21. MCNEILL 1997; NICHOLLS 2003; SMITH 2000, 47.
22. Ó DANACHAIR 1977-1979.
23. NÍ LOINSIGH 1995; NEILL 2009, 475-480.
24. SHERLOCK 2011, 122-125.
25. O'CONOR 1998, 102; O'SULLIVAN 2001; BRADY & O'CONOR 2005.

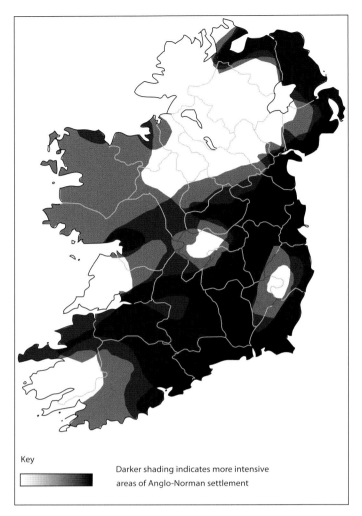

Fig. 2 – Map of Anglo-Norman involvement in Ireland from 1169 to the 15th century. Map G. Eadie.

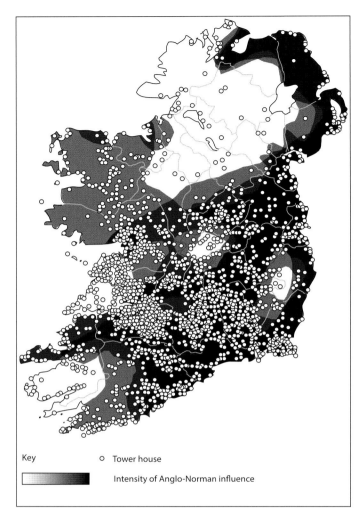

Fig. 3 – Distribution map of tower houses set against the backdrop of Anglo-Norman involvement in Ireland from 1169 to the 15th century. Map G. Eadie.

evidence from the 17th-century English campaigns in Ulster[26]. He argues that the skill required to construct such buildings would argue for their presence in Ulster prior to the political upheavals of the early 17th century[27]. This raises the possibility that the distribution map of tower houses in Ulster is skewed by the lack of surviving evidence of timber structures. Of course, there is no reason why timber structures should have been limited to Ulster, but it is clear that something different was happening in Ulster to the rest of Ireland. This must have been in some way related to the political situation and to social differences between Gaelic Ulster and the cultural melting pot that was the rest of Ireland.

The distribution of towers on a national scale, therefore, highlights some evidence of cultural difference across the island and moving to a regional scale, this paper will focus on towers located in areas that experienced several of the key political movements outlined above (fig. 5) which should provide a well-rounded overview of cultural expression within these buildings.

5. Study areas

The eastern study areas are Counties Down, Louth and Wexford. Down lies on the edge of the Anglo-Norman colony in Ulster, where interaction with the Gaelic lineage of the O'Neills would have been commonplace. By the 15th century, the Anglo-Norman Earldom of Ulster had collapsed and the main family in Down were the Savages of the Ards peninsula[28]. They were loyal to the English crown, but were Gaelicised by this date[29]. County Louth, to the south, was slightly more secure in

26. Donnelly 2007.
27. *Ibid.*, 24.

28. Smith 2000, 47.
29. Nicholls 2003, 156-160.

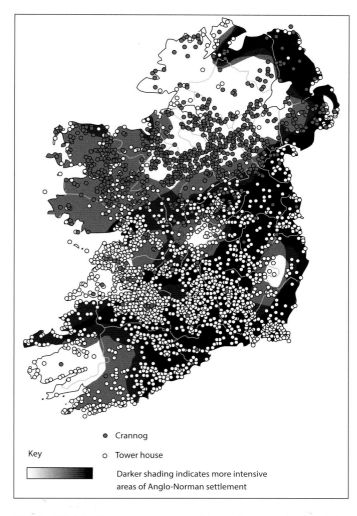

Fig. 4 – Distribution of crannogs and tower houses set against the backdrop of Anglo-Norman involvement in Ireland from 1169 to the 15th century. Map G. Eadie.

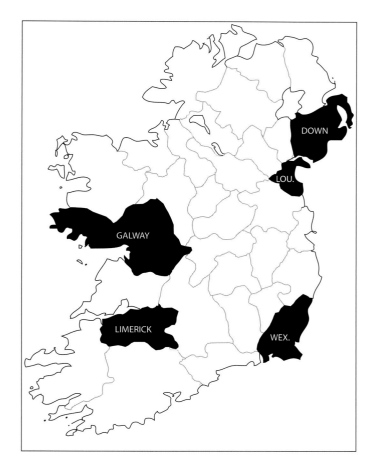

Fig. 5 – Map of the study areas used in the present paper. Map G. Eadie.

its overlordship, with the southern half of the county contained within the Pale[30]. By the 15th century, however, large portions of Louth were considered to be in the marches, a situation that led to the famous £10 subsidy for castle-building in this county and in Dublin, Meath, Kildare and Wicklow[31]. Wexford, in South-West Ireland, was in a similar situation, although it had survived the upheavals of the 14th century relatively unchanged. By the 15th century, the lordship was a small pocket largely cut off from the rest of the colony by the expansion of the Gaelic MacMurroughs in Carlow and North Wexford[32].

The western study areas are Counties Galway and Limerick. Galway is the most Gaelic and Gaelicised area of the study as the lands of William De Burgh, the Anglo-Norman lord of Connacht, were divided between the Gaelicised De Burgh lords, Edmond and William, in the 14th century[33]. Edmond, who remained nominally loyal to the English, was granted an area known as Clanricarde in South Galway, whilst the rest of Connacht was essentially Gaelic[34]. In Limerick, the 14th century was a time of attacks by the native Gaelic lords of Thomond, but when the 6th earl of Desmond took charge in 1411, he improved the strength and wealth of the earldom using a Gaelic form of taxation[35]. The 7th earl of Desmond then supported the Yorkist cause and was appointed governor of Ireland in the 1460s, a move that was criticised by the Anglo-Normans of the Pale who claimed that he was too immersed in Gaelic customs[36].

30. For a condensed introduction to Irish history, see DUFFY 1997.
31. DAVIN 1983, 167; LEASK 1941.
32. NICHOLLS 2003, 202.
33. FITZPATRICK 1994, 22.
34. *Ibid.*; NICHOLLS 2003, 175.
35. DONNELLY 1995, 85-87.
36. *Ibid.*, 91.

6. The priorities behind tower house construction

This paper attempts to view the tower houses within these regions in a way that is largely unconnected with their architectural form, since it is clear that the architectural form of tower houses is intensely regional in character and that this is likely to be a product of the local building industry[37]. Previous attempts to label certain architectural features of tower houses as Gaelic or Anglo-Norman, such as Loeber's suggestion that mural staircases were Anglo-Norman[38] have been shown to be inaccurate[39] and this study therefore focuses on identifying the priorities behind the construction of these buildings, and any differences in the balance of these priorities across the areas studied.

The most basic purpose of tower houses, as we understand them, can be described as defence, domesticity and display and it is these aspects that form the focus of the current paper; effectively testing how well designed the tower houses were in order to perform these functions.

To investigate the importance of defence, the study drew on evidence from near-contemporary literature. For tower house studies, this generally takes the form of travellers' accounts of Ireland in the 16th and 17th centuries[40]. However, using sources such as this, written or drawn by external visitors to Gaelic or Gaelicised Ireland, is problematic since these visitors were generally disposed to present the Irish in a derogatory tone, showing them as at odds with the civilised English population.

Tower houses clearly place importance on the presentation of defensive features and were viewed as castles by contemporary observers[41]. However, scholars are agreed that the actual scale of threat to a tower house would have been small-scale raiding and thievery[42]. As such the towers' defences should have been designed to either keep people at a distance from the structure, where it assumed that portable wealth would be stored, and also to keep people outside of the entrance. This would form two systems of defence and we can analyse each of the individual defensive features of the tower, and how they worked together, in order to assess the level of priority placed on defence in the tower's design stages.

In general the results indicate that the level of importance placed on systematic defence was low and in many cases the defence of the tower rested upon the strength of its doorway. An experimental archaeology project was carried out on two reproduction tower doorways, however, and, without any active defence, the door could be breached with a battering ram in less than 60 strikes and took around 50 minutes to burn through[43].

Regardless of the low level of importance placed on systems of defence, however, towers were well adorned with defensive features, particularly at roof level where they would be seen from the furthest distance. The "show of strength" was therefore more important than the real ability to defend. It can also be no coincidence that the roof-level was the focus of a tower's decorative defensive scheme, making use of the distinctive Irish stepped-battlements. Harold Graham Leask dates these to the 15th century onwards[44], and they would therefore set the tower house apart from earlier stone castles, perhaps invoking architecturally the association between the tower house and a new system of landownership and family prosperity.

To investigate domesticity, the study looked at everyday tasks such as cooking and dining, using evidence from contemporary and near-contemporary finds[45], literature on cooking[46] and known social dining practices[47]. It also looked at how space would be organised within the tower house in order to carry out these tasks, including the use of theoretical furniture layouts to determine how many people could be accommodated in different dining scenarios (fig. 6). The zoning of features was also an important element, looking at associations between fireplaces, cupboards and slop sinks that can indicate a cooking or reheating area.

This analysis also sought to define the private areas of the tower by assessing which tasks would be deemed private in late-medieval Ireland and then looking at ways to locate these tasks within the tower[48]. Using a modified form of access analysis to show firstly that the majority of towers were ostensibly private buildings, lacking any public/private divide, but also showing that there were some activities, particularly bodily functions, which were deemed more private than others and which took place within clearly demarcated and standardised spaces.

---

37. CURTIS 1932-1943, vol. 5, 22-23 (cited in DONNELLY 1999, 36), gives a specification for the construction of a building that could be described as a tower house and gives some impression as to the level of stylistic control given to the mason in 1547.
38. LOEBER 2001, 297.
39. SHERLOCK 2006.
40. See, for example, the descriptions and depictions of the Irish in DERRICKE 1581.
41. See, for example, the descriptions of such buildings by Richard Stanihurst in 1584 quoted in LENNON 1981, 91; and those by Luke Gernon c. 1620, quoted in FALKINER 1904, 360-361, where the term "castle" is used throughout.
42. See CAIRNS 1984, 46; MCAULIFFE 1992, 135; DONNELLY 1995, 201; MCNEILL 1997, 225-226; O'CONOR 1998, 102-104 for the general consensus, and SIMMS 1975, 104 and MCNEILL 1994, 130 for discussion of raiding tactics in the lead up to the development of the tower house in Ireland.
43. BERRYMAN 2009.
44. LEASK 1941, 88.
45. See, for example, the bronze cauldron dating to the 14th century in SIMPSON 1983, 162-164.
46. See O'SULLIVAN 2004; SIMMS 1978; BREARS 2008; POWER 1928; CROSSLEY-HOLLAND 1996.
47. O'SULLIVAN 2004; BREARS 2008; GIROUARD 1978.
48. EADIE 2010.

Finally in assessing the importance of display at tower houses, the study obviously looked at the distribution of decorative features throughout the structures, taking note of those areas where the decorative scheme is concentrated, such as at the roof line, as mentioned previously, but also within the tower's principal chambers. It also looked at the importance of hospitality within the structures and whether they would be capable of hosting typical entertainments. Again this made use of theoretical furnishings arranged to reflect the established formal layout of tables in a medieval hall (fig. 6).

These entertainments would also require servants so a full assessment of working and serving areas was also conducted in an attempt to identify any clearly defined servants' areas and their function. Again this section drew on contemporary or near contemporary sources such John Derricke's derogatory engravings[49], as well the famous descriptions of Irish hospitality from Richard Stanihurst and Luke Gernon, which are often cited in connection with Irish tower house studies[50]. Richard Stanihurst describes entertainments in an exterior hall of clay and thatch, whilst Luke Gernon describes entertainments in the uppermost room of a tower-like structure[51].

The results generally show that as the arrangements for entertaining become more complex, i.e. from the level of everyday dining towards a great feast, fewer towers are able to accommodate this activity and all would need an external kitchen in order to provide even the most basic entertainments. Irish tower houses seldom contain halls, being entirely private buildings[52] and generally small in size in comparison to other hall structures. What we currently refer to as halls within these buildings should really be referred to as principal chambers; clearly the finest chambers within the tower, but more intimate than a hall, used for everyday occasions and small entertainments of an invitation-only nature.

7. The role of the tower house

Figure 7 summarises the results of the investigation into the role of tower houses across the five study areas (fig. 7). It illustrates the level of importance of each activity in each region represented by changes in colour gradient.

Reading figure 7 from left to right demonstrates something of the role of tower houses on the national scale. A clear gradient emerges from black to white across the chart and the emerging pattern indicates that defensive display, privacy and familial dining were the most important aspects of the tower house. These were followed by hospitality, with low levels of importance given to systematic defence, display in the route through the building and service. Tower houses were therefore the intimate, private reserve of the *familia* and were not fulfilling the same role as larger baronial castles, where publicity, hospitality and systematic defence would likely be among the most important activities.

Reading figure 7 from top to bottom, what is also clear is that each county has its own unique balance of priorities with no two counties placing an emphasis on exactly the same things. Towers were built to a common set of ideas, rather than a set ideal and within this there are certain relationships that stand out as worthy of further discussion particularly with regard to the focus of this paper; can we see differences in purpose across the tower houses of Ireland? If so, can these differences in purpose be linked to Ireland's status as a divided country?

8. Differences in priorities and cultural biases

Figure 6 demonstrates that Counties Down and Galway place a similar emphasis on defensive display in terms of the priorities behind their construction and this is interesting because these are the two counties that are farthest from direct English control within the study (fig. 6)[53]. This is perhaps where interactions between families of Gaelic and Anglo-Norman descent would be at their highest. The correlation between this and a heightened desire for the display of defensive strength is therefore telling and shows that antagonism was a real factor within late-medieval Irish society. At the same time, however, the defensive systems were not given the same level of importance, as it was found that defensive features did not work well together to provide a system of defence. It is therefore the "show of strength" that is the more important factor, regardless of the actual effectiveness of these features. This is consistent with the symbolic nature of Gaelic warfare described by Katharine Simms[54], although in this instance it coincides with the adoption of a predominately Anglo-Norman symbolic architectural language.

County Limerick was the next in line with regards to the importance it placed on the display of defensive strength. This can perhaps be linked to feelings of anxiety and insecurity within the colony. It remained in the overlordship of the earls of Desmond who had taken on Gaelic Irish customs by the 15th century, but were still loyal to the English crown[55]. Added to this, the 14th-century retraction of the Anglo-Norman colony had left Limerick as a marginalised outpost surrounded by areas no longer subject to English rule[56]. This conflict of interests may have had the potential to escalate into real conflict and the use of defensive display, together with the clever adoption of Gaelic traditions, may have been the means by which the colony alleviated this threat. In saying this, however,

---

49. Richard Stanihurst in 1584, quoted in Lennon 1981, 91; Luke Gernon c. 1620, quoted in Falkiner 1904, 360-361.
50. For recent examples, see Manning 2009 and Sherlock 2011.
51. Richard Stanihurst in 1584, quoted in Lennon, 1981, 91; Luke Gernon c. 1620, quoted in Falkiner 1904, 360-361.
52. Eadie 2010.
53. See above, section 5.
54. Simms 1975; Simms 1987; Simms 1996.
55. Lydon 1972, 269.
56. Smith 2000, 47.

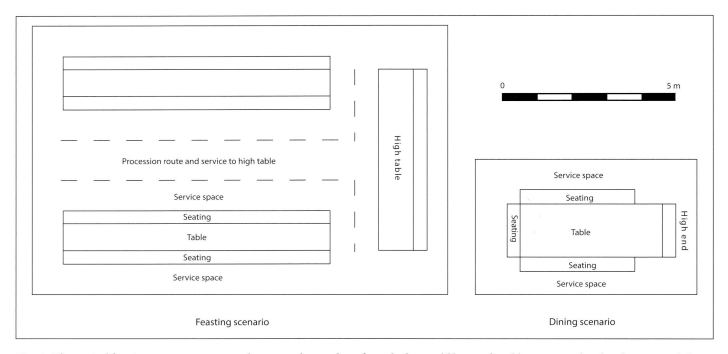

Fig. 6 – Theoretical furniture arrangements used to assess the number of people that could be comfortably accommodated in the principal chamber of the tower house under different dining scenarios. Doc. G. Eadie.

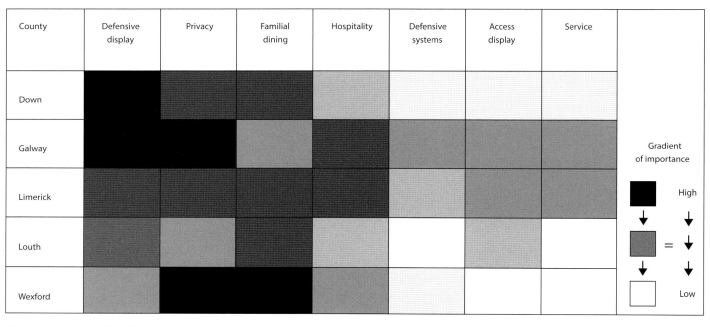

Fig. 7 – Summary table of the level of importance placed on certain functions across the tower houses of the study area. The darker areas are those where the level of importance was high, as opposed to the lighter areas where the level of importance was much lower. Doc. G. Eadie.

we must note the importance placed on useable defensive systems was much lower; it was the "show of strength" that was important.

The final two counties, Louth and Wexford, were the areas closest to the direct English rule of the Pale[57] and they placed the least importance on the display of defensive strength. The lack of emphasis on defensive display in these English-controlled zones highlights that the outward display of strength was only deemed necessary when there would be someone appropriate to be intimidated by it. Clearly this was less of a

57. See above, section 5.

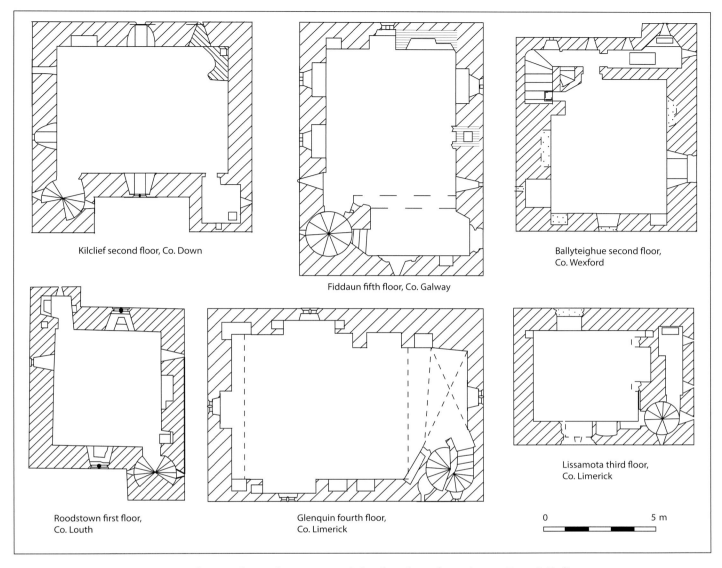

Fig. 8 – Selection of tower house principal chambers from the study area. Doc. G. Eadie.

concern to the inhabitants of Counties Louth and Wexford than those of Counties Galway and Down.

Moving on to hospitality, it was clear throughout the study that the principal chambers of tower houses vary in both size and sophistication across the country (fig. 8). Nevertheless, figure 7 indicates that Counties Galway and Limerick were linked in the level of importance they placed on providing hospitality (fig. 7). This can be related to the generally larger size of the towers in these areas and their greater degree of internal sophistication[58]. This ties in with the evidence from Rory Sherlock's structural or typological study of the "east-west" divide, where the principal chambers in western towers are generally located on the uppermost room over a vault[59]. Here they can accommodate a central hearth and posture towards the old communal halls of the ancient days[60]. These areas were the most Gaelicised areas in the study area and Gaelic culture has been shown by Elizabeth FitzPatrick[61] to have been purposefully anachronistic in its selection of religious and inauguration sites throughout the Gaelic Resurgence. That the same anachronisms were applied to the placement of the principal chamber within Gaelic and Gaelicised tower houses, either consciously or otherwise, is not out of the question. There are towers, such as at Lackeen in County Tipperary, where the walls of the principal chamber

---

58. See above, section 2.
59. Sherlock 2011.
60. R. Sherlock, pers. comm.
61. FitzPatrick 2001.

are riddled with doors; at the low end leading to nominal service areas which could never actually serve that function; and at the high leading to cupboards or tiny mural chambers rather than a solar. At Lackeen a high end is even created by the use of a fine window set within a blind arcade, however the room is still too small in size to have ever served the function of a hall. In a sense these chambers are almost a pastiche of a hall and again it becomes clear that when tower houses act as anything over and above the private home of the lord and his *familia*, they were all about the "show".

The larger towers of the western counties are also the only structures within the study where clearly demarcated guest or servant rooms and even small suites of rooms could be identified. Possible guest suites have been identified at Fiddaun in County Galway, for instance, where a bedchamber, under the vault, a latrine, and a small subsidiary chamber like an office are provided, all of which can be closed off from the staircase from the inside[62].

Hospitality was much less important in the towers of the eastern counties, as figure 7 shows (fig. 7), and these towers tend to be of a smaller size than those in the western counties. This may be related to wealth or the system of landownership within the colony which placed these lords further down the social scale than those in the west. This could mean that they would not necessarily need to host entertainments. An investigation of the system of landholding and its social implications would be beyond the scope of the current paper, but it hints at a fundamental difference in social organisation between the various groups that comprised the late-medieval Irish elite and one that may be tied to deep-rooted differences in culture, tradition and law[63].

The pattern of the level of importance placed upon display unsurprisingly matches that of hospitality where the towers of Counties Galway and Limerick are seen to invest more in decorative features within their towers. Although it must be said that the amount of decoration is generally quite low across all tower houses, the towers of the western counties were seen to have more decorative pointed and rounded doorheads, placed in those areas where they would be seen by the largest number of observers. This is generally directly off the main staircase when the principal chamber is right at the top of the structure, it appears, however, that the sophistication of the doorhead is unrelated to the status of the chamber it is gives access to, such as the pointed doorways leading to latrine chambers[64] in Glenquin, County Limerick. This again highlights the element of show within these buildings where the illusion is not always matched by the reality.

Finally with regards to service, which can also be viewed as a form of display and publicity, the towers of the western counties have a more convoluted method of gaining access to a tower, than those in the eastern counties. The eastern counties show evidence of a porter stationed in the ground floor main chamber who can oversee entry into the tower or bawn and who would work closely with the owner of the tower who we assume would usually be stationed in the principal chamber on the floor above.

In the western counties the evidence indicates that this arrangement changes with the role of the porter being divided between two servants; one stationed on the ground floor, the porter; and one, possibly the steward, stationed in a first-floor subsidiary chamber. At Anbally in County Galway, this chamber contained a fireplace, had a window overlooking the door and contained a murder hole in its floor which was rebated to carry a timber trap door. In some instances, such as at Glenquin in County Limerick and Cahererillan in County Galway, the "steward's" chambers had access to a private latrine and/or bedchamber. At Aughnanure in County Galway, the ground-floor room traditionally interpreted as a guard's chamber has no features that would allow a porter to assess who should be admitted to the tower. This decision would have to be made by an individual in the first-floor subsidiary chamber and was likely communicated to the porter *via* the murder hole.

These different arrangements have implications on how we view the status of these servants, since the porter in the western counties is a lowlier figure than in the eastern counties where he would work directly with the owner in the principal chamber on the first floor. In the western counties the principal chamber is usually on the top floor of the structure, so the porter and steward are much more remote from the owner and would have a higher degree of autonomy. This would create a difference in how the tower would be viewed by visitors, since the increase in ceremony in the western arrangement and the delay that would be caused in gaining access to the owner would be an important status indicator to anyone visiting the structure[65]. This again shows a heightened concern for display in these western counties.

9. Conclusion

We have been able to see that tower houses from across Ireland generally place the most importance on defensive display, familial dining and privacy, but within this we can see that

---

62. Eadie 2010.
63. See Nicholls 2003 for a comprehensive discussion of Gaelic culture, tradition and law.
64. This is worthy of note because latrine chambers were found to be highly standardised spaces in terms of the arrangement of their associated features and were usually accessed *via* plain, square-headed doorways even when entered from the main staircase.
65. For the discussion on the symbolic aspect of the control of access to the tower or lord, see Dixon 1990; Dixon 1996; Marshall 2002, 142.

they are highly nuanced buildings that were regionally and individually serving differing sets of priorities or levels of emphasis. The towers of the western counties, in Gaelic and heavily Gaelicised areas, tend to place more emphasis on hospitality, display and service than those closer to the English administration and whilst there can be a multitude of reasons behind this, such as wealth, chronology, regional style and personal preference, we can also consider that custom and social preferences were a factor as well.

The fact that such structures even exist in Gaelic and Gaelicised areas is a testament to cultural assimilation around 170 years post-colonisation, but the evidence appears to suggest that important social differences still existed that may have been purposefully expressed in the more ostentatious nature of Gaelic and Gaelicised towers when compared to their Anglo-Norman counterparts. It is also important to note, however, that these are not two distinct nations, the pattern of levels of emphasis placed on certain activities is not black and white; it is various shades of grey, and this represents the multifaceted nature of late-medieval Irish society and its expression in elite architecture.

Acknowledgements

This paper is drawn from research conducted during the author's doctoral studies at Queen's University Belfast with funding from the NIEA Department of Employment and Learning. Thanks are due to Dr Tom McNeill and Dr Mark Gardiner for supervising this research and to Archaeological Research Services Ltd for funding attendance at the Château Gaillard conference in Denmark.

Bibliography

Barry T. (1987), *The Archaeology of Medieval Ireland*, London, Routledge.

Berryman D. (2009), "Home Security: how Strong Was a Tower House Door?", *Archaeology Ireland*, 23/2, 8-10.

Bradley J. & Murtagh B. (2003), "Brady's Castle, Thomastown, Co. Killkenny: a 14th-Century Fortified Town House", in *The Medieval Castle in Ireland and Wales. Essays in honour of Jeremy Knight*, J. R. Kenyon & K. O'Conor (eds.), Dublin, Four Courts Press, 194-216.

Brady N. & O'Conor K. (2005), "The Later Medieval Usage of Crannogs in Ireland", *Ruralia*, 5, 127-136.

Brears P. C. D. (2008), *Cooking and Dining in Medieval England*, Totnes, Prospect Books.

Cairns C. T. (1984), *The Tower Houses of County Tipperary*, Unpublished Ph.D. thesis, Trinity College, Dublin.

Crossley-Holland N. (1996), *Living and Dining in Medieval Paris. The Household of a Fourteenth-Century Knight*, Cardiff, University of Wales Press.

Curtis E. (ed.) (1932-1943), *Calendar of Ormond Deeds (1172-1603)*, vols. 1-6, Dublin, Stationery Office.

Davin A. K. (1983), *The Tower Houses of the Pale*, Unpublished M.Litt. thesis, Trinity College, Dublin.

Derricke J. (1581), *The Image of Irelande with a Discoverie of Woodkarne*, London [University of Edinburgh].

Dixon P. (1990), "The Donjon of Knaresborough: the Castle as Theatre", in *Château Gaillard 14*, Caen, Centre de recherches archéologiques médiévales, 121-139.

– (1996), "Design in Castle-building: the Controlling of Access to the Lord", in *Château Gaillard 18*, Caen, Centre de recherches archéologiques médiévales, 47-56.

Donnelly C. (1995), *The Tower Houses of County Limerick*, Unpublished Ph.D. thesis, Queen's University, Belfast.

– (1999), "A Typological Study of the Tower Houses of County Limerick", *Journal of the Royal Society of Antiquaries of Ireland*, 129, 19-39.

– (2007), "Timber Castles and Towers in Sixteenth-Century Ireland: some Evidence from Ulster", *Archaeology Ireland*, 21/2, 22-25.

Duffy S. (1997), *Ireland in the Middle Ages*, Basingstoke, Palgrave MacMillan (British History in Perspective).

Eadie G. (2009), *A New Approach to Identifying Functions in Castles. A Study of Tower Houses in Ireland*, Unpublished Ph.D. thesis, Queen's University, Belfast.

– (2010), "Detecting Privacy and Private Space in the Irish Tower House", in *Château Gaillard 24. Château et représentation*, P. Ettel, A.-M. Flambard Héricher & T. E. McNeill (eds.), Caen, Publications du CRAHM, 69-73.

Falkiner C. L. (1904), *Illustrations of Irish History and Topography, mainly of the Seventeenth Century*, London, Longmans.

FitzPatrick E. (2001), "Assembly and Inauguration Places of the Burkes in Late Medieval Connacht", in *Gaelic Ireland (c. 1250-c. 1650). Land, Lordship and Settlement*, P. J. Duffy et al. (eds.), Dublin, Four Courts Press, 357-374.

FitzPatrick M. (1994), *A Survey of the Tower Houses in South-West County Galway*, Unpublished MA thesis, University College Galway.

Frame R. (1998), *Ireland and Britain (1170-1450)*, London, Hambledon Press.

Girouard M. (1978), *Life in the English Country House. A Social and Architectural History*, London, Yale University Press.

Glasscock R. E. (1987), "Land and People, *c.* 1300", in *A New History of Ireland*, vol. 2: *Medieval Ireland, 1169-1534*, A. Cosgrove (ed.), Oxford, Oxford University Press, 203-239.

Hodkinson B. (2005), "Thom Cor Castle: a 14th-Century Tower House in Limerick City?", *Journal of the Royal Society of Antiquaries of Ireland*, 135, 119-129.

Jope E. M. (ed.) (1966), *An Archaeological Survey of County Down*, Belfast, HMSO.

Leask H. G. (1941), *Irish Castles and Castellated Houses*, Dundalk, Tempest.

Lennon C. (1981), *Richard Stanihurst the Dubliner (1547-1618). A Biography*, Blackrock, Irish Academic Press.

Loeber R. (2001), "An Architectural History of Gaelic Castles and Settlements, 1370-1600", in Duffy *et al.* 2001 (eds.), 271-314.

Lydon J. F. M. (1972), *The Lordship of Ireland in the Middle Ages*, Dublin, Gill & Macmillan.

Mallory J. & McNeill T. E. (1991), *The Archaeology of Ulster. From Colonization to Plantation*, Belfast, Institute of Irish Studies, Queens's University of Belfast.

Manning C. (2009), "Irish Tower Houses", *Europa Nostra Bulletin*, 63: *Towers and Smallers Castles*, 19-30.

Marshall P. (2002), "The Ceremonial Function of the Donjon in the Twelfth Century", in *Château Gaillard 20*, P. Ettel, A.-M. Flambard Héricher & T. E. McNeill (eds.), Caen, Publications du CRAHM, 141-151.

McAuliffe M. (1992), *The Tower Houses of County Kerry*, Unpublished Ph.D. thesis, Trinity College, Dublin.

McNeill T. (1994), "Castles of Ward and the Changing Pattern of Border Conflict in Ireland", in *Château Gaillard 17*, Caen, Centre de recherches archéologiques médiévales, 127-133.

– (1997), *Castles in Ireland. Feudal Power in a Gaelic World*, London/New York, Routledge.

Neill K. (2009), *An Archaeological Survey of County Armagh*, Belfast, The Stationery Office.

Nicholls K. W. (1999), "World's Apart? The Ellis Two-Nation Theory on Late Medieval Ireland", *History Ireland*, 7/2, 22-26.

– (2003), *Gaelic and Gaelicised Ireland in the Middle Ages*, 2nd ed., Dublin, Lilliput Press.

Ní Loinsigh M. S. (1995), *The Castles of North Donegal and their Relationship to the Landholding Structure of Late Medieval Gaelic Lordships*, Unpublished M.Phil. thesis, Queen's University, Belfast.

O'Conor K. (1998), *The Archaeology of Medieval Rural Settlement in Ireland*, Dublin, Royal Irish Academy (Discovery Programme Monographs; 3).

Ó Danachair C. (1977-1979), "Irish Tower Houses and their Regional Distribution", *Béaloideas*, 45-47, 158-163.

O' Keeffe T. (2004), "Barryscourt Castle and the Irish Tower House", in *Medieval Ireland: the Barryscourt Lectures I-X*, Cork, Barryscourt Trust, 1-31.

O'Sullivan A. (2001), "Crannogs in Late Medieval Gaelic Ireland, *c.* 1350-*c.* 1650", in Duffy *et al.* 2001 (eds.), 397-417.

O'Sullivan C. (2004), *Hospitality in Medieval Ireland (900-1500)*, Dublin, Four Courts Press.

Power E. (1928), *The Goodman of Paris: a Treatise on Moral and Domestic Economy by a Citizen of Paris, c. 1393*, London, Routledge (Broadway Medieval Library).

Sherlock R. (2006), "Cross-Cultural Occurrences of Mutations in Tower House Architecture: Evidence for Cultural Homogeneity in Late Medieval Ireland?", *Journal of Irish Archaeology*, 15, 73-91.

– (2011), "The Evolution of the Irish Tower House as a Domestic Space", *Proceedings of the Royal Irish Academy*, 111C, 115-140.

Simms K. (1975), "Warfare in the Medieval Gaelic Lordships", *The Irish Sword*, 12, 98-108.

– (1978), "Guesting and Feasting in Gaelic Ireland", *Journal of the Royal Society of Antiquaries of Ireland*, 108, 67-100.

– (1987), *From Kings to Warlords. The Changing Political Structure of Gaelic Ireland in the Later Middle Ages*, Woodbridge (Suffolk), Boydell Press (Studies in Celtic History; 7).

– (1996), "Gaelic Warfare in the Middle Ages", in *A Military History of Ireland*, T. Bartlett & K. Jeffery (eds.), Cambridge/New York, Cambridge University Press.

Simpson M. L. (1983), "A Cast Bronze Cauldron from Downpatrick, County Down", *Ulster Journal of Archaeology*, 46, 162-164.

Smith B. (2000), "The Conquest of Ireland", in *Atlas of Irish History*, 2nd ed., S. Duffy (ed.), Dublin, Gill & Macmillan, 32-48.

Sweetman D. (1999), *The Medieval Castles of Ireland*, Cork, Collins Press.

– (2004), "The Origin and Development of the Tower House in Ireland", in *Medieval Ireland: the Barryscourt Lectures I-X*, Cork, Barryscourt Trust, 257-287.

Castles and Borders in England after 1066

Richard Eales*

Any discussion of castles and borders, or "borderlands", is almost inevitably drawn into issues of methodology and definition: these are both ambivalent and relative terms. Even a well-documented castle, situated in what political historians acknowledge to be a border zone, with the reasons for its construction there apparently clearly identified in the sources, may not be as straightforward as it seems. Castles were always multi-functional structures and the balance of functions was liable to change over time, all the more so in contested regions or landscapes. And most early castle construction is not nearly so well documented as this, or often even reliably dated to within close limits. This renders conclusions about such castles' status much more conjectural, dependent in many cases on an input of initial assumptions, such as the supposed need for borders to be constantly defended, which are themselves open to challenge.

Awareness of such problems is not of course new. Even when castles were commonly analysed in much more military terms, before the revisionist debates of the last 50 years fully developed, it was perceived that military purposes were complex and cannot be isolated from their wider context. Already in the 1950s, R. C. Smail criticised earlier writers who had argued that Frankish castles in the crusading states of the Holy Land were built "mainly as a means of defending a frontier" and interpreted distribution maps of sites on that basis. Instead he argued that these castles or their defenders could almost never block the passage of enemy forces of any size or maintain a linear frontier[1]. Views of that kind were essentially anachronisms, back-projections of the way in which modern border defences were intended to work, or derived from the way in which Roman frontier defences were then supposed to have worked[2]. Modern analysis has cast doubt on such assumptions for other periods too, but the almost universal lack of large garrisons or standing armies makes them untenable for the medieval west. R. C. Smail's analysis has been influential, and it is interesting that he also suggested that in the early phase of crusader settlement, "the ruling class among the Franks were a military aristocracy whose position in Syria was in many ways comparable with that of the Normans in England after 1066"[3].

Accordingly, it might seem redundant to restate these arguments now, but similar views about castles and borders do keep reappearing, and not just in popular writing. In his *Castellarium Anglicanum* of 1983, David James Cathcart King assessed castles in the south-east of England under the heading "The Invasion Coast", a concept clearly influenced by the events of the 1940s, and described Dover as "a vast castle overlooking a rather small if very important harbour", a special case of a fortress "completely interrupting a route of invasion"[4]. The narrative facts do not bear this out. In the event French plans to attack southern England in the later Middle Ages never actually amounted to more than brief localised raids, though massive invasion scares show that the threat was still taken very seriously at times. But the very earliest of these raids on any scale, in 1295, was directed at Dover, and succeeded in pillaging the town and its priory,

---

* Honorary senior research fellow, University of Kent, United Kingdom.
1. Smail 1956, 60-62, 204-244, quotation at 204.
2. The literature on Roman frontier defences across Europe is huge, with many competing theories still being advanced. In Britain, 19th-century ideas of Hadrian's Wall as an impermeable military barrier were challenged by R. G. Collingwood as early as the 1920s. See Crow 2004, 129-131.
3. Smail 1956, 60.
4. King 1983, vol. 1, li-liv.

notwithstanding the existence of the castle, then at its fullest extent as a fortress[5]. More recently, Stuart Prior, in his *Norman Art of War*, at least constructed a case for the primacy of military considerations in the siting and distribution of early Norman castles in Britain after 1066 (rather than just assuming it). But his argument is still scattered with sweeping general claims, such as that Norman castles in Somerset gave their lords "complete territorial control" or that "the castles literally ring the county, effectively fencing in the native Saxon population", not so different from the views contested by R. C. Smail 50 years before[6].

If recurrent assumptions about the role of castles in border areas can be brought into question even by a reassessment of the military factors involved, this is still more apparent when full weight is given to all the other admitted functions of castles (administrative, residential, symbolic and so on) which might come into play in the context of borderlands. Military history itself shows that borders, however conceived, did not exist just in order to be defended. Castles were as valuable as bases of offensive operations on expanding borders as of defensive ones on borders coming under threat. Perhaps more typically they functioned as centres for implementing a whole range of responses to challenges in areas barely under effective control. By their mere presence in the landscape, often a deliberately modified landscape, castles might deter opposition or confer apparent permanency on a new dispensation[7]. However exploitative the means by which resources, such as labour, were initially procured to build them, castles might in time become integral elements in their local society and economy. As central places: *foci* of markets, communities and rural or urban settlement, they might soon create vested interests much wider than those of their own lords[8]. In England after 1066, it is a commonplace that the military success of the Norman Conquest was made possible by the fact that those among the native population who rebelled were too few, too limited in their regional bases of support and too lacking in ability to work together, to form an effective national resistance. But this outcome in turn was influenced by broader issues than just military and political leadership. A large proportion of the population in effect tacitly accepted the new regime, whether as the Judgement of God or merely as inevitable, so making it easier to defeat those who did not. A similar contest of loyalties must have been repeated many times at the local level around centres of Norman power and settlement, such as castles.

But when this analysis is pursued at the level of local examples, the inevitable problem is one of precise dating: exactly when the castles were actually built. A typology of structures can provide only a very partial answer to the question. It might seem plausible to see rapidly-constructed fortifications of earthwork and timber as characteristic of campaign building, a process conducted in parallel with the military operations of conquest, while stone castles, expensive and slow to erect, were added later. One sort of castle, on this model, was instrumental in achieving victory, another in confirming and perpetuating it; perhaps even, as in the case of ceremonial halls and Great Towers, celebrating its completion. Thus, the Great Tower at Chepstow Castle, once regarded as one of the very earliest Norman secular buildings in England and pre-dating 1071, has now been reassessed as a more ceremonial addition to the castle closer to 1080 in date, designed to show off the establishment of effective royal control over the South Wales border region[9]. But there is no absolute certainly about this and even for such important and relatively well-recorded sites, it is rare to be able to date building phases with real confidence. Modern recording and scientific analysis has certainly brought that goal closer, as with the recent collaborative study of the White Tower published in 2008. But even there, while the two phases of construction of the tower, with a building break in the 1080s, can now be demonstrated beyond doubt by this major research, some of the key dates still remain approximate[10]. For lesser sites, the uncertainties are commensurately larger. In the case of the Norman Conquest and settlement, uncertain building dates between (say) 1067, 1077 or 1087 cover dramatic political changes across the country, and more specifically, changes in which areas can be regarded as borderlands.

Aside from the problem of dating, it is hard even in conceptual terms – what we should be looking for in the sources – to achieve a separation between "Castles of Conquest", "Feudal Strongholds" or "Castles of Lordship", all of them terms in frequent use. If every castle was to some degree multi-functional, the same also applies to individual design features within them, which have to be interpreted on a case-by-case basis. Some early earthwork castles in Norman England might have had a surprisingly low level of material culture, as has been convincingly argued by the excavators of Hen Domen Castle near Montgomery on the Mid-Wales borders[11]. Others might not, or at least did not, carry connota-

---

5. HAINES 1930, 242-249. A modern study of this event would be valuable. The evidence is much increased because a monk killed in the raid, Thomas of Hales, was subsequently locally canonised.
6. PRIOR 2006, 68-109 on Somerset, quotation at 106.
7. The "legitimising" effect of castles is implicit in much of the literature, but has been further developed in recent work on castles and landscapes, e.g. CREIGHTON 2002; CREIGHTON 2009; LIDDIARD 2005; HANSSON 2006.
8. THOMPSON 1991, 131-156, is a summary introduction to the large literature on the relationship of English castles with (old and new) towns, and their association with churches and monasteries. See also THOMPSON 1986; THOMPSON 1998; CREIGHTON 2007; CREIGHTON & HIGHAM 2005 for general discussion and bibliographies. Note 26 below is a striking example.
9. TURNER et al. 2004, 223-317; TURNER et al. 2006, 23-42. See also BATES 2006, 15-22, accepting the revised dating.
10. IMPEY 2008 reports all the findings. The early dating evidence is summarised in HARRIS 2008, 30-45.
11. BARKER & HIGHAM 1982; HIGHAM & BARKER 2000.

tions of lower residential status just because of their building materials[12]. Conversely, great stone towers built at leisure, and apparently unrelated to immediate military needs at the time of their construction, might be pressed into active service in changed circumstances, as was the Norman keep of Rochester, completed in about 1135, in the later sieges of 1215 and 1264. In each case, it was the last part of the castle to resist attack, and in 1264 successfully so; a significant fact, whatever we may judge to have been the intentions of the original designers of the tower in the early 12th century[13]. It is reasonable though to base research on probable links between the forms of castles and their functions, even if this has to be tested in individual cases. Sites with short occupation periods are likely to have served more transient purposes, and not to have been adopted as part of a lasting political or economic system. Site shifts, or regional reductions in the number of castle sites, perhaps involving concentration on a smaller number of major ones, are likely to reflect changes in the hierarchy of lordship and political or economic power[14]. Successive phases of development on castle sites – stone replacing timber, towers added to enclosures and so on – may be clues to shifts in function as well as changes in taste or the continuing availability of resources and patronage. All or any of these might interact with other factors, such as being located in a "borderland".

Borders and borderlands

This in turn raises a second set of definitional issues, about the status of borders in the Middle Ages. Medieval political frontiers are often characterised as vague and unstable, fluctuating with the loyalties of local lords. There is much truth in this, but there are also important exceptions. Without modern mapping techniques, or for that matter barbed wire fences, early medieval societies often went to great lengths to define local boundaries in forms of words, as evidenced by the boundary clauses of charters. Behind these must in every case have lain a body of precise oral knowledge[15]. But larger-scale borders were contested in different ways, even when precise definition was attempted. Contemporaries were themselves aware of the complexity of these issues; seeing for instance that some inherited features in the landscape, like Hadrian's Wall and the Offa's Dyke earthwork in Mid-Wales, which had once acted as extensive border markers no longer did so[16]. In 1245 a report came to the English king Henry III from "his faithful servant Hugh of Bolbec" describing a recent attempt to agree on one section of the Anglo-Scottish border. Both sides, English and Scottish, nominated a committee of six knights sworn to make a true perambulation of the division between the two realms, only for each committee unanimously to insist that its line of march was the correct one. "Since", Hugh continued, "the knights of Scotland were to blame that the perambulation could not take place", he settled for a declaration on oath from the English ones as to what were "the true and ancient bounds and frontiers (*marchias et divisas*)", which he then recorded[17]. Such evidence can be interpreted in detail as showing a complex mixture of topographical knowledge and political negotiability.

The evidence for Norman England leaves much scope for debate over which castles were built or remained active within what can be described as border zones. Most castles which can be characterised in this way were not sited precisely on geographical frontiers at any time, but acted as centres of border lordships composing the local balance of power. Marches or borderlands might be conceived in some cases as quite narrow strips of territory, but could also be very extensive, perhaps as the result of shifts over time or the wider spread of border-related tenurial obligations. On the Anglo-Welsh marches the sheer number of castle sites evident on distribution maps is better interpreted as the product of site shifts in contested areas, repeated destructions and rebuildings which can sometime be verified archaeologically, rather than defence in depth by large numbers of simultaneously-active castles, as was once commonly supposed[18]. Later a more legalistic definition of border status became possible in this region, with the written codification of various Marcher customs in Wales from the 13th century onwards. But, especially after Edward I completed his conquest of Wales between 1277 and 1283, these texts self-evidently fossilised the dynamics of earlier border arrangements[19]. Such sources can add extra complexity to the definition of borderlands rather than clarifying them, as theory and practice tended to diverge.

Another set of definitional problems arises from the fact that borders can be conceived as many things other than political dividing lines. There were also topographical boundaries, as between highland and lowland zones; cultural boundaries, as between distinct areas of custom or language; economic boundaries, as between different types

---

12. HIGHAM & BARKER 1992 remains the best discussion of the evidence, including some well-known "literary" descriptions of elaborate timber structures at 114-121.
13. ASHBEE 2006; GOODALL 2006. See EALES 2003b for the context of the famous 1215 siege. The interesting and well-documented 1264 one is much less studied.
14. EALES 2003a is one general discussion of these issues focusing on Norman England.
15. The methodology of interpreting these texts has been developed in a series of studies by D. Hooke and others. See FLANAGAN & GREEN 2005 for charter scholarship generally.
16. See BARROW 1973; BARROW 1989; DAVIES 1987, 3ff.; DAVIES 1989. For Wales, Domesday Book supports the narrative sources in showing English and Welsh settlement on both sides of the Offa's Dyke line, even as it was overtaken by Norman incursions much further west.
17. STONES 1970, 54-57, gives a text and translation of this document.
18. See, for example, SPURGEON 1987 and KENYON 2003 for modern reappraisals.
19. DAVIES 1978 and DAVIES 1987 remain the classic accounts of the complexity of these changes.

of agriculture or trading networks. Often these coincided, and all could also interact with political divisions. Castles could stand on any or all of them with varying degrees of planned intent and consequences. Thus in Wales the areas of persistent native lordship were also, as was to be expected, those of Welsh law, language and economic organisation. As these became more confined to upland zones, Norman settlement conversely progressed in the increasingly-manorialised lowlands. In some cases, when independent Welsh lordships were incorporated into the Anglo-Norman tenurial system, as happened in Glamorgan in South Wales in the 13th century, their Welsh lords took on the personal status of feudal tenants under English law[20]. But a distinction still existed between English-settled areas and those which remained culturally "purely Welsh" (*pura Wallia* is a contemporary term). A castle situated at the junction of these zones, like the great fortress of Caerphilly in Glamorgan, might later no longer be on a militarised frontier, as it was when first built in the 1270s, but it was still evidently in a borderland, though of a different kind[21].

Castles and the Norman Conquest

The case study of the Norman Conquest of England gives an opportunity to examine the application of these general arguments in distinctive and exceptional circumstances. Though the main issues for explaining the conquest process have been discussed by historians for a very long time, many (perhaps not surprisingly, given the incompleteness of the evidence) are still matters of debate. One is the question of how in 1066 a Norman/French army of less than 10,000 men could invade and conquer the Kingdom of England, with a probable population of about 2 millions and an effective system of government, at least by 11th-century standards. Another is how the leaders of the conquest, reinforced by at most a few tens of thousands of immigrants from France over the following 20 years, succeeded in suppressing native resistance, extending their rule to the limits of the Anglo-Saxon kingdom (the Welsh and Scottish borders), and displacing the existing English ruling nobility by confiscating and regranting most of its lands. The narrative of William's own leadership and vigorous campaigning provides one kind of answer, but broader underlying explanations are also both possible and necessary. They include the partial success of the Norman claim that William I had been shown to be the rightful king by judgement of battle and should be accepted as such once he had been given the blessing of the Church in coronation on Christmas Day 1066[22]. There were also critical internal divisions within England before and after the Battle of Hastings. These acted horizontally, between the native ruling class and the mass of the population, in a way that was common in medieval Europe and facilitated takeovers by new rulers in other countries too, but also vertically, between different regions and their leaders[23]. One explanation less commonly emphasised now, though very popular 100 years ago, is that the Normans simply possessed radically superior military technology and organisation. The tendency now is to see the gap as a small one; the Battle of Hastings itself was a "close-run thing"[24]. But it cannot be discounted altogether, and one key element in the enforcement of conquest following 1066 was the Norman programme of castle building. The historian Orderic Vitalis famously wrote that from 1068 onwards King William

> rode to all the remote parts of his kingdom and fortified strategic sites (*opportuna loca*) against enemy attacks. For the fortifications called *castella* by the Normans were scarcely known in the English provinces and so the English – in spite of their courage and love of fighting – could put up only a weak resistance to their enemies[25].

Orderic wrote in the 1120s, but he based this part of his history closely on the lost final section of the contemporary life of the Conqueror by his chaplain William of Poitiers, so it has some claim to be an opinion held by the Norman leaders themselves.

The central issue is again one of chronology. The achievement of territorial conquest or submission, settlement (the establishment of new lords at regional and then more local levels) and castle building were closely-linked and usually sequential. A notional map of the whole process at national level shows Norman control and occupation of lands moving from the South in 1066-1067 to the South-West from 1068, and then decisively into the Midlands and East Anglia in the early 1070s. Settlement in the North, as opposed to theoretical lordship, took much longer, not becoming really effective until after about 1080. Only then were Norman castle boroughs set up at each end of the Hadrian's Wall line across the country: Newcastle-upon-Tyne to the east in 1080, Carlisle to the west in

---

20. DAVIES 1978, 86ff.; SMITH 1958.
21. SPURGEON *et al.* 2000, 51-104, is now the fullest account of Caerphilly. See also ALTSCHUL 1965, 122ff.
22. As Orderic Vitalis later put it (see note 25 below) although large numbers rebelled, "many of the same people kept their faith to God and revered the king established by him, as the apostle commands when he says, Fear God, honour the king" (CHIBNALL 1969, 206-207). For modern discussions, see WILLIAMS 1995; THOMAS 2003.
23. Witness the fact that resistance tended to peak in the Midlands in 1068 and 1071, but in the North in 1069-1070, as all sources indicate.
24. This is now very much the consensus conclusion. R. A. Brown was the last influential historian who tried to argue the undiluted older view, polemically so in BROWN 1973.
25. CHIBNALL 1969, 218-219, and Introduction, xv, for a likely date of composition *c.* 1125. The surviving manuscript of William of Poitiers ends shortly before this, but Orderic tells us that the fuller text he was using ended only in 1071. In this instance, I cannot agree with the view advanced in LIDDIARD 2000, 4, that this passage "relates to a single campaign and specific sites", so is no basis for wider conclusions. See note 32 below.

1092[26]. Such an overview of the twenty-year period of upheaval and change is naturally generalised and approximate, glossing over many local complexities and reversals, only some of which can be reconstructed in detail, as it proceeded. Though the sources are in many respects exceptionally good they still have clear limitations, which make uncertainties inevitable.

The most important element in this has been analysis of the data provided by the Domesday Book, in over 100 years of research, more recently enhanced by digital technology[27]. This royal survey, unique in its scale for 11th-century Europe, lists and describes in its approximately 2 million words over 13,000 individual land holdings across most of England and enumerates about 300,000 people. It gives very full information about who held land and lordship at the time it was compiled about 1086, and much (though less) information about these men's late Saxon predecessors. Yet, even aside from issues of accuracy and inconsistencies in the conduct of the survey from one region to another, the intended focus on those two dates: "Now" and the "Time of King Edward" (*Tempus Regis Edwardi*), meaning 1066, gives a "before and after" account of the changes brought about by the process of conquest and settlement. It tells us much less about how this was achieved in the course of the crucial 20 years. The problem is compounded by the survival of only about 300 royal charters from the 20 years of William I's reign, many approximately dated, and the unevenness of the chronicle sources for England, which provide several accounts of the king's campaigns between 1067 and 1071, including references to castle building, but are extremely thin for the following 15 years[28]. Accordingly, modern historians who have tried to establish the chronology of grants and occupations (beyond the broad regional pattern already referred to) and to answer other questions, such as the geographical principles on which the new lordships were created or how closely the king and subsequent grantors kept control of the whole process, have been obliged to work with probable inferences from the incomplete sources. Even the most thorough exploitation of the Domesday data and full attention to the local influence of topography and the pre-conquest inheritance in individual cases can only in part overcome the unevenness of the evidence; for instance the fact that the best-documented land disputes concern church possessions[29]. All of these methodological problems carry over into assessments of when (and where and why) castles were set up in the process of Norman settlement.

Turning to the direct evidence for castle-building, the limitations of the written sources are again apparent. Domesday Book made no systematic attempt to record castle sites in 1086, so that even some very important ones are mentioned only incidentally. About 50 are explicitly named or implied in the text[30]. Ella Armitage in 1912 listed 84 pre-1100 "English" castles in all available documents, and another century of research has added few more[31]. Even with the inclusion of Norman castles in Wales mentioned in Welsh sources, it is hardly possible to take the total beyond a hundred. There is clearly an element of chance documentary survival behind these lists, as a significant number of major sites first recorded in 12th-century records, and many minor ones, must have existed before 1100 too. Nevertheless, the early-documented sites are mostly the larger and more important ones, typically built by the king and other major lords early in the conquest process, though this cannot be proved in every case.

A more restricted category of castles is that tied, usually by narrative sources, to King William himself and his campaigns after 1066, hence their wide geographic spread and location in key urban centres. Most of them were in existence by 1070. William of Poitiers explicitly states that the Norman army occupied Pevensey and Hastings as fortifications before the Battle of Hastings "as a refuge for themselves and a defence for their ships". He also refers to the strength of the site at Dover, which was refortified by William soon after the battle, as the victorious Normans moved east to secure Kent before advancing on London, and went on to describe his construction of fortifications in London "as a defence against the inconstancy of the numerous and hostile inhabitants" and Winchester "which can quickly receive help from the Danes", before and after his coronation[32]. In 1067, when King William returned to Normandy to seek reinforcements, "Bishop Odo and Earl William stayed behind and built castles far and wide throughout the country" according to a version of the Saxon Chronicle[33]. Once returned to England, the king put down rebellions through 1068 and 1069, setting up castles as he went at Exeter, then in the Midlands and as far north as York. Calculations of risk and allocations of scarce resources – where to put castles and leave troops to hold them – on the

---

26. FLEMING 1991 is an important attempt to analyse the general progress of Norman settlement. On the north, see KAPELLE 1979; AIRD 1998. Newcastle arose from a campaign provoked by the murder of Walcher, bishop of Durham, also in 1080. A passage in the Saxon Chronicle (WHITELOCK 1961, 169) refers to William II going to Carlisle "with a great army" in 1092 and after erecting and garrisoning the castle, sending "many peasant people there with their wives and cattle to live there to cultivate the land".
27. Domesday Book has been the subject of pioneering statistical and spatial mapping research since MAITLAND 1897, and the long series of Domesday Geography volumes edited by H. C. Darby (1952-1977), up to the latest PACE Domesday Database.
28. BATES 1998 is the modern edition of William I's charters; the Index Verborum includes all standard castle terms.
29. On lawsuits and land disputes in Domesday England, see FLEMING 1998; and for a range of texts printed in full, VAN CAENEGEM 1990, vol. 1, 1-89.
30. DARBY 1977, 313-317, lists castles "in connexion with forty-eight places, of which twenty seven were boroughs". See also HARFIELD 1991.
31. ARMITAGE 1912. Her "Schedule of English castles known to date from the eleventh century", at 396-399, lists 42 as "in towns" and 42 "in manors".
32. DAVIS & CHIBNALL 1998, 114-115 (Pevensey and Hastings); 142-145 (Dover); 148-149 and 160-163 (London); 164-165 (Winchester). These passages in which Poitiers comments on castles strengthen the likelihood that the judgement later recorded by Orderic Vitalis (note 25 above) does derive from him.
33. WHITELOCK 1961, 145.

limits (or on the borders) of the Norman-controlled areas must have been made repeatedly. When the men of York submitted to William in 1068 he was according to Orderic Vitalis "very doubtful of their loyalty" so "he fortified a castle in the city and left trustworthy knights to guard it"[34]. When the castle came under attack early in 1069, he returned in force to relieve the siege and reinforced Norman control there with a second castle. Further north in Durham an opposite decision was taken when the Norman lord sent to take possession was massacred with all his men in January 1069. Here William chose to grant the earldom instead to Waltheof, a native lord with local support, at least until Waltheof rebelled in 1075, by which time William was in a strong enough position to implement more direct rule in the far North[35]. By one definition at least the borderland of Norman settlement and control had moved in those few years.

Some sort of close dating, and even a narrative context, is therefore possible for a significant number of early-documented major castles. But there is no doubt, from archaeological evidence, that many hundreds of undocumented lesser castles were also built in England after 1066. Very few have been recently or systematically excavated, so independently reliable dates from archaeology are rare, and almost never precise in relation to political events. Any estimate of the total numbers of castles in existence at a given date is therefore approximate, even conjectural. It is complicated by the awareness, not present in all studies, that there was turnover in castle sites: some were passing out of use even while others were being constructed, as regional conditions and borders shifted. In a fuller discussion first published in the 1980s, I estimated a total of up to 1,150 castle sites for England and Wales before 1200, but with far fewer "active" sites at any one time – a peak of 800 or less, reached already in the late 11th century[36]. This compares with the total of 327 in Allen Brown's classic list of all English castles documented in written sources for 1154-1216, first published 50 years ago. Allen Brown considered that the much fuller royal records of that period had captured a "high proportion" of occupied sites, and that his figure might equate to the real existence then of 400 castles[37]. More discussion of these provisional estimates would be welcome, but as they stand they suggest some conclusions. First, the chronology of early castle development in England was very distinctive compared with most of continental Europe: rising rapidly from almost nothing to a maximum number in the decade or two after 1066, then declining over the 12th century. Second, all of the total numbers of castles proposed are still extremely low compared with those recorded for many provinces of France, a difference that has yet to be fully addressed by comparative research.

The present discussion more specifically of castles and borders in England after 1066 suggests another hypothesis, especially for regional and local enquiry. In England during this period of political transition between 1066 and 1086, or later in some areas, there were very exceptional border conditions. Temporary lines of demarcation came successively into existence across the country as Norman settlement spread, primarily from south to north but including all the local variations already referred to. Such divisions lay between areas of Norman and continuing English lordship, but also between zones of relatively strong and weak or contested lordship, and between local societies disrupted by violent change, like Yorkshire after the campaigns of 1069-1070, and those which had experienced more peaceful transition[38]. In these respects much of England successively experienced the creation and temporary operation of "borderland" conditions. They were not confined to the Welsh and Scottish borders in the way that textbook writers routinely suppose. It follows that many castles were built and sited in this period to meet circumstances that turned out to be transitory, located in relation to borders that (especially in political terms, but sometimes in others too) soon ceased to be borders. A predictable consequence of this in the archaeological record would be many site shifts and briefly-occupied castle sites in early Norman England. A more persistent effect was that, despite subsequent modifications, the geographical pattern of castle sites laid down to meet the needs of the late 11th century exercised a significant influence over political and social developments in later periods, when those conditions had long ceased to apply. Work in progress on Kent and the south-east strongly suggests that dispositions of estates and major castle sites there made very early after 1066 played a key role in shaping later politics, despite some subsequent modifications[39].

Recent publications on early Norman castles in England do of course take into account the wider context of the conquest process, but in local and regional studies especially, this has tended to be subsumed into analysis of the choice of sites within landscapes and within the territorial composition of estates as they emerge from Domesday Book and subsequent evidence. The many uncertainties about the transition of 1066-1086 outlined above are one reason for adopting a cautious approach, as a few examples might show. In his study of sites in Norfolk before 1200, Robert Liddiard's 2000 monograph,

---

34. CHIBNALL 1969, 218-219.
35. KAPELLE 1979; AIRD 1998, 60ff., 91-94 on Waltheof as earl of Northumbria.
36. EALES 2003a, 46-53.
37. BROWN 1989, 327, total figure at 90, quotation at 100; BROWN 1976, 215, for estimate of 400 castles.
38. This last example is valid even if one accepts the case made by some historians that much of the "waste" widely recorded in the Domesday Book for Yorkshire can be explained (against the chronicle evidence) as disruption rather than actual destruction. But this is not accepted by everyone: PALMER 1998 argues strongly that the violence and devastation were entirely real.
39. For example, the arrest and dispossession of Odo of Bayeux in 1082 (and again in 1088) left the baronial estates of his subtenants largely untouched. See EALES forthcoming.

"Landscapes of Lordship". Norman Castles and the Countryside in Medieval Norfolk, 1066-1200, began with an introduction on the county's pre-conquest inheritance, the Norman takeover and the resultant balance of political and economic power, which is a model of its kind. But its conclusions are not much integrated into the analysis of landscape and castle functions which follows, being treated more as background, soon overtaken by other influences[40]. John Hunt's similarly titled 1997 study, *Lordship and the Landscape. A Documentary and Archaeological Study of the Honor of Dudley, c. 1066-1322*, pointed out that this Midland lordship appears from Domesday Book to be placed "in a region away from a vulnerable frontier" but actually owed its origin "to a particular situation that was affecting the west midlands in the early 1070s" when it was "an area only recently pacified". His brief discussion (in a longer-period study) also suggested that might be a rewarding approach to the study of other major midland lordships and castles[41]. Andrew G. Lowerre's 2005 work on the South-Eastern Midlands, *Placing Castles in the Conquest. Landscape, Lordship and Local Politics in the South-Eastern Midlands, 1066-1100*, which focuses explicitly on the period 1066-1100, takes this much further, with a full examination of all the relevant political interactions within his selected region. His conclusions are extremely cautious, relying heavily on Robin Fleming's influential thesis that antecessorial Norman grants (conveying the land of a named pre-conquest holder) are usually "early" and those defined in territorial terms relatively "late", often making no attempt to go beyond that bipartite distinction. Again, he regarded topographical and landscape conclusions, which were capable of statistical testing, as more robust[42]. But such caution is salutary and this remains a benchmark study in its methods of analysis. Stuart Prior's 2006 book, *A Few Well-Positioned Castles. The Norman Art of War*, is markedly less cautious, explicitly pressing the evidence into service to make a case for the siting of early Norman castles in accordance with military planning ahead of all other considerations. In his case study of Somerset, for instance, he attempted to reconstruct otherwise undocumented military campaigns of the late 1060s almost entirely from the siting of castles which are themselves not closely dated except by reference to those campaigns, a purely circular argument[43]. This might serve as a warning that the linkage of political history and spatial analysis being proposed has to be conducted with care.

It is in no way the intention here to argue for a "remilitarisation" of the study of castles on traditional lines. But castles are significant precisely because they reflect so many defining aspects of medieval societies and (an appropriately sophisticated account of) political tensions and violence should not be omitted or underplayed amongst them. In the specific case of the Norman Conquest, the concept of England between 1066 and the 1080s as a country of a whole series of fluid and rapidly-evolving "borderlands" further emphasises just how exceptional was the political context in which castles were introduced there.

---

40. LIDDIARD 2000, 20ff. on "the Norman impact".
41. HUNT 1997, quotations at 11, 14, 28.
42. LOWERRE 2005, e.g. at 11, "usually it is only possible to suggest 'early' or 'late' for the date of acquisition of a Norman's collection of lands" and "a Norman who took possession of his antecessor's lands in, say, 1070 could well have waited until 1086 or even later to build his castle", though it is hard to see that as typical. LOWERRE 2007 is a useful summary. FLEMING 1991 is the starting point for the argument.
43. PRIOR 2006, 74-82. It should be said that much of the well-informed analysis of local conditions can be accepted, even if the overstated conclusions are not.

Bibliography

AIRD W. M. (1998), *St Cuthbert and the Normans. The Church of Durham (1071-1153)*, Woodbridge/Rochester, Boydell Press (Studies in the History of Medieval Religion; 14).

ALTSCHUL M. (1965), *A Baronial Family in Medieval England. The Clares (1217-1314)*, Baltimore, The John Hopkins Press.

ARMITAGE E. S. (1912), *The Early Norman Castles of the British Isles*, London, Murray.

ASHBEE J. (2006), "The Medieval Buildings and Topography of Rochester Castle", in *Medieval Art, Architecture and Archaeology at Rochester*, T. AYERS & T. TATTON-BROWN (eds.), Leeds, British Architectural Association/Maney (British Archaeological Association Conference Transactions; 28), 250-264.

BARKER P. & HIGHAM R. (1982), *Hen Domen, Montgomery: a Timber Castle on the English-Welsh Border*, vol. 1, London, Royal Archaeological Institute.

Barrow G. W. S. (1973), "The Anglo-Scottish Border", in *The Kingdom of the Scots. Government, Church and Society from the Eleventh to the Fourteenth Century*, London, Arnold, 139-161.

– (1989), "Frontier and Settlement: which Influenced which? England and Scotland, 1100-1300", in *Medieval Frontier Societies*, R. Bartlett & A. MacKay (eds.), Oxford, Clarendon Press, 2-21.

Bates D. (ed.) (1998), *Regesta Regum Anglo-Normannorum. The Acta of William I (1066-1087)*, Oxford, Clarendon Press.

– (2006), "William the Conqueror, William fitz Osbern and Chepstow Castle", in *Chepstow Castle. Its History and Buildings*, R. Turner & A. Johnson (eds.), Almeley, Logaston, 15-22.

Brown R. A. (1973), *Origins of English Feudalism*, London, Allen and Unwin.

– (1976), *English Castles*, 3rd ed., London, Batsford.

– (1989), "A List of Castles 1154-1216", in R. A. Brown, *Castles, Conquest and Charters: Collected Papers*, Woodbridge, Boydell Press, 90-121 [Reprinted from: *English Historical Review*, 74, 1959, 249-280].

Chibnall M. (ed.) (1969) *The Ecclesiastical History of Orderic Vitalis*, vol. 2, books 3 & 4, Oxford, Clarendon Press.

Creighton O. H. (2002), *Castles and Landscapes*, London, Continuum.

– (2007), "Castles and Castle Building in Town and Country", in *Town and Country in the Middle Ages: Contrasts, Contacts and Interconnections (1100-1500)*, K. Giles & C. Dyer (eds.), Leeds, Maney (The Society for Medieval Archaeology Monograph; 22), 275-292.

– (2009), *Designs upon the Land: Elite Landscapes of the Middle Ages*, Woodbridge, Boydell Press.

Creighton O. H. & Higham R. (2005), *Medieval Town Walls. An Archaeology and Social History of Urban Defence*, Stroud, Tempus.

Crow J. (2004), "The Northern Frontier of Roman Britain", in *A Companion to Roman Britain*, M. Todd (ed.), Oxford, Blackwell (Blackwell Companions to British History), 114-135.

Darby H. C. (1977), *Domesday England*, Cambridge, Cambridge University Press.

Davies R. R. (1978), *Lordship and Society in the March of Wales (1282-1400)*, Oxford, Clarendon Press.

– (1987), *Conquest, Coexistence and Change. Wales 1063-1415*, Oxford, Clarendon Press.

– (1989), "Frontier Arrangements in Fragmented Societies: Ireland and Wales", in Bartlett & MacKay 1989 (eds.), 77-100.

Davis R. H. C. & Chibnall M. (eds.) (1998), *The Gesta Guillelmi of William of Poitiers*, Oxford/New York, Clarendon Press/Oxford University Press (Oxford Medieval Texts).

Eales R. (2003a), "Royal Power and Castles in Norman England", in *Anglo-Norman Castles*, R. Liddiard (ed.), Woodbridge, Boydell Press, 41-67 [Reprinted from: *The Ideals and Practice of Medieval Knighthood III*, C. Harper-Bill & R. Harvey (eds.), Woodbridge, Boydell Press, 1990, 49-78].

– (2003b), "Castles and Politics in England, 1215-1224", in Liddiard 2003 (ed.), 367-388 [Reprinted from: *Thirteenth-Century England II*, P. R. Coss & S. D. Lloyd (eds.), Woodbridge, Boydell Press, 1988, 23-43].

– (forthcoming), "Castles in Kent, 1066-c. 1220", in *Early Medieval Kent (the Kent History Project)*, Woodbridge, Boydell Press.

Flanagan M. T. & Green J. A. (eds.) (2005), *Charters and Charter Scholarship in Britain and Ireland*, Basingstoke, Palgrave Macmillan.

Fleming R. (1991), *Kings and Lords in Conquest England*, Cambridge, Cambridge University Press (Cambridge Studies in Medieval Life and Thought).

– (1998), *Domesday Book and the Law. Society and Legal Custom in Early Medieval England*, Cambridge, Cambridge University Press.

Goodall J. (2006), "The Great Tower of Rochester Castle", in Ayers & Tatton-Brown 2006 (eds.), 265-299.

Haines C. R. (1930), *Dover Priory*, Cambridge, Cambridge University Press.

Hansson M. (2006), *Aristocratic Landscape. The Spatial Ideology of the Medieval Aristocracy*, Stockholm, Almqvist & Witsell International (Lund Studies in Historical Archaeology; 2).

Harfield C. G. (1991), "A Hand-List of Castles Recorded in the Domesday Book", *English Historical Review*, 106/419, 371-392.

Harris R. B. (2008), "The Structural History of the White Tower, 1066-1200", in *The White Tower*, E. Impey (ed.), New Haven/London, Yale University Press, 29-93.

Higham R. & Barker P. (1992), *Timber Castles*, London, Batsford.

– (2000), *Hen Domen, Montgomery. A Timber Castle on the English-Welsh Border: a Final Report*, Exeter, University of Exeter Press in Association with the Royal Archaeological Institute.

Hunt J. (1997), *Lordship and the Landscape. A Documentary and Archaeological Study of the Honor of Dudley, c. 1066-1322*, Oxford, BAR (BAR. British Series; 264).

Impey E. (ed.) (2008), *The White Tower*, New Haven/London, Yale University Press.

Kapelle W. E. (1979), *The Norman Conquest of the North. The Region and its Transformation, 1000-1135*, London, Croom Helm.

Kenyon J. (2003), "Fluctuating Frontiers: Normanno-Welsh Castle Warfare, c. 1075 to 1240", in Liddiard 2003 (ed.), 247-257 [Reprinted from: *Château Gaillard 17*, Caen, Centre de recherches archéologiques médiévales, 1996, 119-126].

King D. J. C. (1983), *Castellarium Anglicanum. An Index and Bibliography of the Castles in England, Wales and the Islands*, New York/London, Kraus, 2 Vols.

Liddiard R. (2000), *"Landscapes of Lordship". Norman Castles and the Countryside in Medieval Norfolk, 1066-1200*, Oxford, BAR (BAR. British Series; 309).

– (2005), *Castles in Context. Power, Symbolism and the Landscape, 1066 to 1500*, Macclesfield, Windgather Press.

Lowerre A. G. (2005), *Placing Castles in the Conquest. Landscape, Lordship and Local Politics in the South-Eastern Midlands, 1066-1100*, Oxford, J. and E. Hedges (BAR. British Series; 385).

– (2007), "Why Here and not There? The Location of Early Norman Castles in the South-Eastern Midlands", *Anglo-Norman Studies*, 29, 121-144.

Maitland F. W. (1897), *Domesday Book and Beyond. Three Essays in the Early History of England*, Cambridge, University Press.

Palmer J. J. N. (1998), "War and Domesday Waste", in *Armies, Chivalry and Warfare in Medieval Britain and France. Proceedings of the 1995 Harlaxton Symposium*, M. Strickland (ed.), Stamford, Watkins (Harlaxton Medieval Studies; 7), 256-275.

Prior S. (2006), *A Few Well-Positioned Castles. The Norman Art of War*, Stroud, Tempus.

Smail R. C. (1956), *Crusading Warfare, 1097-1193*, Cambridge, University Press (Cambridge Studies in Medieval Life and Thought. New Series; 3).

Smith J. B. (1958), "The Lordship of Glamorgan", *Morgannwg*, 2, 9-38.

Spurgeon C. J. (1987), "Mottes and Castle-Ringworks in Wales", in *Castles in Wales and the Marches. Essays in Honour of D. J. Cathcart King*, J. R. Kenyon & R. Avent (eds.), Cardiff, University of Wales Press, 23-49.

Spurgeon C. J. et al. (2000), *An Inventory of the Ancient Monuments in Glamorgan. Medieval Secular Monuments: the Later Castles from 1217 to the Present*, Aberystwyth, Royal Commission on the Ancient and Historical Monuments of Wales.

Stones E. L. G. (ed.) (1970), *Anglo-Scottish Relations, 1174-1328. Some Selected Documents*, 2nd ed., Oxford, Clarendon Press (Oxford Medieval Texts).

Thomas H. M. (2003), *The English and the Normans. Ethnic Hostility, Assimilation and Identity, 1066-c. 1220*, Oxford/New York, Oxford University Press.

Thompson M. W. (1986), "Associated Monasteries and Castles in the Middle Ages: a Tentative List", *Archaeological Journal*, 143, 305-321.

– (1991), *The Rise of the Castle*, Cambridge, Cambridge University Press.

– (1998), *Medieval Bishops' Houses in England and Wales*, Aldershot, Ashgate.

Turner R. et al. (2004), "The Great Tower, Chepstow Castle, Wales", *The Antiquaries Journal*, 84, 223-317.

– (2006), "The Norman Great Tower", in Turner & Johnson 2006 (eds.), 23-42.

Van Caenegem R. C. (1990), *English Lawsuits from William I to Richard I*, vol. 1: *William I to Stephen (Nos 1-346)*, London, Selden Society (Publications of the Selden Society; 106-107).

Whitelock D. (ed.) (1961), *The Anglo-Saxon Chronicle. A Revised Translation*, London, Eyre and Spottiswoode.

Williams A. (1995), *The English and the Norman Conquest*, Woodbridge, Boydell Press.

Ungarnburgen in Süddeutschland im 10. Jahrhundert

Peter Ettel*

Fünfzig bis sechzig Jahre lang, bis 955, haben die ungarischen Reiterscharen wiederholt die Regionen des Ostfränkischen Reichs im heutigen Deutschland, Italien, Frankreich und Spanien überfallen und als „Geißel des Abendlandes" große Not und Schrecken hervorgerufen. Davon zeugen die historischen Berichte, z.B. des Regino von Prüm und des Widukind von Corvey. Die Ungarn waren wegen ihrer für Reitervölker typischen Kampfesweise und Bewaffnung gefürchtet. Sie waren auf den Kampf zu Pferde spezialisiert, der es ihnen ermöglichte, im Gefecht und bei Überfällen schnell und wendig zu sein, nach erfolgtem Angriff sich schnell zurückziehen und große Entfernungen zurücklegen zu können. Der Reflexbogen versetzte sie zudem in die Lage, einerseits aus dem Sattel heraus, andererseits aus relativ großer Distanz den Gegner zu beschießen, z.B. auch mit Brandpfeilen Siedlungen und Klöster, Städte sowie Befestigungen und Burgen anzugreifen[1].

Historische Überlieferung zum Befestigungsbau gegen die Ungarn

Welche Art von Burgen haben die Ungarn auf ihren Zügen im ostfränkischen Reich nun angetroffen und angegriffen? Stellen die sogenannten Ungarnrefugien oder -wälle ihrerseits als Reaktion auf die Ungarneinfälle indirekt einen archäologischen Nachweis der Ungarneinfälle dar? Sicherlich besaßen die Burgen weder eine einheitliche Bauart noch einen genormten Grundriss, wie früher noch vermutet. So sollten nach der Wormser Burgenbauordnung zur Abwehr der Ungarn die bereits vorhandenen Burgen ausgebaut werden, ständig besetzt und mit Proviant versehen sein. Aber es sollten auch ganz neue Befestigungen errichtet werden, die vor Jahrzehnten in der Forschung mit den sog. Heinrichsburgen über- und falsch bewertet wurden[2]. In Süddeutschland wurden, von Paul Reinecke angeregt, hohe Wälle als typische Ungarnburgen bzw. -refugien herausgestellt, die bis heute in der Forschungsgeschichte eine wichtige Rolle spielen[3].

Best bekanntes, auch historisch belegtes Beispiel für ein Ungarnrefugium ist St. Gallen (Abb. 1.1). Hier wurde 926 nach dem Bericht von Ekkehard IV. im Zuge der Ungarngefahr ein Wall mit Graben und Verhau, die Waldburg bei Häggenschwil aufgeschüttet, die aber von den Ungarn dann doch nicht angegriffen wurde[4]. Sie diente mit etwa 1,4 ha Umfang als Refugium für die mehr als 100 Mönche des ca. 6,5 km entfernt liegenden Klosters St. Gallen, in dessen Kapelle auch Kreuze, Kapseln mit den Totenverzeichnissen und der Klosterschatz gebracht wurden.

Eichstätt wurde 741 von dem heiligen Willibald als Benediktinerkloster gegründet und schon bald, zwischen 741 und 750, zum Bistumssitz erhoben, der allerdings nicht, wie die etwa zeitgleich gegründeten Bistumssitze Würzburg, Büraburg mit oder gar auf einer Burg eingerichtet, sondern erst 908 im Zuge der Ungarngefahr befestigt wurde. Bischof Erchanbald erhielt 908 für Eichstätt von König Ludwig dem Kind die Erlaubnis, bei seinem Kloster einen Markt einzurichten mit Zoll- und Münzrecht sowie einen befestigten Ort herzustellen – *urbem que construere contra paganorum*

---

* Bereich für Ur- und Frühgeschichte, Friedrich-Schiller-Universität Jena, Deutschland.
1. Zu Ungarn allgemein: Anke *et al.* 2008; Schulze-Dörrlamm 2007.
2. Jankuhn 1965.
3. Reinecke 1930; Reinecke 1952.
4. Eccardus/Helbling 1958; Schwarz 1989.

incursus moliri. Grabungen 1984 und 1985/86 erbrachten ein stellenweise wohl zweiphasiges Grabenwerk von 12 m Breite mit zweifacher Abtreppung und 4 m breiter Sohle sowie einen Palisadenzaun, der im Abstand von durchschnittlich 1 m von der inneren Grabenkante verlief und von der Grabenseite her abgestützt war[5]. Anzunehmen, aber nicht belegt ist, dass der Grabenaushub als Wall aufgeschüttet wurde (Abb. 1.2 & 1.3). Diese Befestigung von ca. 700 m Länge und auffallend runder Form wird mit der Nennung von 908 in Zusammenhang stehen und unter Bischof Erchanbald entstanden sein.

Archäologisch untersuchte Ungarnburgen

Die inzwischen seit Paul Reinecke über 80 Jahre andauernde Forschung zu Abwehr- und Befestigungsmaßnahmen gegen die Ungarn zeigt deutlich, dass in erster Linie topographische Merkmale zur Definition dieser Befestigungen und Burgen herangezogen wurden. Dazu gehören hohe, geschüttete Wälle, teils ältere Befestigungen überlagernd mit vorgelagertem Graben. Charakteristisch scheinen geschüttete, heute teils noch 4-6 m hoch erhaltene Wälle. Die Gräben sind bei diesen Wallanlagen mit einer durchschnittlichen Breite von 10-12 m sehr groß dimensioniert. Kennzeichnend ist oftmals ein mehrfach gestaffeltes Wallgrabensystem, das, meist als Abschnittsbefestigung ausgeführt, Spornlagen abriegelt. Ringwälle sind hingegen untypisch[6]. Den Zugang zum Innenraum stellten einfache Tordurchlässe oder solche mit einbiegenden Torwangen am Rand der Befestigung bzw. am Steilhang dar. Von den in der Literatur als Ungarnburgen angesprochenen Anlagen wurden jedoch nur wenige wie Karlburg und Veitsberg tatsächlich mit Grabungen archäologisch untersucht.

Die zunächst königliche Burg Karlburg befand sich seit 751/753 im Besitz der Würzburger Bischöfe. In der ersten Hälfte des 10. Jahrhunderts wurde die karolingische Befestigung aufgegeben, der Graben eingefüllt und planiert, als man eine neue, größere Anlage auf bisher ungenutztem Gelände davor errichtete, die jetzt mit 170 x 120 m eine vergrößerte Innenfläche von 1,7 ha besaß[7]. Auch die neue Befestigung grenzte den Sporn bogenförmig ab (Abb. 2). Die Befestigung setzte sich aus einem mit Steinen und Erdreich geschütteten Wall von etwa 9-10 m Breite und einem ohne Berme vorgelagerten Graben zusammen. Nach den 14C-Daten aus dem Pfostenhaus am Wallfuß dürfte der Wall tatsächlich in der Ungarnzeit errichtet worden sein. Zu dieser Befestigungsphase gehört vermutlich der nördlich in 100 m Entfernung vom Osthang abgehende, bogenförmige, kleine Wall mit Graben von etwa 150 m Länge. Der 5,5 m breite und noch 0,8 m hoch erhaltene Wall mit dem ohne Berme vorgelagerten Graben von 5,5 m Breite und 1,7 m Tiefe ist ebenfalls geschüttet und so in gleicher Art und Weise wie der große Wall mit Graben ausgeführt. Nochmals 100 m vorgelagert befindet sich eine weitere Wall-Graben-Sperre von noch 40 m erhaltener Länge. Beide Sperren stellen auf dem nach Norden hin ansteigenden Vorgelände wirksame Annäherungshindernisse gerade für Reiter dar.

Wie Karlburg ist wohl auch Salz, Bad Neustadt a. d. Saale aus einem Königshof als Mittelpunkt eines *fiscus* hervorgegangen. Mit seiner Konzentration von frühmittelalterlichen Anlagen, darunter drei Burgen, zugehörigen Siedlungen im Tal sowie einem Gräberfeld, ist der Ort als mehrgliedriger Siedlungskomplex ausgewiesen. Mehrfache Herrscheraufenthalte sind belegt und zeigen die Bedeutung dieser Pfalz, allein Otto der Große hielt sich 940 bis 948 viermal in Salz auf. Seit 2010 wird der Veitsberg als mutmaßlicher Standort der Pfalz, auf jeden Fall fortifikatorischer Mittelpunkt des Pfalzkomplexes, in einem Projekt mit geophysikalischen Prospektionen, Luftbild- und Laserscananalysen sowie weiteren Ausgrabungen untersucht, die schon 1983 bis 2006 eine komplexe Innenbebauung u.a. mit mehreren Bauten und einer jüngeren Turmburg, erbrachten[8]. Die laufenden Grabungen (Abb. 3) bestätigen das Bild, dass hier eine Burg mit ausgeprägter mehrphasiger Befestigung stand – wobei die relative Abfolge und insbesondere die Datierung der einzelnen Bauphasen noch geklärt und abgesichert werden müssen –, darunter ein Erdwall, bei dem es sich ebenfalls um eine ungarnzeitliche Befestigung wie auf der Karlburg handeln könnte.

Annäherungshindernisse bei Burgen

Annäherungshindernisse spielten als wirksame Abwehr gegen die Reiterheere der Ungarn sicherlich eine wichtige Rolle. Dies wurde in der Forschung auch in den letzten Jahrzehnten mehrfach herausgestellt. Dazu gehören dem Abschnittswall vorgelagerte Annäherungshindernisse, so etwa einfache Gräben mit Wall dahinter, wie auf der Karlburg, bzw. vorgelagerte Grubenfelder, wie bei Schäftlarn, oder Erdriegel wie bei der Haldenburg, deren Interpretation, insbesondere Zeitstellung allerdings ohne Grabungen bislang noch nicht endgültig gesichert ist.

Das Kloster Schäftlarn wurde zwischen 760 und 764 im Isartal im Voralpenland gegründet. Auf der gegenüberliegenden Isarseite liegt im Wald, etwa 1 km nördlich des Klosters die Birg (Abb. 4.2). Hierbei handelt es sich um einen auf drei Seiten steil abfallenden 90 m hoch aufragenden Bergsporn, der zur Befestigung nahezu prädestiniert ist. Der Innenraum von ca. 8 ha wird durch eine 300 m lange Abschnittsbefestigung geschützt, die sich aus einem 10 m hoch erhaltenen Wall mit doppeltem Grabenwerk und einer im Südwesten vorgelagerten Zone aus in mehreren Reihen versetzt angeordneten Gruben zusammensetzt[9].

---

5. RIEDER 1987; RIEDER 2010.
6. ETTEL 2001, 227, Abb. 84 und 206.
7. *Ibid.*, 32ff.; ETTEL 2012, 55f.
8. WAMSER 1984; ETTEL et al. 2011.
9. HABERSTROH 1999; SCHWARZ 1971 mit weiterer Literatur.

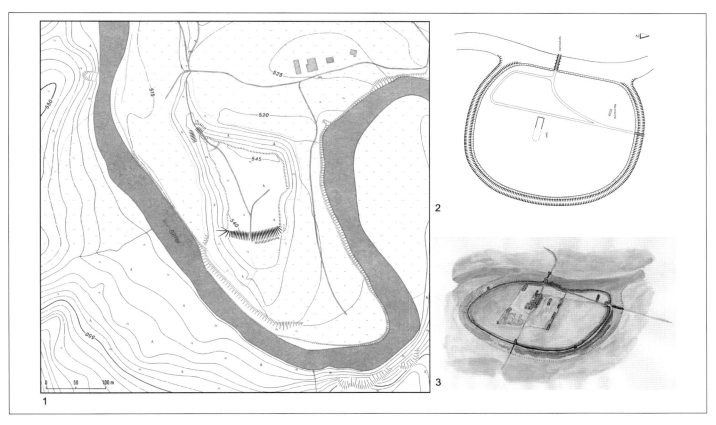

Abb. 1 – 1) Topografischer Plan der Waldburg bei Häggenschwil (SCHWARZ 1975, Beil. 40,6); 2) Eichstätt: Plan der Befestigung im 10. Jahrhundert nach 908 (RIEDER 1987, 44); 3) Rekonstruktion von Eichstätt im 10. Jahrhundert (RIEDER 2010, 8, Abb. 6).

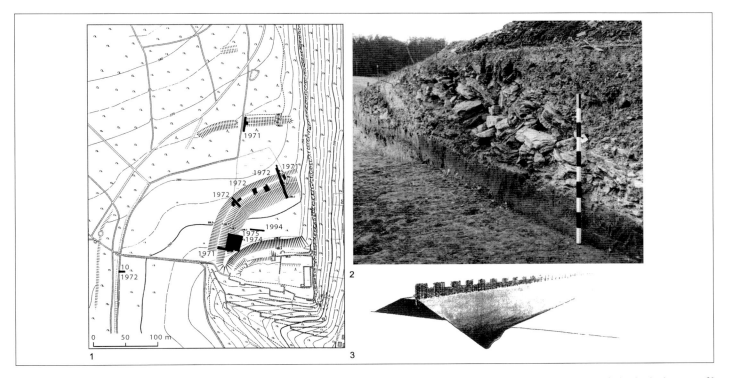

Abb. 2 – Karlburg: 1) Topografischer Plan mit den Grabungsflächen von 1971-1972, 1974-1975 und 1994 (ETTEL 2001, Taf. 1); 2) Fläche 4 Profil 8, Mittelteil der Wallschüttung (von Ost nach West) (ETTEL 2001, Taf. 249,2); 3) Rekonstruktionen der karolingischen Mauer (Dokument P. Ettel).

Abb. 3 – 1) Veitsberg: Gesamtplan der Befestigung mit Grabungsflächen 1983-2012. Luftbild BLfD-Luftbilddokumentation, Aufnahmedatum 20.06.2000; Foto K. Leidorf, Archiv-Nr. 5726/029, Dia 8264-20; Kartographie P. Wolters, Universität Jena; 2) Veitsberg: Digitales Geländemodell (Geobasisdaten Bayerische Vermessungsverwaltung 2010 Hillshade, Beleuchtung Azimuth 270 Grad, Altitude 25 Grad). Kartographie L. Werther, Universität Jena.

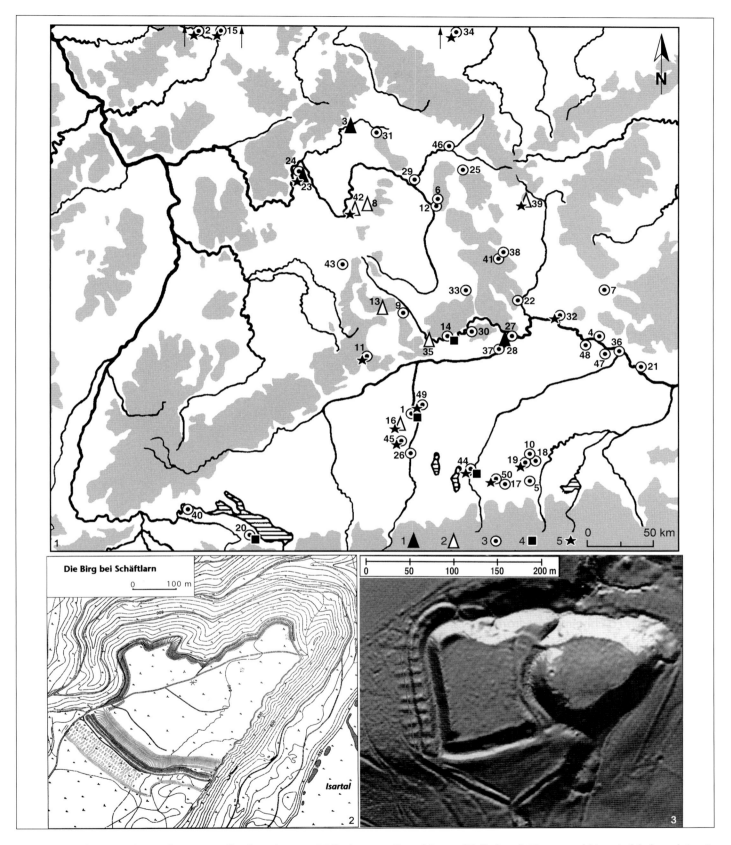

Abb. 4 – 1) Verbreitung der geschütteten Wälle: 1) geschütteter Wall; 2) eventuell geschütteter Wall; 3) nach Literatur; 4) historisch belegt; 5) Annäherungshindernisse. Kartierung P. Ettel; 2) „Birg" bei Hohenschäftlarn (HABERSTROH 1999, 114); 3) Haldenburg (Geobasisdaten Bayerisches Landesamt für Vermessung und Geoinformation). Bearbeitung H. Kerscher, Bayerisches Landesamt für Denkmalpflege.

Die Haldenburg mit ihren ausgeprägten Erdriegeln (Abb. 4.3) reiht sich in eine Gruppe von Burgen mit gestaffelten Annäherungshindernissen ein[10] (Abb. 4.1). Vergleichbare Erdriegel finden sich auf dem Buschelberg, in Kleinhöhenkirchen und Aiterndorf. 2011 wurden solche auch am Ringwall Vogelherd (Kruckenberg) mittels eines digitalen Geländemodells entdeckt, die an der höchsten Stelle des Geländerückens als hohlwegartige Rinnen der Befestigung im Norden vorgelagert sind. Die Reihe von 1 m hohen Erdrippen verlaufen im Abstand von 10 m bei einer Länge von 20-30 m. Auffallend ist die identische Ausführung dieser Erdrippen oder Erdriegel, auch als Reitergassen bezeichnet, die schon nahezu genormt wirken.

Schluss

Die neuere Forschung (Abb. 4.1) zeigt, dass von den etwa 50 in der Literatur teilweise seit langem postulierten Ungarnwällen nur eine Handvoll von Burgen übrigbleibt, die man nach den Grabungsergebnissen tatsächlich als geschütteten Wall interpretieren und dazu mit großer Wahrscheinlichkeit auch in die Zeit der Ungarneinfälle, ausgehendes 9. und v.a. erste Hälfte 10. Jahrhundert datieren kann[11]. Karlburg, der Veitsberg und wohl auch der Wolfgangswall über Weltenburg gehören dazu, schon andere Befunde vom Schwanberg, Castell, Mörnsheim, Rauher Kulm und Buschelberg lassen Fragen offen. Die große Mehrzahl der sogenannten Ungarnwälle, muss auch infolge fehlender archäologischer Untersuchungen bislang in ihrer Deutung und Datierung unsicher bleiben, einige Fundplätze sind ganz sicher zu streichen.

Die Interpretation der Anlagen als ein gegen die Ungarneinfälle errichtetes System von Burgen ist schon seit der Diskussion um die sächsischen Rundwälle abzulehnen. Eher wird man überlegen müssen, dass geschüttete Wälle und Annäherungshindernisse als befestigungstechnische Elemente, eine zeitspezifische Reaktion auf die Ungarnbedrohung waren, die leicht und schnell, ohne große Vorkenntnisse zu bewältigen war. Eine wichtige Rolle in diesem Prozess spielten möglicherweise Klöster bzw. die klösterlichen Schutzmaßnahmen gegen die Ungarneinfälle – auf St. Gallen mit der Schilderung von Wall, Graben und Verhau ist zu verweisen. Die Deutung als Ungarnrefugien ist ebenfalls kritisch zu sehen und jeweils im Einzelfall zu prüfen. Karlburg, Veitsberg und auch Weltenburg sind von ihrer Bedeutung sowie den zahlreichen Siedlungsbefunden und Funden im Innenraum her mit Sicherheit nicht nur Refugien in Notzeiten gewesen. Topographische Merkmale wie hohe Wälle reichen jedenfalls für eine Interpretation als Ungarnrefugium auf keinen Fall aus. Im Analogieschluss zur historischen Schilderung von St. Gallen alle Burgen mit geschütteten Wällen[12] und Annäherungshindernissen in die Ungarnzeit zu datieren und als Refugium zu interpretieren, ist sicherlich zu einfach, zumal wenn keine archäologischen Untersuchungen im Befestigungs- und Innenbereich vorliegen. Auf der anderen Seite ist die Existenz von Ungarnburgen unzweifelhaft, sie ist aber im Einzelfall mit entsprechenden Grabungen zu prüfen und zu belegen.

---

10. Schneider 1977; Kerscher 2010; Sage 1990.
11. Ausführliche Darstellung in: Ettel 2012.
12. Geschüttete Wälle waren in der gesamten Vor- und Frühgeschichte, gerade zu Beginn und auch in den jüngeren Perioden, noch gebräuchlich und kennzeichnen sicherlich kein fortschrittliches Element in der Entwicklung der frühmittelalterlichen Befestigungstechnik, sondern eher das Gegenteil, wenn man sich die zeitgleiche Entwicklung im 10. Jahrhundert mit Errichtung von Mörtelmauern und Türmen vor Augen hält.

Literatur

Anke B. et al. (2008), *Reitervölker im Frühmittelalter. Hunnen, Awaren, Ungarn. Archäologie in Deutschland Sonderheft*, Stuttgart, Theiss.

Eccardus/Helbling (1958), *Die Geschichten des Klosters St. Gallen. Gesamtausgabe 3*, Köln, Böhlau.

Ettel P. (2001), *Karlburg – Rossthal – Oberammerthal. Studien zum frühmittelalterlichen Burgenbau in Nordbayern*, Rahden, Leidorf (Frühgeschichtliche und provinzialrömische Archäologie. Materialien und Forschungen; 5).

– (2012), „,Ungarnburgen – Ungarnrefugien – Ungarnwälle'. Zum Stand der Forschung", in *Zwischen Kreuz und Zinne. Festschrift für Barbara Schock-Werner zum 65. Geburtstag*, T. Bitterli-Waldvogel (hrsg.), Braubach, Deutsche Burgenvereinigung (Veröffentlichungen der Deutschen Burgenvereinigung, Reihe A; 15), 45-66.

Ettel P. et al. (2011), „Der Veitsberg – Forschungen im karolingisch-ottonischen Pfalzkomplex Salz, Stadt Bad Neustadt a.d. Saale, Landkreis Rhön-Grabfeld, Unterfranken", *Das archäologische Jahr in Bayern*, 2011, 129-131.

HABERSTROH J. (1999), „,Birg'. Ringwallanlage und Abschnittsbefestigung", in *Burgen in Bayern. 7000 Jahre Burgengeschichte im Luftbild*, K. LEIDORF & P. ETTEL (hrsg.), Stuttgart, Theiss, 114-115.

JANKUHN H. (1965), „,Heinrichsburgen' und Königspfalzen", in *Deutsche Königspfalzen. Beiträge zu ihrer historischen und archäologischen Erforschung. Zweiter Band*, Göttingen, Vandenhoeck und Ruprecht (Veröffentlichungen des Max-Planck-Instituts für Geschichte; 11/2), 61-69.

KERSCHER H. (2010), „Gegen die Steppenreiter? – Neue Beobachtungen am Ringwall Vogelherd bei Kruckenberg. Gemeinde Wiesent, Landkreis Regensburg, Oberpfalz", *Das archäologische Jahr in Bayern*, 2010, 113-116.

REINECKE P. (1930), „Spätkeltische Oppida im rechtsrheinischen Bayern", *Bayerischer Vorgeschichtsfreund*, 9, 29-52.

– (1952), „Der Ringwall Staffelberg bei Staffelstein", *Archiv für Geschichte und Altertumskunde von Oberfranken*, 36, 12-32.

RIEDER K. H. (1987), „Eichstätt", *Führer zu archäologischen Denkmälern in Deutschland*, 15, 36-45.

– (2010), „Neue Aspekte zur ,Urbs' der Eichstätter Bischöfe", in *Verwurzelt in Glaube und Heimat. Festschrift für Ernst Reiter*, K. KREITMEIR & K. MAIER (hrsg.), Regensburg, Pustet (Eichstätter Studien; 58), 1-21.

SAGE W. (1990), „Auswirkungen der Ungarnkriege in Altbayern und ihr archäologischer Nachweis", *Jahresbericht der Stiftung Aventinum*, 4, 5-41.

SCHNEIDER O. (1977), „Frühe Burganlage ,Haldenburg' bei Schwabegg", in O. SCHNEIDER et al., *Archäologische Wanderungen um Augsburg*, Stuttgart, Theiss (Führer zu archäologischen Denkmälern in Bayern. Schwaben; 1), 54-58.

SCHULZE-DÖRRLAMM M. (2007), „Spuren der Ungarneinfälle des 10. Jahrhunderts", in *Heldengrab im Niemandsland. Ein frühungarischer Reiter aus Niederösterreich*, F. DAIM (hrsg.), Mainz, Römisch-Germanisches Zentralmuseum (Mosaiksteine; 2), 43-63.

SCHWARZ K. (1971), „Die Birg bei Hohenschäftlarn – eine Burganlage der karolingisch-ottonischen Zeit", in *Führer zu vor- und frühgeschichtlichen Denkmälern*, Bd. XVIII: *Miesbach, Tegernsee, Bad Tölz, Wolfratshausen, Bad Aibling*, Mainz, Von Zabern, 222-238.

– (1975), „Der frühmittelalterliche Landesausbau in Nordostbayern – archäologisch gesehen", in *Ausgrabungen in Deutschland*, Teil II: *Römische Kaiserzeit im Freien Germanien, Frühmittelalter*, Mainz, Verl. des römisch-germanischen Zentralmuseums (Monographien des Römisch-Germanischen Zentralmuseums; 1), 338-409.

– (1989), *Archäologisch-topographische Studien zur Geschichte frühmittelalterlicher Fernwege und Ackerfluren im Alpenvorland zwischen Isar, Inn und Chiemsee*, Kallmünz/Opf, Lassleben (Materialhefte zur bayerischen Bodendenkmalpflege. Reihe A; 45).

WAMSER L. (1984), „Neue Befunde zur mittelalterlichen Topographie des fiscus Salz im alten Markungsgebiet von Bad Neustadt a. d. Saale, Landkreis Rhön-Grabfeld, Unterfranken", *Das archäologische Jahr in Bayern*, 1984, 147-151.

Burgen im österreichisch-ungarischen Grenzraum im 12. und 13. Jahrhundert

◆

István Feld*

Der Grenzraum des mittelalterlichen Königreiches Ungarn und der östlichen Gebiete des Deutsch-Römischen Reiches – d.h. die westlichen Komitate des heutigen Ungarn sowie Burgenland, Ost-Steiermark und Ost-Niederösterreich – ist besonders reich an oft gut erhaltenen, aber archäologisch noch ungenügend erforschten Burganlagen. Wann sie entstanden und inwieweit sie als „Grenzburgen" zu interpretieren sind, gehört zu den meist diskutierten, aber immer noch offenen Fragen sowohl der österreichischen als auch der ungarischen Geschichtsforschung bzw. der Burgenkunde dieser Regionen.

Es steht nämlich fest, dass nach der 896 erfolgten Landnahme der ungarischen Stämme im Karpatenbecken eine spezielle Berührungszone zwischen der Ostmark und dem neuen ungarischen Fürstentum entstand. Mangels eindeutiger Angaben sind aber weder die zeitliche bzw. räumliche Ausdehnung noch der Charakter dieser Zone genauer festzustellen. Man findet daher darüber recht unterschiedliche und oft unbegründete Hypothesen in der österreichischen und ungarischen Literatur. Einer Auffassung nach sollte anfangs westlich von den eigentlichen ungarischen Siedlungsgebieten bis zu den Flüssen Leitha, Fischa und March eine spärlich bewohnte, 30-60 km tiefe Zone existieren. Davor bildeten natürliche und künstliche Geländehindernisse eine Grenzschutzzone mit Grenzwächtern und mit ihren vorgeschobenen Posten (sog. Warten), die auch als Grenzöde bezeichnet und als Teil des sog. Grenzgürtels (ungarisch *gyepű*) interpretiert wird. Man spricht noch von einer Einflusszone westlich dieses Gebiets, so sollte z. B. „der westlichste Einzugsbereich des Grenzgürtels […] nicht über die Flüsse Kamp und Traisen"[1] hinausreichen. Es ist aber auch von einem „menschenarmen Grenzödland (gyepüelve)" oder einen „Grenzverhau(gyepű)system" zu lesen – ohne dass diese Begriffe eindeutig definiert wären[2].

In der neuesten Forschung wird aber immer mehr betont, dass man mit genau festgestellten Grenzlinien im Frühmittelalter noch kaum rechnen dürfe – und das betrifft auch das besprochene Gebiet. Die oft durch die geographischen Bedingungen bestimmten und meist durchlässigen Zonen bildeten keine gut bestimmbaren Trennlinien. Die aufgrund der archäologischen Funde zusammengestellten Verbreitungskarten geben uns sonst vor allem über die Siedlungsgebiete Auskunft. So wird neuerdings von Kulturgrenzen von Verbindungszonen gesprochen, die als Grenzgebiet/Grenzraum die Möglichkeit einer ethnischen bzw. politischen Umwälzung in sich bergen[3].

Der ungarische Begriff *gyepű* hat also keine eindeutige (bzw. eindeutig geklärte) Bedeutung, man versteht aber darunter meist ein komplexes territoriales System, das zuerst nach Westen, ab 955 aber nach Osten verschoben wurde, bis sich „die Grenze" ab dem Ende des 10. bis Mitte des 11. Jahrhunderts an der Leitha- bzw. südlich davon an der Lafnitz-Linie fixierte. Parallel dazu erfolgte eine kontinuierliche Besiedlung des besprochenen Gebietes aus den beiden Richtungen[4].

Eine immer noch offene Frage ist, inwieweit die Burganlagen – vor allem großräumige Burgwälle mit Holz-Erde-Befestigung – in diesem „Gyepüsystem" eine Rolle spielten. Wenn wir die ungarische Situation kurz zusammenfassen, ist darauf hinzuweisen, daß die westlichen Komitatsburgen – Wieselburg (Moson), Ödenburg (Sopron), Lutzmannsburg

---

* Lehrstuhlleitender Universitätsdozent, Ungarn.
1. Thorma 2008, 171.
2. *Ibid.*; Sallai 2002; Gömöri 2002.
3. Brather 2004; Pohl et al. 2008, 131; Hardt 2000.
4. Kristó 1994; Kühtreiber & Kühtreiber 2007.

(Locsmánd), Eisenburg (Vasvár) – des um 1000 gegründeten Königreiches Ungarn in den Quellen zwar als „Grenzkomitatsburgen" vorkommen, ihre Funktion[5] aber mit derjenigen der anderen „innerländischen" Anlagen übereinstimmte – abgesehen davon, daß die in den einzelnen Siedlungen ansässigen Grenzwächter unter der Oberhoheit des Komitatsgespanns des Königs standen. Das Verhältnis der Grenzwächter zu den Burgen ist aber für uns unbekannt, und das gilt auch für die weiteren, nicht allzu zahlreichen und bislang kaum genauer datierbaren Anlagen mit Holz-Erde-Strukturen – so Draßburg (Darufalva), Burg (Pinkaóvár) oder Szentvid –, die nicht als Komitatszentren funktionierten und daher in der Literatur (ohne nähere Begründung) oft als „Grenzburgen" angesprochen wurden[6]. Es ist aber kaum zu belegen, dass diese Befestigungen zur Verhinderung von Eroberungsversuchen der deutschen Kaiser errichtet wurden[7]; sie spielten vor allem in der Verwaltung des Landes eine wichtige Rolle. Auch die chronologische Einordnung weiterer sog. Grenzschutzeinrichtungen wie Verhaagungen und langer Wallbauten ist noch unsicher (Abb. 1)[8].

Was die Situation in Österreich anbelangt, erfolgte hier ab der Mitte des 11. Jahrhunderts die Kolonisation des Grenzgebietes. Im Bereich des Wiener Beckens und des Pittener Gebietes sind bayrische Hochadlige mit ihrer Gefolgschaft erschienen, später kamen u.a. die Stubenberger aus der Steiermark und ließen die Burg Landsee (Lánzsér) direkt an der Grenze zu Ungarn bzw. eigentlich schon auf ungarischem Gebiet errichten. Die damals erbauten Befestigungen sind aber kaum näher bekannt, Verhaagungen kennen wir aus Niederösterreich nicht[9]. Der nach der älteren burgenländischen Fachliteratur seit der zweiten Hälfte des 12. Jahrhunderts an der steierischen und österreichischen Grenze errichtete „Burgengürtel" als organisiertes Grenzschutzsystem – hierher sollten u.a. Ebreichsdorf, Bruck an der Leitha, Riegersburg, Pitten, Seebenstein, Kirchschlag, Neudau und Fürstenfeld gehören – ist heute schon als eine kaum beweisbare Hypothese zu bewerten[10].

Obwohl die Chronologie der frühen ungarischen Grenzverteidigung noch nicht geklärt ist – aus der Zeit nach 1100 stehen uns allerdings kaum Angaben über das Weiterleben der alten Strukturen zur Verfügung – rechnen sowohl österreichische als auch ungarische Forscher mit der Existenz des Gyepüsytems bis zum Ende des 12. Jahrhunderts[11]. Es steht

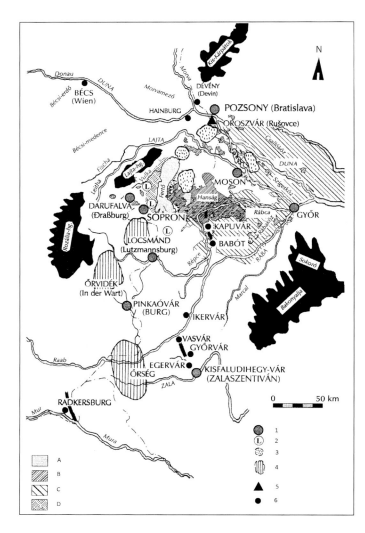

Abb. 1 – Der österreichisch-ungarische Grenzraum zwischen Bratislava und Radkersburg im 10.-11. Jahrhundert: A) Flüsse und Teiche; B) Wasserfläche; C) Hochwassergebiet; D) sumpfige Gebiete; 1) Burgen mit sogenannten Brandwällen; 2) auf Grenzwächter hinweisende Ortsnamen; 3) Petschegene; 4) Székler; 5) Russen; 6) weitere Burgen (GÖMÖRI 2002, 34, Abb. 11).

aber fest, dass die meisten erwähnten Komitatsburgen auch noch Mitte des 13. Jahrhunderts eine wichtige militärische Funktion hatten[12].

---

5. Siehe dazu zuletzt: FELD 2012.
6. Auch in einigen neuen Zusammenfassungen wird eine ganze Reihe von Befestigungen hypothetisch als „Grenzburg" bezeichnet, so neben den erwähnten Anlagen noch Bad Deutsch Altenburg (?), Egervár, Győr-Bácsa, Győrvár, Ikervár, Kapuvár/Babót, Körmend, Oroszvár, Sárvár und Szombathely. Siehe dazu mit weiterer Literatur: BÓNA 1998; GÖMÖRI 2007.
7. BUZÁS 2006; TAKÁCS 2006; dagegen: FELD 2012.
8. Zu dieser Frage: KISS & TÓTH 1987.
9. KÜHTREIBER 2007. Die sonst nicht eindeutig lokalisierbare früheste Anlage von Landsee kam später unter näher nicht bekannten Umständen zu Ungarn. Siehe dazu den Beitrag von T. Kühtreiber und M. Jeitler in diesem Band.
10. Siehe dazu als Beispiel: MEYER 1990, 113.
11. So z. B. BUNZL 1990, 177: „nach Aufgabe des Gyepüsystems, eines Grenzverhaues durch Béla III. erfolgt im 12. Jh. der Bau von gemauerten Burgen zur Sicherung der Landesgrenze".
12. Auf die Auflösung des Systems deutet aber schon die Tatsache hin, dass Lutzmannsburg (Locsmánd) 1210 dem Adligen Nikolaus aus dem Szák-Geschlecht geschenkt wurde (GÖMÖRI 2002).

Die ab dem 12. Jahrhundert in sehr großer Zahl errichteten, sonst aber recht unterschiedlichen Befestigungen sind daher auf den beiden Seiten der „Grenze" schon immer mehr als Adelsburgen zu bestimmen – ein königlicher bzw. landesherrlicher Bauherr ist selten nachzuweisen. Wenn wir aber den Burgenbau des österreichisch-ungarischen Grenzraumes in der zweiten Hälfte des 12. und in der ersten Hälfte des 13. Jahrhunderts anhand von schriftlichen und archäologischen Quellen analysieren möchten, kommen wir zu einem überraschenden Ergebnis. Im heutigen südöstlichen Niederösterreich existierten nach den neuesten Forschungen schon um 1150 fast 50 Adelsburgen[13], dagegen rechnet man auf den östlich direkt benachbarten Gebieten des Königreiches Ungarn vor 1200 kaum mit einem privaten Burgenbau – die auch hier in großer Zahl vorhandenen Anlagen sind meist frühestens in das 13. Jahrhundert datiert[14].

Es stellt sich die Frage, ob dieses Bild der historischen Wirklichkeit entspricht d.h. ob die politisch-gesellschaftliche Entwicklung der beiden Gebiete wirklich so große Unterschiede aufwies und sich die Adelsburg als historisches Phänomen in Ungarn erst so verspätet verbreitete. Lässt sich mit den unterschiedlichen Herrschaftsprinzipien der Landesherren der österreichischen bzw. ungarischen Gebiete vielleicht erklären, dass sich die Adeligen des Königreiches Ungarn gegenüber ihrem Herrscher erst viel später durchsetzen konnten[15]? Oder handelt es sich nur um ein Problem einer unterschiedlichen Quellenlage, der Forschungsmethoden bzw. der Traditionen historisch-archäologischer Forschung beider Länder?

Bei der Durchsicht der neuesten Ergebnisse der Burgenforschung im niederösterreichischen Alpenvorland – im sogenannten Pittener Raum als einer typischen Berg- und Hügellandschaft – finden wir schon mehrere, zum Teil hypothetische frühe Adelssitze, die anhand historischer Angaben bzw. aufgrund von Oberflächenfunden in das 11. Jahrhundert datiert werden. Zu diesen gehört der Hausstein bei Grünbach, eine sehr früh abgesetzt gelegene, kleinräumige Höhenburg[16].

Ab 1100 ist dann eine Burgengründungswelle festzustellen, auch wenn direkte Baubefunde und archäologische Untersuchungen nur für einige Fälle vorliegen[17]. Eine Ausnahme bildet der 1992-2002 fast vollkommen ergrabene Dunkelstein, eine in der ersten Hälfte des 12. Jahrhunderts als Turmburg errichtete Anlage der Ministerialen des steierischen Markgrafengeschlechts, der Otaker. Er wurde bald um einen Wohnbau erweitert und um 1200 stand hier schon eine „klassische Adelsburg" (Turm/*Palas*/Kapelle) (Abb. 2)[18]. Nur aufgrund der Mauerwerkstrukturen nahm man an, dass die Burg Starhemberg in der gleichen Zeit entstanden sei, desgleichen die etwas später datierte Gutenbrunn, eine auffallend regelmäßige Anlage mit feldseitiger Bergfried[19].

Nördlich von Pitten sind ab 1100 vor allem Niederungsburgen bekannt, die aber bisher archäologisch nur teilweise untersucht wurden. In Möllersdorf, südlich von Wien, errichtete in der ersten Hälfte des 12. Jahrhunderts ein Ministerialengeschlecht eine Anlage mit regelmäßiger Ringmauer – man rechnet hier mit innerer Holzbebauung – die dann nach 1200 mit neuem Graben und mit einem Steinturm befestigt wurde[20] (Abb. 3). Ein ähnlicher Bau entstand etwas später, im dritten Drittel des 12. Jahrhunderts: die Veste Rohr, die dem Herren „de Rote" gehörte. Hier war die gleiche Tendenz festzustellen: eine gewisse Anpassung an die neuen militärischen Anforderungen und die „Versteinerung" der Wohnbauten[21].

Aus der Steiermark stehen uns nur spärliche archäologische Angaben zur Verfügung. Auf dem Kurutzenkogel bei Fehring wird ein Steinturm aus dem 11. Jahrhundert vermutet, auf dem Alt-Gleichenberg deuten nur Streufunde auf die 1170 erbaute Anlage der Herren von Wildon[22].

Da das Urkundenmaterial über Westungarn im Vergleich zu den ostösterreichischen Gebieten viel spärlicher ist, kennen wir die hiesigen Besitzverhältnisse – also die Verteilung des königlichen, kirchlichen und privaten Besitzes – vor dem 13. Jahrhundert kaum. In dieser Hinsicht ist der Zustrom des west- und mitteleuropäischen Adels nach Ungarn erwähnenswert. Unter diesen *hospites*, die sich oft in der Elite des Landes etablieren konnten, sind die – früher in der deutschsprachigen Literatur irrtümlicherweise „Güssinger" genannten[23] – Günser aus dem Héder-Geschlecht besonders wichtig, da sie ab der Mitte des 12. Jahrhunderts in der Grenzregion wahrscheinlich größere Besitzungen erwerben konnten. Die frühere historische Forschung schreibt ihnen traditionell die Errichtung einer hölzernen Burg in Güssing (Németújvár) schon zu dieser Zeit zu[24].

---

13. Kühtreiber & Kühtreiber 2007. Unter den von den Autoren bearbeiteten sieben Burgen des 11. Jahrhunderts im südlichen Niederösterreich sind nur drei, bei denen wo auch Funde aus dieser Zeit vorliegen, in den weiteren Fällen sind nur historische Angaben (Geschlechtername bzw. Adelsbesitz im Ort) bekannt. Unter den weiteren 36 Befestigungen, d.h. Burgen und Ansitzen, die in die Zeit bis etwa 1158 datiert werden können, kennen wir nur aus Lanzenkirchen, Hausstein von Muggendorf, Siedling-Tanzboden und vielleicht Thernberg gesicherte Funde der besprochenen Zeit. In Klamm und Tachenstein-Wulfingstein weist noch das Mauerwerk auf das 12. Jahrhundert hin. In allen anderen Fällen liegt uns nur die urkundliche Nennung des ortsässigen Adelsgeschlechts vor (unser Dank gehört Herrn Kühtreiber für die Bereitstellung seiner Datensammlung!). So kann man natürlich nicht ausschließen, dass in einigen Fällen nicht mit Burgen sondern nur mit Herrenhöfen zu rechnen ist. Zu diesem Thema siehe noch: Kühtreiber et al. 1998-2003; Kühtreiber & Kühtreiber 1999.
14. Siehe Dénes 2000; Dénes 2008; Vándor 1990.
15. Zu dieser Frage jüngst Horváth 2011 sowie der Beitrag von T. Kühtreiber und M. Jettler in diesem Band.
16. Kühtreiber & Kühtreiber 2007.
17. Siehe Anm. 13. Die Frage nach der Verbindung der adeligen Familien- bzw. Burgennamen auf den österreichischen bzw. ungarischen Gebieten verdient noch eine tiefergehende historische Untersuchung.
18. Kühtreiber 2005.
19. Kühtreiber & Kühtreiber 2007.
20. Hofer 2007.
21. *Ibid.*
22. Tiefengraber 2007.
23. Meyer 1989, 209.
24. Bunzl 1990; Prickler 1972, 58-59.

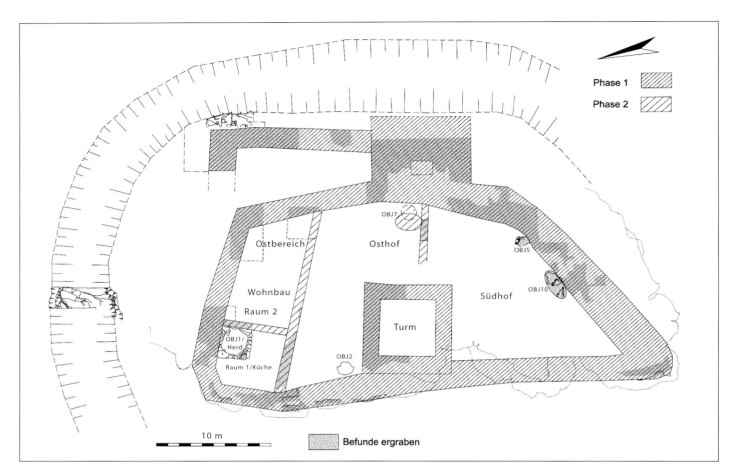

Abb. 2 – Die Burg Dunkelstein zwischen 1100 und 1150 (Kühtreiber & Kühtreiber 2007, 273, Abb. 6).

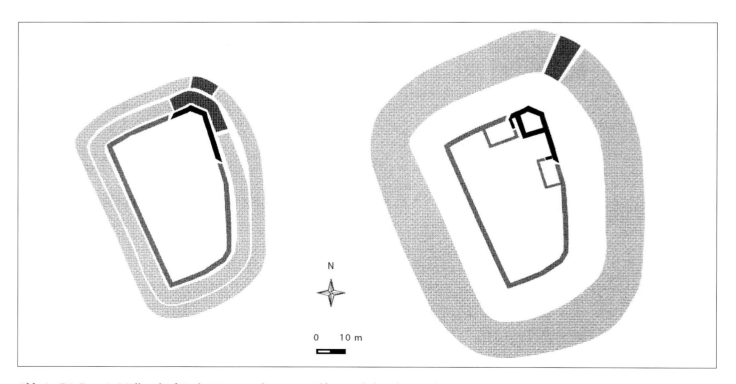

Abb. 3 – Die Burg in Möllersdorf. Links: Bauperiode zweite Hälfte 12. Jahrhundert; Rechts Bauperiode 13. Jahrhundert (Hofer 2007, 252, Abb. 2).

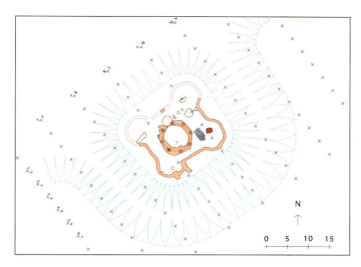

Abb. 4 – Die Burg Gór: Ausgrabungsgrundriss (Dénes 2011, 45, Abb. 5).

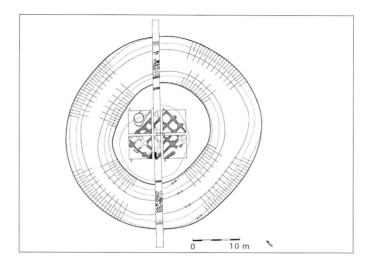

Abb. 5 – Die Burg Zalak bei Sorkifalud (Kiss 1995, 212, Abb. 1).

Wenn wir aber das Urkundenmaterial näher untersuchen – eine moderne, komplexe Bearbeitung der Geschichte dieses Herrengeschlechtes steht gleichwohl noch aus[25] – kommen wir zu der Überzeugung, dass hier nur die Gründung eines Benediktinerklosters im Jahre 1157 gesichert ist. Wo dieser Bau genau stand, wann und wie er vielleicht zur Burg umgebaut wurde – als Bauherr kommen König Béla III., Andreas II. und der Adlige Demeter aus dem Csák-Geschlecht in Frage, eine Befestigung stand hier aber wahrscheinlich schon vor 1235 – muss zukünftig geklärt werden[26]. Erst jüngst fanden begrenzte archäologische Forschungen auf dem ausgedehnten Plateau des Burgberges statt, ältere Baureste – kleinteiliges Bruchsteinmauerwerk in geringem Umfang – wurden früher im Verlauf der südlichen Ringmauer der Hochburg vermutet[27].

Hölzerne Burgenbauten – die aber mit ihren einfachen Strukturen (in Form von Pfostenreihen archäologisch überlieferten Palisaden) stark von den mächtigen Konstruktionen der erwähnten Komitatsburgen abweichen – kennen wir aus modernen Ausgrabungen vom Gebiet des heutigen ungarischen Komitates Vas. In Gór wurde in der Nähe der mittelalterlichen Dorfkirche eine Turmburg mit einem auffallend kleinen Durchmesser von 15 Meter freigelegt (Abb. 4). Ob es mit dem in einer unsicheren Urkunde von 1238 erwähnten *castrum Guor* identisch ist, steht noch offen. Der Besitz gehörte jedenfalls schon 1279 den erwähnten Günsern. Zu dieser Zeit wurde die Anlage wahrscheinlich nicht mehr genutzt – nach der bisherigen ^{14}C-Datierung soll sie zwischen 1105-1131 erbaut worden sein. Das noch nicht vollständig veröffentlichte Fundmaterial weist aber eher auf eine spätere Zeit – erste Hälfte des 13. Jahrhunderts? – hin[28].

Die horizontale Grundkonstruktion einer weiteren hölzernen Turmburg sowie unsichere Reste einer äußeren Umwehrung fand man auf der in der sumpfigen Umgebung von Sorkifalud erbauten Zalak (Abb. 5). Die Funde, darunter die Münzen von Béla IV. (1235-1270) und Ottakar II. (1251-1276) stammen aus dem 13. Jahrhundert. Hier wurde 1278 schon ein *locus castri* erwähnt, der Besitz gehörte ab Mitte des 13. Jahrhunderts den Mitgliedern des Adelsgeschlechtes Herman. Der Ausgräber, der einen Rekonstruktionsversuch aufgrund der rezenten Volksarchitektur der Umgebung vorschlug, interpretiert aber die Anlage nicht als Adelsburg sondern als einen noch vor dem Mongolensturm von 1241 errichteten Stützpunkt des Gyepü-Systems[29]. Ob diese Annahme zutrifft, ist ohne weitere Untersuchungen nicht zu entscheiden, fest steht aber, dass es sich nicht um eine Motte handelt. Künstlich aufgeschüttete Burganlagen aus dem 12.-13. Jahrhundert konnte man bisher in Westungarn archäologisch nicht nachweisen[30].

Auf dem Gebiet des heutigen Burgenlandes gab es bisher wenig Burgenarchäologie. Als eine wichtige Ausnahme ist Leithaprodersdorf (Lajtapordány) zu erwähnen, wo der in der unmittelbaren Nähe des Grenzflusses, am Dorfrand erbaute Bau 1232 als Burg des Peters aus dem Adelsgeschlecht Gut-Keled erwähnt wurde. Die schon 1273 zerstörte Anlage war hier auch eine – aber schon steinerne – Turmburg[31] (Abb. 6), deren Grundriss viele Ähnlichkeiten mit den genannten Anlagen in Möllersdorf und Veste Rohr auf der „österreichischen" Seite aufweist. Dies ist freilich vor allem durch die sehr ähnlichen geographischen Gegebenheiten bedingt, doch sollte man auch persönliche Kontakte der adeligen Burgenbauer nicht ausschließen. Sonst geht es hier um eine

---

25. Siehe eine neuere Arbeit über die „Spätphase" der Familiengeschichte: Zsoldos 2010.
26. Zu den Quellen: Hervay 2001.
27. Bunzl 1990; Krenn et al. 2009.
28. Die neueste Veröffentlichung der Grabungsergebnisse: Dénes 2011.
29. Kiss 1995.
30. Feld 2007.
31. Hofer & Sauer 2011.

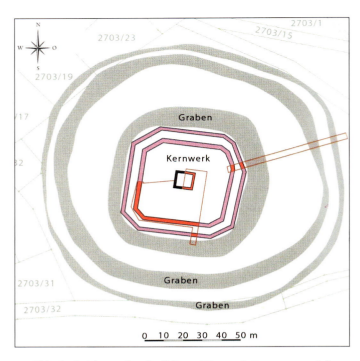

Abb. 6 – Leithaprodersdorf, Burg (Hofer & Sauer 2011, 60).

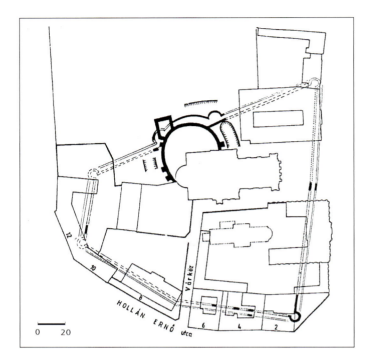

Abb. 7 – Szombathely, die Reste der bischöflichen Burg und der Stadtbefestigung. Unpublizierte Zeichnung von J. Dénes.

überall auffindbare Grundform, die nicht unbedingt aus einer einzigen Quelle abzuleiten ist.

Daher ist die bislang vorgeschlagene frühe Datierung[32] der ovalförmigen Burganlage des Bischofs von Győr (Raab) in Szombathely (Steinamanger) (Abb. 7) kaum zu akzeptieren. Das Fundmaterial der hier durchgeführten Altgrabung – wobei man sich eher auf die tiefer aufgefundenen römischen Bauten konzentrierte – ist unbekannt, die Schriftquellen erwähnen die Burg erst in der zweiten Hälfte des 13. Jahrhunderts[33].

Eine bewusste Nachahmung kann man sich aber nicht nur bei den Flachland- bzw. Niederungsburgen vorstellen. Der einzige Vertreter des in Österreich sehr verbreiteten (aber zusammenfassend noch nicht analysierten[34]) Burgtyps „Festes Haus" ist in Ungarn oberhalb der Stadt Kőszeg (Güns) – die als Namengeber der erwähnten Günser gilt – als Höhenburg aufzufinden. Die Burg Óház (Altes Haus) war die früheste Günser Burganlage, die Schriftquellen zufolge schon vor 1241 existierte. Die Funde der hier unlängst durchgeführten, leider nicht fachgerechten Ausgrabungen erlauben uns keine eindeutige Datierung. Der in der Literatur meist angenommene königliche Bauherr ist aber nur eine mögliche Hypothese, die Anlage könnte unserer Meinung nach auch als eine der frühesten adligen Steinburgen Westungarns, vielleicht als eine Gründung der Günser entstanden sein[35].

Eine weitere, aber nur teilweise freigelegte Höhenburg liegt südlich von Kőszeg, in Velemszentvid. Die über den Resten der Hallstatt- und La Tène-zeitlichen befestigten Siedlung bzw. auf den Spuren einer Holz-Erde-Konstruktion des 11.-12. Jahrhunderts (?) errichtete, mehrteilige Steinanlage wird in den Quellen zwischen 1270 und 1288 als eine Befestigung der Günser genannt, ihre genauere Bauzeit ist aber unbekannt[36].

Im heutigen Burgenland – am West- bzw. Nordrand des Günser-Gerbirges, auf dessen östlichen Gipfeln auch die beiden zuletzt erwähnten Befestigungen erbaut wurden – befinden sich zwei weitere wichtige Burgen, auf denen aber noch keine archäologischen Geländearbeiten durchgeführt wurden. Bernstein (Borostyánkő) existierte schon während der Regierung Andreas II. (1205-1235), sie ging später wiederum an die Günser; ihre Erbauer und Form sind unbekannt[37]. Einmalig ist unter den Burgenbauten des ehemaligen Königreiches die Burg Lockenhaus (Léka) (Abb. 8), die anlässlich der Kämpfe von 1241 schon erwähnt wurde. Der Stil der Bauteile des Kapellenturmes bzw. der zweischiffigen Halle im Erdgeschoss des Palastbaus weist auf das zweite Viertel des 13. Jahrhundert

32. Kiss et al. 1998.
33. Siehe die Rezension von J. Dénes in Vasi Szemle, 54, 2000, 147-150.
34. Über diesen Bautyp berichteten N. Hofer und M. Krenn auf der 11. Castrum Bene Konferenz im Jahre 2009, siehe Castrum, 10, 2009, 21.
35. Bakay 1996; Feld 2006. Der Grundriss der Burg zuletzt: Feld 2012, 166, Abb. 9.
36. Fekete 2007.
37. Nach der Bauaufnahme von A. Klaar sollte ein Teil der Außenmauer noch aus dem Mittelalter stammen: Prickler 1972.

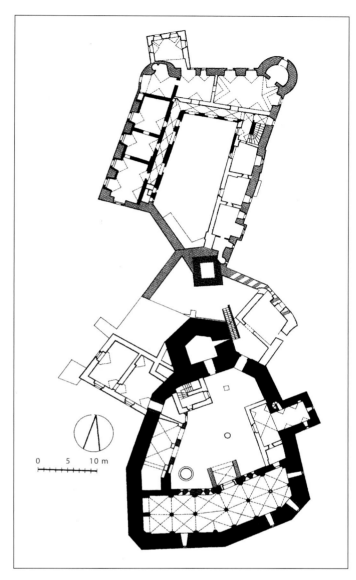

Abb. 8 – Lockenhaus. Grundriss der Burg mit Markierung der ältesten Bauphase. Unpublizierte Zeichnung von M. Feld.

hin. Es handelt sich hier um eine, auf einem 30 x 30 m großen unregelmäßigen Grundriss errichtete Anlage mit großem Turm, Palast und Kapelle, die in dem westlichen Mitteleuropa als typische Adelsburg gelten würde. Ihr architektonischer Reichtum findet zwar kaum Parallelen in anderen Gebieten des Königreiches – solche Details kommen nur bei den großen königlichen Bauten des 13. Jahrhunderts, in Spissky Hrad (Zipser Burg) oder in Visegrád vor –; das kann aber kaum als eindeutiger Beweis für eine landesherrliche Gründung dienen. Weiterführende Angaben lassen sich aber nur von Grabungs- bzw. Bauforschungen erwarten[38].

In der ungarischen Forschung wird neuerdings die Frage diskutiert, in wie weit die einfachen, in den Quellen oft nicht erwähnten Befestigungsanlagen des (12.-)13. Jahrhunderts wirklich als Burgen, und nicht als siedlungsnahe oder -innere Herrenhöfe zu interpretieren sind. Diese Möglichkeit ist im Falle des erwähnten Baus von Gór nicht auszuschließen. Gleiches gilt für Kobersdorf (Kabold) im Burgenland, wo die herrschaftliche Anlage von Pósa aus dem Geschlecht Szák 1229 nicht als *castrum* (= Burg) sondern als *castellum* (= Schloss im spätmittelalterlichen Wortgebrauch in Ungarn) bezeichnet wurde. Dieses Gebäude sucht man auf dem Gebiet des heutigen Renaissance-Schlosses, wo aber bisher noch keine systematischen Grabungen durchgeführt wurden[39]. Die für uns bisher bekannten Angaben reichen noch nicht aus, um eine (in der Wirklichkeit vielleicht nie vorhanden gewesene) eindeutige Grenze zwischen den erwähnten beiden Bautypen zu ziehen.

Wenn wir unsere bisherigen Erörterungen zusammenfassen möchten, kommen wir kaum zu eindeutigen Ergebnissen. Ob die auf der österreichischen Seite erbauten adligen Anlagen wirklich viel früher zu datieren sind als die ähnlichen Bauten auf dem Gebiet der ungarischen Komitate, ist mangels zuverlässiger archäologischer Angaben kaum mit Sicherheit festzustellen. Die schriftlichen Quellen reichen dazu nicht aus, man braucht weitere komplexe bauarchäologische Untersuchungen sowohl bei den bestehenden als auch bei den zerstörten Anlagen. Auch eine vergleichende Auswertung des bisher gewonnenen Fundmaterials könnte zu neuen Ergebnissen führen.

Es ist aber schon heute eindeutig, dass die meisten Adelsburgen auf dem Gebiet des mittelalterlichen Königreiches Ungarn im 13. Jahrhundert, vor allem nach dem Mongolensturm von 1241-1242 errichtet wurden, in einer Zeit, als König Béla IV. oft die Adeligen zum Burgenbau zwang, in der Hoffnung, dadurch der breiten Bevölkerung Schutz zu bieten. Die zu dieser Zeit entstandenen privaten Befestigungen waren aber dafür nicht geeignet, sie dienten vielmehr als Machtstützpunkte, als Herrschaftsbildungskerne ihrer Eigentümer. Die kriegerischen Ereignissen des österreichisch-ungarischen Grenzraumes, die seit etwa 1230 ständig anhaltenden Kämpfe zwischen den ungarischen und österreichischen Herrschern führten dazu, dass fast ein jeder Adelige – aus Sicherheits- wie auch aus Repräsentationsgründen – eine Burganlage für sich erbauen ließ. Endlich konnten sich die größten Burgbesitzer, darunter vor allem die Günser, ab 1270 fast selbständig machen und unabhängig von den „Grenzen"

---

38. *Ibid.*, 91; Fügedi 1977, 161; Schöbel 2005. M. Tóth (Tóth 1974, 76-77) nahm früher nur aufgrund der reichen Bauformen an, dass die Burg erst zwischen 1254 und 1260 als Sitz für den späteren König Stefan V. errichtet wurde.

39. Prickler 1972; Koppány 1999.

mit den Herrschern der benachbarten Gebiete Kämpfe führen oder Frieden schließen. Unter den Auseinandersetzungen ist besonders die sog. „Güssinger Fehde" von 1289 hervorzuheben, bei der der Habsburger Herzog Albrecht wenigstens 30 Burganlagen der Günser und ihrer Verbündeten erobern und zum Teil zerstören konnte. Dieser Feldzug ist – dank des darüber erhalten gebliebenen reichen schriftlichen Quellenmaterials[40] – besonders geeignet, die Burganlagen und ihre Bekämpfungsweise detailliert kennenzulernen. Leider sind die sonst meistens gut identifizierbaren Bauten selbst kaum archäologisch untersucht – eine große Ausnahme stellt die Stadtburg von Kőszeg (Güns) dar[41]. Entsprechend sind die um 1990 durchgeführten ersten umfangreichen Interpretationsversuche[42] nur als der Anfang einer weiteren, über die Typologie hinausreichenden komplexen Untersuchung zu bewerten. Als ein sehr wichtiges Ergebnis ist aber zu nennen, dass über die meisten Anlagen dieser Zeit von den beiden Seiten der heutigen Staatsgrenze moderne Vermessungen zur Verfügung stehen[43].

Zum Abschluss kurz zu der Frage, ob es in der untersuchten Region im 12.-13. Jahrhundert spezielle „Grenzburgen" gab. Für eine eindeutige Antwort benötigt man zweifellos noch weitere Untersuchungen. So sollte z. B. näher analysiert werden, in wie weit es zu dieser Zeit eine zentral gelenkte, vom König organisierte ungarische Grenzverteidigung gab. Wir sind aber der Meinung, dass die bekannten Burganlagen in den oben erwähnten kriegerischen Auseinandersetzungen kaum (oder nur temporär) als Stützpunkte einer direkten Grenzsicherung dienten. Sie spielten vielmehr als Machtfaktoren der verschiedenen Gruppen der Elite auf beiden Seiten der „Grenze" (König, Landesherr, Großadlige, Mittelschicht) eine Rolle[44].

---

40. Zu diesem Thema sind die Aufsätze des Tagungsbandes „Die Güssinger" (Wissenschaftliche Arbeiten aus dem Burgenland, 79, Eisenstadt, Das Landesmuseum, 1989) grundlegend.
41. Holl 1992.
42. Meyer 1989; Meyer 1990.
43. Meyer 1984; Meyer 1990; Vándor 1990; Dénes 2008.
44. Als Beispiel für eine andere, eindeutig historisierende frühere Auffassung: Prickler 1972, 58-59.

Literatur

Bakay K. (1996), *Castrum Kwszug. A kőszegi felsővár és a milléniumi kilátó*, Kőszeg, Kőszeg Városi Múz.

Bóna I. (1998), *Az Árpádok korai várai. 2., erweiterte Auflage*, Debrecen, Ethnica.

Brather S. (2004), *Ethnische Interpretationen in der frühgeschichtlichen Archäologie. Geschichte, Grundlagen und Alternativen*, Berlin/New York, De Gruyter (Reallexikon der germanischen Altertumskunde. Ergänzungsbände; 42).

Bunzl F. (1990), „Burg Güssing, Baugenese und Restaurierung", in *Die Ritter. Burgenländische Landesausstellung 1990. Burg Güssing, 4. Mai-28. Oktober 1990*, H. Prickler (hrsg.), Eisenstadt, Amt der Burgenländischen Landesregierung, Landesarchiv, Landesbibliothek, 176-181.

Buzás G. (2006), „11. századi ispáni várainkról", in *„Gondolják, látják az várnak nagy voltát". Tanulmányok a 80 éves Nováki Gyula tiszteletére*, G. Kovács & Zs. Miklós (hrsg.), Budapest, Castrum Bene Egyesület, 43-54.

Dénes J. (2000), „Az Árpád-kori kisvárak kérdései", *Vasi Szemle*, 54, 55-64.

– (2007), „Vas és Sopron megye középkori várainak kutatástörténete", *Savaria*, 31/2, 8-30.

– (2008), *Vasi várak. Segédanyag helytörténeti kirándulások szervezőinek*, Szombathely, M. Művel. és Ifj. Közp.

– (2011), „Gór, egy feltárt favár (*castrum ligneum*)", in *Várak nyomában. Tanulmányok a 60. éves Feld István tiszteletére*, G. Terei et al. (hrsg.), Budapest, Castrum Bene Egyesület, 43-48.

Fekete M. (2007), „Szentvid vára", *Savaria*, 31/2, 77-156.

Feld I. (2006), „Kőszeg-Óház", *Castrum*, 5, 147-150.

– (2007), „Die Frage der Motten in Ungarn", in *Motte-Turmhügelburg-Hausberg. Zum europäischen Forschungsstand eines mittelalterlichen Burgentypus*, S. Felgenhauer-Schmiedt (hrsg.), Wien, Österreichische Gesellschaft für Mittelalterarchäologie (Beiträge zur Mittelalterarchäologie in Österreich; 23), 289-305.

– (2012), „Die Burgen des Königreiches Ungarn im 11-12. Jahrhundert", in *Château Gaillard 25. L'origine du château médiéval*, P. Ettel, A.-M. Flambard Héricher & K. O'Conor (hrsg.), Caen, Publications du CRAHM, 159-169.

FÜGEDI E. (1977), *Vár és társadalom a 13-14. századi Magyarországon*, Budapest, Akadémiai Kiadó.

GÖMÖRI J. (2002), *Castrum Supron. Sopron vára és környéke az Árpád-korban*, Sopron, Scarbantia Társaság.

– (2007), „A nyugati határvidék korai sáncváriról, különös tekintettel Sopronra", *Savaria*, 31/2, 187-216.

HARDT M. (2000), „Linien und Säume, Zonen und Räume an der Ostgrenze des Reiches im frühen und hohen Mittelalter", in *Grenze und Differenz im frühen Mittelalter*, W. POHL & H. REIMITZ (hrsg.), Wien, Verl. der Österr. Akad. der Wiss. (Forschungen zur Geschichte des Mittelalters; 1), 39-56.

HERVAY J. (2001), „Küszén", in *„Paradisum plantavit". Bencés monostorok a középkori Magyarországon*, I. TAKÁCS (hrsg.), Pannonhalma, Pannonhalmi Bencés Főapátság, 499.

HOFER N. (2007), „Hochmittelalterlicher Burgenbau im ostösterreichischen Flachland", *Savaria*, 31/2, 247-265.

HOFER N. & SAUER F. (2011), *Leithaprodersdorf – von der Frühbronzezeit zum Mittelalter*, Horn, Berger (Fundberichte aus Österreich. Materialhefte, Reihe A, Sonderheft; 16).

HOLL I. (1992), *Kőszeg vára a középkorban: az 1960-1962. évi ásatások eredménye*, Budapest, Akadémiai Kiadó (Fontes archaeologici Hungariae).

HORVÁTH R. (2011), „Várépítés engedélyezése az Árpád-kori Magyarországon", in *Várak nyomában. Tanulmányok a 60. éves Feld István tiszteletére*, G. TEREI et al. (hrsg.), Budapest, Castrum Bene Egyesület, 79-93.

KISS G. (1995), „A 13. századi zalaki vár fatornya", in *Nyugat-Dunántúl népi építészete*, M. CSERI (hrsg.), Szentendre/Szombathely, Szabadtéri Néprajzi Múzeum/Szombathely Savaria Muzeum, 211-217.

KISS G. & TÓTH E. (1987), „A vasvári ‚Római sánc' és a ‚Katonák útja' időrendje és értelmezése", *Communicationes Archaeologiae Hungariae*, 1987, 101-137.

KISS G. et al. (1998), *Szombathely története a város alapításától 1526-ig*, Szombathely, Szombathely Megyei Jogú Város Önkormányzata (Szombathely története; 1).

KOPPÁNY T. (1999), *A középkori Magyarország kastélyai*, Budapest, Akadémiai Kiadó (Művészettörténeti Füzetek; 26).

KRENN M. et al. (2009), „Güssing", *Fundberichte aus Österreich*, 47, 14.

KRISTÓ G. (1994), „Gyepű", in *Korai magyar történeti lexikon (9-14. század)*, G. KRISTÓ (hrsg.), Budapest, Akadémiai Kiadó, 242.

KÜHTREIBER K. (2005), „Burg Dunkelstein. Ergebnisse der archäologischen Untersuchungen eines Hochmittelalterlichen Adelssitzes", *Burgen und Schlösser*, 2005/1, 48-51.

KÜHTREIBER K. & KÜHTREIBER T. (1999), „Der Beitrag der Archäologie zur Burgenforschung im südlichen Niederösterreich", in *Österreich im Mittelalter. Bausteine zu einer revidierten Gesamtdarstellung*, W. ROSNER (hrsg.), St. Pölten, Niederösterreichisches Institut für Landeskunde (Studien und Forschungen aus dem Niederösterreichischen Institut für Landeskunde; 26), 205-252.

– (2007), „Frühe Herrschaftsbildung und Burgenbau im südlichen Niederösterreich", *Savaria*, 31/2, 267-285.

KÜHTREIBER K. et al. (1998-2003), *Wehrbauten und Adelssitze Niederösterreichs*, Bd. I-II, St. Pölten, Institut für Landeskunde.

MEYER W. (1984), „Wehranlagen im Burgenland – Gedanken zum gegenwärtigen Stand ihrer Erfassung", *Burgenländische Heimatblätter*, 46, 145-167.

– (1989), „Der Burgenbau zur Zeit der Herren von (Güssing)-Güns im heutigen Burgenland", in *Die Güssinger. Beiträge zur Geschichte der Herren von Güns/Güssing und ihrer Zeit, 13.-14. Jahrhundert*, H. DIENST & I. LINDECK-POZZA (hrsg.), Eisenstadt, Das Landesmuseum (Wissenschaftliche Arbeiten aus dem Burgenland; 79), 209-352.

– (1990), „Burgenlands Burgenbau vom 13. bis zum 15. Jahrhundert", in PRICKLER 1990 (hrsg.), 112-123.

POHL W. et al. (2008), *Eastern Central Europe in the Early Middle Ages. Conflict, Migrations and Ethnic Processes*, Bucuresti/Braila, Editura Academiei Române/Istros (Florilegium magistrorum historiae archaeologiaeque Antiquitatis et Medii Aevi; 3).

PRICKLER H. (1972), *Burgen und Schlösser im Burgenland*, Wien, Birken-Verlag.

SALLAI J. (2002), „A gyepürendszer térképe", in *Központok és falvak a honfoglalás és kora Árpád-kori Magyarországon*, J. CSEH (hrsg.), Tatabánya, Tatabányai Múzeum (Tatabányai Múzeum/Tudományos füzetek; 6), 273-282.

SCHÖBEL J. (2005), „Burg Lockenhaus", in *Die Kunstdenkmäler des politischen Bezirkes Oberpullendorf*, J. SCHÖBEL, U. STEINER & P. SCHRÖCK (hrsg.), Horn, Berger (Österreichische Kunsttopographie; 56), 356-412.

Takács M. (2006), „A Ménfőcsanak-Szeles dűlői lelőhelyen 1990-91-ben feltárt Árpád-kori veremházak", *Arrabona*, 44/1, 537-567.

Thorma B. (2008), „Das Kriegswesen der Ungarn im Spiegel der Schlacht bei Pressburg im Jahre 907", in *Im Schnittpunkt frühmittelalterlicher Kulturen. Niederösterreich an der Wende vom 9. zum 10. Jahrhundert*, R. Zehetmayer (hrsg.), St. Pölten, Niederösterreichisches Institut für Landeskunde (Mitteilungen aus dem Niederösterreichischen Landesarchiv; 13), 169-193.

Tiefengraber G. (2007), „Zum Burgenbau im Oststeiermark", *Savaria*, 31/2, 285-306.

Tóth M. (1974), *Árpád-kori falfestészet*, Budapest, Akadémiai Kiadó (Művészettörténeti Füzetek; 9).

Vándor L. (1990), „A várépítészet kezdetei Zala megyében", *Castrum Bene*, 1989, 56-67.

Zsoldos A. (2010), „A Henrik-fiak", *Vasi Szemle*, 64, 651-661.

Moated Sites in County Roscommon, Ireland: a Statistical Approach

Thomas Finan*

Moated sites in Ireland have been variously defined as Anglo-Norman lower status agricultural settlements and higher status Gaelic timber fortifications. Graham noted in his article on medieval settlement in Roscommon that there are a number of moated sites that exist in regions where there was no significant Anglo-Norman settlement[1], a fact that has led Kieran Denis O'Conor and Tom Finan, using evidence from Bardic poetry and the historical sources, to argue that these moated sites were in fact constructed by Gaelic lords in the late 13th and 14th centuries[2]. At the same time Tadhg O'Keeffe has cautioned against the idea of assigning ethnic identities to particular monuments, a point actually first made by Graham[3]. Rather than rehash that discussion, this research will apply a different statistical model in an effort to place those moated sites within a particular landscape context. This survey is part of a wider survey of field monuments that will not only consider the morphology of the monuments in question (i.e. the size, dimensions, or materials used to construct them) but will also define the relationship between those monuments and other monuments and landscape features.

An intensive survey of the Dublin region in the Middle Ages has argued that within the context of medieval Dublin and its environs, moated sites are likely more emblematic of Anglo-Norman farmsteads that were not further associated with parish churches or more intensive manorial settlement[4]. Following Tom E. McNeill and Kieran Denis O'Conor, Margaret Murphy and Michael Potterton further postulate that these sites could be the remains of minor Anglo-Norman gentry and prosperous peasant settlement, particularly since the distribution of the sites around Dublin tends towards the more marginal hinterlands near the region's borders[5].

Ringworks and mottes have arguably been used to designate likely Anglo-Norman settlement, but the same cannot be said of moated sites. The pattern of distribution of moated sites throughout Roscommon in particular does not match known Anglo-Norman settlement. While the argument of Tom Finan and Kieran Denis O'Conor in a study of the moated site at Cloonfree (i.e. that many of these moated sites may in fact be suggestive of high status Gaelic settlement) holds in relation to the distribution of known moated sites in Roscommon, the distribution is still vexing[6]. Their distribution reflects a general lowland orientation. They do not seem to respect the differences in soil type in the county, with an equal distribution of sites being located on soil with poor drainage towards bog, as well as on soil that is well drained and ideal for agriculture. 30 of the 53 moated sites are located within 100 metres of the medieval road network into and out of Roscommon or are beside navigable rivers. In short, the pattern of settlement of moated sites in the Dublin and Roscommon regions are vastly different.

The other notable issue with moated sites is that in an Anglo-Norman context they are generally seen as agricultural centres within frontier settlements[7]. They are not really defensive, or, perhaps more precisely, they are not militaristic in nature. They were not constructed by high status Anglo-Norman lords, and many may even have been built

---

* Assistant professor of History, Associate director of the Center for Medieval and Renaissance Studies, Saint Louis University, United States.
1. Graham 1988.
2. O'Conor 2000, 92-96.
3. O'Keeffe 2004, 3-9.
4. Murphy & Potterton 2012, 202-207.
5. *Ibid.*, 202-203; McNeill 1997, 148-149; O'Conor 1998, 61-62.
6. Finan & O'Conor 2002, 72-87.
7. O'Conor 2000, 93-94.

by higher status peasants brought to Ireland in the early 13th century, mainly from Western England or the English settlements in South Wales. Yet the same structure built by a Gaelic lord (as at Cloonfree in the early 14th century) takes on the characteristics of a militaristic sort of settlement. In the poems describing Cloonfree, the features that are most impressive are the timber towers, walls, and battlements that would actually seem to make it more comparable to a very well defended motte. There is very little discussion in the poems about the economic sustenance of the moated site, so we don't find a good picture of whether the site was used as an agricultural centre or not.

For this study the moated sites of Roscommon were assembled in a geodatabase, and were then clustered using the Ward Method. The best-fit model created 5 types of clusters based upon the means of several different measurable categories. Archaeologists are familiar with the notions of clustering and nearest-neighbour analysis in so far as it relates to defining whether artefacts and features are grouped in a particular manner in the archaeological landscape. The drawback to these basic procedures is that they are effectively uni-dimensional, and cannot consider weighted or multiple variables in the computation. Cluster analysis has been used to study the Irish ringfort with some success by Matthew Stout[8]. In this study, the latter placed a sample of ringforts within their likely medieval landscape by bringing together multiple variables such as size and proximity to churches. While Matthew Stout's modelling might be questioned, particularly as it relates to early Irish laws on status and landholding, the method itself provides a much more rigorous model of statistical analysis than has often been appreciated.

The method employed through this study is the Ward Method of Clustering within the SPSS Statistical Package. The Ward Method is often used in archaeological analysis because it tends to assume that examples *should* be placed within a cluster, while other methods might tend towards assuming that examples should be independent. The Ward Method is effective in an archaeological context because of the presumption that archaeological features identified as a given type are actually similar. This clustering model simply defines how similar they actually might be. This also means that the groupings in the Ward Method tend to be larger than other methods, which is an acceptable by product of the method. The Hierarchical Clustering method begins by taking examples and putting them with other examples, until the clusters themselves represent a statistically significant grouping based upon the mean of particular variables that define that cluster. Therefore it is possible, for instance, to imagine 2 clusters with similar mean interior areas, but the first cluster might be more remote and the second cluster could be more centrally located.

The moated sites in Roscommon broke down into 5 clusters, with the most significant factors in the clustering being the internally enclosed area, the distance to a church, and the distance to a transportation network. The other factors considered (soil quality, shape and elevation) were not as significant, while the distance of the moated site from the townland centre was of mixed significance. Upon consideration of the spatial distribution of the moated sites in relation to other monument types, another category was added, distance to crannog, which proved to be a further significant factor in the location of several of the clusters.

Cluster 1 moated sites are of average size internally relative to the other clusters. They tend to be located more towards the borders of the townlands within which they are found, but these 30 moated sites are more characterized by proximity to transportation and proximity to a crannog. The Cluster 2 moated sites are nearly identical in mean values except that they are located at a much greater distance on average to transportation networks. So, in short, they are more remote, but nevertheless of similar size to Cluster 1. The Cluster 3 moated sites are also very distant from transportation networks, but they are also on average very remote from crannogs. The final 2 clusters (consisting of a total of 8 moated sites) were across the board more remote than even the Cluster 3 moated sites, but were also the smallest on average (figs. 1 & 2).

Kieran Denis O'Conor has argued that in some cases these moated sites in Roscommon are likely to be some of the *longphorts* mentioned in the Irish Annals, and, perhaps more importantly, that the moated site at Cloonfree (a Cluster 1 moated site in this study) is a known high-status Gaelic settlement[9]. The bulk of Cluster 1 moated sites are found in the central part of the King's Cantreds extending into Moylurg, and from all accounts these regions were never settled by Anglo-Normans. Hence, it would seem that, again, Kieran Denis O'Conor, Tom Finan and Brian J. Graham are correct in noting that there is no doubt that these moated sites (like the one at Cloonfree) were constructed by Gaelic lords, and not Anglo-Normans or, for that matter, English tenants of the latter.

The other important issue to consider is that while the moated site at Cloonfree was described in somewhat militaristic terms in Bardic poetry, such descriptions are potentially hyperbolic, and we may lose sight of the true nature of these Gaelic moated sites. Another site mentioned in the Irish Annals, the moated site on the shores of Lough Key facing the Rock of Lough Key (the island fortress that functioned as the centre of the powerful MacDermot lordship of Moylurg), appears to have been the principal settlement within a market town of some sort, and at least a hub for economic activity in relation to the main lordly site on the Rock[10]. This moated site at Rockingham is also one of these Cluster 1 moated sites. None of these moated sites has been excavated, so it is very

---

8. Stout 1991, 201-210.
9. O'Conor 1998.

10. O'Conor *et al.* 2010, 15-40.

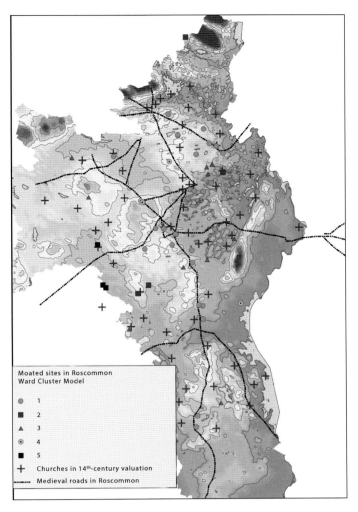

Fig. 1 – Moated sites in Roscommon – Ward Cluster Model.

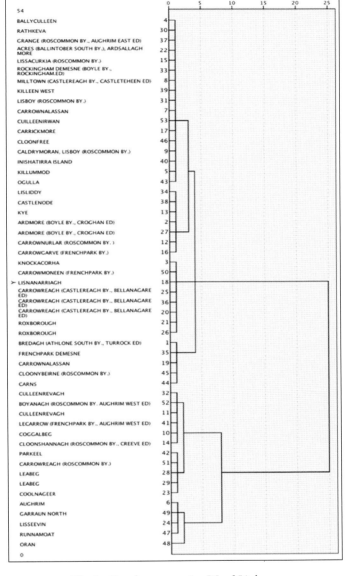

Fig. 2 – Dendrogram using Ward Linkage.

difficult to reach any conclusions about how these features functioned within Gaelic society. If we trust the Annals, some of these sites were in fact used as semi-permanent military settlements on the part of higher status Gaelic lords. As at Lough Key, the moated site associated with the Rock may be seen as the landward component of a lordly settlement, and this connection between moated site and crannog or island or *inis*-type settlement needs to be explored in greater detail. As well, some of these sites may have been constructed earlier in the 13th century than Cloonfree, which was likely built at the very end of the 13th or beginning of the 14th century[11]. For instance, in 1230, after one of the major de Burgo raids into North Roscommon, the "Foreigners of Ireland" (i.e. an Anglo-Norman force) retreated south-westwards from Slieve Anieren in modern County Leitrim to the shores of Lough Key[12]. It could just as easily be the case that the Anglo-Normans stopped at Lough Key because it was a convenient half-way-point on the route to Elphin and Roscommon; however, they stayed at this location for 9 days celebrating. There is no mention of MacDermot countering this stop near Lough

---

11. FINAN & O'CONOR 2002, 74.

12. FREEMAN 1944, 39.

Key, but we might assume the army would have needed provisioning of some sort for that nine-day block, and it would therefore seem likely that the provisioning came from some type of settlement on the shores of the lake. The Rockingham moated site is a likely location for that spot.

By using the Hierarchical Clustering Method this article has placed moated sites within a wider landscape context, and hence argues that this kind of landscape might be construed as a particularly Gaelic landscape. The moated sites in Roscommon, while morphologically similar to their counterparts in Anglo-Norman regions of Ireland, are very different because of their location and relationship to other monuments in the landscape. A further step to this survey and analysis would be to analyze a smaller sub-set of moated sites and to define the relationships between those moated sites and monuments that have been assumed as early medieval or post-medieval in date. It will likely be the case that these moated sites (which characterise 13th- and 14th-century settlement in a Gaelic context) are economically and socially connected to other forms of Gaelic settlement such as ringforts and ecclesiastical sites. Hence, by drawing these connections, we should be able to redefine the economic and social relationships of Gaelic Roscommon while placing moated sites in the area into their true context as high status Gaelic fortifications.

Bibliography

Finan T. & O'Conor K. (2002), "The Moated Site at Cloonfree, Co. Roscommon", *Journal of the Galway Archaeological and Historical Society*, 54, 72-87.

Freeman A. M. (ed.) (1944), *The Annals of Connacht*, Dublin, Dublin Institute for Advanced Studies.

Graham B. J. (1988), "Medieval Settlement in County Roscommon", *Proceedings of the Royal Irish Academy*, 88c, 19-38.

McNeill T. E. (1997), *Castles in Ireland. Feudal Power in a Gaelic World*, London/New York, Routledge.

Murphy M. & Potterton M. (2012), *The Dublin Region in the Middle Ages. Settlement, Land-Use and Economy*, Dublin, Four Courts Press.

O'Conor K. D. (1998), *The Archaeology of Medieval Rural Settlement in Ireland*, Dublin, The Royal Irish Academy (Discovery Programme Monographs; 3).

– (2000), "The Ethnicity of Irish Moated Sites", *Ruralia*, 3, 92-101.

O'Conor K. D. *et al.* (2010), "The Rock of Lough Cé", in *Medieval Lough Cé: History, Archaeology and Landscape*, T. Finan (ed.), Dublin, Four Courts Press, 15-40.

O'Keeffe T. (2004), *The Gaelic Peoples and their Archaeological Identities, AD 1000-1650*, Cambridge, University of Cambridge.

Stout M. (1991), "Ringforts in the South-West Midlands of Ireland", *Proceedings of the Royal Irish Academy*, 91c, 201-243.

Les derniers acquis des recherches sur le Château Ganne

◆

Anne-Marie Flambard Héricher*

À LA LIMITE DES DÉPARTEMENTS du Calvados et de l'Orne, sur l'actuelle commune de La Pommeraye[1], au sud de Caen[2] et 20 kilomètres à l'est du château ducal de Falaise[3] se dressent les vestiges du Château Ganne, possession, au Moyen Âge central, des seigneurs de La Pommeraye[4]. Le site qui a été abondamment décrit par les Antiquaires au milieu du XIXe siècle n'avait jamais été l'objet de recherches scientifiques : sa morphologie et son organisation restaient inconnues, à l'image de la famille dont il dépendait, peu présente dans les sources normandes.

Les toutes premières recherches, entreprises principalement dans la documentation écrite, ont été présentées au colloque « Château Gaillard » d'Houffalize en 2006[5]. Quant aux résultats préliminaires des fouilles, ils ont été évoqués lors d'une communication présentée au colloque « Château Gaillard » de Stirling en 2008, dont le thème a permis d'évoquer la légende attachée aux lieux.

Le château est un site fossoyé bien conservé composé de trois enceintes successives. La basse cour principale, qui constitue l'enceinte intermédiaire, est fouillée depuis 2004[6]. Les recherches ont permis de mettre au jour dans ce périmètre protégé par un rempart de terre surmonté d'une courtine, des bâtiments et aménagements aux fonctions bien identifiées (chapelle, bâtiment domestique avec fournil, cuisine et deux résidences successives, éléments de fortification) et de préciser leur chronologie. Les toutes premières installations : constructions sur poteaux et premiers bâtiments sont édifiés dès le Xe siècle, les bâtiments se multiplient durant les trois siècles suivants avant l'abandon du site au début du XIVe siècle.

La haute cour et la tour porche – de dimensions et d'un type exceptionnels –, qui permet d'y pénétrer, restent à étudier dans le détail et à dater.

Au terme de ces huit années de fouille, il est possible de faire le point sur l'ensemble des résultats obtenus. Dans ce but, il est nécessaire de rappeler brièvement les acquis de la première tranche de travaux qui n'ont pas été remis en question par les découvertes suivantes – ils concernent les constructions situées au nord de la basse cour – puis de présenter les résultats des quatre dernières années de recherches qui portent sur le sud de la basse cour. En conclusion, nous aborderons les questions qui se posent encore au sujet du site ; nous nous interrogerons notamment sur l'organisation et le rôle de la haute cour.

1. Les constructions situées au nord de la basse cour (fig. 1)

Le Château Ganne, qui tire son nom actuel de la légendaire *Chanson de Roland*, a été implanté dans une région au relief fortement accidenté, au contact du Massif armoricain et du Bassin parisien. Des plissements importants ont créé des reliefs vifs qui ne sont pas sans rappeler les paysages de montagne, d'où le nom « Suisse normande » habituellement donné à la région. Il est difficile d'imaginer l'aspect du château primitif mais le choix de son emplacement, sur une barrière rocheuse longue et étroite dominant de plus de 50 mètres les voies de circulation voisines, révèle le rôle défensif qu'on entendait

---

* Professeur émérite d'archéologie et histoire médiévales, GHRIS (EA 3831)/CRAHAM (UMR 6273), université de Rouen, France.
1. Canton de Thury-Harcourt, département du Calvados, France.
2. Département du Calvados, France.
3. Département du Calvados, France.
4. FLAMBARD HÉRICHER 2010a, 94, fig. 1.
5. FLAMBARD HÉRICHER 2006, 139-148.
6. FLAMBARD HÉRICHER 2010a.

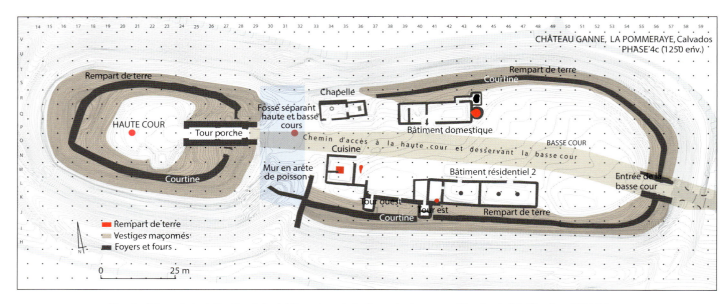

Fig. 1 – Plan général du site et des bâtiments qui s'y dressaient en 1250. Dessin A.-M. Flambard Héricher.

lui faire jouer. Cette installation a nécessité un très important aménagement du terrain pour créer vers le sud une terrasse artificielle appuyée sur l'arête rocheuse qui correspond à la partie nord du site. Au fil du temps, les travaux se sont multipliés visant à conserver, consolider et élargir cette terrasse dominant le fossé creusé au sud, pour isoler le château et assurer sa défense.

La basse cour principale, longue de 150 mètres, était divisée en deux dans le sens de la longueur par le chemin qui reliait l'entrée de la basse cour à la tour porche. Cette dernière contrôlait l'entrée sur la haute cour (fig. 1). Après avoir franchi une première entrée donnant sur la basse cour, le visiteur traversait un espace ouvert, où aucune trace de bâtiment n'a pu être mise en évidence, qui constituait la cour du château. Face à lui, de part et d'autre du chemin, se dressaient deux alignements d'édifices : au nord c'était d'abord un bâtiment domestique, puis, après un intervalle dépourvu de construction, une chapelle.

1.1. Le bâtiment domestique (fig. 2)

La fouille du bâtiment domestique, dont le plan avait été mis en évidence en 2006, a été achevée en 2007 et celle du puits qui le flanque, en 2008.

Les vestiges les plus anciens découverts à cet emplacement sont des structures en creux et un foyer. Ce dernier était inscrit dans un arc de cercle formé par une rigole creusée dans le rocher et débouchant dans deux fosses. Sa fonction était clairement de protéger le foyer des eaux de ruissellement. Au nord de cet aménagement quatre trous de poteau alignés, partiellement recouverts par le mur postérieur, ont été découverts. On peut supposer qu'ils appartenaient à un aménagement destiné à supporter une toiture abritant le foyer. Une datation ^{14}C a permis d'en faire remonter la construction à la fin du Xe siècle[7].

Dans la phase finale (XIIIe siècle), deux portes s'ouvraient dans le mur de façade (mur latéral sud). La porte orientale donnait sur une large pièce avec, en pignon, à l'est, un vaste four saillant. Le mur latéral nord était percé d'une ouverture étroite permettant d'accéder à un couloir longeant le bâtiment pour aboutir à une petite construction quadrangulaire, accolée à l'angle nord-est du bâtiment, qui, extérieurement, voisinait avec le four. Cette petite construction, dépourvue d'ouverture donnant sur l'extérieur, abritait un puits dont l'usage, dans la dernière phase d'occupation, était réservé aux occupants du bâtiment. Un plancher, posé sur des lambourdes fichées dans les quatre angles de la maçonnerie et percé d'une ouverture centrale, permettait de puiser l'eau. La seconde pièce, qui occupait l'extrémité occidentale du bâtiment, était plus petite que celle que nous venons de présenter. Dans la dernière phase d'occupation elle était divisée en deux par un refend sud-nord, appuyé contre le mur latéral sud et laissant un passage auprès du mur nord de la pièce. La petite pièce du fond, au sol très propre, devait servir de zone de stockage tandis que la pièce précédente, au sol jonché de débris culinaires, de débris de céramique et d'objets métalliques, semble avoir été utilisée comme zone d'habitat et comme zone de travail. C'est à cette époque que la terrasse et la courtine semblent avoir été aménagées nécessitant, pour maintenir les terres, la construction du couloir et du petit édicule qui protège le puits.

La stratigraphie, le mobilier métallique et l'étude de la céramique permettent de définir quatre périodes d'occupation. La première doit se situer au début du Xe siècle, elle se traduit par des structures creusées dans le rocher, la deuxième, qui voit

---

7. Datation AMS ETH-34442 : probabilité que la date calibrée soit située entre 733 cal AD et 985 cal AD, 100 %.

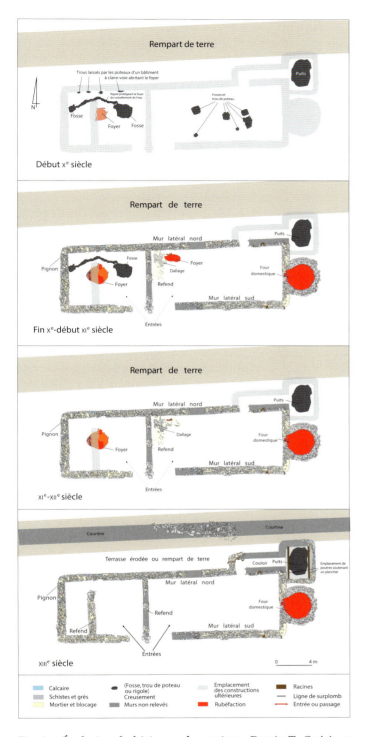

Fig. 2 – Évolution du bâtiment domestique. Dessin T. Guérin et A.-M. Flambard Héricher.

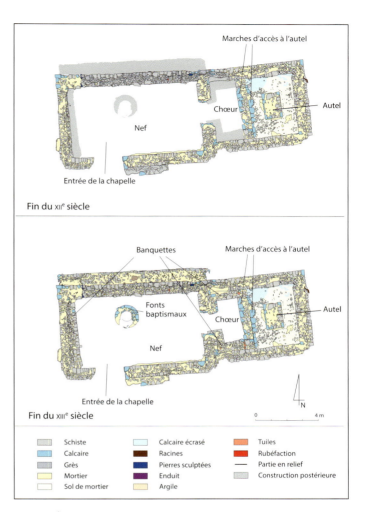

Fig. 3 – Évolution de la chapelle. Dessin T. Guérin et A.-M. Flambard Héricher.

1.2. La chapelle (fig. 3)

On trouve la trace de la chapelle dans le cartulaire de l'abbaye du Val, fondée en 1125 par Gosselin de La Pommeraye. C'est, en effet, le seul bâtiment du château mentionné par les textes. La chapelle est citée à trois reprises : en 1167, 1254-1261 et 1273 dans trois confirmations des biens donnés à l'abbaye[8]. Si elle n'apparaît pas dans la charte initiale, alors que de nombreux édifices religieux sont mentionnés, c'est probablement qu'elle n'existait pas encore. La présence, dans le mur latéral nord, de

les premiers aménagements (renforcement ou construction du rempart) tout en conservant une partie des structures en creux, correspond aux Xe-XIe siècles. La troisième voit l'édification des bâtiments maçonnés aux XIe-XIIe siècles et la quatrième correspond à l'aménagement simultané de la terrasse et de la courtine au début du XIIIe siècle.

---

8. ARNOUX 2000b, 207-237 et 347-362, ainsi que ARNOUX 2000a, 5-64 et plus particulièrement 28 : acte n° 5, daté de 1167 (Henri, évêque de Bayeux, ratifie la donation par le jeune Henri de La Pommeraye des églises qu'il possédait tant en Angleterre qu'en Normandie), p. 37, n° 20, 1254-1261 (confirmation des biens de l'abbaye par le pape Alexandre IV : parmi ces biens se trouve la chapelle du château de La Pommeraye), et p. 38, n° 23 (Grégoire X confirme les biens et possessions de l'abbaye y compris cette chapelle). Voir aussi FLAMBARD HÉRICHER 2005, 615-633.

pierres sculptées romanes en remploi, provenant, très probablement, de la première *aula* détruite, confirme cette hypothèse[9].

Le plan de la chapelle n'a pas varié au fil du temps. L'unique entrée perçait le mur gouttereau sud et donnait accès au bas de la nef rectangulaire, séparée du chœur, plus étroit, par un arc triomphal. Le long du mur pignon de la nef s'allongeait une banquette maçonnée basse[10] qui permettait aux fidèles de s'asseoir. À proximité de cette banquette, dans l'angle nord-ouest, on observait la trace de fonts baptismaux identifiables à la présence d'un cercle de pierres en calcaire taillé, de 1,48 mètre de diamètre, entourant un arrachement de forme circulaire imprimé dans le rocher, de 0,66 mètre de diamètre. Leur présence suggérait que la chapelle pouvait avoir un statut paroissial, mais, bien que des recherches aient été effectuées, aucun texte, à notre connaissance, ne mentionne ou ne laisse entendre que la chapelle du château avait ce statut.

À l'autre extrémité de l'édifice, dans le chœur, deux marches maçonnées menaient à l'autel rectangulaire dont ne subsistaient qu'une à deux assises de pierres. Une banquette périphérique, comparable à celle de la nef, venait s'attacher sur la plus haute marche de l'autel après avoir longé le mur de séparation intérieur et les murs gouttereaux. Le sol était aménagé : tantôt le rocher était aplani, tantôt, pour régulariser le niveau, un lit de mortier, une couche de calcaire écrasé ou encore un rechapage d'argile venaient combler les cavités.

Le décor peint devait occuper une grande place dans la chapelle, tant à l'intérieur qu'à l'extérieur, toutefois peu de traces subsistaient sur les murs, à l'exception de quelques fragments de dimensions très limitées. En revanche, d'innombrables fragments ont été découverts au pied des murs démontrant la présence de motifs peints souvent géométriques, et parfois figuratifs. À l'extérieur, un décor très coloré (rouge et bleu de lapis-lazuli) était probablement visible depuis le pied du château. Certains fragments, montrant deux couches d'enduit superposées portant chacune une couche de peinture, témoignaient de la réfection du décor et de sa transformation[11].

Les murs n'étaient pas conservés sur une hauteur suffisante pour garder la trace des ouvertures qui éclairaient l'édifice. Des pierres calcaires taillées, aux angles soulignés d'un décor peint en rouge, semblent avoir constitué des ébrasements pouvant appartenir à des fenêtres. Il pouvait y en avoir deux de chaque côté de la nef, et sans doute une, de part et d'autre du chœur. Des croisillons de plomb destinés au maintien des vitraux et des morceaux de verre plat, très corrodés en surface et devenus totalement noirs dans l'épaisseur, indiquent que les fenêtres étaient munies de vitrages[12].

Plusieurs blocs de calcaire taillé et sculpté témoignent d'aménagements architecturaux actuellement disparus. Aucun d'entre eux n'a été découvert en place. Certains étaient contenus dans les remblais, d'autres en réemploi dans les murs. Tous se rattachent à la période romane[13].

La stratigraphie, le bâti et le mobilier ont permis d'élaborer une chronologie relative de l'édifice. Trois phases se dessinent ; la première phase n'est que virtuelle. En effet, si les découvertes d'éléments sculptés prouvent l'existence d'un bâtiment à l'architecture soignée dès la fin du XIe siècle, rien ne permet d'affirmer que celui-ci se trouvait à l'emplacement de la chapelle. La mise en évidence, lors des dernières campagnes, du déplacement de l'*aula*, permet de penser que ces éléments sculptés réemployés dans le mur initial de la chapelle peuvent provenir de cette *aula* disparue.

La chapelle a sans doute été construite au XIIe siècle, soit par Henri Ier de La Pommeraye, soit par son fils Henri II, immédiatement avant la confirmation faite à l'abbaye du Val. L'édifice ne possède alors ni banquette, ni fonts baptismaux qui seront ajoutés dans la troisième phase environ un siècle plus tard. Il n'est pas possible de dater avec précision la construction du mur qui vient doubler le mur gouttereau nord mais il faut souligner que ce dernier, bien que de facture extrêmement grossière, était orné de peintures murales richement colorées et particulièrement visibles de l'extérieur.

2. Les constructions situées au sud de la basse cour

Au sud du chemin, au-delà de la partie vide constituant la cour, un long ensemble bâti se dressait de manière continue sur près de 80 mètres de long. En se dirigeant vers la tour porche, le visiteur dépassait successivement : un vaste bâtiment résidentiel, un espace central dévolu aux aménagements défensifs et enfin une très vaste cuisine. La fouille a révélé que l'espace central avait connu d'importants réaménagements probablement dus à des désordres architecturaux imprévus. Du fait de la pente du rocher, tout cet espace a été construit sur une terrasse artificielle difficile à stabiliser – le pendage actuel considérable des assises de pierre de la cuisine montre l'instabilité du sol. Pour cette raison, les travaux entrepris au XIe siècle ont dû avoir pour objectif : autant la stabilisation des terres de soutènement que le renforcement de l'enceinte. La démolition partielle d'un premier bâtiment résidentiel a entraîné le réaménagement de la cuisine, l'installation d'une zone à vocation défensive et la construction d'un second bâtiment résidentiel destiné à remplacer le premier. Nous les découvrirons successivement.

---

9. Flambard Héricher 2005, 623-627 ; Flambard Héricher 2008b, 85.
10. Flambard Héricher 2008a, 127-154 ; Flambard Héricher 2008b, 72-89 ; Flambard Héricher 2009, 129.
11. Flambard Héricher 2008b, 82-83.
12. *Ibid.*, 84-85 ; pour le détail des fragments de plomb recueillis et les indications qu'ils livrent sur le vitrage, voir Flambard Héricher 2012a, 62-66.
13. Flambard Héricher 2010, 97-98 ; Flambard Héricher 2007, 68-69.

2.1. Un bâtiment résidentiel du XIIIe siècle (fig. 4)

Sous le niveau d'occupation peu marqué du bâtiment, des couches riches en mobilier céramique, métallique et osseux, ont été découvertes ainsi que des foyers et de nombreuses traces de charbons situées à des altitudes diverses. Ces artefacts témoignent d'une occupation intense antérieure à la construction du bâtiment. C'est également à cette occupation antérieure qu'il faut rattacher les scories découvertes et l'horizon brun-rouge à forte granulométrie apparu au pied du mur nord. Ce dépôt évoque des déchets de grillage de minerai de fer dont la région est particulièrement riche.

Dans l'espace correspondant aux futures pièces A et B du bâtiment, le rocher sous-jacent plonge rapidement vers le sud. Plusieurs trous de poteau (tous situés sous la pièce A) ont été découverts à sa surface. Ils ont été aménagés dans le rocher et parfois la silhouette du poteau se distinguait nettement dans le comblement. En outre, une rigole a été mise au jour. Elle circonscrivait, dans la pièce B, un dôme rocheux et se prolongeait dans la pièce A en passant jusqu'à l'un des trous de poteau (fig. 4). Aucun réceptacle n'étant présent à l'une ou à l'autre extrémité et en l'absence de pente, il ne peut s'agir d'une rigole de drainage comparable à celle qui a été mise en évidence au nord, dans le bâtiment domestique, mais plutôt d'une tranchée de calage des planches d'une palissade. Faute de niveau d'occupation correspondant à cet aménagement, on ne peut que faire l'hypothèse d'une installation au Xe ou début du XIe siècle.

La phase d'occupation suivante, à la fin du XIe siècle ou au tout début du XIIe siècle, se caractérise par la mise en place d'un important rempart de terre maintenu à sa base, vers le nord, par une rangée de poteaux enfoncés dans le rocher. Un muret nord-sud, rasé pour installer le bâtiment résidentiel, semble avoir servi à maintenir les terres.

Sur le rocher, contre la base du rempart, une très importante scorie coulée a été découverte. En raison de son poids (plus de 30 kg), elle n'a vraisemblablement pas été déplacée à longue distance. Elle confirme l'existence sur le site d'une activité métallurgique contemporaine de l'accumulation du rempart.

Après la démolition des murs nord et est du premier bâtiment résidentiel, le sol est aplani (fin du XIIe siècle ou au début du XIIIe siècle) et l'on édifie un nouveau bâtiment résidentiel de 40 mètres de long comprenant un étage. Tandis que l'étage devait constituer l'*aula* à laquelle on accédait par une porte percée dans le pignon est, le rez-de-chaussée était divisé en trois pièces de dimensions inégales. Celle de l'est devait abriter des réserves tandis que les deux autres avaient peut-être une fonction plus résidentielle. Celle de l'ouest, munie d'une cheminée à contrecœur incurvé, aux murs recouverts d'enduit, devait être un lieu de vie.

Parallèlement à la construction de ce bâtiment, des tours sont installées au sud du mur conservé du bâtiment résidentiel.

C'est au XIVe siècle que, pour compléter la défense, on installe une courtine maçonnée sur le rempart de terre préalablement rehaussé.

2.2. Un premier bâtiment résidentiel (fig. 5)

La densité des structures découvertes au sud-ouest de la basse cour n'a pas permis d'ouvrir de fenêtre suffisante pour mettre en évidence une éventuelle occupation ancienne, contemporaine des bâtiments sur poteaux dont les traces ont été découvertes sous le bâtiment domestique au nord de la basse cour et sous le bâtiment résidentiel du XIIIe siècle. Une longue tranchée nord-sud a cependant été réalisée jusqu'au substrat, mais dans un secteur où les dépôts avaient été décaissés jusqu'au rocher ce qui n'a permis de mettre en évidence que : la forte plongée vers le sud de ce dernier, un replat correspondant à l'assise du mur nord d'un bâtiment résidentiel initial et un unique trou de poteau probablement en lien avec ce même mur.

Dans ce secteur, les vestiges construits découverts correspondent au château de pierre tel qu'il se met en place au début du XIIe siècle sous l'impulsion de Gosselin de La Pommeraye, fondateur de l'abbaye du Val en 1125[14]. Ils se composent de deux bâtiments jointifs, mais dont les façades donnant sur le chemin sont légèrement décalées l'une par rapport à l'autre. Le premier bâtiment est l'ancienne *aula*, le second est la cuisine qui la dessert.

Il ne reste de cette première *aula* que deux murs orthogonaux, liés l'un à l'autre par un arrondi : le mur latéral sud et le pignon ouest, mitoyen avec la cuisine. Le mur latéral sud est remarquable et révèle le statut exceptionnel du bâtiment. Plus large que tous les autres, il est en effet percé sur toute sa longueur de quatre fentes de jour recouvertes d'enduits et de trois portes étroites donnant vers le sud : l'une située au centre, entre les fentes de jour, les deux autres à chacune des extrémités. Ces passages, dont les seuils se situent à des niveaux différents, n'ont pas été conçus dès la construction du mur, mais percés après coup. L'orientation des fentes de jour indique clairement l'existence d'un bâtiment se développant vers le nord. Les tentatives destinées à mettre en évidence le mur gouttereau nord sont restées relativement infructueuses, cependant une pierre calcaire bien appareillée à l'extrémité du mur pignon ouest, le ressaut du rocher et le trou de poteau mentionné plus haut, ont permis d'évaluer la largeur du bâtiment qui atteint 13 mètres hors œuvre. L'emplacement du pignon nord a été mis en évidence grâce à la variation de l'épaisseur du mur latéral sud : l'*aula* mesurait donc 25,70 mètres de long. L'importante élévation encore conservée de l'extrémité est du mur à ébrasements permet d'affirmer que ce premier édifice possédait, tout comme la seconde *aula*, un étage.

La mise en évidence de ce bâtiment peut être rapprochée du tailloir à décor d'étoiles découvert en remploi dans la chapelle toute proche et daté de la fin du XIe siècle ou du début XIIe. Il est très possible qu'il ait fait partie de l'ornementation de l'édifice. Ses dimensions, son organisation, les fentes de

---

14. Arnoux 2000a et 2000b.

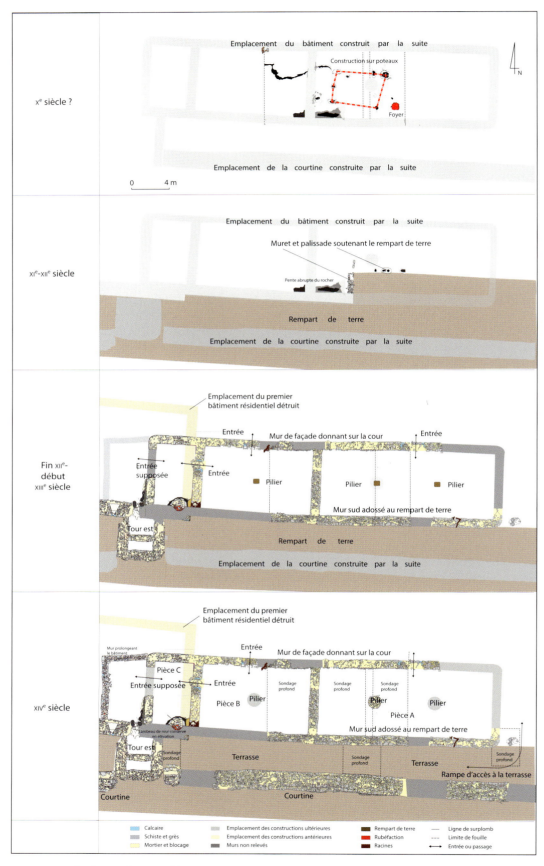

Fig. 4 – Évolution du second bâtiment résidentiel. Dessin T. Guérin et A.-M. Flambard Héricher.

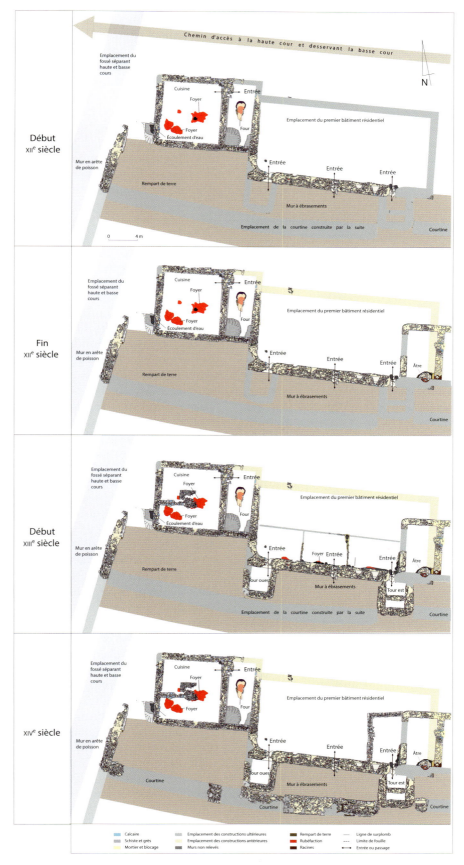

Fig. 5 – Évolution du secteur du premier bâtiment résidentiel et de la cuisine. Dessin T. Guérin, A. Painchault et A.-M. Flambard Héricher.

jour, les enduits muraux confortent l'hypothèse d'un édifice de prestige.

Pour des raisons que la fouille n'a pas révélées mais qui pourraient être des désordres architecturaux liés à l'affaissement de la plateforme de terre supportant la partie sud du bâtiment, celui-ci est partiellement démoli sans doute dès la fin du XIIe siècle. Le mur nord dépourvu de fondation est totalement démonté, le pignon sud, qui s'enfonce profondément vers le sud, est arasé, diminuant peut-être, de ce fait, la partie couverte de la cuisine. Immédiatement après cette démolition, d'importants travaux de soutènement sont entrepris : deux tours sont plaquées contre le mur à ébrasements, elles traversent le rempart de terre et permettent, immédiatement après leur construction, de renforcer le rempart. Toutes deux sont creuses à l'origine, cependant la base de la tour ouest est immédiatement comblée de débris de démolition, de carcasses d'animaux et de cadavres de chiens de chasse appartenant sans doute à une meute, tandis que la tour ouest reste vide, un arc permettant de ménager une petite salle souterraine. Des traces de poutres indiquent, dans les deux cas, la présence d'un plancher au niveau du seuil de l'entrée. Les tours devaient avoir également un rôle défensif, mais rien ne permet de savoir comment leur partie supérieure était aménagée.

Dans le même temps, le mur à ébrasement est transformé en adéquation avec les nouvelles fonctions du secteur : il est percé de portes donnant vers les tours et le rempart tandis que les fentes de jours sont obstruées. Trois petites pièces possédant chacune son foyer sont installées le long du mur. Ce sont des installations légères en bois et torchis.

Enfin dans un dernier temps, au XIVe siècle, ces constructions sont démontées, le rempart de terre est rehaussé et on construit la courtine doublée d'un chemin de ronde. Dans l'angle formé par le mur à ébrasement et le pignon du second bâtiment résidentiel, une petite construction assez grossière et liée à l'argile est installée. Sa fonction reste énigmatique.

2.3. *Une large cuisine (fig. 5)*

Attenante à l'*aula*, la cuisine se présentait à l'origine comme un bâtiment rectangulaire de 14,5 mètres de long sur 10 mètres de large divisé en deux parties inégales par un refend nord-sud. On y accédait par une porte située dans l'angle nord-est. La pièce orientale étroite et allongée abritait un petit four dont la fonction exacte n'a pu être déterminée. Il s'ouvrait vers le sud où se trouvaient deux fosses dépotoir. La pièce occidentale, carrée, était organisée autour de plusieurs foyers centraux. D'importantes traces de rubéfaction et la quantité de mobilier découvert pour toutes les époques montrent qu'elle fut fréquemment et abondamment utilisée. L'arasement du mur est ne modifia en rien le fonctionnement de la cuisine carrée,

mais un peu plus tard, au début du XIIIe siècle, elle connut des modifications importantes avec l'installation d'un foyer central, puis celle d'un demi-refend et d'un nouveau foyer central en dalles de schiste. Un écoulement d'eau ménagé dans l'angle sud-ouest de la pièce permettait de déverser les eaux sales dans une fosse extérieure creusée à la base du rempart de terre.

Les fosses à déchets installées à l'intérieur de la cuisine, le long du mur sud, se sont peut-être accentuées du fait du tassement naturel des terres. L'étude du mobilier qui y a été recueilli donne une bonne idée de l'approvisionnement, des activités et de l'alimentation des habitants d'un château entre le XIIe et le début du XIVe siècle[15].

Conclusion

Avant de conclure de manière définitive sur l'organisation du Château Ganne, on ne peut omettre la dernière enceinte du château, la haute cour (fig. 6). Alors qu'elle constitue le cœur emblématique du monument avec sa tour porche encore bien conservée et ses hauts remparts de terre, sa cour exiguë qui ne dépasse 400 m², dominée par de hauts reliefs, ne laisse guère la place à d'imposants bâtiments. Une fouille aurait été souhaitable mais n'a pas été possible. La prospection radar entreprise pour tenter de détecter d'éventuelles traces de murs n'a rien décelé. Les seules constructions qui ont pu exister devaient donc se situer au pied du rempart de terre et leurs vestiges éventuels peuvent avoir été recouverts par les débris engendrés par l'érosion de ce dernier. Une dépression, au sud, pourrait correspondre à l'emplacement d'une cavité.

Au sommet du rempart de terre se dresse une courtine continue qui semble prendre appui sur la tour porche. Il est tentant de considérer que la courtine a été construite, comme celle de la basse cour, assez tardivement, c'est-à-dire dans la dernière phase d'occupation du site au début du XIVe siècle, mais rien ne permet de l'affirmer[16]. Il n'a pas été possible d'observer le contact entre la courtine et la tour porche en raison des grillages de sécurité installés sur le site. La tour porche elle-même, qui repose sur le rocher, n'a pu être archéologiquement datée. Ses caractéristiques architecturales : l'appareil en arête de poisson et la forme circulaire de la baie qui s'ouvre sur la haute cour[17] plaident en faveur d'une date haute et d'une construction réalisée en une fois, préalablement à l'accumulation du rempart même qui l'enserre. Ces critères permettraient donc d'en situer l'édification dès le XIe siècle, simultanément à l'installation du bâtiment domestique.

Quelle que soit la date à laquelle la courtine est érigée, elle est dotée d'un dispositif qu'il convient de mentionner. Il s'agit d'une ouverture correspondant à une porte ménagée au sommet du rempart, juste à côté de la tour porche. Il est tentant d'y voir une entrée pour les piétons, ce qui suppose

---

15. Borvon 2011, 71-130 ; Bisson 2012, 9-145 ; Painchault 2010, 64-94, et Painchault 2012, 145-191.

16. Flambard Héricher 2011, 42-63.
17. Flambard Héricher 2012, 298-299.

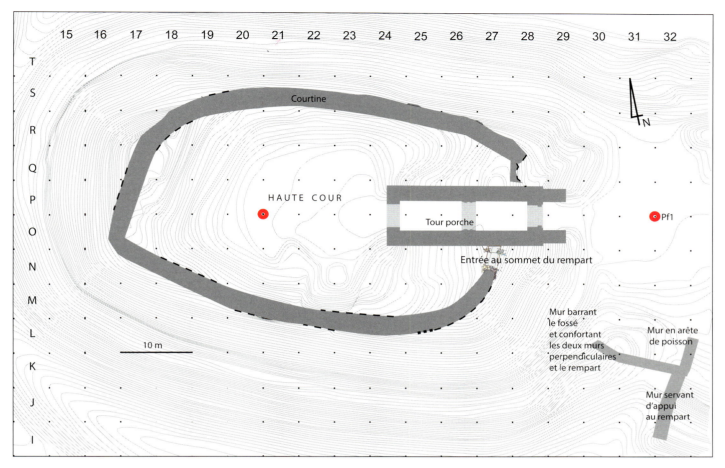

Fig. 6 – Plan de la haute cour. Dessin T. Guérin, A. Painchault et A.-M. Flambard Héricher.

un aménagement de la pente du rempart afin d'y accéder. La tour porche ne présente en effet qu'une entrée monumentale destinée aux chevaux ou aux charrettes, sans accès spécifique pour les piétons. À l'étage, elle devait être divisée en deux parties inégales comme le suggère la disposition des arcs conservés. La fonction précise de ces pièces n'est pas perceptible ; traditionnellement, elles assuraient une fonction de surveillance. La haute cour aurait donc rempli un rôle défensif, servant au stockage des denrées les plus précieuses et à la surveillance des abords du château tandis que la basse cour constituait le véritable lieu de vie du château.

Une reconstitution assez fidèle des bâtiments conservés dans la basse cour et la description de leur évolution sont donc possibles (fig. 7, p. 190). Tandis que l'installation primitive sur le site apparaît relativement ténue et composée de bâtiments de faible prestige, dès le Xe siècle et surtout dès le début du XIe siècle, les constructions maçonnées se multiplient et se différencient les unes des autres. Quoique le château apparaisse à son apogée au début du XIVe siècle, lorsque tous les bâtiments sont édifiés et qu'une courtine maçonnée surmonte le rempart de terre, la période durant laquelle la vie est la plus intense correspond au moment où le premier édifice résidentiel est en usage. Le mobilier piégé sous les niveaux de construction du second bâtiment résidentiel l'atteste[18].

---

18. Bisson 2012, 9-145 ; Painchault 2010, 64-94, Painchault 2012, 145-191, et surtout Painchault 2007, 172-232.

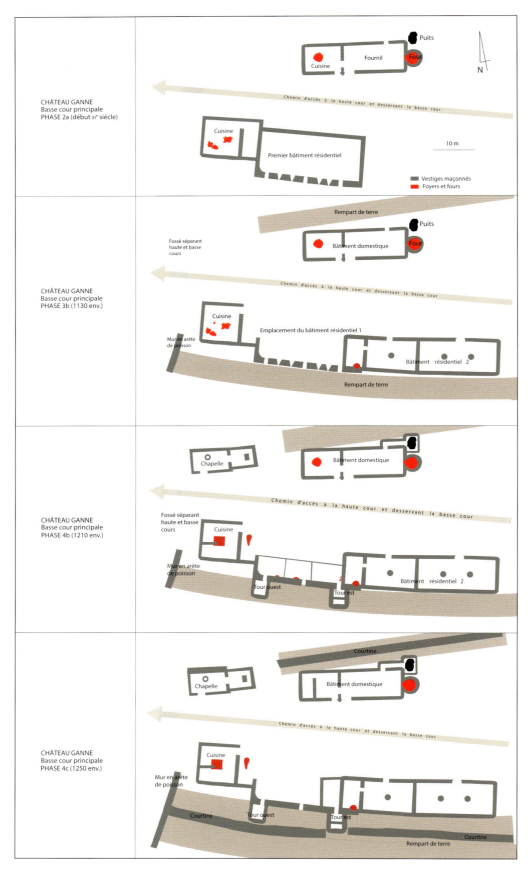

Fig. 7 – Évolution des structures bâties de la basse cour du XIe au XIIIe siècle. Dessin A.-M. Flambard Héricher.

Bibliographie

Arnoux M. (2000a), « Actes de l'abbaye Notre-Dame-du-Val », *Le pays bas-normand*, n° 1-2 [n° 237/238] : *Deux abbayes de Basse-Normandie : Notre-Dame-du-Val et le Val-Richer (XIIe-XIIIe siècles)*, M. Arnoux et C. Maneuvrier (dir.), 5-64.

– (2000b), « L'abbaye Notre-Dame-du-Val aux XIIe et XIIIe siècles », in *Des clercs au service de la réforme. Études et documents sur les chanoines réguliers de la province de Rouen*, M. Arnoux (dir.), Turnhout, Brepols (Bibliotheca victorina ; 11), 207-237 et 347-362.

Bisson É. (2012), « Le mobilier métallique », in Flambard Héricher 2012a, 9-145.

Borvon A. (2011), « L'étude archéozoologique », in Flambard Héricher 2011, 71-130.

Flambard Héricher A.-M. (2005), « Un monde en couleurs. Les enduits peints médiévaux extérieurs du Château Ganne (Calvados) », in *Dieu(x) et hommes. Histoire et iconographie des sociétés païennes et chrétiennes de l'Antiquité à nos jours : mélanges en l'honneur de Françoise Thelamon*, S. Crogiez-Pétrequin (éd.), Mont-Saint-Aignan, Publication des universités de Rouen et du Havre (Publication des universités de Rouen et du Havre ; 379), 615-633.

– (2006), « Les seigneurs de La Pommeraie, le Château Ganne et le peuplement du territoire de La Pommeraye/Saint-Omer (Normandie) au XIIe siècle », in *Château Gaillard 22. Château et peuplement* (Actes du XXIIe Colloque international de Voiron, 28 août-4 septembre 2004), P. Ettel, A.-M. Flambard Héricher et T. E. McNeill (éd.), Caen, Publications du CRAHM, 139-148.

– (2007), « Le Château Ganne à La Pommeraye (Calvados) », rapport de fouille programmée 2005-2007 déposé au Service régional de l'archéologie de Basse-Normandie, 2 vol. (vol. I : 283 p. ; vol. II : 300 p).

– (2008a), « Le Château Ganne à la Pommeraye (Calvados). Bilan des recherches 2004-2007 » (CLXV^e Congrès de Condé-sur-Noireau, 2007), *Annuaire des cinq départements de la Normandie*, 127-154.

– (2008b), *Le Château Ganne. Premiers résultats de la fouille archéologique*, Caen, Publications du CRAHM (Lieux communs).

– (2009), « Le Château Ganne à La Pommeraye à l'époque de la bataille de Tinchebray d'après les premières recherches archéologiques », *Le pays bas-normand*, n°s 271-272 et 273/274 : *Tinchebray 1106-2006* (Actes du Colloque de Tinchebray, 28-30 septembre 2006), V. Gazeau et J. Green (dir.), 123-138.

– (2010a), « Entre légende et réalité : le vrai visage du Château Ganne (La Pommeraye, Calvados) », in *Château Gaillard 24. Château et représentations* (Actes du XXIVe Colloque international de Stirling [Écosse], 30 août-5 septembre 2008), P. Ettel, A.-M. Flambard Héricher et T. E. McNeill (éd.), Caen, Publications du CRAHM, 93-103.

– (2010b), « Le Château Ganne à La Pommeraye (Calvados) », rapport de fouille programmée déposé au Service régional de l'archéologie de Basse-Normandie, 163 p.

– (2011), « Le Château Ganne à La Pommeraye (Calvados) », rapport de fouille programmée pluriannuelle 2008-2010, rapport intermédiaire 2010, déposé au Service régional de l'archéologie de Basse-Normandie, 186 p.

– (2012a), « Le Château Ganne à La Pommeraye (Calvados) », rapport de fouille programmée déposé au Service régional de l'archéologie de Basse-Normandie, 290 p.

– (2012b), « Les représentations du Château Ganne au XIXe siècle : légendes et réalité », *Annales de Normandie*, 62e année, n° 2 : *Mélanges offerts à Catherine Bougy*, 291-301.

Painchault A. (2007), « Étude de la céramique », in Flambard Héricher 2007, 172-232.

– (2010), « Compléments à l'étude de la céramique », in Flambard Héricher 2010b, 64-94.

– (2012), « Les objets non métalliques remarquables », in Flambard Héricher 2012a, 145-191.

The *Burgward* Organisation in the Eastern Marches of the German Realm

Frontier Mentality and Inculturation

◆

Christian Frey*

The relationship of castles and borders was versatile during the Middle Ages. For generations, scholars of disciplines with an historical interest have conducted research on this topic, with very different results. Historical borders and their organisational form were especially the focus of past work; comparisons to their present shape often influenced researchers' results. New findings and methods, however, make it necessary to reconsider older theories. The aim of this paper is to examine the phenomenon of *burgwardi*, an administrative construct that utilised castles to develop lordship in the border region in the German East from the 10th to the 12th century and to rediscuss some of the older research results[1].

How different historical and present concepts of borders can be seen in the development of language. The German word *Grenze*, for example, derives from the Slavonic word *Granize* that was used for the limit or boundary between two agricultural fields[2]. Before it found its way into the German language in the late Middle Ages, there was no word and also no concept of a linear division of areas. And even since its first use, the understanding of the word *Grenze* has evolved, as we learn from Jacob and Wilhelm Grimms' dictionary:

> *während der eigentliche Begriff der grenze im ursprünglichen sinne auf der vorstellung eines raumes diesseits und jenseits der scheidelinie fuszt, entwickelt sich seit dem 18. jh. ein gebrauch, der von dem raum jenseits der grenze mehr oder weniger absieht und das wort so den bedeutungen "schranke, abschlusz, ziel, ende" nähert* [...][3].

Our present understanding of space is significantly influenced by the limits of certain areas – our everyday contact with maps and satellite-pictures shapes our perception. The medieval mind was different. Not only did they lack forms of spatial display, like maps, but also the difference in the conceptual interpretation of lordship and power had a remarkable impact on the landscape. Lordship did not end at abstract lines of conventions, it even was not tied to space itself[4]. Lordship spanned the network of people that formed a certain group – in that implementation it had only an oblique connection to space. Therefore, it had no sharp distinction to its spatial surroundings, it ended in border areas known as marches. Lordship phased and faded out the farther it was from the lord himself.

A very good example for this resulting kind of border situation can be seen in the east of the German realm from the year 800 to about 1200. Here the river Elbe and its tributaries formed the landscape where Saxons and Franks on the western and Slavonic tribes on the eastern side came together. There, personal networks merged and formed a special kind of society, a cultural emulsion, which had a great influence on cohabitation in the marches.

Helmold of Bosau reports on one Count Adolf II that he ruled the tribes of Holsten, Stormarn and the *markomanni*[5]. Helmold states that these *markomanni* are the inhabitants of the borderland. According to his evidence, the latter came from a lot of different places to settle on the frontier. An

---

* TU Braunschweig, Germany.
1. This paper is based on results of my dissertation thesis *Burgen als Handlungsorte im Spannungsfeld der Grenzen im nordöstlichen Elbraum des früheren Mittelalters*, that was submitted in January 2011 to the Technical University of Brunswick, Germany.
2. LexMA, vol. 4, 1700-1701, "Grenze, Grenzbeschreibung".
3. Grimm & Grimm 1991, vol. 9, 134f.
4. Pohl 2000, 16.
5. Helmold von Bosau, *Chronica Slavorum*, 67, 28: "*Fueruntque parentes mandato eius plebes Holzatorum, Sturmariorum atque Marcomannorum. Vocantur autem usitato more Marcomanni gentes undecumque collectae, quae marcam incolunt*".

appropriate translation for the word *markomanni* seems to be "frontiersmen" or, perhaps, "men of the marches". Widukind of Corvey gives another insight of this special group of inhabitants. He writes about the legion of Merseburg:

> This legion was set together by robbers. King Henry was strict with foreigners, but mild with members of his own nation. When he heard of a robber, that he was a brave man and ready for war, he pardoned him, sent him to the castle of Merseburg, gave him weapons and land, ordered him to spare the citizens but to undertake as much raids to the barbarians, as he pleases[6].

This shows that not only settlers from all over the German realm but also violent criminals with a mission were coming to the marches. This type of borderland inhabitants is termed "frontier-warriors" by the German scholar Bertram Turner[7]. He identifies certain aspects of these groups, which are common among all similar frontiers. Avoiding the much stressed frontier-society-theory, which has its origins in the book of Frederick Jackson Turner on settlement in the American West, the frontier-warriors are located on the sill between two different cultures, not at the edge between civilisation and the wild[8]. Bertram Turner discovered that in these societies the level of aggression and violence was high and that its members were establishing their own lordships and trying to become as independent as possible from the centre. The narratives of the borderlands, such as the works of Thietmar of Merseburg, Widukind of Corvey and Helmold of Bosau, tell us the stories of these special spaces – with castles as the places where most of the actions took place.

One of the main features of medieval borderlands was the large number of castles in them. This phenomenon can be observed all over Europe. From Northern and Eastern Saxony to Spain, to England, Scotland, Ireland and Wales: the space between the spaces was highly fortified by castles of all kinds[9].

Based on the observations of the German sociologist Georg Simmel, who stated that the border is a sociological fact that becomes manifest in a spatial way – and not the other way around[10] –, castles were one way to declare the transition from one territory to another. They can be found in large numbers in the borderlands as archaeological sites – and in the medieval historiographic texts that narrate the story of the interactions between the societies of the Middle Ages.

Not only do archaeological findings prove that a landscape was filled with fortifications, but also written sources of that time use castles significantly often as settings for events. The narrated wars mostly took place around castles – and along with the achievements of kings and other great lords, the events at these places fill the biggest part of the historiographic works. All of the texts are full of violent happening in the border-area – here the density of action was much greater than in the main lands. But not only stories of sieges and captures of castles were told, often enough they were used as monuments of the past. Also, castles served as housing for the nobility or as geographical markers and more. The variety of themes about castles in these chronicles was wide.

The reality of war around castles in the border region was different than the older research assumed. The English scholar Robert Liddiard observed that the dense castle network in the northern and western marches of the English realm could not preserve England from being attacked[11]. Aggressors just took a way around to avoid contact with a castle. The same can be stated of the marches in the German East. The dense castle network could not hold back hostile armies from attacking the west; battles like the one at Lechfeld had to be undertaken to avert the danger of invasion[12]. And the mostly wooden fortifications were not always an effective defence: they caught fire easily and burned down fast – as Carl Schuchhardt stated 80 years ago, they died their occupational death[13].

The builders of the castles in the marches were the nobles who had settled in the borderlands. The marches were extremely attractive for the nobility, especially the function of margrave. The margraves became the most powerful group in the borderlands. They fought their own battles, raised their own taxes and tried most of the time to become as independent as possible from royal control[14]. This behaviour often aroused the suspicion of the king, who tried to stabilise his power in the outskirts of his realm, which he badly needed as buffer-zones against the dangers of violence and foreign attacks. But the main interest of the nobles in at the border was a more selfish one: here they could make a fortune. Helmold of Bosau, for example, mentions the greed of the margraves several times. He accuses not only the margrave Dietrich as treating the Slavs badly[15], but also criticises the highly-acclaimed Billunger Bernhard. Helmold says that the latter was corrupted by his own greediness and interfered with the mission, because he raised too high taxes[16].

The great numbers of settler nobility was the cause of the high density of castles in the marches. They built castles as their appropriate housing, demonstrating their status as warriors in a mostly hostile environment. Around those castles administrative districts were established, like everywhere all

---

6. Widukind von Corvey, II/3, 69: "*Erat a namque illa legio collecta ex latronibus. Rex quippe Heinricus cum esset satis severus extraneis, in omnibus causis erat clemens civibus; unde quemcumque videbat furum aut latronum manu fortem et bellis aptum, a debita poena ei parcebat, collocans in suburbano Mesaburiorum, datis agris atque armis, iussit civibus quidem parcere, in barbaros autem in quantum auderent latrocinia exercerent*".
7. Turner 2005.
8. See, for example, Burns 1989, 314f.
9. See, for example, Liddiard 2005, 82; Creighton 2002, 46.
10. Simmel 1958, 467.
11. Liddiard 2005, 23f.; Kenyon 1997, 119ff.
12. See Bowlus 2006.
13. Schuchhardt 1931, 228.
14. Stieldorf 2012.
15. Helmold von Bosau, *Chronica Slavorum*, 16, 33f.
16. Ibid., 18, 38.

over Europe. But only at the eastern border of the *christianitas* were they were named *burgward*.

The creation of administrative districts around castles was nothing new. In fact, it was a common way to establish a new lordship[17]. During the Frankish conquest of Saxony, one can observe the same mechanism of territorial power – for example, at the monastery of Hersfeld, several surrounding castles with all their attached farms and villages were obliged to give tithes to it[18].

The unique term of *burgward* and other observations led to the assumption in the earlier research that during the Ottonian colonisation, a special law was applicable, the so-called "Burgwardverfassung"[19]. But the scholars stating this were never able to support their argument with historical facts – it remained an idea following the "Verfassungsgeschichte" during the 1960s. Nevertheless, a lot of effort was made to find examples of the mechanisms behind castles and their administrative districts. This research showed that a typical *burgward* consisted of 10 to 20 villages, a timber castle as its centre and a network of rights and duties. The distribution area of *burgwardi* ranged from the river Havel in the north to the Sorbic settlements in the south[20].

Walter Schlesinger showed that the tradition had its origins in the Frankish realm. Very early castles there developed as centres that had a network of rights and income. The term *municipium* is one of the first to be used in the written sources for castle districts[21]. They bundled court, dues and rights together; it is known for example that persons in Francia without military obligations had to help in building lordly infrastructure – in the form of castles, bridges or dykes.

Since the 9th century, special rights were given to vassals with the agreement of the margraves in the eastern marches. The recipients had to do guard service or help building castles in return. There was still a significant difference to the core areas of the realm, where the relationship of a village or farm to a castle was fixed in a so-called *Burgbann*. This form of organisation seems to have existed all over the German realm and its parts in similar forms[22].

After the military conquest of the areas by the river Elbe, Slavonic castles were also reused by the Saxons. New dendrochronological evidence shows that these castles had their origins in the 10th century[23]. The old doctrine assumed the building of these castles dated to the time of the Slavonic settlement. The older theories on Slavonic lordship were based on that assumption – and now have to be considered wrong[24]. For example, earlier research came to the conclusion that the *burgward* was some kind of Saxon adoption of a Slavonic conception of lordship and castles. New research, however, shows that the opposite is the case: Slavonic tribes learned to build castles during the contact with the Saxons, and they began to use castles as tools of lordship as well.

One has to assume that *burgward* is a Saxon phenomenon. The word is German in language in the written sources and has no Latin translation. It is only used for castle districts in Eastern Saxony and the marches that have mixed settlement. Its appearance seems to correlate with the situation at the border, similar to the marches.

Since the digital humanities opened the way to new methods of text analysis that were unthinkable before the digitalisation of the medieval written sources, a new approach to old questions can be undertaken. A full search in the DMGH (Digital Monumenta Germaniae Historica) allows an overview on the use of the term *burgward*. Considering all possible forms of writing, all possible forms of declension and possible mistakes in the digitalisation, a truncated search was conducted on the text corpus of the MGH. Covering historiographic, diplomatic and legal sources, one can gain results on a broad basis.

The outcomes of this research were that the first usage of the word *burgward* in the sources was in the middle of the 10th century and its last occurrence was in the 12th century. Only limited use in historiographic texts on the one hand and extended use in diplomatic sources are accompanied by only one use in legal writings. The geographical use of the word was restricted to Eastern Saxony and the marches.

Why is the usage of *burgward* limited to the border region of the east? What makes it interesting to modern castle research?

Originally the term seems not to have meant a lordly castle district. The second part of the Saxon compound *burgward*, the word *-ward/-wart* is the term used for the function of a warden or a steward. This meaning is still alive in the English language. We know this usage from Saxon texts like the Heliand[25]. In this text, written to help in the Christianisation of the pagan Saxons, the stories of the New Testament of the Bible are renarrated and the plot is relocated into a Saxony-like environment. All cities have become castles in that text: *Rûmûburg* is Rome, *Nazarethburg* is Nazareth, *Bethleêmaburg* is Bethlehem and so on. This was done in order to make the story understandable for its audience – cities like the ones in the biblical setting were unknown to the Saxons. In the text, Salomon is the lord of Jerusalem, the warden of the castle: *the burges uuard – Salomon the cunning*[26]. From the function of a warden or steward, the name *burgward* could have spread over the districts belonging to them; the individual-related power structure was transferred from the person to the castle

---

17. CREIGHTON 2002, 89ff.; KERBER 1999.
18. WEIRICH 1936, vol. 1, no. 37: "*cum viculis suis et omnibus locis ad se pertinentibus*".
19. SCHLESINGER 1961, 178.
20. LexMA, vol. 2, 1101-1103.
21. SCHLESINGER 1961, 160ff.
22. *Ibid.*, 177.
23. HENNING 2002, 132.
24. See, for example, SCHLESINGER 1961, 176.
25. See SCHUCHHARDT 1913, 351-357.
26. BEHAGEL 1984, 65.

and its district and took the name with it. Also as a man's name, we find *Burgward* or something like this – this is also an indication for its origin.

It is charters that hold the most information about *burgwardi* – here the trading of the districts or rearrangement of rights are chartered. The first mentioning of the term can be found in a charter that was issued on April 23, 961, in Wallhausen. From that time on, the term had a firm position in the repertoire of the notaries in the royal chancellery. Mostly complete districts were denoted in that manner, the allocation of rights inside a certain *burgward* was less common, but not unusual.

While the most legal sources do not mention *burgward* as a definition, only one single use can be found. The Sachsenspiegel, Lehnrecht 65, § 22 orders a lord to take a *burgward* from his liege in case of a fight, because it is a higher fief than a village or farm:

> De herre scal sek underwinden des gudes dat deme manne verdelet is, sunderleke swar it leget. Sint dar aver dorp oder huve de in ene borchwart oder in enen hof horet, swar de herre sek des hoves underwint, dar mede hevet he sek underwunden al der huve unde al der borchwere de in den hof horet[27].

We can see that it had a place in feudal law and it had a certain definition; the singularity of its use, however, makes further interpretations impossible.

A charter of the year 961 gives more insight into the contemporary definition of a *burgward*[28]. Luckily this charter has survived in two different versions. The first version names a *burgward* called Zpuitneburg and all the rights that belonged to the castle[29]. The second version of the charter offers a different and shorter version. Here only the castle with all its benefits is mentioned[30]. Both versions mean one thing – the *burgward* of Zpuitneburg. Although the versions differ in wording, we can see that *burgward* in that time meant everything that belonged to the castle – a feudal unit that could be given. The term *municipium* here is used as a synonym to *burgward*, we can assume no significant difference between them. But why is the term *burgward* then in use? What makes it special and applicable for the border region?

Another charter, also available in two versions, allows an answer to that question. The charter gives the tithe of the Slavs in the districts of the castles of Magdeburg, Frohsa, Barby and Calbe to the monastery of the Holy Mauritius in Magdeburg:

> […] *Omnibus sanctae dei ecclesiae fidelibus nostrisque presentibus scilicet et futuris notum sit, qualiter nos ob amorem dei regnique aeterni mansionem, insuper etiam pro salute nostra ac stabilitate regni remidioque anime nostre dilecteque nostre coniugis Adelheidae atque amantissime prolis et aequivoci nostri Ottonis ad sanctum Mauricium in Magadaburg donavimus atque tradidimus decimam quam Sclavani ad eandem urbem Magadaburg pertinentes persolvere debent, nec non et etiam omnium Sclavanorum decimam ad civitatem Frasa pertinentium, insuper etiam et illam decimam quam Sclavani persolvere debent ad Barbogi civitatem pertinentes, similiter etiam omnem decimam Sclavanorum ad civitatem que dicitur Caluo pertinentium ex integro donamus atque tradimus ad sanctum Mauritium in Magadaburg. Hoc instantissime iubemus ut omnes Sclavani qui ad predictas civitates confugium facere debent, annis singulis omnem addecimacionem eorum plenissime ad sanctum Mauritium persolvant* […][31].

The second version extends this donation by the tithe of the German population in the *burgwardi*. The separation of both cultural groups makes *burgwardi* unique. While the German population was growing by settlement of farmers from the western parts of the realm, the Slavonic population had to suffer from being displaced, sold or murdered. Thietmar of Merseburg gives an insight into the situation of the Slavs in his times, by commenting on the property of Merseburg. This was "spread miserably, like Slavonic families, that were accused and dispersed by being sold"[32].

The castles had also another function for the surrounding villages and farms. The population, both Slavonic and German, had to work at fortifying the castles. In return, the castles granted safety to both groups in times of war, and this had an explicit validity for the Slavs: "*omnes Sclavani qui ad predictas civitates confugium facere debent*" had to give the tithe in the aforementioned charter[33].

In conclusion, the castles in the marches rearranged their surrounding landscapes[34]. While earlier research assumed a mainly military function for the *burgwardi* in terms of frontier guarding[35], we now can see a different picture. Castles in the marches were the centres of the local communities[36], more than they were in other parts of the medieval realms. Here different population groups came together for events that stimulated community building, like markets, court days or church service. This was in effect for all groups living in the marches, Saxons, Slavs or *markomanni* alike.

Since the Hungarian wars and the efforts in castle building of Henry I, the benefits of castles and their effect on communities was well known to the *potentes*. The fortifications were constructed to shelter the *agrarii miltes* from the attacks of Hungarian riders. Along with the kingly order to build these

---

27. Eckhardt 1956, 90.
28. Sickel 1879, no. 222, 304ff.
29. "*Municipium etiam vel burgwardum urbis Zpuitneburg in pago Nudzici site cum omnibus ad eadem urbem iure et legaliter pertinentibus*".
30. "*Urbem Zputinesburg sitam in pago Nudzici cum omnibus que ipse in beneficium habet*".
31. Sickel 1879, no. 232A, 318.
32. Thietmar von Merseburg, *Chronicon*, III/16, 116: "[…] *divisa sunt miserabiliter, Sclavonicae ritu familiae, quae accusata venundando dispergiur*".
33. Sickel 1879, no. 222.
34. Creighton 2002, 65.
35. Schlesinger 1961, 177.
36. Frey 2010, 50ff.

castles, came the order to utilize them in everyday community life: all markets, all court days and all feasts should be held in these fortifications. This what made them local centres which had an immense impact on local communities. Castles like this had great advantages: in the collaborative effort of building and maintaining the fortification, the community was strengthened. Also lordship was made visible to the people, as castles were the most common and durable architectural symbol for power. Shelter in times of war was combined with a central market place – it can be assumed that these castles became very important central places for the surrounding population, a place of identification and identity.

Castles in general consisted of much more than just their architectural structure. The concept of a castle included the surrounding district more and more during the Middle Ages. One has to consider the *municipium* when thinking of a castle, like the contemporaries did. In all charters, castles with their rights and benefits are mentioned; the castle itself is nearly without value. And often the complex of property stayed together with the name of the castle in the later Middle Ages – even if the fortification was destroyed and only a ruin[37]. This has an impact on castle war. They were nearly useless in frontier defence and were, therefore, not targeted by invaders from the outside. Sieges and attacks on castles took place by competing lords trying to gain the property of another or to damage or destroy it.

The *burgwardi* of the German East were points of inculturation – and that is their unique feature. In a mostly hostile environment of constant violence and threat, the border castles in the marches offered not only protection and shelter, but also appropriate housing for the warriors. The warriors of the marches cultivated a certain kind of mind-set that could be called a frontier mentality. This had its basis in a warrior culture, which resulted in a healthy self-consciousness, an adventurousness that bordered on recklessness and a strong will to rule. This culture also included a greedy entrepreneurship – in the marches free land could be developed with new settlements and Slavonic areas could be conquered. This attracted a lot of people that tried their best to make a fortune in the east. All persons mentioned in the contemporary narrations of the marches have these characteristics.

For the Ottonian and Salian kings, the border regions in the east and north were an important part of their territories. Here they could not only show their will to widen their territory and their efforts at Christianisation, but also their warrior-skills. In the fights with foreign enemies, a society constituted itself that was shaped by warrior-ship and violence. The defence of the western parts of the German realm on the one hand and the expansion into the east on the other formed a special landscape. The most important tool in rearranging the landscape was the castles which became nodes in a network of centres. New settlements were positioned around the castles and proto-urban structures developed. A wide range of socio-cultural change took place because of and at the castles; their impact in the marches was immense. They proved to be to a most versatile tool in colonisation and transported power even into the lowest ranks of society – and into different cultural groups, like the *burgwardi* did.

---

37. MEYER 2010, 16f.

Bibliography

BEHAGEL O. (ed.) (1984), *Heliand und Genesis*, Tübingen, Niemeyer.

BOWLUS C. R. (2006), *The Battle of the Lechfeld and its Aftermath, August 955. The End of the Age of Migrations in the Latin West*, Aldershot, Ashgate.

BURNS R. I. (1989), "The Significance of the Frontier in the Middle Ages", in *Medieval Frontier Societies*, R. J. BARTLETT & A. MACKAY (eds.), Oxford, Clarendon Press, 307-330.

CREIGHTON O. H. (2002), *Castles and Landscapes. Power, Community and Fortification in Medieval England*, London, Equinox (Studies in the Archaeology of Medieval Europe).

ECKHARDT K. A. (ed.) (1956), *Sachsenspiegel. Lehnrecht*, Göttingen, Musterschmidt (MGH Fontes iuris Germanici antiqui, nova series; I, 2).

FREY C. (2010), "Burgen König Heinrichs I. – 'urbes ad salutem regni'", in *Die Burg. Wissenschaftlicher Begleitband zu den Ausstellungen "Burg und Herrschaft" und "Mythos Burg"*, G. U. GROSSMANN & H. OTTOMEYER (eds.), Dresden, Sandstein, 50-55.

GRIMM J. & GRIMM W. (eds.) (1991), *Deutsches Wörterbuch*, vols. 1-33 [photomechanical reprint], München, Deutscher Taschenbuch Verlag.

HENNING J. (2002), "Der slawische Siedlungsraum und die ottonische Expansion östlich der Elbe: Ereignisgeschichte – Archäologie – Dendrochronologie", in *Europa im 10. Jahrhundert. Archäologie einer Aufbruchszeit*, J. HENNING (ed.), Mainz, Von Zabern, 131-146.

Hirsch P. (ed.) (1935), *Die Sachsengeschichte des Widukind von Korvei*, Hannover, Hahn (MGH SS rerum Germanicarum in usum scholarum; 60).

Holtzmann R. (ed.) (1935), *Die Chronik des Bischofs Thietmar von Merseburg und ihre Korveier Überarbeitung*, Berlin, Weidmann (MGH SS rerum Germanicarum. Nova series; 9).

Kerber D. (1999), "Die Burg als Element des Landesausbaus", in *Burgen in Mitteleuropa. Ein Handbuch*, vol. 2: *Geschichte und Burgenlandschaften*, H. W. Böhme et al. (ed.), Stuttgart, Theiss, 68-72.

Kenyon J. R. (1997), "Fluctuating Frontiers: Normanno-Welsh Castle Warfare, c. 1075 to 1240", in *Château Gaillard 17*, Caen, Centre de recherches archéologiques médiévales, 119-126.

Liddiard R. (2005), *Castles in Context. Power, Symbolism and Landscape, 1066 to 1500*, Macclesfield, Windgather Press.

Meyer W. (2010), "Burg und Herrschaft – Beherrschter Raum und Herrschaftsanspruch", in Grossmann & Ottomeyer 2010 (eds.), 16-25.

Pohl W. (2000), "Soziale Grenzen als Spielräume der Macht", in *Grenze und Differenz im frühen Mittelalter*, W. Pohl & H. Reimitz (eds.), Wien, Verlag der Österreichischen Akademie der Wissenschaften (Denkschriften – Österreichische Akademie der Wissenschaften. Philosophisch-historische Klasse; 287), 11-18.

Schlesinger W. (1961), *Mitteldeutsche Beiträge zur deutschen Verfassungsgeschichte des Mittelalters*, Göttingen, Vandenhoeck und Ruprecht.

Schmeidler B. (ed.) (1937), *Helmolds Slavenchronik*, Hannover, Hahn (MGH SS rerum Germanicarum; 32).

Schuchhardt C. (1913), "Über den Begriff der Burg im Heliand", in *Opuscula archaeologica Oscarii Montelio septuagenario dicata d. IX. m. Sept. a. MCMXIII*, Stockholm, Haeggstroem, 351-357.

– (1931), *Die Burg im Wandel der Weltgeschichte*, Potsdam, Akademische Verlags Gesellschaft Athenaion.

Sickel T. (ed.) (1879), *Die Urkunden Konrad I., Heinrich I. und Otto I.*, Berlin, Weidmann (MGH. Diplomata regum et imperatorum Germaniae; 1).

Simmel G. (1958), *Soziologie. Untersuchungen über die Formen der Vergesellschaftung*, Berlin, Duncker und Humblot.

Stieldorf A. (2012), *Marken und Markgrafen. Studien zur Grenzsicherung durch die fränkisch-deutschen Herrscher*, Hannover, Hahnsche Buchhandlung (MGH. Schriften; 64).

Turner B. (2005), "Überlappende Gewalträume. Christlich-islamische Gewaltwahrnehmung zwischen Polemik und Alltagsrationalität", in *Gewalt im Mittelalter. Realitäten – Imaginationen*, M. Braun & C. Herberichs (eds.), München, Fink, 225-250.

Weirich H. (ed.) (1936), *Urkundenbuch der Reichsabtei Hersfeld*, Marburg, Elwert.

Burgen und Territorialgrenzen in den rheinischen Kurfürstentümern

◆

Reinhard Friedrich*

Das Bild des Mittelrheintales wird von den beidseitig des Flusslaufs auf hohen Felsen gelegenen, zahlreichen Burgruinen geprägt, so dass es heute als klassische Burgenlandschaft weltbekannt ist. Zweifellos weist das Mittelrheintal zwischen Bingen und Bonn eine hohe Burgendichte von noch dazu höchst prominenten Anlagen auf. Insgesamt sind in der Rheinzone und den Seitentälern ca. 150 Burgen vorhanden. Zwar entstanden die meisten Burgen am Mittelrhein während der Stauferzeit (Mitte 12. bis Mitte 13. Jahrhundert), aber auch im 14. Jahrhundert sind noch neue Anlagen errichtet worden, häufig als Landesburgen im Zusammenhang mit Zollerhebung und territorialer Grenzsicherung.

Denn von den sieben deutschen Kurfürstentümern hatten gleich vier Anteile am Mittelrheintal mit seinem bedeutenden Verkehrsweg, dem Rhein. Dies waren die kirchlichen Kurk Kurtrier, Kurmainz und Erzbistümer Köln sowie die weltliche Kurpfalz. Aber auch andere mächtige Landesherren wie die Grafen von Katzenelnbogen oder die Grafen von Nassau waren bestrebt, ihr Territorium Richtung Mittelrheintal auszuweiten, um in den Vorzug der dortigen Zolleinnahmen zu gelangen. Diese Mächte betrieben im 13. und in der ersten Hälfte des 14. Jahrhunderts im Mittelrheingebiet den Burgenbau als Mittel zur Herausbildung und Abrundung geschlossener Herrschaftskomplexe (Territorien).

Als ein Beispiel hierfür kann Burg Ehrenfels bei Rüdesheim gelten (Abb. 1), die sich unmittelbar am Eingang zum Engtal des Mittelrheins an einem steilen Hang ca. 80 m oberhalb des Flusses erhebt[1].

Eine erste Burganlage war zu Anfang des 13. Jahrhunderts auf dem Grund und Boden des Mainzer Erzbistums errichtet worden, dem sie 1222 überlassen wurde. Um 1356 – mittlerweile war hier eine wichtige Mainzer Zollstätte eingerichtet worden – erfolgte eine völlige Umgestaltung der Burganlage beim Ausbau zum kurmainzischen Hoflager.

Burg Ehrenfels bildet somit ein gut erhaltenes Beispiel einer imposanten Burganlage, wie sie Mitte des 14. Jahrhunderts von einem finanzkräftigen Bauherrn, in diesem Fall dem Erzbischof von Mainz, aufgeführt werden konnte. Das wichtigste und markanteste Bauwerk ist die bergseitig aufragende, mächtige Schildmauer von rund 4,6 m massiver Mauerstärke und rund 20 m Höhe. Sie wird an beiden Enden von zwei runden Türmen flankiert. Ihr vorgelagert war ein tiefer Halsgraben. Die Kernburg hat einen fast quadratischen Grundriss, an der Südseite zum Rhein hin erhob sich der Palas. 1987 wurden bei Grabungen im Innenbereich die Reste einer aufwendig gestalteten Filterzisterne freigelegt, die sich an der Nordseite des Innenhofes unmittelbar vor der Schildmauer befand und auf die gehobene Ausstattung dieser wichtigen Mainzer Zollanlage hinweist. 1689 wurde die Burg zerstört.

Das Tagungsthema „Burgen im Grenzland" lässt sich am besten am Beispiel des Territoriums der Pfalzgrafschaft verfolgen (Abb. 2), die sich im Raum Bacharach zu beiden Seiten des Rheins erstreckt[2]. Zwar waren die rheinischen Besitzungen der Pfalzgrafschaft, deren Hauptterritorium sich seit dem 13. Jahrhundert weiter südlich mit Heidelberg als bedeutendem Zentrum befand, nur von relativ bescheidener Ausdehnung. Hier lagen aber die für den Pfalzgrafen ungemein wichtigen Zollstellen als bedeutende Einnahmequelle, die entsprechend gegen die umliegenden Territorien geschützt werden mussten.

---

* Institutsleiter, Europäisches Burgeninstitut, Einrichtung der Deutschen Burgenvereinigung e.V., Braubach, Deutschland.

1. Herchenröder 1965, 334-336; Stauth 1970; Struck 1989; Sattler 1992.
2. Schaab 2000, 27, Karte 3.

Abb. 1 – Burg Ehrenfels. Foto Europäisches Burgeninstitut, Braubach: DBV-Archiv, Fotosammlung.

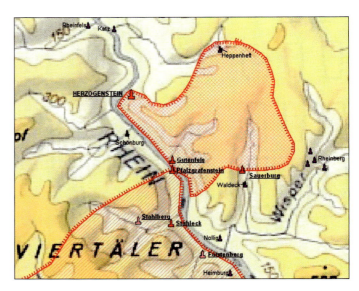

Abb. 2 – Pfalzgräfliches Territorium. Die Karte zeigt den Territorialbestand der Pfalzgrafschaft bei Rhein im Jahre 1329. Plan Verfasser (nach SCHAAB 2000, Anm. 2); Europäisches Burgeninstitut, Braubach: DBV-Archiv, Fotosammlung.

Abb. 3 – Burg Stahleck. Foto Europäisches Burgeninstitut, Braubach: DBV-Archiv, Fotosammlung.

Abb. 4 – Burg Fürstenberg. Foto Europäisches Burgeninstitut, Braubach: DBV-Archiv, Fotosammlung.

Hierzu bediente man sich vor allem der Burgen, die entweder erworben oder neu errichtet wurden.

Zentral im linksrheinischen Territorium erhob sich mit Burg Stahleck eine der ältesten pfalzgräflichen Burgen (Abb. 3). Sie war zusätzlich durch die in pfalzgräflicher Lehnsabhängigkeit stehenden Burgen Stahlberg und Fürstenberg gesichert.

Die auf einem Sporn über dem Rhein gelegene Burg Stahleck über Bacharach wurde 1135 erstmals erwähnt. 1142 wurde Herrmann von Stahleck zum Pfalzgrafen bei Rhein erhoben. Seitdem war Stahleck bis ins 14. Jahrhundert eine der wichtigsten pfalzgräflichen Burgen am Rhein. 1689 ist sie durch Sprengung zerstört und im 19. Jahrhundert weitgehend eingeebnet worden. Ab 1925 wurde sie durch Ernst Stahl wieder aufgebaut[3].

Das rechteckige Burgareal wird an der Rheinseite vom wieder aufgebauten Palas und an der Nordseite von einem ehemaligen Wirtschaftsgebäude begrenzt. Frei im Hof, aber nahe der gefährdeten Westseite, erhebt sich der runde Bergfried. Die Kernburg wird bergseitig von einer im 14. Jahrhundert erbauten Schildmauer mit vorgelagertem Halsgraben abgeriegelt.

Die linksrheinisch gelegene Burg Fürstenberg über Rheindiebach (Abb. 4) wurde als südlichste Burg des Kurkölner Territoriums unter Erzbischof Engelbert I. zwischen 1217 und

---

3. BORINGER 1988; FUHR & STRAETER 2002, 40-43; STÜBER 2004.

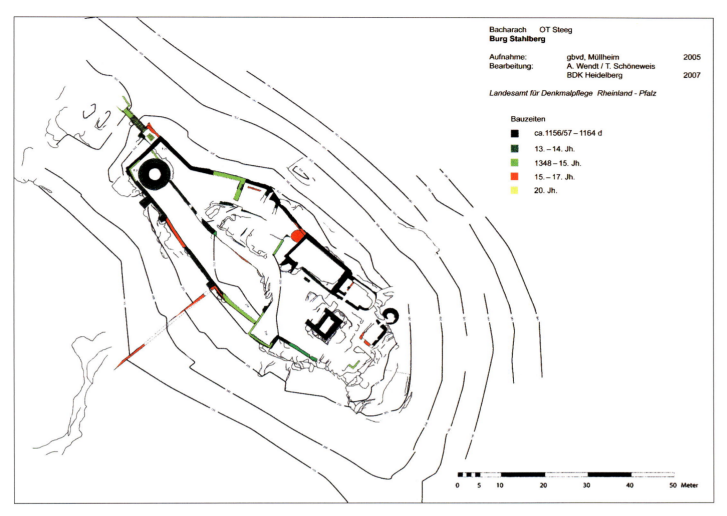

Abb. 5 – Stahlberg, Bauphasenplan. Nach Heberer & Wendt 2007, 24; wie Anm. 5.

1219 errichtet, um hier eine kölnische Exklave zu sichern[4]. Sie kam aber bereits 1230 zunächst als Pfand, ab 1242 als Lehen in den Besitz des Pfalzgrafen. Unterhalb der Burg ist seit der Mitte des 13. Jahrhunderts ein Land- und Schiffszoll nachzuweisen. Im Pfälzischen Erbfolgekrieg teilte Burg Fürstenberg das Schicksal zahlreicher Rheinburgen und wurde 1689 von den französischen Truppen zerstört. Seitdem ist sie Ruine.

Die Burg weist einen polygonal-dreieckigen Grundriss auf. Zum Hang im Westen war sie durch einen Halsgraben und eine hohe Schildmauer gesichert, die durch einen dreiviertelrunden Flankenturm verstärkt war. Gut erhalten ist der runde, 26 m hohe und sich nach oben deutlich verjüngende (konische), fensterlose Bergfried mit originalem Zinnenkranz. Rheinseitig erhoben sich der Nordbau aus dem 13. Jahrhundert und der jüngere Palas.

Die im Steeger Tal westlich von Bacharach gelegene Burg Stahlberg (Abb. 5) war in der zweiten Hälfte des 12. Jahrhunderts (dendrochronologische Daten um 1157/1158) errichtet worden[5]. Auch sie befand sich zunächst in der Verfügungsgewalt des Kölner Erzbischofs. 1243 gab dieser sie als Lehen an die rheinischen Pfalzgrafen, die somit neben Fürstenberg auch Stahlberg als Vorposten bzw. Grenzscherung ihres linksrheinischen Kleinterritoriums einfügen konnten.

Die eindrucksvolle, langgezogene Ruine liegt auf einem länglichen, spornartigen Bergausläufer. Markant sind die Reste ihrer beiden Haupttürme. Der eine, viereckige steht auf einem abgearbeiteten Schieferfelsklotz in der Oberburg. Der zweite, runde Hauptturm erhebt sich an der westlichen Angriffsseite direkt hinter der Frontmauer am Halsgraben, in die das Tor zur Hauptburg integriert ist. Zum ältesten romanischen Baubestand gehören außer den beiden Haupttürmen und Teilen der Ringmauer Reste eines Wohnbaus sowie einer Kapelle.

Von besonderem Interesse ist nun der rechtsrheinische Teil des pfalzgräflichen Territoriums (Abb. 2). Dieses Gebiet

---

4. Stanzl 2003; Stanzl 2005; Krienke 2007, 584-586.

5. Parzer 2005; Heberer & Wendt 2007; Wendt 2005.

Abb. 6 – Gutenfels. Foto Europäisches Burgeninstitut, Braubach: DBV-Archiv, Fotosammlung.

Abb. 7 – Pfalzgrafenstein. Foto Europäisches Burgeninstitut, Braubach: DBV-Archiv, Fotosammlung.

hatte Pfalzgraf Ludwig II. 1277 erworben. Es war zwar nur klein, aber wegen des Ortes Kaub und den damit verbundenen Zollrechten eminent wichtig. Die Zollstelle, die sich im Ort direkt am Rhein befand, wurde durch die oberhalb gelegene Burg Gutenfels gesichert.

Die um 1220/1230 erbaute, 1260 erstmals als *castrum Cube* erwähnte Kernburg (Abb. 6) ist in Aufbau und Gesamtanlage ausgesprochen symmetrisch[6]. In der Mitte der Ostseite deckt der fast quadratische Bergfried die bergseitige Angriffsseite. Dahinter schließt sich der wie ein Kubus wirkende, nahezu quadratische (21,6 x 21,1 m) Gebäudetrakt an. Neben einem als Mittelachse dienenden Innenhof steht rheinseitig der mit einer beeindruckenden Schauseite versehene Palas, während sich an der anderen Seite ein Wirtschaftsbau erhebt. Die Burganlage wurde von einem mehrteiligen Mauerbering umfasst.

Um die Zollanlage weiter auszubauen, ließ Pfalzgraf Ludwig der Bayer im Sommer des Jahres 1327 auf einer Rheininsel unterhalb von Burg Gutenfels einen fünfeckigen Turm errichten. Trotz Ächtung durch den Papst wurde die Anlage von 1339 bis 1342 erweitert, wobei um den Turm herum noch eine sechseckig verlaufende Ringmauer erbaut wurde (Abb. 7), die bis heute nahezu unverändert erhalten ist[7].

Das kleine rechtsrheinische Territorium der Pfalzgrafschaft mit dieser wichtigen Zollanlage grenzte zwar im Westen und Norden an den Rhein, aber an den beiden Landseiten war es von anderen, machtbewussten Territorialherren bedrängt und musste entsprechend gesichert werden. Der im Süden angrenzende Rheingau gehörte zum Erzbistum Mainz, in dessen Abhängigkeit die grenznah im Wispertal gelegenen Burgen geraten waren. Unmittelbar jenseits dieser Grenze lag die wahrscheinlich schon im 12. Jahrhundert entstandene Burg Waldeck[8]. Spätestens seit 1211 sind die Herren von Waldeck als Mainzer Lehnsmänner nachgewiesen, Burg Waldeck diente somit auch als eine Mainzer Grenzfeste zur Sicherung des Rheingaus.

Um sein wichtiges Unteramt Kaub gegen das Erzbistum Mainz zu sichern, hatte Pfalzgraf Ruprecht der Ältere daher wohl kurz vor Mitte des 14. Jahrhunderts die Sauerburg (erste Nennung 1355) als pfalzgräfliche Landesburg und Gegenburg zur Waldeck im Sauerthal erbaut[9]. Sie liegt nur wenige 100 Meter von der Mainzischen Waldeck entfernt.

Die Kernanlage der Sauerburg ist von einem trapezförmigem Bering umschlossen. In seine nördliche Angriffsseite ist beherrschend der über 22 Meter hohe, quadratische Hauptturm eingestellt, der sechs Geschosse aufweist (Abb. 8).

An der Nordostseite der Kernburg stand an Stelle des heutigen Wohnbaus ehemals ein dreistöckiger Palas. Die Südostseite wird durch eine hohe, schildmauerartige Ringmauer mit zwei runden, auf Rundbogenfries vorkragenden Ecktürmchen gegen die Unterburg gesichert.

Der Kernburg südlich vorgelagert befindet sich die ungefähr rechteckige Unterburg (erste Vorburg), die ebenfalls von einer gut erhaltenen Ringmauer umgeben ist. Die östlich vorgelagerte zweite Vorburg hat eine dreieckige Form und ist wohl jünger. Im 16. und 17. Jahrhundert wurde das Vorgelände der Burg durch eine Bastion im Südwesten und ein Geschützrondell im Norden verstärkt.

Nachdem die Sauerburg 1389 Amtmännern anvertraut wurde, war sie ein Nebensitz des Amtes Kaub, später auch Mittelpunkt einer kleinen adeligen Herrschaft.

Im Nordosten grenzte an das pfalzgräfliche Gebiet das Territorium der expandierenden Grafen von Katzenelnbogen. Vielleicht schon um 1360 errichteten diese die Burg Neu-Katzenelnbogen am Rhein, die mit der Weihung der Kapelle 1371 erstmals sicher genannt wird[10].

---

6. COHAUSEN 1891; LUTHMER 1914, 57-62; BACKES 1991.
7. BACKES 2003; SEBALD 2006a; SEBALD 2006b; LORENZ 2006.
8. LUTHMER 1914, 142f.; HERCHENRÖDER 1965, 53.
9. LUTHMER 1914, 130-134; SEBALD 2006c.
10. LUTHMER 1914, 34-37; CUSTODIS & FREIN 1981; FUHR & STRAETER 2002, 102.

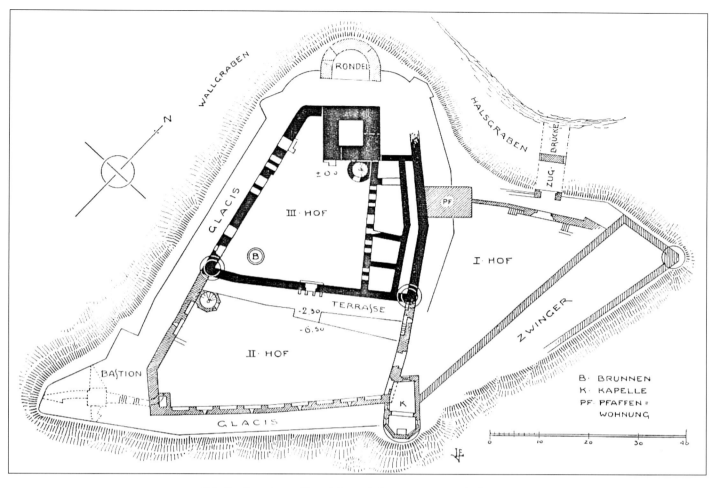

Abb. 8 – Sauerburg. Grundriss nach LUTHMER 1914, wie Anm. 9.

An der nordwestlichen Grenze des pfalzgräflichen Territoriums befinden sich auch die Reste von Burg Heppenheft, von der sich nur noch wenige Mauerreste und ein mächtiger Halsgraben erhalten haben. Als die Herren von Heppenheft im Laufe des 12. Jahrhunderts erstmals in den Urkunden erwähnt werden, sind sie zum Erzbistum Mainz orientiert, denn mehrmals treten sie in Urkunden als Zeugen des Mainzer Erzbischofs auf[11]. Auch erhält Ritter Friedrich von Heppenheft 1280 die Hälfte der Burg Rheinberg im Wispertal als Mainzer Lehen. Es könnte somit gut sein, dass auch die nahe gelegene, zum Erzbischof von Mainz orientierte Burg Heppenheft Mitte des 14. Jahrhunderts als bedrohlich für das pfalzgräfliche Kleinterritorium eingeschätzt wurde.

Möglicherweise auf Grund dieser Bedrängung durch die Burgen Katz und Heppenheft plante Pfalzgraf Ruprecht bald nach der Mitte des 14. Jahrhunderts den Bau einer Burg unmittelbar an der nordwestlichen Grenze seines Territoriums. Der Bauplatz auf einem Felssporn direkt am Rhein war nahezu ideal, fiel die östliche Flanke dieses Sporns doch direkt in das die Grenze bildende Urbachtal ab.

Baubeginn dieser in zeitgenössischen Quellen „Herzogenstein", später auch „Rhineck" genannten Anlage war wohl noch im Jahre 1359[12]. Aufgrund von Protesten der auf der anderen Rheinseite gelegenen Stadt (Ober)Wesel, die diese zusammen mit dem Trierer Erzbischof Boemund II. vorbrachten, wurde der Bau am 6. Januar 1360 vertraglich bis Pfingsten desselben Jahres unterbrochen. In den Streitigkeiten vermittelte schließlich Kaiser Karl IV. und bewog den Pfalzgrafen offenbar zur Einstellung seiner Bauabsichten. Bereits im Burgfrieden vom 14. August 1361 sind die Burgen Kaub/Gutenfels, Pfalzgrafenstein und Sauerburg genannt, Herzogenstein hingegen nicht mehr.

Hier bietet sich also das interessante Phänomen einer begonnenen, aber nicht vollendeten Burganlage am Mittelrhein. Ein auf dem Sporn direkt am Rhein gelegenes Plateau von ca. 80 x 200 m bot ausreichend Platz für eine umfangreiche

---

11. ROSER 1992; GENSICKE 1997; FRIESE & GÖTTERT 2007; www.ebidat.eu, „Heppenheft".

12. SCHMIDT 1916-1917; FUHR & STRAETER 2002, 107; FRIEDRICH 2006.

Burganlage. Ein den Sporn abriegelnder Halsgraben scheint erstaunlicherweise noch nicht begonnen worden zu sein. Jedoch erhebt sich an der schmalsten Stelle, ca. 140 m vom Spornende entfernt, ein heute noch ca. 5 m hoher Hügel, an dessen Außenseite Reste von Mauerlagen aus Bruchstein auszumachen sind (Abb. 9). Wie ebenfalls erhaltene Mauerinnenseiten an der Hügeloberfläche nahelegen, handelt es sich offenbar um die verstürzten Reste eines viereckigen, turmartigen Gebäudes, dessen Innenfläche recht sicher auf ca. 10 x 9,3 m zu bestimmen ist.

Die gesamte übrige Innenfläche ist ausgesprochen plan, was auf eine bewusste Abarbeitung hindeutet. Berücksichtigt man seitlich etwas Raum für eine Berme, so kommt man auf eine nutzbare Fläche für den Platz einer Burg von vielleicht 60 x 120 m (7.200 m²), was in seiner Grundfläche ungefähr der kurz zuvor durch den Pfalzgrafen errichteten Sauerburg entspricht. Von den wenigen Informationen, die man über den möglichen Grundriss der geplanten Burg gewinnen kann, scheint zumindest gesichert, dass eine Frontturmburg geplant war. Damit würde sich Burg Herzogenstein gut in das Grundkonzept der beiden anderen benachbarten pfalzgräflichen Burgen Gutenfels und Sauerburg einfügen.

Abb. 9 – Herzogenstein. Foto Europäisches Burgeninstitut, Braubach: DBV-Archiv, Fotosammlung.

Insgesamt sollte dieser Überblick vor allem aufzeigen, wie im 14. Jahrhundert Burgen als Mittel der Grenzsicherung bei den rheinischen Territorien der Kurfürsten dienten. Insbesondere am Beispiel des rechtsrheinischen Gebietes des Pfalzgrafen konnte dies verdeutlicht werden.

Literatur

Backes M. (1991), *Pfalzgrafenstein*, Mainz, Landesamt für Denkmalpflege Rheinland-Pfalz (Führer der Verwaltung der Staatlichen Burgen, Schlösser und Altertümer Rheinland-Pfalz; 11).

– (2003), *Burg Pfalzgrafenstein und der Rheinzoll*, Regensburg, Schnell und Steiner (Edition Burgen, Schlösser, Altertümer Rheinland-Pfalz; 11).

Boringer U. (1988), *Geschichte und Wiederaufbau der Burg Stahleck*, Bacharach, Verein für die Geschichte der Stadt Bacharach und der Viertäler (Kleine Schriftenreihe; 4).

Cohausen A. (von) (1891), „Burg Gutenfels am Rhein", *Annalen des Vereins für Nassauische Altertumskunde und Geschichtsforschung*, 23, 91-104.

Custodis P. G. & Frein K. (1981), *St. Goarshausen mit Burg Katz und Patersberg*, Neuss, Gesellschaft für Buchdruckerei (Rheinische Kunststätten; 258).

Friedhoff J. (2006), „Die Sauerburg im Wispertal (Gem. Sauerthal). Eine pfalzgräfliche Burggründung des späten Mittelalters", *Nassauische Annalen*, 117, 17-47.

Friedrich R. (2006), „Herzogenstein – begonnener, aber nicht vollendeter Bau einer Burg Mitte des 14. Jahrhunderts im Mittelrheintal", *Castrum Bene*, 9, 87-98.

Friese G. & Göttert M. (2007), *Die Niederadeligen von Heppenheft*, Braubach, Bericht im Dokumentations archiv des Europäischen Burgeninstitutes.

Fuhr M. & Straeter H. (2002), „Wer will des Stromes Hüter sein?" *40 Burgen und Schlösser am Mittelrhein. Ein Führer*, Regensburg, Schnell und Steiner.

Gensicke H. (1997), „Die von Rheinberg", *Nassauische Annalen*, 108, 269-297.

Heberer P. & Wendt A. (2007), „,…in vergangenen kriegsläufen versöhret…' Zur Geschichte der Burg Stahlberg bei Bacharach", *Baudenkmäler in Rheinland-Pfalz*, 2005, Jahrgang 60, 23-27.

Herchenröder M. (1965), *Der Rheingaukreis*, München, Dt. Kunstverl. (Die Kunstdenkmäler des Landes Hessen; 3).

Krienke D. (2007), *Kreis Mainz-Bingen*, Worms, Wernersche Verlagsgesellschaft (Kulturdenkmäler in Rheinland-Pfalz; 18, 1), 584-586.

Lorenz F. (2006), „Die Baugeschichte des Pfalzgrafenstein", *Burgen und Schlösser*, 2006/3, 143-153.

Luthmer F. (1914), *Die Bau- und Kunstdenkmäler des Regierungsbezirkes Wiesbaden*, Bd. V: *Die Kreise Unter-Westerwald, St. Goarshausen, Untertaunus und Wiesbaden Stadt und Land*, Frankfurt, Keller.

Parzer S. (2005), „Die Burglehen der Pfalzgrafen bei Rhein", *Zeitschrift für die Geschichte des Oberrheins*, 153, 233-240.

Roser W. L. (1992), „Die Burgen der Rheingrafen und ihrer Lehnsleute zur Zeit der Salier im Rheingau und im Wispertal", *Nassauische Annalen*, 103, 1-26.

Sattler S. (1992), „Burg Ehrenfels bei Rüdesheim. Neue Erkenntnisse zur frühen Baugestalt", *Nassauische Annalen*, 103, 27-61.

Schaab M. (2000), „Zeitstufen und Eigenart der pfälzischen Territorialentwicklung im Mittelalter", in *Mittelalter. Der Griff nach der Krone. Die Pfalzgrafschaft bei Rhein im Mittelalter. Begleitpublikation zur Ausstellung der Staatlichen Schlösser und Gärten Baden-Württemberg und des Generallandesarchivs Karlsruhe*, V. Rödel (hrsg.), Regensburg, Schnell und Steiner (Schätze aus unseren Schlössern. Eine Reihe der Staatlichen Schlösser und Gärten Baden-Württemberg; 4), 15-36.

Schmidt F. A. (1916-1917), „Herzogenstein, eine verschollene Burg am Rhein (1359-1361)", *Nassauische Heimatblätter*, 20, 52-59.

Sebald E. (2006a), „Der Pfalzgrafenstein und die Kauber Zollstelle im Kontext der Zoll- und Territorialpolitik der Pfalzgrafen bei Rhein", *Burgen und Schlösser*, 2006/3, 123-136.

– (2006b), „Denkmalpflegerische Überlegungen zur Sanierung der Ringmauer des Pfalzgrafenstein", *Burgen und Schlösser*, 2006/3, 136-142.

– (2006c), „Eine Burg mit Kegelbahn und Schwimmbad? Die Sauerburg über Sauerthal", *Baudenkmäler in Rheinland-Pfalz*, 59, 46-47.

Stanzl G. (2003), „Bauforschung und Instandsetzung an der Burgruine Fürstenberg in Rheindiebach", *Jahresberichte des Landesamtes für Denkmalpflege Rheinland-Pfalz 1997-2001*, 56-76.

– (2005), „Der Erzbischof liebte Rot – Der Bergfried der Fürstenberg. Oder: Über das Anmalen von Architektur", *Burgen und Schlösser*, 2003/4, 208-214.

Stauth W. (1970), „Vermessung und Beobachtung an Burgruinen (Ruine Ehrenfels und Ruine „Landskron"-Oppenheim)", *Burgen und Schlösser*, 1970/2, 61-66.

Struck W. H. (1989), „Vom Zoll und Verkehr auf dem Rhein bei Burg Ehrenfels im Mittelalter", *Nassauische Annalen*, 100, 17-53.

Stüber H. (2004), *Burg Stahleck über Bacharach. Von der Stauferburg zur Jugendherberge*, Bacharach, Verein für die Geschichte der Stadt Bacharach und der Viertäler.

Wendt A. (2005), „Die Burgruine Stahlberg. Erste Ergebnisse der Bauforschung", *Rheinische Heimatpflege*, 42/4, 245-255.

Later Medieval Aristocratic Landscapes in Scandinavia

Martin Hansson*

1. Introduction

During the last couple of decades it has been shown that the medieval aristocracy used space and landscape to strengthen their position in society. It has become obvious that the aristocracy created elite landscapes around their castles and residences. This type of research has for a long time been restricted to a European context, mainly in the British Isles, but the purpose of this paper is to discuss the presence of late medieval elite aristocratic landscapes in Scandinavia. The castles and landscapes around Bergkvara in Småland in medieval Sweden and Glimmingehus in Scania and Gurre on Zealand, both in medieval Denmark, are used as examples (fig. 1).

The landscape surrounding the castle was important for emphasising lordship. It was in the castle and its vicinity that the aristocratic life took place: courtly love in the garden, hunting in the park, processional routes approaching the castle, tournaments, jousts, and so on. The castle and its surrounding landscape materialised lordship and were intended to impress visitors and create an aristocratic setting. So far the discussion of medieval designed landscapes has mainly been a concern of English scholars, but there can be no doubt that the same type of landscapes also existed in other parts of Europe[1].

Aristocratic life materialised in a number of features that when found together can indicate the presence of an aristocratic milieu. Various types of aristocratic elements have been presented in scholarly literature. They vary from architectural elements, economic-functional features as well as immaterial values. What unites these elements – some of which are listed in table 1 – is the fact that they often are found in and around castles and residences (table 1)[2]. Sometimes all of them are present, on other occasions fewer, or just a single feature, are found. These features all materialised important parts of aristocratic life. For example, moats, walls and crenellations symbolised the martial dimension of knighthood and aristocracy, while the ornamental garden was the location for courtly love, often described in chivalric literature. The view and scenery of the castle from the outside, as well as the scenery from the inside of the castle when looking out over the landscape, contributed to enhancing dominion and lordship. The watery setting of the castle strengthened this impression. Mills and dovecotes were in a medieval European context visible evidence of feudal grants, while deer parks were perhaps the highest form of conspicuous consumption of arable land. Dovecotes, fishponds and rabbit warrens are other features that often are found in the vicinity of a castle or residence, being used both as a constant supply for fresh meat, but also as feudal symbols, placed in prominent positions in the castle area. A church or an abbey is also something that often can be found, instigated by the lord of the castle and functioning as a family memorial. The power to transform the agrarian landscape, to enclose pasture land and reorganize arable land and tenant settlements are other elements in this development that need to be taken in to consideration[3].

---

* Department of Archaeology and Ancient History, Lund University, Sweden.
1. See Hansson 2006.
2. For this discussion, see Liddiard 2000; Taylor 2000; Johnson 2002, 136ff.; Creighton 2002, 65ff.; Creighton 2009; Hansson 2006, 129ff.; Hansson 2009.
3. See Hansson 2006; Hansson 2009.

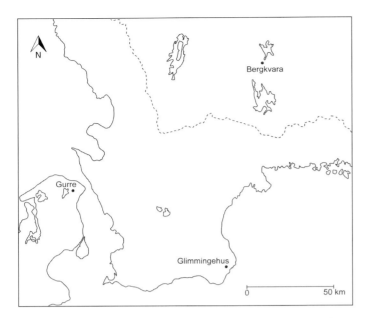

Fig. 1 – Position of Bergkvara, Glimmingehus and Gurre in Southern Scandinavia. The dotted line is the medieval border between Sweden and Denmark. Map M. Hansson.

Moats
Crenellations and walls
Ornamental gardens
Watery setting
Scenery
Fishponds
Mills
Rabbit warren
Deer park
Dovecote
Religious institution – abbey/monastery

Table 1 – List of possible aristocratic elements often found at castles and in their vicinity.

It must be stressed that these types of features and elements can of course be present without implying aristocratic connotations, but when found grouped together the aristocratic implications must be considered. The elements presented in table 1 are very disparate. Some of the elements are highly material (walls and moats), while others are rather immaterial (scenery). What unites them, however, was their importance for various parts of the chivalric life, and that they emphasise different aspects of this culture. Searching for the presence of these features and elements is one way of localising aristocratic landscapes.

2. The aristocratic landscape of Bergkvara

Bergkvara is a late medieval castle situated west of the medieval town of Växjö (Småland, South Sweden). The manor and estate is known in written documents since the middle of the 14th century[4]. The castle and stone house at Bergkvara was according to written sources built around 1470, shortly after the previous manorial complex had been burnt (fig. 2). The builder Arvid Trolle was at this time one of the richest men in Scandinavia with large estates in both Sweden and Denmark. The substantial remains of the castle, together with later descriptions and images, make it possible to reconstruct what the castle looked like. With the aid of old maps in the archive of the manor, it also becomes possible to cast light on the surroundings of the castle[5].

The stone house was originally a six-storey building, 20 m x 15 m large. The preserved walls are about 20 m high, and one can still see that the house had 4 protruding turrets in each corner[6]. Judging by the measurement of the building, each floor had an area of almost 300 m². According to a description from 1746, the entrance to the building was on the second floor on the northern side of the building. The preserved masonry does not give many clues to how the building was used, but it is evident that the many fireplaces in the upper part of the building show that this part was the living quarters of the noble family, while the lower part probably was used for storage and a kitchen[7].

Judging by the masonry and a picture, dated to 1707, one can see differences in how the windows were placed in the building. It is evident that the northern façade of the building had few and small windows. The northern façade faced land and this side of the building gave a heavy, military impression. The eastern and southern façade, facing the lake, had large windows, which must have given these floors both light and a splendid view of the lake from the inside. Here we can see a completely different architecture, where comfort is put before military needs. In this aspect Bergkvara is an interesting mix between older castles where military needs are structuring the architecture, and the later Renaissance palaces, where comfort and light are emphasised. The importance of the scenery looking out from castles is an aspect that has recently been emphasised[8].

The impression of the castle in Bergkvara was further underlined by the landscape setting. The castle lies on a spur

---

4. Larsson 1974; Hansson 2005.
5. See *ibid.*
6. *Ibid.*; Menander et al. 2008.

7. *Ibid.*, 10. This is also mentioned by Carl Linneus in 1746 when he described the then recently ruined stone-house.
8. Creighton 2009, 168ff.

Fig. 2 – Ruined tower house of Bergkvara. Photo J. Ludwigsson, Kulturparken Småland (Sweden).

Fig. 3 – Parts of a map from 1858-1861 showing the former main road passing Bergkvara while making a noticeable bend: 1) the tower house; 2) the mill at Örsled; 3) the smithy; 4) mechanical industry. Drawing P. Lönegård, after an original in the manorial archive.

in a lake. A bit to the east of the castle, the Mörrum River runs into this lake. At the outlet of the river lies Örsled's mill. The mill has belonged to the estate since the 14th century. The castle also lies near the main road from Växjö towards Scania. This road passes Örsled, where today the remains of the road can be seen in a pasture land. From this road a traveller on his/her way to Bergkvara had to turn west at Örsled, and passing the river in order to reach the castle. It is interesting to notice two things here.

The first is the bend the road makes in the pasture land (fig. 3). This bend takes the traveller closer to the river valley. The bend is not caused by any topographical hinder, the road could just as well have continued straight on (as the modern road does). But by forcing the travellers closer to the river, the great castle became visible in the distance on the other side of the lake. And to the east the medieval church tower at the parish church in Bergunda was also visible. The western tower of the church is dated to the late 15th century and was most likely instigated and perhaps financed by the Trolle family[9]. For a by passer on the main road, it must have been clear that they now entered a very special type of landscape of power, seeing the large stone house in the west and the church tower in the east. The profane and spiritual powers were united and guarded the landscape.

Secondly, when a traveller to Bergkvara came to Örsled and turned westwards, he or she got the great castle in focus in the distance when passing the river at the mill. All the way towards the castle, a traveller would see the impressive great stone house on the other side of the lake in front of him/her. On a day when the lake was calm, the castle became even larger as the masonry was reflected in the water. The impression of the castle becomes even greater when we consider that this was one of very few stone buildings in the region in the late Middle Ages[10].

By analysing a map of the manor from the 1680s, it also becomes possible to get an impression of what the traveller met when he/she arrived at the castle (fig. 4). The great stone house lay protected behind two moats, of which only the inner one is visible today. Bergkvara was a castle with an inner part that housed the living quarters of the lord, and a relatively large bailey with various economical functions. Before entering the castle, a traveller had to pass a large geometrical garden that judging by the map gives a Renaissance impression. It is not possible to date the garden, but since no lords resided at Bergkvara after c. 1580, it is more probable that the garden was created by the middle of the 16th century at the latest, than later. We cannot rule out that the garden was actually created by Arvid Trolle at the same time as he had the stone house built.

Another typical aristocratic feature that can be seen is the two fishponds by the shore of the lake. It is interesting to find fishponds by a lake, which in itself is a large natural

9. Liepe 1984, 40ff.

10. Hansson 2001, 210ff.

fishpond. The digging of fishponds can thus be seen as something unnecessary from a strictly functional point of view. One can always argue that the fishponds were useful when large parties of visitors were coming and that fish could be stored here, waiting to be used. But similar fish-storing could be done in wooden boxes in the lake. The fishponds should rather be seen as an aristocratic element, something that *should* exist at a castle of this type, they belonged to the aristocratic concept. And the fishponds were also needed if the lord was breeding foreign fish, like carp. The two fishponds were filled in during the 1740s[11].

A large number of the previously mentioned aristocratic elements can thus be found in the landscape around Bergkvara. The residence was defended by two moats and a bailey, and by lying inaccessible in the landscape, the castle gave an impression of power and lordship. By forcing the main road to make the bend, the glory of the lord of the castle became visible even for passers-by, and for travellers to Bergkvara this became even more obvious, where the garden and the fishponds fulfilled the place's aristocratic ambitions.

There is of course a problem with the dating of many of the elements discussed above, but I would argue that most of them probably have a late 15th- or early 16th-century date. Different maps from the 1680s show that the layout of the manor, with the garden, the fishponds, road system and the location of the mill, existed at this time. The fact that no lord resided at Bergkvara between the 1580s and 1732 is in my opinion circumstantial evidence that the elements in question probably date to a period earlier than 1580. It seems rather unlikely that an absent lord would spend resources on creating gardens and digging fishponds at a manor which he/she hardly ever visited. Most probably the landscape of Bergkvara was created sometimes between 1470 and 1580.

3. The aristocratic landscape of Glimmingehus

Another place where an aristocratic landscape might be found is Glimmingehus in Scania. The standing well-preserved castle is the result of the transformation of an older castle made by the knight Jens Holgersen (Ulfstand) in 1499 according to a stone tablet above the entrance to the castle. Jens Holgersen was also son-in-law to Arvid Trolle, and had as such certainly visited Bergkvara. Glimmingehus lies in South-Eastern Scania in a shallow valley, today surrounded by a small moat[12].

This is not the place to present the history of Glimmingehus in detail, just to point to some indices that there probably existed some kind of aristocratic landscape around the castle c. 1500. The starting point can be the earliest picture of Glimmingehus from 1680 by Gerhard Burman (fig. 5). The picture shows the castle from a bird's-eye perspective, lying surrounded by a small lake. In the lake, apart from the castle

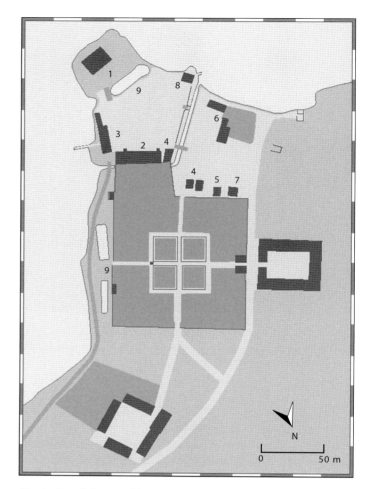

Fig. 4 – Detailed map of the Bergkvara around 1700: 1) the stone house; 2) main building; 3) kitchen; 4-7) storage houses; 8) bathhouse; 9) fishponds. Drawing P. Lönegård, after an original in the manorial archive.

island, is another island called *Trädgårdsholmen* – the Garden Island. Today, neither the lake nor this garden island is visible. The water level in the lake was created by a dam wall east of the castle. A minor excavation of the dam wall has shown that it was constructed in two phases. In an earlier phase, the wall was only one meter high, which none the less must have created a watery setting for the castle and ensured that water was kept in the moats. In the 17th century the wall was raised and the watery setting seen on Burman's picture was created. When the water level was raised, the moat was flooded, as is seen on the picture. The dating rests on the findings of fragments of clay pipes and a shard of faience in the wall. According to Anders Ödman, the wall was probably raised to strengthen the defenses of the castle during the Scanian wars in 1675-1677[13].

There is no dating of the initial phase of the dam wall, which means that it can be of late medieval origin. If that is the case, some kind of artificial watery setting was created at the

---

11. HANSSON 2005.
12. ÖDMAN 2004, 28ff.

13. ÖDMAN 1999, 123.

Fig. 5 – Glimmingehus and its surroundings *c.* 1680. Drawing G. Burman (from G. Burman & A. Fischer, *Prospecter af åtskillige märkvärdige Byggnader, Säterier och Herre-Gårdar uti Skåne*, 1756). Note the lake and the "Garden Island" by the castle.

same time as the present castle was built. There is however a problem with how this "lake" would have been able to coexist with the moat in their present appearance, since the moats would have been flooded by this lake[14].

Another indicator for an elite landscape surrounding the castle is the so-called "garden table", that today can be found sitting in a window niche in *Frustugan* on the second floor (fig. 6). The garden table is an octagonal tablet with an inscribed knight and two coats-of-arms in the middle, and an inscription following the edge of the tablet. The coat-of-arms are those of the Ulfstand and Brahe families, probably commemorating Jens Holgersen and his first wife, Holmgerd Axelsdatter (Brahe). An English translation (by the author) of the inscription reads: "I am a great and strong fighter, I went from Gotland to Scania in 1487". In the eight corners of the tablet and incorporated in the inscription, small figures can be seen, such as some grapes, a swine, a rose, a hare/rabbit, a lily, a deer, a unicorn and a hand in a blessing gesture[15].

The tablet has caused much scholarly debate. It is obvious that it is not sitting in its original position. In 1487 Jens Holgersen was lord of Gotland and according to the other stone tablet at the entrance, the present castle was first built in 1499. It has recently been confirmed that the castle had a predecessor[16], and the tablet could have functioned in that context, or it can have been moved to its present position later on. The function of the tablet has also been debated. One scholar has argued that the tablet originally had been sitting over the entrance to the older castle, while others suggested that it functioned as a garden table[17].

Octagonal tables like this can be seen on medieval images having being present in gardens which makes the latter inter-

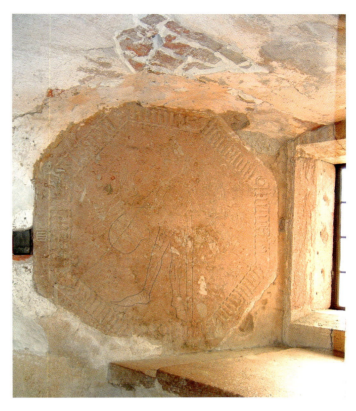

Fig. 6 – Garden Table in its present position. Photo M. Hansson.

pretation reliable[18]. The table with its figures and inscription can be seen as symbols of the aristocratic life and culture centered on the knight. The coat-of-arms emphasizes the importance of lineage, while the small figures symbolize different important aspects of the aristocratic life; the deer (hunting), the rose, grapes and lily (the garden, courtly love), the rabbit/hare (the warren or, perhaps if a hare, hunting again), the blessing hand (the lord's position in society sanctioned by God). Together with the existence of the Garden Island, this becomes at least circumstantial evidence of the presence of an ornamental garden at Glimmingehus in Jens Holgersen's days. When one considers the social position of Jens Holgersen in medieval Denmark[19], and the impression given by the castle as a whole, it would be rather surprising if a garden was not present.

The modern landscape surrounding Glimmingehus is completely transformed, which makes it difficult to discuss its late medieval presence. Some remarks of the castle's location in the landscape can however be made. Glimmingehus lies in the parish of Vallby, and the castle seems to have been built on the outfields of the village of Vallby. Originally the castle appears to have been called Glimminge which indicates that there

14. *Ibid.*, 123.
15. Nilsson 1999, 67ff.
16. Ödman 1999.
17. Nilsson 1999, 69.
18. *Ibid.*
19. See Skansjö 1999.

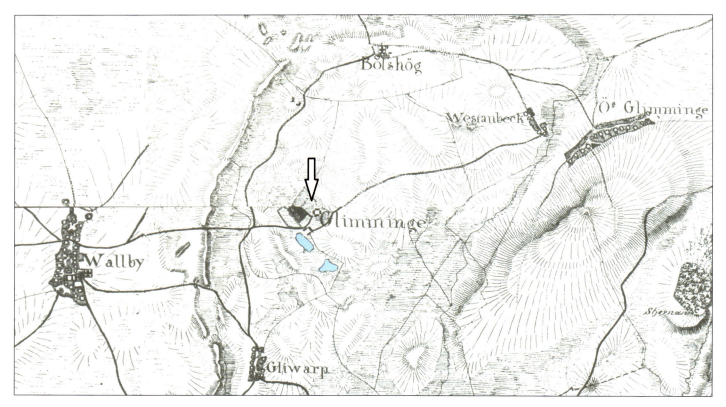

Fig. 7 – *Skånska rekognosceringskartan*, c. 1810, giving an impression of the landscape setting of Glimmingehus. The arrow points to the castle. Map from Krigsarkivet (the Military Archives), Stockholm (Sweden).

must have been a connection with the village of Glimminge in the neighboring parish of Bolshög. In the only preserved document made by Jens Holgersen, the castle is called *Stora Glimminge*[20]. In the village of Glimminge, east of the castle, both Jens Holgersen and his ancestors owned farms and it is possible that the family originally had a manor in this village. Perhaps this manor was moved from the village and fortified in the 14th century, a development that has been noticed on several occasion in a Scandinavian context[21]. If a move took place, it meant that the manor not only left the village and was fortified; it also meant that it moved to another parish. This indicates that the lord of the manor probably had a strong position in the local society as a landowner in both parishes.

The new location of the manor/castle at Glimmingehus meant that the castle became secluded from local society in the landscape, which is typical for the aristocratic spatial ideology of the Middle Ages[22]. Judging by the cadastral maps, the land of the castle was separated from both Vallby and Glimminge. *Skånska Rekognosceringskartan*, a map from *c.* 1810, shows that the castle was situated between the villages of Vallby, Glivarp, Bolshög and Glimminge (fig. 7). One can also notice the straight road from Vallby, where the church was, to the castle. The lord of the castle could go straight to church if and when he/she needed. This road system is also present on the earliest map of Vallby, from 1777, and has probably a medieval origin. A similar straight connection between the castle and the church can be found in Krapperup in North-Western Scania, where a manor was moved from a location beside the parish church, to a new site where it was turned into a castle in the early 14th century[23]. In neither case do we know the dating of these roads, but it cannot be ruled out that they are of a late medieval origin, ensuring a swift passage or journey from the castle to the church.

Even if the evidence for an aristocratic landscape at Glimmingehus can be seen as weak, I would argue that there are some interesting indices that could be looked into in the future. At least, the move from one parish to another is a strong indication that the lord both had the power and need to transform the landscape to make it fit his/her needs. The power of transforming and ordering the landscape was as an important part of the spatial ideology of the medieval aristocracy[24].

4. The aristocratic landscape of Gurre

While both Bergkvara and Glimmingehus are connected to the Scandinavian high aristocracy, the castle of Gurre in the

---

20. Skansjö 1999, 39; Ödman 1999, 123.
21. Hansson 2006, 106f.

22. See *ibid.*, 105ff. for further discussion.
23. Carelli 2003.
24. Hansson 2006, 129ff.

north-eastern part of Zealand was a Danish royal castle. Gurre is another example where an aristocratic landscape hypothetically existed already in the 14th century. The origin of the castle might go back to the second half of the 12th century. Gurre was transformed and enlarged by the Danish king Valdemar Atterdag in the middle of the 14th century. This is also where he eventually died in 1375. Excavations in the years 2000-2005 have revealed a lot of new information about the place (fig. 8)[25].

During the reign of King Valdemar, the area outside the central part of the castle was heavily transformed. Large brick buildings, as well as timber houses, were erected on artificially constructed islets in the bog. Being situated in a bog between two lakes definitely gave the castle a watery setting, despite the absence of a moat. Main access to the castle area was from the east, by a paved roadway on a partly artificial embankment. The nearby village church in Gurre, St Jacob, became attached to the castle in this period. The church was perhaps originally a parish church built around 1200, which later on became a castle chapel. Most likely the villagers were subordinate to the lord of the castle[26].

Apart from the castle chapel, the Cistercian abbey in Esrom, *c.* 10 km north-west of Gurre, perhaps should be seen as part of the aristocratic setting of the castle in a wider landscape context. The abbey was already old when King Valdemar transformed Gurre, but written documents show the close connections between the castle and the abbey. During the last years of her life, Valdemar's queen, Helvig, chose to withdraw and live in the abbey. When she died in 1374, she was buried in front of the main altar in Esrom[27].

That huge efforts were made to transform the landscape surrounding the castle is evident. The water level of the lakes were regulated, something that also facilitated the construction of a water-driven mill in the vicinity[28]. The castle was situated in a wooded landscape, and written sources mention that large forests belonged to the castle, at least in the 16th century[29]. Woodlands were suitable places for royal hunts and that hunting took place is also shown by the archaeological finds from the excavations of the castle as well as the many local histories of the king's hunts that still exist in the local society[30].

In the vicinity of the castle, some undated earthen banks have been found. The functions and dating of these banks are not known and they can of course be earlier or later than the castle. However, some of the banks north of Gurre Sø, one called "King Valdemar's bank", connect bogs and watery areas, thus demarcating parts of the landscape[31]. These banks could, at least hypothetically, be remains of a park pale, demarcating a royal hunting ground. A similar interpretation has been put forward for the earthen banks in Dalby Söderskog outside Lund in Scania, which have been seen as the remains of a royal deer park[32].

This short overview of Gurre shows that, even if much of the discussion have been rather hypothetical, considerable efforts were made in the middle of the 14th century to transform and organize the landscape around the castle. Being one of the King Valdemar's favorite castles, it would be rather surprising if, for example, an ornamental garden was not in place. So far there are no traces of such a garden, but a report from a local priest in 1743 talks among other things of the "king's garden", which shows that a garden can have existed[33].

The lavish interiors of the castle show that much effort was spent to create an appropriate and up-to-date living quarter for the king. The same kind of efforts most likely also created an aristocratic landscape around the castle. Perhaps some of these hypotheses about Gurre, presented above, can be confirmed by future research.

5. Conclusion

This short presentation of three late medieval Scandinavian castles has shown that many aristocratic elements can also be found in a Scandinavian context. As usual in this type of analysis, secure dating of the individual elements in the discussed landscapes does not exist. This means that the discussion perhaps is seen as too hypothetical for some. But the absence of secure dating should not deter us from contextualising the castle and its landscape. We must acknowledge that life in a castle also took place outside the walls, if we are to fully understand the meaning and importance of castles. Future research and new dating will either strengthen or falsify some of the interpretations made in this text. However, there is no doubt that the Scandinavian aristocracy used the landscape around their castles to fulfil their aristocratic lifestyle and I would argue that we here have Scandinavian versions of the aristocratic landscapes that we find elsewhere in Europe. We have fortified castles in watery settings, with moats, fishponds, gardens and mills, churches and in the case of Gurre, perhaps even the abbey at Esrom should be included in a wider landscape context. The possibilities to hunt must have been good in the surrounding forested landscape at Bergkvara and Gurre. So far, few landscapes of this type have been identified in Scandinavia but future research into this matter will certainly find other examples as well. It is however important when searching for aristocratic landscapes in Scandinavia to realise that they were not copies of their European cousins, rather adjusted to local circumstances.

---

25. ETTING *et al.* 2003; ETTING 2010, 120f., 172ff.
26. ETTING *et al.* 2003, 44f.; ETTING 2010, 151, 174.
27. ETTING *et al.* 2003, 27f., 47.
28. *Ibid.*, 12.
29. *Ibid.*, 14f.
30. *Ibid.*, 18, 153f.
31. *Ibid.*, 19f.
32. ANDRÉN 1997.
33. See ETTING *et al.* 2003, 81.

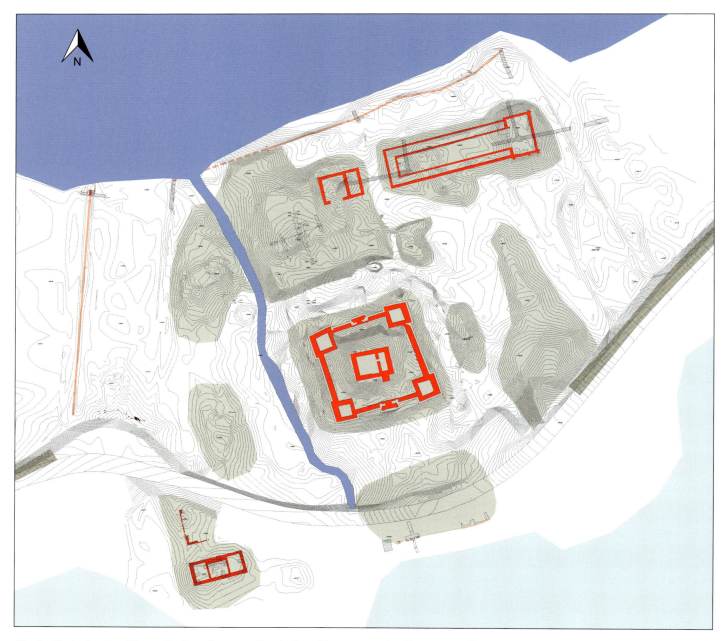

Fig. 8 – Central parts of Gurre Castle and surrounding bailey with numerous buildings on artificial islets in the bog. Drawing N. C. Clemmensen, Skov-og Naturstyrelsen (Denmark). Scale *c.* 1:1000. © The National Museum of Denmark, Copenhagen.

The castles discussed in this article lay in different countries even if the countries during the time discussed partly formed a union with a common sovereign. The border question has not been discussed at all in this article, mainly because it seems to have been a non-issue to the persons involved. Instead similar types of aristocratic landscapes can be found on either side of the medieval Swedish/Danish border. The Scandinavian high aristocracy had contacts, family relations and often also land in the neighbouring country. Many of the great castles were related to each other by their owners[34]. For this group of individuals, the perhaps most important border was the one towards other groups in society, peasants, merchants and the lesser nobility. In this way the castles and their landscapes guarded borders of a more social and mental importance, rather than the physical border of the country. The aristocratic landscape at Bergkvara, Glimmingehus and Gurre were tangible materialisations of a high aristocratic medieval culture in a Scandinavian version.

34. Ödman 2004, 7.

Bibliography

ANDRÉN A. (1997), "Paradise Lost: Looking for Deer Parks in Medieval Denmark and Sweden", in *Visions in the Past. Trends and Traditions in Swedish Medieval Archaeology*, H. ANDERSSON et al. (eds.), Stockholm, Almqvist & Wiksell (Lund Studies in Medieval Archaeology; 19), 469-490.

CARELLI P. (2003), *Krapperup och det feodala landskapet. Borgen, bygden och den medeltida bebyggelseutvecklingen i en nordvästskånsk socken*, Nyhamnsläge, Gyllenstiernska Krapperupstift (Historia kring Krapperup).

CREIGHTON O. (2002), *Castles and Landscapes. Power, Community and Fortification in Medieval England*, London, Equinox (Studies in the Archaeology of Medieval Europe).

– (2009), *Designs upon the Land. Elite Landscapes of the Middle Ages*, Woodbridge, Boydell Press.

ETTING V. (2010), *The Royal Castles of Denmark during the 14th Century. An Analysis of the Major Royal Castles with Special Regard to their Functions and Strategic Importance*, Copenhagen/Odense, National Museum of Denmark/University Press of Southern Denmark.

ETTING V. et al. (2003), *Gurre slot. Kongeborg og sagnskat*, Copenhagen, Sesam.

HANSSON M. (2001), *Huvudgårdar och herravälden. En studie av småländsk medeltid*, Stockholm, Almqvist & Wiksell International (Lund Studies in Medieval Archaeology; 25).

– (2005), "Gods människor och landskap: Bergkvara under 700 år", Smålands Museum Rapport 2005:23, Växjö.

– (2006), *Aristocratic Landscape. The Spatial Ideology of the Medieval Aristocracy*, Stockholm, Almqvist & Wiksell International (Lund Studies in Historical Archaeology; 2).

– (2009), "The Medieval Aristocracy and the Social Use of Space", in *Reflections. 50 Years of Medieval Archaeology, 1957-2007*, R. GILCHRIST & A. J. REYNOLDS (eds.), Leeds, Maney Publishing (Society for Medieval Archaeology Monograph; 30), 435-464.

JOHNSON M. (2002), *Behind the Castle Gate. From Medieval to Renaissance*, London/New York, Routledge.

LARSSON L-O. (1974), "Utsikt mot ett gods: Bergkvara under sju sekler", in *Bergunda. Utgiven av Öja Hembygds- och Kulturminnesförening*, S. ALMQVIST et al. (eds.), Växjö, Utgiven av Öja Hembygds- och Kulturminnesförening, 57-129.

LIDDIARD R. (2000), *"Landscapes of Lordship". Norman Castles and the Countryside in Medieval Norfolk, 1066-1200*, Oxford, Archaeopress (BAR. British Series; 309).

LIEPE A. (1984), *Medeltida lantkyrkobygge i Värend. Ett försök till relationsanalys kyrka-bygd*, Växjö, Kronobergs läns hembygdsförbund (Kronobergsboken; 1984-1985).

MENANDER H. et al. (2008), "Byggnadsarkeologisk förundersökning av Bergkvara stenhus", Riksantikvarieämbetet UV Öst Rapport 2010:3.

NILSSON S.-Å. (1999), "Stenarna talar 2", in NILSSON & LANDEN 1999 (eds.), 67-74.

NILSSON S.-Å. & LANDEN A. (1999) (eds.), *Glimmingehus 500 år. Tretton texter*, Lund, Lund University Press (Skånsk senmedeltid och Renässans; 17)

ÖDMAN A. (1999), "De arkeologiska undersökningarna", in NILSSON & LANDEN 1999 (eds.), 115-126.

– (2004), *Glimmingehus*, Stockholm, Riksantikvarieämbetet (Svenska kulturminnen; 7).

SKANSJÖ S. (1999), "Jens Holgersen, aktör i Östersjörummet", in NILSSON & LANDEN 1999 (eds.), 27-40.

TAYLOR C. (2000), "Medieval Ornamental Landscapes", *Landscapes*, 1/1, 38-55.

„Grenzburgen" in Böhmen und die Problematik ihrer Vorburgen

Josef Hložek*

Burgen, die entlang der mittelalterlichen Grenzen erbaut wurden, stellen ein äußerst breites Spektrum von Objekten unterschiedlicher Gestalt und unterschiedlichen Qualitätsniveaus dar. Sie wurden besonders in den Grenzgebirgen und an den Trassen bedeutender Fernwege angelegt. Bei einem Teil dieser Objekte handelt es sich um mehr oder weniger monofunktionale Anlagen überwiegend mit Wachfunktion, wobei die Funktion als Stützpunkt gegenüber der Wohnfunktion im Vordergrund stand. Diese Burgobjekte dienten vor allem als landesherrschaftliche Stützpunkte und werden zusammenfassend als „Bergburgen" bezeichnet[1]. Einige dieser Burgen wurden jedoch auch von ausreichend vermögenden und ehrgeizigen Mitgliedern des Adels[2] oder als Grundbesitzstützen der Ritterorden angelegt[3]. Viele sollten keine langfristige Wohnfunktion erfüllen, sondern waren meist, besonders im Falle kleinerer königlicher Stützpunkte, Objekte mit kurz angelegter Nutzungsdauer, die nur einer kleinen Besatzung einen grundelementaren Wohnstandard bieten konnten. In diese Burggruppe gehört auch die höchstgelegene böhmische Burg auf dem Gipfel Ostrý in einer Höhe von 1293 m ü. N.N., durch deren Areal heute die deutsch-tschechische Staatsgrenze verläuft[4]. Einige der Burgen, die zu den königlichen Stützpunkten entlang der tschechischen Grenzen oder entlang von Fernwegen gehören, besonders die so genannten Bergburgen[5], wurden noch im Laufe des Mittelalters aufgrund ihrer fehlenden Entwicklungsperspektiven aufgegeben.

Einige der ursprünglich königlichen Stützpunkte wurden jedoch weitergenutzt, und dies oft als Eigentum neuer Besitzer aus den Adelsreihen. In diesem Fall konnten jedoch die unterschiedlichen Ansprüche an einen königlichen Wach- und Stützpunkt und an eine Adelsburg des späten Mittelalters und der frühen Neuzeit in größerem Maße deutlich werden. Bei diesen Objekten können die baulichen Veränderungen an der ursprünglichen Burganlage nachvollzogen werden, die aufgrund des Bedarfs an wirtschaftlichen und betrieblichen Komponenten notwendig wurden und meist die Form einer Vorburg annahmen.

Eine etwas andere Ausgangslage zeigt sich im Falle der Adelsburgen. Die einzelnen Objekte wurden im Rahmen von Herrschaftsgebieten mit oft komplizierten Netzen wirtschaftlicher und betrieblicher Verbindungen angelegt. Diese durchlebten jedoch, ähnlich wie die Burgen selbst, bereits im Mittelalter und in der frühen Neuzeit eine oft sehr stürmische Entwicklung. Einige der Adelsburgen konnten daher in der Zeit ihrer Entstehung bedeutende Stützen sich stabilisierender Grenzen des adeligen Grundbesitzes darstellen. Eine Identifikation dieser Objekte mit Stützen der Grundbesitzgrenzen kann jedoch auch sehr problematisch sein. Eine gewisse Lösung ist hier nur eine weitergehende Bewertung der möglichen zeitgenössischen besitzrechtlichen Verhältnisse. Diese stößt jedoch in vielen Fällen durch mangelnde Belege in den schriftlichen Quellen schnell an ihre Grenzen.

Versuchen wir nun, uns auf drei grundsätzlich unterschiedliche Burglokalitäten zu konzentrieren, die aufgrund ihrer Gestalt in unterschiedliche Qualitätsklassen der mittelalterlichen Burgen fallen. Bei allen drei Burgarealen lassen sich

---

* Západočeská univerzita v Plzni, Katedra archeologie, Tschechische Republik.
1. Kubů & Zavřel 1994; Durdík 2000, 167.
2. *Ibid.*, 598-599; Durdík 2003; Durdík 2011b, 182.
3. Hejna 1974.
4. Fröhlich 1996; Durdík 2000, 413.
5. *Ibid.*, 167.

die verschiedenen Ansprüche verfolgen, die an mittelalterliche Burgen im königlichen Umfeld auf der einen und im adeligen Umfeld auf der anderen Seite gestellt wurden.

Ein Beispiel, um dies zu illustrieren, ist die Burg Kynžvart im Egerland (Abb. 1). Sie wurde auf einem hohen Sporn über der gleichnamigen Stadt erbaut. Die Burg verrät schon durch ihren Namen ihren Ursprung als königlicher Stützpunkt. Dieser entstand offensichtlich bereits am Ende der ersten Hälfte des 13. Jahrhunderts über einem der Zugangswege nach Böhmen. Der Bauherr war wahrscheinlich Wenzel I. oder Ottokar II. Přemysl. In der zweiten Hälfte des 13. Jahrhunderts ging die Burg in den Besitz der Hartenberger über, wobei sie in den Titeln einiger der Angehörigen dieser Familie auftauchte. Im Jahr 1347 wurde die Burg als Rückzugsort von Räubern und Anhängern des Kaisers Ludwigs des Bayern durch Johann von Luxemburg erobert und wurde danach für einen längeren Zeitraum nicht erneuert. Die Burg wurde erst nach dem Jahr 1398 auf der Grundlage einer Erlaubnis durch Wenzel IV. durch Hyncík Pluh von Rabstein repariert. Die Erneuerung der Burg bedeutete ihren Neuaufbau sowie eine deutliche Vergrößerung ihrer Grundfläche. Bereits im Jahr 1400 wurde die Burg jedoch durch Hyncík Pluh von Rabstein an den Leuchtenberger Landgraf Johann verkauft, von dem die Burg weiter in die Hände der Herren von Plauen gelangte. Am Ende des 15. Jahrhunderts wechselten sich auf der Burg für kurze Zeit die Geschlechter Schlik und Gutštejn ab. Als Folge von Besitzstreitigkeiten zwischen ihnen wurde die Burg im Jahr 1509 erneut erobert. Die Herren von Gutštejn waren in Folge dieser Situation gezwungen, die Burg an Vladislav II. abzutreten, der die Burg an die Herren von Rabstein verpachtete. Am Anfang des 16. Jahrhunderts geriet die Burg in die Hände der Schwanberger, die sie im Jahr 1561 umbauten. Nach dem Wechsel mehrerer Eigentümer blieben die Burg und ihr Herrschaftsgebiet bis ins 20. Jahrhundert im Besitz der Familie Metternich. Die Burg besaß fast während ihrer gesamten Nutzungszeit große militärische Bedeutung, und dies auch trotz der wiederholten Eroberungen. Sie wurde in verteidigungsfähigem Zustand gehalten und spielte noch während des Dreißigjährigen Krieges eine bedeutende Rolle, als sie durch das kaiserliche und das schwedische Heer eingenommen wurde. Die letzte Eroberung im Jahr 1648 besiegelte das Schicksal der Burg[6]. Während ihrer ältesten, königlichen Lebensphase stellte die Burg ein einteiliges, durch einen Graben und einen Wallkörper gesichertes Objekt dar. Auf der nördlichen Zugangsseite handelte es sich wahrscheinlich um eine doppelte Befestigung. Die kleine, von einer hohen Ringmauer begrenzte Burg war über ein viereckiges turmartiges Tor in der nordöstlichen Ecke der Kernburg zugänglich. Teil der ältesten Burgphase war auch ein zweiräumiger Bau, offensichtlich mit dem Charakter eines turmartigen *Palas* oder eines Wohnturms, im südöstlichen Teil der Kernburg. Es kann nicht mit Sicherheit gesagt werden, ob die Kernburg

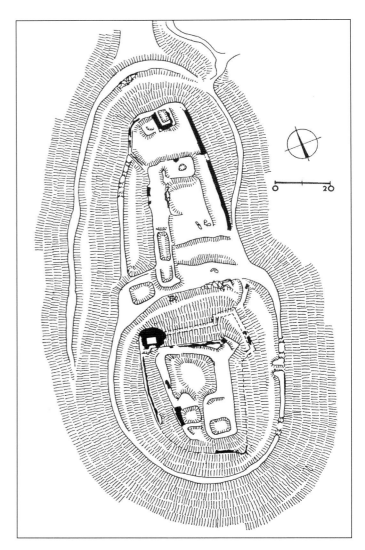

Abb. 1 – Kynžvart Bez. Karlovy Vary. Grundriss der Burganlage. Nach MENCLOVÁ 1972, Bd. II, 183; beabeitet nach DURDÍK 2000, 314.

schon zu dieser Zeit durch einen Zwinger geschützt war. Die kleine Burg kann in dieser Gestalt auf Grund ihrer überwiegenden Wachfunktion und des Charakters ihrer das Umland dominierenden und von anderen Siedlungen entfernten Lage der Gruppe der so genannten Bergburgen zugeordnet werden[7].

Das heutige Aussehen des Burgareals ist zu einem großen Teil das Ergebnis der Erneuerung der Burg am Ende des 14. Jahrhunderts. Die Bauaktivitäten Hyncík Pluhs von Rabstein konzentrierten sich hauptsächlich auf zwei Aspekte. Die einteilige Burg erlebte eine deutliche Veränderung und wurde zum Kern eines weit größeren Objekts. Der ältere *Palas*-Teil der Kernburg wurde in westlicher Richtung erweitert. Mit Blick auf den Charakter der noch heute obertägig sichtbaren Baustrukturen könnte man vielleicht auch von

---

6. Zur Geschichte der Burg siehe z. B. SEDLÁČEK 1905, Teil XIII, 59-63; DURDÍK 2000, 315-316; DURDÍK & SUŠICKÝ 2005, 92-93; KAREL et al. 2009, 99-100.

7. DURDÍK & SUŠICKÝ 2005, 95.
8. Zu diesem Burgtyp siehe z. B. DURDÍK 2000, 56-58; DURDÍK 2002.

zwei Palastrakten ausgehen. Spätestens in dieser Bauphase war die Kernburg bereits durch einen Zwinger geschützt. An seiner nordwestlichen Ecke wurde ein halbkreisförmiger Turm erbaut, allerdings mit rechtwinkligen Innenräumen. Der Turm war nur an seiner südöstlichen Ecke mit der Hauptmauer der Kernburg verbunden. Seine Stirnseite ragte an der Außenseite der Zwingermauer hervor. Obwohl man den Turm nicht für einen vollwertigen Bergfried halten kann, ließe sich seine Lage an der Stirnseite der Kernburg mit einiger Vorsicht als ein gewisser Anklang an den Grundaufbau der Kernburgen des Bergfriedtyps auffassen[8], bei der ein großer Turm an der Stirnseite der Kernburg weitere, im am besten geschützten Teil der Kernburg gelegene Gebäude wenigstens teilweise abschirmt. In diesem Fall hätte der Turm jedoch eher den Charakter einer großen Bastei[9].

Die Burganlage wurde des Weiteren in nördlicher Richtung durch eine ausgedehnte Vorburg erweitert, die durch eine komplizierte Bauentwicklung geformt wurde[10]. Die Stirnseite der Vorburg wurde durch einen neuen Halsgraben und einen Wall geschützt, welcher parallel zur Westseite der Vorburg verlief. Zeitgleich mit der Anlage der Vorburg kam es zur Verfüllung eines Teils des Grabens der Kernburg, der jedoch noch zur Zeit des Mittelalters infolge der Absackung des aufgefüllten Materials sichtbar war. Die Westseite der Vorburg wurde von einem rechteckigen, offenbar als Wirtschaftsgebäude genutzten Flügel eingenommen, dessen Südseite bereits im Bereich des aufgefüllten Grabens angelegt worden war. In einer weiteren Bauphase kam es zur erneuten Erweiterung der Vorburg in nördlicher Richtung, wodurch sie eine fünfseitige Grundfläche bekam. Der Halsgraben wurde aufgeschüttet und die Burg wurde auf der Zugangsseite durch einen neuen Graben geschützt, vor dessen Außenseite ein Wall aufgeschüttet war. Dieser sicherte die Westseite der Vorburg und einen Teil der Westseite der Kernburg. Hinter der neuen Ringbefestigung im Nordteil der Vorburg entstand ein offenbar turmartiger, in die Vorburg hineingezogener Bau mit quadratischer Grundfläche, der eventuell den Zugang zum Burgareal schützte. Diese jüngste der Befestigungsanlagen erfüllte ihre Aufgabe jedoch auch noch weit später, als zur Zeit des Dreißigjährigen Krieges in den Wallkörper an der Stirnseite des Burgareals Geschützlöcher eingegraben wurden.

Am Beispiel der Burg Kynžvart lässt sich die Verwandlung eines ursprünglich kleinen königlichen Stützpunkts in eine ausgedehnte Adelsburg verfolgen, an die im Vergleich mit einem eher monofunktionellen königlichen Wach- und Stützpunkt gänzlich andere Ansprüche gestellt wurden, und zwar sowohl im wirtschaftlichen und betrieblichen als auch im militärischen und gesellschaftlichen Bereich[11].

Auch im adeligen Umfeld lassen sich bedeutende, als Stützen ausgedehnter Herrschaftsgebiete erbaute Objekte finden, und dies in Bauformen der höchsten Qualität. Als Beispiel kann die südböhmische Burg Přibenice dienen, die auf einem langgezogenen, vom Fluss Lužnice umflossenen Sporn erbaut wurde (Abb. 2 und 3). Die Burg wurde offensichtlich als Objekt mit Macht- und Demonstrationsfunktionen am Nordrand des ausgedehnten Wittigonen-Gebiets angelegt, welches neben einem außerhalb des böhmischen Königreichs gelegenen Gebiet einen großen Teil Südböhmens umfasste.

In den schriftlichen Quellen taucht die Burg im Jahr 1243 zum ersten Mal auf. Die stürmischste Lebensetappe des Komplexes spielte sich unter Ulrich von Rosenberg ab, der im Jahr 1420 in Konflikt mit den Taboriten geriet. Auf den Rosenberger Burgen kam es nach und nach zur Gefangennahme hussitischer Geistlicher. Auf der Burg Přibenice wurde im Jahr 1420 Václav Koranda gefangen genommen. Dieses Ereignis wird traditionell mit der Eroberung der Burg in Verbindung gebracht. Auf der Grundlage einer Vereinbarung zwischen den Taboriten und Ulrich von Rosenberg aus dem Jahr 1437 wurde die Burg samt *Latrane* – einer angegliederten Agglomeration städtischen Typs – abgerissen[12].

Die Burg Přibenice stellt das anspruchsvollste wittigonische Bauunternehmen im 13. Jahrhundert dar. Die Kernburg (Abb. 4) zerfällt im Prinzip in vier Teile, die auf einem mehr oder weniger stufenartig bearbeiteten Felsuntergrund lagen. Der südwestliche Teil der Kernburg wurde von einem frei stehenden, achteckigen Turm dominiert[13], der aus Bruchsteinmauerwerk bestand und in den Ecken durch mächtige behauene Quader gefestigt wurde[14]. Hinter dem Turm breitet sich ein kleinerer, ursprünglich wohl leerer Hof ohne bedeutendere Bebauungsspuren aus. Der Mittelteil der stufenartig nach Südwesten abfallenden Kernburg wurde von einem ausgedehnten, mehrflügeligen Palaskomplex eingenommen, der einen engen, über eine Durchfahrt im Nordflügel zugänglichen Innenhof umgab. Der nordöstliche Teil der Kernburg wurde durch einen viereckigen Turm mit einer rechteckigen Grundfläche von ca. 12 x 8 m dominiert. Die Kernburg war über einen engen Korridor erreichbar. Dieser führte entlang der südwestlichen Seite in den Bereich des am niedrigsten gelegenen ersten Hofes, von dem man in den in der Mitte der Kernburg gelegenen Palaskomplex gelangte. Auf der Südwestseite war hinter der Kante des zweiten Grabens an diesen Korridor die Befestigung der unter der Burg liegenden *Latrane* angeschlossen. In der ersten Hälfte des 14. Jahrhunderts war die Kernburg mit einer Kapelle ausgestattet. Es widerspricht der Logik der mittelalterlichen Fortifikationssysteme, dass die Nordostseite der Kernburg durch einen Zwinger mit zwei viereckigen

---

9. Durdík 2000, 315.
10. Zur Problematik der Vorburgen in Böhmen zuletzt Hložek 2012.
11. Zu dieser Problematik stichprobenhaft z. B. Austin 1984; Hložek 2012; Zeune 1996.
12. Sedláček 1890, Teil VII, 75.
13. Menclová 1972, 178-181.
14. Zu den weiteren Zusammenhängen polygonaler Türme in Böhmen zuletzt Durdík 2011a, 13.

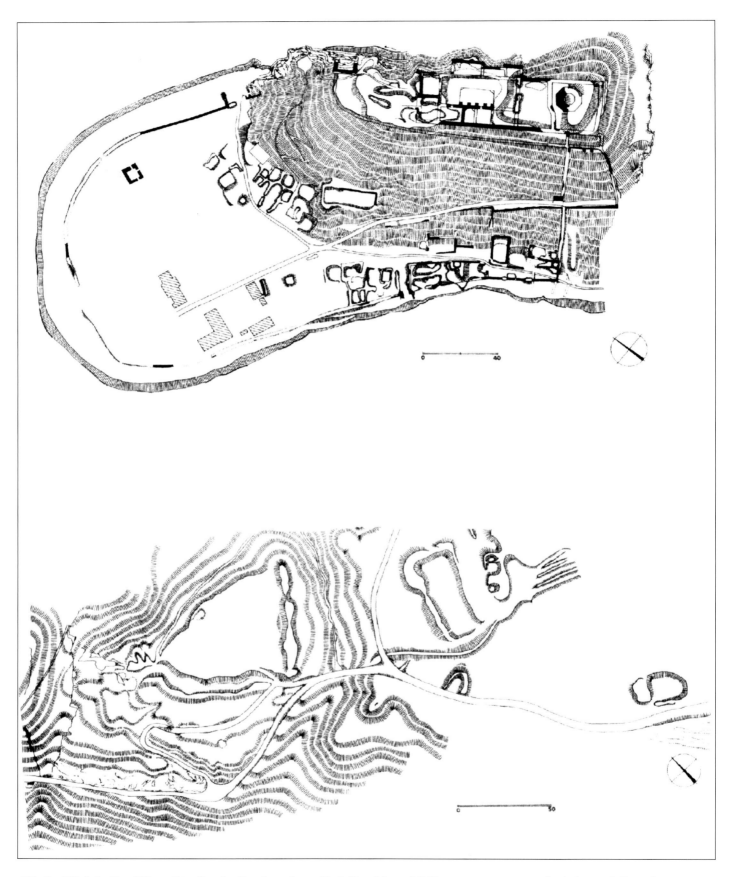

Abb. 2 – Příběnice Bez. Tábor. Situation des Burgkomplexes. Nach Dvořáková & Hilmera 1947, 124-125; beabeitet nach Durdík 2005, 87.

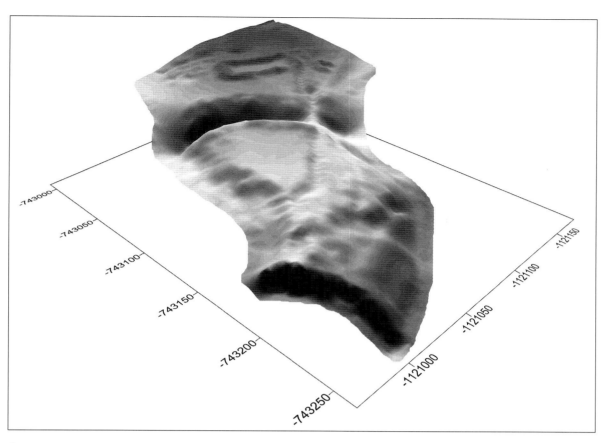

Abb. 3 – Příběnice Bez. Tábor. 3D Modellierung des Vorburgareals mit dem Programm Surfer 8 (Golden software) aus Richtung Nordost. Im Vorfeld des Vorburgareals sind Terrainrelikte der Belagerngsobjekte sichtbar. Nach HLOŽEK 2011, 213.

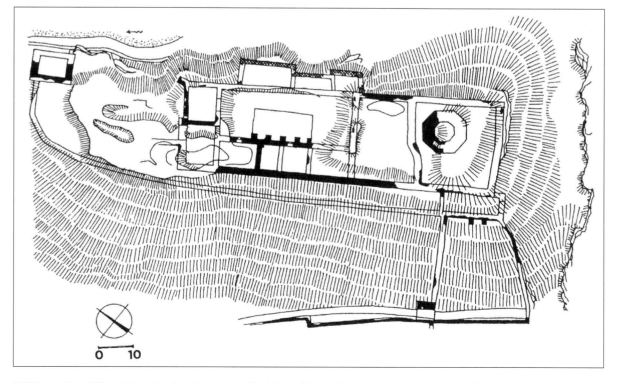

Abb. 4 – Příběnice Bez. Tábor. Situation des Burgkerns. Nach DVOŘÁKOVÁ & HILMERA 1947, 124-125; bearbeitet nach DURDÍK 2000, 459.

Basteien über einer fast senkrecht abfallenden Felswand befestigt war. Mit Rücksicht auf die Geomorphologie des Geländes in diesem Teil der Burganlage lässt sich die Hauptbedeutung dieser Befestigung im Bereich der Demonstrationsarchitektur verorten[15], vorausgesetzt dass sie keinen anderen Sinn hatte, der uns bisher entgangen ist. In baulicher Hinsicht ist die Burg Přibenice mit anspruchsvollen königlichen Bauunternehmen aus dem Kontext der Burgen mit Ringbebauung vollkommen vergleichbar[16]. Die Burg stellte im Rahmen der Rosenberger Besitztümer keine Ausnahme dar. Ähnlich wie bei anderen Adelsburgen, und besonders bei Rosenberger Adelsburgen, wurde auch im Fall der Burg Přibenice die wirtschaftliche Rolle des Objekts sehr betont. Ebenfalls Teil der Burg war eine spezifische Siedlungsagglomeration städtischen Typs am Fuß der Burg, die *Latrane*[17], eine ausgedehnte Vorburg und ein Wirtschaftshof im Burgvorland[18].

Vor der Stirnseite der Kernburg lag eine geräumige Vorburg mit einer Fläche von 3650 m² ohne stärkere Bebauungsspuren[19]. Dieses befestigte Areal stellte den Zugang zur Kernburg und zur *Latrane* unter der Burg sicher. Entlang der Kommunikationslinien sind im Bereich der Vorburg deutlich sichtbare, teils in den Felsuntergrund eingesenkte Hohlwege erhalten geblieben. Die Vorburg, vor der bereits im Mittelalter ein ausgedehnter Wirtschaftshof entstand, erfüllte hier also neben der gewöhnlichen Verteidigungs- und Betriebsfunktion auch eine entscheidende Aufgabe als Hauptkommunikationsknoten des gesamten Siedlungskomplexes der Burg und der Latrane.

Eine nicht weniger bedeutende Rolle spielten auch weitere Adelsburgen, die an den sich oft schnell ändernden Grenzen des adeligen Grundbesitzes erbaut worden waren. Wenn wir die weiteren Funktionen der mittelalterlichen Adelsburg, wie die Residenz-, Verwaltungs-, Militär-, Zentrums- und Symbolfunktion, für einen Moment vernachlässigen, können wir auch die im 14. Jahrhundert in der Region Tachov erbaute Burg Falštejn (Falkenštejn) als Beispiel einer solchen Burg betrachten (Abb. 5).

Auf der Grundlage des gefundenen archäologischen Materials lassen sich die Anfänge der Burg nur grob auf das 14. Jahrhundert datieren. Die erste indirekte historische Erwähnung der Burg stammt erst aus dem Jahr 1460[20]. Aus dem Jahr 1497 stammt ein weiterer historischer Bericht, der jedoch nur die Existenz der Burg bestätigt. Im Jahr 1566 wird Falštejn im Urbar des Herrschaftsgebiets Bezdružice ausdrücklich als verwaistes Schloss aufgeführt[21].

Die Burganlage wurde auf einem Sporn erbaut, der von einem stark gegliederten, steil ins Tal des Flusses Úterský potok abfallenden Felsgebilde abgeschlossen wird. Sie war an ihren Standort, einen durch zwei Felsblöcke abgeschlossenen

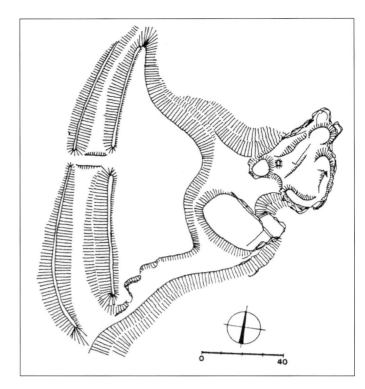

Abb. 5 – Falštejn Bez. Tachov. Grundriss der Burganlage. Nach Procházka & Úlovec 1988, 40, bearbeitet nach Durdík 2000, 132.

Sporn, stark angepasst. Die ausgedehnte Vorburg mit einer Fläche von ca. 600 m² weist keine sichtbaren Bebauungsspuren auf und war vom Vorland der Burg durch einen auf beiden Seiten von Wallkörpern flankierten Graben getrennt. Die deutlich kleinere Kernburg mit einer Fläche von ca. 180 m², die von der Vorburg durch einen weiteren Graben getrennt wurde, zerfiel in zwei Höhenebenen auf den frei stehenden Felsblöcken. Auf der ersten Felsebene, deren Oberfläche in der Zeit der Erbauung der Burg bearbeitet worden war, sind heute keine Bebauungsspuren sichtbar. Es ist jedoch wahrscheinlich, dass über diese Fläche der Zugangsweg zum hinteren, durch eine Kluft natürlichen Ursprungs abgeschnittenen und durch die Geländemorphologie am besten geschützten Felsplateau führte. Das größere, hintere Felsplateau wurde von einer Steinmauer umgeben und war offenbar aus südwestlicher Richtung zugänglich. Es trug eine gemauerte Bebauung, was durch Mauerreste belegt wird, die besonders in den Felsspalten erhalten geblieben sind. Dieser Teil des Burgareals war über ein einfaches Torobjekt erreichbar, dessen Fundament in den Felsuntergrund gebrochen worden war. Die in der Geländeform andeutungsweise erhaltene Hauptbebauung der Kernburg zog sich an der

---

15. Zu dieser Problematik Durdík 2003.
16. Zur Typologie der böhmischen Burgen siehe z. B. Durdík 1976; Durdík 1981; Durdík 1998.
17. Durdík 2006.
18. Dvořáková & Hilmera 1947.
19. Zu diesem Teil der Lokalität zuletzt Hložek 2012.
20. Sedláček 1905, Teil XIII, 56.
21. Profous 1954, 534; Kohout 2012, 9.

Westseite des Felsplateaus entlang. Die typologische Einordnung des Objekts ist allerdings mit Rücksicht auf den Erhaltungszustand der Baustrukturen in der Kernburg recht problematisch. Die Bebauung der Kernburg erstreckte sich besonders an der nordwestlichen, durch eine steile Felswand geschützten Seite. Mit Blick auf analoge Situationen kann man eine Einordnung in den Burgtyp mit *Palas* als Hauptverteidigungs- und Wohnbau in Betracht ziehen[22]. Auch die mögliche Existenz eines Turms im südwestlichen Teil der Kernburg kann nicht ausgeschlossen werden. Dieser könnte mit seiner Masse den kleineren, an der nordwestlichen Seite der Kernburg gelegenen *Palas* abgeschirmt haben. In diesem Fall hätte die Kernburg eher dem Schema der Burgen des Bergfriedtyps entsprochen[23]. Mit Rücksicht auf den Erhaltungszustand der Kernburg können jedoch auch andere Bebauungsformen nicht ausgeschlossen werden.

Falštejn stellt eine kleinere Burg dar und kann durch ihre Ausführung eher den sparsam gestalteten Objekten zugeordnet werden, welche in keiner Weise aus dem Kontext der zeitgenössischen adeligen Burgbauten ausbrachen, die ein eher mittelmäßiges Bauniveau erreichten. Hinsichtlich der Interpretation der Burg scheinen jedoch die weiteren geographischen und besitzrechtlichen Zusammenhänge entscheidend zu sein. Die Burg wurde an der Grenze verschiedener Herrschaftsgebiete einiger bedeutender Adelsgeschlechter angelegt, die in Westböhmen über ausgedehnten Grundbesitz verfügten: die Gutštejner, die Schwanberger und die Herren von Bezdružice[24]. Die wahrscheinlichen Erbauer der Burg sind die Herren von Schwanberg oder die Herren von Gutštejn.

Beide Adelsfamilien zeigten bereits im 13. Jahrhundert starke Kolonisierungsaktivitäten in der Region. In Verbindung mit den Herren von Gutštejn wird die Burg außerdem zum ersten Mal historisch erwähnt[25]. Für die These, dass die Burg als Kolonisierungsstützpunkt am Kollisionspunkt verschiedener Grundbesitze fungierte, spricht in begrenztem Maße auch die Tatsache, dass sie in den zeitgenössischen Adelstiteln nicht als Familiensitzobjekt auftaucht.

Obwohl alle drei Burgen an heute mehr oder weniger sichtbaren Grenzen erbaut wurden (den Grenzen des tschechischen Staates und den Grenzen der Grundbesitzdomänen der Adelsgeschlechter), ist offensichtlich, dass die Ansprüche, die an eine als landesherrlicher Stützpunkt erbaute mittelalterliche Burg gestellt wurden, sich von den Ansprüchen an die Adelsburgen unterschieden, obwohl diese in der Zeit ihrer Entstehung in vielerlei Hinsicht ähnliche Funktionen erfüllten. Diese Erscheinung kann besonders an den Vorburgarealen und den etwas anderen wirtschaftlich-betrieblichen Vernetzungen dieser Objekte beobachtet werden, die sich sowohl von den königlichen Anlagen als auch von Burgen, welche durch kirchliche Institutionen erbaut worden waren, unterscheiden[26]. Letztere konnten sich besonders in der vorhussitischen Zeit auf die umfangreichen kirchlichen Wirtschaftsstrukturen stützen. In der Form und der Ausrüstung dieser Burgobjekte und in ihren Verbindungen zu zeitgenössischen Siedlungs- und Kommunikationsnetzen und zu weiteren Strukturen spiegelten sich vor allem die verschiedenen wirtschaftlich-betrieblichen Beziehungen, aber auch die unterschiedlichen Ansprüche an diese Burgen wider.

---

22. Zu diesem Burgtyp siehe z. B. Durdík 1977; Durdík 2000, 173-174.
23. Zu diesem Burgtyp siehe z. B. *ibid.*, 56-58; Durdík 2002.
24. Kohout 2012, 61.

25. Sedláček 1905, Teil XIII, 56; Kohout 2012, 61.
26. Durdík & Bolina 1996.

Literatur

Austin D. (1984), „The Castle and the Landscape: Annual Lecture to the Society for Landscape Studies", *Landscape History*, 6, 69-81.

Durdík T. (1976), „Současný stav, potřeby a výhledy výzkumu hradů v Čechách – *Stand, Bedarf und Aussichten der Burgenforschung zur Zeit in Böhmen*", *Archeologické rozhledy*, 28, 172-180.

– (1977), „Zaniklý sídlištní komplex Řebřík – *Die Wüstung Řebřík*", in *Středověká archeologie a studium počátků měst*, M. Richter (hrsg.), Praha, Československá akademie věd, 231-235.

– (1981), „Problematika výzkumů hradů v Čechách – *Zur Problematik der Burgenforschung in Böhmen*", *Archaeologia historica*, 6, 7-17.

– (1998), *Hrady kastelového typu 13. století ve střední Evropě*, Praha, Academia.

– (2000), *Ilustrovaná encyklopedie českých hradů*, Praha, Libri.

– (2002), „Velká věž hradu Velešína – *Der große Turm der Burg Velešín*", *Castellologica bohemica*, 8, 409-416.

– (2003), „Hrad Vítkův Hrádek (Vítkův Kámen)", *Muzejní a vlastivědná práce – Časopis Společnosti přátel starožitností*, 41/111, 51-54.

– (2005), *Ilustrovaná encyklopedie českých hradů. Dodatky 2*, Praha, Libri.

– (2006), „Latran – ein spezifischer Typ der befestigten Unterburgsiedlungen in Böhmen – *Latran: un type spécifique de peuplements castraux en Bohème – Latran: a Specific Type of Castral Population in Bohemia*", in *Château Gaillard 22. Château et peuplement*, P. Ettel, A.-M. Flambard Héricher & T. E. McNeill (hrsg.), Caen, Publications du CRAHM, 109-118.

– (2011a), „K problematice možného ovlivnění středoevropské hradní architektury křížovými výpravami do Svaté země – *Zur Problematik einer möglichen Beeinflussung der mitteleuropäischen Burgenarchitektur durch die Architektur der Kreuzfahrten ins Heilige Land*", Archaeologia historica, 36, 7-25.

– (2011b), „Rožmberské hrady", in *Rožmberkové. Rod Českých velmožů a jeho cesta dějinami*, Praha, Národní památkový úústav, 182-195.

Durdík T. & Bolina P. (1996), „Hrady pražského biskupství (arcibiskupství) – *Die Burgen des Prager Bistums (Erzbistums)*", Archaeologia historica, 21, 291-306.

Durdík T. & Sušický V. (2005), *Zříceniny hradů, tvrzí a zámků. Západní Čechy*, Praha, Agentura Pankrác.

Dvořáková V. & Hilmera J. (1947), „Rožmberský latrán pod Příběnicemi", *Zprávy památkové péče*, 7, 121-126.

Fröhlich J. (1996), „Hraniční horský hrádek na Ostrém na Šumavě – *Die Gebirgsgrenzfeste am Berge Osser im Böhmerwald*", Castellologica bohemica, 5, 101-106.

Hejna A. (1974), „Bradlo u Hostinného nad Labem. Příspěvek k výzkumu opevněných sídel v severovýchodních Čechách", *Památky archeologické*, 65, 365-418.

Hložek J. (2011), „Pozůstatky obléhacích prací v předpolí hradu Příběnice, okr. Tábor – *Remains of Siege Features in Foreland of the Příběnice Castle, Tábor District*", Archeologické výzkumy v jižních Čechách, 24, 209-225.

– (2012), „Předhradí středověkých hradů v Čechách – Proč právě předhradí? – *Baileys of the Middle Age Castles in Bohemia*", Časopis společnosti přátel starožitností, 2012/1, 36-47.

Karel T. et al. (2009), *Panská sídla západních Čech, Karlovarsko*, České Budějovice, Veduta.

Kohout M. (2012), *Hrad Falštejn a jeho bezprostřední hospodářské zázemí*, Die Diplomarbeit welche im Archiv der Westböhmische Universität in Pilsen ablegen ist.

Kubů F. & Zavřel P. (1994), „Terénní průzkum české části Zlaté stezky", *Zlatá stezka*, 1, 54-76.

Menclová D. (1972), *České hrady*, Teil II, Praha, Odeon (České dějiny; 45).

Procházka Z. & Úlovec J. (1988), *Hrady, zamky a tvrze okresu Tachov 1*, Tachov, Okr. muzeum (Mládež a kultura. Historická řada; 2).

Profous A. (1954), *Místní jména v Čechach I. Jejich vznik, původní význam a změny*, Praha, Nakl. Československé akad. věd.

Sedláček A. (1882-1927), *Hrady, zámky a tvrze království Českého 1-15*, Praha, Tiskem a nákladem knihtiskárny František Šimáček.

Zeune A. (1996), *Burgen – Symbole der Macht. Ein neues Bild der mittelalterlichen Burg*, Regensburg, Pustet.

The Border Castles of the Bishopric of Utrecht c. 1050-1528

From Military Strongholds to Seats of Power and Authority

◆

Hans L. Janssen*

1. Introduction

During the Middle Ages the largest part of the present Netherlands belonged to the diocese of the bishop of Utrecht. Mainly by extensive donations of the German emperor, parts of this diocese developed into a secular state from the 10th/11th century onwards. Here the bishop of Utrecht wielded temporal power until he transferred it to Emperor Charles V in 1528. In this secular state, the episcopal castles played an important role as military strongholds and as centres of power and seats of the judicial and administrative organisation in the territory[1]. The subject of this paper is the function of these episcopal castles as border castles of the bishopric.

As episcopal castles, I consider the bishop's own castles, built or administered by the bishop and his officials, in contrast to the castles of his vassals, over which he had very little effective control. The sources for this study are written documents of all sorts and some cartographic, topographical and archaeological evidence. The buildings themselves have vanished with the exception of two examples of which substantial ruins exist.

We know the territory of the bishopric mainly from the boundaries it had reached around 1300. It consisted then of two parts: the Nedersticht in the west and the Oversticht in the east (fig. 1). The neighbouring territory in the west was the county of Holland and Zeeland. To the east lay the county (from 1339, the duchy) of Guelders, in part of which was the Veluwe area, which separated the two parts of the bishopric from the end of the 12th century onwards.

Mostly border castles are defined as castles built to guard territorial borders or vital elements of them at the time of the functioning of these castles. Following this definition, almost all episcopal castles originally were border castles, as they were built to protect specific trouble spots at the borders of the territory.

Though the more theoretical concept of border castles as a safeguard of the state or nation against enemy attacks may appear in the 14th century, it does not seem to have existed in the bishopric of Utrecht during the 12th and 13th centuries. Then the princely episcopal castles were seen as the jewels in the crown, so to speak, to safeguard the territory as a whole, rather than the borders in a narrow sense. In charters, chronicles and especially on epitaphs, the founding and building of castles is declared to be a great virtue for the defence of the church and the territory as a whole. An often repeated formula in the archbishopric of Cologne and the bishopric of Utrecht is that castles had to be built for the strengthening and defence of the bishopric ("…*ad munimen et defensionem episcopatus…*") and in defence of the church ("*in defensionem ecclesie*"), the castles of which are the advanced posts ("*propugnacula*")[2].

---

* Leiden University, Netherlands.
1. The importance of the episcopal castles for the administrative development of the episcopal state has been discussed in Janssen 1977.
2. See Janssen 1976, 296 for the terminology in charters, issued by the archbishop of Cologne and authors in his entourage (for instance, Caesarius van Heisterbach) during the 12th and early 13th century. For the bishopric of Utrecht, the phrase "*ad munimen et defensionem episcopates*" was also used by the early 13th-century writer of the *Narratio* in the case of the building of the castle at Hardenberg: see Van Rij 1989, 67. In a general vein, the Utrecht bishop Godfried van Rhenen (1156-1178) was praised in contemporary sources, annals and epitaphs for having enriched his church with 4 castles ("*Godefridus…decoravit astra, quia struxit bis duo castra…*" and "*Godefridus…ecclesiam suam…castris bonis et firmis decoravit…*"):

Fig. 1 – Map of the Netherlands *c.* 1300 with the episcopal castles in Nedersticht and Oversticht. The castles are numbered in chronological order: 1) Ysselmonde (1076); 2) Schulenborg (1123-1228); 3) Randenburg, one of a number of place-names with the suffix *-burg* (Zvadenburg, Middelburg, Grensburg, etc.) in this neighbourhood, possibly indicating a number of 12th-century episcopal walled enclosures; 4) Lexmond (1133); 5) Hunenborg (12th century); 6) Bentheim (1146-1178/1196); 7) Coevorden (1139/1150-1522); 8) Ter Horst (1178-1528); 9) Woerden, *c.* 1160; 10) Montfoort (1156/1178-1297); 11) Vollenhove (before 1169-1528); 12) Gein (1228); 13) Hardenberg (1228-1393); 14) Goor (*c.* 1250-1394/1421); 15) Vreeland (1258/1260-1528); 16) Lage (1266-1528); 17) Dullenborch (1312/1318); 18) Stoutenburg (1315/1316-1459); 19) Diepenheim (1331-1528); 20) Arkelstein (1347-1528); 21) Ter Eem (1347/1348-1527); 22) Waardenborg (1378/1382-1528); 23) Kuinre (1407-1528); 24) Venebrugge (before 1413-1500); 25) Slingeborg (1399-1461); 26) Neuenhaus (1418/1429-1435); 27) Blankenham (before 1434-1528); 28) Enschede (1433-1437/1455); 29) Blankenborg (1449-1528); 30) Duurstede (1449-1528); 31) Abcoude (1449-1528). Drawing Cartografisch Bureau MAP (Amsterdam, Netherlands).

The aim of this paper is to analyse the actual development of the military, territorial and administrative functions of the border castles of the bishopric of Utrecht throughout its existence as a secular state, which can be divided in three successive stages. These are:

– *c.* 1050-1200, development of territorial power;
– *c.* 1200-1350, weakening authority of the bishop;
– *c.* 1350-1450, consolidation of territorial power and completion of the territory.

For each period, castle-building policies and castle architecture will be reviewed as well as the relationship between military and residential function, the garrisoning and the administrative and territorial function of the castles.

2. The episcopal border castles during the development of the territorial power, *c.* 1050-*c.* 1200

During the 11th and the early part of the 12th century, the prince-bishop of Utrecht was undoubtedly the most powerful feudal prince in the Northern Netherlands. Most of the Northern Netherlands belonged to the diocese where he wielded spiritual power, and over more than half of this area he wielded temporal power as well.

The main factor behind this temporal power was the general policy of the German kings and emperors to counterbalance the tendencies towards independence by secular princes, by giving extensive secular powers to the bishops of the realm. They appointed the bishops and enlarged the bishoprics with gifts of large estates, legal rights and privileges and permanent support during political troubles. The Concordat of Worms (1122) ended this policy, but the ties between the bishop of Utrecht and the Emperor remained close until the end of the 12th century. At that time the main outline for the later territorial state had been formed.

The territorial authority of the bishops as a kind of imperial viceroys in the Northern Netherlands was undisputed during the 11th century. It was expressed by a number of prestigious visits paid by the emperors to the residence of the bishop in Utrecht[3]. The importance and status of the bishop were also apparent in the stone buildings of his residence, a rare feature in this area, as stone had to be imported from the Eifel region. The Utrecht residence was located inside an old Roman fort and contained an impressive tufa stone palace and cathedral. The bishop's palace also had defensive features: a tower, the *turris episcopalis*, is mentioned in 1122 and 1159, in which the bishop was besieged by his own citizens. The residence had also a separate palace, called *Lofen*, for the visiting emperor[4].

Probably the bishop had another stone palace built in Deventer[5], his second residential town and it has been suggested recently the bishop may also have been responsible for another excavated 11th-century stone palace, a *Pfalz*, in Zutphen that functioned as the capital of a county, donated to the bishop by the emperor in 1046[6]. The architecture of this palace has much in common with the German royal palaces in Goslar and Paderborn.

2.1. Building policies, function and architecture

In their territorial authority the bishops were only occasionally challenged during the 11th century. Therefore, there was no reason to build permanent border castles, certainly not in stone. During the second half of the 11th and the beginning of the 12th century, the bishops reacted to challenges by constructing earth and timber constructions, probably temporary motte castles, at strategic points, such as river and road crossings.

The written sources mention two examples: the *firmissimum castrum* in Ysselmonde[7] in the west, somewhere on the estuary of the river Yssel, built shortly before 1076, and the castle of Schulenborg in the east, mentioned in 1123 because of a siege[8]. Schulenborg can possibly be identified with a large unexcavated earthwork near Almelo. Firstly, this construction was thought to have been a walled enclosure, but a recent careful survey of the site showed it to have been a large, now-eroded motte and bailey castle (fig. 2)[9]. Traces of tufa suggest a stone building, possibly a tower, on top of the motte. It probably existed until 1228, when timber and other building materials were brought to Hardenberg and used for the newly built episcopal castle there.

The exact location and character of the construction at Ysselmonde are unknown. The terminology used suggests a heavily fortified castle, possibly also a motte. It played a role in the perennial conflict between the bishop and the count of Holland over the possession of the reclaimed areas, between the later Nederstricht and the high sand ridges along the dunes in the extreme west of Holland[10]. During this conflict, the bishop was supported by the Emperor, but suffered defeat at the hands of the count in 1076. The castle was burned and the bishop himself was captured[11].

MULLER 1888, 493; VAN RIJ 1989, 6. The 14th-century chronicler Johannis de Beke is the first to add that the bishop built his 4 castles to defend the territory against its neighbouring enemies, respectively the counts of Holland, Guelders, the Frisians and internal rebels: BRUCH 1973, 127.
3. LABOUCHÈRE 1930.
4. DE BRUIJN 1995, 429-432; KOOPMANS 1989; for a recent reconstruction of the episcopal palace in Utrecht, see HUNDERTMARK 2012, esp. 53-54, 60, 62.
5. Partly excavated. See SARFATIJ 1973, 377-391. For a reconstruction of the ground plan, see SPITZERS 1992, 18-26.
6. GROOTHEDDE 2013.
7. *Annales Egmundenses*: see OPPERMANN 1933, 133; BRUCH 1973, 89.
8. WAITZ 1844, 759.
9. VERLINDE & HAGENS 2002.
10. HENDERIKX 1997.
11. *Annales Egmundenses*: see OPPERMANN 1933, 133; HENDERIKX 1997, 122-124.

It does not seem Ysselmonde had been part of a planned line of fortifications guarding the border with Holland. Nevertheless there probably have been many more episcopal fortifications in this area during this period. A late example may have been Lexmond, mentioned as an episcopal stronghold in 1133[12]. There are, however, a number of place-names with the suffix *-burg* such as Randenburg, Middelburg, Zvadenburg, Grensburg etc.[13] near Reeuwijk and Zwammerdam just to the west of the later western boundary of the Nedersticht. The *-burg* names suggest episcopal fortifications, possibly circular walled enclosures in the reclaimed peat areas. Roughly, however, it can be stated that after the major setback in 1076, noted above, the bishop's territory in the west shrank to the present province of Utrecht, the Nedersticht.

The process of the development of the territorial power succeeded much better in the eastern part of the bishopric. Although it was very laborious to weld an untidy bundle of newly acquired rights and possessions into a homogeneous whole, there were not many powerful opponents in the east, so here eventually a coherent territory emerged: the Oversticht, which consisted of the present provinces of Overijsel, Drente and the town of Groningen. The curious gap between both parts of the territory originated in 1196 from the loss of the interjacent Veluwe area to the count of Guelders in what was a complicated conflict.

The castle of Schulenborg near Almelo, besieged by the Emperor in 1123 during a conflict with the bishop, was probably not positioned at the borders at that time, but rather guarded a road crossing along a trade route. Another fortification, the Hunenborg, further to the east, was better positioned to be called a border castle. This castle is not clearly identified by name in the written sources[14], but early excavations in 1916 have shown it to have been a walled enclosure, possibly dating from the 11th or early 12th century[15]. A stone building (constructed of tufa and Bentheim sandstone) within the enclosure, constructed on top of the earlier wall structure and recent dendrochronological dating, point to a reuse of this old fortification by the bishop during the mid-12th century[16].

Shortly before the middle of the 12th century, Bishop Hartbert (1139-1150), himself originating from the Oversticht, built and took over castles at the borders there. He succeeded in subjugating the important territorial dynast of Bentheim, probably in 1146, who handed over his own ancestral castle at Bentheim to the bishop, who gave it back to him as a fief. The bishop, however, reserved parts of the castle, such as the hall, kitchen, chapel and granary, specifically mentioned in

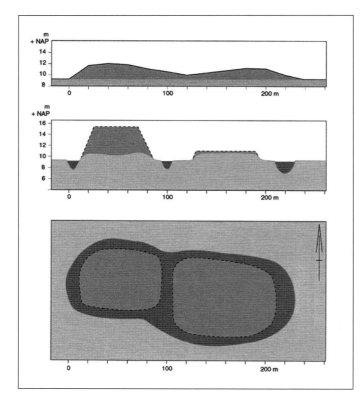

Fig. 2 – Site of Schulenborg Castle (Almelo), mentioned in 1123 (during a siege) and (during demolition) in 1228, originally (c. 1970) reconstructed as walled enclosure. At present it is thought to have been an eroded motte and bailey castle. Above and under: present situation; middle: possible reconstruction 12th century. After VERLINDE & HAGENS 2002, 246.

a charter from 1165, as a personal residence[17]. The still-extant castle is situated on a rocky outcrop. The present oval ground plan shows loosely grouped buildings along the curtain wall, partly still dating from the Middle Ages.

Even more important was the building of the castle of Coevorden, possibly before 1141[18]. It was strategically located on a high, narrow strip of land between vast peat bogs, commanding all traffic between the northern part and the rest of the bishopric. Excavations have shown the castle to have been a (later levelled) motte, having a diameter at its base of 40 m (fig. 3). As the military commander of the castle, Hartbert appointed his half-brother[19]. He also appointed another brother as *prefectus* in Groningen. Probably no castle was built there, but it is supposed that the walled enclosure around the

---

12. Mentioned in 1133 by the *Annales Egmundenses* as "Lakesmunde", an "*urbs episcope*": see OPPERMANN 1933, 148. The early 14th-century chronicler Melis Stoke calls Lexmond a "*veste*": Stoke, *Rijmkroniek*: see BURGERS 2004, 58.
13. VAN DER LINDEN 1956, 263-266.
14. VAN RIJ 1989, 5, note 9, identifies the Hunenborg with "Walstat", mentioned by the *Narratio* (*ibid.*, 4) as a battleground in 1146.
15. HOLWERDA 1917.
16. JANSSEN 1996, 24, 27, 33.
17. VEDDELER 1970, 39-41; sources: *Narratio*: VAN RIJ 1989, 4; KOCH 1970, no. 159 (charter 1165). The charter mentions "*...domum et capellam et granarium et coquinam...*". The "*domus*" from the charter is probably the same as the "*palatium*" in the *Narratio*.
18. In 1141 a "Fredericus de Cuvorden" is mentioned, possibly a castellan: MULLER *et al.* 1920-1959, vol. 1, no. 381.
19. *Narratio*: VAN RIJ 1989, 2, 4; JANSSEN 2009, 103-104.

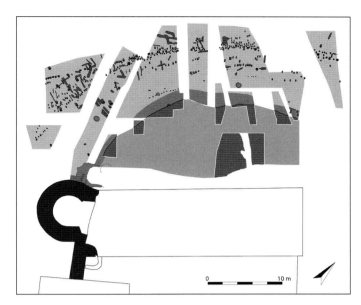

Fig. 3 – Coevorden Castle, result of excavations in 1958 and 1968. Originally built as motte castle, which had a base diameter of *c.* 40 m. Rebuilt after reconquest in 1395, when the motte was levelled and the castle was rebuilt as a square castle with four round towers at the corners. Three towers were demolished before *c.* 1545. Drawing I. Cleijne, BAAC ('s-Hertogenbosch, Netherlands), after JANSSEN 2009, 104.

settlement of Groningen functioned as a fortification[20]. It is beyond doubt that Coevorden Castle had a primarily military function. It can be called a border castle as it had to defend the borders of the new territory, but simultaneously its function was to pacify the interior.

Hartbert's policy was continued even more forcefully by Bishop Godfried van Rhenen (1156-1178), the greatest castle-builder among the early bishops. He not only built castles in the eastern part, but also in the shrunken western part of his territory. According to 14th-century written sources, he built 4 castles: Montfoort, Ter Horst and Woerden, as border castles to protect the borders of the Nedersticht against the counties of Holland and Guelders, and the castle of Vollenhove near the coast of the Zuiderzee to protect the vulnerable north of the Oversticht against the Frisians. The contemporary 12th-century sources are much less specific[21]. Among these castles, Ter Horst was a special case, as it was Bishop Godfried's own ancestral home, which he donated to the bishopric on his deathbed.

For Vollenhove and Montfoort, we have a rough idea about their physical appearance, as there are reliable 17th- and 18th-century drawings (figs. 4 a-b & 5) and fragmentary archaeological observations[22]. It is clear that these castles, like Bentheim, were round or oval court-yard castles, which also had a residential function. Loosely grouped around the court-yard were the chapel, a tower, and a representative hall, a *palas*. Ter Horst, probably built a few decades earlier as a private castle, might have been a variation on this theme. Archaeological observations during the levelling of the site in 1942 have shown this castle to possess a polygonal curtain wall (*c.* 42 m x 58 m), while from written sources, the existence of a large 12th-century, tufa-built tower within the curtain wall is known[23]. Clearly the bishop had these castles built, apart from their obvious military function, as his private residences also. Typologically these court-yard castles were the forerunners of a range of round, oval or polygonal castles built by the princes and the high nobility of the territories in the Low Countries during the 13th century[24].

2.2. Garrisoning

The main function of the early castles of the bishop was a military one. Probably standing garrisons were maintained in most cases, consisting of *borgmannen*, mostly under the command of a castellan or *burggraaf*. In Germany the institution of *borgmannen* is common, especially in the bishoprics. Generally these *borgmannen* were *ministeriales* of the bishop, who in exchange for one or more fiefs belonging to the castle, called *borglenen*, were obliged to live in or near the castle and to defend the castle as members of the garrison. The institution is already mentioned in the 12th century for Bentheim[25] and Ter Horst[26], although most sources date from the 13th and 14th centuries. It seems certain that the system of *borgmannen* was also used for episcopal residences like Deventer[27] and defensible settlements like Groningen[28].

2.3. Administrative and residential functions

Bishop Hartbert must have realised the important pacifying role of Coevorden, as he gave far-reaching legal and administrative powers in the county of Drenthe to the military commander of the castle. In Groningen he did the same. So, in fact, the earliest mention of a real permanent border

---

20. GOSSES 1946, 175-181; NOOMEN 1990, 123-132.
21. MULLER 1888, 493; *Johannis de Beke*: BRUCH 1973, 127; *Narratio*: VAN RIJ 1989, 6. For the detailed motivation see also note 2. It is possible that the late 12th-century castle at Kuinre, although not specifically mentioned as such, was also built as an episcopal castle: suggested (with references) by JANSSEN 1977, 151, note 48. See also for general background DE BOER & GEURTS 2002, 17-19.
22. SARFATIJ 1991 for Montfoort. See also NOORDAM 1995. Vollenhove has completely vanished during the enlargement of the harbour from 1821-1823 onwards.
23. RENAUD 1995a. It is intriguing that in the scarce documentation – except in the case of the older tower at Ter Horst – only brick and no tufa stone is mentioned as building material for the castles built by Godfried van Rhenen. Therefore, the question could be asked: whether these castles have not been built in brick from the beginning and in that case did belong to the earliest constructions in brick in the Netherlands?
24. JANSSEN 1996, 45-56.
25. KOCH 1970, no. 159.
26. MARIS 1954, 146, note 11.
27. BENDERS 2005, 115, note 3.
28. NOOMEN 1990, 129-132.

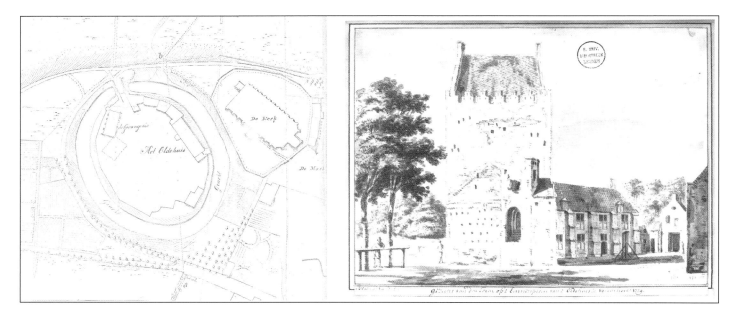

Fig. 4 – Vollenhove Castle. Border castle and episcopal residence in the Oversticht, 1169-1528, now vanished: A) plan c. 1820, during demolition (Rijksarchief Overijsel [Zwolle], Kaartenverzameling, inv. nr. 1227); B) drawing of great tower A. De Haen, 1729. Oval stone castle, with buildings (tower, hall and chapel) along curtain wall. After JANSSEN 1996, 48.

Fig. 5 – Montfoort. Episcopal border castle, 12th century, presently vanished. Drawing R. Roghman in 1646/1647 from the south-east. Round court-yard castle with (partly) later medieval buildings such as chapel, living quarters and (at the back) a large square tower. After NOORDAM 1995, 318.

castle built by the bishop coincides with the first mention of a permanent official with military, judicial and administrative powers, residing outside the residence of the bishop. A major problem was introduced, however, by creating the positions of castellan and sheriff as hereditary.

From Godfried van Rhenen's episcopate onwards, Ter Horst developed into the main private residence of the bishop in the western part, as did Vollenhove in the eastern part. The earliest charter, given by the bishop in Vollenhove, dates from 1169[29]. The functioning of these residences, however, can only be gathered from later sources.

3. The episcopal border castles in a period of weakening authority, c. 1200-c. 1350

After the death of Bishop Godfried van Rhenen (1178), a period of gradual decline followed in the territorial power of the bishop during the 13th century and especially the first half of the 14th century. The most obvious reason for this was the loss of the support of the Emperor after the Concordat of Worms (1122). This resulted in a power struggle during every election of a new bishop by the canons of the bishopric. Consequently the rival powers to the bishop, especially the neighbouring princes of Guelders and Holland, in ever-changing coalitions, tried to wring concessions and bribes from the unfortunate candidate-bishop. The resulting need to buy off the various rivals led in the long run to a serious depletion of the episcopal treasury.

3.1. Building policies, function and architecture

During the 13th century most bishops were not able or willing to pursue an active policy of castle building and strengthening borders. An exception might seem the building of a new border castle at Hardenberg in 1228. The building of this castle, however, was not a proof of strength, but on the contrary an illustration of the essentially weak position of the bishop. The castle had to be built in order to neutralize the power of the former border castle of Coevorden, where the episcopal functionary, supported by his hereditary position,

---

29. MULLER *et al.* 1920-1959, vol. 1, no. 463.

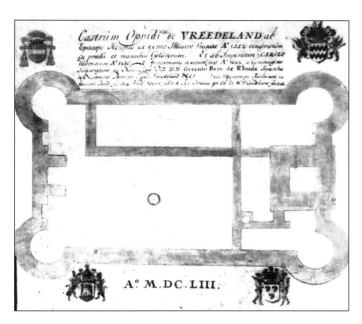

Fig. 6 – Vreeland Castle. Ground plan after excavation of the foundations in 1653 by the then owner of the site, Godard, lord of Reede, meant to acquire a seat in the Estates of the province. Originally built c. 1260 by Bishop Hendrik van Vianden (1249-1267). To this period probably belongs the square tower at the right. Probably rebuilt into a rectangular castle when it was mortgaged to the count of Holland (1327-1353). Presently vanished. Photo W. H. M. Bouts, after JANSSEN 1993, 52.

had made himself a nearly independent dynast, who went so far as to support rebellions against the bishop, finally defeating and killing the bishop in battle in 1227. The new bishop, Willebrand of Oldenburg (1227-1233), built the new castle a few miles to the south on the same ridge that ran through the marshes as Coevorden, cutting off all traffic between the latter castle and the eastern part of the bishopric. The building of Hardenberg was only possible with the financial support of the town of Zwolle. It was the first time a town supported the bishop in saving the territorial integrity of the bishopric[30]. Unfortunately we have no information about the physical appearance of this castle. Vague indications in the written sources suggest a motte.

During the 13th century the hereditary position of the castellans had led to the same problems with the castles of Montfoort and Woerden, which in an almost identical manner to Coevorden, had passed out of the control of the bishops.

So generally speaking, no new castles were built during the 13th and first half of the 14th century. Some of the bishops, however, were able to add a few feudal lordships and existing castles to the territory of the Overstict: Goor (1248/1250)[31], the *castrum* of Lage just before 1266[32] and the addition of the lordship and castle of Dalen and Diepenheim in 1331[33], all situated on the eastern border of the Overstict. Unfortunately we do not have any information about the physical appearance of these castles at that time. Probably these were not important military fortifications, but smaller private castles, perhaps with the exception of Lage.

However, during this long period of decline, there were two bishops, Hendrik of Vianden (1249-1267) and Guy of Avesnes (1301-1317), who were able to pursue an active policy of castle building. The Nederstict was the focus of their attention. Here the main enemies were the count of Holland to the west, the count of Guelders to the east and insurgent nobility within. Hendrik of Vianden was one of the ablest rulers among the 13th-century bishops. In the western part of his territory, Bishop Hendrik built the castle of Vreeland between 1258 and 1260, soon after followed by the creation of a new borough close to the castle. So Vreeland was not in the first place meant to defend the outer borders, but as the name, given by Hendrik himself, implies a castle to "free the land" – that is to pacify the interior[34]. Bishop Guy of Avesnes was another able ruler who in between two disastrous episcopates had temporarily been able to restore territorial power to the bishopric. He built a new castle, the Dullenborch, in the extreme south in a wet, contested area along the Rhine near Rhenen, possibly meant as a toll-house, shortly after 1312[35]. He rebuilt the derelict castle of Goor[36] and also bought and rebuilt the feudal castle of Stoutenburg in 1315/1316, which was potentially useful for the defence of the eastern border of the Nederstict against Guelders[37].

Almost nothing is known of the physical appearance of these castles. We may surmise from the later ground plan (fig. 6) that during the 13th century the most important part of Vreeland was a square tower. Stoutenburg was probably a round court-yard castle, originally built c. 1260 by the episcopal governor of Amersfoort as his private castle, possibly as a smaller imitation of the episcopal castles of Montfoort, Ter Horst and Vollenhove. However, only a part of the curtain wall could be excavated[38]. Perhaps with the exception of Vreeland, the military aspects of both castles do not seem to have been very prominent.

---

30. *Narratio*: VAN RIJ 1989, 66; MULLER *et al.* 1920-1959, vol. 2, no. 803.
31. *Johannis de Beke*: BRUCH 1973, 197; BRUCH 1982, 129; SNUIF 1930a, 253-254.
32. The castle is mentioned as *domus* in 1266 and as *castrum* in 1270: VEDDELER 1970, 89; HULSHOFF 1957, 41.
33. BERKELBACH VAN DER SPRENKEL 1937, nos. 960, 961, 973, 974, 984, 986, 990, 1001.
34. MULLER *et al.* 1920-1959, vol. 3, nos. 1527, 1532, 1681, 1717. For discussion: JANSSEN 1993, 31-34.
35. *Johannis de Beke*: BRUCH 1973, 281; IMMINK & MARIS 1969, 237-238. In later medieval sources the castle is called Tollenburg: VAN ITERSON 1960, 14-16.
36. *Johannis de Beke*: BRUCH 1973, 281.
37. BERKELBACH VAN DER SPRENKEL 1937, nos. 318, 319, 340. For discussion, see JANSSEN 1990, 121-122.
38. HULST 2006. For written information about the castle buildings, see JANSSEN 1990, 132-135.

3.2. Garrisoning

The garrisons of the castles during the 13th and 14th centuries still generally consisted of *borgmannen*. For this period, they are known from the castles of Ter Horst[39], Goor[40], Lage[41], Diepenheim[42] and the Dullenborch[43], and probably Coevorden and Hardenberg[44]. The institution can also be traced in Vollenhove[45], Montfoort[46] and the Schulenborg[47]. A curious extension of the institution of *borgmannen* can be found in the founding charter of the chapter of secular canons at Ter Horst in 1347, where it is stipulated that they also had to serve as armed knights[48].

3.3. Administrative and residential functions

Despite sometimes difficult circumstances, the function of Ter Horst and Vollenhove as episcopal residences appeared from the bishops issuing charters there on a regular basis – in Ter Horst, for instance, from at least 1227 onwards[49] – and appointing and discharging officials. In addition, Ter Horst and Vollenhove both functioned as episcopal record offices. Later, in 1347, a chapter of secular canons was founded at Ter Horst[50], from which clerks could be recruited.

Although not much is known about the organisation of the military and administrative tasks of the castellans, there are glimpses of a more modern form of organisation during the episcopate of Bishop Guy of Avesnes (1301-1317). He seems to have been the first bishop to introduce an administrative structure, based upon dischargeable officials with clearly defined districts, mostly residing in episcopal castles[51]. He seems to have done so at least for the most important officials of the episcopal territory, the sheriffs and stewards, who were given an episcopal castle as a residence.

4. The 14th- and 15th-century episcopal border castles in Nedersticht and Oversticht: consolidation of territorial power and completion of the territory

Two episcopates, those of Jan van Nassau (1267-1290) and Jan van Diest (1323-1340), were instrumental in bringing about the complete breakdown of the temporal power of the bishop. Both ended their reigns with such heavy debts, that almost all castles and offices had to be mortgaged, partly to local noblemen, partly to the counts of Holland and Guelders. After the death of Jan van Diest in 1340, there was no money left to pay off the debts. So there was a real danger that these mortgaged possessions would be annexed by the neighbouring counties of Holland and (since 1339) the Duchy of Guelders or would develop into independent lordships or robber baronies.

During the episcopate of the new bishop Jan van Arkel (1342-1364), however, the foundations were laid for the restoration of law and order and a new balance of power. An able ruler himself, the bishop was much helped by internal strife in the principalities of Holland and Guelders. The main factor, however, in the restoration of the territorial power of the bishopric were the towns, i.e. the city of Utrecht in the Nedersticht and the three Hanseatic towns of Zwolle, Kampen and Deventer in the Oversticht. Until this period, the towns had generally tried to take as much advantage as possible of the fundamentally weak position of the bishop. The trade interests of the towns, however, would certainly not benefit from the dissolution of the episcopal state. So the towns changed their policy and allied themselves with the new bishop.

4.1. Building policies, function and architecture

4.1.1. Nedersticht

In the Nedersticht, the city of Utrecht cleared up the mess. By a combination of paying off the bishop's debts, mediating in quarrels between the bishop and his creditors and the use of occasional military force, the city succeeded in saving the territorial integrity of the Nedersticht. By paying the mortgage for Vreeland Castle in 1353, the city also brought back this important castle into the territory of the Nedersticht[52], where it then functioned as the border castle in the north. In 1354 the city even took Ter Eem Castle, built a few years earlier by an ecclesiastical functionary of the bishop. The castle had an important strategic position, near the mouth of the river Eem, with access to the Zuiderzee[53]. Ter Eem Castle became the main harbour for the bishop in travelling from the Nedersticht to his residence Vollenhove in the Oversticht, thus evading the often hostile Veluwe area, belonging to Guelders.

We know the ground plan of Ter Eem Castle from careful and exact measurements dating from 1529 – as part of a not realised plan for the extension of the castle with artillery bastions (fig. 7 a) – and a cartographic depiction from 1628 within

---

39. Muller 1909.
40. Snuif 1930a.
41. Hulshoff 1957, 41, 44.
42. Snuif 1930a, 261-262.
43. Immink & Maris 1969, 237.
44. Benders 2005, 20, esp. note 7.
45. *Ibid.*, 19-20.
46. Muller *et al.* 1920-1959, vol. 5, no. 2803.
47. Verlinde & Hagens 2002, 249.
48. Kuys 2008, 96; Muller 1909, 120.
49. Muller *et al.* 1920-1959, vol. 3, nos. 762-763 (1227); 883 (1235); 1005 (1243); 1174 (1248); 1299 (1253); 1330 (1254); 1458 (1258); 1532 (1260); 1569, 1576, 1579 (1270). Probably more charters were issued in Horst, but in most cases the place of issue of the charter is not mentioned. For Vollenhove, see also Gevers *et al.* 2004, 13-14, 58ff.
50. Kuys 2008.
51. Maris 1954, 104.
52. Janssen 1993, 38.
53. Janssen 1995, 187-188.

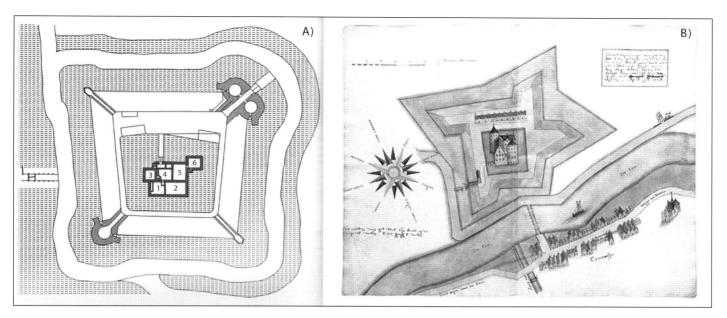

Fig. 7 – Ter Eem Castle, built 1347/1348. Until 1528, it was the main Northern border castle of the Nedersticht, now vanished: A) ground plan of castle measured and drawn by R. Keldermans in 1529 within designed, but not realised, artillery bastions. Scale approximately 1:1050. Numbers in ground plan according to an inventory of 1478: 1) kitchen; 2) hall; 3) castellan's chamber; 4) court-yard; 5) unknown; 6) Bishop's chamber. After JANSSEN 1996, 110. B) cartographic depiction of the castle from a military atlas, dated 1618, within later fortifications. Photo J. A. Bakker, with the kind permission of Mr S. Hesselink.

later realized fortifications (fig. 7 b). It shows a characteristic, probably 14th-century private castle (c. 22 m x 27 m) – perhaps with some minor later additions – with connected towers and halls with only a small internal court-yard and no open stretch of curtain wall. The large, protruding square tower on the north-eastern corner may be a later addition[54]. Typologically it is a compact tower-hall castle, characteristic for the second half of the 14th and first half of the 15th century[55].

The ground plan of the castle of Vreeland is known from a remarkable, but reliable document, dating from 1653, the result of an excavation by the then owner of the site. It shows a rectangular castle (43 m x 29 m) with 4 round corner towers, a square internal gate tower and a larger square, possibly older keep (fig. 6). This castle looks more like a modern 14th-century military fortification than the private castle of Ter Eem. Probably its plan originated from an extensive rebuilding between 1327 and 1353.Vreeland was at that time mortgaged to the count of Holland, who had intended to use it as his most advanced post against Utrecht[56]. So the "modern" appearance of Vreeland Castle in the 14th century was not the result of the episcopal building policy, but of that of his arch-enemy, the count of Holland.

From the middle of the 14th century onwards, only a few minor changes occurred in the number of episcopal castles of the Nedersticht. Stoutenburg lost its position as a border castle to Ter Eem and was abandoned as an episcopal castle in 1457[57]. The only additions to the territory were the forced purchase of the castles and lordships of Duurstede and Abcoude from the lord of Gaasbeek in 1449[58]. This was, however, an isolated event, rather than the result of a deliberate policy.

Nevertheless both castles, situated at the borders, were useful additions to the territorial structure of the Nedersticht. Abcoude was an old 13th-century polygonal castle[59] which by 1449 was militarily somewhat outdated but still useful because of its position on the northern border of the Nedersticht. Duurstede, on the southern border, was rebuilt by Bishop David of Burgundy (1449-1496), the illegitimate son of Duke Philip the Good, and turned into a luxurious residence for him from 1459 onwards. Later the castle was further extended by David's half-brother Bishop Philip of Burgundy (1517-1524)[60].

54. Ibid., 189-191; JANSSEN 1996, 109-110. The plan of the proposed fortifications and – probably – measurement of the existing castle is by Rombout Keldermans by order of the emperor Charles V. The fortifications were not executed in this form: JANSSEN 1981. The bird's-eye view of Ter Eem Castle, dated April 3, 1618, is no. 1 of a military atlas of 80 maps and plans of fortifications (c. 1612-1629), presently in the possession of the "Antiquariaat Forum" (Mr S. Hesselink): Catalogue no. 107, no. 458. The atlas (deriving possibly via the Library of Blenheim Palace from the "Theological Library of Connecticut", US) was kindly brought to my attention by Dr J. A. Bakker, Baarn (Netherlands).

55. JANSSEN 1996, 91-93.
56. JANSSEN 1993, 49-52, 55-61. The general correctness of the ground plan, drawn in 1653, has been confirmed by an auger analysis in 1978: ibid., 51 and a resistivity survey in 1995: EXALTUS & ORBONS 1995, 23-28.
57. JANSSEN 1990, 125-126.
58. MULLER 1917-1922, vol. 2, nos. 3422-3431, 3485, 3497, 3500, 3518-3519, 3561-3562, 3576; vol. 3, 3801, 3803-3804; ZILVERBERG 1951, 23-25.
59. RENAUD 1995b, 99-101. The polygonal ground plan was confirmed by a geophysical investigation: EXALTUS & ORBONS 1995, 10-17.
60. RENAUD 1995c.

Fig. 8 – Duurstede, oldest surviving part of the 13th-century tower-house is to the right, which was built by an episcopal vassal, then enlarged in 14th or 15th century into a more or less square castle. Seized by the bishop in 1449. Further enlarged and rebuilt by Bishop David of Burgundy (1456-1496) to be his new residence. Most remarkable surviving part of this rebuilding is the (restored) so-called Burgundian tower to the left. Photo L. Smals.

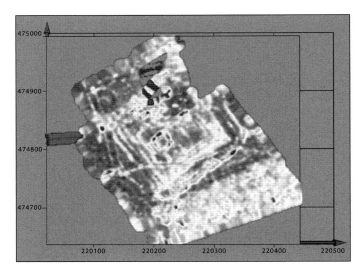

Fig. 9 – Arkelstein Castle, built as a border castle against Guelders shortly before 1360. All visible building phases date from the 14th to the 16th century. Ground Tracer survey, 2007. By kind permission of E. Mittendorff, project manager, Archaeology, Municipality of Deventer (Netherlands).

It took over the function as episcopal residence from the castle of Ter Horst.

Duurstede today still has extensive ruins (fig. 8). It was enlarged from a large tower-house inside a curtain wall with some annexes into a large, more or less square castle (c. 40 m x 45 m) with 4 round corner towers, one of which was an enormous 41 m high, round tower (c. 15 m diameter and 4 m in thickness) with extensive machicolations. Although the design has a French character, the architect is not known[61].

The episcopal castle building activities in the Nederstricht during the 14th and 15th centuries seem to have been rather limited and mostly restricted to repairs. It reflects the general absence of outward threats. Most functioning episcopal border castles were conquered or redeemed from mortgages and originally built by members of the nobility or, in the case of Vreeland, the count of Holland. The only exception was Duurstede Castle which was enlarged and rebuilt under the supervision of the bishop himself and – possibly – French architects into a splendid "Burgundian" square castle.

4.1.2. Oversticht

In the Oversticht the three towns of Deventer, Kampen and Zwolle, operating together, had a similar role in the restoration of episcopal power. However, the town of Deventer went much farther. At the instigation of Deventer and probably paid by the town but with the approval of the bishop, a new line of defence was built along the southern border of the Oversticht with Guelders, which included two new episcopal castles, Arkelstein, named after the then bishop Johan van Arkel (1342-1364), between 1347 and 1360, and Waardenborg, built between 1378 and 1382, and restored and rebuilt between 1401 and 1415[62]. The Waardenborg, built at a junction on the trade routes to Deventer, also functioned as a toll-house.

The town of Deventer also built its own fortifications: the so-called *Koerhuis* and a free-standing round watchtower within a curtain wall, called the Swormer tower[63]. These towers and both episcopal castles were embedded in a *Landweer*, a more than 20 km-long fortification running along the castles and towers to Deventer. It consisted of an earthen wall, provided with a continuous palisade and planted with thornhedges and bushes. The wall had defended passages and moats on both sites, parallel to a canalised river, the *Schipbeek*, running along the border. In the excavated sections, the width of the moats varied between 4 m and 6 m[64]. This *Landweer* type of fortification occurs often in Northern Germany. Deventer built this *Landweer*, including the two castles, with a dual function: to protect the border of the Oversticht with Guelders and to protect their trade routes from the east, which ran along this border.

---

61. Top 2000; Wevers 2004. In the episcopal accounts and registers, Mr Jacob van der Borch, the architect of the Utrecht "Dom", is appointed in 1466 as episcopal architect to oversee the repairs of the episcopal castles. Apart from him a Bohemian, Przilyk Behem van Kossenberch, is mentioned as an architect (State Archives Utrecht, Bisschoppelijk Archief, inv. no. 12, fol. 16; inv. no. 373, fol. 176). There is, however, no indication that they designed (parts of) Duurstede.
62. Janssen & Verlinde 1977.
63. Lubberding 1996.
64. Vermeulen 2002, 8-10.

Arkelstein Castle was surveyed by a ground tracer in 2007. Roughly, it shows the plan of a square castle with round corner towers and a large square tower in the middle (fig. 9)[65]. The medieval castle in the centre seems to be surrounded by a number of earthen ramparts with moats on both sides. In the north-western corner, a round structure suggests an artillery tower. Parts of these traces could well be the remains of the fortifications erected by Charles, Duke of Guelders, after the capture of the castle in 1521[66].

Waardenborg Castle was summarily excavated in 1972. The ground plan shows a square castle with obliquely placed square corner towers and a square keep annex gate-tower (fig. 10). In the excavation no living quarters were identified. If we assume that these quarters (a hall and chamber?) were situated to the south and the west side under a "massive debris layer", where no open curtain wall was present, a remarkable resemblance comes to light with the ground plan of Lechenich Castle, built by the archbishop of Cologne during the first half of the 14th century and finished around 1360[67]. A common characteristic of both castles is the square obliquely placed corner towers, which are rare in the Netherlands and occur only in castles in the Lower Rhine area[68]. The major differences with Lechenich are the position of the keep (not at a corner but in the middle of a side) and the smaller size of the castle as a whole: Lechenich *c.* 33 m x 35 m, without the large tower of 15 m x 11 m; Waardenborg *c.* 25 m x 30 m. The resemblance between both castles is so striking, that it possible that the Waardenborg may have been modelled after Lechenich Castle, which makes sense as the bishop responsible for building the Waardenborg, Florens van Wevelinkhoven (1379-1393), began his career as a canon at Cologne Cathedral in 1343, where he undoubtedly had come in contact with the building of Lechenich Castle[69].

After securing the southern border by building the *Landweer* and the new castles Arkelstein and the Waardenborg, there were still many unreliable areas and nearly independent enclaves, especially on the northern and eastern borders. The new collaboration of bishop and towns was directed mainly at the solution of these problems by an active policy of conquest, castle-building and -buying. The first action was undertaken against the almost independent dynast of Coevorden in 1395, who was subjected and his castle conquered, bringing back the administration of Drente to the bishopric[70]. The castle of Coevorden was immediately rebuilt as a new border castle.

After the abandonment of Hardenberg Castle (last mention in 1393), two small new castles, the Venebrugge and the Slingeborg, were built a few miles to the east of Hardenberg in order to command the main land route through peat bogs to the east, roughly at the border. Both castles were also part of a *Landweer* and functioned as toll-houses. Both are mentioned for the first time in 1399 (Slingeborg) and 1413 (Venebrugge)[71].

After the conquest of Coevorden, the main remaining problem was the independent position of the castle and lordship of Kuinre in the north. As a pirates' nest, it was seriously hindering the maritime trade to Kampen. To end this danger, the castle and lordship were purchased by bishop and towns in 1407 and a new border castle was built here[72]. To round off with the north, a small castle, Blankenham, was newly built during the first half of the 15th century[73].

A few minor territorial problems in Twente were left to deal with. The castle of Diepenheim, functioning as a border castle against the then enemy, the bishop of Münster, was enlarged and possibly refortified between 1436 and 1438[74], the castle of Blankenborch with the lordship of Haaksbergen was bought in 1449[75]. In 1418 a joint action of bishop and towns resulted in the conquest of the ex-territorial castle of Neuenhaus in the county of Bentheim, which removed a dangerous obstacle to trade along the eastern rivers[76]. The ex-territorial castle of Lage, which had been mortgaged since 1346, was redeemed in 1445, then rebuilt and fortified[77].

These castles were all situated at the borders and came to function as the new border castles of the territory. However, we do know little about their physical appearance, so we cannot fully assess their military strength. There is, however, some information about the architecture of Coevorden, Kuinre, Lage and perhaps Slingeborg and Venebrugge.

Partial excavation and written documentation have shown the motte of Coevorden to have been lowered at the beginning of the 15th century and probably transformed into a more or less square castle (possibly *c.* 30 m/35 m x 30 m/35 m) with 4 round towers at the corners and a long hall along its north side[78]. The excavation showed that only the remains of one

---

65. Bartels et al. 2007, 98-103. The dimensions of the castle according to the excavators are surprisingly large: *c.* 90 m x 95 m.
66. Janssen et al. 2000, 131.
67. Friedhoff 2001, 134-36. For the ground plan of Lechenich Castle, see Wildeman 1954, 77. For the excavation of Waardenborg, see Janssen & Verlinde 1977.
68. Janssen 1996, 62-63, 71.
69. Huiting 1992.
70. Heringa et al. 1985, 193-201.
71. First mention of Slingeborg is in 1399: Elte & Berkenvelder 1970, 71. Commissions for the sheriffs and castellans, for Venebrugge (before 1413-1500): State Archives Utrecht, Bisschoppelijk Archief, inv. no. 371, fol. 201x v.-202x (1413, 1419); inv. no. 372-I, fol. 42 v.-43 (1429); inv. no. 373, fol. 27-27 v. (1458), 59-60 (1459), 218-218 v. (1477, 1485), 26x-26x v. (1493); inv. no. 280, fol. 62 v.-64 (1500). For Slingeborg (1411-1461): State Archives Utrecht, Bisschoppelijk Archief, inv. no. 95-2 (1411); inv. no. 372-I, fol. 102 v. (1416, 1441); inv. nos. 329 and 372-II, 11 v. (1446); inv. no. 373, fol. 80 v.-81 (1461).
72. De Boer & Geurts 2002, 69.
73. Commissions of sheriff and castellan between *c.* 1430-1513: State Archives Utrecht, Bisschoppelijk Archief, inv. no. 372-I, fol. 42-42 v.; inv. no. 372-II, fol. 26; inv. no. 373, fol. 91, 229; Officiatorum 1872, 69-70, 423-424.
74. Benders & Bloemink 1996.
75. Snuif 1930b, 66-74; Ter Kuile Jr 1959, 180, 182-183.
76. Hulshoff 1957, 50-52; Veddeler 1970, 78-79.
77. Hulshoff 1957, 59; Veddeler 1970, 92.
78. Janssen 2009, esp. 105-112.

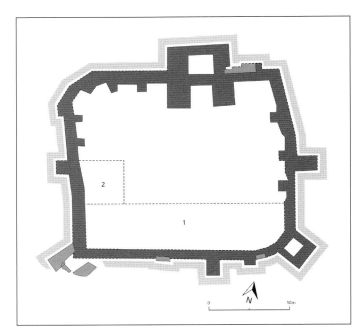

Fig. 10 – Waardenborg Castle, built as a border castle and toll-house by the bishop and the town of Deventer in 1378-1382, restored and rebuilt 1400-1415. At the spaces 1 and 2, the possible living quarters (hall and chamber) were situated. Drawing E. Krijgsman, BAAC ('s-Hertogenbosch, Netherlands), after JANSSEN & VERLINDE 1977, 15.

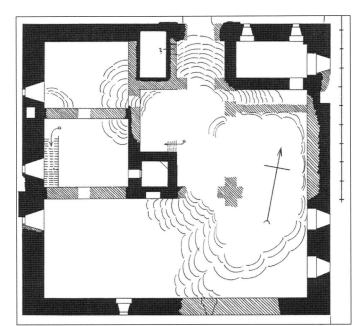

Fig. 11 – Lage Castle, ex-territorial episcopal border castle, first mentioned in 1266, completely rebuilt shortly after 1445. Ruins still existing. Square block with internal towers (including a gate tower) and halls. Internal yard with staircase tower. After NÖLDEKE 1919, 163.

round corner tower were preserved (fig. 3). The other towers were demolished before 1545, as the earliest cartographic map of Coevorden and 16th-century inventories show. This probably happened between 1522 and 1536[79].

Kuinre, existing from the late 12th century onwards as a round castle on a raised platform, was, according to excavations in 1951 and 1999, rebuilt at some distance in the same round form, albeit somewhat larger (c. 45 m x 45 m). The ground plan of the new castle could have been determined by the last dynast of Kuinre, who had started the rebuilding and who may have chosen a larger copy of his old castle. Bishop and towns enlarged and refortified this large round castle between 1407 and 1421. As it turned out, no foundations were present during the excavation. The plan of the castle could only be determined roughly by the imprint of the mass of earth in the subsoil[80].

The 15th-century written commissions of the castellans of Blankenham, the Slingeborg and the Venebrugge suggest that these castles consisted of separate towers (*berchvreden*). In the case of the Slingeborg the tower was accompanied by living quarters (*huysinge*), while the complex as a whole was provided with two moats. In 1446 the bishop paid the castellan of the Slingeborg, mentioned in 1411 as still an exclusively timber construction, to provide the tower with a brick foundation (and basement?), using between 20,000 and 30,000 bricks in order to make the tower habitable[81].

Finally, the castle of Lage still exists in the form of ruins. Written sources prove the castle to have been almost completely rebuilt shortly before 1445[82]. It consists of a square block of around 30 m by 30 m with internal, not projecting, towers (fig. 11). Typologically it belongs to the group of compact tower-hall castles, which in the Netherlands are characteristic for the second half of the 14th and the first half of the 15th century[83]. It is a castle type which is characteristic for Northern Europe and the Baltic area in general.

In spite of the limited information, it seems clear that Coevorden and Kuinre were relatively large, militarily strong, castles, comparable with the earlier Waardenborg and Arkelstein. The small towers of Slingeborg and Venebrugge had a more modest military function, which was to secure the trade route from Coevorden to the east at the border. The castle of Lage, however, was not primarily a military stronghold, but rather proto-typical of a late medieval private castle with a combined defensive and residential function. Generally

79. JANSSEN 2009, 113-115, 118.
80. DE BOER & GEURTS 2002, 24-28, 47-63.
81. Mentioned in the commissions of the castellans, see notes 71 and 73. The commission for the castellan of the Slingeborg in 1446 mentions it as "…*enen gueden stenen voet…*" under the *berchvrede*.

82. NÖLDEKE 1919, 161-163, states, probably erroneously, that the castle has been built in 1576. In 1445, however, an enormous building operation was finished in which a total amount of 665,700 bricks was used. This seems enough to have built a new or at least a substantial part of a new castle. See also HULSHOFF 1957, 60-61.
83. JANSSEN 1996, 91-93.

speaking, it was a remarkable development, that not only was the territorial integrity of the episcopal state saved by the city and towns, but that especially the Hanseatic towns of the Oversticht had built two new lines of defence along the border of the territory with a number of really militarily strong border castles on it. For the towns, the defence of the border meant also the defence of their trade routes, which ran along this border.

4.2. Garrisoning

The new castles built from the middle of the 14th century onwards were also garrisoned in a more modern manner. The old system of hereditary castellans and *borgmannen* with feudal fiefs was abandoned and replaced with paid dischargable castellans appointed for a fixed period. The castellans were responsible for employing paid servants, soldiers and watchmen to guard the castle. Generally the required number of servants for each castle varied between 2, 3 (Waardenburg, Vreeland), 5 (Ter Horst) or 6 men (Abcoude). There were always a gate-keeper and a stableman among them. During wartime, the paid garrison could rise to 12 (Arkelstein, 1380), 18 (Arkelstein, 1523), 25 (Kuinre, 1427) or even 33 (Vollenhove, 1425) soldiers[84].

4.3. Administrative functions[85]

It is clear that the tottering structure of the territorial episcopal state had been saved by the towns of the bishopric around the middle of the 14th century. In close collaboration with the bishop, they had done so firstly by militarily crushing the power of their opponents, secondly by designing, building and paying for new castles along the borders and reorganising the structure of the castle's garrisons. What they still lacked was the guarantee of law and order and a secure administrative organisation in the territory of the bishopric.

Therefore, the city of Utrecht and the towns of the Oversticht demanded an important influence upon the administration of the castles and their dependent offices. Firstly, they acquired a number of general guarantees in order to safeguard them from damage, caused by misconduct of the commanders of episcopal castles. Secondly, they were granted the right that every new castellan of a castle had to be a citizen of a specific town. The city of Utrecht acquired this right for the castles of Ter Eem (1354) and Vreeland (1369) in the Nedersticht, the three towns in the Oversticht together for the castle of Arkelstein (1381), the town of Deventer on its own for Waardenborg Castle in 1383.

Bishop and towns kept the administrative structure, probably introduced by Bishop Guy of Avesnes half a century earlier, based upon dismissible officials with clearly defined districts and fixed terms of office. The most important offices were the sheriffs (called *maarschalken* in the Nedersticht and *drosten* in the Oversticht). There were 2, later 3, of these sheriffs in the Nedersticht and 3 in the Oversticht, each with their own district. Only slightly less important than the sheriffs were the stewards (*rentmeesters*), the main financial officers. Sometimes the offices of sheriff and steward were combined in specific districts. Generally all officials were also appointed as castellans of their residences.

According to this hierarchy of offices, the most important castles in the Oversticht were the newly built castle of Arkelstein, which immediately after 1360 became the seat of the *drost* of Salland, and the rebuilt castle of Coevorden, which after its reconquest in 1395, became the seat of the combined office of sheriff and steward of Drente. Only slightly less important was the residence of the sheriff of Twente at the castle of Goor and the seat of the sheriff of Vollenhove at the castle of that name.

In the Nedersticht the first of the two sheriffs came to reside at the castle of Vreeland, the second one at the castle of Stoutenburg, later transferred to the castle of Ter Eem. The steward of the Nedersticht resided from 1404 onwards in the castle of Ter Horst. The castle of Lage in the Oversticht functioned, after its rebuilding shortly after 1445, alternately as the seat of the sheriff or the steward of Twente.

The residence of the bishops themselves, the castle of Ter Horst, was at the top of the castle hierarchy until this position was taken over by the castle of Duurstede shortly after 1459. The castle of Vollenhove functioned as a second residence of the bishop, which made it the most important castle in the Oversticht.

For contemporaries, the episcopal castles and the offices attached to them were indivisible and two sides of the same coin. This is for instance evident from the terminology in the *Landbrieven*, the first codifications of the regular functioning of the political bodies, known as the Three Estates of which the earliest example comes from the Nedersticht and dates from 1375. In this document, the castles and the offices (*sloten ende ambochten*) are always mentioned as one unit[86], which was from then on considered as the basis for the episcopal state.

5. Conclusion

The concept of border castles as strongholds guarding the frontiers of the territory against attacks does not seem to have existed in the bishopric of Utrecht during the 11th and 12th centuries. Rather the castles were considered as the symbols of the power of the bishops and the church in general.

---

84. Janssen & Verlinde 1977, 29.
85. For a detailed annotation and more detailed history of the administrative function of the border castles, see Janssen 1977, 152-156.
86. Enklaar 1950, 224-228.

The power of the bishops, strongly supported by the Emperor, was not seriously threatened during this period. There seem to have been only incidental conflicts and the building of castles was limited to trouble spots at road- and river-crossings, not necessarily at the borders. As far as is known, motte castles were used for this function.

During the formation of the territory in the 12th century, the first permanent episcopal castles were built. Although they were situated at the borders, they had a residential character and were partly built for the bishop's representation. Most of them were round or oval stone court-yard castles with loosely grouped buildings along the curtain wall. Garrisoning of the castles was organised by means of *borgmannen*, "*ministeriales*" of the bishop with a hereditary fief. Commanders were *borggraven* or castellans, who generally exercised administrative and judicial functions as well. A built-in problem, however, was that all these functions were hereditary.

The 13th and the first half of the 14th century saw a serious decline in episcopal power. A fundamentally weak political and financial position, an insurgent nobility, powerful towns and mighty neighbouring princes led to a disintegration of the territorial power of the bishop. In the border areas no big new episcopal castles were built, only some smaller feudal castles and lordships were added to the territory of the bishopric, while the hereditary position of the castellans and the dependent offices had led to the loss of a number of old episcopal castles.

Around 1340 almost all castles and offices were mortgaged and the territorial integrity of the episcopal state was collapsing. At this stage, the situation was saved by the towns of the bishopric, the city of Utrecht in the Nedersticht and the Hanseatic towns of Deventer, Kampen and Zwolle in the Oversticht. They could not tolerate anarchy and needed law and order for their trade interests. By a combination of paying off the bishop's debts, mediating in quarrels between the bishop and his creditors and the occasional use of military force, the city and towns succeeded in saving the territorial integrity of the bishopric. Moreover, the towns and bishop reorganized the military and administrative structure of the episcopal state.

Militarily, the bishop, city and towns did so by financing the building of a new line of defence along the borders, with a number of strong castles, generally on a square plan, and crushing, conquering and rebuilding the castles of insurgent border lords. Secondly, they changed the garrisoning of the castles from hereditary *borgmannen* to paid soldiers and servants, who were employed by the castellan. Thirdly, they changed the administrative structure of the bishopric from hereditary offices to dismissible officials with clearly defined districts, fixed terms of office and who – generally – had an episcopal castle as their residence.

Bibliography

Bartels M. H. *et al.* (2007), "Arkelstein, het grootste kasteel in de Sallandse landweer", *Overijssels erfgoed. Archeologische en Bouwhistorische kroniek 2006*, 87-112.

Benders J. F. (2005), "Uit de schaduw van het kasteel: Vollenhove van de 12de eeuw tot omstreeks 1400", in *Vollenhove, stad en vermaarde zonen. Negen opstellen bij de viering van 650 jaar stadsrecht*, J. Mooijweer (ed.), Kampen, Stichting IJsselacademie (Publikaties van de IJsselacademie; 180), 19-41, 115-126.

Benders J. F. & Bloemink J. W. (1996), "Het Utrechts Schisma en een Twents kasteel: de versterking van het huis Diepenheim 1436-1438", *Deventer Jaarboek 1996*, 6-21.

Berkelbach van der Sprenkel J. W. (ed.) (1937), *Regesten van oorkonden betreffende de bisschoppen van Utrecht uit de jaren 1301-1340*, Utrecht, Broekhoff (Werken Historisch Genootschap 3[e] serie; 66).

Burgers J. W. J. (ed.) (2004), *Melis Stoke, Rijmkroniek van Holland (366-1305)*, Den Haag, Instituut voor Nederlandse Geschiedenis (Rijks Geschiedkundige Publicatiën. Grote serie; 251).

Bruch H. (ed.) 1973, *Chronographia Johannis de Beke*, 's-Gravenhage, Nijhoff (Rijks Geschiedkundige Publicatiën. Grote serie; 143).

– (1982), *Johannes de Beke, Croniken van den Stichte van Utrecht ende van Hollant*, 's-Gravenhage, Nijhoff (Rijks Geschiedkundige Publicatiën. Grote serie; 180).

De Boer P. C. & Geurts A. J. (2002), *Oude Burchten in het nieuwe land. De middeleeuwse kastelen van Kuinre in de Noordoostpolder*, Lelystad, Stichting Uitgeverij De Twaalfde Provincie/ Sociaal Historisch Centrum voor Flevoland (Publikaties van het Sociaal Historisch Centrum voor Flevoland; 74).

De Bruijn M. W. J. (1995), "De Burcht Trecht", in *Kastelen en ridderhofsteden in Utrecht*, B. Olde Meierink *et al.* (eds.), Utrecht, Stichting Utrechtse Kastelen, 429-432.

Elte S. & Berkenvelder F. C. (eds.) (1970), *Maandrekening van Zwolle 1399*, Zwolle, Gemeentelijke Archiefdienst (Uitgaven van de Gemeentelijke Archiefdienst van Zwolle; 1).

ENKLAAR D. T. (1950), *De Stichtse Landbrief van 1375*, Amsterdam, Noord-Hollandsche uitgevers Maatschappij (Mededelingen der Koninklijke Nederlandsche Akademie van Wetenschappen, Afd. Letterkunde. Nieuwe Reeks 13; 8), 183-228.

EXALTUS R. P. & ORBONS P. J. (1995), *Provincie Utrecht. Archeologisch Onderzoek op de kasteelterreinen Slot van Abcoude, Huis te Vreeland en Huis Ter Eem*, Amsterdam, Stichting RAAP (RAAP-Rapport; 116) [Report].

FRIEDHOFF J. (2001), "Burg Lechenich im Kontext der spätmittelalterlichen Residenzentwicklung im Erzstift Köln", *Annalen des historischen Vereins für den Niederrhein*, 204, 125-155.

GEVERS A. J. et al. (2004), *De havezaten in het land van Vollenhove en hun bewoners*, Alphen aan den Rijn, Canaletto Repro Holland (Adelsgeschiedenis; 2).

GOSSES I. H. (1946), "De bisschop van Utrecht, het Domkapittel en de Groninger prefect", in I. H. GOSSES et al., *Verspreide Geschriften*, Groningen, Wolters, 152-207.

GROOTHEDDE M. (2013), *Een vorstelijke palts te Zutphen? Macht en prestige op en rond het plein 's-Gravenhof van de Karolingische tijd tot aan de stadsrechtverlening*, Zutphen, Gemeente Zutphen (Zutphense Archeologische Publicaties; 77) [Ph.D. Leiden University, 2013].

HENDERIKX P. A. (1997), "De bisschop van Utrecht en het Maas-Merwedegebied in de 11e en 12e eeuw", in *De kerk en de Nederlanden. Archieven, instellingen, samenleving*, E. S. C. ERKELENS-BUTTINGER et al. (eds.), Hilversum, Verloren, 99-128.

HERINGA J. et al. (eds.) (1985), *Geschiedenis van Drenthe*, Meppel/Amsterdam, Boom.

HOLWERDA J. H. (1917), "De Huneborg in Twente", *Verslagen en Mededeelingen van de Vereeniging tot beoefening van Overijsselsch Regt en Geschiedenis*, 33, 1-31.

HUITING J. H. (1992), "Floris van Wevelinghofen", *Utrechtse Biografieën*, 1, 189-192.

HULSHOFF A. (1957), "Het slot te Lage en het Sticht te Utrecht", *Verslagen en Mededeelingen van de Vereeniging tot beoefening van Overijsselsch Regt en Geschiedenis*, 72, 39-62.

HULST R. A. (2006), "Selectierapport Inventariserend Veldonderzoek Plangebied Heerlijkheid Stoutenburg", Amersfoort [Report].

HUNDERTMARK H. (2012), "Naar Adelbolds voorbeeld. De kerken van bisschop Bernold", in *De nalatenschap van de Paulusabdij in Utrecht*, H. VAN ENGEN & K. VAN VLIET (eds.), Hilversum, Verloren (Middeleeuwse studies en bronnen; 130), 37-68.

IMMINK P. W. A. & MARIS A. J. (eds.) (1969), *Registrum Guidonis. Het zogenaamde register van Guy van Avesnes, vorst-bisschop van Utrecht (1301-1317). Met aansluitende stukken tot 1320*, Utrecht, Kemink (Werken der Vereeniging tot Uitgave der Bronnen van het Oud-Vaderlandsche Recht; 23).

JANSSEN H. L. (1977), "The Castles of the Bishop of Utrecht and their Function in the Political and Administrative Development of the Bishopric", in *Château Gaillard 8*, Caen, Centre de recherches archéologiques médiévales, 135-157.

– (1981), "De fortificaties van Ter Eem 1528-1553 en het ontwerp van Rombout Keldermans", in *Liber Castellorum. 40 variaties op het thema kasteel*, T. J. HOEKSTRA et al. (eds.), Zutphen, Walburg, 302-318.

– (1990), "Het verdwenen bisschoppelijk kasteel Stoutenburg bij Amersfoort (1259-1543)", *Castellogica. Verkenningen en Mededelingen van de Nederlandse Kastelenstichting*, 2 (1988-1992), 120-139.

– (1993), "Het bisschoppelijk kasteel Vreeland ca. 1258-ca. 1700", *Castellogica. Verkenningen en Mededelingen van de Nederlandse Kastelenstichting*, 3 (1993-1999), 31-72.

– (1995), "Ter Eem", in OLDE MEIERINK et al. 1995 (eds.), 187-191.

– (1996), "Tussen woning en versterking. Het kasteel in de middeleeuwen", in *1000 jaar kastelen in Nederland. Functie en vorm door de eeuwen heen*, H. L. JANSSEN et al. (eds.), Utrecht, Matrijs, 15-111.

– (2009), "Het kasteel Coevorden. 15e en 16e eeuwse inventarissen als bron voor de bouwgeschiedenis", in *Middeleeuwse kastelen in veelvoud. Nieuwe studies over oud erfgoed*, H. L. JANSSEN & W. LANDEWÉ (eds.), Wijk bij Duurstede, Nederlandse Kastelenstichting (Academic Studies Series; 2), 101-131.

JANSSEN H. L. & VERLINDE A. D. (1977), *Holten, het bisschoppelijk kasteel de Waardenborg*, Amersfoort/Bussum, Fibula-Van Dishoeck/R.O.B. (Archeologische monumenten in Nederland; 6).

JANSSEN H. L. et al. (2000), "Fortification of Castles in the Northern Netherlands during the Gelre-Habsburg Conflict (1492-1543)", in *Château Gaillard 19*, Caen, Centre de recherches archéologiques médiévales, 123-148.

JANSSEN W. (1976), "Burg und Territorium am Niederrhein im späten Mittelalter", in *Die Burgen im deutschen Sprachraum. Ihre rechts- und verfassungsgeschichtliche Bedeutung*, vol. 1, H. PATZE (ed.), Sigmaringen, Thorbecke (Vorträge und Forschungen; 19), 283-324.

KOCH A. C. F. (ed.) (1970), *Oorkondenboek van Holland en Zeeland tot 1299*, vol. 1: *Eind van de 7e eeuw tot 1222*, 's-Gravenhage, Nijhoff.

Koopmans B. (1989), *Lofen. Een elfde-eeuws keizerlijk paleis in Utrecht*, Utrecht/Zutphen, Clavis/De Walburg Pers (Clavis kleine kunsthistorische monografieën; 9).

Kuys J. (2008), "Het kapittel in de Pancratiuskapel op kasteel Ter Horst", in *Geschiedenis van Rhenen*, J. Vredenberg *et al.* (eds.), Utrecht, Matrijs (Historische Heuvelrug Reeks; 15), 94-101.

Labouchère G. C. (1930), "De bezoeken der Duitsche koningen en keizers aan de stad Utrecht gedurende de Middeleeuwen", *Jaarboek Oud-Utrecht 1930*, 31-65.

Lubberding H. (1996), "De Swormertoren", *Westerheem. Tijdschrift voor de Nederlandse archeologie*, 45, 57-62.

Maris A. J. (1954), *Van voogdij tot maarschalkambt, Bijdrage tot de geschiedenis der Utrechts-bisschoppelijke staatsinstellingen, voornamelijk in het Nedersticht*, Utrecht, De Vroede.

Muller S. (ed.) (1888), "Drie Utrechtse Kroniekjes vóór Beka's tijd", *Bijdragen en Mededeelingen van het Historisch Genootschap*, 11, 460-508.

– (1909), "De borchluden van Ter Horst", *Verslagen en mededelingen Oud-Vaderlandsch Recht*, 5/2, 118-127.

– (ed.) (1917-1922), *Regesten van het Archief der bisschoppen van Utrecht (722-1528)*, Utrecht, Oosthoek, 3 vols.

Muller S. *et al.* (eds.) (1920-1959), *Oorkondenboek van het Sticht Utrecht tot 1301*, Utrecht/'s-Gravenhage, Oosthoek/Staatsdrukkerij, 5 vols.

Nöldeke A. (1919), *Die Kunstdenkmäler der Provinz Hannover. Die Kreise Lingen und Grafschaft Bentheim*, Hannover, Selbstverlag der Provinzialverwaltung.

Noomen P. N. (1990), "Koningsgoed in Groningen. Het domaniale verleden van de stad", in *Groningen 1040. Archeologie en oudste geschiedenis van de stad Groningen*, J. W. Boersma *et al.* (eds.), Bedum/Groningen, Profiel, 97-144.

Noordam C. (1995), "Montfoort", in Olde Meierink *et al.* 1995 (eds.), 318-324.

Officiatorum (1872), *Officiatorum referendissimi Frederici de Baden (1496-1516)*, Deventer, De Lange (Werken Overijsselsch Regt en Geschiedenis; 9).

Oppermann O. (ed.) (1933), *Fontes Egmundenses*, Utrecht, Kemink (Werken Historisch Genootschap. 3ᵉ serie; 61).

Renaud J. G. N. (1995a), "Ter Horst", in Olde Meierink *et al.* 1995 (eds.), 259-260.

– (1995b), "Abcoude", in Olde Meierink *et al.* 1995 (eds.), 96-101.

– (1995c), "Duurstede", in Olde Meierink *et al.* 1995 (eds.), 180-186.

Sarfatij H. (1973), "Digging in Dutch Towns: Twenty-Five Years of Research by the ROB in Medieval Town Centres", *Berichten van de Rijksdienst voor het Oudheidkundig Bodemonderzoek*, 23, 367-420.

– (1991), "Het kasteel van Montfoort (U)", *Castellogica. Verkenningen en Mededelingen van de Nederlandse Kastelenstichting*, 2 (1988-1992), 258-260.

Snuif C. J. (1930a), "Het borgmansrecht van Goor", in *Verzamelde Bijdragen tot de geschiedenis van Twenthe*, M. G. Snuif (ed.), Amsterdam, De Spieghel, 244-264.

– (1930b), "Haaksbergen en de Blanckenborg", in Snuif 1930 (ed.), 66-74.

Spitzers T. A. (1992), "De ontwikkeling van Deventer als kerkelijke vestigingsplaats tot aan de bouw van de zogenoemde Bernoldkerk", in *De Grote of Lebuinuskerk te Deventer. De "Dom" van het Oversticht veelzijdig bekeken*, A. J. J. Mekking (ed.), Zutphen, Walburg Pers (Clavis kunsthistorische monografieën; 11), 11-28.

Ter Kuile Jr G. J. (1959), "Heerlijkheden in Overijsel onder het 'Ancien Régime'", in *Dancwerc. Opstellen aangeboden aan prof. dr. D. Th. Enklaar ter gelegenheid van zijn vijfenzestigste verjaardag*, Groningen, Wolters, 176-187.

Top R. J. (2000), "De bouwgeschiedenis van kasteel Duurstede", in *Wijk bij Duurstede 700 jaar stad. Ruimtelijke structuur en bouwgeschiedenis*, M. A. Van der Eerden-Vonk *et al.* (eds.), Hilversum, Verloren, 137-164.

Van der Linden H. (1956), *De cope. Bijdrage tot de rechtsgeschiedenis van de openlegging der Hollands-Utrechtse laagvlakte*, Assen, Van Gorcum.

Van Iterson W. (1960), *De stad Rhenen. De resultaten van een rechtshistorisch onderzoek*, Assen, Van Gorcum.

Van Rij H. (ed.) (1989), *Quedam narracio de Groninghe, de Thrente, de Covordia et de diversis aliis sub diversis episcopis Traiectensibus*, Hilversum, Verloren (Middeleeuwse studies en bronnen; 1).

Veddeler P. (1970), *Die territoriale Entwicklung der Grafschaft Bentheim bis zum Ende des Mittelalters*, Göttingen, Vandenhoeck und Ruprecht (Studien und Vorarbeiten zum Historischen Atlas Niedersachsens; 25).

Verlinde A. D. & Hagens H. (2002), "Almelo, de Schulenborg, een motte-kasteel onder een eenmans-es", *Overijsselse Historische Bijdragen*, 117, 245-250.

Vermeulen B. (2002), *Het middeleeuwse tolhuis en de middeleeuwse landweer aan de Snipperlingsdijk te Deventer*, Deventer, RMW-VHMZ (Rapportages Archeologie Deventer; 10) [Report].

Waitz G. (ed.) (1844), *Annalista Saxo*, Hannover, Impensis Bibliopolii Hahniani (MGH. Scriptores; 6, 553-777).

Wevers L. (2004), "Duurstede. Eine Residenz des Utrechter Bischofs David von Burgund", *Forschungen zu Burgen und Schlössern*, 8, 59-68.

Wildeman T. (1954), *Rheinische Wasserburgen und Wasserumwehrte Schlossbauten*, Neuss am Rhein, Gesellschaft für Buchdruckerei.

Zilverberg S. B. J. (1951), *David van Bourgondië, Bisschop van Terwaan en van Utrecht (c. 1427-1496)*, Groningen/Djakarta, Wolters (Bijdragen van het Instituut voor Middeleeuwse Geschiedenis der Rijks-Universiteit te Utrecht; 24).

Rouelbeau : un château en bois du XIVe siècle aux frontières du Faucigny (Suisse)

◆

Michelle Joguin Regelin, Jean Terrier*

Dernier vestige d'un château médiéval conservé en élévation, le château de Rouelbeau se situe au cœur de la campagne genevoise, sur la rive gauche du lac Léman. Ce bâtiment fait l'objet d'un vaste projet d'étude et de restauration entrepris depuis plusieurs années qui devrait prendre fin dans le courant de l'année 2014. Classé monument historique en 1921, le château était alors laissé à l'abandon, à la merci d'une nature qui avait progressivement repris ses droits, mettant en péril la conservation des maçonneries[1].

1. Aperçu des sources historiques

Si l'on se réfère à la chronique du prieuré de Saint-Victor de Genève, l'édification du château de Rouelbeau fut achevée par le chevalier Humbert de Choulex, le 7 juillet 1318[2]. Au cours de l'année suivante, Hugues Dauphin, sire de Faucigny, acquit cette bâtie qui devint sans doute le siège d'une châtellenie. Cette position fortifiée jouait alors un rôle stratégique de premier ordre, ayant pour mission la défense de la route qui menait à la ville neuve d'Hermance, unique débouché sur le lac pour les seigneurs de Faucigny, dont les terres formaient ici un étroit couloir principalement délimité par les possessions des comtes de Genève. Pour cette raison, le château fut édifié en plaine, au milieu des marécages, et non sur une hauteur, selon la tradition des châteaux défensifs (fig. 1). Le château continue à jouer ce rôle jusqu'en 1355, date à laquelle la Savoie annexe le territoire du Faucigny et rend caduque la présence

Fig. 1 – Tours et courtine sud du château de Rouelbeau avec le fossé en eau au premier plan. Photo M. Delley, Service cantonal d'archéologie de Genève (Suisse).

d'un bâtiment militaire sur un territoire dont la stabilité est désormais assurée par sa réorganisation géopolitique. Le château passe de mains en mains par le jeu des héritages jusqu'en 1536, où il se trouve dans la maison de Genève-Lullin et sera détruit. À la fin du XVIIIe siècle, propriété des Loys et désormais en ruine, ses pierres seront vendues aux habitants de Meinier pour construire leurs maisons.

En 1339, Hugues Dauphin, désireux de vendre certaines de ses possessions au pape, envoie son procureur afin d'effectuer

---

* Archéologues, Service cantonal d'archéologie de Genève, Suisse.
1. Cette communication a pu être présentée en anglais au colloque d'Aabenraa grâce à la traduction avisée de M. Louis Nermann, architecte que nous remercions.
2. Les données historiques présentées dans cet article proviennent essentiellement d'un rapport dactylographié fourni par M. de La Corbière (La Corbière 2001), à qui nous exprimons notre profonde gratitude.

un inventaire et de prendre des mesures aussi fidèles que possible des bâtiments. Cette source d'archives est un témoignage primordial pour la connaissance du château de Rouelbeau qui y est décrit comme une bâtie en bois. Même s'il faut se méfier quelque peu – le procureur du Dauphin ayant tout intérêt à valoriser le capital à vendre –, ce texte est évidemment très précieux. À cette époque, la bâtie est décrite comme édifiée au sommet d'une motte environnée de marais. L'ouvrage est constitué d'une enceinte palissadée de plan quadrangulaire, dont seulement trois angles sont défendus chacun par une tour en bois comprenant deux niveaux. À l'intérieur de cette enceinte se dresse une *domus plana*, maison dépourvue d'étage, abritant une *aula*, une cheminée en bois et une chambre, le tout au-dessus d'un cellier et d'une étable « charmurée ». Cette position fortifiée est protégée par un double fossé en eau entourant la plateforme, traversé par un pont en bois pour accéder à la porte du château. Toutes les dimensions des bâtiments ainsi que celles des structures de défenses sont connues et indiquées en toises et en pieds dans le procès-verbal de la visite de la bâtie. Après le dépouillement des sources d'archives, deux informations essentielles ont été retenues pour amorcer l'étude archéologique des vestiges de Rouelbeau : en premier lieu, le château primitif a été édifié en bois en 1318, puis remplacé par une forteresse maçonnée dans un second temps ; en second lieu, le chantier de construction de cette forteresse maçonnée serait postérieur à 1339 et assurément antérieur à 1355 pour les raisons historiques mentionnées plus haut.

2. Permanence des fortifications de terre et de bois au bas Moyen Âge

En Suisse occidentale, certaines découvertes fournissent un éclairage nouveau sur l'utilisation du bois au cours du bas Moyen Âge dans l'architecture militaire[3]. Les sources sont également précieuses pour attester du maintien de cette tradition[4]. C'est cependant l'édification de bâties, ouvrages fortifiés implantés dans les zones frontières durant toute la période du conflit delphino-savoyard, qui nous intéressera tout particulièrement pour aborder les vestiges découverts à Rouelbeau[5]. Il s'agit de positions essentiellement dévolues au logement temporaire de garnisons et au stockage d'engins de guerre permettant de défendre une nouvelle ligne de frontière dans les plus brefs délais. Un exemple est donné par la fouille de la bâtie de Gironville située dans le Bugey, à 20 kilomètres au nord-est de Lyon[6]. Cette bâtie fut édifiée à la hâte par le comte de Savoie durant la fin de l'année 1324 et le début de l'année suivante. Elle fait partie d'une ligne de retranchements rendue nécessaire par la politique d'expansion menée en direction du nord par la maison de Savoie au détriment du comte de Genève, vassal du Dauphin. Essentiellement militaire, la bâtie n'a pas vocation à devenir le chef-lieu d'une châtellenie et elle sera rapidement abandonnée lorsqu'elle aura perdu tout intérêt stratégique après la signature du premier traité de paix entre le Dauphiné et la Savoie.

Les fouilles ont mis en évidence le plan d'un bâtiment dont le sol est partiellement aménagé avec de la terre battue[7]. Cette pièce comporte un foyer ouvert, dont la sole est réalisée avec des carreaux de terre cuite ; les parois étaient édifiées sur des sablières de bois. La présence de petites cavités creusées dans le sol, dont l'une conservait encore un fond entier de céramique, ainsi que la proximité d'un puits, incitent à considérer cette pièce comme la cuisine. Les sondages effectués à plusieurs reprises n'ont révélé aucune trace de palissade. Cette observation laisse penser que les fossés en eau constituaient, avec les façades arrières des bâtiments, une protection suffisamment efficace contre les attaques de cavalerie. Les observations réalisées à partir de ces vestiges peuvent être mises en perspective grâce à l'apport fourni par un compte de châtellenie savoyarde qui décrit de façon détaillée le déroulement du chantier de construction de la place forte[8]. L'effort principal est porté sur la réalisation des fossés et l'aménagement de la plateforme surélevée à l'aide du matériau provenant des terrassements. Les fossés sont alimentés en eau par le détournement d'un petit ruisseau et la seconde ligne est séparée de la première par un rempart de terre. Les constructions comprennent quatre tours, une cuisine et deux autres bâtiments ; elles présentent toutes une architecture à pans de bois avec un hourdis fait de clayonnage enduit de torchis. Seules les tours s'élèvent sur trois niveaux, alors que les autres bâtiments ne comportent pas d'étage, et toutes les toitures sont couvertes de tuiles. Aucune indication n'est consignée concernant les dimensions des bâtiments et du système défensif.

Un autre exemple est donné par un document relatant la fondation de la ville de Rolle sur les bords du lac Léman par Amédée V de Savoie[9]. Dans ce cas, il s'agit de la création d'une enceinte préfabriquée, entièrement en bois, destinée à délimiter les terrains réservés à la future agglomération projetée à proximité du château bâti dans les années 1260. Les informations contenues dans ce compte illustrent les préparatifs et la mise en œuvre d'une telle entreprise, réalisée quelques mois après la construction de la bâtie de Rouelbeau. Ainsi, dès la mi-novembre de l'année 1318, on s'attelle à la préparation de cette enceinte fortifiée qui devait s'étendre sur près de 750 mètres de longueur, enceinte comprenant une série de tours et d'échauguettes, ainsi qu'une porte aménagée à chacune de ses deux extrémités. Pour la mise en œuvre de ce projet, une commande de bois provenant de l'ensemble du pourtour lémanique est passée. Une partie de ce matériau est

---

3. Menna 2009, 18-26.
4. Raemy 2004, 141-143.
5. La Corbière 2002, 329-335.
6. Poisson 1986a, 253-260.
7. Poisson 1986b, 225-236.
8. Cattin 1979, 2-18.
9. Bissegger 2008, 167-179.

transportée par barques à Évian, où une équipe de charpentiers doit bâtir des éléments préfabriqués qui retraverseront le lac pour être stockés dans la cour du château de Rolle. Sans entrer dans les détails de ce document, on retiendra que les couvertures des toitures sont réalisées à l'aide de tavillons et que la palissade, haute de 5,80 mètres, est constituée de pieux supportant une série de claies superposées. L'ensemble est défendu par un chemin de ronde reposant sur des chevalets de chêne ainsi que par douze tours de 12 mètres de haut et dix échauguettes de 5,60 mètres de haut. Il semble bien que cette fortification impressionnante soit montée en un temps record, entre le 5 et le 12 janvier, par une armée de tâcherons. L'aspect temporaire de ce type de défense en bois est bien mis en évidence dans le cas de Rolle où les portes, ainsi qu'une partie de l'enceinte, seront démontées une année seulement après leur édification.

3. Les fouilles archéologiques

3.1. La bâtie en bois

Lors de la première campagne de fouilles archéologiques qui débuta au printemps 2001, plusieurs décapages furent effectués à l'intérieur et dans l'angle sud-ouest de la place forte. Aucune fondation ayant pu appartenir à des constructions contemporaines de la forteresse maçonnée n'était alors visible en surface. C'est finalement à près de 1,60 mètre de profondeur qu'un niveau d'occupation apparut et mit en évidence des structures révélant l'existence d'une architecture de bois (fig. 2, A)[10]. Des alignements de trous de piquets de modestes dimensions indiquaient la présence d'une palissade formant un angle identique à celui constitué par les courtines du château maçonné. Des alignements de pierres ayant servi pour le calage au sol de poutres, dont l'une était encore conservée sous la forme de bois calciné, s'organisaient perpendiculairement les uns par rapport aux autres. Le relevé précis de tous ces éléments permit de restituer le plan d'une construction carrée de 4,50 mètres de côté, aménagée dans l'angle de la palissade. Ce bâtiment présentait une architecture à pans de bois, dont les parois nord et est reposaient sur des sablières basses, alors que les parois sud et ouest étaient constituées par la palissade elle-même. La grande quantité de clous découverts dans cet espace indique certainement la présence d'une couverture de bois, faite en tavillons. Néanmoins, ces structures n'étaient pas très convaincantes en tant que système défensif, alors que dans le texte de 1339 il est fait état d'une palissade composée de poteaux de 30 à 40 centimètres de largeur, culminant à près de 6 mètres de hauteur. Il fut alors décidé d'étendre la surface de fouille à l'ensemble de la partie sud de la plateforme[11]. L'exploration de ces nouvelles zones permit de mettre au jour des trous de poteaux correspondant à la description de 1339 et de comprendre l'organisation de la palissade. Il fallait se rendre à l'évidence : la fouille de la première campagne n'avait pas été assez profonde et n'avait mis au jour que la partie supérieure des poteaux. Le flanc sud de la palissade présente une longueur de 30 mètres ; les côtés est et ouest, partiellement fouillés, s'étendent respectivement sur 12 et 19 mètres (fig. 3). Aujourd'hui, la palissade défensive du château en bois est constituée de plus de 155 trous de poteaux.

En observant la stratigraphie, nous avons pu comprendre comment avait été édifiée cette palissade : les poteaux, dont l'extrémité est plate, furent implantés à environ 1,20 mètre sous le niveau d'occupation, au sein d'une tranchée un peu plus large, creusée dans le remblai constituant la motte artificielle. Un espace dont la dimension fluctue entre 5 et 15 centimètres les sépare les uns des autres, comme s'ils avaient été attachés par des cordages.

La description de 1339 mentionne l'existence de trois tours, il n'était donc pas nécessaire de défendre les quatre angles de la bâtie. À l'angle sud-est ont été retrouvées les structures d'une tour imposante (fig. 2, C), puisque les trous de poteaux sont liés avec une sablière basse d'environ 30 centimètres d'épaisseur, formant ainsi une tour de 6,50 mètres de côté. Le texte précise d'ailleurs qu'elle comportait deux planchers et devait culminer à plus de 10 mètres de hauteur. Le bâtiment mis au jour au début des travaux (fig. 2, A) n'est aucunement comparable et on peut affirmer que cet angle était dépourvu de tour défensive. Deux massifs constitués d'une seule assise de gros boulets posés directement sur l'argile de la plateforme ont été mis au jour le long de la palissade. L'un, au sud (fig. 2, D), est placé tout contre les pieux de la paroi fortifiée ; l'autre, à l'ouest (fig. 2, E), est disposé légèrement en retrait. Ces dispositifs s'apparentent à des socles ou des bases et la question se pose de savoir s'ils n'étaient pas destinés à recevoir des chevalets soutenant un chemin de ronde comme pour la fortification de Rolle.

Proche de la palissade sud, un petit bâtiment quadrangulaire de 3,50 sur 4,20 mètres (fig. 4), contemporain du château en bois, a été mis au jour. Ce bâtiment est constitué de quatre trous de poteaux aux angles reliés par une sablière basse et des clayonnages en guise de parois. Le sol était recouvert de plusieurs couches de cendres, sans qu'un foyer (ou une zone rubéfiée) n'ait été découvert, l'argile restant uniformément ocre sur le sol. Une concentration de trous de piquet pourrait indiquer l'existence d'une crémaillère installée à l'entrée d'un four aujourd'hui démantelé. Une série de fragments de céramique culinaire noire, ainsi que des restes de faune,

---

10. Terrier 2002, 378-379.

11. Les résultats obtenus au cours de ces campagnes de fouilles ont été régulièrement présentés dans différents articles. Voir Joguin 2003, 271-272 ; Joguin Regelin 2006, 189-194 ; Terrier 2003, 323-329 ; Terrier 2004, 157-182 ; Terrier 2006, 325-364 ; Terrier 2008, 150-152 ; Terrier & Joguin Regelin 2009, 54-63.

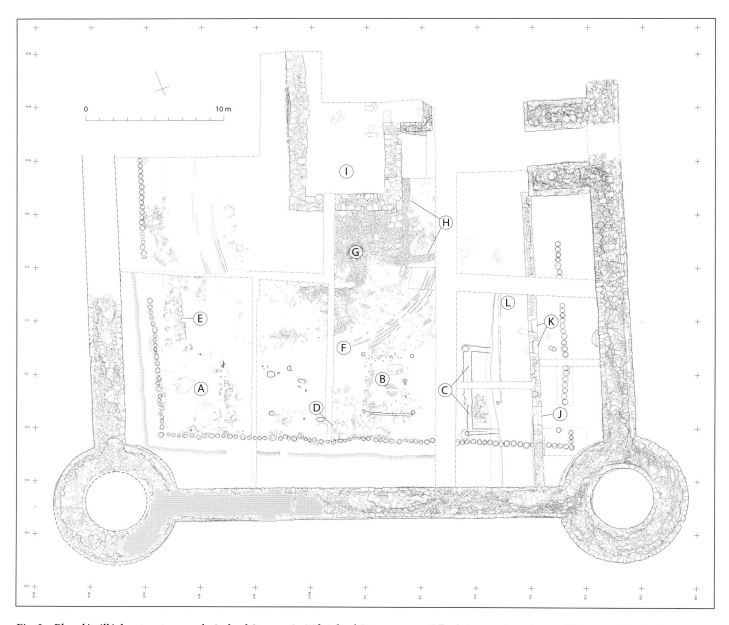

Fig. 2 – Plan détaillé des structures en bois du château primitif et du château maçonné (les lettres majuscules se réfèrent aux descriptions contenues dans le texte). Doc. P. Ruffieux, Service cantonal d'archéologie de Genève (Suisse).

confirment l'usage domestique de cet espace couvert qui est sans doute la cuisine de la bâtie. Le fait qu'elle soit détachée de l'enceinte fortifiée et séparée de la *domus plana* pourrait renforcer cette hypothèse, sachant que les cuisines étaient souvent tenues à l'écart dans les sites castraux médiévaux[12]. Une série de traces d'ornières parallèles imprimées dans l'argile atteste du passage de charrois (fig. 2, F). Cet axe de circulation venant sans doute de la porte de la bâtie tourne autour de l'espace central de la plateforme.

Dans le texte de 1339, il est également fait mention d'une *domus plana* de 42 mètres de pourtour. Selon ce document, cette maison, dépourvue d'étage et localisée au centre de la plateforme, comprenait un cellier et une étable « charmurée » aménagés sous les pièces d'habitation composées d'une *aula* et d'une cheminée, permettant aux chevaliers de la garnison de se loger.

Au centre de la plateforme, le haut d'une dépression a été mis en évidence dès les premières années de fouilles. En contrebas, un épandage de boulets assez impressionnant, interprété comme le vide sanitaire de la maison, a été découvert (fig. 2, G). Autour de cet amas de boulets se détache une structure faite de pierres rondes de plus petites dimensions et organisées différemment. Il s'agit là de drains qui devaient

12. Levalet 1978, 225-244.

Fig. 3 – Vue de l'angle sud-ouest de la palissade défensive du château en bois. Photo M. Berti, Service cantonal d'archéologie de Genève (Suisse).

Fig. 4 – Cuisine de la bâtie en bois : le plan est défini par les poteaux d'angle, les traces des sablières basses et les alignements de piquets, ainsi que par la couche de cendres épandue sur tout l'espace. Photo M. Joguin Regelin.

Fig. 5 – Vue générale de la *domus plana* : les drains sont visibles au premier plan, puis l'élévation du « charmur » dont les négatifs de poutres sont perceptibles sur la façade et à l'angle. Photo M. Joguin Regelin.

Fig. 6 – Détail de l'élévation du « charmur », les négatifs de la structure en bois apparaissant distinctement sur la façade ouest : la poutre verticale est maintenue par deux bras de force, reposant eux-mêmes sur un carrelet. Photo M. Joguin Regelin.

courir le long des fondations de la *domus* et permettre à l'eau qui s'accumulait dans ce creux d'être évacuée (fig. 2, H). À l'angle sud-est, un autre drain amorce une pente en direction du fossé est, rendant ainsi possible l'évacuation de l'eau hors de la bâtie.

Ces drains donnent quelques indices quant à la mise en œuvre de l'édification de toute la bâtie : en effet, les fossés ont été creusés en premier, permettant d'avoir de la matière première pour créer un tertre artificiel. Ces travaux, très coûteux et longs à accomplir, étaient indispensables pour la protection de la nouvelle construction contre d'hypothétiques assaillants. Néanmoins, il semble que l'aménagement de la *domus* et le drainage aient été prévus dès l'origine et qu'une sorte d'anneau fut créé dans ce but tout autour du vide sanitaire et de la partie inférieure de la *domus* qui devait rester visible.

Le « charmur » (fig. 2, I et fig. 5) a été installé directement sur les boulets du vide sanitaire. Ce mur impressionnant, de près de 1,20 mètre d'épaisseur, est bâti avec d'énormes pierres pour les parements et avec des boulets plus petits pour le remplissage, le tout lié avec peu de mortier. En nettoyant la façade sud, deux négatifs de poutres verticales ont été mis au jour, témoins de l'existence d'une structure en bois. Sur la façade ouest, des piliers verticaux étaient stabilisés dans la diagonale par des bras de force, eux-mêmes fixés sur un carrelet (fig. 6). Sur la façade est, conservée sur quelques assises de hauteur, les mêmes négatifs de poutres ont été observés, en plan cette fois-ci. L'édification de la charpente de bois et de la construction de pierre semble bien participer à la mise en œuvre du même chantier de construction. Le mur ouest s'élève à près de 1,60 mètre de hauteur et a une arase très régulière qui pourrait bien être le niveau à partir duquel s'élevait la partie exclusivement édifiée en bois. La stratigraphie montre que la base de ce bâtiment n'a été remblayée qu'au moment où la décision de reconstruire tout le château en maçonnerie a été prise.

3.2. Le château maçonné

Paradoxalement, aucun document d'archive ne relate le début des travaux de maçonnerie : le château était encore en bois en 1339 et, en 1355, la Savoie ayant annexé le territoire du Faucigny, il n'y avait plus de raison d'édifier un bâtiment à vocation militaire à cet endroit. En conséquence, le parti de reconstruire le château en pierres a dû être pris entre 1340 et 1355.

Si leur maintien se justifie, les bâties en bois implantées en zone frontalière vont être remplacées, peu de temps après leur édification, par des châteaux maçonnés[13]. Rouelbeau appartient à cette catégorie et les courtines de la nouvelle fortification vont être édifiées dans le flanc du fossé, tout le long et à l'extérieur des palissades de la bâtie antérieure. Au cours de ces travaux, un épandage constitué de déchets de taille de molasse, matériau utilisé pour les parements des maçonneries, est venu recouvrir les structures de la bâtie dont les bâtiments ont été alors progressivement démantelés. Les palissades de bois vont être maintenues à l'intérieur de la nouvelle enceinte fortifiée jusqu'à l'achèvement de cette dernière, comme l'indique l'accumulation de ces débris de taille de molasse venant buter contre les alignements de pieux de la bâtie. Les charrois empruntaient toujours le même tracé et les empreintes laissées par leurs roues sont perceptibles en surface de ce niveau.

Le château forme un rectangle de 52 mètres sur 39, doté à chaque angle de tours circulaires saillantes dont le diamètre atteint près de 9 mètres. Les murs, d'une épaisseur de 2,30 mètres, possèdent des parements en molasse couvrant un blocage de boulets liés au mortier. Le plan de cette nouvelle place forte reprend celui de la bâtie en bois avec des dimensions légèrement supérieures.

La tour sud-ouest située à l'autre extrémité de la courtine est bien conservée, la partie la plus élevée se développant sur plus de 6,50 mètres de hauteur. Les parements intérieurs de cette tour sont appareillés de pierres liées au mortier pour leur partie inférieure, alors qu'un appareil de blocs de molasse revêt leur partie supérieure. Une série de trous de poutres, visibles à mi-hauteur, marque sans doute l'existence d'un plancher dont les solives étaient fixées dans le mur.

Une découverte intéressante a été faite à la base de la courtine orientale où une série de négatifs de poutres noyées dans la maçonnerie sont apparus. Ces éléments de bois disposés perpendiculairement à l'axe de la courtine appartiennent à un système destiné à renforcer la construction des murs, ce qui a déjà été observé sur d'autres sites à vocation militaire[14].

Fig. 7 – Deux ouvertures du corps de logis construit en même temps que le château maçonné. Photo M. Joguin Regelin.

Au cours des premières campagnes de fouilles, aucune trace en lien avec une phase d'utilisation de la forteresse maçonnée n'avait été repérée sur la plateforme à l'intérieur de l'enceinte. La question se posait alors de savoir si le chantier de construction du château maçonné avait bien été mené jusqu'à son terme. La découverte d'un corps de logis adossé contre la courtine orientale, entre la porte du château et la tour sud-est, apporte une réponse définitive à cette question. Cette construction (fig. 7) présente un plan rectangulaire de 21,50 mètres sur 5 ; le mur de sa façade ouest, d'une épaisseur de 60 centimètres, préservé par endroits jusqu'à près de 1 mètre de hauteur, est appareillé à l'aide de galets liés au mortier. Une grande porte (fig. 2, J) de 1,30 mètre de largeur est ouverte dans la partie sud de cette façade, alors que deux autres portes (fig. 2, K) de 80 centimètres de largeur sont aménagées l'une à côté de l'autre en son centre. Un montant montre encore un congé plat et le départ d'un chanfrein droit, alors que le montant lui faisant face est bien altéré et que seule l'extrémité du congé est encore visible.

L'intérieur du bâtiment n'a conservé aucune trace de cloison indiquant l'ordonnance de cet immense espace qui était sans doute subdivisé en plusieurs pièces. Le sol devait être en terre battue ; peut-être recouvert, en certains endroits, d'un plancher dont aucun élément n'aurait alors subsisté. En l'absence d'indices permettant de restituer la fonction de ces espaces intérieurs, on se contentera de proposer l'existence d'entrepôts et de réserves au rez-de-chaussée, alors que le premier étage devait être dévolu au logis[15]. Ce bâtiment est légèrement encaissé par rapport au niveau de circulation de la bâtie en bois et une galerie courait le long de sa façade[16]. En effet, une bande d'un peu plus de 2 mètres de largeur prolonge ce niveau encaissé devant le bâtiment ; elle est délimitée par une planche d'épicéa, dont la trace est conservée sur plus de 11 mètres de longueur (fig. 2, L). Une analyse radiocarbone a été effectuée sur un échantillon de ce bois et la date fournie est comprise entre 1280 et 1410, le centre de la fourchette

---

13. Kersuzan 2005, 123-131.
14. Estienne 2003, 257-261.
15. Raynaud 1992, 71-80.
16. Pour la présence de portique ou de galerie dans ce contexte, voir Raemy 2004, 347-349.

Fig. 8 – Niveau d'épandage des tuiles correspondant au démantèlement du corps de logis. Photo M. Joguin Regelin.

chronologique se situant en 1345[17]. En l'absence d'autres éléments de datation absolue, nous retiendrons l'hypothèse de la mise en œuvre de ce corps de logis dès la construction du château qui intervient certainement peu avant 1355.

Une épaisse et impressionnante couche de tuiles correspondant au démantèlement du bâtiment a été mise au jour à l'intérieur de ce dernier (fig. 8). La zone située à proximité de la tour comprenait une grande majorité de tuiles plates de forme trapézoïdale provenant de la couverture de cette construction circulaire. La partie plus éloignée comprenait essentiellement des tuiles creuses ayant de toute évidence servi à la couverture du corps de logis. Une étude par thermoluminescence de deux échantillons prélevés dans chacun des deux ensembles décrits ci-dessus a fourni des datations intéressantes[18]. Les tuiles canal du corps de logis dateraient ainsi de 1415, plus ou moins 50 ans, alors que les tuiles plates seraient légèrement plus récentes, puisqu'elles seraient attribuées à l'année 1450, plus ou moins 50 ans.

Ces analyses, fournissant des éléments de datation absolue conjuguées avec les résultats des fouilles et les sources historiques, permettent de proposer l'hypothèse de l'édification du château maçonné de Rouelbeau peu avant 1355, le corps de logis étant construit au cours du même chantier. À l'origine, le bâtiment devait être recouvert de tavillons, tout comme la tour sud-est, près de laquelle aucun fragment de tuile n'a été mis au jour, et ce n'est que dans un second temps que le corps de logis a été doté d'une couverture de tuiles, celle de la tour étant mise en place encore plus tard.

4. Le matériel

Les objets proviennent principalement du niveau correspondant à l'utilisation de la bâtie en bois. On retient en particulier la mise au jour de grandes quantités de clous de tavillons, des séries de carreaux d'arbalète de différents types, quelques tessons d'une cruche en céramique à glaçure plombifère appartenant à de la vaisselle de table et plusieurs fragments de récipients en terre cuite noire utilisés pour la cuisson des aliments. Parmi les fragments de céramique, des éléments de trompes d'appel à pâte orangée doivent en outre être mentionnés. Dans les remblais de l'intérieur de la *domus plana*, ce sont deux clés qui ont été découvertes avec un petit couteau dont le manche en os avait été décoré. Une trentaine de monnaies, dont un denier anonyme de l'évêché de Lausanne frappé entre la fin du XIIIe siècle et la première moitié du XIVe siècle et deux gros tournois probablement frappés par Philippe V entre 1316 et 1322[19], complètent cet inventaire. Notons encore l'étonnante découverte d'une bulle du pape Innocent IV – dont le pontificat dura de 1243 à 1254 – qui, en 1247, autorisa Aimon II de Faucigny à édifier des chapelles dans les bourgs d'Hermance et de Monthoux, lieux situés à proximité du château de Rouelbeau. La présence de cette bulle témoigne peut-être de l'existence d'archives des Faucigny conservées dans un coffre du château.

Conclusion

D'ores et déjà, l'étude du château de Rouelbeau apporte une importante somme de connaissances relatives à la construction de bois au cours du bas Moyen Âge. Au-delà de l'organisation de la bâtie et des techniques de construction adoptées, c'est surtout la rapidité d'exécution avec l'emploi de matériaux faciles à mettre en œuvre et accessibles dans un environnement proche ou éloigné qui est intéressante. Ce phénomène doit certainement trouver des échos dans d'autres types de constructions, tels que, par exemple – si l'on tient compte des sources historiques –, les églises en bois que l'on pouvait observer en territoire genevois jusqu'à une période récente.

---

17. Analyse ETH-36758 réalisée par l'Institute of Particle Physics du Swiss Federal Institute of Technology, Zurich (Suisse).
18. Cette étude par thermoluminescence a été réalisée par ARCHEOLABS TL, référence : A-09-31-02-TL.
19. L'identification finale est encore à déterminer entre Philippe IV (1284-1316) et Philippe V (1316-1322).

Bibliographie

Bissegger P. (2008), « Une opération coup de poing sur La Côte : la fondation de Rolle en 1319 », *Études lausannoises d'histoire de l'art*, n° 7, 167-179.

Cattin P. (1979), « Le compte de la construction de la bastide de Gironville près d'Ambérieu-en-Bugey (1323-1325) », *Cahiers René de Lucinge*, n° 22, 2-18.

Estienne M.-P. (2003), « Les chaînages de bois du donjon de Verclause (Drôme) », in *Le bois dans le château de pierre au Moyen Âge* (Actes du colloque de Lons-le-Saunier, 23-25 octobre 1997), J.-M. Poisson et J.-J. Schwien (dir.), Besançon, Presses universitaires franc-comtoises (Annales littéraires de l'Université de Besançon. Architecture ; 2), 257-261.

Joguin M. (2003), « Meinier GE, Château de Rouelbeau », *Annuaire de la Société suisse de préhistoire et d'archéologie*, vol. LXXXVI, 271-272.

Joguin Regelin M. (2006), « Le château de Rouelbeau (Meinier, Suisse) », in *Château Gaillard 22 : études de castellologie médiévale. Château et peuplement* (Actes du colloque international de Voiron, 28 août-4 septembre 2004), P. Ettel, A.-M. Flambard Héricher et T. E. McNeill (éd.), Caen, Publications du CRAHM, 189-194.

Kersuzan A. (2005), *Défendre la Bresse et le Bugey. Les châteaux savoyards dans la guerre contre le Dauphiné (1282-1355)*, Lyon, Presses universitaires de Lyon (Collection d'histoire et d'archéologie médiévales ; 14), 123-131.

La Corbière M. (de) (2001), *La « Bâtie-Souveyro », ou « Bâtie-Roillebot », au Moyen Âge (1318-1536). Pré-rapport historique*, Genève, Inventaire des Monuments d'art et d'histoire du canton de Genève/Service cantonal d'archéologie.

– (2002), *L'invention et la défense des frontières dans le diocèse de Genève. Étude des principautés et de l'habitat fortifié (XIIe-XIVe siècle)*, Annecy, Académie salésienne (Mémoires et documents publiés par l'Académie salésienne ; 107-108), 329-335.

Levalet M. (1978), « Quelques observations sur les cuisines en France et en Angleterre au Moyen Âge », *Archéologie médiévale*, t. VIII, 225-244.

Menna F. (2009), « Un ouvrage défensif médiéval (1307-1308) à Champagne-Le-Moulin (VD) », *Zeitschrift des Schweizerischen Burgenvereins*, n° 1, 18-26.

Poisson J.-M. (1986a), « Une fortification de terre et de bois édifiée en 1324. La bastide de Gironville à Ambronay (Ain) », in *La maison forte au Moyen Âge* (Actes de la table ronde de Nancy – Pont-à-Mousson, 31 mai-3 juin 1984), M. Bur (dir.), Paris, Éd. du Centre national de la recherche scientifique, 253-260.

– (1986b), « Recherches archéologiques sur un site fossoyé du XIVe siècle : la bastide de Gironville ("Fort-Sarrazin", Ambronay, Ain) », in *Château Gaillard 12. Études de castellologie médiévale* (Actes du colloque international tenu à Oostduinkerke et à Floreffe, Belgique, 3-9 septembre 1984), Caen, Publications du CRAHM, 225-236.

Raemy D. (de) (2004), *Châteaux, donjons et grandes tours dans les États de Savoie (1230-1330). Un modèle : le château d'Yverdon*, vol. I : *Le Moyen Âge. Genèse et création*, Lausanne, Association pour la restauration du château d'Yverdon-les-Bains (Cahiers d'archéologie romande ; 98).

Raynaud F. (1992), *Le château et la seigneurie du Vuache. Haute-Savoie, 74*, Lyon, Service régional de l'archéologie (Documents d'archéologie en Rhône-Alpes ; 6), 71-80.

Terrier J. (2002), « Découvertes archéologiques dans le canton de Genève en 2000 et 2001 », *Genava*, t. L, 378-379.

– (2003), « Les vestiges d'une bastide en bois du XIVe siècle découverts sous les ruines du château de Rouelbeau à Genève », in *ConstellaSion. Hommage à Alain Gallay*, M. Besse, L.-I. Stahl Gretsch et P. Curdy (dir.), Lausanne, Cahiers d'archéologie romande (Cahiers d'archéologie romande de la Bibliothèque historique vaudoise ; 95), 323-329.

– (2004), « Découvertes archéologiques dans le canton de Genève en 2002 et 2003 », *Genava*, t. LII, 157-182.

– (2006), « Découvertes archéologiques dans le canton de Genève en 2004 et 2005 », *Genava*, t. LIV, 325-364.

– (2008), « Rapport intermédiaire sur les fouilles du château de Rouelbeau à Meinier GE. La découverte d'une bastide en bois du XIVe siècle », *Annuaire d'archéologie suisse*, vol. XCI, 150-152.

Terrier J. et Joguin Regelin M. (2009), « Rouelbeau : un château en bois édifié en 1318 au sommet d'un tertre artificiel », *Archéologie suisse*, n° 32, 54-63.

Hochmittelalterliche Herrschaftsbildung und Burgenbau in Grenzsäumen des heutigen Ostösterreich
Fallstudien im Vergleich

◆

Thomas Kühtreiber*, Markus Jeitler**

1. Methode und Fragestellungen

Die Rolle der Burgen als Herrschaftsmittelpunkte im Zusammenhang mit dem sogenannten Landesausbau wird von der österreichischen Forschung seit langem durchaus kontrovers diskutiert[1]. Als methodische Ansätze dienen der Geschichtswissenschaft im Wesentlichen die als überholt geltende sogenannte „besitzgeschichtlich-genealogische Methode"[2] bzw. dem gegenüber die Verbindung zwischen Personenverband und Territorialisierung[3]. Während erstere Methode von jüngsten Besitzverhältnissen ausgehend ältere Zustände zu rekonstruieren versucht und dergestalt festgefügte Lösungen anbietet, geht die andere Methode von weitaus flexibleren und durchlässigeren Vorgängen aus. Für die Landwerdung und damit auch die herrschaftliche Durchdringung von Grenzregionen, die eine spezifische und sensible Rolle spielen, sind diese Denkansätze und Modelle vor allem für die Länder Oberösterreich und Niederösterreich aufgrund der intensiven Forschungen der vergangenen Jahre sehr gut nachweisbar[4]. Die betreffenden Verhältnisse haben zwar in erster Linie wegen der verbesserten Quellenlage für das Spätmittelalter Gültigkeit[5], doch lassen sie sich mit Hilfe vieler Indizien auch für das Hochmittelalter anwenden[6]. Demnach wäre das „Land" und somit auch dessen Entstehung sowie Expansion in Grenzräume als vielschichtiger Personenverband zu betrachten, der als Interessengemeinschaft lokaler Machthaber mit der von ihnen als übergeordnet anerkannten Instanz des Landesherrn kooperiert[7]. Die Existenz als lokaler Machthaber war daher also nur im Verein mit dessen Standesgenossen möglich und man musste sich auf jeden Fall einem entsprechenden Personenverband einordnen[8]. Auf diese Weise bekundete man in weiterer Folge durch die Teilnahme an den Landesversammlungen unter Vorsitz des Landesherrn seine Zugehörigkeit zum „Land" und akzeptierte gleichzeitig das dort geltende Landrecht[9]. Dieser Herrschaftspraxis stand jedoch ein seit dem 11./12. Jahrhundert bestehendes und auf zentralistischen Herrschaftsprinzipien beruhendes Landesverständnis in den benachbarten Ländern Böhmen, Mähren und Ungarn gegenüber, wie die dort betriebene Forschung hinreichend herausgearbeitet und postuliert hat[10].

Anhand ausgewählter Burganlagen aus dem niederösterreichisch-böhmisch-mährischen sowie dem niederösterreichisch-steirisch-westungarischen (heute burgenländischen) Grenzraum soll versucht werden, die Folgen für den „Burgenbau

---

* Institut für Realienkunde des Mittelalters und der frühen Neuzeit, Interdisziplinäres Zentrum für Mittelalterstudien, Universität Salzburg, Österreich.
** Österreichische Akademie der Wissenschaften, Kommission für Kunstgeschichte, Österreich.
1. Zur Forschungsgeschichte dieses Themas siehe Zehetmayer 2012, 83-84.
2. Zu deren Methode samt ausführlicher Kritik siehe Kupfer 2009, 28-31; Weltin 2006c, 399-401.
3. Brunner 1939; Brunner 1990.
4. Birngruber et al. 2012; Zehetmayer 2012.
5. Weltin 2006c, 403-404.
6. Ibid., 406.
7. Ibid., 404.
8. Ibid.
9. Ibid.
10. Zur Diskussion vgl. Feld 1994; Feld 2012; Györffy 1976; Jan 2012.

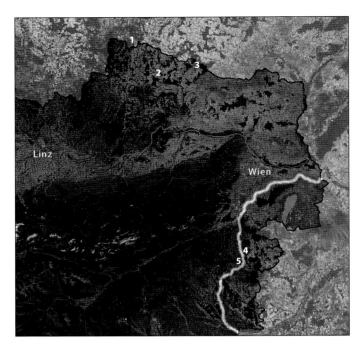

Abb. 1 – Überblickskarte zu den im Text behandelten Burgen: 1) Landšteijn/Landstein; 2) Raabs; 3) Hardegg; 4) Landsee; 5) Kirchschlag. Weiße Linie: Grenze zwischen Heiligem Römischen Reich und Königreich Ungarn. Hervorgehoben das heutige Staatsgebiet von Österreich. Kartierung Autoren; Kartengrundlage M. Schmid.

Abb. 2 – Burg Raabs, Niederösterreich. Luftbild G. Scharrer, VIAS, Universität Wien.

an der Grenze" als Beispiel dieser Vorgänge und gegensätzlichen Meinungen vorzustellen und zu diskutieren.

2. Raabs an der Thaya

Das erste Fallbeispiel beschäftigt sich mit der Burg Raabs an der Thaya in Niederösterreich, deren älteste Baugeschichte in das 11. Jahrhundert zurückreicht (Abb. 1.1 & Abb. 2). Die gut nachvollziehbaren historischen Hintergründe dieser zwischen dem Herzogtum Böhmen und der babenbergischen Markgrafschaft Österreich entstandenen Burg und Herrschaft sind besonders interessant, zumal sich der tschechische Name für Österreich, *Rakousko*, von Raabs ableitet. Während für die nahe gelegene Vorgängeranlage auf der Flur Sand, die zwischen circa 900 und 950 existierte und offenbar gewaltsam zerstört wurde[11], jegliche historischen Belege fehlen, sind wir über die herrschaftlichen Verhältnisse in jener Gegend ab der Mitte des 11. Jahrhunderts besser informiert. Demnach galt der Großteil des als „Nordwald" bezeichneten Gebietes als praktisch offenes, nahezu siedlungsfreies Land, um das sich sowohl die Herzogtümer Bayern (mit der Babenbergermark) und Böhmen bemühten und selbst ungarische Interventionen nachweisbar sind[12]; nominell verfügte über das herrenlose Land jedoch der König. 1041 eroberten und zerstörten Markgraf Adalbert und sein Sohn Leopold II. im Zuge eines kriegerischen Konfliktes mit Herzog Břetislav von Böhmen eine *in terminis marcharum Boiemiae ac Boiariae* gelegene *urbs*, die Adalbert zuvor „entrissen" worden war[13]. Diese Anlage konnte jedoch trotz vielerlei Versuchen bislang immer noch nicht schlüssig lokalisiert werden[14].

Im Jahre 1055 begegnet in einer Königsschenkung der Name *marchia Boemia*, der zur viel diskutierten Annahme einer eigenständigen „böhmischen Mark" geführt hat[15]. Eine neuere These meint nun, dass hier die Babenbergermark gemeint sei, die sich inzwischen deutlich nach Norden aus-

---

11. Felgenhauer-Schmiedt 2000, 49-77; Felgenhauer-Schmiedt 2002, 381-395; Felgenhauer-Schmiedt 2012, 57-82.
12. Annales Altahenses Maiores, a. 1042, 29-30; Weltin 2006d, 345.
13. Annales Altahenses Maiores, a. 1041, 28.
14. Weltin 1993, 81, Anm. 246; Brunner 1994, 463f., Anm. 153; Niederösterreichisches Urkundenbuch I, 432.
15. Lechner 1947, 93-96; Bosl 1965, 418-426.

gedehnt hatte (die Schenkung lag im nordöstlichen Niederösterreich), und für die offenbar bald die Thaya von beiden Seiten als Grenzfluss anerkannt wurde[16]. Rund 20 Jahre später erhielten die Babenberger Markgrafen Ernst (1074) und Leopold II. (1076) von Kaiser Heinrich IV. schließlich 40 bzw. 60 Hufen *in silva Rŏgacs* zu Eigen, die mit einem großen Teil des heutigen Raabser Waldes ident sind[17]. Die beiden Babenberger kamen allerdings wegen ihrer gregorianischen und somit antikaiserlichen Haltung während des Investiturstreits nicht mehr dazu, diese umfangreichen Schenkungen zu nutzen: Der Abfall Markgraf Leopolds II. 1081 und seine Niederlage in der Schlacht bei Mailberg 1082 ermöglichten, dass sich in diesem Raum der Edelfreie Gottfried von Nürnberg festsetzen konnte, der vermutlich an der Seite des böhmischen Herzogs Vratislav II. mitkämpfte und die Waldschenkungen vom König erhielt[18]. Im Jahr 1100 hatte er den Aufzeichnungen des Cosmas von Prag zufolge Leutold, den Sohn Konrads von Znaim bei sich aufgenommen, der jedoch nächtliche Überfälle in Mähren beging und sich sogar der Burg Raabs bemächtigte, sodass Gottfried fliehen und bei Herzog Břetislav und dessen Bruder Bořivoj Hilfe suchen musste[19]. Nach der Eroberung des *castrum Racouz* durch die herzoglichen Truppen erhielt Gottfried seine Burg wieder zurück[20]. Die Episode zeigt, dass Gottfried sich dem Personenverband des Leutold von Znaim verpflichtet fühlte und sich nach dessen Verrat an den Herzog von Böhmen wandte, nicht aber an den Markgrafen von Österreich. Das heißt, dass das Raabser Gebiet zu Mähren zählte[21]. Die Edlen von Raabs und seit 1105 Burggrafen von Nürnberg sind somit bezeichnenderweise nicht auf den Landesversammlungen der folgenden Jahrzehnte anzutreffen. Erst nach 1140 wird Graf Konrad (I.) in der Umgebung des Markgrafen Heinrich II. genannt, was möglicherweise auf verwandtschaftliche Verbindungen zurückzuführen ist[22]. Die Gefolgsleute des Grafen Konrad (II.) von Raabs (gest. 1191), etwa die Zöbing-Weikertschlager, finden sich zudem auch auf böhmischem Gebiet verteilt, was nochmals die ursprüngliche Herrschaftsbildung beweist[23]. Außerdem leiteten die Babenberger trotz der aufbewahrten Königsschenkungen der *silva Rŏgacs* nie Ansprüche auf die Herrschaft Raabs ab, sondern sollen sie erst unter Herzog Leopold VI. (reg. 1194/1198-1230) erkauft haben[24]. Die Burg selbst wurde archäologischen Forschungen zufolge vermutlich bereits in der ersten Hälfte des 11. Jahrhunderts errichtet[25], woraus sich nun vier mögliche Szenarien ergeben: 1. eine ehemalige Burg der Babenberger geriet in die Hand der Vorfahren Gottfrieds; 2. es handelte sich ursprünglich um eine „mährische" Burg; 3. die Vorfahren Gottfrieds hatten hier schon vorher Besitz; 4. eine ältere Burg unbekannter Besitzer geriet in die Hände Gottfrieds oder schon seiner Vorfahren. Dabei sind die beiden ersten Varianten jedoch eher auszuschließen, da die Babenberger sicher Regressforderungen gestellt hätten, was sie aber wie wir anhand der beiden Königsschenkungen erfahren haben, unterließen. Eine „mährische" Burg wäre ebenfalls problematisch, da es sich bei Raabs eindeutig um eine „Burg westlichen Typs" handelt, d. h. eine klassische Mauerburg. Es bleiben also die beiden letzten Optionen übrig, allerdings fehlen zu dieser Frage jegliche schriftlichen Quellen.

3. Hardegg

Weiter östlich von Raabs, ebenfalls im nördlichen Niederösterreich, führten die aus Salzburg stammenden Grafen von Plain mit ihren Ministerialen im Raum Hardegg seit Beginn des 12. Jahrhunderts eine umfangreiche Herrschaftsbildung durch, wobei sie herrenloses Land sukzessive in Besitz nahmen; seit 1187 nennt sich die Familie nachweislich auch nach Hardegg (Abb. 1.3 & Abb. 3)[26]. Im Gegensatz zu ihrem Raabser Nachbarn nahmen sie aber an den Landesversammlungen der babenbergischen Markgrafen teil und taten damit ihre Zugehörigkeit zur Mark kund, gleichzeitig unterhielten sie enge Kontakte nach Böhmen[27]. Im Spätmittelalter glückte der Herrschaft sogar der Aufstieg zur Reichsgrafschaft[28].

4. Landstein/Landštejn

Ein vergleichsweise spätes Beispiel für die Frage der Rolle von Burgen an der österreichisch-böhmischen Grenze stellt die Burg Landstein/Landštejn dar (Abb. 4). Die heute noch als imposante Ruine erhaltene Burg befindet sich knapp 10 km westlich von Slavonice/Zlabings bzw. 4,5 km von der heutigen Staatsgrenze entfernt auf tschechischem Staatsgebiet (Abb. 1.1). Sie geht im Kern auf eine romanische Doppelturmanlage mit eingestelltem *Palas* und einen im Westen einen Hof umfassenden Bering zurück, deren Mauerwerksstruktur und Architekturdetails auf Basis gut datierter Vergleichsbeispiele eine Errichtung im Zeitraum zwischen 1190 und

---

16. NIEDERÖSTERREICHISCHES URKUNDENBUCH I, 343; KUPFER 2009, 138.
17. MGH DH IV 271 bzw. NIEDERÖSTERREICHISCHES URKUNDENBUCH I, Nr. 36; MGH DH IV 285 bzw. NIEDERÖSTERREICHISCHES URKUNDENBUCH I, Nr. 36a.
18. NIEDERÖSTERREICHISCHES URKUNDENBUCH I, 433-434; ZEHETMAYER 2012, 85.
19. COSMAE PRAGENSIS CHRONICA BOEMORUM, 172-173.
20. *Ibid.*; ZEHETMAYER 2012, 86. Die Quellen lassen den Schluss zu, dass Gottfried zudem nicht als Gefolgsmann des Herzogs sondern als mehr oder weniger gleichrangig angesehen wurde.
21. WELTIN 2006a, 246.
22. WELTIN 2006b, 514.
23. ZEHETMAYER 2012, 86-87.
24. NIEDERÖSTERREICHISCHES URKUNDENBUCH I, 434-435.
25. FELGENHAUER-SCHMIEDT 2006, 15-50.
26. WELTIN 2006a, 242-246; WELTIN 2006b, 513-514; ZEHETMAYER 2012, 93.
27. WELTIN 2006a, 246-248.
28. *Ibid.*, 251-252.

Abb. 3 – Burg Hardegg, Niederösterreich. Foto P. Schicht.

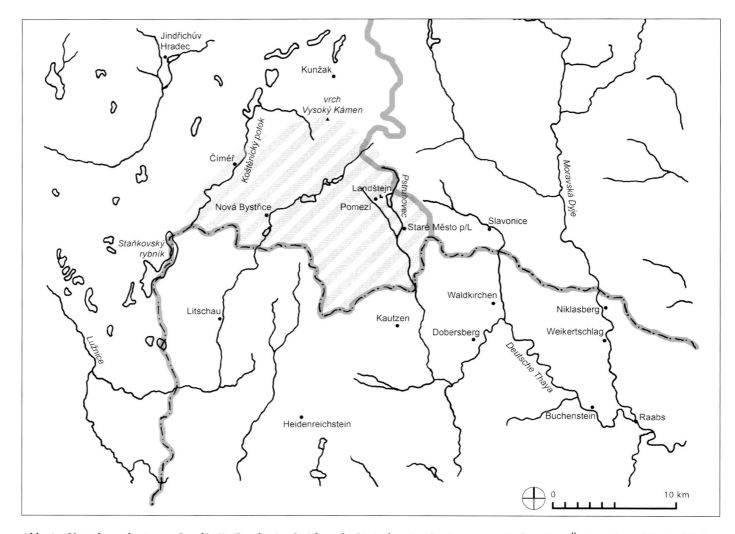

Abb. 4 – Umgebungskarte von Landšteijn/Landstein. Strichpunkt-Linie: heutige Staatsgrenze zwischen Rep. Österreich und Tschechischer Republik, Volle graue Linie: böhmisch-mährische Landesgrenze vor 1949, Schraffierte Fläche: ungefähres Gebiet, das zwischen 1179 und dem zweiten Drittel des 13. Jahrhunderts zu Österreich gehörte. Plan aus Razím 2011, 32, Abb. 32. Plangrundlage V. Razím; Ausführung V. Tutr.

1230/1240 indizieren[29]. Diese Datierung wird durch die Erstnennung eines Adeligen nach Landstein 1231 aus dem Umfeld bzw. Gefolge der Zöbinger bzw. ihrer Erben, der Herren von Gutrat, unterstützt[30].

Die Errichtung eines steinernen Monumentalbaus auf heutigem tschechischem Staatsgebiet hat insbesondere die ältere tschechische Burgenforschung dazu veranlasst, in Burg Landstein eine Gründung durch die böhmische Herrscherdynastie der Přemysliden zu postulieren, zumal der adelige Burgenbau in Böhmen um 1200 noch nicht entwickelt gewesen sei[31]. Dem widerspricht die – zugegebenermaßen spärliche – Quellenlage des späten 12. bis zur Mitte des 13. Jahrhunderts: Spätestens seit der zweiten Hälfte des 12. Jahrhunderts war die siedlungs- und herrschaftsmäßige Durchdringung des Gebietes sowohl von böhmischer als auch von österreichischer Seite so weit fortgeschritten, dass daraus entstandene Grenzstreitigkeiten durch Kaiser Friedrich I. am Hoftag zu Eger 1179 geschlichtet werden mussten[32]. Zwar sind einige der im Friderizianum genannten Grenzpunkte heute nicht mehr lokalisierbar, das in den Quellen fassbare Auftreten österreichischer und bayerischer Adelsgeschlechter in der Region, wie den Grafen von Hirschberg-Raabs, den Herren von Zöbing, sowie dem Bistum Passau, legen aber eine Zugehörigkeit des Gebietes zu Österreich bis um die Mitte des 13. Jahrhunderts nahe. Erst unter Otakar II. Přemysl, der ab den 1250er Jahren bis 1278 auch Herzog von Österreich war, zeichnet sich eine Inkorporation des Gebietes in das böhmische Königreich ab, zumal ab 1260 die Wittigonen im Besitz von Burg Landstein waren[33]. Vladislav Razím postulierte in der jüngsten Arbeit zu Landstein 2011, dass der Name programmatisch als landesherrliche Grenzburg gedeutet werden könnte und schlug als möglichen Bauherrn das Ministerialengeschlecht der Zöbinger im Auftrag der österreichischen Herzöge vor. Letztere hatten gemäß dem Landbuch von Österreich und Steier von 1278/1280 im Jahr 1200 Teile der Besitzungen der Grafen von Raabs erworben, wozu möglicherweise auch Burg und Herrschaft Landstein gehört haben könnten[34]. Dem ist entgegen zu halten, dass auf österreichischer Seite, wie bereits Folker Reichert betonte, kein bedeutendes österreichisches Ministerialengeschlecht Herrschafts- und Stadtgründungen vor der Mitte des 13. Jahrhunderts im Auftrag der jeweiligen Landesherren vornahm, sondern immer nur aus ihrer eigenen Machtfülle heraus[35]. Dazu kommt, dass auch andere Burgen mit „Land" als Teil ihres Namens zwar bisweilen in Grenznähe lagen – auf Landsee an der österreichisch-ungarischen Grenze wird noch zurückzukommen sein – aber keine dieser Anlagen landesfürstlich war oder der Quellenlage nach im landesfürstlichen Auftrag errichtet wurde. Vielmehr vermittelt die Burg in Verbindung mit einer zu ihren Füßen gelegenen Stadtwüstung namens Markl/Pomezí[36] den Eindruck einer hochmittelalterlichen Herrschaftsbildung „auf wilder Wurzel" eines nicht sicher identifizierbaren, aber wohl österreichischen Adelsgeschlechts. Ob diese Gründung nun auf Betreiben, Duldung oder ohne Rücksichtnahme auf territoriale Herrschaftspolitik der jeweiligen Landesfürsten „hüben und drüben" erfolgte, geht aus den Quellen nicht hervor und war – entsprechend dem vorhin Ausgeführten – möglicherweise auch unerheblich.

5. Burgenbau, Herrschaftsbildung und Territorialisierung im österreichisch-ungarischen Grenzgebiet

Wenden wir uns im zweiten Teil des Vortrages einer anderen Grenze zu, nämlich jener zwischen dem Königreich Ungarn und den Markgrafschaften und späteren Herzogtümern Österreich und Steier. Im Gegensatz zum österreichisch-böhmischen Grenzgebiet lassen sich hier relativ früh lineare Grenzziehungen fassen: So wird beispielsweise zunächst im frühen 11. Jahrhundert die Fischa und um 1043 letztendlich die Leitha im südlichen Wiener Becken zur Reichsgrenze und bleibt dies mit wenigen Ausnahmen bis zur Angliederung des Burgenlandes an Österreich 1921[37]. Weitaus weniger klar ist die Grenzbildung weiter südlich, wo das bewaldete Hügelland der Buckligen Welt zunächst wohl einen wenig besiedelten Grenzsaum bildete, dessen westliches Randgebiet zumindest bis zur Mitte des 13. Jahrhunderts zur Steiermark gehörte und unter dem örtlichen Stammsitz der Grafen von Formbach, Pitten, als „Pittener Gebiet" in der Forschung geläufig ist[38]. Südlich davon bildete auf dem Gebiet der heutigen Steiermark ab der Mitte des 11. Jahrhunderts die Lafnitz die „nasse Grenze" zu Ungarn[39]. Im 12., spätestens aber in der ersten Hälfte des 13. Jahrhunderts ist mit dem „Ungarbachtal" östlich von Kirchschlag in der Buckligen Welt auch hier eine lineare Grenze fassbar, die gleichzeitig die siedlungs- und herrschaftsmäßige Erschließung dieser Region innerhalb von 100-150 Jahren anzeigt[40].

Damit sind wir allerdings schon bei der zentralen Frage: Von wem wurde dieser Grenzraum erschlossen und was bedeutete dies für die territoriale Entwicklung? Ungarische Quellen des 11. und 12. Jahrhunderts belegen, dass Angehörige „deutscher" Adelsfamilien auf Betreiben verschiedener

---

29. KÜHTREIBER 2011.
30. *Ibid.*, 77-78; RAZÍM 2011, 31-32.
31. Die ältere Forschung kritisch zusammenfassend *ibid.*, 35-42.
32. Zur Diskussion aus Sicht der österreichischen Forschung TOMASCHEK 1979; zur Quelle: BUB IV/1, Nr. 861 und 862.
33. RAZÍM 2011, 34.
34. *Ibid.*, 63-64.
35. REICHERT 1985, 353-354.
36. KÜHTREIBER 2011, 83; RAZÍM 2011, 31.
37. WELTIN 1999, 262.
38. WELTIN 1998, 19-26.
39. WELTIN 1999, 262-263.
40. WELTIN 1998, 29.

ungarischer Könige zur militärischen und organisatorischen Unterstützung ins Land geholt wurden, wobei die Bezeichnung *hospites*, was mit „Gäste" übersetzt werden kann, einen rechtlichen Sonderstatus andeutet[41]. Viele Angehörige dieser Familien wurden mit Gütern in den nördlichen, westlichen und südlichen Grenzgebieten des Königreiches abgegolten, einigen gelang es rasch, auch in der weitaus zentraleren ungarischen Herrschaftsstruktur Karriere zu machen und als *comites*, d.h. Gespane zeitweise Amtsträger über ungarische Burgbezirke mit deren zentralen Gespanschaftsburgen zu werden[42]. Eine der bedeutendsten Familien waren die Herren von Güns-Güssing, die der Urkundenlage nach spätestens um die Mitte des 12. Jahrhunderts als *hospes* nach Ungarn kamen. Ihre Herkunft ist bis heute umstritten, nach Heinz Dopsch erscheint eine Identifizierung mit den Edelfreien von Au-Erlach auf Grund ihrer Leitnamen Wolfger und Heidenrich sowie auf Grund ihres Engagements im ungarischen Grenzgebiet im Raum Hainburg im 12. Jahrhundert am wahrscheinlichsten[43]. Während ein Wolf(g)er um die Mitte des 12. Jahrhunderts über schriftliche Quellen mit einer frühen Holzburg in Güssing in Verbindung gebracht wird, macht sein Bruder Hederich/Heindricus Karriere am Hof Gézas II. und nimmt 1162 mit der Palatinswürde das höchste Hofamt ein[44]. Dennoch ist von archäologisch-bauhistorischer Seite kaum etwas über den frühen Burgenbau der Güssinger bekannt[45]. Die Blütezeit der Güssinger ist um die Mitte des 13. Jahrhunderts erreicht, als es aufgrund einer Schwächephase des ungarischen Königtums verschiedenen Adelsfamilien am Rande des Reiches gelingt, mehr oder weniger autonome Herrschaftsterritorien aufzubauen. Heinrich II. gelang es in diesem Zeitraum bis zu seinem Tod 1274, nicht weniger als elf Burgherrschaften unter sich zu vereinigen, von denen neben Besitzungen in Slawonien und Slowenien vor allem die Burgen Bernstein, Köszeg/Güns, Gaas, St. Veit/Szentvid, Neuhaus, Schlaining die Grundlage für das mehr oder weniger geschlossene Grenzterritorium bildeten[46]. Gerade in der zweiten Hälfte des 13. Jahrhunderts, als mit König Otakar II. Přemysl als Herzog von Österreich ab den 1250er Jahren den ungarischen Königen ein neuer politischer Akteur gegenüber stand, verstand es Heinrich II., durch wechselnde Parteigängerschaft sich trotz mehrfacher militärischer Auseinandersetzungen auch auf seinen Herrschaftsterritorien eine weitgehende Unabhängigkeit zu sichern[47]. Diese Machtbasis wurde erst unter dem Habsburger Albrecht I. im Rahmen der vom Steirischen Reimchronisten wortreich geschilderten „Güssinger Fehde" 1289/1290 durch Erobern und Besetzen aller Burgen der Güssinger im Grenzgebiet gebrochen, auch auf ungarischer Seite war damit der Niedergang dieses bedeutenden Herrschergeschlechts im Laufe der ersten Hälfte des 13. Jahrhunderts besiegelt[48]. Welche Rolle ist dabei den Burgen zuzubilligen? Unserer Ansicht nach bildeten sie auch hier die zentralen Elemente der örtlichen Burgherrschaften, d.h. der Legitimierung und Absicherung des Besitzes durch die Adelsfamilie. Auch wenn, wie im Fall von Köszeg oder Schlaining, die topographische Bezugnahme zu einem Altweg wahrscheinlich gemacht werden kann, ist in keinem Fall die vorrangige Sicherung einer linear zu denkenden Grenze nachvollziehbar. Vielmehr zeigen die chronikalen Quellen zu den militärischen Auseinandersetzungen auf Güssinger Gebiet in den 1270er Jahren sowie um 1289/1290, dass zur Durchsetzung der politischen Ziele eine Burg nach der anderen belagert wird: Es geht nicht um Eroberung von Territorium durch Besetzung, sondern durch Einnahme der Burg, an der die herrschaftlichen Rechte haften[49].

Damit kommen wir zum Schluss noch auf ein letztes Beispiel zu sprechen, nämlich die Errichtung von Burgherrschaften durch österreichisch-steirische Adelige im ungarischen Niemandsland ohne königlich-ungarische „Einladung" bzw., wie die Quellen zeigen, im ausdrücklichen Gegensatz dazu[50]. Wie bereits oben dargestellt, war insbesondere das Hügelland der Buckligen Welt im frühen 12. Jahrhundert noch weitgehend unbesiedelt, und zwar sowohl auf „österreichischer", als auch auf „ungarischer" Seite. Bereits um die Mitte des 12. Jahrhunderts versuchte aber das Kloster Reichersberg am Inn, Zehentrechte auf Besitzungen der Grafen von Formbach *ultra vallem Ungaricum*, womit wohl das Ungarbachtal östlich von Kirchschlag gemeint ist, zu erstreiten[51]. Ungefähr gleichzeitig nannten sich erste Angehörige der steirischen Adelssippe der Stubenberger nach Landesere, der heute „Landsee" genannten großen Burganlage deutlich östlich besagten Ungarbachtales und somit auf ungarischem Gebiet (Abb. 1.4). Es verwundert daher nicht, dass die Burg 1263 bereits Teil der Gespanschaft Lutzmannsburg war und wohl im Zuge militärischer Auseinandersetzungen an Ungarn fiel[52]. Explizit wird dies im gleichen Zeitraum für die nicht weit entfernt gelegene Burg Kirchschlag fassbar, deren Erstnennungen ausgerechnet in ungarischen Belohnungsurkunden für Verdienste rund um die Belagerung der Burg genannt wird (Abb. 1.5 & Abb. 5). Hier waren es Angehörige der steirischen Wildonier, die in der ersten Hälfte des 13. Jahrhunderts herrschaftsbildend aufgetreten sind. Die Bedeutung Kirchschlags ist unter anderem in der Nennung einer *strata publica* 1279, die u.a. die Burgen Lockenhaus und Kirchschlag mit einander verbindet,

---

41. WELTIN 1999, 263; DOPSCH 1989, 186, Bezug nehmend auf Simon de Kéza, Gesta Hungarorum, absatz 52.
42. WELTIN 1999, 263-267.
43. DOPSCH 1989, 194.
44. LINDECK-POZZA 1989, 60-61.
45. Vgl. den Beitrag von I. Feld in diesem Band.
46. LINDECK-POZZA 1989, 67.
47. WELTIN 1999, 267.
48. *Ibid.*, 268-269 mit weiterführender Literatur.
49. Vgl. dazu KÜHTREIBER 2009, 56; 83; 86.
50. Vgl. zum Folgenden WELTIN 1999, 263-264.
51. WELTIN 1998, 29, Anm. 72.
52. WELTIN 1999, 264.

Abb. 5 – Das westungarische Grenzgebiet im 12./13. Jahrhundert. Plan aus WELTIN 1999, 265.

erschließbar, sodass hier noch am ehesten eine Rolle als „Grenzburg" im weitesten Sinne plausibel erscheint. Im Gegensatz zu Landsee gelang es aber hier, Burg und Herrschaft dauerhaft zu behaupten und letztendlich – wohl auch aufgrund der Lage westlich des Ungarbaches – als zunächst in steirisches und in weiterer Folge österreichisches Landesgebiet zu integrieren[53]. Zusammenfassend lässt sich aber auch hier konstatieren, dass von österreichischer Seite keine übergeordnet gesteuerte Strategie der Erweiterung territorialer Ansprüche, geschweige denn Grenzsicherung durch Burgenbau nachvollziehbar ist. Vielmehr sind es Initiativen einzelner, bisweilen potenter Familien, die in Grenzsäumen ihre Machtbasis zu erweitern versuchen. Hingegen scheint die Reaktion von ungarischer Seite zumindest im 13. Jahrhundert zentral gelenkt, wie die königlichen Belohnungsurkunden für an der Belagerung von Kirchschlag beteiligte Personen anzeigen. Möglicherweise stießen hier zwei unterschiedliche Herrschaftskonzepte auf einander.

6. Fazit

Die geschilderten Beispiele haben gezeigt, dass Herrschaftsbildungen und damit einhergehender Burgenbau im betreffenden Grenzraum sowohl auf geordneten wie auch ungeordneten rechtlichen Verhältnissen aufbauen konnten. Die jeweilige Zugehörigkeit zu einem „Land" war von der entsprechenden Ausrichtung der herrschaftsbildenden Familien abhängig, wobei im Falle der Babenbergermark, speziell deren Frühzeit, zu beachten ist, dass die „Mark als werdendes Land" vorstellbar ist[54]. Der Bau von Burgen ist nun speziell in Grenzregionen eng mit diesen Herrschaftsbildungen verbunden, die auch Auswirkungen auf übergeordnete Einflusssphären und Landesgrenzen haben konnten. Im Lauf der Geschichte fügten sich die Grenzen dieser Herrschaften erst zu etablierten überregionalen Territorialgrenzen, doch können sie auch heutzutage noch für manch grotesk anmutende Dispute zur „Landeszugehörigkeit" sorgen.

53. WELTIN 2003, 66-68.

54. BRUNNER 1994, 235.

Literatur

ANNALES ALTAHENSES MAIORES, Hannover, Hahn (MGH SS rerum Germanicarum in usum scholarum; 4), 1891.

BIRNGRUBER K. *et al.* (2012), „Adel, Burg und Herrschaft im unteren Mühlviertel. Ein interdisziplinärer Versuch zum mittelalterlichen Adels-, Burgen- und Grenzbegriff", *Studien zur Kulturgeschichte von Oberösterreich*, 34, 13-40.

Bosl K. (1965), „Die Markengründungen Kaiser Heinrichs III. auf bayerisch-österreichischem Boden", in *Zur Geschichte der Bayern*, K. Bosl (hrsg.), Darmstadt, Wissenschaftliche Buchgesellschaft, 364-442.

Brunner K. (1994), *Herzogtümer und Marken. Vom Ungarnsturm bis ins 12. Jahrhundert. Österreichische Geschichte*, Bd. II, Wien, Ueberreuter, 1994.

Brunner O. (1939), *Land und Herrschaft. Grundfragen der territorialen Verfassungsgeschichte „Südostdeutschlands" im Mittelalter*, Baden bei Wien, Rohrer (Veröffentlichungen des Österreichischen Instituts für Geschichtsforschung; 1).

– (1990), *Land und Herrschaft. Grundfragen der territorialen Verfassungsgeschichte Österreichs im Mittelalter*, Darmstadt, Wissenschaftliche Buchgesellschaft.

Cosmae Pragensis Chronica Boemorum, Berlin, Weidmann (MGH SS rerum Germanicarum Nova Series; 2), 1923.

Dopsch H. (1989), „Die Hengistburg, Wildon und die Herkunft der Grafen von Güssing", in *Die Güssinger. Beiträge zur Geschichte der Herren von Güns/Güssing und ihrer Zeit (13./14. Jahrhundert)*, H. Dienst et al. (hrsg.), Eisenstadt, Das Landesmuseum (Wissenschaftliche Arbeiten aus dem Burgenland; 79), 185-194.

Feld I. (1994), „Der Beginn der Adelsburg im mittelalterlichen Königreich Ungarn", in *Château Gaillard 16*, Caen, Centre de recherches archéologiques médiévales, 189-205.

– (2012), „Die Burgen des Königreichs Ungarn im 11.-12. Jahrhundert", in *Château Gaillard 25. L'origine du château médiéval*, P. Ettel, A.-M. Flambard Héricher & K. O'Conor (hrsg.), Caen, Publications du CRAHM, 159-169.

Felgenhauer-Schmiedt S. (2000), „Die Burg auf der Flur Sand und die Burg Raabs in Niederösterreich", *Beiträge zur Mittelalterarchäologie in Österreich*, 16, 49-77.

– (2002), „Herrschaftszentrum und Burgenbau des 10. Jahrhunderts in Niederösterreich. Neue archäologische Forschungen im nördlichen Grenzgebiet", in *Europa im 10. Jahrhundert. Archäologie einer Aufbruchszeit*, J. Henning (hrsg.), Mainz, Von Zabern, 381-395.

– (2006), „Archäologische Forschungen in der Burg Raabs an der Thaya, Niederösterreich", *Beiträge zur Mittelalterarchäologie in Österreich*, 22, 15-49.

– (2012), „Herrschaftszentren und Adelssitze des 10. bis 13. Jahrhunderts im nördlichen Waldviertel – der Beitrag der Archäologie", *Studien zur Kulturgeschichte von Oberösterreich*, 34, 57-82.

Györffy G. (1976), „Die Entstehung der ungarischen Burgenorganisation", *Acta Archaeologica Academiae Scientiarum Hungaricae*, 28, 323-358.

Hageneder O. (1957), „Die Grafschaft Schaunberg. Beiträge zur Geschichte eines Territoriums im späten Mittelalter", *Mitteilungen des oberösterreichischen Landesarchivs*, 5, 189-264.

Jan L. (2012), „Zur Frage der Entstehung des böhmisch-mährischen Adels und der Entstehung großer Herrschaftskomplexe in Grenzgebieten", *Studien zur Kulturgeschichte von Oberösterreich*, 34, 107-118.

Kühtreiber T. (2009), „Die Ikonologie der Burg", in *Die imaginäre Burg*, O. Wagener et al. (hrsg.), Frankfurt am Main, Lang (Beihefte zur Mediävistik; 2), 53-92.

– (2011), „Der Gründungsbau der Burg Landštejn. Überlegungen zur zeitlichen Einordnung aus bauhistorischer Sicht", *Průzkumy Památek*, 18/1, 71-84.

Kupfer E. (2009), *Krongut, Grafschaft und Herrschaftsbildung in den südöstlichen Marken und Herzogtümern vom 10. bis zum 12. Jahrhundert*, St. Pölten, Niederösterreichisches Institut für Landeskunde (Studien und Forschungen aus dem Niederösterreichischen Institut für Landeskunde; 48).

Lechner K. (1947), „Die Gründung des Klosters Maria-Zell im Wiener Wald und die Besitzgeschichte seiner Stifterfamilie", in *Ausgewählte Schriften*, K. Lechner (hrsg.), Wien, Phönix Verlag, 69-100.

Lindeck-Pozza I. (1989), „Die Herren von Güssing im Lichte der Urkunden", in Dienst et al. 1989 (hrsg.), 59-84.

Niederösterreichisches Urkundenbuch I: 777-1076, St. Pölten, Verein zur Förderung von Editionen Mittelalterlicher Quellen Niederösterreichs (Publikationen des Instituts für Österreichische Geschichtsforschung; 8/1), 2008.

Razím V. (2011), „K počátkům Hradu Landštejna", *Průzkumy Památek*, 18/1, 31-70.

Reichert F. (1985), *Landesherrschaft, Adel und Vogtei. Zur Vorgeschichte des spätmittelalterlichen Ständestaates im Herzogtum Österreich*, Köln/Wien, Böhlau (Beihefte zum Archiv für Kulturgeschichte; 23).

Tomaschek J. (1979), „Die Grenzziehung von 1179", *Das Waldviertel*, 28, 213-224.

Urkundenbuch zur Geschichte der Babenberger in Österreich, IV/1: *Ergänzende Quellen (976-1194)*, Wien, Oldenburg, 1997.

WELTIN M. (1993), „Probleme der mittelalterlichen Geschichte Niederösterreichs unter besonderer Berücksichtigung des Hollabrunner Bezirkes", in *Vergangenheit und Gegenwart. Der Bezirk Hollabrunn und seine Gemeinden*, E. BEZEMEK & W. ROSNER (hrsg.), Hollabrunn, Verein zur Förderung der Heimatkundlichen Forschung im Bezirk Hollabrunn, 47-96.

– (1998), „Das Pittener Gebiet im Mittelalter", in *Wehrbauten und Adelssitze Niederösterreichs. Das Viertel unter dem Wienerwald I*, St. Pölten, Niederösterreichisches Institut für Landeskunde (Studien und Forschungen aus dem Niederösterreichischen Institut für Landeskunde; 1), 19-35.

– (1999), „Der Kampf um das westungarische Grenzgebiet – das heutige Burgenland", in *Die Länder und das Reich. Der Ostalpenraum im Hochmittelalter. Österreichische Geschichte (1122-1178)*, H. DOPSCH (hrsg.), Wien, Ueberreuter, 262-269.

– (2003), „Kirchschlag – Geschichte", in *Wehrbauten und Adelssitze Niederösterreichs*, St. Pölten, Niederösterreichisches Institut für Landeskunde (Das Viertel unter dem Wienerwald; 2), 66-72.

– (2006a), „Böhmische Mark, Reichsgrafschaft Hardegg und die Gründung der Stadt Retz", *Mitteilungen des Instituts für Österreichische Geschichtsforschung Ergänzungsband*, 49, 233-253.

– (2006b), „Landesfürst und Adel – Österreichs Werden", *Mitteilungen des Instituts für Österreichische Geschichtsforschung Ergänzungsband*, 49, 509-564.

– (2006c), „Der Begriff des Landes bei Otto Brunner und seine Rezeption durch die verfassungsgeschichtliche Forschung", *Mitteilungen des Instituts für Österreichische Geschichtsforschung Ergänzungsband*, 49, 384-409.

– (2006d), „Ascherichsbrvgge – Das Werden einer Stadt an der Grenze", *Mitteilungen des Instituts für Österreichische Geschichtsforschung Ergänzungsband*, 49, 338-374.

ZEHETMAYER R. (2012), „Zur Struktur des Adels im nördlichen Wald- und Weinviertel bis um 1150", *Studien zur Kulturgeschichte von Oberösterreich*, 34, 83-106.

"Lost and Forgotten": the Castles of Eric of Pomerania (King of Denmark, 1396-1439) in the Duchy of Schleswig

Heidi Maria Møller Nielsen*

1. Introduction

During the reign of King Eric of Pomerania (1396-1439) two political goals remained crucial for him: these were to strengthen Danish dominance of the Baltic and to regain control of the Duchy of Schleswig, the southern part of the Jutland Peninsula. In order to accomplish these ambitions Eric built, rebuilt or acquired several castles in various ways. Moreover, he abandoned a couple of older castles no longer of any use and reassigned their responsibilities to other royal castles. In reality, the system of royal castles was rationalized and restructured at this time – a fact which turned out to be of great importance in the longer term[1]. Nevertheless, Eric of Pomerania never gained a reputation as a great castle builder or castle organizer.

So far scholars have focused on Eric's more famous castles along the shores of Øresund and on Gotland. That is: Krogen at Elsinore, founded around 1400; Visborg on Gotland, founded in 1411; and the new castle in Malmø, founded in 1434[2]. It can however also be established that several royal castles were reinforced and extended during the reign of King Eric. The most important among these was the castle of Copenhagen, an apple of discord between the King and the Bishop of Roskilde until 1417, when Eric succeeded in a legally recognized take over which became of great significance as Copenhagen gradually became the administrative centre of the Kingdom and the castle of Copenhagen grew to be the main residence of its kings[3]. The central subject of this paper is however to present an outline of Eric's castle building in the border province of Schleswig. This has been rather unnoticed and neglected from an archaeological point of view, a fact which is first and foremost due to a very small amount of knowledge about these castles which have almost totally disappeared.

Altogether the King initiated the building of at least seven castles, at a minimum two siege works and reinforcements or rebuilds of several castles in Schleswig (fig. 1). The duchy was lost to Germany in 1864 but the northern part, roughly speaking the area from the stream of Kongeåen to the present border, was reunited with Denmark in 1920. Ribe however was never part of Schleswig and remained with the Kingdom all the time. This means that only a couple of King Eric's castles in Schleswig are situated within present Danish borders and traditionally most of the castles south of the border are not described in Danish castle literature at all. They are in a double sense "lost and forgotten" and it is indeed worthwhile to shed what little light is possible on the appearance, purpose and destiny of these castles. Such a study has to be based primarily on studies of the standing structures and the landscape, written sources, maps and various other records as almost no excavations or proper surveys have been carried out.

When Eric was crowned and the Kalmar Union founded in 1397, all three Scandinavian kingdoms, Denmark, Norway and Sweden, then including Finland, Iceland, all inhabited islands north of Scotland and formally also Greenland, were brought together under one Crown. However, the control of the Duchy of Schleswig had in reality slipped away to Holstein

---

* Aarhus University, Denmark.
1. Møller Nielsen 2011, 92-93.
2. Møller Nielsen 2008, 322-323; Reisnert 2001, 162ff.
3. Olesen 1994, 149; Møller Nielsen 2011, 92-93, Olsen 2011, 68-69.

and the counts of Schauenburg who held even Gottorp, the most important castle in the duchy just outside the town of Schleswig (fig. 1).

Until her death in 1412, Queen Margaret I (1387-1412) reigned with her foster son Eric, and mainly by means of diplomacy and redemption of mortgages, the two of them succeeded in getting hold of several important strongholds in Northern Schleswig. This however resulted in a lasting armed conflict which deeply affected the rest of Eric's reign. Control of the castles in Schleswig and thus the balance of power was constantly changing[4].

Exactly how important the struggle was is clearly stated by the unique design of the King's coat-of-arms at Krogen, the new royal castle in Elsinore, as the four main quarters of the royal insignia represent not only the traditional emblems of Denmark, Norway and Sweden but also Schleswig[5]. The royal coat of arms is literally blessed and is thus symbolically legitimized by the image of the "Arma Christi" which crowns the decoration. The heraldic murals were painted in the splay of a circular window in the King's audience chamber at some time during the 1420s when the war in Schleswig reached its culmination and it is clearly an important manifestation of the King's confidence and political agenda regarding this matter[6].

2. Duborg

In 1409 Eric of Pomerania and Queen Margaret succeeded in getting hold of the important town of Flensburg. In the years to follow a castle, later known as Duborg, was built on the Marienberg hillside situated at the north-western perimeter of the town and a late medieval reinforcement of the town defences is attributed to Eric as well[7]. The construction must have been progressing rapidly as King Eric referred to "our castle in Flensburg" less than a year later and according to later complaints by the counts of Holstein, the castle was largely completed within 5 years[8]. In October 1412 Eric and Margaret made their official entry and the Queen was paid tribute to in Flensburg. It was then, at the zenith of her power, that she fell ill and died on her ship in the harbour by the end of the latter month. Continuing building works were probably carried out on the castle during the years of war, and in 1419 a reinforcement of both the outer works and the buildings was discussed[9].

Today nothing is left above ground of the castle which became the base of Danish power in Schleswig and very often served as a royal residence for the kings of Denmark. It was mostly demolished during the 18th century but the last remains

Fig. 1 – Castle building during the reign of King Eric of Pomerania (1396-1439) in Southern Jutland and bordering areas. Map H. M. Møller Nielsen.

of the huge curtain wall were broken down, in fact blown up, as late as the turn of the 19th century. In the 1920s the still-existing Duborg School was built on the castle mound which all things considered still might represent a great archaeological potential.

Based on various documentary records, images and a sequence of excavations during the 1920s and early 1940s it is however possible roughly to reconstruct the layout of the medieval castle (fig. 2)[10]. The excavations were carried out by the local artist and historian Erwin Nöbbe who documented the results in a series of reports and small newspaper articles, first and foremost in the local paper *Flensburger Nachrichten*.

The castle consisted of a rectangular brick-built curtain wall, measuring approximately 53 m by 70 m, surrounded by ramparts and moats. The main building (within which was The Great Hall) had two storeys, above at least a partial basement. It was placed along the east wall and at least one lighter building stood in the south-east corner of the courtyard. In this area remnants of some wooden constructions have been found outside the curtain wall but they have not been dated and might be older than the castle. The curtain wall had a small corner tower facing south-east and a gate

---

4. La Cour *et al.* 1937-1939, 55-58.
5. Illustrated in Møller Nielsen 2008, fig. 10.
6. In all probability the audience chamber at Krogen also served as an assembly hall for the Royal order founded by Eric of Pomerania in the early 15th century. Reitzel-Nielsen 1976, 39; Møller Nielsen 2008, 321.
7. Presbyter Bremensis 1903, 111; Wolff 1882, 116-119; Poulsen 1988, 41-42; Pelc 2001, 25-28.
8. Diplomatarium Danicum/Danmarks Riges Breve 2002-2003, no. 123; Diplomatarium Flensborgense 1865-1873, vol. 1, 296, no. 79.
9. Erslev 1901, 111; La Cour *et al.* 1937-1939, 60.
10. Haupt 1905; Nöbbe 1926-1929; Rohling 1955, 284-290; La Cour 1971.

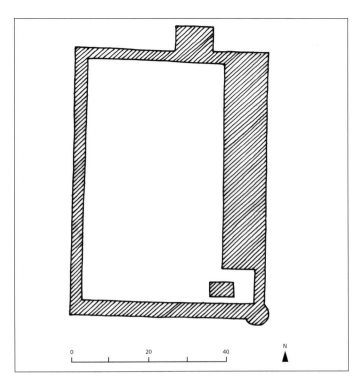

Fig. 2 – Reconstructed plan of Duborg c. 1475 (drawing H. M. Møller Nielsen) and painting of the castle in 1591 seen from the southeast. Section of the epitaph of Georg Beyer in St Mary's Church in Flensburg (after ROHLING 1955).

tower or gatehouse in the north wall. There must have been additional buildings to the west and north where sadly, no excavations have been registered. Buildings here are not documented until the 16th century. 15th-century documents and inventories mention the chapel (1440)[11], the "Knights Chamber", the new gate (1452), an inner and outer gate and the bridge (1450s), the hall, the kitchen, the bakery, the powder magazine (1473), the gatehouse (1487) and a spiral staircase of stone in the "Great House" (1487/1488)[12].

Though there are great differences in size, the same type of layout, a rectangular or square curtain wall with separate buildings alongside it, a spacious, open courtyard and a projecting gate tower, is also seen in Eric's castles along Øresund and on Gotland: Krogen, Malmø and Visborg[13]. Due to the character of the landscape, the natural angle of attacks on the castle in Flensborg was from the south and so the curtain wall facing south was about 4 m thick whereas the other walls were about 2 m thick. Similar conditions and measures are seen at Krogen in Elsinore where the northern and eastern walls facing the sea are about 2 m thick while the southern and western walls facing Elsinore and the mainland are almost 4 m thick. A painting of Duborg from 1591 indicates that the castle might also have had a vaulted gallery circling the curtain wall as seen on Krogen (fig. 2)[14]. Even more similarities are recognised and based on their character, it seems fair to suggest that the two castles were designed and constructed by the same builders.

3. Nyhus

In the autumn of 1411 the Grand Master of the Teutonic Order received information from his emissary that not one but two castles were under construction at Flensburg[15]. This message doubtlessly referred not only to Duborg but also to Nyhus to the north of the town just south of the present Danish-German border.

Originally, Nyhus was built in the 14th century in order to secure Flensburg against the Danes but now it was reinforced by King Eric. The castle was strategically positioned by Hærvejen, the main north/south road in Jutland, which passed right beside the place. A partly levelled moated site is all that remains of the castle. No excavations are registered but fragments of medieval bricks are scattered all over the location (fig. 3)[16].

---

11. DIPLOMATARIUM FLENSBORGENSE 1865-1873, vol. 1, no. 123.
12. *Ibid.*, vol. 2, no. 828; ROHLING 1955, 288-289.
13. Plans are illustrated in MØLLER NIELSEN 2011, fig. 2.
14. Krogen is illustrated in MØLLER NIELSEN 2008.
15. DIPLOMATARIUM DANICUM/DANMARKS RIGES BREVE 2002-2003, no. 298.
16. DÄHN 2001, 353.

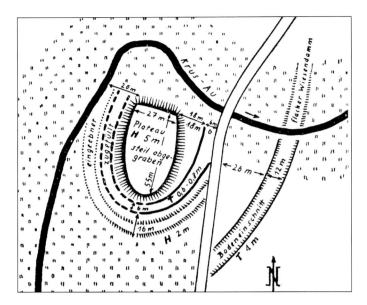

Fig. 3 – Nyhus, sketch of the site (after Dähn 2001).

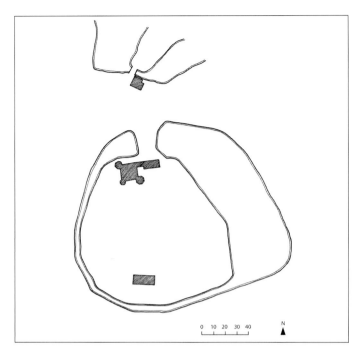

Fig. 4 – Brundlund, plan of the site. Doc. H. M. Møller Nielsen.

4. Brundlund

The same year, in 1411, Margaret and Eric managed to obtain the town and castle of Åbenrå from the widow of the duke of Schleswig. The castle then situated in the midst of the town was demolished and a new castle was built by the King in the swampy areas to the south-west of the settlement. Of this new castle which was later to be named Brundlund, only the huge artificially built, moated site measuring 120 m by 140 m, with moats up to 45 m wide has survived (fig. 4).

The present building and the unique fortified mill to the north of the manor date from the 1520s and later, and though excavations have revealed a few remains of older foundations and cobblestone paving, the layout of the original 15th-century constructions is unknown. However, records of 1523 mention at this time buildings, such as stables, barns and a bakery, were to be found at the moated site itself[17].

5. Schwabstedt and Stubbe

In order to control the waterway of the Schlei and to conquer Gottorp and the town of Schleswig, King Eric established a line of strongholds across Schleswig in 1415 (fig. 1). As opposed to Duborg and Brundlund which had long term significance, these emergency strongholds were less complex structures and were quickly built[18]. Nevertheless, it was a major project financed by an extraordinary warfare tax collected in Denmark, as well as in Norway and Sweden. The chain of fortifications had its starting point in two older castles which were in the possession of the bishop of Schleswig. The bishop was loyal to the King and had handed over his castles to him: Schwabstedt close to the southern border of Schleswig and Stubbe at the southern bank of the Schlei but both of them had been partly destroyed by respectively the Frisians and the Holsteiners. The two castles were rebuilt and armed by the King but the present state of decay of the remains and the lack of excavations do not allow any valid suggestions as to what changes were made (figs. 5 & 6)[19].

6. Schwonsburg, Arnis and Lindau

In 1415 the mouth of the Schlei was fortified on both sides. To the south a stronghold was allegedly established on a former small island, Schwonsburg or Schwonsberg, and to the north a castle was constructed at the point of Arnis. Only a vague rise is visible at Schwonsburg and the actual existence of a castle has been debated as it is not mentioned in any contemporary sources. Remains of late medieval earthworks were however found at the site in 1903[20].

---

17. Trap 1967, 813; Hertz 1986, 86ff., 93-94; Kristensen 2000.
18. Olsen 2011, 186.
19. Erslev 1901, 25; Poulsen 1988, 41; Slevogt 1998, 115; Poulsen et al. 2003, 604.
20. Loewe 1998, 4.

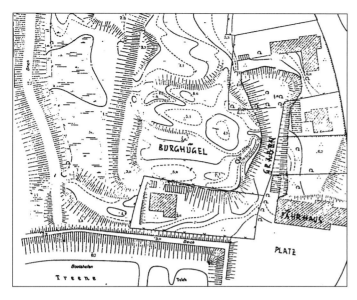

Fig. 5 – Remains of Schwabstedt (after Dähn 2001).

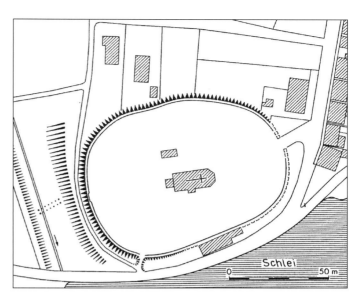

Fig. 7 – Arnis. Plan of the "Kirchberg" (after Loewe 1998).

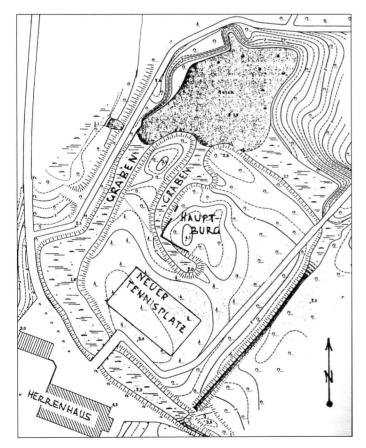

Fig. 6 – Remains of Stubbe (after Dähn 2001).

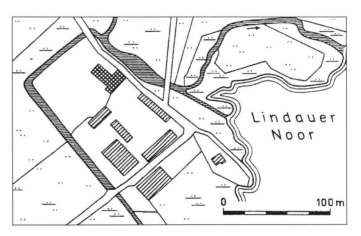

Fig. 8 – Lindauhof, plan based on a land register sketch of 1781 and the present landscape (after Loewe 1998).

its summit and the site was transformed into a churchyard and was thus greatly disturbed (fig. 7). Further up the waterway at the point of Lindau, just opposite the bishop's castle at Stubbe, on the southern shore of the Schlei, yet another castle was established in 1415. The present manor house of Lindau is of the 16th- or 17th- century date but is situated on a rectangular, partly moated site, surrounded by marshland, that might be relics of the medieval earthworks (fig. 8). Proper excavations have never been carried out at either place[21].

At Arnis a quite large oval-shaped moated site is preserved on the edge of the Schlei. The mound which is partially lined with granite boulders roughly measures 70 m by 100 m and is up to 3 m high. In the 17th century a church was built right on

21. Diplomatarium Flensborgense 1865-1873, vol. 1, 265, no. 76; 296, no. 79; Ellger & Teuchert 1957, 379-388; Loewe 1998, 4, 188.

7. Königsburg

The fourth castle which King Eric built in 1415 was Königsburg on a small promontory at the southern bank of the Schlei at its narrowest passage. The irregular earthwork at the edge of the water is very large, approximately 220 m by 150 m. It is surrounded by moats, 10 m wide and 3 m deep. In the early 20th century, traces of a tower-like building of bricks were apparently found on an inner, also moated, castle mound, measuring 50 m by 50 m, but a house was built on the site. Today also the outer bailey is marked by various buildings and a rather dense growth of trees. On the whole, however, the site is relatively well preserved (fig. 9)[22]. In 1416 Königsburg, which was by far the most complex of the emergency strongholds in the Schlei region, was suggested by King Eric as the setting for a court of arbitration regarding the Schleswig matter, involving representatives of the Holsteiners, the King and allies of both parties besides a number of Hanseatic towns[23].

8. Wellspang (Vedelspang)

The fifth royal fortification of 1415 was built on the crossing between a lake and the Wellspang stream to the north of the town of Schleswig (fig. 1). An important road from Flensburg to the Mysunde ferry at the Schlei passed the place, which according to written sources seems to have been a garrisoned earthwork or bulwark rather than a permanently garrisoned ordinary castle. It was supposedly destroyed the following year, rebuilt by the King and once again destroyed by the enemy in 1426 when 60 men, including arms and 40 horses, were captured. Traces of the medieval earthworks were still visible in the mid-19th century when the crossing was once again fortified during the Danish-German War of 1848 to 1850[24].

A famous artefact, the so-called Vedelspang-gun, was found at this site. It is traditionally dated to the early 15th century and is regarded the oldest existing handgun in Denmark. The gun could well have been used in the numerous captures of the fortification[25].

9. Friesenburg

King Eric's sixth castle of 1415, Friesenburg or Freesenburg, was built at the River Treene further west (fig. 1). At the site of the present farmstead of Harenburg, very slight remains of earthworks are seen but fragments of medieval bricks appear all over the place. Friesenburg was not only aimed at the Holsteiners but also at the Frisians who were from time to

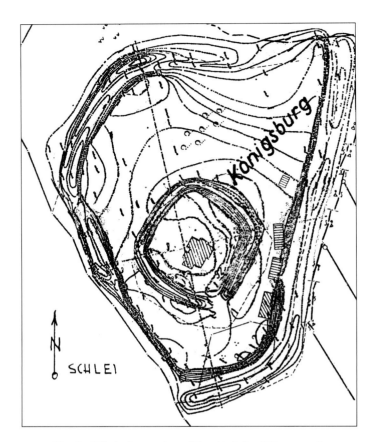

Fig. 9 – Königsburg, plan of the site (after DÄHN 2001).

time allied with the Holsteiners and were also enemies of the King of Denmark[26]. According to written sources, the castle was in fact destroyed by Frisians the following year[27].

10. The siege work Hattensburg at Gottorp and the attempts to conquer the town of Schleswig

With his string of castles, King Eric practically controlled a frontier across Southern Jutland in 1415. The Schlei was guarded by castles in pairs where the river grew narrower and in 1416 the Danes were finally ready to attack the town of Schleswig. The siege was however soon raised as both Wellspang and Friesenburg were captured by the enemy, as mentioned above[28].

The following year, in 1417, King Eric returned with a large army and a fleet, later said to be of 2,000 ships. Schleswig was finally taken and Gottorp Castle was besieged which in itself

---

22. JENSEN undated; OBERDIECK et al. 1950, 33; DÄHN 2001, 320-321.
23. HEDEMANN 2007, 48.
24. PRESBYTER BREMENSIS 1903, 116-117; SCRIPTORES RERUM DANICARUM MEDII ÆVI 1772-1878, vol. 5, 507; LOEWE 1998, 350.
25. BLOM 1872.
26. DIPLOMATARIUM FLENSBORGENSE 1865-1873, vol. 1, 265, no. 76; 296, no. 79; ERSLEV 1901, 27; LOEWE 1998, 384; DÄHN 2001, 370.
27. SCRIPTORES RERUM DANICARUM MEDII ÆVI 1772-1878, vol. 1, 322.
28. ERSLEV 1901, 27; LA COUR et al. 1937-1939, 66.

was a great victory. With much ceremonial the municipal charter of Schleswig was confirmed, something no Danish king had been able to accomplish for more than a century. Later that year, Gottorp was however relieved by unexpected German forces and at the same time Königsburg and Stubbe were attacked by the Holsteiners. Königsburg withstood the siege while the episcopal Stubbe was demolished. King Eric had to reach a compromise and the siege of Gottorp was raised[29]. The idea that retreating royal troops completely destroyed the town of Eckernförde at the eastern coast of Jutland to the south of Schleswig and that the King built a new castle at the site around this time dies hard (fig. 1). The new castle in Eckernförde was in fact built by the Holsteiners to counterbalance Königsburg[30].

Almost 10 years of on-and-off warfare went by before King Eric in 1426 made a final attempt to capture Gottorp. On the hillside of Kleiner Hesterberg to the east of the castle he established a siege work known as Hattensburg or Owensburg (Avindsborg) which, according to a 15th-century chronicler from Holstein, the so-called Presbyter Bremensis, had double moats and ramparts with palisades[31]. The hillside was a natural attack position and had been used as such on more than one occasion thus Hattensburg might have had its origin in earthworks from the King's previous siege in 1416 or even older remains. As the remnants of the fortification continued to be a military threat to Gottorp, it was eventually completely destroyed in the 1630s and it gradually sank into oblivion. Until recently the exact location of the fortification has in fact been widely misunderstood[32].

On November 2, 1426 the Holsteiners managed to capture the Hesterberg position after a short ceasefire and King Eric's siege of both Gottorp and Schleswig failed once again. The Hanseatic League had joined forces with Holstein and a group of Hanseatic towns declared war on Denmark. In the years to come Hanseatic fleets savaged and plundered the Danish coasts[33].

11. The siege work at Tørning

Hattensburg was not the only siege work built by the King. The great magnate Claus Limbek had been loyal to the crown but a growing dissatisfaction with the behaviour of the royal bailiffs operating on his estates in Southern Jutland eventually caused a conflict and made him change sides to the counts of Holstein in 1421. This meant that a large part of Northern Schleswig was suddenly controlled by the enemy. In 1422 the main castle of Claus Limbek, Tørning, was besieged several times by the King who built a siege work in the shape of two bulwarks in front of it (fig. 1). Tørning was however relieved by a large force belonging to the counts of Holstein. When the parties reached a settlement in 1423, it was agreed that Tørning as well as the siege work should remain untouched for the time being and nothing was ever heard of the latter since[34].

Remains of two earthworks, in all about 200 m by 120 m, which were first discovered in 1921, are preserved on each side of a small stream in the woods a couple of hundred meters to the north of the huge moated site of Tørning. They have been convincingly interpreted as the siege works of 1422 (fig. 10)[35]. The western construction is of rectangular shape surrounded by moats. It has a small circular mound in the south-west corner and an inner moat and rampart. The oval eastern construction is also surrounded by moats and has a small rectangular mound in the south-east corner. Especially the Central and southern parts of the earthworks have been destroyed and levelled by a road and gravel pits. A sketch from 1922 is the only image of the site which has never been excavated or properly surveyed.

12. Haderslev

Based on recent dendrochronological dates, the 1420s also saw a reinforcement of the outer defences of both town and castle in nearby Haderslev which was to become completely surrounded by water. By building a huge dam (present Sønderbro) the King initiated a redesign of the system of moats enclosing the town and the otherwise almost unknown late 13th-century castle which was entirely demolished in the 16th century[36]. At the same time, the King started a major rebuild of the town church of Our Lady in order to compete with the standards of the cathedral in Schleswig. He intended to establish a new diocese centred in Haderslev which was to be independent from the diocese of Schleswig[37]. War was not only fought on the earthly battlefield!

13. Glambek Castle and the fight for Fehmarn

Although "the scorched-earth policy" never became common practise, both parties used acts of terrorism such as extorting contributions, cattle raids and more or less random violence and burning on a regular basis. The terror was exercised from the castles. The province of Schleswig was harried by this kind

---

29. ERSLEV 1901, 40-41; LA COUR et al. 1937-1939, 66-68.
30. DIPLOMATARIUM FLENSBORGENSE 1865-1873, vol. 1, 266, no. 76; 322, no. 79; UNVERHAU 2001.
31. PRESBYTER BREMENSIS 1903, 146; SCRIPTORES RERUM DANICARUM MEDII ÆVI 1772-1878, vol. 5, 507.
32. LORENZEN 1859, 94; ERSLEV 1896; ERSLEV 1901, 27; LAUR 1964, 16, 18; HOPPMANN 1997, 39, 44-45; RATHJEN 2005, 24-25; HOPPMANN 2007, 137-138.

33. LA COUR et al. 1937-1939, 78; POULSEN 2008, 145.
34. JØRGENSEN 1889-1892, 108-109; LA COUR et al. 1937-1939, 71.
35. ULDALL 1921.
36. L. Madsen, Museum Sønderjylland (Denmark), Arkæologi Haderslev, pers. comm.
37. POULSEN 2008, 149.

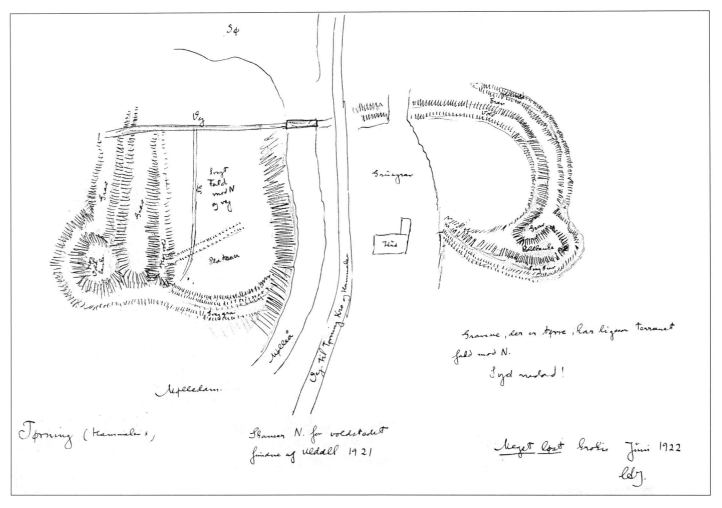

Fig. 10 – Siege work at Tørning (north is upwards). A gravel pit with a small house is seen in the centre. Rough sketch by C. A. Jensen, June 1922, by courtesy of the National Museum of Denmark.

of war, causing the civilian population to suffer immensely. Several generations later, written sources still spoke frequently of settlements, farms, mills and manors that were laid waste and deserted during the war[38].

The worst assaults and outrages committed by the troops seem to have taken place on the island of Fehmarn in the Baltic near the coast of Holstein. In 1416 the Danes conquered the island and the castle of Glambek (fig. 1). The castle was first built in the early 13th century by King Valdemar the Victorious (1202-1241) as a brick curtain wall, 54 m by 38 m, with two diagonally placed corner towers and buildings in the opposite areas. According to Presbyter Bremensis, King Eric reinforced the castle with ramparts but later that year the Holsteiners recaptured the lot[39].

In 1420 the Danes returned with allegedly 700 ships, taking the castle and ravaging, plundering and killing half the population. Presbyter Bremensis, the chronicler from Holstein, later described the assault as follows:

> They ruthlessly killed the male population with the sword but some escaped into the churches, particularly in the town Burg. After dragging them out of the churches and stripping them of their clothes, they were taken to the churchyard naked and crying and killed with much cruelty. Whit these outrageous atrocities they – alas! – desecrated the sacred places, churches and churchyards along with the sacraments and the Holy Body of Christ, and they ravaged the whole country as they plundered all houses and eventually burned down all houses and cottages in the whole country. They left no one behind but captured all surviving males, women, virgins and children of which many – alas! – were degraded by destitution as the men became pirates and the women and virgins became adulteresses and harlots. Such inhumanity is unheard of among heathens and barbarians but was executed in this country by those who call themselves Christians[40].

38. Poulsen et al. 2003, 501-506.
39. Presbyter Bremensis 1903, 118; Erslev 1901, 32; Selch Jensen 2007, 19ff.
40. Translation of Presbyter Bremensis 1903, 135, by the author.

Undoubtedly the anti-Danish description of the events is much exaggerated but the massacre is in fact mentioned in several sources and it seems that some 300 people who had sought refuge in a church were actually slaughtered. 4 years later, in 1424, the Holsteiners recaptured the island. Ethnic cleansing of the unreliable islanders was executed in favour of peasants from the Ditmarches, and the professional pirates, the so-called "Vitalie Brothers", were summoned in order to seize Glambek. Archaeological results indicate that the ravaged castle was rebuilt in the late Middle Ages, presumably by the pirates who used it as a base for exploitation of both Fehmarn and the Baltic for several decades[41].

14. The siege of Duborg 1431

Similar war crimes were committed by the Holsteiners in the Åbenrå area when Brundlund Castle was captured in 1429 after a four-week siege. As a consequence, the northern supply line to the castle in Flensborg, which had successfully withstood sieges in 1422 and 1427, was cut off[42].

When Duborg was once again besieged in 1431, the 600 men defending the castle were totally dependent on supplies from the seafront as 800 Frisians who were very skilled in the art of dike building joined the army of Holstein and helped it build bulwarks around the castle in order to cut off all mainland supplies. After a few months a fleet managed to bring in provisions as a small part of the town protected by a "barde", apparently some kind of bulwark or perhaps a tower, was still under royal command but the Holsteiners succeeded in taking the town and cutting off the harbour with ships and barrages. The totally encircled Duborg endured the siege for more than 6 months from March to September when only 140 men, barely surviving on dogs and horses, were still alive. Eventually the castle surrendered and the lord lieutenant negotiated a safe departure for the survivors provided that they left behind all arms and equipment. Shortly after Nyhus to the north of Flensburg also fell into enemy hands and was destroyed and in the meantime the royal troops were long since forced to leave the last castle in the Schlei region[43].

With the loss of Flensburg and Duborg, the very base of Danish power in Southern Jutland, King Eric was forced to give up his ambition of winning Schleswig back. Both in 1415 and again in 1424 his cousin, Emperor Sigismund, had passed judgement that Schleswig be part of the Kingdom of Denmark but in spite of these imperial arbitrages in favour of Denmark, Eric never managed to regain control of the duchy[44]. It underlines that enforcement of law whether imperial or not meant very little in this bitter conflict.

At the request of the Emperor and the Grand Master of the Teutonic Order, Denmark, Holstein and the Hanseatic League entered into peace negotiations in 1432. The Holsteiners were allowed to keep what land they had conquered and in 1435 the King had to conclude a humiliating treaty, the so-called Vordingborg-peace-treaty, which forced him to relinquish all claims to the Duchy of Schleswig except the town and castle of Haderslev, the small island of Ærø and some estates on the islands of Föhr and Sylt (fig. 1)[45].

15. Postscript

Though the politics and wars of Eric of Pomerania did not always work out successfully – he was in fact dethroned a few years later – it is indeed appropriate to reassess his role in medieval castle-building and castle-organizing. In this respect he is often overlooked in favour of former kings such as the Valdemars (the Great [1157-1182], the Victorious [1202-1241]), Erik Menved (1286-1319) and his own great-grandfather Valdemar Atterdag (1340-1375). Considering the volume, number and importance of Eric's new castles as well as his purchases and rebuildings of older castles, any similar activity in this field was hardly seen to this extent before in Denmark and certainly never again during the Middle Ages. Moreover several of his new castles would turn out to be of great importance also after the era in question. It is apparent that Eric should be remembered, therefore, as a castle builder of note.

---

41. Poulsen *et al.* 2003, 501; Selch Jensen 2007, 19, 25-26.
42. La Cour *et al.* 1937-1939, 82; Poulsen *et al.* 2003, 502.
43. Koppmann 1875; Wolff 1891, 248ff.; Erslev 1901, 267; La Cour *et al.* 1937-1939, 83-84; Schütt 1996, 322.
44. La Cour *et al.* 1937-1939, 63, 76; Hedemann 2007.
45. Erslev 1901, 273-278; La Cour *et al.* 1937-1939, 86-87; Poulsen 2008, 146.

Bibliography

Blom O. (1872), "Lodbøssen fra Vedelspang. Et Bidrag til Haandskydevaabnenes Historie i det 15de Aarhundrede", *Aarbøger for Nordisk Oldkyndighed og Historie*, 229-256.

Dähn A. (2001), *Ringwälle und Turmhügel. Mittelalterliche Burgen in Schleswig-Holstein*, Husum, Husum Verlag.

Diplomatarium Danicum/Danmarks Riges Breve (2002-2003), 4. række, bind 12, Det Danske Sprog- og Litteraturselskab (ed.), Copenhagen, Reitzel.

Diplomatarium Flensborgense (1865-1873), *Samling af Aktstykker til Staden Flensborgs Historie indtil Aaret 1559*, vols. 1-2, H. C. P. Sejdelin (ed.), Copenhagen, Gyldendal.

Ellger D. & Teuchert W. (1957), *Die Kunstdenkmäler des Landskreises Schleswig*, Munich/Berlin, Deutscher Kunstverlag (Die Kunstdenkmäler des Landes Schleswig-Holstein; 8).

Erslev K. (1896), "Det saakaldte Slag paa Hesterbjærg 1325. Jydernes Angreb paa Gottorp", *Historisk Tidsskrift*, 6/6, 389-400.

– (1901), *Danmarks Historie under Dronning Margrethe og Erik af Pommern II. Erik af Pommern, hans Kamp for Sønderjylland og Kalmarunionens Opløsning*, Copenhagen, J. Erslev.

Haupt R. (1905), "Das königliche Schloss zu Flensburg", *Zeitschrift der Gesellschaft für Schleswig-Holsteinische Geschichte*, 35, 56-75.

Hedemann M. (2007), "Ofendommen 28. juni 1424. Politiske forudsætninger og juridisk strategi", *Historisk Tidsskrift*, 107, 34-70.

Hertz J. (1986), "Brundlund – et næsten ukendt slot", *Nationalmuseets Arbejdsmark*, 84-103.

Hoppmann J. (1997), "Der Schleswiger Hesterberg – 'vor den Toren Gottorfs'", *Beiträge zur Schleswiger Stadtgeschichte*, 42, 37-49.

– (2007), "Hvor lå Sliesthorp? Og hvem anlagde de glemte volde nord for Slien?", *Sønderjysk Månedsskrift*, 4, 132-141.

Jensen C. A. (undated), *Foredrag i Oldskriftselskabet. Sønderjyske Voldsteder*, Unpublished manuscript in the library at Antikvarisk-Topografisk Arkiv, National Museum of Denmark.

Jørgensen A. D (1889-1892), "Klavs Lembeks Frafald 1421", *Danske Magazin*, 5/2, 108-119.

Koppmann K. (1875), "Zur Belagerung Flensburgs im Jahre 1431", *Hansische Geschichtsblätter*, 5, 127-129.

Kristensen T. R. (2000), *Kloakering ved Brundlund Slot (HAM 3452)*, Unpublished excavation report.

La Cour V. (1971), "Duborg", *Sønderjysk Månedsskrift*, 47/7, 233-252.

La Cour V. et al. (eds.) (1937-1939), *Sønderjyllands Historie II*, Copenhagen, Reitzel.

Laur W. (1964), "Zum Namen der Hattesburg", *Beiträge zur Schleswiger Stadtgeschichte*, 9, 16-18.

Loewe G. (1998), *Kreis Schleswig (seit 1974 Kreis Schleswig-Flensburg)*, Neumünster, Wachholtz (Archäologische Denkmäler Schleswig Holsteins; 8).

Lorenzen C. C. (1859), "De sydslesvigske Befæstningsværker i og fra Oldtiden og Middelalderen", *Annaler for Nordisk Oldkyndighed og Historie*, 3-125.

Mackeprang M. (1932), "En Skjoldefrise fra Erik af Pommerns Tid paa Krogen Slot", *Fra Nationalmuseets Arbejdsmark*, 78-80.

Møller Nielsen H. M. (2008), "Krogen: the Medieval Predecessor of Kronborg", in *Château Gaillard 23. Bilan des recherches en castellologie*, P. Ettel, A.-M. Flambard Héricher & T. E. McNeill (eds.), Caen, Publications du CRAHM, 315-328.

– (2011), "A Network of Power: the Royal Castles of Denmark in the 15th Century – Ein Netzwerk der Macht: Dänische Königsburgen im 15. Jahrhundert", in *Die Burg im 15. Jahrhundert*, vol. 12, J. Zeune (ed.), Braubach, Deutschen Burgenvereinigung/Europäischen Burgeninstitut, 91-101.

Nöbbe E. (1926-1929), *Beobachtungen auf Duburg 1926, 1927, 1928, 1929*, Unpublished excavation reports, drawings, etc., Stadt Archiv, Flensburg.

Oberdieck G. et al. (1950), *Die Kunstdenkmäler des Kreises Eckernförde*, Munich/Berlin, Deutsche Kunstverlag (Kunstdenkmäler der Provinz Schleswig-Holstein; 5).

Olesen J. E. (1994), "Erik af Pommern og Kalmarunionen. Regeringssystemets udformning 1389-1439", in *Danmark i senmiddelalderen*, P. Ingesman & J. V. Jensen (eds.), Aarhus, Aarhus universitetsforlag, 143-165.

Olsen R. A. (2011), *Danske middelalderborge*, Aarhus/Copenhagen, Aarhus universitetsforlag.

Pelc O. (2001), "Burg, Tor und Mauer. Die Befestigung der schleswig-holsteinischen Städte im Mittelalter", in *Landesgeschichte und Landesbibliothek. Studien zur Geschichte und Kultur Schleswig-Holsteins. Hans F. Rothert zum 65. Geburtstag*, D. Lohmeier (ed.), Heide, Boyens, 21-45.

Poulsen B. (1988), *Land – by – marked. To økonomiske landskaber i 1400-tallets Slesvig*, Flensburg, Studieafdelingen ved Dansk Centralbibliotek for Sydslesvig.

– (2008), "Hertugdømmets dannelse 700-1544", in *Sønderjyllands Historie 1. Indtil 1815*, H. S. Hansen, L. N. Henningsen & C. P. Rasmussen (eds.), Aabenraa, Historisk samfund for Sønderjylland, 41-186.

Poulsen B. et al. (2003), *Det Sønderjyske Landbrugs Historie. Jernalder, vikingetid og middelalder*, Haderslev, Haderslev Museum.

Presbyter Bremensis (1903), *Holstenerpræstens Krønike*, A. Hude & Selskabet til Historiske Kildeskrifters Oversættelse (trans.), Copenhagen, Schønberg.

Rathjen J. (2005), *Schleswig im Spätmittelalter 1250-1544*, Husum, Husum Druck- und Verlagsgesellschaft.

Reisnert A. (2001), "The City of Malmö and the Castle Malmöhus", in *Castella Maris Baltici 3-4*, Turku/Tartu/Malbork, The Society for Medieval Archaeology in Finland/Malbork Castle Museum, 159-166.

Reitzel-Nielsen E. (1976), *The Danish Order of Saint John since the Reformation*, Copenhagen, Krohn.

Rohling L. (1955), *Die Kunstdenkmäler der Stadt Flensburg*, Munich/Berlin, Deutscher Kunstverlag.

Schütt H. F. (1996), "Die als Steinbau errichtete Turmbau in Flensburg", *Offa – Berichte und Mitteilungen zur Urgeschichte, Frühgeschichte und Mittelalterarchäologie*, 53, 317-325.

Scriptores rerum Danicarum medii ævi (1772-1878), *Partim hactenus inediti, partim emendatius editi, qvos collegit, adornavit, et publici juris fecit Jacobus Langebek*, vols. 1-9, Hafniæ, Godiche.

Selch Jensen C. (2007), "Krigen om Femern", *Skalk*, 4, 18-27.

Slevogt H. (1998), *Eckernförde. Die Geschichte einer deutschen Kaufmannsstadt in Herzogtum Schleswig*, vol. 1: *Von den Anfängen bis zur Reformation*, Husum, Husum Druck- und Verlagsgesellschaft.

Trap J. P. (1967), *Danmark. Åbenrå-Sønderborg Amter*, Copenhagen, Gad.

Uldall K. (1921), *Tørning*, Unpublished report, Danish National Museum.

Unverhau H. (2001), "Die angebliche Zerstörung Eckernfördes im Jahre 1416/17", in *700 Jahre Stadt Eckernförde. Beiträge zur Erforschung und Beschreibung der Geschichte der Stadt aus den Schriften und Veröffentlichungen der Heimatgemeinschaft*, Eckernförde, Heimatgemeinschaft (Schriftenreihe der Heimatgemeinschaft Eckernförde; 13), 67-78.

Wolff A. (1882), "Flensburg's alte Stadtmauern", *Zeitschrift der Gesellschaft für Schleswig-Holstein-Lauenburgische Geschichte*, 12, 115-129.

– (1891), "Flensburg's Belagerung im Jahre 1431", *Zeitschrift der Gesellschaft für Schleswig-Holstein-Lauenburgische Geschichte*, 21, 235-264.

The Post-Medieval Fortifications of Earth and Timber in Hungary

◆

Maxim Mordovin*

1. General

The end of the Middle Ages in Hungary can be connected with the disastrous Battle of Mohács that took place in 1526 between the Ottoman forces and the Hungarian army. King Louis II's death in this battle resulted in a civil war between the supporters of two different claimants to the Hungarian throne. The Ottomans took the advantage of this situation and in 1541 the capital of the Kingdom of Hungary became the seat of their northernmost province. The conquest of Buda made the occupation of the central part of Hungary permanent[1].

The main consequence of these events was the formation of a new, more-or-less, stable border. Most of the castles situated in this zone were simple, medieval, noble or royal fortifications not suitable for accommodating large garrisons, nor for withstanding serious attack, especially against an Ottoman army equipped with heavy artillery. This whole situation forced the Habsburgs (now the new kings of Hungary), on the one hand, to try to transform the old medieval castles on the new border into fortifications that would meet the needs of modern warfare. On the other hand, the Ottomans had to secure their newly conquered territories by defending the border – thus, they faced quite similar problems to the Habsburgs, their opponents[2].

Since both of the opposing sides did not have sufficient financial resources nor had they enough time to construct large, modern fortresses on the constantly changing and disturbed borderline, an urgent need arouse to find a cheap and fast way to secure the borders. The solution appeared in the form of castles, whose main defences consisted of the so-called *Hungarian Wall*. Since most of the military written sources in this period were German, this term was usually written as *Ungarische Mauer* in contemporary sources[3]. This type of fortification gained its name from the territory where it was most widely used but – certainly – it was adapted not only along the Hungarian-Ottoman borderland, but was used even further afield, on different newly constructed and endangered existing sites. This included not only castles but these defences were also used in the fortification of existing churches and monasteries of an earlier date.

The fortification itself is known in the Turkish and Hungarian languages as *palánk* and this name also got into the German tongue as *palanken*. There is no special term for this feature and architectural solution in English but it can be described as an earthwork with a specific inner wooden structure. Even if any two fortifications that used these *palánk* defences were not exactly similar, the basic concept of their architecture was the same and had ancient traditions all across Europe[4]. In all cases, these defences consisted of at least two rows of stakes placed loosely or tightly next to each other in a foundation ditch. These posts were then interwoven with twigs and branches, which created a wattle fence. The ditch and the space between the wattle-lines were filled with lime and clay. This wall was supported on its inner side by a fence-like vertical wooden wall and mostly defended against the artillery fire from the outside by a splayed embankment. In some

---

* Eötvös Loránd University, Hungary.
1. Parry 1976, 42-60.
2. Buzás *et al.* 2003, 380-383.
3. Domokos 2006, 48.
4. Higham & Barker 1992, 17-26; Etting 2010, 69-72.

cases, both sides of such fortifications were simply plastered and had no scarps[5].

Earlier research, mostly based on Vidor Pataki's study, regarded these post-medieval fortifications as cheap, quickly-erected structures, which were only used temporarily. Also, it was believed that such fortifications dated narrowly and mainly to period from 1541 to 1556 and rarely to the second half of the 16th century. This earlier research connected them with a particular phase of the Hungarian-Ottoman wars preceding the reorganisation of the Habsburg military administration, which ended in the establishing of the Court Council of War (the *Hofkriegsrat*) in 1556[6]. Fortunately enough, recent archaeological and historical research has clearly demonstrated that this earth and timber military architecture was at least as complex as stone-masonry building and required experience and the same comparative level of skills to erect[7].

There are quite a few sites in Hungary with such fortifications that have been investigated so far, especially during the last 10 to 20 years. There are several articles that give preliminary overviews of the latest results. The most recent was compiled by Gábor Tomka who collected the evidence from the main post medieval fortified sites investigated in Hungary between 1995 and 2005[8]. The excavations of such monuments in a much smaller region were discussed and described by Gyöngyi Kovács. She carried out archaeological, historical and environmental investigations in the Dráva valley, which was a border zone between the Kingdom of Hungary and Ottoman Empire during the 16th and 17th centuries[9]. There is also a more popular synthesis written by her on the same topic[10]. Certainly, there is still huge amount of data about these fortifications waiting to be published. Hopefully this paper decreases this scientific debt by discussing some of the results from the recent excavations carried out in Szécsény.

These monuments can be divided in three main groups according to which side constructed them: royal, Ottoman and unclear. Since the length of the paper is limited, the present writer will mention only the major recognised examples of this type of fortification.

The earliest such examples are known from the 1540 to the 1560s. An Italian military engineer, Giulio Turco, made detailed surveys of different castles in Western Hungary. Many of these surveys clearly indicated that these fortresses had *Hungarian Wall*-type defences. The sites depicted on his plans are very diverse. Some were modernised medieval castles, while a significant group was fortified ecclesiastical buildings. First of all, the greater monasteries such as Zalavár and Tihany were fortified. Larger churches situated on the weakest sections of the new border zone were also modified and transformed into more-or-less defendable fortifications. The most notable of them is the one at Fonyód just on the southern shore of the Lake Balaton. This former medieval church gained a double defence line made of two concentric ditches and palisades. This little stronghold, with these defences, was able to withstand minor Ottoman attacks from 1540s until 1575. Some other less significant sites like Csákány, Somogyzsitfa-Szöcsénypuszta or Somogyzsitfa-Szöcsénypuszta had very similar constructions (fig. 1)[11]. According to the archaeological excavations at the latter site, the defence line there consisted of a single stockade or palisade combined with wattle. The corners were fortified using circular earth platforms[12]. All of these sites sooner or later were occupied by the Ottomans and finally destroyed.

From the royal Habsburg side, there is only one wholly excavated post-medieval fortification in Hungary – the castle of Bajcsa. This late 16th-century star-shaped fortress consisted of ramparts of post structure, reinforced at a later date using brick curtain walls. Due to its unfortunate static location, the site was abandoned already before 1610[13]. Another investigated royal fortress was situated in Zalaegerszeg. Some parts of its ramparts and a circular bastion were excavated in 2002-2003. Its walls had an inner post-wattle structure, common for this period. Its construction must have been started about the mid-16th century and it was in use until the end of the Ottoman wars[14]. The fortified city of Pápa was among the most important royal border castles in North-West Hungary. Its fortifications were constructed during the 1560s and then renewed several times. Despite the high importance of the site, its earth and timber ramparts were never replaced by stone or brick defences[15]. A smaller medieval castle of much less significance at Várgesztes was reinforced and rebuilt in the same period. Its destroyed stone curtain walls were replaced by earthworks with an inner post structure and a new circular bastion was constructed in the same manner[16]. A relatively late earth and timber fortification was built in castle of Boldogkő. The appearance of such an architectural solution in a medieval stone castle located on the top of a rock is very unusual. The lower terrace of the rock was fortified using a palisade integrating a semicircular bastion. This structure must have been built as late as *c.* 1680[17].

This earth and timber military architecture was used not only in case of secondary or provisional castles but also on the constructions of very important central strongholds. Certainly, as soon as the financial situation of the state improved, this enabled those parts or sections defended in such a way at these places to be replaced with more durable structures.

---

5. Buzás *et al.* 2003, 381.
6. Pataki 1931, 98-133.
7. Domokos 2000, 21.
8. Tomka 2010, 596-620.
9. Kovács 2010, 757-781.
10. Buzás *et al.* 2003, 380-383.
11. Magyar & Nováki 2005, 40-41, 126-127, 237, 241-242.
12. *Ibid.*, 237.
13. Vándor & Kovács 2002, 47-62; Kovács & Vándor 2003, 109-113.
14. Vándor 2003; Havasi 2004.
15. Ilon 1988; Ilon 1997.
16. Feld 2004, 313.
17. Fülöp & Koppány 2006, 109.

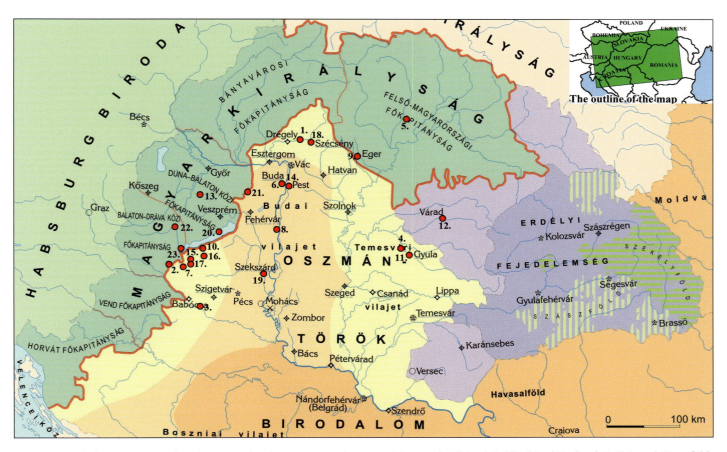

Fig. 1 – Fortified sites mentioned in the paper: 1) Balassagyarmat; 2) Bajcsa; 3) Barcs; 4) Békés; 5) Boldogkő; 6) Buda; 7) Csákány; 8) Dunaföldvár; 9) Eger; 10) Fonyód; 11) Gyula; 12) Nagyvárad; 13) Pápa; 14) Pest; 15) Somogysámson; 16) Somogyvár; 17) Somogyzsitfa; 18) Szécsény; 19) Szekszárd; 20) Tihany; 21) Várgesztes; 22) Zalaegerszeg; 23) Zalavár. Doc. M. Mordovin.

This process can be clearly traceable in Eger and Nagyvárad (Oradea). Both of these places were the seats of bishoprics and were already fortified before the Ottoman wars, primarily to represent the power of the Church. However, their defences were not suitable to withstand any significant sieges. The complete reconstruction of these castles started in the 1540s and in both cases this was carried out under the supervision of prominent Italian architects. The construction of Eger was finished during the 1570s but the modernisation of Nagyvárad (Oradea) lasted much longer. Its last polygonal bastion was only finished in 1618[18]. The earth and timber fortification of these castles are known from pictorial sources. Eger was depicted by the architects Pietro Ferrabosco in 1568 and Franz von Poppendorf and Ottavio Baldigara in 1572[19]. The best drawing illustrating the complexity of the star-shaped post medieval fortress at Nagyvárad (Oradea) was made by Georg Houfnagel in 1617[20].

On the Ottoman side there are two main and many smaller excavated sites. The first relatively well-known and well-investigated site is castle of Barcs, which was in existence from the mid-16th century until the 1660s[21]. Some remains of an Ottoman timber fortification datable to the second half of the 16th century were investigated in the centre of Békés[22]. The castle of Szekszárd-Jenipalánka is among the most spectacular of the excavated Ottoman sites in Hungary. This small rectangular fortress had 4 circular bastions on its corners. It was built during the Long War and was destroyed in the late 17th century. Its ramparts were made of earth and timber with an inner post and wattle structure[23]. A huge Ottoman timber and earth bastion was identified during rescue excavations in Budapest along the medieval city walls of Pest. Its construction can be dated to the late 17th century[24]. Further remains of partly-investigated Ottoman fortifications include Somogyvár and Dunaföldvár. In both cases, medieval Benedictine abbeys

18. Domokos 2000, 31-37; Balogh 1982, 325.
19. Domokos 2000, 130-138.
20. Balogh 1982, ill. 108.
21. Kovács & Rózsás 2010.
22. Gerelyes 1980.
23. Gaál 2003.
24. Írás-Melis 2003.

were re-used for military purposes. In Somogyvár traces of burnt timber and earthen defences were found[25]. The Ottoman castle of Dunaföldvár, however, had at least one stone tower surrounded by huge earthworks[26].

In some cases, it is still hard to decide which of the opposing sides constructed the earliest fortifications at certain places or rebuilt existing medieval structures at others. This is the situation in Balassagyarmat. Its medieval fortified parts and its post-medieval rampart were investigated but have not been published yet. Due to this, the precise dating of its construction is still questioned[27]. In another case, namely in Gyula, the confusing stratigraphic situation hinders the precise understanding of who exactly constructed its ramparts. The excavated parts of the fortification can be dated to the 1560s but unfortunately this is the decade when the castle was conquered by the Ottoman forces. According to the 16th-century plans, the castle gained its general layout just before the siege that took place here in 1566. The remains of the burnt wattle defences and piling found on the site may belong either to a pre-Ottoman structure destroyed during the above-mentioned siege or to an Ottoman reconstruction set on fire at a later date during the Long War around 1600[28].

2. Timber-and-earth fortifications in Szécsény

The reconstruction of the historical city of Szécsény in 2005 and 2010-2011 allowed the possibility to investigate the remains of its post-medieval fortifications known from contemporary sources[29]. We were only able to conduct rescue excavations and thus we could not reach the subsoil. Due to this, the recognised, uncovered stratigraphy almost exclusively represents activity from the early Modern period.

The post-medieval topography of Szécsény can be reconstructed based on the written sources and two available drawings dating to the 1650s, which were redrawn by Gerhard Graaß in 1666 (fig. 2)[30]. According to this data, the fortification of Szécsény consisted of two main parts: its castle and its city ramparts. The castle itself is of medieval origin and must have been built in the first half of the 15th century. Now it is incorporated into the 18th-century Forgách Château. The structure of the ramparts is worth mentioning since its three parts were constructed using different techniques. The plan clearly differentiates these differences. The eastern and south-eastern sections of the defences were built of brick and had two circular bastions – most probably cannon towers. There was an eastern gate tower attached to the northern bastion (fig. 3). According to recent but unpublished excavations, this bastion was built of brick and had two entrances. From here the brick wall continued southward until it came to the second bastion. On the 17th-century plan, the southern part of this wall was not finished but it seems to have been constructed not much later after than the latter drawing. Today this wall is largely preserved in the southern façades of 18th- and 19th-century houses. This section connected the south-eastern bastion to the gate-tower. This gate-tower was built in the late 16th century according to the results of the excavations carried out at this spot in 2011[31]. The south-western section of the ramparts had an earth-and-timber structure and seemingly was also planned to be replaced by a brick wall, also with a more advanced star-shaped bastion. This rebuilding project, however, had never been realised and defences always remained of earth and timber. The last, western and north-western sections of the defences surrounded the Franciscan friary and consisted of a traditional stone wall. This wall had not been yet investigated and thus its dating is unknown. Most likely, it can be connected to the late 15th-century reconstruction and modernisation of the friary. Most of the brick and some parts of the stone wall have survived to the present day. The earthworks were almost completely destroyed leaving no visible remains on the surface.

A detailed excavated area, investigated by the present writer and others, is situated on the southern line of the ramparts of timber and earth, about 20 m west of the stone gate tower. The remains of the fortification were traced across 6 different excavated sections here (2005/3-4, 2010/I-II, 2010/V and 2010/XIV [fig. 4]). The sections 2005/3-4, 2010/I-II and 2010/XIV covered the whole width of the earthwork. In the smaller trench, 2010/V, only the inner (northern) post row of the defences was reached. The largest and best preserved remains of the post-medieval defences were documented in the sections 2005/3-4 and 2010/I-II. Not only was the base of the foundation trench reached by excavation but also the burnt timbers of the upper part of the rampart were excavated.

Two large-scale building phases of the ramparts were distinguished on this investigated site. The line of the fortification did not change during the whole time of its existence. The second phase had largely destroyed the traces of the earlier one. The description of these phases is given according to the stratigraphy observed in sections 2005/3-4 and 2010/I-II.

Since there was no possibility to reach the subsoil, we have neither archaeological evidence regarding the late medieval topography of this place nor the evidence for a supposed 15th-century predecessor of the post-medieval defences. At the same time, a significant burnt layer beneath the first phase of the 16th-century fortification clearly shows that the site was

---

25. BAKAY 1988.
26. KOZÁK 1970; KOZÁK 1973.
27. MAJCHER 2001; FÜREDI 2004.
28. SZATMÁRI & GERELYES 1996; GERELYES & FELD 2004; GERELYES & FELD 2005.
29. The excavations in 2005 were led by G. Tomka (Hungarian National Museum) and they were coordinated in 2010 by B. F. Romhányi but led by the present writer.
30. SZABÓ 2010, 58.
31. MORDOVIN 2012, 17.

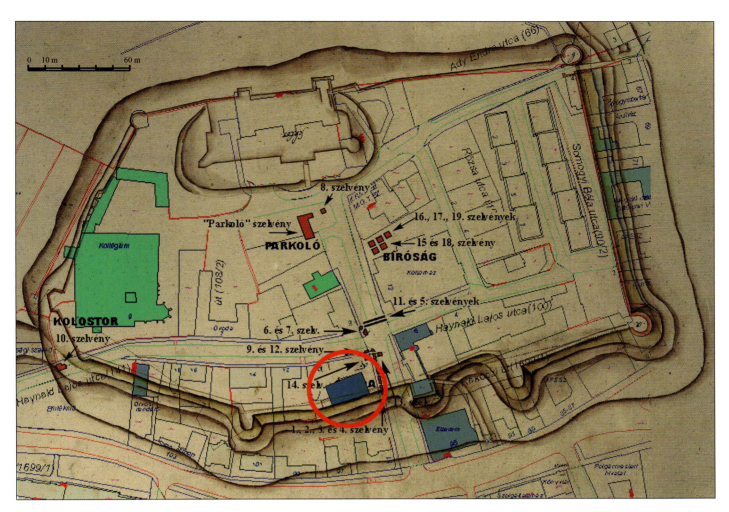

Fig. 2 – Gerhard Graaß's survey of Szécsény adjusted to the present-day city plan and showing the location of the investigated area. Doc. M. Mordovin.

Fig. 3 – North-eastern cannon tower at Szécsény, showing traces of the demolished gate tower. Photo M. Mordovin.

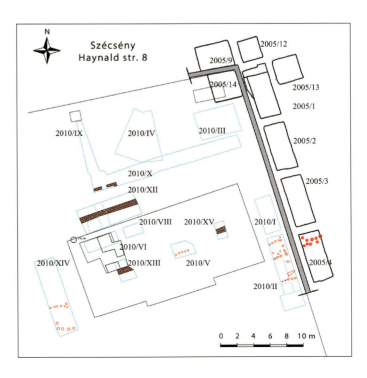

Fig. 4 – Excavations at Szécsény, Haynald str. 8, trench layout. Doc. M. Mordovin.

Fig. 5 – Trench 2010/II, view from south on the post holes of the rampart. Photo M. Mordovin.

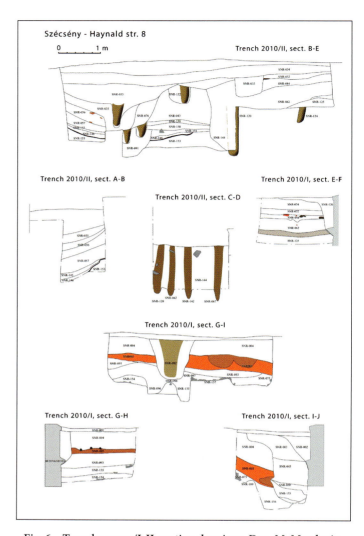

Fig. 6 – Trenches 2010/I-II, section drawings. Doc. M. Mordovin.

not empty and that significant activity had taken place there. This layer was partly destroyed by the posts of the ramparts[32].

Only the outer (southern) part of the first phase of the fortification could be observed. This consisted of double row of posts (palisades). The posts were placed in a 30 cm-60 cm wide foundation trench and were 25 cm-30 cm in diameter. The latter trench had a flat bottom and had a maximum depth of 2.30 m. The posts might have been pulled out because unlike other such features, their places had filled up and contained no wooden remains. The relative chronology of the above-mentioned two post-rows is not clear. Since for the general structure of the rampart, the contemporary existence of the two rows was not necessary and so they might have followed each other. Similar structures can be observed in the second phase. In this case, one of the rows may be a "sub-phase" showing traces of an earlier repair of the defences. The core of the rampart must have been of similar structure to the second phase (figs. 5 & 6). The observation made in section 2010/XIV that the later posts were situated exactly above the earlier confirms this assumption.

The second phase or at least its foundation level can be reconstructed more precisely. It seems that there was no levelling preceding the reconstruction of the ramparts. The new foundation trench was dug into the filling of the earlier defence structure. In this case, the central part was made of double row of 25 cm-40 cm thick, wooden piles placed vertically into a 2.5 m wide trench that was at least 1.5 m-1.7 m in depth. There were no traces of wattle but the situation of the posts suggests its probable existence. The posts slightly narrowed toward the bottom of the trench but their lower end was cut flat. The foundation trench was filled and tamped with clay and daub up to the former surface. A large amount of huge rough stones was observed in the central part of the fillings. The structure was stabilised using perpendicular post rows connected to the two longitudinal ones, creating smaller "boxes". The distance between such perpendicular walls was at least 2 m (fig. 7).

32. The drawings were made in 2005 by I. Nagy, É. Nagy and the present writer; and in 2010 by S. Guba, M. Vargha, E. Varga, E. Szalai, K. B. Bognár, B. Bárdi, L. A. Nagy and, again, the present writer.

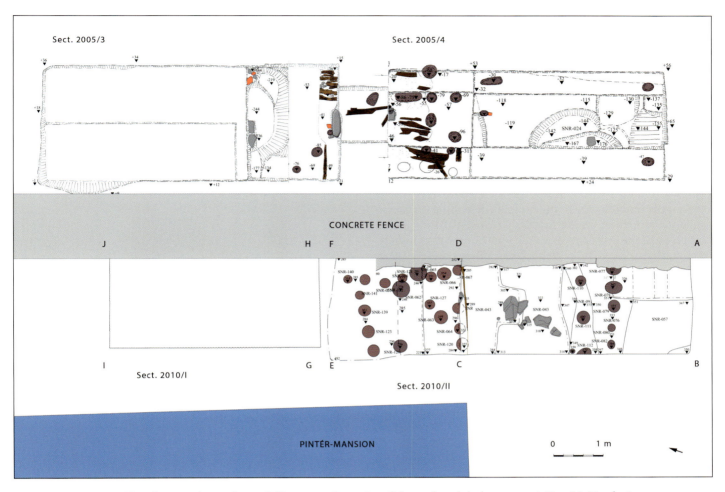

Fig. 7 – Trenches 2005/3-4 and 2010/I-II, excavated remains of the earth and timber rampart. Doc. M. Mordovin.

Above the former ground surface, the structure of the rampart was more complex. The outer and the inner "façades" of the rampart were covered with horizontally placed timbers or planks used, on the one hand, to keep the infilling within the wattle boxes and, on the other, to stabilise the timber structure. In some places, the remains of cross-binding beams were found. It seems that these were used inside the rampart only above the contemporary surface. The upper part of the fortification was filled up with the same clay-like earth as its lower part. The 15th- to 17th-century pottery found indicates that the filling most probably originated from the moat surrounding the city. Some human bones found in the section 2010/II clearly indicate at the same time that earth from a burial ground was also used for construction of the ramparts. This fact indirectly helps understand the historical background for the period of the building of the ramparts. This could have happened when the Christian burials were out of use or when the authorities in the town did not care about the contents of a graveyard being used in the construction of town defences. In both scenarios, this is more likely to have happened during the Ottoman occupation.

An interesting fact is that no nails were used in the construction of ramparts at Szécsény, making it somewhat different from similar contemporary examples known from Dunaföldvár, Szekszárd-Jenipalánk or Gyula[33].

Very shallow traces of another row of posts were documented in the upper filling layers of the rampart. According to contemporary architectural plans, these posts must have belonged to the parapet. Many remains of burnt planks and timber found not much higher than these posts confirm that this part was not buried and was set on fire during a siege. On the inner side of the parapet in the section 2005/3-4, a group of planks placed perpendicularly to the direction of the rampart were found. These burnt planks were found lying on the reddish blackened filling of the fortification (fig. 7). This c. 90 cm wide "covering" belonged to the inner platform. Most probably its width could change according to the function of the defence structure.

The stakes of the parapet were regularly connected with the inner wall of the rampart using 10 cm-15 cm thick perpendicular horizontal timbers. This most likely compensated for the shallow foundation of the parapet, the piles of which,

---

33. Kozák 1970, 203; Kozák 1973, 195; Gaál 2003, 101; Gerelyes & Feld 2005, 101.

despite these supports, leaned in towards the city under the pressure from the outer embankment (fig. 6, section B-E, SNR-124). The structure of the parapet can be reconstructed based on the contemporary drawings since there is no way to define the original height of the three outer rows of posts. The closest analogy can be seen on Jacob von Hols's etching, datable to 1660, which shows the castle of Tokaj. According to this drawing, the two outer rows of posts were of similar height. The "binding" cross beams observed in the lower layers of filling might have continued up to the uppermost parts, creating a stable timber-framed structure, which was completely filled in[34]. A huge embankment could have partly covered the outer façade of the rampart defending it against artillery. Something similar must have existed already in the first phase of the fortification at Szécsény but it was definitely rebuilt at least once. The earlier double palisade was replaced by a simple one placed into a 20 cm-30 cm wide foundation trench. The diameter of the used stakes was defined by the width of the ditch. The width of the whole rampart could have reached 6 m-6.5 m.

The distance between the defences of the city and the houses was surprisingly little. The closest houses stayed only 1.8 m-2.4 m away from the inner face of the rampart. Even if there is no clear evidence for direct attaching of houses to the ramparts, we cannot exclude this possibility in some cases. During the excavations, we did not reach or find the edge of the moat. However, even if there is no archaeological data concerning it, according to Graaß' drawing, it started in distance 4 m-5 m from the ramparts, was at least 6 m-7 m deep and was filled with water.

The visual reconstruction of this part of the defences at Szécsény made from the archaeological data cannot be ideal due to the lack of large pieces of information, most of all concerning the upper part of the rampart (fig. 8). Moreover there is no possibility to define the inclination of the embankment surface. The reconstruction in this case uses contemporary pictorial and written sources. Most of the post-medieval earth and timber castles in Hungary had no such embankments on the outer sides of their ramparts. However, on the one hand, Graaß's ground plan of Szécsény actually depicts a scarp and; on the other hand, there are some known examples found in Hungary with this feature, namely at Dunaföldvár[35] and probably at Gyula[36]. According to a 17th-century description the ideal inclination of this outer scarp was 45°[37].

The archaeological dating of the rampart was possible thanks to dendrochronology. Some well-preserved wooden samples were taken from the inner structure of the first phase of the rampart beside the southern gate tower and from under

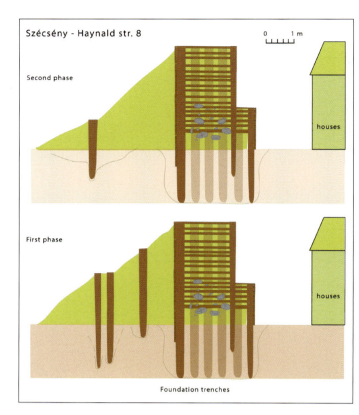

Fig. 8 – Visual reconstruction of the rampart at Szécsény. Doc. M. Mordovin.

the south-eastern circular bastion. The investigated trunks must have been cut down not earlier than 1562[38]. This perfectly corresponds to the historical and other archaeological data. The city of Szécsény was first besieged by the Ottomans in 1544 but taken only in 1552. The latest archaeological finds from the filling layers of the ramparts cannot be dated before the mid-16th century. At the same time, the first mention of the city's fortifications is from a description in 1596, 3 years after Szécsény was retaken by the royal forces. The first half of the 17th century was used for modernising the castle and ramparts, replacing the earthworks with brick walls. This process, however, was interrupted by the second Ottoman occupation in the period from 1663 to 1683. During the whole period of the Hungarian-Ottoman wars, Szécsény played an important role as a border castle with a garrison of between 500 and 800 soldiers, regardless of who controlled it. In 1683 Polish troops lead by King John Sobieski, on the way home from Vienna, finally liberated the city from the Ottomans[39].

---

34. Détshy 1995, 86.
35. Kozák 1973, 195.
36. Szatmári & Gerelyes 1996, 117.
37. Domokos 2006, 59.

38. The evaluation of the samples was made by A. Grynaeus. I am very grateful to him for the results.
39. Hegyi 2007, vol. 1, 106, 126, 135, 153.

Bibliography

Bakay K. (1988), "Elégett palánk nyomai a somogyvári várfalak mentén" ["Traces of a Burnt Palisade along the Ramparts of Somogyvár"], *Soproni Szemle*, 42, 128-135.

Balogh J. (1982), *Varadinum. Várad vára* [*Varadinum. Castle of Várad*], vols. 1-2, Budapest, Akadémiai Kiadó (Művészettörténeti füzetek; 13).

Buzás G. et al. (2003), "Castles, Forts and Stockades – Medieval and Ottoman Period Military Architecture", in *Hungarian Archaeology at the Turn of the Millennium*, Z. Visy (ed.), Budapest, Ministry of National Cultural Heritage, 377-383.

Détshy M. (1995), *A tokaji vár története* [*History of Castle of Tokaj*], Tokaj, Önkormányzat (Borsodi Kismonográfiák; 37/Tokaj és Hegyalia; 15).

Domokos G. (2000), *Ottavio Baldigara. Egy itáliai várfundáló mester Magyarországon* [*Ottavio Baldigara. An Italian Castle Architect in Hungary*], Budapest, Balassi Kiadó (A Hadtörténeti Intézet és Múzeum milleniumi könyvtára; 2).

– (2006), "Újabb adatok a szatmári erődítmény építéstörténetéhez az 1660-1670-es években" ["New Data Regarding the Construction of the Fortress of Szatmár in 1660-1670"], *Castrum*, 4, 47-70.

Etting V. (2010), *The Royal Castles of Denmark during the 14th Century. An Analysis of the Major Royal Castles with Special Regard to their Functions and Strategic Importance*, Copenhagen/Odense, National Museum of Denmark/University Press of Southern Denmark (Publications from the National Museum. Studies in Archaeology and History; 19).

Feld I. (2004), „Várgesztes, Gesztes vára" ["Várgesztes, Castle of Gesztes"], *Régészeti kutatások Magyarországon*, 313.

Fülöp A. & Koppány A. (2006), "Building Technologies of Natural Rock Surfaces in Hungarian Castles", in *Castrum Bene 9. Burg und ihr Bauplatz*, T. Durdík (ed.), Prague, Archeologický ústav AV ČR, 99-120.

Füredi Á. (2004), "Balassagyarmat, Bástya utca 12", *Régészeti kutatások Magyarországon*, 155-156.

Gaál A. (2003), "Turkish Palisades on the Tolna-County Stretch of the Buda-to-Eszék Road", in *Archaeology of the Ottoman Period in Hungary*, I. Gerelyes & G. Kovács (eds.), Budapest, Hungarian National Museum (Opuscula Hungarica; 3), 105-108.

Gerelyes I. (1980), "Előzetes jelentés a Békés-Kastélyzugi törökkori palánkvár ásatásáról 1975-1978" ["Preliminary Report on the Excavations of the Turkish Castle in Békés-Kastélyzúg, in 1975-1978"], *Archaeologiai Értesítő*, 107, 102-111.

Gerelyes I. & Feld I. (2004), "Gyula, Vár" ["Gyula Castle"], *Régészeti kutatások Magyarországon*, 224-225.

– (2005), "A gyulai külső vár 2004. évi ásatása" ["The 2004 Excavation of the Outer Bailey of Castle of Gyula"], *Castrum*, 1, 100-101.

Gerő L. (1955), *Magyarországi várépítészet* [*Hungarian Castle Architecture*], Budapest, Művelt Nép.

– (1968), *Magyar várak* [*Hungarian Castles*], Budapest, Műszaki Kiadó.

Havasi B. (2004), "Zalaegerszeg, Vár, Batthyány utca 9", *Régészeti kutatások Magyarországon*, 295-296.

Hegyi K. (2007), *A török hódoltság várai és várkatonasága* [*Castles and Soldiers of the Period of Ottoman Occupation*], vols. 1-3, Budapest, MTA Történettudományi Intézete (História könyvtár Kronológiák, adattárak; 9).

Higham R. & Barker P. (1992), *Timber Castles*, London, Batsford.

Ilon G. (1988), "Pápa város keleti palánkjának szondázása" ["Trial Excavation of the Earthworks of the City of Pápa"], *Communicationes Archaeologicae Hungariae*, 159-167.

– (1997), "Pápa", *Régészeti Füzetek*, 1/49, 114.

Írás-Melis K. (2003), "Pest during the Ottoman Era", in Gerelyes & Kovács 2003 (eds.), 161-172.

Kovács G. (2010), "A magyarországi oszmán-török régészet új eredményei: áttekintés a Dráva menti kutatások kapcsán" ["New Findings in the Ottoman-Turkish Archaeology in Hungary: Topics Highlighted by Research Work along the River Drava"], in *A középkor és a kora újkor régészete Magyarországon* [*Archaeology of the Middle Ages and Early Modern Period in Hungary*], vol. 2, E. Benkő & G. Kovács (eds.), Budapest, Magyar Tudományos Akadémia Régészeti Intézete, 757-781.

Kovács G. & Rózsás M. (2010), "A barcsi török vár és környéke" ["The Ottoman-Turkish Castle at Barcs and its Surroundings"], in Benkő & Kovács 2010 (eds.), vol. 2, 621-642.

Kovács G. & Vándor L. (2003), "Remarks on Archaeological Investigations into Smaller Ottoman-Era Palisades in Hungary", in Gerelyes & Kovács 2003 (eds.), 109-113.

Kozák É. (1970), "Régészeti és műemléki kutatások a dunaföldvári Öregtoronynál" ["Archaeological and Architectural Research on the Old Tower of Dunaföldvár"], *A Szekszárdi Béri Balogh Ádám Múzeum Évkönyve*, 1, 181-208.

– (1973), "A dunaföldvári (Tolna m.) öregtorony régészeti feltárása" ["Archaeological Excavation of the Old Tower of Dunaföldvár (Tolna Co.)"], *Műemlékvédelem*, 17, 193-198.

Magyar K. & Nováki G. (2005), *Somogy megye várai a középkortól a kuruc korig* [*Castles in the Middle Ages in the Province of Somogy*], Kaposvár, Somogy Megyei Múzeumok Igazgatósága.

Majcher T. (2001), "Balassagyarmat", *Régészeti kutatások Magyarországon*, 126.

Mordovin M. (2012), "Az erődítés maradványai a város déli oldalán" ["Remains of the Fortifications on the Southern Side of the Town"], in *Szécsény évszázadai*, Z. Galcsik & S. Guba (eds.), Szécsény, Múz. Baráti Köre Szécsényi Helyi Csop., 15-18.

Parry J. V. (1976), "The Reign of Sulaiman the Magnificent, 1520-1566", in *A History of the Ottoman Empire to 1730*, M. A. Cook (ed.), Cambridge/London/New York, Cambridge University Press, 79-102.

Pataki V. (1931), "A XVI. századi várépítés Magyarországon" ["16th-Century Castle Architecture in Hungary"], *A Bécsi Magyar Történeti Intézet Évkönyve*, 1, 98-133.

Szabó A. P. (ed.) (2010), *A szécsényi seregszék jegyzőkönyve (1656-1661)* [*The Military Register of Szécsény (1656-1661)*], Salgótarján, Nógrád Megyei Levéltár (Adatok, források és tanulmányok a Nógrád Megyei Levéltárból; 59).

Szatmári I. & Gerelyes I. (1996), *Tanulmányok a gyulai vár és uradalma történetéhez* [*Studies on the History of Gyula Castle and its Demesne*], Gyula, Békés Megyei Levéltár (Gyulai Füzetek; 8), 111-120.

Tomka G. (2010), "Kora újkori erődítések régészeti kutatása 1996-2006 között" ["Archaeological Research of Post-Medieval Fortifications"], in Benkő & Kovács 2010 (eds.), vol. 2, 596-620.

Vándor L. (2003), "Zalaegerszeg, Vár", *Régészeti kutatások Magyarországon*, 239.

Vándor L. & Kovács G. (2002), "Bajcsavár régészeti kutatása" ["Archaeological Research on Bajcsa Castle"], in *Bajcsa-vár. Egy stájer erődítmény Magyarországon a 16. század második felében* [*Bajcsa Castle. A Styrian Fortification in Hungary in the Second Half of the Sixteenth Century*], G. Kovács (ed.), Zalaegerszeg, Göcseji Múzeum, 47-62.

Enniscorthy Castle, Co. Wexford:
an Elizabethan Castle on the Borderland with Gaelic Ireland

◆

Ben Murtagh*

1. Introduction

The present castle is a turreted building, which is three storeys in height beneath the roof and battlements (fig. 1). It has a prominent location in the town of Enniscorthy, which is in the centre of Co. Wexford in the south-east corner of Ireland (fig. 2). The earliest part of the building consists of a fortified house, which is devoid of vaulting. It has an oblong central block, measuring around 14 m by 11.5 m, with four flanking three-quarter round towers or turrets at the corners. It was extensively renovated in the early 20th century (fig. 3)[1]. A local tradition reflected on a plaque above the entrance states that the castle was built in the 12th century by Raymond le Gros, one of the leaders of the first Anglo-Normans to arrive in Ireland in 1169/1170[2]. It is now clear however that this dating is far too early. Instead, Raymond may have built an earth and timber predecessor, which was replaced by a masonry one in the 13th century[3]. The medieval castle was strategically located in the centre of the largest fief or manor in the county[4]. From around the 1170s until the early 17th century, the castle was located on or near the frontier or borderland between the Anglo-Norman or English colony and lands of the Gaelic Irish in this part of south-east Ireland.

The presumption that the present castle was Anglo-Norman in date persisted until recently. In the early 20th century, for example, one view was that it dated to the first half of the 13th century[5]. This view was initially challenged by Philip Herbert Hore, who argued that it had been completely rebuilt by an English official and planter, Sir Henry Wallop, in the late 16th century[6]. He then changed his view and argued that the other dating was correct after all[7]. Moreover, he compared it to a group of similar-looking Anglo-Norman stone castles in the south-east of the country, which included those of Carlow and Wexford, together with nearby Ferns just to the north-east of Enniscorthy (fig. 2 B). The similarity in design between the latter and Enniscorthy was noticed as far back as the 18th century (fig. 4)[8]. Harold Graham Leask also saw the architectural similarity between the latter and this group of 13th-century castles, which he called "towered keeps". He however noted that Enniscorthy was smaller in size and had thinner walls than the other castles. This led him to conclude that it was a late 16th-century rebuilding of "an obsolete plan" based on old walls or foundations[9]. The 13th-century dating for the castle even persisted into the late 20th century[10]. By that time, however, wider opinion held that the present building dates from the late 16th century[11].

---

*   Buildings archaeologist, Kilkenny, Ireland.
1. Hore 1911, 336-337.
2. Grose 1791-1795, vol. 1, 48; Lewis 1837, vol. 1, 602.
3. Murtagh 2010, 103.
4. Colfer 2010, 90.
5. Grattan-Flood 1904, 380.
6. Hore 1905, 74.
7. Hore 1911, 344-345.
8. Grose 1791-1795, vol. 2, pls. 111 & 113.
9. Leask 1937, 176; Leask 1951, 27, 51.
10. Johnson 1985, 7; Reeves-Smyth 1995, 176.
11. Craig 1982, 63; Moore 1996, 154, no. 1437; McNeill 1997, 118; Salter 1993, 61; Sweetman 1999, 77; Whelan 1994, 73.

Fig. 1 – South-west view of Enniscorthy Castle. Photo B. Murtagh, 2012.

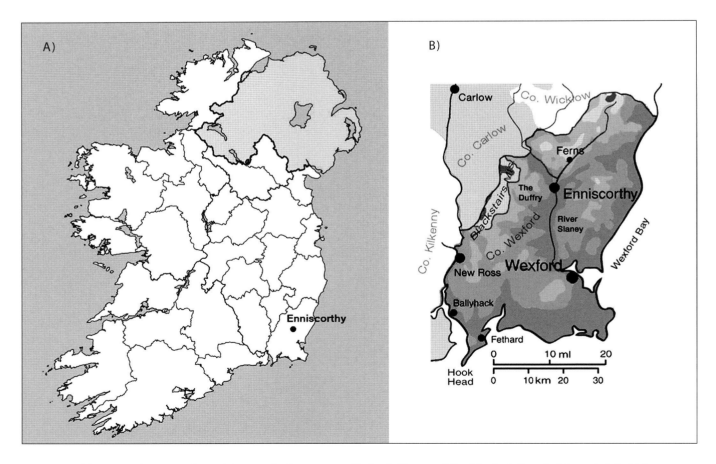

Fig. 2 – A) location of Enniscorthy and Co. Wexford on a map of Ireland; B) map of Co. Wexford. Doc. B. Murtagh & P. McInerney.

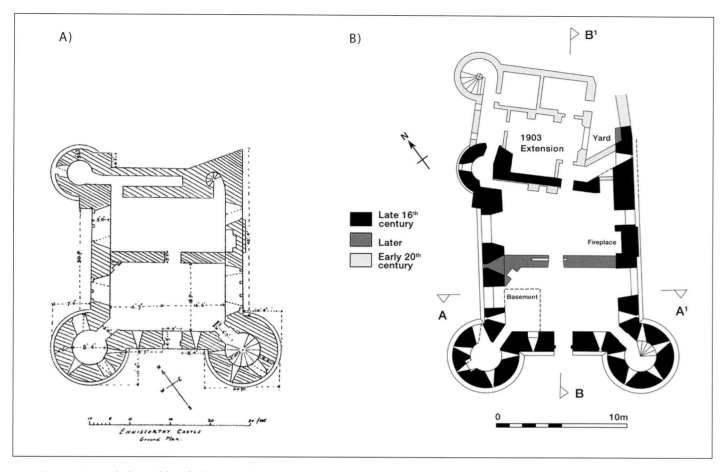

Fig. 3 – Ground plans of fortified house: A) 1903 plan in Hore 1911, 338; B) current phased plan (doc. B. Murtagh & P. McInerney).

Renovations to the castle in 2010 provided the writer with the opportunity to study its fabric. It confirmed the view that the primary phase is not medieval, but instead dates to the late 16th century[12]. This was a time when Enniscorthy had become both a base for English expansion into the Gaelic part of Co. Wexford and an industrial centre, which developed into the town that exists today. It would seem that the present castle is located on either the site or in the vicinity of the medieval one. The present one has been used as an armoury, barracks, residence, store, and has latterly served as the county museum. It is now a Protected Structure and together with its adjoining ground is listed in the Sites and Monuments Record[13].

2. Location and setting of the castle

The castle is built on sloping ground on a rocky promontory that rises above the west side of the River Slaney, which divides the town in two (figs. 1 & 5). Here the medieval river crossing or ford was located at the end of the tidal waterway of the lower part of the river, which linked Enniscorthy to Wexford town and the sea beyond (fig. 2 B). There is a commanding view from the castle's battlements of the fording point on the river, where there is now a bridge (fig. 5). The latter gives access to the eastern suburb called Templeshannon and is the oldest part of the town, which developed around the early medieval church and monastery of St Senan or *Teampell Senáin* (fig. 6)[14]. On the west side of the river, the town developed around the medieval castle (fig. 6)[15]. Up to the early 17th century, the hilly country to the west of and north-west of Enniscorthy and extending as far as the Blackstairs Mountains, was covered by oak woodlands or forests and was known as the Duffry (fig. 2 B)[16]. This derived from its Irish name *Dubh Tír*, meaning black or dark country from the dense tree cover[17]. It provided a refuge for the native or Gaelic Irish who opposed the Anglo-Normans and later the Elizabethan English settlers that dwelt on the borderland in and around the castle and town

---

12. Murtagh 2010, 106.
13. WX020-031003.
14. Culleton 1999, 127; Hore 1911, 335-336; Moore 1996, 137, no. 1301.
15. Murtagh 2010, 105.
16. St John Brooks 1950, 137, note 1.
17. Colfer 2010, 85; Whelan 1994, 71.

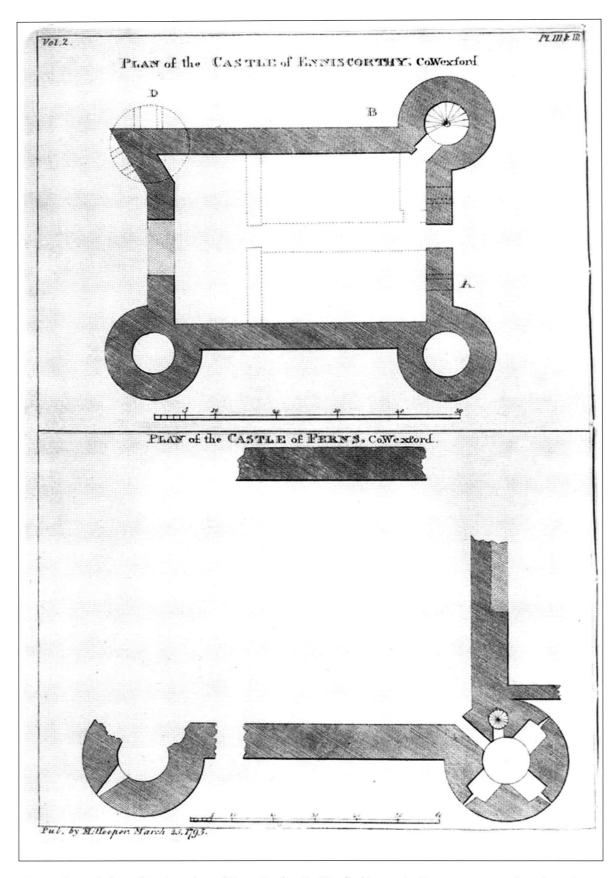

Fig. 4 – Ground plans of Enniscorthy and Ferns Castles, Co. Wexford in 1780 in Grose 1791-1795, vol. 2, pls. 111 & 113.

Fig. 5 – Views of Enniscorthy Bridge and Castle: A) GROSE 1791-1795, vol. 2, pl. 110; B) current view (photo B. Murtagh, 2012).

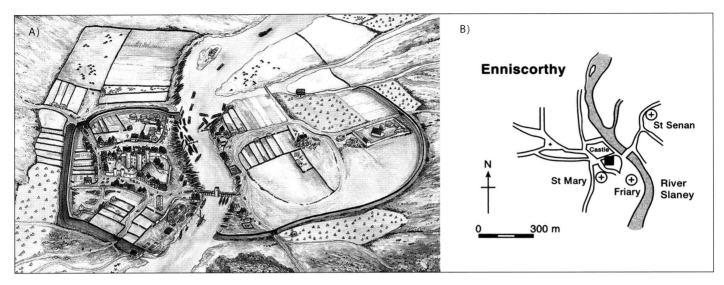

Fig. 6 – Town of Enniscorthy: A) view of *c.* 1600 from south by U. Hogerzeil; B) plan of town (doc. B. Murtagh & P. McInerney).

of Enniscorthy. The immediate environs of the present castle are now surrounded by a dense urban landscape, consisting of the rear end of properties that are fronted by high terraced houses and other buildings, which date from the late Georgian period onwards (fig. 5 B).

3. The medieval castle

The nature, extent and dating of the original castle is still unclear. It is possible that the Anglo-Norman Raymond le Gros constructed an earth and timber fortress, such as a ringwork, as he had custody of the adjoining fief in the 1170s and 1180s, during the minority of an heiress, Maud de Quency[18]. In 1190, she married Philip de Prendergast, whose family held a number of large fiefs in the county, and they established themselves at Enniscorthy[19]. During the first half of the 13th century, they and their son, Gerald, developed the town and surrounding fief[20]. It is likely that it was during this period of prosperity and expansion that they built a stone castle, perhaps within an earlier earth and timber fortress[21]. The castle is first mentioned in 1372-1373 when it was taken into the hand of the English King Edward III, following the death of the last descendant of the Prendergasts, and it was given to Mathew FitzHenry[22]. This was at a time when the Anglo-Norman colony had been in decline. The 14th century saw a resurgence in the power of the Gaelic Irish, in particular the MacMurrough Kavanaghs, descendants of the old kings of Leinster. They resumed their old kingship and sought to recover their ancestral lands in north and central Co. Wexford[23]. The castle must have been a substantial and strongly defended fortress to have held out for so long against the Gaelic Irish. Mathew FitzHenry held the castle until the close of the century, when it fell to Art Mór MacMurrough Kavanagh, king of Leinster[24]. It then became a stronghold and seat of his family until the end of the Middle Ages, during which time they founded a Franciscan friary nearby (fig. 6)[25]. The town appears to have survived around the castle under their rule and may have functioned as a pragmatic interface between the Gaelic Irish and the colonists in times of relative peace[26].

4. The castle and the arrival of the New English, 1534-1611

The end of the Middle Ages in the 1530s saw the English King Henry VIII extending his government's control and laws beyond the Pale around Dublin, followed by his Reformation and the dissolution of the monasteries. This new English conquest included a move against the outlying Gaelic lordships in Leinster, such as the Kavanaghs, whose lord, Cahir McInncross, was forced to conclude a treaty that curbed his power[27]. A report in 1537 noted that the castle or "strong house" and town of Enniscorthy were in a state of disrepair and it recommended that they be "builded" (i.e. repaired) and that it, together with Ferns and other places, would have garrisons

18. Hore 1911, 341-342; Murtagh 2010, 103-104; Orpen 1892, lines 3036-3039.
19. Colfer 2010, 84-85; Orpen 1892, lines 2823-2825; St John Brooks 1950, 130-131.
20. Colfer 2010, 85, 88, 90; Hore 1911, 342-344; St John Brooks 1950, 136-138.
21. Colfer 2010, 90; Murtagh 2010, 105.

22. Hore 1911, 351; St John Brooks 1950, 141.
23. O'Byrne 2007, 173-192.
24. Hore 1911, 352.
25. O'Byrne 2003, 136; Moore 1996, 154.
26. Colfer 2010, 92.
27. Brewer & Bullen 1867, 93-94, no. 77; O'Byrne 2011, 71-72.

placed in them under the command of English gentlemen[28]. Henry VIII dissolved the two religious houses at Enniscorthy and confiscated their possessions, so that they could be leased to English tenants[29]. Cahir McInncross was then forced to hold the castle and manor of Enniscorthy from the English crown, which in 1548 took possession of them and placed a garrison in them, as well as at other centres in lands of the Kavanaghs[30]. This method of controlling the Irish continued into the Elizabethan period and initially had the desired effect[31]. Meanwhile, the manor was leased out to various English tenants. For example, in 1568 it, along with the friary, was given to one Thomas Stuckley, an English soldier, around the same time as the town was granted a market in recognition of its growing economic importance[32].

In 1569, however, disaster struck when the Butlers of Ormond arrived "with great force of horsemen" and took the castle and house of Enniscorthy, sacked the town, committed "horrible atrocities", then "spoilt" and burnt the castle[33]. During the following years, while the disaffected Kavanaghs remained a serious threat to the colony in Co. Wexford from their densely forested heartland, the English continued to hold and garrison Enniscorthy[34]. It is not known however if the soldiers were billeted in the castle or nearby friary or both. In 1585 Sir Henry Wallop acquired the lease of Enniscorthy[35]. This Englishman, who had arrived in Ireland in 1579, served as a Lord Justice and Vice-Treasurer of the country[36]. He was an ideal representative of the New English, being a planter, soldier, administrator, landowner and businessman[37]. From his base at Enniscorthy, he embarked upon a long campaign to push back the borderland with the Gaelic Irish in Co. Wexford, which he outlined in a letter of 1586[38]. He set about exploiting the great economic potential of the Duffry oak forests, thus eliminating the military advantage enjoyed by Gaelic Irish in their woodland environment and transforming much of it into good farmland[39]. Such encroachments into their heartland naturally led to further hostility and conflict with the Kavanaghs[40].

It was in this environment that Wallop embarked upon the task of building a new castle on the rocky promontory, apparently replacing the earlier structure or "house of Enniscorthy". In a letter of 1587, Wallop mentions "his houses at Enniscorthy"[41]. These may refer to his new castle and a manor house that he built at the nearby-dissolved friary (fig. 6)[42]. In petitioning the Queen in 1594 for the fee farm of the manor, he reminded her of his building, fortifying "and strengthening your Ma[ties] House of Ennescorthie which at such time as I toke the same was utterly ruined & defaced"[43]. In this case, he was referring to the castle, or rather the original and dilapidated one and its replacement with the new one. In 1595 the Queen granted him the fee farm "in consideration of his great & expences in the structure & building of the Castle of Eniscorthy, & the better fortification of it, & defence of her faithful subjects in those parts [.....]grants & confirms to the said Sir Henry Wallop, his heirs &c., forever, the Abbey of Eniscorthy, appurtenances, also the Castle of Eniscorthy"[44]. This grant would confirm the architectural evidence in the present building, which indicates that a new castle was constructed on the site between 1585 and 1595.

Wallop's grant coincided with the beginning of the Nine Years War (1594-1603), which started when the Gaelic Irish of Ulster rose up against the encroachment of the English State and the rebellion spread throughout the rest of the country, eventually reaching the borderland in Co. Wexford[45]. Wallop and the colonists at Enniscorthy soon came under military pressure from the Irish. He complained to the Queen in 1596 that the garrison of troops had been removed from Enniscorthy, presumably from the castle and were sent off to fight elsewhere. Wallop felt that things were so bad that his force of woodcutters would "leave waste their dwellings" and return to England[46]. In 1598, after he and the settlers were defeated by the Gaelic Irish outside the town, he remained defiant as he reported that there was a "good store of corn" at Enniscorthy and furthermore, the townsmen of Wexford had "built a strong barge", armed with cannon and muskets, which could travel up and down the river "to victual at all times the garrison"[47]. Soon afterwards however, Wallop and his force suffered yet another defeat outside Enniscorthy, after which the Kavanaghs burnt some of the town[48]. It was the end of the road for Wallop, as he died around this time[49]. Despite these reverses, however, the garrison and settlers held out. The centre of their resistance would have been the new castle on the promontory.

In June 1599 the earl of Essex arrived at Enniscorthy with an army to relieve the garrison and settlers[50]. He opened negotiations with the Kavanaghs, who had assembled their forces

---

28. COLFER 2010, 92; HORE 1905, 75; HORE 1911, 345, 359.
29. COLFER 2010, 92.
30. BREWER & BULLEN 1867, 236, no. 200; O'BYRNE 2011, 86, 91.
31. BREWER & BULLEN 1867, 337, no. 236.
32. COLFER 2010, 93.
33. *Ibid.*; HORE 1911, 372-375.
34. HAMILTON 1867, 198, no. 35 ; 310, no. 16. iv.
35. COLFER 2010, 93.
36. HAMILTON 1867, 437, no. 53; 513, nos. 35 & 41.
37. WHELAN 1994, 73.
38. HAMILTON 1877, 5, no. 15.
39. WHELAN 1994, 73.
40. HAMILTON 1877, 266, no. 49; O'BYRNE 2003, 211-212.
41. HAMILTON 1877, 259, no. 43.
42. WHELAN 1994, 74-75.
43. HORE 1905, 75.
44. HAMILTON 1890, 317, no. 81; HORE 1905, 75.
45. O'BYRNE 2003, 224, 229-230.
46. ATKINSON 1893, 46-47, no. 40.
47. ATKINSON 1895, 150, no. 39; 457, no. 15 ii.
48. *Ibid.*, 506, no. 119.
49. BREWER & BULLEN 1869, 290, no. 119.
50. *Ibid.*, 308, no. 305.

nearby under Domhnall Spainneach (Spanish) "their King of Leinster", but these came to nothing[51]. It seems that Essex considered abandoning the castle and town, as he regarded Ferns Castle "a fitter place for a garrison than Eniscorty, were it not that the want of a navigable river"[52]. The latter was significant, as the strategically located new castle at Enniscorthy could be supplied by boat from Wexford town, such as by the armed barge, mentioned above. Furthermore, the castle was strongly defensible with its circular flanking towers and state-of-the-art gun-ports or loops. In the end, Essex must have been swayed by these factors as he left six companies of soldiers behind to garrison the castle and town[53].

When the tide of the war changed in favour of the English by 1601, Domhnall Spainneach, chief of the Kavanaghs, made peace with them by agreeing to settle down and become a landowning country gentleman in the English style[54]. It seems that he was slow to abandon his old ways, as Enniscorthy had to be provided with a garrison in 1602 to defend it against his renewed raiding[55]. In the following year, Sir Henry Wallop Junior, who had inherited the place from his father, pleaded with the government not to withdraw the garrison, as Domhnall Spainneach "takes our cattle, mows our meadows, spoils our houses, kills our people". Moreover, he argued that "to obtain the withdrawal of the ward [garrison] which I have for my castle of Enniscorthy in the co. of Wexford, which would injure me and the common good of the county"[56]. It is clear that Wallop had used these government soldiers to garrison his castle, which played a key role in the defence of the borderland. With the new Stuart king in England, James I, a more drastic and permanent solution was adopted in dealing with troublesome Gaelic Irish in Co. Wexford, which involved their removal and plantation of settlers throughout their lands[57]. This resulted in Enniscorthy Castle no longer having a borderland to defend.

5. Description of the Elizabethan castle

Work to date by the writer points to Wallop's castle consisting of two main parts: firstly, his fortified house and, secondly, the adjoining walled enclosure or bawn, located to the north-west. It was a garden from at least the 18th century until it was built upon in the 1960s. The eastern side is still delineated by a stone wall, now largely overgrown. This runs north from the north-east corner of the fortified house to a circular tower or flanker, which was located at the north-east corner of the garden. A drawing of the castle in 1780 from within the garden by John James Barralet shows both the wall and flanker[58]. The latter is also depicted with a conical roof on an 18th-century view from across the river (fig. 5 A). The cliff that is located to the east of the fortified house continues north to skirt the outside of wall and flanker, emphasising the defensive nature of the enclosure. Although some of the wall has been rebuilt, an intact section at the south end has an original gun-port where it is conjoined with the north-east corner of the fortified house (fig. 3 B). The enclosing wall appears to have run west before returning south-west from the flanker towards Castle Street and returning east to the south-west tower of the fortified house. The north-west side of the enclosure may have originally been delineated by the rock-cut ditch that was found to the west of the castle in the 1890s.

The fortified house is constructed mainly of the same stone as the bedrock on which it is built, a greenish volcanic rock outcrop. Although stone may have been reused from the earlier castle, the exposed quarried face at the base of the south-east exterior of the fortified house would suggest that new stone was also quarried on site (fig. 7 A-A1). Moreover, the basement inside was quarried into the bedrock (fig. 7). Angular and roughly dressed blocks and slabs of this stone were used in the construction, bonded with a course lime mortar. The faces of the building were constructed mainly of these stones, horizontally laid in irregular courses, except for example where they were used inside as voussoirs in the construction of rear arches. Features that were constructed of dressed stones, such as window and door surrounds, used light grey-white granite, which came from the mountains to the north-west of Enniscorthy (figs. 8 & 9 A).

There is a base-batter on the exterior of the building at ground-storey level, most noticeably on the south-west and south-east exteriors, which were located outside the defensive enclosure. This was punctuated with gun-loops with dressed granite surrounds on the outside, which are splayed in the inside (fig. 9 B). Some were destroyed by the insertion of large windows in the 1903 renovations (fig. 3). The flanking south-west and south-east turrets are the same in size, but are larger than the other two (figs. 1 & 3). They, together with the gun-loops, protected the entrance doorway, which gives access to the ground-storey interior (figs. 8 B & 9 A). The doorway surround on the outside, which formerly had an iron grate, is constructed of dressed granite and is covered by a Tudor-style hood moulding. A similar-style doorway can be seen reconstructed in Lett's brewery to the south of the castle. It may have come from the demolished manor house of Wallop, which was built down at the medieval friary or from a blocked-up doorway on the ground floor in the north-east wall of the fortified house, which would have given access to the walled enclosure (figs. 3 B & 4). In addition to loops, there were larger windows on the first and second storeys, which had granite surrounds and hood mouldings on the outside. There

---

51. ATKINSON 1899, 52, no. 74.
52. BREWER & BULLEN 1869, 309, no. 305.
53. ATKINSON 1899, 77, no. 101.
54. O'BYRNE 2003, 240.
55. PENTLAND-MAHAFFY 1912, 492.
56. *Ibid.*, 552-553.
57. BREWER & BULLEN 1873, 299-302, no. 153; WHELAN 1994, 74.
58. GROSE 1791-1795, vol. 1, pl. 127.

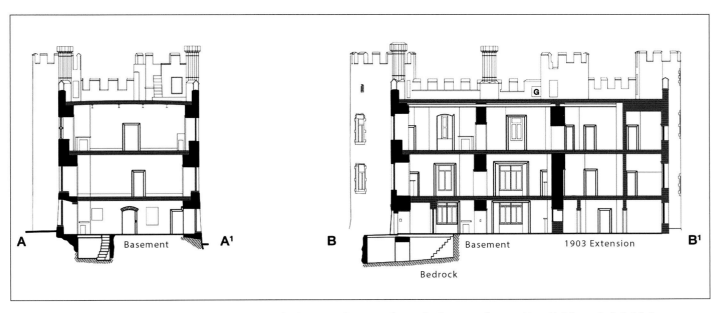

Fig. 7 – Cross-sections of the fortified house: A-A1 looking north-east and B-B1 looking north-west. Doc. B. Murtagh & P. McInerney.

Fig. 8 – Original external features with granite surrounds: A) single-light windows; B) entrance doorway. Photos B. Murtagh, 2012.

Fig. 9 – Original gun-loops: A) south-east stair-turret (photo B. Murtagh, 2012); B) internal view at ground entrance to stair-turret (photo B. Murtagh, 2010).

are two single-light examples on the north-west exterior, which have transoms. A mid 19th-century drawing of the building by George Victor Du Noyer shows original larger windows in the south-west exterior, which were enlarged in 1903[59].

Internally, the main block of the building consisted of a single, large rectangular chamber on each of the three main floors beneath the roof. These were later sub-divided by a spine wall (figs. 3, 4 & 7). The north-east wall has been narrowed on the inside (figs. 3 A & 7 B-B1). Original fireplaces in the side walls heated the chambers and most of these have been in-filled with smaller Edwardian ones. A fine original example, however, can still be seen on the ground storey in south-east wall (fig. 3)[60]. A chimney-breast on the exterior of the building rises from the base-batter to roof level (fig. 10 A). A projecting chute on the north-west exterior beside the north-west turret would appear to have served now-concealed garderobes (fig. 3). One can still be seen, however, in the parapet on roof level (G on fig. 7 B-B1). There is a basement beneath the ground storey of the building, which was excavated into the bedrock and is known as the oubliette (figs. 3 B & 7). It consists of two compartments: a rectangular one beneath the main block and the second in the base of the south-west turret, in which there is an Elizabethan-style figure or graffito incised into the wall plaster[61].

The sharp angle at the north-east corner of the building on the ground and first storeys, which is conjoined with the bawn wall, underlies the north-east turret (figs. 3, 4 & 10 A). Moving to the far end of the building, a spiral stairwell rises up through the south-east turret giving access from ground to roof (figs. 3 & 4). Access is made on ground to second floors through pointed or Gothic-headed doorways (fig. 9 B). From top of the stairwell, access is made onto the 1903 roof of the main block, around which the parapet survives on three sides (figs. 7 & 10 B). The circular turrets at each corner rise up a storey higher in the form of cap-houses (figs. 1 & 7). The parapets of both the main block and turrets, which are crenellated with simple merlons of the English fashion of the period, are capped with dressed granite (figs. 1, 7 & 10). Although some of the merlons have been rebuilt, many of them are original. The three surviving sections of parapet around the main block are divided midway by tall Tudor-style, brick-built chimney-stacks (figs. 1, 7 & 10). Although they show evidence of repairs, they date from the primary phase of construction and emphasize the English nature of the building.

6. Interpretation

During the late medieval period and for much of the 16th century, when the "old English" colony of south Co. Wexford

Fig. 10 – Views of battlements and roof: A) from north-east (photo B. Murtagh, 2012); B) south-east stair turret (photo B. Murtagh, 2010).

was under pressure from the Kavanaghs and the Gaelic Irish of Leinster, the descendants of the Anglo-Norman settlers built stone castles to defend themselves. Many consisted of a principal building, such as a tower or tower house, often with an attached hall, as well as a walled or defendable enclosure or bawn, such as at Rathmacknee[62]. In addition to this, the gentry of south Co. Wexford constructed fortified houses[63]. Such buildings consist of a main block, usually three storeys in height beneath the roof and stepped battlements with a service tower at one angle. Late medieval examples include Ballymagir, Fethard and Slade[64]. Later ones than these can be seen at Coolhull and Dungulph[65]. Although Enniscorthy Castle is contemporary with the later fortified houses in the south of the county, the latter belong to a local type of fortified building, the origins of which lie in the Middle Ages. Wallop's building, however, should be seen as a new type of castle associated with Elizabethan conquest, followed by plantations and settlements by the Protestant New English throughout the country. In the case of Enniscorthy, Wallop, as the senior English official and entrepreneur in the area, built the new castle to defend the town and settlers, together with his industrial interests, on the

---

59. MURTAGH 2010, fig. 3.
60. *Ibid.*, fig. 6.
61. HORE 1911, 340.
62. MOORE 1996, pl. 6b.
63. *Ibid.*, 165; MURTAGH 2004, 6; SWEETMAN 1999, 100.
64. MOORE 1996, 181, no. 1564; MURTAGH 2004; O'CALLAGHAN 1980-1981, 5-7, 15-20.
65. MOORE 1996, 180-181, nos. 1560 & 1561; O'CALLAGHAN 1980-1981, 22-31.

borderland with the Gaelic Irish. It was used to house garrisons of English soldiers, which were regularly under threat of being withdrawn by the government. The Wallops would have normally resided in their manor house at the nearby dissolved friary, but could retreat to castle when the town was being attacked. Even during the height of the Nine Years War, when the surrounding countryside had been overrun and town partly burnt, the castle still held out. The Kavanaghs obviously did not risk attacking the fortified house with its compact design, flanking towers and gun-ports, manned by a well-armed and provisioned garrison. In the early 17th century, when the war was over and the New English were in the ascent, they were able to move from Enniscorthy and the borderland into lands of the Gaelic Irish and plant them with settlers, by which time the castle would have served its purpose.

Henry Wallop appears to have built his castle within the precinct of the medieval one on the strategic promontory. The nature and development of the earlier fortress is still unclear. So is the matter of whether the fortified house resembled the earlier "house" and if this was an Anglo-Norman "towered keep". It is peculiar that there are no remains of it incorporated into the fabric of the present building. One possibility is that it was at another or nearby location and was used as a quarry for the construction of Wallop's castle. Future archaeological excavation might throw light on the earlier castle and answer some questions in regard to the later one, such as the full extent of the defensive enclosure and if it, as well as the fortified house, were in part at least enclosed by a rock-cut ditch.

Whatever resemblance it may have had to "towered keeps", Wallop's fortified house ought to be viewed as a building of its time and in the context of other colonial or plantation castles that were built by New English in Ireland during the Elizabethan and Jacobean periods. For example, it fits into one group of such castles that Eric Klingelhofer has categorized by their "x-plan", which consist of a central block with flanking towers at each corner[66]. Flankers were often square or even trapezoidal "spear shape"[67]. A fine example of the latter is Rathfarnham, Co. Dublin, which is roughly contemporary with Enniscorthy and interestingly was built by Adam Loftus, the Protestant, New English, Archbishop of Dublin, who had served with Wallop as Lord Justices in Ireland during the 1580s[68]. The circular flankers on the Enniscorthy building were a defensive improvement on the other two flanker-types, particularly when they had gun-loops. These, together with the central block and circular flankers, made the fortified house ideally suited to have been defended by a small garrison or ward on the borderland of the English colony. This design was later used for the construction other English colonial and plantation castles, such as Ballinafad, Co. Sligo, and Roughan, Co. Tyrone[69]. Wallop's fortified house also has affinities with an example of another form of plantation castle, such as the one seen at Mallow, Co. Cork, such as English-style crenellations, transom windows, gun-ports and flanking towers[70]. In a wider context, these flankers, together with the style of crenellations, tall brick-built chimneystacks and windows of the Enniscorthy building might be compared to those of contemporary castles or "mock castles" that were built in Elizabethan England, such as Lulworth, Dorset or the gate house at Kenilworth Castle[71]. Such affinities would merely emphasize the English nature of the castle that was built by an Elizabethan planter and entrepreneur, who was determined to defend his interests on the borderland with Gaelic Ireland.

Acknowledgements

I would like to thank Patrick McInerney for his work on the illustrations, Uto Hogerzeil for figure 6 A and Kieran Costello for his assistance in regard to my work at the castle.

---

66. KLINGELHOFER 2010, 90.
67. KERRIGAN 1995, 65 & fig. 35; KLINGELHOFER 2010, 90-91.
68. CRAIG 1982, 116-117, figs. 72-74.
69. KERRIGAN 1995, 64; SALTER 1993, 28-29, 158.
70. SWEETMAN 1999, 180 & figs. 51-52.
71. GOODALL 2011, 443, 481 & pls. 328, 358; KLINGELHOFER 2010, 139 & figs. 6.5, 6.7.

Bibliography

ATKINSON E. G. (ed.) (1893), *Calendar of State Papers Relating to Ireland*, vol. 6: *1596-1597*, London, Longman.

– (1895), *Calendar of State Papers Relating to Ireland*, vol. 7: *1598-1599*, London, Longman.

– (1899), *Calendar of State Papers Relating to Ireland*, vol. 8: *1599-1600*, London, Longman.

BREWER J. S. & BULLEN W. (eds.) (1867), *Calendar of the Carew Manuscripts, Preserved in the Archepiscopal Library at Lamberth*, vol. 1: *1515-1574*, London, Longman.

– (1869), *Calendar of the Carew Manuscripts, Preserved in the Archepiscopal Library at Lamberth*, vol. 3: *1589-1600*, London, Longman.

– (1873), *Calendar of the Carew Manuscripts, Preserved in the Archepiscopal Library at Lamberth*, vol. 6: *1603-1624*, London, Longman.

COLFER B. (2010), "Medieval Enniscorthy: Urban Origins", in *Enniscorthy. A History*, C. TÓIBÍN & C. RAFFERTY (eds.), Wexford, Wexford County Council Public Service Library, 83-97.

CRAIG M. (1982), *The Architecture of Ireland from the Earliest Times to 1880*, London/Dublin, Batsford.

CULLETON E. (1999), *Celtic and Early Christian Wexford. AD 400-1166*, Dublin, Four Courts Press.

GOODALL J. (2011), *The English Castle, 1066-1650*, New Haven/London, Yale University Press.

GRATTAN-FLOOD W. H. (1904), "Enniscorthy in the Thirteenth Century: who Built the Castle?", *Journal of the Royal Society of Antiquaries of Ireland*, 34/4, 380-383.

GROSE F. (1791-1795), *The Antiquities of Ireland*, E. LEDWICH (ed.), London, Hooper, 2 vols.

HAMILTON H. C. (ed.) (1867), *Calendar of State Papers Relating to Ireland*, vol. 2: *1574-1585*, London, Longman.

– (1877), *Calendar of State Papers Relating to Ireland*, vol. 3: *1586-1588*, London, Longman.

– (ed.) (1890), *Calendar of State Papers Relating to Ireland*, vol. 5: *1592-1596*, London, Longman.

HARBISON P. (2004), "Barralet and Beranger's Antiquarian Sketching Tour through Wicklow and Wexford in Autumn of 1780", *Proceedings of the Royal Irish Academy*, 104c/6, 131-190.

HORE P. H. (1905), "Enniscorthy Castle (Notes on the Ancient and Present Buildings)", *Journal of the Royal Society of Antiquaries of Ireland*, 35/1, 74-76.

– (1911), *History of the Town and County of Wexford*, vol. 6, London, Stock.

JOHNSON D. N. (1985), *The Irish Castle*, Dublin, Eason (Irish Heritage Series; 49).

KERRIGAN P. M. (1995), *Castles and Fortifications in Ireland, 1485-1945*, Cork, Collins Press.

KLINGELHOFER E. (2010), *Castles and Colonists. An Archaeology of Elizabethan Ireland*, Manchester/New York, Manchester University Press.

LEASK H. G. (1937), "Irish Castles: 1180 to 1310", *Archaeological Journal*, 93, 143-199.

– (1951), *Irish Castles and Castellated Houses*, Dundalk, Dundalgan.

LEWIS S. (1837), *A Topographical Dictionary of Ireland*, vol. 1, London, Lewis.

MCNEILL T. E. (1997), *Castles in Ireland. Feudal Power in a Gaelic World*, London/New York, Routledge.

MOORE M. (1996), *Archaeological Inventory of County Wexford*, Dublin, Stationery Office.

MURTAGH B. (2004), *Fethard Castle. A Manorial Centre and Episcopal Residence in County Wexford*, Bray, Archaeology Ireland (Archaeology Ireland. Heritage Guide; 25).

– (2010), "The Medieval Castle of Enniscorthy", in TÓIBÍN & RAFFERTY 2010 (eds.), 100-109.

O'BYRNE E. (2003), *War, Politics and the Irish of Leinster, 1156-1606*, Dublin, Four Courts Press.

– (2007), "The MacMurroughs and the Marches of Leinster, 1170-1340", in *Lordship in Medieval Ireland. Image and Reality*, L. DORAN & J. LYTTLETON (eds.), Dublin, Four Courts Press, 160-192.

– (2011), "The Tudor State and the Irish of East Leinster, 1535-54", in *Dublin and the Pale in the Renaissance c. 1540-1660*, M. POTTERTON & T. HERRON (eds.), Dublin, Four Courts Press, 68-92.

O'CALLAGHAN J. (1980-1981), "Fortified Houses of the Sixteenth Century in South Wexford", *Journal of the Wexford Historical Society*, 8, 1-51.

ORPEN G. H. (1892), *The Song of Dermot and the Earl*, Oxford, Clarendon Press.

PENTLAND-MAHAFFY R. (ed.) (1912), *Calendar of State Papers Relating to Ireland*, vol. 11: *1601-1603*, London, Longman.

REEVES-SMYTH T. (1995), *Irish Castles*, Belfast, Appletree.

SALTER M. (1993), *Castles and Stronghouses of Ireland*, Malvern, Folly Publications.

ST JOHN BROOKS E. (1950), *Knights' Fees in Counties Wexford, Carlow and Kilkenny (13th-15th Century)*, Dublin, Stationery Office.

SWEETMAN D. (1999), *The Medieval Castles of Ireland*, Cork, Collins Press.

WHELAN K. (1994), "Enniscorthy", in *Irish Country Towns*, A. SIMMS & J. H. ANDREWS (eds.), Cork/Dublin, Mercier Press in Association with Radio Telefís Éireann, 71-82.

The Fort on the Ridge in the Marches of the Pale: Dundrum Castle, Co. Dublin

David Newman Johnson*

1. Introduction and history

The castle of Dundrum was located on the edge of the Pale between Dublin and the Wicklow mountains to the south, in a region that was a particular flash-point for antagonism since the mountainous lands remained a Gaelic-Irish stronghold of the O'Tooles, who constantly raided the more prosperous region round Dublin (fig. 1). Following King Henry II's direct intervention in Ireland in 1171, the Anglo-Normans began to fully occupy the province of Leinster, building a network of fortifications to secure the lands.

Castles were the strength behind the Anglo-Norman colonisation and castle builders favoured focal points and pre-existing defensive sites, like Dundrum (from the Irish *Dun Droma* – the fort on the ridge). In 1172 King Henry II personally granted Dundrum directly to Sir John de Clahull, the Marshal of the Lordship of Leinster. The lands went to his sons John and Hugh, followed by John's son-in-law and then passed to Sir Robert Bagod of Baggotrath. At the beginning of the 13th century the broadlands of Meath and Louth were among the most encastelleated parts of Europe[1]. The castle and lands were found to be in the possession of Alexander de Bicknor, an archbishop of Dublin from 1317-1349, around 1330[2]. King Edward III complained in 1344 that Eustace Le Poer, who had acquired Dundrum from the Bagods, had held the manor of Dundrum *in capite* from him and transferred it to the archbishop without licence. But on consideration of Alexander's service in fighting the King's enemies, the offence was pardoned. Before he died in 1349, he conveyed Dundrum to the Fitzwilliam family[3].

During the upheavals of the early- to mid-14th century, the Fitzwilliams attempted to lease the perilously located Dundrum to various tenants but with little success and the condition of the castle at this time could not have been good. During the 15th century, the castle and lands were granted to their chaplains for the first 40 years. In 1463 the Harolds, a family of Anglo-Norman descent, who were supposed to be protecting the marches, descended on the lands of Dundrum, and after killing 8 of the King's lieges decamped with 600 cows, 40 plough horses and 100 sheep[4]. A few years after this, the Pale ditch was begun.

The Fitzwilliams retained possession of Dundrum throughout the 16th century and in 1565 an Exchequer Return assigns to "Thomas Fitzwilliams of Dondrom, having his chief mansion house at Dondrom, all his lands of Dondrom…"[5]. The following year, due to a boundary dispute between the lands of Dundrum and Cheverstown, it was recorded that "the usurpation on FitzWilliam began by the waste of his manor town of Dondrome where in time past he had but 3 cottiers to inhabit"[6]. The Will of Richard FitzWilliam, who died in 1595, gave "all his tenants of Dundrum dwelling there at the time of his building and assisting him, to be forgiven the term rents due next after his death"[7]. Here there is direct evidence of building work at the castle. The castle continued

---

*   Independant scholar and architect, Dublin, Ireland.
1.   Murphy & Potterton 2010, 264.
2.   Erlington-Ball 1903, 67.
3.   McNeill 1950, 197.
4.   Erlington-Ball 1905, 5.
5.   Pembroke and Montgomery 1891, 82.
6.   *Ibid.*, 83.
7.   *Ibid.*, 94.

Fig. 1 – Location map. The boundary of the Pale is indicated by a broken line. It is based on the places mentioned in the Acts of 1488 and 1495. The Dublin area map is reproduced from Hiberniae Delinatio, Province of Leinster, 1686. The important castle of Dundrum is depicted on the summit of its steep ridge.

in the possession of the Fitzwilliams into the 17th century and was noted during the 1640s as a centre of disaffection. In 1646 the Fitzilliams finally left, ending the family occupation of Dundrum.

In 1653 Dundrum was leased to Lt Col Isaac Dobson, an officer of the Parliamentary Army, who restored it. The Civil Survey of 1654-1656 lists the proprietor as Col Oliver Fitzwilliam and the buildings as "one Castle slated & a Barne, one garden plott & a small orchard"[8]. After the restoration, King Charles II granted a pardon and restoration of his family premises to Oliver Fitzwilliam subject to "saving the rights of Isaac Dobson to a lease of Dundrum". The Dobsons remained in possession of Dundrum into the 18th century and the property was greatly improved at this time, the castle being well maintained and furnished, and the grounds laid out down to the river although subsequent lessees let it deteriorate. This is shown in sketches made in 1765 by Gabriel Beranger, who also shows a new five-bay mansion to the south-west[9].

By the later 19th century the main structure was a roofless garden ornament for Dundrum House. In the early 20th century the Goff family lived in Dundrum House, using part of the castle as a butcher's shop in the 1920s[10]. In the 1940s part of the castle was converted into a cow byre by a local dairyman.

In 1984 following a failed attempt to remodel the castle into modern offices, the writer approached the developer and purchased it for more authentic restoration. An archaeological summer school excavation was carried out over 5 seasons from 1987 to 1991 under the direction of Elizabeth O'Brien. A preliminary result was the confirmation of an earlier castle underlying the late medieval one. The finds from the, as yet, unpublished excavation included large quantities of Leinster Ware with occasional shards of imported Saintonge Ware and many metal objects including items of horse harness and arrow heads. A macabre Modern Murder Mystery occurred when the battered frontal part of a skull was found in the castle (location shown on plan) in 1987. This caused a local sensation and the forensic report indicated that the man had been killed during the Irish Civil War, thus the castles history begins and ends in violence, since the face of the skull was torn off to avoid recognition.

2. The architecture

It is likely that the castle was built over a pre-existing fort, as at Dunamase, Co. Laois, where the early dry-stone walling could be of 9th-century origin[11]. The ridge is a highly defensive location, with its precipitous drops to the north and east to the river Slang.

The buildings of the castle are generally aligned north-east to south-west or, to be more precise, 40 degrees to the east of true north. The following architectural account of Dundrum can be followed on the plans and section (fig. 2). The stonework of the castle can be divided into three major periods: firstly, the remains of the Anglo-Norman fortress; secondly, the twin towers built in the later medieval period; thirdly, a late 17th-century extension to the north-west, now mainly reduced to a low wall.

2.1. The Anglo-Norman fortress

Before excavation the presence of the remains of an early castle was not verified although stonework of a different period, possibly earlier, could be identified to the north-east of the junction of the two towers. It was initially decided to excavate the possible cesspit under the exit from the garderobe chutes in the north-east wall of the moat tower. This began to reveal unexpected items, firstly the occurrence of a ditch or moat, secondly stone walls that were part of a major gateway into the castle from the north-west side, and opposite the gateway, the projecting pier to receive the end of the drawbridge. Further work revealed two slots, later three, in the masonry on the castle side which accommodated the counter-balance beams of the drawbridge. These were the first to be identified as such in Ireland. Further excavation to the north-east revealed an early wall, 2 m wide, with a flared or battered base to the moat and with a garderobe chute at its northern end, which was flushed at its base by a spring with two openings into the moat. Dendrochronological dating of an oak shuttering found in the chute exits revealed a date of 1187 + or - 9 years. This dates the building work to the De Clahull ownership. It would appear that this north-west wall was the first build on the site and would date from after 1187. As a length of this battered wall runs under the gate tower and is traceable through the central beam slot. It would appear that the gate tower is later and could date to around 1200. The base of the central beam slot expands considerably outwards and downwards – 1.75 m – to the level of the bottom of the moat. This corbelled subterranean chamber had two extensions running under the adjacent beam slots. As water seeps into its base, it could have been a shallow well or a damp dungeon. The original gate through this early wall could have been just to the south-west of the gate tower, where an excavation in front of the later fireplace found no walling. At the western corner of the later main tower, some walling could be early and suggests a rounded corner originally.

The foundations of the gate-tower project forward some 2 m into the moat area and are some 5.50 m wide, indicating that this was a substantial tower rather than just a gateway. Furthermore, the remains of the south-west jamb of the main entrance gateway and part of the arch above the springer, now blocked, are visible at the upper levels above the

---

8. NOLAN 1985, 9.
9. HARBISON 1998, 75.
10. NOLAN 1985, 9.
11. HODKINSON 1996, 53.

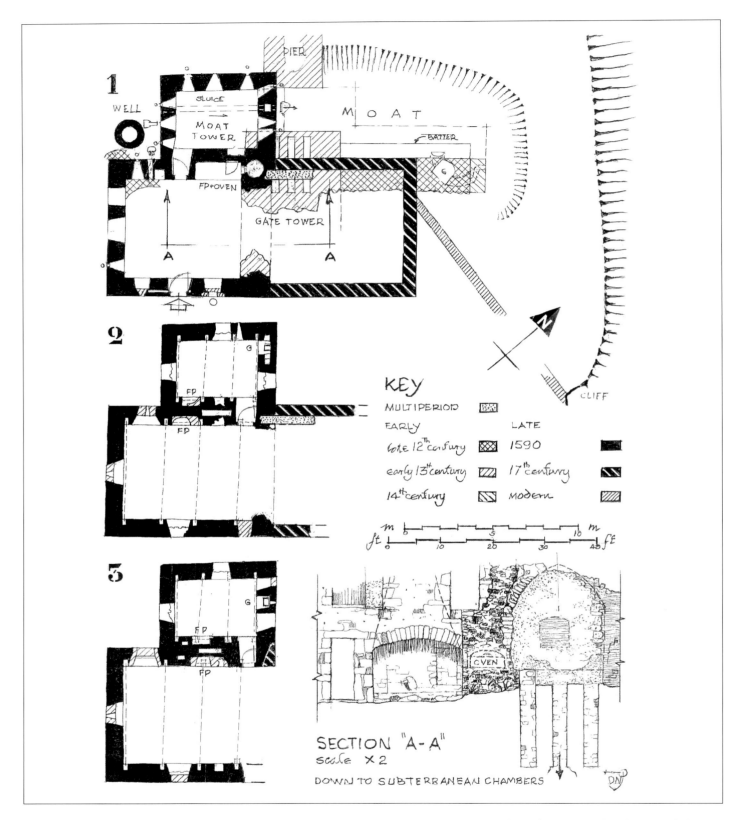

Fig. 2 – Floor plans of the castle. The base of the 1187 wall is battered on the exterior down to the base of the moat, which has been fully excavated along the foot of this wall and between the gate-tower and drawbridge pier. The remaining moat area (beyond the broken line) has been partially excavated. Over the three drawbridge slots the stippled wall is composite consisting of the remains of the original wall arch and its blocking, which also includes a blocked window (see Section A-A). FP stands for fireplace; G for Garderobe. Drawing D. Newman Johnson.

counter-balance slots. This was visible pre-excavation, as noted (see section, fig. 2). There are indications of a portcullis groove.

Gate-towers of this early period were rectangular structures enclosing the entrance passage, the familiar gatehouse with projecting circular towers flanking the gate being developed in the 13th century, with the first one dating to the 1190s. Small rectangular gate towers were common during this period in England, and the remains of a castle at Egremont, Cumbria[12], somewhat resemble the situation at Dundrum. The stonework is dated to the late 12th century[13], and it shows that gate-towers of this type could occur among the earliest Anglo-Norman fortresses to be built here[14]. Brough Castle, Cumbria, *c.* 1200, is of similar type. Both Brough and Egremont had a stone-vaulted entrance passage. This was usual, to prevent attack by fire and to provide convenient murder holes overhead, strengthening security. At Dunamase, Co. Laois, there is an early simple rectangular gatehouse dating to the late 12th century, which could be the work of Meiler FitzHenry in the 1180s, or even earlier[15]. Fairly close to Dundrum, there is an example of a similar type of gate-tower at Macdermot's Castle, Co. Wicklow, where the projection is 2.5 m in length and 6 m in width making it slightly larger. It had stone vaulting which has now collapsed. It was built on the summit of a low hill and forms the entrance to a rectangular moated site, attributed to the 13th century[16].

Counter-balance slots occur in England in the 12th century, the great donjon at Dover Castle possessing three on the upper side of the drawbridge pit in the fore-building protecting the stairs to the main entrance on the second floor. Since the discovery of the counter-balance slots at Dundrum, five other examples have been recognised in Ireland. They are found, firstly, in the forebuilding to the donjon at Clonmacnoise, Co. Offaly[17], secondly, in the barbican gate at Dunamase, Co. Laois[18], and, thirdly, in the gatehouse at Nenagh, Co. Tipperary[19]. All of these are early 13th century in date, while the remaining two examples are later in the century, being in the earlier period of the development of the castles of Roscrea, Co. Tipperary and Roscommon. Of the various drawbridge systems, the one used at Dundrum is called a turning bridge and uses the counterweighted deck as a pivot, the three counterweights sinking into internal pits inside the door while the deck rises to close the entrance. This is an early arrangement as the more advanced systems, or bascule bridges, elevate the deck by means of overhead beams or rainures.

The architectural details support the dendrochronological date of 1187 for the earliest castle at Dundrum. That there were walls and a strong tower fronting the drop on the north-east side of the ridge is known since they are shown on Gabriel Beranger's north view and his south-west view shows high ruined walls on the north-east side (fig. 3). The details of a possible great tower and, indeed, the rest of the early castle presumably still remain under modern terrace houses built in the 1980s.

2.2. The later medieval castle

Most of the upstanding stonework of the castle that is visible today dates from this building period which belongs to the Fitzwilliam ownership and dates to the 1590s. The details can be followed on the plans (fig. 2). Of note, on the ground floor between the two towers is a fine large fireplace 2.85 m wide, with circular oven 1.22 m in diameter in the right hand jamb. In the rear of the fireplace, at the right hand side next to the oven, was a fire-door, the iron hooks for which still remain, which when open would shield people using the oven from the heat of the fire. To the left of the connecting door in the main tower is an aumbry and next to this is a slop sink and conduit leading to the exterior. Adjacent to the slop sink exit is a sink and conduit leading into the castle. This is adjacent to the castle well and was obviously for transferring water into the interior of the castle. The garderobe exit in the north-east wall of the moat tower for the two garderobes was flushed out in similar fashion by a sluice running through the tower from a vent near the well in the south-west wall. The towers were strongly fortified; on the ground floor they were plentifully supplied with gun-ports, having two in each side at a low level near the corners with gun-loops in between. The loop in the centre of the south-west side of the smaller moat tower is a stirrup-loop for a small cannon and this has been previously described and illustrated[20]. The north-west gun-port and loop in the south-west wall of the main tower have been widened to form large window openings, while the gun-ports in the south-east wall of this tower have been altered, the two ports to form windows and the centre loop to form a door. It is square-headed with a bar-hole, suggesting a 17th-century date. The south-west wall of the gate-tower is 2.8 m thick, to probably accommodate a straight mural stair which would be typical of an early gate tower. It has been largely destroyed but parts of this wall still remained in 1898 together with a small blocked door at ground level[21]. The castle was turned into a garden folly for Dundrum House when iron hooks were hammered into the outside walls to encourage the growth of creepers and the like and these hooks still remain, extending up to the top of the walls.

Of the original architectural features remaining, some dating can be attempted. Gun-ports began to be used in Irish castles in the later 15th century, an early example being Aughnanure, Co. Galway, *c.* 1500, while stirrup-loops for

---

12. RENN 1968, fig. 31.
13. GOODALL 2011, 138.
14. NEVELL 2012, 258.
15. HODKINSON 1995, 18-21.
16. JOHNSON 1982.
17. MANNING 1994, 35.
18. HODKINSON 1995, 18-21.
19. HODKINSON 1999, 164.
20. KERRIGAN 1995, 27, fig. 13; 28.
21. DIX 1897-1898, 27-28.

Fig. 3 – Illustrations of the castle before its decay. Top: Gabriel Beranger, 1765 (after HARBISON 1998, 73), first view (from the south-east), indicating the drop in level to the northeast and showing the remains of a tall wall or tower on the extreme right; middle: Gabriel Beranger, 1765 (after HARBISON 1998, 75), second view (from the north-west), showing the north-east end of the main building in a state of collapse. Through the trees on the left can be made out a high north-east wall terminating in a strong tower or donjon; bottom: Dundrum Castle in 1802 (from a plate in *The Literary and Masonic Magazine*, after ERLINGTON-BALL 1903, 70). If this is not a reproduction of a much earlier sketch, it shows the castle fully restored after the collapse shown in the Beranger view above.

Fig. 4 – Recent watercolour of the south-west view of the castle by Dr T. Ryan, PPRHA (Ireland), showing a survey in progress by D. Newman Johnson (D. Newman Johnson's collection).

cannon occur at Caher, Co. Tipperary, in the 15th century[22]. Large kitchen fireplaces with an adjacent circular oven began to be built in the later towers which began to expand laterally under the pressure to provide better living accommodation. These can be dated to around 1600. An early tower with a "T" shaped plan remains at Bremore, Co. Dublin[23], and dates from c. 1546, a kitchen wing being added half a century later, incorporating a similar fireplace and oven. The later medieval buildings at Dundrum also formed a "T" plan with the moat tower the short stem of the "T". That this tower is built over the remains of the early moat is singular and indicates that the moat had fallen out of use. From its position, it would have been able to provide flanking fire along the north-west front. The upper floors of the towers are provided with loops and small windows, and one can be seen, blocked, on the north-west side of the moat tower at first floor level. A further loop in this tower at the second-floor level in the re-entrant angle with the gate-tower suggests the presence of a spiral stair. The thickness of some of the walls, the mural garderobes, the gun-ports and the fact that the stepped battlements are fully operational all round the castle would suggest a 16th-century date, while the lack of stone vaulting, the overall "T" shaped plan and the large fireplace with oven would tend to place the building period towards the end of this century.

22. Kerrigan 1995, 26.

23. Johnson 2007, 251, fig. 3; 253.

2.3. Post-medieval building

The third building phase is post-medieval and much smaller in extent. Only the lower courses remain, except where it is attached to earlier work and the overall thickness is a constant 0.76 m. It is attached to the north and east corners of the main tower and extends over the remains of the gate-tower and the early original wall towards the north-east. The filling in of the window in the entrance passage blocking could be of this period. There are no dating features but it was probably built in the Dobson period when they carried out building works.

2.4. Later alterations and additions

More recent work to the existing castle includes the breaking through of large windows at the upper levels in the centre of each wall and the extending of the gable ends of the attic rooms to include the battlement in the room space and then inserting windows in the resulting gables. These changes, probably due to Dobson, obviously affect the castle, giving it a more residential aspect. A circular window high up on the ground floor in the north-east end of the south-east wall of the main tower indicates that at a later period there once was a staircase in this corner.

It is possible by studying the later views (fig. 3) and descriptions to give an account of the final years of the castle. The first sign of decay is the collapse of the north-east wall, together with some of the north-west wall. This is clearly shown in the 1765 view from the north by Gabriel Beranger where the roof is shown missing to the north-east, but still remains on the gate tower. However, Austin Cooper visited the castle on April 16, 1780, and reported:

> The Case of Dundrum three Miles S. of Dublin, is inhabited & in excellent Repair, at the N.E. End of it are the remains of a much Older Building than the present Castle, which is visibly a modern Addition, in Comparison to the Old Remains. There is but very little of this ancient part remaining. Some of the Walls are 6 feet thick. About the Castle are sevl. traces of Old Walls Avenue's &c., proving it to have been once a very complete Habitation. The whole is on the Summit of a small Hill, surrounded with Ash Trees, with a handsome Rivulet running at its foot, but this Shelter will soon be removed, as they are cutting away the Trees[24].

The term "excellent repair" does not agree with Gabriel Beranger and suggests that repair work had been carried out. This is borne out by a view from a plate (fig. 3) in "The Literary and Masonic Magazine" of 1802[25], which shows the north-east wing repaired and re-roofed, with a crow-stepped gable butting against the gate tower. Sadly, during the 19th century rather inexplicably the castle became uninhabited though the Ordnance Survey of 1837 indicates that is was still roofed. Eventually it fell into ruin, ending up in the condition that it is in today (fig. 4).

Two recent developments in the vicinity of the castle are of interest. During the making of the Wyckham bypass road round the base of the ridge on which the castle stands, cuttings into the base exposed medieval artifacts which had probably fallen from above. Secondly, during the building of apartments in a field to the north-west of the castle, a wide medieval ditch or moat was discovered which seemed to have run round the outside of the castle complex at a distance of about 50 m. Part of this was excavated but is unpublished. Both developments emphasis the importance of the site as a whole, of which the buildings described here are only the gate tower complex.

Acknowledgements

Grateful acknowledgments are necessary for valuable assistance from several people, Mia Johnson, Anne Henderson, Ben Murtagh and Elaine Irwin.

---

24. PRICE 1942, 48.

25. ERLINGTON-BALL 1903, 70.

Bibliography

DIX E. R. M. (1897-1898), "The Lesser Castles in the County Dublin", *The Irish Builder*, articles 27 & 28.

ELRINGTON-BALL F. (1903), *A History of the County Dublin. The People, Parishes and Antiquities from the Earliest Times to the Close of the Eighteenth Century*, part 2, Dublin, University Press.

– (1905), *A History of the County Dublin. The People, Parishes and Antiquities from the Earliest Times to the Close of the Eighteenth Century*, part 3, Dublin, University Press.

GOODALL J. (2011), *The English Castle, 1066-1650*, New Haven/London, Yale University Press.

Harbison P. (ed.) (1998), *Drawings of the Principal Antique Buildings of Ireland*, Dublin, Four Courts in Association with the National Library of Ireland.

Hodkinson B. J. (1995), "The Rock of Dunamase", *Archaeology Ireland*, 9/2, 18-21.

– (1996), "Rock of Dunamase", in *Excavations 1995. Summary Accounts of Archaeological Excavations in Ireland*, I. Bennett (ed.), Bray, Wordwell, 18-21.

– (1999), "Excavations in the Gatehouse of Nenagh Castle, 1996 and 1997", *Tipperary Historical Journal*, 162-182.

Johnson D. N. (1982), *The Medieval Fortification of County Wicklow*, Unpublished MA Thesis, University College, Dublin.

– (2007), "A Renaissance Doorway Architrave from the Elizabethan Period at Bremore Castle, County Dublin", in *From Ringforts to Fortified Houses. Studies on Castles and Other Monuments in Honour of David Sweetman*, C. Manning (ed.), Bray, Wordwell, 249-260.

Kerrigan P. M. (1995), *Castles and Fortifications in Ireland, 1485-1945*, Cork, Collins Press.

Manning C. (1994), *Clonmacnoise*, Dublin, Stationery Office.

McNeill C. (ed.) (1950), *Calendar of Archbishop Alen's Register, c. 1172-1534*, Dublin, Royal Society of Antiquaries of Ireland.

Murphy M. & Potterton M. (2010), *The Dublin Region in the Middle Ages. Settlement, Land-Use and Economy. A Discovery Program Monograph*, Dublin, Four Courts Press.

Nevell R. (2012), "Castle Gatehouses in North West England", *The Castle Studies Group Journal*, 26, 257-281.

Nolan J. (1985), *Changing Faces*, Dublin, Dundrum Brass and Reed Band.

Pembroke and Montgomery (Earl of) (1891), *Calendar of Ancient Deeds and Muniments Preserved in the Pembroke Estate Office, Dublin*, Dublin, University Press, Sections 247, 249 & 286.

Price L. (1942), *An Eighteenth-Century Antiquary. The Sketches, Notes and Diaries of Austin Cooper (1759-1830)*, Dublin, Falconer.

Renn D. F. (1968), *Norman Castles in Britain*, London, Baker.

Russian Medieval Fortresses in the Light of New Discoveries

Konstantin S. Nossov*

1. Introduction

Before getting down to the topic proper, the present writer would like to specify its chronological confines. Different things show that the end of the Middle Ages can be dated differently for different regions. In Russia medieval fortification did not become a thing of the past until the end of the 17th century. Certainly samples of bastion fortification appeared in Russia during the 16th and 17th centuries, but they only fully replaced classic medieval forms of fortification in the epoch of Peter the Great. The fortress in Smolensk built between 1596 and 1602 is one such medieval fortification. Thus the chronological confines of this paper cover the period from the 10th century, when we find the earliest examples of specifically Russian fortification, up to the 17th century.

As it is impossible to show the evolution of the Russian fortification in detail in such a short paper, the present writer will concentrate on several aspects of it that have seen reinterpretation and re-evaluation in recent years.

2. A new approach to earthen ramparts

Perhaps the main revolutionary event, which has begun to change views on medieval Russian fortification, was the recent criticism of the conception of wooden intra-rampart structures offered by Yuri Yurievich Morgunov.

From the 19th century, scholarship regarded ramparts as one of the main features of the protective enceintes around the towns of Old Russia. They were assigned a crucial role in defence. High ramparts and steep slopes were considered the main elements of Old Russian fortification. A log wall or just a stockade atop a rampart was deemed sufficient. That is why all the reconstructions of Old Russian towns made during the Soviet era always looked the same. These reconstructions always depicted high ramparts running along the perimeter of a town, encircling the built-up area, with hypothetically reconstructed wooden defences on top of them. Such reconstructions can still be seen on display in some Russian museums.

When they excavated through these earthen ramparts, researchers often discovered the remains of wooden structures inside. And now the most interesting thing! How do you think they explained the appearance of wood inside earthen ramparts? From the 1940s to the 2000s, these archaeologists agreed with the work of Alexandr Lvovich Monguite[1] who believed that these were intra-rampart wooden structures, which were needed to strengthen the earthen ramparts and make their slopes steeper. It was believed that without these wooden log cells placed inside these ramparts, the latter would sag and that their slopes could not be made steep enough.

Moreover, researchers tried to put even abnormal phenomena into the confines of the theory of intra-rampart structures. For instance, the remains of coal, charred logs or burnt clay in the filling, more than once discovered inside these ramparts, seem to offer certain evidence of fire before the defences fell down[2]. However, to fit the theory, this was explained as representing the deliberate baking of these log

---

* Director of the History of Fortification Study Centre, Moscow, Russia.
1. Монгайт [Monguite] 1947.
2. Раппопорт [Rappoport] 1961, 104-106, 110; Раппопорт [Rappoport] 1967, 118, 120.

cells, before they were filled up with earth, to preserve them from decay[3]. And the bent walls of some log cells in the rampart were considered to be a regional peculiarity[4], instead of supposing that a log cell could have slanted at the moment it was falling.

A few years ago, Yuri Yurievich Morgunov proposed and proved a revolutionary idea, arguing that ramparts dating from the 10th to 13th centuries are mostly the ruins of wooden walls that had earthen cores. Originally they were surface walls, not purposely raised ramparts, and it was only with time, in the process of decay, that they turned into earthen ramparts that can be seen today[5]. The idea was so novel that not every scholar has acknowledged it or has agreed with it as yet. Earthen ramparts with the rotten remains of logs inside look so different from vertically standing wooden walls that many scholars traditionally continue to call them earthen ramparts and refuse to believe they represent examples of a very different structure. The present writer must admit that he, too, held the old rampart version and has only recently changed his opinion.

Let us consider the arguments in favour of the new theory. First, 60% of all recognised medieval Russian settlements are surrounded by very low (0.5 m-1.5 m in height) and up to 1.5 m-wide ramparts. Even considering that with time the ramparts have lost their form, these structures could hardly have offered any serious protection against attacking troops. Meanwhile, the making of a log frame and its covering with earth was highly labour-consuming, unworthy of so ineffective a fortification. Secondly, raising ramparts along the edge of high riverbanks seems pointless. It would have been sufficient to scarp such banks to turn them into powerful barriers. A wooden defence of some type (a stockade, fence or log wall) could have been put along their edges, but an earthen rampart was obviously unnecessary. However, such low ramparts are common. Hence, this is one reason for believing that they are remains of a different structure. Thirdly, intra-rampart log cells would make a poor foundation: infiltrating atmospheric water would cause the logs to rot, which could not be replaced, eventually causing the foundation to suddenly sag and bring down the surface palisade. At the same time, wooden walls were more efficient in these situations: the coating of the logs and the roofing of the walls did not allow water to penetrate into the earthen filling. Once dry, the earthen filling remained dry and did not cause the logs of the cells to rot. Moreover, the rotten ends of the logs in surface structures could have been easily replaced. Fourthly, direct evidence of the collapse of log walls has been discovered inside some ramparts. For instance, at Ekimauts human skeletons were discovered under the collapsed walls and in Voin' the remains of a 28 m-long stretch of a collapsed wall was found under the ridge of the rampart[6]. Nothing but parts of surface structures could be found above the corpses as the tradition of burying people within ramparts never existed in Rus'. Last but not least, it has been proved from an engineering point of view that log cells covered with earth neither strengthened the rampart nor influenced the steepness of its slopes[7] – and these were the main arguments of the advocates of intra-rampart structures.

Now, how could wooden walls have turned into ramparts? Most wooden fortifications were burned down. Chronicles are full of references to numerous fires that burned down houses and "towns" (and the word "town" in medieval Russia was applied to a stronghold or fortification itself). The many kilometres long Zmievy Valy were also destroyed by fire. When a wooden wall with an earthen core caught fire, the upper part was the first to burn down. No longer supported by anything, the earth poured from above and buried the lower parts of the wall, which also became charred. When excavated, these ruins create an illusion of intra-rampart structures (fig. 1).

Everything that has just been said does not, however, mean that in Rus' there were never purposely built earthen ramparts with defences on top. Earthen ramparts as fortification elements certainly existed. Walls were erected straight on the ground only where there had never been other defences.

Moreover, it cannot be excluded that a sloping earthen widening or bank was sometimes added to the front wall of log cells filled with earth; it played the part of a talus protecting the bottom of the wall from the battering of a ram or from undermining and eliminated the dead ground at the foot of the wall. This structure may be functionally close to the fortifications that have mud-brick front layers. The latter has been found in many of Old Russia's fortresses.

The same structure can be seen in all cases. Excavation of ramparts reveal the remains of wooden log cells fronted with a layer of mud-brick put inside wooden frames. With the inner side of the mud-brick layer being next to the log cells, the outer side could be strictly vertical or stepped (from one to five steps can be followed). Clay was used for binding, sometimes mixed with a bit of sand.

Fortifications with mud-brick layers were only used in Rus' for a short period of time, from 988 to 1015, when Vladimir Svyatoslavich carried out his programme for the protection of Rus' from the Pechenegs. The peculiarity of the structure and the short period of its usage gave rise to the opinion that it was brought to Rus' by foreigners. But the question of the sources of influence is still under discussion.

Also under discussion is the question of the original look of the fortification with a mud-brick facing layer. For a long time it was considered that, like wooden intra-rampart struc-

---

3. Голубева [Golubeva] 1949, 140; Раппопорт [Rappoport] 1961, 106.
4. Раппопорт [Rappoport] 1961, 110.
5. Моргунов [Morgunov] 2007, 15; Моргунов [Morgunov] 2009, 52-55.
6. Моргунов [Morgunov] 2009, 53-55, 66.
7. Борисевич [Borisevich] 1987, 181. In this work, G. V. Borisevich for the first time advanced an opinion that intra-rampart structures were useless and that earthen widenings to the walls were harmful as they only make it easier for the enemy to assault the fortress.

Fig. 1 – Log cells with earthen cores in the process of collapse, which caused the creation of ramparts having wooden remains inside. Drawing V. V. Golubev, after Yu. Yu. Morgunov.

tures, this building technique was designed to keep the steep front slope of the rampart from slipping down[8]. However the technique seems too labour-consuming for the task. The result is also doubtful – frames filled with mud-brick could hardly increase the steepness of a rampart. Therefore, Yuri Yurievich Morgunov's opinion seems more valid as he claims that originally these were vertical walls erected on the ground surface and they turned into ramparts as the log cells filled with earth broke down[9].

A question arises: what was the mud-brick front layer for? It is well known that defences made of mud-brick are fire-resistant, less susceptible to damage by earthquakes and cannot be broken by a ram. But rams were not used in the 10th-century Rus' and earthquakes were rare. So fire-resistance is the only advantage for mud-brick front layers.

Thus, mud-brick masonry in front of a timber-earth wall formed a vertical fire-resistant layer or a sloped talus (the steps between the frames were filled with clay). The result formed a powerful defensive structure (fig. 2).

Why wasn't mud-brick widespread in Rus' and only used for a very short period? In the present writer's opinion, it can be explained by the climate. A considerable quantity of precipitation falling in Russia would inundate defences made of unbaked brick (which in fact is just foundry clay dried in the sun). It is not for nothing that fortifications made of mud-brick only survived in regions where the level of rainfall is insignificant (Mesopotamia, Central Asia, Egypt, etc.). Not a single mud-brick fortification has been preserved in regions with a more or less high level of rainfall, such as Greece or Asia Minor, although it is well-known that mud-brick was used there. In Rus' surface walls made of mud-brick would be short-lived and would require yearly renovation. Their preservation inside ramparts tells us that they had not lasted long as surface structures and were soon buried under the ruins of the walls with the earthen core.

3. The interpretation of the words *byk* and *roskat*

The second aspect the present writer would like to touch upon in this paper is the interpretation of the terms *byk* and *roskat*.

Until recently scholars usually understood these terms as synonyms for the word "bastion" (the latter word appeared in Russia only as late as the time of Peter the Great[10]). This led to problems with the interpretation of written sources: any mention of *byk* or *roskat* was understood as an indication of an angled bastion. However, recent studies of sources by the present writer show that the terms *byk* and *roskat* had several different meanings and did not always mean "bastion". So the use of any of these terms in the sources cannot in itself be considered as a proof of the existence of a bastion[11].

The term *byk* had three different meanings in fortification. Firstly, the word could mean a buttress or a strengthening lean-to structure, added to towers or more rarely to curtain walls. They could be made of wood or stone. They usually had a roof and sometimes had loopholes. They were not common narrow vertical projections, but rather stretched, stout and

---

8. Раппопорт [Rappoport] 1956, 91.
9. Моргунов [Morgunov] 2009, 78.
10. Каменных [Kamennyh] 1985, 14.
11. Носов [Nossov] 2008b; Носов [Nossov] 2009b, 36-55.

roofed lean-tos. A *byk*-buttress could be added to a tower in two ways: either as a separate annexe or one built all along the side of the tower at its foot. Secondly, a *byk* could be earth-and-wood defences built out from fortifications to face the enemy. *Byks*, however, differed considerably from West European bastions. Not only bastion-type projections but also any earthen projections of considerable size were called *byks*. They were also revetted in wood while West Europeans preferred stone facing or left their earthen fortifications uncovered. Also, a *byk* was often topped not only with a breastwork that had loopholes but, also, with wooden towers and walls, which must have considerably increased the general firepower of the fortification. Thirdly, a *byk* was also the word sometimes used for a stout, tower-like wooden structure. These were usually called *otvodnoy byk*, not just *byk*. This type of *byk* had two or more floors and a roof. On each floor there were several openings for cannon and a lot for handguns, which puts *otvodnoy byk* closer in its form to a tower-*roskat*. However, unlike the latter type of tower, an *otvodnoy byk* was detached from the fortress' walls. It was also more stout and had fewer loopholes for cannon (fig. 3).

The term *roskat* also had three meanings during the 17th century. Firstly, it could mean a lean-to against a curtain, or sometimes a tower, and were designed to mount artillery and therefore increased a fortress' firepower. It could be made of stone, brick or wood. Annexe-type *roskats* could differ widely in size. They were usually built at to the base of a tower but sometimes at its top. Secondly, a *roskat* could be a tower-like building built of wood or stone. They could be rectangular, octagonal or round in shape, but other forms are known. Rectangular and octagonal structures of such are known. Like ordinary towers, they were usually covered with a hipped roof. *Roskats* could differ in height: they were sometimes as high as the fortress towers or even a bit higher, but more often they were much higher. There were several times as many loopholes for cannon in *roskats* as in wooden towers. So it seems that this type of *roskat* was a more powerful structure than common wooden towers, which made it possible to put considerably more cannon on them. Thirdly, *roskat* can also mean an earthen bastion. The word was only used with this meaning from the very late 17th and early 18th centuries, when the term "bastion" was not yet common (fig. 4).

4. The Italian influence on fortifications of the late 15th to 17th century

The third important peculiarity of fortification of the late 15th to 17th century is the Italian influence. Foreign influence was not spoken of in the Soviet Union; every achievement was ascribed only to Russian masters. But in the post-Soviet time the subject was opened up and developed. It is now well known that a lot of Italian masters arrived in Russia at the invitation of Ivan III and Vasily III. They did not work there long – for about 60 years (from the last quarter of the 15th century to about the first third of the 16th century). Nev-

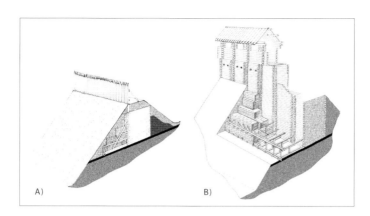

Fig. 2 – Different reconstructions of the defences of the city of Belgorod, as it looked during the 10th century: A) after V. V. Khvoika (1909). This researcher believed the remains of log cells and a mud-brick layer that he found in the rampart were intra-rampart structures. In addition, he mistakenly dated the remains of a 17th-century stockade on the top of the rampart to the 10th century. As a result, for several decades, there existed an absurd reconstruction of the fortification system consisting of a most complex intra-rampart structure and the simplest wooden defences on the ridge of a rampart. B) after M. V. Gorodtsov & B. A. Rybakov. Having corrected one of the shortcomings of V. V. Khvoika's reconstruction, these scholars erected a hypothetical log surface wall but put it on top of the same rampart with a complex intra-rampart structure of log cells and mud-brick masonry. The present writer believes that the mud-brick masonry was not covered with earth but, levelled with clay, forming a fire-resistant talus.

ertheless, they contributed to the building of many Russian kremlins of which the Moscow and Novgorod Kremlins were the first.

Italian masters introduced many elements of Italian fortification to Russian military engineering: the wide use of brick, merlons in the form of a swallow tail, machicolations, white-stone belt, widening down socle of the walls, an arcade on the inner side of the wall, loopholes at ground level, bridgehead towers, drawbridges[12]. Some of those innovations were purely decorative, others were significant as they increased firepower, fortification resistance to destruction or eliminated the dead ground at base of fortress walls. The subject of Italian influence is vast and would take a lot of time to examine. So we shall only touch upon the three most striking innovations.

The first and most important innovation is the wide use of baked brick in the building of Russian fortresses. It was only with the arrival of Italian masters that mass production of brick was developed in Russia and fortresses made entirely of brick appeared. Brick had considerable advantages in comparison with stone where building was concerned. First of all, clay fit for brick making was a more widespread material than the stone fit for construction. Secondly, as was recently

---

12. Below are the features of Italian influence given in short. For details, see Носов [Nossov] 2009b, 91-98, 104-108.

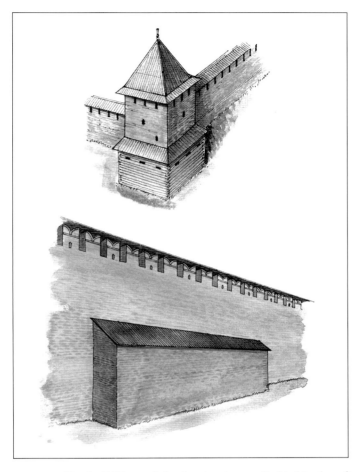 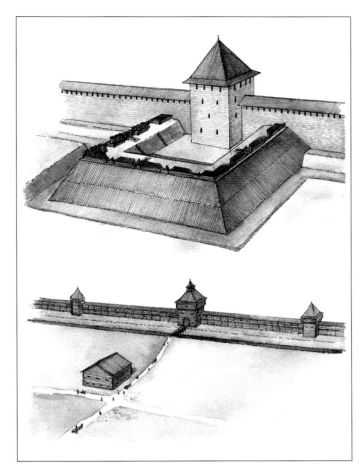

Fig. 3 – Different defensive structures called *byk* in the 17th century. Reconstruction K. S. Nossov; drawings V. V. Golubev.

proved, building in brick was about ten times cheaper than in stone (because of difficulties in transporting stone and the cost of quarrying and dressing it)[13]. Brick fortresses were much less labour-consuming than stone ones[14].

Swallow-tailed shaped merlons are a notable element of Italian influence in Russia. In Italy this shape of a merlon meant that the owner of the castle belongs to Ghibellines, meaning that they were adherents of the German Emperor and opponents of the Papacy. The appearance of such merlons on the walls of Russian fortresses was undoubtedly an important political step made with Ivan III's consent as a consequence of the theory "Moscow is the Third Rome". The shape of these merlons had no practical function, it was purely decorative (fig. 5).

Machicolations were another element of Italian architecture introduced in Russia at the end of the 15th century. In 15th-century Italy machicolations were constructed not only on towers but very often on walls (curtains) too. Moreover, they were sometimes put on towers in two tiers. In Russia machicolations were usually made on towers (only one tier under the parapet as a rule) and very rarely on the walls. Despite their obvious advantages, machicolations did not become common in Russia and they did not feature on many kremlins built at that period (fig. 6).

In spite of this strong Italian influence, Russian fortresses were not just a copy of Italian castles. They preserved their originality in their decor, the shape of loopholes and the covering of walls and towers with planked roofs (the walls and towers of Italian castles were either roofed with tile or left uncovered). The whitewashing of fortification, which became widespread in Russia in the 17th century, made the contrast between Russian and Italian fortifications even more striking.

The influence of Italian forms of the 15th century turned out to be wonderfully strong. Russian builders liked them so much that these forms were present in the fortresses constructed not only at the end of the 15th and the beginning of the 16th century but even in the fortresses of the late 16th and early 17th centuries. Built on the basis of Italian fortification principles of the late 15th century were the walls of the Kazan Kremlin, the Bely-Gorod in Moscow (1586-1593), the kremlin

---

13. Заграевский [Zagraevskii] 2002, 19-20, 141-143.

14. Носов [Nossov] 2008a, 100.

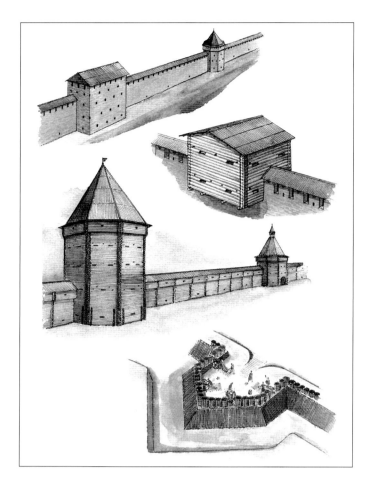

Fig. 4 – Different defensive structures called *roskat* in the 17th century. Reconstruction K. S. Nossov; drawings V. V. Golubev.

Fig. 6 – Beklemischevskaya Tower of the Moscow Kremlin. Photo K. Nossov.

Fig. 5 – Merlons in the form of a swallow tail. The Tula Kremlin. Photo K. Nossov.

Fig. 7 – Orel Tower of Smolensk Fortress. This frontier fortress was built at the turn of the 16th to 17th centuries and was a fighting fortress. Note the brick, the machicolations and the merlons in the shape of a swallow tail. Photo K. Nossov.

of Astrakhan (1582-1589), Boris Godunov's residence-castle at Borisov-Gorodok (founded in 1598), and the frontier fortresses of Smolensk (1596-1602) and Mozhaisk (1624-1626), to say nothing of numerous monastic enceintes of the 16th and 17th centuries. In other words, the Italian influence on Russian fortification lasted until the end of the 17th century, although the last Italian master left Russia in 1538 (fig. 7).

There can be only one explanation for this long adherence to Italian forms of the late 15th century – in Russia the image of a fortress was firmly linked to medieval towers and walls. Bastion-shaped fortresses were considered unimposing and not sufficiently safe from the point of view of defence. This is confirmed by several refusals to build angle-bastioned fortifications, which were given up in favour of archaic stone-brick ones. For instance, in 1653 the already-started work on fortifying Kirillo-Belozersky Monastery with earthen bastions was suspended because the monks appealed to Tsar Aleksey Mikhailovich to allow them to build high stone walls and towers instead of bastions, which was in the end carried out in 1654-1680[15]. After Smolensk was returned to Russia in 1654, commanders of the Russian army more than once offered to level the pentagonal King's bastion there built by the Poles to the ground and put a stone wall on the site[16]. And even in those places where a bastion-like fortification was built, a wooden or stone wall was erected in addition (e.g. Ladoga, the Maly Zemlyanoy Gorod of Novgorod, the Zemlyanoy Gorod in Moscow, the Archbishop's house in Rostov). This outlook was completely revised only as late as the 18th century, when Russian fortification gave up medieval forms and turned to polygonal fortresses with pointed bastions.

---

15. Кирпичников [Kirpichnikov] & Хлопин [Hlopin] 1972, 120-124.

16. Кирпичников [Kirpichnikov] 1979, 498, footnote 152.

Bibliography

Борисевич Г. В. [Borisevich G. V.] (1987), "Сооружения городища Слободка", in Никольская Т.Н. *Городище Слободка XII-XIII вв.*, Москва, Наука, 180-187 ["The Structures of the Ancient Settlement of Slobodka", in T. N. Nikolskaya, *The Ancient Settlement of Slobodka in the Twelfth to Thirteenth Centuries*, Moscow, Nauka, 180-187].

Голубева Л. А. [Golubeva L. A.] (1949), "Раскопки в Верейском кремле", *Материалы и исследования по археологии СССР*, 12, 134-143 ["Excavations in the Kremlin of Vereya", *Materials and Studies in the Archaeology of the USSR*, 12, 134-143].

Каменных М. Г. [Kamennyh M. G.] (1985), *К истории наименований фортификационных сооружений в русском языке*, Тбилиси, Издательство Тбилисского университета [*Concerning the Names of Fortifications in the Russian Language*, Tbilisi, Publishing House of the Tbilisi University].

Кирпичников А. Н. [Kirpichnikov A. N.] (1979), "Крепости бастионного типа в средневековой России", in *Памятники культуры. Новые открытия. Письменность. Искусство. Археология. Ежегодник 1978*, Москва, Наука, 471-499 ["Fortresses of Bastion Type in Medieval Russia", in *Monuments of Culture. New Discoveries. Literary Texts. Art. Archaeology. Year-Book 1978*, Moscow, Nauka, 471-499].

Кирпичников А. Н. & Хлопин И. Н. [Kirpichnikov A. N. & Hlopin I. N.] (1972), *Великая Государева крепость*, Ленинград, Художник РСФСР [*The Great Fortress of the Sovereign*, Leningrad, Artist of RSFSR].

Монгайт А. Л. [Monguite A. L.] (1947), "Древнерусские деревянные укрепления по раскопкам в Старой Рязани", *Краткие сообщения Института истории материальной культуры*, 17, 3-33 ["Old Russian Wooden Fortifications on the Basis of the Excavations in Old Ryazan", *Brief Reports from the Institute of the History of Material Culture*, 17, 3-33].

Моргунов Ю. Ю. [Morgunov Yu. Yu.] (2007), *Фортификация Южной Руси X-XIII вв.: Автореферат дисс. ...*, докт. ист. наук, Москва [*Southern Rus' Fortification in the Tenth to Thirteenth Centuries: Abstract of the Dissertation...*, Doctor of History, Moscow].

– (2009), *Древо-земляные укрепления Южной Руси X-XIII веков*, Москва, Наука [*Timber-Earth Fortifications of Southern Rus' of the Tenth to Thirteenth Centuries*, Moscow, Nauka].

Носов К. С. [Nossov K. S.] (2008a), "Опыт расчета трудозатрат на строительство Смоленской крепости 1596-1602 гг", in *Проблемы отечественной истории*, Москва, Издательство РАГС, 74-100 ["An Attempt in Accounting Labour Expenses for Building Smolensk Fortress in 1596-1602", in *Problems of National History*, Moscow, Izd-vo RAGS, 74-100].

– (2008b), "Особенности русского оборонного зодчества XVII в.: бык и роскат", *Альманах центра общественных экспертиз*, 1, 161-176 ["Peculiarities of Russian Defensive Architecture of the Seventeenth Century: *byk* and *roskat*", *Almanac of the Centre of Public Expert Opinion*, 1, 161-176].

– (2009a), *Русские крепости конца XV-XVII в.*, Санкт-Петербург, Нестор-История [*Russian Fortresses of the Late Fifteenth to Seventeenth Century*, St Petersburg, Nestor-Istoriia].

– (2009b), *Терминология оборонительного зодчества на Руси в XI-XVII вв.*, Москва, Изд-во РАГС [*Terminology of Defensive Architecture in Rus' in the Eleventh to Seventeenth Centuries*, Moscow, Izd-vo RAGS].

Раппопорт П. А. [Rapoport P. A.] (1956), "Очерки по истории русского военного зодчества X-XIII вв.", *Материалы и исследования по археологии СССР*, 52 ["Studies in the History of Russian Military Architecture of the Tenth to Thirteenth Centuries", *Materials and Studies in the Archaeology of the USSR*, 52].

– (1961), "Очерки по истории военного зодчества Северо-Восточной и Северо-Западной Руси X-XV вв.", *Материалы и исследования по археологии СССР*, 105 ["Studies in the History of Military Architecture of North-East and North-West Rus' of the Tenth to Fifteenth Centuries", *Materials and Studies in the Archaeology of the USSR*, 105].

– (1967), "Военное зодчество западнорусских земель X-XIV вв.", *Материалы и исследования по археологии СССР*, 140 ["Military Architecture of West Russian Lands in the Tenth to Fourteenth Centuries", *Materials and Studies in the Archaeology of the USSR*, 140].

Заграевский С. В. [Zagraevskii S. V.] (2002), *Юрий Долгорукий и древнерусское белокаменное зодчество*, Москва, Алеб-В [*Yuri Dolgoruki and Old Russian White-Stone Architecture*, Moscow, Alex-V].

Rindoon Castle, Co. Roscommon

A Border Castle on the Irish Frontier

Kieran O'Conor, Paul Naessens, Rory Sherlock*

1. Introduction

Rindoon (also Rinndown, Rindown or *Rinn Duin*) Castle, a royal castle whose first phase dates to the late 1220s and early 1230s, is situated on the peninsula of St John's Point, which juts out south-westwards from the western shores of Lough Ree, in Co. Roscommon, at this lake's narrowest part (fig. 1)[1]. The castle is located beside the deserted remains of a town that is contemporary with it and whose walls, church, extra-mural hospital and harbour can still be made out. A 13th-century windmill mound and some house foundations can also be seen (fig. 2). All these remains now lie within farmland[2]. Overall, the castle functioned as a royal administrative and military centre in an area that was held directly of the English king, in his role as Lord of Ireland, by the Gaelic-Irish O'Conor kings of Connacht. In effect, the castle and town functioned as an Anglo-Norman/English enclave in a border region (known as the Five Cantreds) that was dominated by a Gaelic-Irish prince, despite attempts by the Dublin government to bring more of the area under its direct control as the 13th century progressed[3].

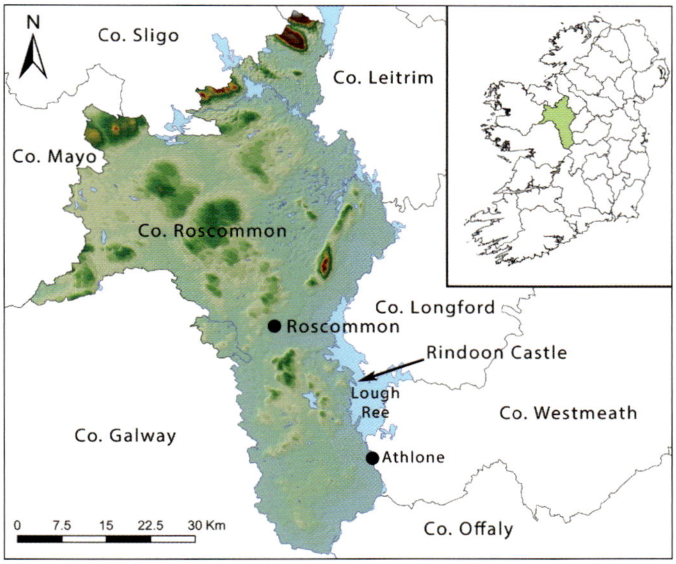

Fig. 1 – Location of Rindoon Castle, Co. Roscommon.

2. Siting

As just noted, Rindoon Castle and its adjacent town were sited on a peninsula jutting out into Lough Ree. This lough is one of a string of great lakes that occur along the Shannon River, which is 222 miles in overall length. This river was navigable during the medieval period from near its source in the Gaelic-Irish territory of *Breifne* down to the Hiberno-Norse and later Anglo-Norman trading city of Limerick, which lay on its estuary. Furthermore, some of the Shannon's tributaries,

---

* National University of Ireland, Galway, Ireland.
1. For previous work on Rindoon, see Fitzpatrick 1935; Bradley & Dunne 1988; Harbison 1995.
2. The best description of the physical remains at Rindoon is in Bradley & Dunne 1988.
3. Fitzpatrick 1935, 178; Harbison 1995, 140; Graham 1988, 22-23; Orpen 2005, 100-110.

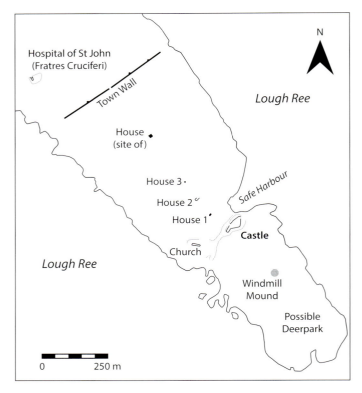

Fig. 2 – Plan showing the location of the principal remains associated with the deserted Anglo-Norman town at Rindoon, including the castle and Safe Harbour (modified from BRADLEY & DUNNE 1988).

Fig. 3 – Aerial photograph of Rindoon Castle, showing its present overgrown state, with Safe Harbour beside it. The remains of the town's church are also visible. Photo P. Naessens.

such as the Boyle River leading into Lough Key, were also navigable in medieval times. A partly-artificial island on the latter lake was the *caput* of the powerful Gaelic territory of Moylurg, which was ruled by the MacDermots, vassal lords of the O'Conors. The evidence also suggests that some form of nucleated settlement with market facilities existed on the shore opposite this island from at least the second quarter of the 13th century onwards[4]. This all shows Rindoon Castle was in an excellent position to control the Shannon waterways in medieval times and to extend its influence right into the heart of the Gaelic-dominated parts of north Connacht. Furthermore, the castle and town's excellent position on a trading route on the Shannon and its tributaries appear to have been of great importance economically.

The castle's siting on St John's Point is also interesting. It is located on a slight eminence right beside a natural inlet, known locally as "Safe Harbour" (fig. 3). The castle is sited so close to this feature that on good days its reflection can be seen on the waters of this inlet. Local boatmen state that the "Safe Harbour" is regarded as the most sheltered place on the whole lake in bad weather, hence its name[5]. Therefore, the castle controls the best natural harbour along this part of the Shannon. A now-broken out postern gate on the eastern side of the castle opens out onto steps that lead down directly to the shores of "Safe Harbour". Furthermore, a disused slipway and a series of collapsed dry-stone built jetties jut out into the inlet along its north-western and south-eastern sides. It is held that these represent the remains of a harbour area associated with the deserted medieval town and castle. Certainly waterborne activity and trade are recorded at Rindoon during the 13th and early 14th centuries and this must be taken as evidence of the presence of an important harbour there[6]. Therefore, the overall evidence suggests that Rindoon Castle dominated and controlled a thriving harbour that literally lay under its walls. There may also have been a symbolic aspect to this choice of siting, as it has been suggested that the "ideal castle" in the medieval mind and in medieval literature was sited beside water, for aesthetic and display reasons as much as for pragmatic, economic ones[7].

3. Pre-Norman Fortification at Rindoon

The first actual reference to Rindoon comes in 1156 during a very cold winter, when it is stated that the navy of Rory O'Conor, the king of Connacht, was able to pull its galleys over the ice that then covered Lough Ree across to place on its western shore called *Rinn Duin*[8]. The Irish place-name *Rinn Duin* (i.e. Rindoon) translates into English as something approximating "the fort of the promontory". This is surely an indication that there was some form of pre-Norman fortification there.

It has been argued that the fortification implied in this place-name was a straightforward promontory fort. It has been

4. O'CONOR *et al.* 2010.
5. R. Collins, St John's House, Lecarrow (Ireland), pers. comm.
6. HARBISON 1995, 142, 144.
7. MORRIS 1998, 74-76; JOHNSON 2002, 44-52.
8. BRADLEY & DUNNE 1988, 62.

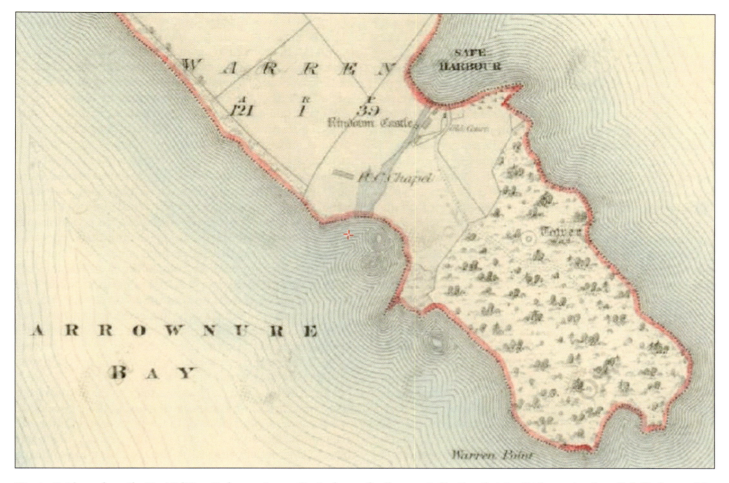

Fig. 4 – Evidence from the First Edition Ordnance Survey Six-Inch map for the area, indicating that the ditch running from Safe Harbour of the peninsula was originally wet. Note the expansion of the ditch at its south-western end. This may represent the remains of a fishpond (by courtesy of the Ordnance Survey of Ireland).

suggested that the defences of this postulated promontory fort consisted of the 250 m long bank and ditch that can be seen today running from the Safe Harbour, past the later castle, right across to the south-western side of the peninsula[9]. Again, the First Edition Ordnance Survey Six-Inch map for the area indicates that this ditch was originally wet (fig. 4). Anyway, it has been argued that this "promontory fort" may have been built by the O'Conor kings of Connacht in the 12th century, as part of their attempts to fortify the borders of their kingdom, or even by the Vikings in the mid-9th century[10].

There are references to a Viking *longphort* or stronghold on Lough Ree during the 9th century but its location has never been definitively identified[11]. Given Rindoon's location on the Shannon system and the excellent harbour facilities offered by Safe Harbour, however, it is fair to say that Rindoon is the most likely location on Lough Ree for such a *longphort*. Furthermore, it is also clear that naval forces were being used along the Shannon by Irish provincial kings during the course of the 11th and 12th centuries[12]. It is also apparent that the O'Conor kings of Connacht were busily fortifying the borders of their kingdom during the course of the 12th century[13]. It is highly probable, therefore, that the O'Conors also had a fortification at Rindoon, given its strategic location on the Shannon system, its border location, its proximity to the Meath shore (a province constantly targeted by the Connachtmen) and the fact that the Safe Harbour would have made an excellent haven for their historically-attested fleet of galleys.

There is much merit, therefore, in the view that there was some form of pre-Norman Viking or O'Conor fortification at Rindoon. It certainly helps explain the place-name *Rinn Duin*.

9. *Ibid.*, 77-79.
10. *Ibid.*, 78.
11. Valante 2008, 39, 42.
12. Flanagan 1996, 62-63.
13. Ó Corráin 1972, 151, 156; Ó Cróinín 1995, 282-283; Flanagan 1996, 61-62; Naessens & O'Conor 2012.

However, is the so-called "promontory fort", seen running across the narrowest part of the peninsula, really one? It seems far too large to be one, as the area enclosed by these defences measures 750 m north-west/south-east by 300 m north-east/south-west. The areas within the overwhelming majority of promontory forts are only a fraction of this[14]. So, if these linear earthworks are not the defences of a promontory fort, what do they represent? A better option may be that they represent the south-western defences of the Anglo-Norman town, being originally surmounted by timber palisades and having a wet ditch. Again, plans of many Anglo-Norman towns in Ireland, founded in the late 12th or 13th century, such as Athenry, Co. Galway, and Kilkenny, show the lord's castle to be located on the edge of the settlement, forming part of the town's defensive enceinte[15]. This location on the edge of the town proper is seen to be indicative and symbolic of a lord's willingness to allow the townsfolk govern their own legal and economic affairs. However, it has also been argued that such a location for a castle was chosen for purely military and defensive reasons[16]. Whatever the reason, if the earthworks between the Safe Harbour and the western shore are taken to mark the south-western boundary defences of the town, Rindoon Castle would have been positioned in exactly the same location as castles in many other towns – on the edge of the original town. Furthermore, to back up this argument, the available evidence suggests that the remainder of the peninsula to the south-east of the linear bank, ditch and castle was open, apparently seigneurial land. Firstly, there are no house foundations to be found in this part of the point, suggesting it was not part of the town. Furthermore, some of the land here, especially that to the immediate south of the castle, seems to have been too wet for occupation. The remains of what appear to be a 13th-century windmill mound occurs on rising ground about 250 m to the south-west of the castle. Mills were a lordly prerequisite throughout medieval times and provided large incomes for their owners[17]. This evidence may suggest that the whole area to the south-east of the castle was directly controlled by its lord, or in this case, his constable.

It might also be added to expand this argument that the townland within which the deserted town and castle of Rindoon are located, along with the area to south-east of the castle, is called Warren or *Coinegeir* in Irish. This place-name is perhaps referring to the possibility that a rabbit-warren once occurred here, maybe as early as the 13th century. It is unlikely that this rabbit warren, if it existed, would have occurred within the town itself. Evidence from England shows that medieval rabbit warrens there occurred beside castles, but were located a little bit away from associated nucleated settlements, like towns, and were not sited within them[18]. This would suggest that the best location for this rabbit warren within the bounds of what is now the modern townland of Warren lay somewhere along the peninsula to the south-east of the castle during medieval times. Like milling, rabbit farming was a lordly privilege during this period[19]. Furthermore, it is also clear that the south-western end of the ditch running across the whole promontory, just argued as cutting off the Anglo-Norman town from the rest of the peninsula, seems to have been modified and expanded at some stage or may even have been constructed like this originally. Certainly this expansion is not a recent feature as it exists on the First Edition Six Inch map for the area, which dates to the 1830s (fig. 4). What does this feature represent? Arguably, it could be the remains of a fishpond, especially as it lies near the castle, which was incorporated into the south-eastern defences and boundary of the town. Again, the right to build and stock fishponds was a lordly right during the medieval period[20]. In England, for example, it has been shown that fishponds, rabbit warrens and, for that matter, mills and planned nucleated settlements were all important elements of deliberately-designed landscapes around medieval castles[21]. The purpose of these deliberately-designed landscapes was to further emphasise the power of the castles' owners.

In all, the evidence, such as it is, suggests that all the rest of the peninsula to the south-east of the royal, 13th-century castle was not part of the associated Anglo-Norman town. Nor was it tenanted land worked by the townsfolk of Rindoon but was instead land directly utilised by the castle, as it has evidence for features within it or on its edges that were associated with lordship and its display. The overall evidence suggests that this whole area to the south-east of the castle and town, which stretched for almost a kilometre until the end of the peninsula, was relatively open demesne land. What was the function of this area, apart from being the place where the royal mill was located and where a possible rabbit warren existed, with a possible fishpond on its edge? The ground is either too rocky or too wet for arable farming. One possibility is that it could have functioned as a royal deer park and as the major part of the deliberately designed landscape, discussed above.

Returning to the main question in this part of the paper, therefore, it is suggested that the so-called pre-Norman "promontory fort" may be better interpreted as being the remains of the south-eastern earth-and-timber defences of the early 13th-century Anglo-Norman town, with the royal castle lying at their north-western end. Also, it is suggested that far from being the interior of a massive, pre-Norman promontory fort, the rest of the peninsula to the south-east of the town and castle seems to have been royal, demesne land associated

---

14. Edwards 1990, 41-43.
15. Bradley 1995, 38.
16. *Ibid.*
17. See, for example, O'Conor 1998, 33.
18. Liddiard 2000, 56-68.
19. Creighton 2002, 177-179; Creighton 2009, 110-114; Murphy & O'Conor 2006, 53, 57-58, 64-66.
20. *Ibid.*, 57.
21. For example, see Liddiard 2000; Creighton 2009.

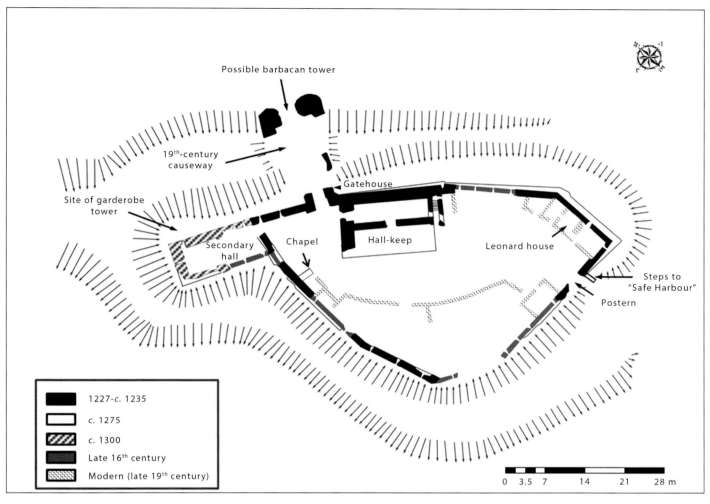

Fig. 5 – Phased plan of Rindoon Castle by the authors (modified from BRADLEY & DUNNE 1988).

with the 13th-century castle, and was perhaps a deliberately designed landscape whose function was to further emphasise the power and control of resources at the disposal of the castle's owner, which was in this case the English king in his role of Lord of Ireland. Where, then, was the pre-Norman fortification implied by the place-name *Rinn Duin*, if it was not a promontory fort?

The answer to this may lie in a more detailed analysis of the 13th-century castle's ground plan. In Ireland, as elsewhere, castles of the first rank built after *c.* 1200 tended, amongst other things, to be far more defensive than those built at earlier dates. These new defensive features could include: twin-towered gatehouses, well equipped with arrow-loops, having provision for heavy wooden gates and portcullises in their passageways; straighter, higher curtain walls, whose battlements included merlons pierced with arrowloops; projecting round towers, also looped for archery, often three storeys in height, occurring on the angles of these straight curtains; projecting half-round towers, again with arrow-loops, found on straight stretches of curtain wall. Keeps cease to function as the most defensive feature in major castles but they still continue to be built. This discussion all shows that the defences of curtain walls and the entranceways to major castles were enhanced from the last years of the 12th century onwards. The arrow-loops set in the sides of these new projecting towers and twin-towered gatehouses allowed bowmen to fire along the bases of adjacent stretches of curtain wall and, therefore, control them. Basically, it could be said that from this time onwards, the defensive emphasis in castles moved to their curtain walls and, amongst other things, the ability to be able to control the bases of these walls became a paramount feature of castle design[22].

It was noted above that the first masonry phase at Rindoon Castle dates to the late 1220s and early 1230s. An analysis of the castle's ground plan shows that its curtain wall runs in a curving fashion for much of its length (fig. 5). There is a rectangular extension to the south-west but it will be shown that this is in fact a secondary hall added on to the castle around 1300. The original castle's curtain wall lacked mural and angle towers as well. The curtain does

22. KING 1988, 62-67, 77-78; McNEILL 2001, 44-45; DE MEULEMEESTER & O'CONOR 2007, 333-334; O'CONOR 2011, 254-256.

not follow the line of the castle ditch in places, especially on its northern side. If Rindoon Castle had been built on a green-field site in the late 1220s, it must be presumed that it would have had straight walls with towers, well looped for archery, at its angles, following the defensive designs then current. The curving nature of the castle's ditch and at least part of the curtain walls strongly suggest that the masonry castle here was built within a pre-existing earthwork and timber fortification. Barry noted this and has suggested that this earlier fortification may well have been an early 13th-century Anglo-Norman ringwork[23]. This is, of course, possible but it is clear that any early thirteenth-century grants to Anglo-Norman knights in this area were effectively speculative and could not really have been taken up due to the military and political strength of Cathal Crovderg O'Conor, king of Connacht until his death in 1224[24]. Given that it is now suggested that the earthworks running across the narrow waist of the peninsula are the remains of the later Anglo-Norman town's defences, is it possible that it was a pre-existing earthwork fortification, evidence for which is seen in the design of the later castle, that gave Rindoon its name in pre-Norman times? It seems likely. Again, only excavation will tell whether this fortification was built by the Vikings in the 9th century or the O'Conors in the 12th century. Of course, it may well be that such an excavation will show that this fortification was first used by the Vikings, as it clearly controlled Safe Harbour, but that it was taken over and rebuilt by the O'Conor kings of Connacht at a later date for partly the same reason.

4. The First Masonry Castle at Rindoon

Henry III's governor in Ireland, the justiciar Geoffrey de Marisco, started to build a masonry castle at Rindoon in 1227[25]. The historical sources suggest that this first phase was completed by around 1236, when it was held successfully by its garrison against an attack by Felim O'Conor, king of Connacht[26].

What features of the castle date to this first phase? It is clear that two-storey hall-keep (which originally had a cap tower at battlement level at each of its four corners and has a first-floor entry) which occurs along the north-western curtain, is original. The single-towered gatehouse, which upon close scrutiny of the evidence appears to have had an attached barbican and drawbridge in front of it, is clearly original, as it is attached to the hall. Indeed, a doorway leads from the first floor of the hall into the first-floor room of the gatehouse (fig. 6). A portcullis groove and bar-holes for a heavy wooden gateway can be seen in the passageway under this room. Other evidence suggests that this gatehouse may have had a third floor or, at least, that its battlements were at more-or-less the same height as those on the hall-keep. This was clearly an impressive, well-defended gatehouse. Indeed, the juxtaposition of the gatehouse and keep made the whole north-western and northern front of the castle very impressive looking. This was no coincidence as the main landward and lake-ward approaches to the castle were from these sides and these buildings were clearly placed here to impress and overawe visitors coming down the main street of the town or sailing into Safe Harbour.

By contrast, the other sides of the castle are not so impressive, as they lack mural and angle towers. Again, at first glance, this suggests that one of the primary considerations of castle defence – control of the base of the curtain wall – was not met by the design of the fortification. It could be said, therefore, on first appraisal, that this suggests that the masonry castle, as built in the late 1220s and 1230s, was poorly defended, despite the complexity of its gatehouse, its deep wet ditch and the fact that it lay on a border region. In fact, certain commentators have implied that Rindoon Castle was not well defended, when built and throughout its subsequent phases[27].

There was another way to control the base of the curtain safely, however, other than building mural or angle towers along its length. An alternative way to achieve this was to place a timber *hourd* on top of a curtain wall[28]. This would allow defenders to safely fire down to the base of the curtain wall at attackers. Evidence of joist holes for a timber *hourd* can be seen along stretches of the primary castle wall (fig. 7). Some of the original merlons can be seen in the fabric of the wall too and at least some of these were looped, allowing downward fire. The original masonry castle at Rindoon, with its well-defended gatehouse and its curtain wall surmounted by a timber *hourd*, was actually far more defensive than it appears on an initial assessment. It helps explain why the Anglo-Norman defenders of Rindoon were able to see off the major attack by Felim O'Conor, king of Connacht, in 1236[29].

One last question needs to be asked. Why were mural or angle towers not built at Rindoon? The decision not to do this may be due to a desire to keep costs down but there may have been other reasons too. As noted, the shape of the 13th-century castle is dictated by the morphology of the earlier pre-Norman fortification. This means that the size of the castle is also dictated by the existence of this earlier fortress. The area enclosed by the defences at Rindoon Castle is quite small. It could be argued that the builders of the castle decided not to build towers along the length of the curtain wall on it south-western to north-eastern sides, as it would have seriously reduced the amount of living space available within it. The decision to surmount the curtain wall with a timber *hourd* at Rindoon was at least partly due to a desire

---

23. BARRY 1987, 52-53.
24. GRAHAM 1988, 22-23; T. Finan, pers. comm.
25. HENNESSEY 1871, vol. 1, 294-295; FREEMAN 1944, 27.
26. BRADLEY & DUNNE 1988, 71.
27. MCNEILL 1997, 125-126; SWEETMAN 1999, 59-60.
28. MCNEILL 1997, 246; LEPAGE 2002, 39-40, 49-52; GRAVETT 2009, 24.
29. HENNESSEY 1871, vol. 1, 335-336, FREEMAN 1944, 61-62.

Fig. 6 – Hall-keep and attached gatehouse at Rindoon Castle. The gatehouse was originally as tall as the hall-keep. Photo K. O'Conor.

Fig. 7 – The lowermost openings in this photograph of the curtain wall at Rindoon Castle are the joist-holes for a timber hourd built during the period 1227-1236 – the castle's first phase. The higher openings represent the joist-holes for a second timber hourd, erected when the curtain wall was considerably heightened in the 1270s. Photo K. O'Conor.

to maximise the amount of space available within the castle. Another possibility is that in 1227 Geoffrey de Marisco, conscious that he was building the castle on a pre-existing earthwork, decided against building masonry towers along most of the curtain because he feared that the ground was not firm enough in places to take them and, therefore, was afraid of subsidence damaging anything built. Both of these explanations suggest that perhaps the existence of an earlier earth and timber fortress not only dictated the size and shape of the later Anglo-Norman castle, it also affected the choice of defences used in it.

5. The second phase of the masonry castle at Rindoon

Rindoon Castle was captured by Aedh (Hugh) O'Conor in 1270 and was then badly destroyed by him in 1272[30]. There are references to considerable building work and repairs being carried out at the castle between 1273 and 1279[31]. What was the nature of this work? Again, an analysis of the standing fabric suggests that this included a heightening of the castle's curtain wall by about 2 m. Again, towers were not built along the curtain and, instead, another timber hourd surmounted this heightening, as the joist holes for one are still visible in places, considerably above the earlier, primary ones (fig. 7).

The castle's ditch was apparently scoured out[32]. We also hear of timber towers being built at the castle[33]. Certainly there is some evidence for earthworks along the whole north-western front of the castle, on the external edge of the ditch. Perhaps this bank was erected at this time and had a palisade and towers built along its top. Alternatively, these earth and timber outer defences on the edge of the ditch at Rindoon date from the primary stone-castle phase and the reference to timber towers in the 1270s was merely referring to the replacement of wooden defences that had been burnt down in 1272. In all, however, the architectural and historical evidence does suggest that Rindoon Castle's defences were considerably strengthened in the 1270s, presumably to counter the growing threat of the local Irish at this early stage of the Gaelic Resurgence.

6. The third phase of the masonry castle

A new hall was begun at the castle in the late 1290s[34]. This hall has been identified by some as being the two-storey building that juts south-westwards from the main castle (fig. 5)[35]. It is clearly later than the earlier phases of the masonry castle, discussed above, as its stonework does not bond into the curtain wall. McNeill also noted that this building was "later" but gives no definite date for it[36]. An analysis of this later building shows it to have two phases in its architecture. The latest phase in the building is probably late 16th century in date and is associated with gunloops, as well as the repair and complete rebuilding of some lengths of the earlier phase's walls. What date is the first phase of this structure? Two narrow rectangular windows occur high up in the wall at

---

30. Hennessey 1871, vol. 1, 467; Hennessey & McCarthy 1887-1891, vol. 2, 347; Freeman 1944, 157.
31. Bradley & Dunne 1988, 70, 72; Harbison 1995, 143.
32. Sweetman 1875-1886, vol. 2, no. 1412.
33. *Ibid.*
34. *Ibid.*, vol. 3, no. 1151; Harbison 1995, 143-144.
35. Fitzpatrick 1935, 178; Bradley & Dunne 1988, 74; Sweetman 1999, 60.
36. McNeill 1997, 126.

ground-floor level at the south-western end of this secondary hall. The stonework of these windows has clear signs of diagonal tooling on them. This suggests that these windows probably date in a general sense to sometime between the late 12th and mid-14th centuries. Furthermore, the arches over the embrasures within which these windows are set are plank centered, again suggesting a general high medieval date for their construction. The best analogy for these windows comes from those in the ground floor of a hall building in the Lower Ward or bailey at Okehampton Castle, Devon, in a phase dating to the very early 14th century. Furthermore, what appears to be a large lancet (now covered in ivy) occurs at the northern end of the north-western wall of this building, again indicating a general high medieval date for this hall. The remains of the joist holes for a timber *hourd* can also be seen along this wall just below original battlement level (fig. 8). Timber hourding as a form of defence was replaced by stone machicolation from the very early 14th century onwards across northern Europe[37]. This physical evidence suggests, therefore, that this building is later than the 1270s and earlier than the very early 14th century. In turn, integrating this conclusion in with the available historical evidence, this does suggest that this structure is the hall mentioned as being constructed at the castle between the late 1290s and 1302. It might be added that the first floor of this hall seems to have been originally lit by a number of fine windows and was heated by one, if not two, fireplaces. It obviously offered some very fine accommodation.

Why was this later hall built at this point? It could have been built elsewhere in the castle. The decision to build the hall where it is seems to have been linked to a desire by the castle's occupants to add to the dramatic facade of the whole north-western side of the castle. Travellers coming into the town, along its main street or sailing into Safe Harbour, would now have seen a gatehouse flanked by not one, but now two fine halls.

One further point needs to be made about this later hall. Two narrow, round-headed doorways (that were later blocked up, with gunloops seen today in the blocking) can be seen at ground- and first-floor level at the southern end of the north-western wall of the building. These doorways correspond to a kink in the fosse, as the ground surface at the base of the building now juts out into the ditch (fig. 5). This seems to indicate that some form of two-storey tower or building existed here that was entered from the hall. However, there is no sign of any stone toothing on the external face of the hall's wall at this point. The wall, as elsewhere, is smooth and unbroken. This evidence suggests that some form of wooden tower or narrow building existed at this point. What was the function of this tower or building?

Fig. 8 – Openings for a timber hourd can also be seen just below battlement level on the second hall at Rindoon Castle, which was built around 1300. Photo R. Sherlock.

Did it offer flanking defence? It seems not, as the provision of timber hourding at battlement level on this later hall meant that such a defensive provision was not needed at this point. Anyway, arrowloops must have existed in the southern side of the original gatehouse 20 m away and these would have covered this whole area anyway. This suggests that this wooden structure, that seems to have been only two storeys in height, had another function. The narrow round-headed doorways most probably led into a garderobe tower/building. The siting of a two-storeyed garderobe tower along the most dramatic-looking, visible side of the castle is interesting. Why was it located here? Why was it not located in a more private, less obvious location, such as 21st-century sensibilities would require? At one level, it could be said that the garderobe structure was located at this point because the flow of water along the main ditch here may have been stronger, as it lay on the direct line between the two shores of the lake (fig. 4). Waste from the tower/building would have been flushed away more efficiently than anywhere on the whole south-eastern side of the castle. Johnson, however, has noted that garderobes in at least some English and Welsh castles were located to be seen from the main approach routes to these places. He has argued that this was all part of a display of conspicuous consumption on behalf of such a castle's owner[38]. In other words, the placing of a garderobe tower at this point around 1300 at Rindoon Castle may have been deliberate and the building was meant to add to the message of power and wealth that this whole north-western facade of the castle was trying to give to the world – a desire that can be traced back to the original erection of the castle in the late 1230s, as already noted.

---

37. For example, see O'CONOR 2011, 256.

38. JOHNSON 2002, 43. T. O'Keeffe has suggested something similar for Ballymoon Castle in Co. Carlow.

7. The fourth (destruction) phase of the masonry castle

The historical sources suggest that the town was deserted by its English inhabitants in the early 14th century, as a result of Gaelic-Irish pressure[39]. The castle itself is clearly in Irish hands by the early 1340s[40]. There is absolutely no mention of the castle in the sources from the mid-14th century until the late 16th century, when it is referred to as a "bare castle"[41]. This seems to suggest that it was in need of great repair at the very least. The physical evidence from the castle suggests that the curtain walls of the castle were completely rebuilt at the end of the latter century (fig. 5).

The complete lack of historical evidence for the occupation of the castle from the 1340s onwards for over two centuries and architectural evidence for massive repairs to the castle in the late 16th century suggests that the local Irish levelled large parts of the castle in the mid-14th century[42]. This included taking down stretches of curtain wall and undermining the keep, causing its south-eastern half to collapse. This destruction of the castle was to prevent its reoccupation by the Dublin government. In this, they seem to have been successful and Rindoon Castle appears to have lain ruined for more than two centuries. This destruction and partial levelling was not unique, as it has been argued that other well-known early Anglo-Norman castles, including Clonmacnoise Castle, Co. Offaly, and Dunamase Castle, Co. Laois, were destroyed and rendered permanently uninhabitable by the local Irish over the course of the 14th century[43].

8. The fifth masonry phase at Rindoon Castle

In 1574 the castle is referred to as the "Bare Castle" and it is mentioned as belonging to the Crown in 1603[44]. The physical evidence from the standing remains of the castle suggests that the destroyed parts of the old 13th-century curtain wall were replaced by a thinner wall that had gunloops in it (fig. 5). Gunloops were inserted into the still-upright remains of the old wall at ground level too and, also, into the second hall, argued above as having been built around 1300.

The best way to interpret this evidence is to suggest that the ruined castle was repaired by the Dublin government at some stage in the late 16th century, as part of the English policy of reconquest. Its strategic location on the Shannon must have been recognised again and so it was refortified and played some sort of role in pacifying Connacht during the latter period, especially during the very bloody Nine Years War of 1594-1603. It is noticeable that the last reference to the castle comes at the end of this war. It must have then fallen into ruin.

9. Conclusions

The castle controlled and dominated one of the best harbours along the Shannon. It was argued that a pre-Norman promontory fort does not exist at Rindoon. Instead, it is suggested that these earthworks represent the south-eastern defences of the later Anglo-Norman town. The pre-Norman fortress implied in the place-name *Rinn Duin* perhaps lies under the later Anglo-Norman masonry castle. It too was sited to control and take advantage of the harbour. This earlier fortification might have been built as a Viking longphort, a later O'Conor fortress or both.

The Anglo-Norman masonry castle was started in 1227. This royal castle has at least five identifiable architectural phases within it. These range in date from the early 13th century through to the very late 16th century. The shape and size of this Anglo-Norman castle were dictated by the morphology of the earlier pre-Norman fortress. The relatively small interior area of the castle meant that a decision was made not to build flanking towers along the length of the curtain wall, as to do so would have reduced the habitable space within it still further. Control of the base of the curtain wall was achieved instead by the use of a timber *hourd*. Defenders could fire down through openings at attackers. This all suggests that the existence of the earlier pre-Norman fortification not only dictated the morphology of the later castle, it also affected the choice of defences used in it.

The use of timber hourding, the well-defended gatehouse, the deep water-filled fosse and the high probability that serious wooden defences occurred around the outer edge of the latter feature all suggest that Rindoon Castle was far stronger in defensive terms than was once thought. This makes some sense as the historical sources suggest that it lay in a relatively turbulent border area, on the frontier between Gaelic- and Anglo-Norman dominated parts of Ireland.

Lastly, the siting of major buildings within the castle suggests that there was a deliberate attempt by its original builders and later occupants to make its whole north-western and northern façades very dramatic looking. These were the sides from which visitors approached the castle from both the main street of the town and from the Safe Harbour. There are also hints, no more, that the castle was framed by what could be described as a designed landscape, which may have included a rabbit warren, a windmill, a fishpond and a deer park. The concentration of the castle's most imposing-looking buildings along the whole north-western front of the castle and this possible designed landscape behind it gave a message of great power to the world and was a form of display. At first glance, given the fact that it was argued above that the defences of the castle were far stronger than was once thought, it may seem a needless exercise for the castle's builders to have

---

39. Bradley & Dunne 1988, 72; Harbison 1995, 144-145.
40. Bradley & Dunne 1988, 73; Harbison 1995, 146.
41. Bradley & Dunne 1988, 73.
42. *Ibid.*, 74.
43. O'Conor & Manning 2002; see Hodkinson 2003, 43.
44. Bradley & Dunne 1988, 73.

created such a display, which was in turn maintained by the fortress's occupants into the early 14th century, especially as the area around Rindoon was troubled and subject to much warfare. Nevertheless, as argued by O'Conor, such a power display was as important in warlike border regions as it was in peaceful areas, if not more so. The control of great resources, wealth and power implied in the construction of a castle with imposing buildings within it, set within a designed landscape, must have acted as a deterrent against military attack, as much as strong defences would have done. Simply, the message would have been that all the power implied in the creation of a great castle and its associated elite landscape could be brought to bear upon an enemy, if he dared attack. Theoretically, any potential attacker, upon seeing such a castle and landscape, would have realised that he could not possibly match the resources of the castellan and so would have desisted from hostile action[45]. The concentration of imposing buildings along the whole north-western front of Rindoon Castle and the hints of a designed landscape behind it were a form of "symbolic violence", a strong message from the Dublin government, that was supposed to have acted as a deterrent against aggression from all potential enemies in the region, in particular the powerful O'Conor kings of Connacht. In reality, as was so often the case, the castle's defences and messages of power proved unable to stop Gaelic-Irish aggression in the 14th century.

45. O'Conor 2008, 335.

Bibliography

Barry T. B. (1987), *The Archaeology of Medieval Ireland*, London/New York, Methuen.

Bradley J. (1995), *Walled Towns in Ireland*, Dublin, Country House.

Bradley J. & Dunne N. (1988), *Urban Archaeological Survey – County Roscommon* [limited distribution], Dublin, Office of Public Works.

Creighton O. (2002), *Castles and Landscapes*, London, Continuum.

– (2009), *Designs upon the Land. Elite Landscapes of the Middle Ages*, Woodbridge/Rochester, The Boydell Press.

De Meulemeester J. & O'Conor K. (2007), "Fortifications", in *The Archaeology of Medieval Europe*, vol. 1: *Eighth to Twelfth Centuries AD*, J. Graham-Campbell & M. Valor (eds.), Aarhus, Aarhus University Press (Acta Jutlandica. Humanistisk serie; 79), 316-341.

Edwards N. (1990), *The Archaeology of Early Medieval Ireland*, London, Batsford.

Fitzpatrick J. E. (1935), "Rinndown Castle", *The Journal of the Royal Society of Antiquaries of Ireland*, 65, 177-190.

Flanagan M. T. (1996), "Irish and Anglo-Norman Warfare in Twelfth-Century Ireland", in *A Military History of Ireland*, T. Bartlett & K. Jeffery (eds.), Cambridge, Cambridge University Press, 52-75.

Freeman A. M. (ed.) (1944), *The Annals of Connacht*, Dublin, Dublin Institute for Advanced Studies.

Graham B. J. (1988), "Medieval Settlement in County Roscommon", *Proceedings of the Royal Irish Academy*, 88c, 19-38.

Gravett C. (2009), *English Castles (1200-1300)*, Oxford/New York, Osprey.

Harbison S. (1995), "Rindown Castle: a Royal Fortress in Co. Roscommon", *The Journal of the Galway Archaeological and Historical Society*, 47, 138-148.

Hennessy W. M. (ed.) (1871), *The Annals of Loch Cé*, London, Longman.

Hennessy W. M. & McCarthy B. (eds.) (1887-1901), *The Annals of Ulster*, Dublin, Stationery Office, 4 vols.

Hodkinson B. (2003), "A Summary of Recent Work at the Rock of Dunamase, Co. Laois", in *The Medieval Castle in Ireland and Wales. Essays in Honour of Jeremy Knight*, J. R. Kenyon & K. O'Conor (eds.), Dublin, Four Courts Press, 32-49.

Johnson M. (2002), *Behind the Castle Gate. From Medieval to Renaissance*, London/New York, Routledge.

King D. J. C. (1988), *The Castle in England and Wales. An Interpretative History*, London/New York, Routledge.

Lepage J.-D. (2002), *Castles and Fortified Cities of Medieval Europe. An Illustrated History*, Jefferson (N.C.)/London, McFarland.

Liddiard R. (2000), *"Landscapes of Lordship". Norman Castles and the Countryside in Medieval Norfolk, 1066-1200*, Oxford, Archaeopress (BAR. British Series; 309).

McNeill T. E. (1997), *Castles in Ireland. Feudal Power in a Gaelic World*, London/New York, Routledge.

– (2001), "Castles", in *Medieval Archaeology. An Encyclopedia*, P. J. Crabtree (ed.), London/New York, Garland, 43-46.

Morris R. (1998), "The Architecture of Arthurian Enthusiasm: Castle Symbolism in the Reigns of Edward I and his Successors", in *Armies, Chivalry and Warfare in Medieval Britain and France*, M. Strickland (ed.), Stamford, Watkins (Harlaxton Medieval Studies. New Series; 7), 63-81.

Murphy M. & O'Conor K. (2006), "Castles and Deer Parks in Anglo-Norman Ireland", *Eolas. The Journal of the American Society of Irish Medieval Studies*, 1, 53-70.

Naessens P. & O'Conor K. (2012), "Pre-Norman Fortification in Eleventh- and Twelfth-Century Connacht", in *Château Gaillard 25. L'origine du château médiéval*, P. Ettel, A.-M. Flambard Héricher & K. O'Conor (eds.), Caen, Publications du CRAHM, 259-268.

O'Conor K. (1998), *The Archaeology of Medieval Rural Settlement in Ireland*, Dublin, Royal Irish Academy (Discovery Programme Monograph; 3).

– (2008), "Castles Studies in Ireland – the Way forward", in *Château Gaillard 23. Bilan des recherches en castellologie*, P. Ettel, A.-M. Flambard Héricher & T. E. McNeill (eds.), Caen, Publications du CRAHM, 329-339.

– (2011), "Fortifications in the North", in *The Archaeology of Medieval Europe*, vol. 2: *Twelfth to Sixteenth Centuries*, M. Carver & J. Klapste (eds.), Aarhus, Aarhus University Press (Acta Jutlandica. Humanistisk serie; 9), 243-260.

O'Conor K. & Manning C. (2002), "Clonmacnoise Castle", in *Clonmacnoise Studies*, vol. 2: *Seminar Papers 1998*, H. A. King (ed.), Dublin, Dúchas, 137-165.

O'Conor K. et al. (2010), "The Rock of Lough Cé, Co. Roscommon", in *Medieval Lough Cé. History, Archaeology and Landscape*, T. Finan (ed.), Dublin, Four Courts Press, 15-40.

Ó Corráin D. (1972), *Ireland before the Normans*, Dublin, Gill and Macmillan (Gill History of Ireland; 2).

Ó Cróinín D. (1995), *Early Medieval Ireland, 400-1200*, London/New York, Longman (Longman History of Ireland).

Orpen G. H. (2005), *Ireland under the Normans*, Dublin, Four Courts Press.

Sweetman D. (1999), *Medieval Castles of Ireland*, Cork, Collins Press.

Sweetman H. S. (ed.) (1875-1886), *Calendar of Documents Relating to Ireland, 1171-1307*, London, Longman, 5 vols.

Valante M. A. (2008), *The Vikings in Ireland. Settlement, Trade and Urbanization*, Dublin, Four Courts Press.

Leisure, Symbolism and War:
Hermitage Castle, Liddesdale and the Anglo-Scottish Border

◆

Richard Oram*

The Anglo-Scottish border is popularly perceived as a militarised frontier, ravaged by warfare and wracked by endemic feud and casual violence. It is difficult to refute that view in a landscape where rival rulers and their magnates invested in castle-building, and where literary tradition has fixed a vision of state-sponsored violence and social disorder in the popular canon of folk-history. It was, however, not always so, for the contested frontier of popular tradition became established only in the 15th century after 150 years of intermittent warfare that saw the border line advance and recede with the fluctuating fortunes of the two kingdoms. Until that warfare began in 1296, the border had been stable for 140 years and, unlike the Welsh March or the frontier between the English and Gaelic Irish, comparatively lightly fortified: there were few major castles in a broad swathe of territory on either side of the frontier.

It is not that there was no need for defence or the construction of symbols of lordship, for this was a "new" border created as two expanding powers – Scotland and England – absorbed a third (Northumbria) that once lay between them. Scottish ambitions to continue to expand southwards were balanced in the 11th century by English domination of Scotland and the forging of personal bonds between their rulers, culminating in the marriage of David, younger brother of the Scottish king, to the heiress of Northumbria. Until 1124, the couple ruled a semi-independent principality where David settled knights drawn from the Norman elite of England. He gave them extensive lordships with privileged jurisdictions, whose economic potential was largely untapped and whose political infrastructure was rudimentary. The new lords began to construct an apparatus of power modelled on Anglo-Norman systems, where castles and their intensively-managed hinterlands projected their lordly authority. Until he succeeded to the Scottish throne in 1124, David had a closer relationship with England than with his homeland to the north, a link strengthened by the familial ties of his knightly colonists. This trend climaxed in 1138-1157, when David annexed much of English Northumbria during a long period of civil war in England. His expanded realm now pivoted on an axis between Roxburgh in South-East Scotland and Carlisle in North-West England; the former border zone had moved from liminality to centrality in an enlarged Scottish state. Although this expanded realm lasted barely 20 years, socio-economic and cultural bonds forged in that brief episode endured into the 13th century and had a powerful influence over how lordly authority was displayed locally.

Of the landholdings created by David, the lordship of Liddesdale is one of the least well documented; all that can be said with certainty is that before c. 1140 he granted Ranulf de Sules the uplands north of the valley of the Liddel Water – the river forming the Anglo-Scottish border on this section of the pre-1138 frontier. No crown charter survives so there is no explicit record of Ranulf's tenurial status, only incidental references in later de Sules' charters. On the basis of Ranulf's gift to Jedburgh Priory of a tenth of all venison caught in Liddesdale, one privilege was possession of a baronial hunting forest[1]. By the same grant Ranulf also gave the parish church of Castleton, which he may have founded and over which he held rights of patronage[2]. A dependent settlement – the "Castleton" from which the parish took its name – is on record by 1275[3].

---

* Professor of Environmental and Medieval History, University of Stirling, United Kingdom.

1. Barrow 1999, no. 167; Gilbert 1979, 21.
2. Barrow 1999, no. 167; RCAHMS 1956, no. 60.
3. Anon. 1843, lxv. RCAHMS 1956, no. 64, states incorrectly that Castleton is recorded in 1220 (Anon. 1843, no. 114).

Fig. 1 – Liddel Castle, bank and ditch of the original caput of Liddesdale. Photo R. Oram.

Fig. 2 – Hermitage, bank and ditch of possible 13th-century hunting-lodge site west of the chapel. Photo R. Oram.

Castleton's name records the location of Liddel Castle, the original de Sules' *caput*, adjacent to the church site (NY509899) (fig. 1)[4]. Only unexcavated earthworks remain of this substantial enclosure castle and little is known of its history beyond the fact that it was still occupied as late as 1298[5]. However, a list of castles that surrendered to the invading Edward I of England in 1296 included "the castle which is called Hermitage of Soules"[6], as distinct from Liddel. The first explicit reference to two castles dates from 1300 when Edward wrote to his keeper of the castles of "Lydel" and "Eremitage-Soules"[7]. The old *caput* was abandoned apparently shortly afterwards in favour of Hermitage, which is located 6 km from Castleton, away from the border.

Despite this late first record, Hermitage may date to the early 1240s when the building of two unnamed castles was amongst factors that brought Scotland and England to the brink of war[8]. No contemporary accounts name the castles involved, but 14th-century sources identify one as Hermitage[9]. These references might imply the presence of an earlier castle beneath the present building, but none of that structure predates the mid-14th century[10]. However, on a terrace between the Hermitage Water and the hillside on the north side of the valley, 500m west of the present castle, are the remains of an early 13th-century chapel, and to its west an earthwork that may mark the site of an older residence (fig. 2)[11]. In the 1950s it was mooted that the earthworks represented the 1240s castle, but that possibility was dismissed since they seemed too slight and their location indefensible[12]; awkwardly crowded onto a cramped terrace overlooked from its north, it was no fortress. A second de Sules' residence so close to Castleton and in use contemporaneously suggests a specialist function. Small-scale, lightly defended and in a secluded location, it was perhaps a hunt-hall within the de Sules' baronial forest.

Why Hermitage supplanted Liddel is unknown, but Liddel's frontier position harked back to a more peaceful age. An opportunity to develop Hermitage as a more securely located alternative occurred in a brief pause in the conflict between 1327 and 1332. Old Hermitage, however, was unsuitable so building commenced on a more spacious site 0.5 km to the east on a broad platform above the river. The new castle was perhaps of earthwork and timber construction, represented now by portions of the bank and ditch enclosure around the present building[13]. At some stage in the mid-14th century, probably during a second episode of relative security when Liddesdale was under English occupation, held by the English Dacre family, a stone-built lodging was erected within the enclosure, with opposed ranges flanking a small courtyard. Confidence in the stability of the prevailing political settlement determined the non-defensive character of this English-style manor-house, the remains of which form the oldest upstanding stonework of the castle (fig. 3).

In its present form, however, Hermitage is a monolith with walls rising sheer to a uniform height, crowned by an oversailing parapet and wall-walk (fig. 4). This uniformity is deceptive: stonework analysis reveals that this appearance evolved piecemeal and received its current finish during heavy-handed restoration in the 1830s[14]. What was produced then was a romantic vision of the grim fortress which Hermitage was believed to have been, and the image of a cheerless, forbidding tower which it projected remains fixed in the popular consciousness, for it typifies the idea of castles as uncompromising fortresses, cold and unyielding to any sense of comfort

---

4. RCAHMS 1956, no. 64.
5. *Ibid.*
6. LUARD 1859, 311-312.
7. BAIN 1884, no. 1165.
8. LUARD 1877, 380.
9. SKENE 1872, 287.
10. RCAHMS 1956, 82, no. 63.
11. *Ibid.*, 75, no. 62.
12. *Ibid.*
13. Http://canmore.rcahms.gov.uk/en/site/67915/details/hermitage+castle/.
14. RCAHMS 1956, 77, no. 63.

Fig. 3 – Hermitage, central courtyard of the mid-14th-century manor-house. Photo R. Oram.

Fig. 4 – Hermitage, general view of the castle from the south-west, showing the parapet and upper works as restored in the early 19th century. Photo R. Oram.

or refinement. This vision of castles in Scotland's past was in the spirit of that age, where buildings were seen to reflect the culture of past eras, rough, isolated from European trends, and lacking in wealth and sophistication, the bleakness compounded by the fact that Hermitage was supposedly a frontier-post built for defence not comfort[15]. Seen stripped of its interior finish, the castle's stark ruin was visual confirmation of the proudly uncouth nature of Scotland's medieval nobility.

Despite present appearances, however, Hermitage challenges that orthodoxy: reanalysis in the 1980s offered a radically different view[16]. That analysis highlighted Hermitage's place as a residence of one medieval Scotland's greatest families – the Douglases – and how from the 1360s when the first Earl of Douglas secured possession it evolved on a grand scale to provide one of the largest volumes of residential accommodation available in any Scottish castle of that era. Of the more than 5,000 square metres of floor space within it, 3,700 was public and private residential space, with the remaining 1,300 service provision. A significant amount of room was needed for the Earl's military retinue[17], but its private space surpasses the accommodation in other Douglas castles. In scale but not plan it matches the earl's main residence at Tantallon; the need, however, was the same. He aspired to be the greatest lord in Southern Scotland and its principal defender against English aggression, commanding the loyalty of lesser families and projecting his power through the scale of his retinue and size of his household. Hermitage's developed form of four towers projecting from the angles of the central block that subsumed the earlier manor-house is, however, the product of the first Earl's illegitimate son George, first Earl of Angus, who competed with his cousin the third Earl of Douglas for

the headship of their kin and the dominant leadership role in the border region enjoyed by the first Earl. Angus constructed a new shell around his predecessors' residence, absorbing the older structure within it in a symbolic act which demonstrated continuity of power and lordship. Hermitage, with its sophisticated suite of semi-public and private chambers for Angus and his immediate family in the keep-like south-west tower (fig. 5), high-quality accommodation in the other angle-towers, multiple halls and ample storage, was designed as a physical setting where he could project those ambitions and where guests would have experienced his splendour and social superiority.

That projection of superiority extended beyond the castle to the organisation, division and exploitation of its environs. Visitors to Hermitage were made aware of the physical organisation of its setting and understood that they were traversing a landscape of economic as well as jurisdictional lordship; landscape features and the functions which they fulfilled were immediately recognisable visual indicators of power and status. Of those indicators, however, the most potent was designation as a hunting forest.

Hunting forests were far from static and economically sterile zones; they were dynamic economic resources exploited for more than simply game-meat[18]. How Liddesdale's status as forest affected its use can be glimpsed in two surveys concerning neighbouring English Liddel, the extent of the baronial forest there and late 13th-century non-hunting-related activity within it. The first is a 1276 inquest listing landed properties and various assarts within the forest[19]. The second is a 1282 survey that records the forest area and the value and use of an associated park[20]. The latter was "half a league in

---

15. MCKEAN 2001, 5-7.
16. TABRAHAM 1988, 267-276.
17. *Ibid.*, 270.
18. GILBERT 1979.
19. BAIN 1884, 19.
20. *Ibid.*, no. 208.

Fig. 5 – Hermitage, exterior of the south-west tower, which contained the principal apartments of the Douglas Earls. Photo R. Oram.

Fig. 6 – Hermitage, the White Dyke. Photo R. Oram.

precinct" (i.e. about 2.4 km around its boundary), and capable of sustaining 60 oxen or cows during the grazing season. The survey is explicit that the park was not for deer; "it being only enclosed for oxen and cows". The forest measured 34 km in length and 14.5 km in breadth for 19.3 km down its length, the remainder narrowing to 4.8 km. Its chief value was not for hunting but for grazing and associated rights. Pannage income, however, could not be extended for few oaks remained to provide the acorns upon which pigs grazed. The grazing of the forest was held by 139 rent-paying free farmers, while the sale of deadwood and windfall yielded further income. It is clear that the assarts were dispersed throughout the forest, were primarily arable clearances, and supported a substantial human population; far from being an unpeopled hunting reserve in a contested frontier zone, Liddel forest was a densely populated agricultural landscape.

Similar assarts can be identified in Scottish Liddesdale in surviving records from the era of Douglas ownership which detail the extent of the Forest of Liddesdale and the presence of parks at both Hermitage and Castleton[21]. A 1376 rental lists the components of the forest and their values; amongst them are *Park de Ermetag* and *Parkis de Casteltoun*[22]. Like the parks in English Liddel, these were cattle-grazing enclosures rather than fenced areas to hold deer as a live larder. In Liddesdale forest assarting was also well established and the 1376 rental names thirty individual examples, several of which have been identified in fieldwork[23].

Although Hermitage park is mentioned in 1376, there is no specific medieval record of deer-management arrangements. If the earthwork west of the chapel was a hunt-hall, a park might have been an associated feature. The first maps of Liddesdale date from only 1718 and show no park enclosure, but in 1750 and 1752 the survey and construction of a dyke for "Hermitage Park" was recorded[24]. That park, however, was not then designated as a "deer park" but in 1863 the first edition Ordnance Survey map labelled as "Deer Park" an area defined by a drystone wall known as the "White Dyke" that runs in an arc across the hillside north of the castle (fig. 6)[25]. Quite distinct in construction from other field walls in the district although built of locally occurring limestone blocks, its better preserved portions survive up to 1.5 m high on a base around 1.2 m wide; the enclosed area extends to 114 ha.

Does this feature define the 1376 park and was it associated originally with the early hunt-hall? The latter is unlikely: but

---

21. Dixon 2009, 27-46.
22. Anon. 1853, lxxiii.
23. *Ibid.*, appendix, no. 17; Gilbert 1979, 202; Dixon 1997, 345-354.
24. Canmore NY49NE 3 (date accessed 6 February 2012).
25. National Records of Scotland, RH4/23/178, 41.

Fig. 7 – Hermitage, the vestigial earthworks of the northern arc of the deer-trap looking south-east towards the castle. Photo R. Oram.

Fig. 8 – Hermitage, view south from the White Dyke over the later medieval park enclosure. Photo R. Oram.

there is reason to see the enclosure as a later development, superimposed on an earlier hunting landscape. The evidence for this is a deer-trap north-west of the castle formed by two arcs of earthen dyke that gradually converge over a distance of 300 m – now only some 0.5 m high but perhaps originally defined by a rail-and-post fence or pale – the space between them narrowing from 600 m at the north-west end to only 10m wide at the south-east (fig. 7)[26]. The converging dykes form a funnel leading to a killing-ground near the castle. The juxtaposition of castle and deer-trap, if contemporary, is a visual statement of the privileged status of Hermitage's lords. The forest rights of the de Sules family had been confirmed to the Douglases and, for a family striving to proclaim its status, the public performance of hunting rights was an important indicator of power. However, the drive to the killing-ground by the castle, from which onlookers could view the virile display of their Douglas lords, probably declined as conflict over possession of the district re-intensified in the late 1300s. Other priorities brought landscape reorganisation, leaving a redundant earthwork as a reminder of activities that once broadcast the status of the castle's owners.

Within the White Dyke boundary the deer-trap is useless; it is too large for an 114 ha-park and is a relic of an unenclosed landscape formalised through the physical presence of the trap structure. To observers from the castle, whose principal chambers overlook the killing-ground, the westwards view was framed by the divergent arms of the trap, but the park enclosure changed that perspective. The wider region remained hunting-ground where the Douglases exercised their hunting rights, but the area around the castle formed a zone of different economic organisation. It is likely that the area bounded by the White Dyke is the 1376 park and, while some sections of the wall are more recent, its course follows an old boundary represented by a bank and ditch continuing downhill from its south-eastern end. It is likely that this park, like those in English Liddel, was an enclosure juxtaposed with the castle to contain the demesne herd or flock: it offered security from both animal and human predators in an increasingly disturbed frontier-land (fig. 8).

What the 1376 rental otherwise records is a crowded and intensively exploited landscape upon which neither the wars nor plagues of the 14th century had made significant impacts. Although unquestionably in a border zone, Hermitage was not surrounded by war-devastated waste but was the thriving hub of a productive economic landscape: a centre of power where the Douglases broadcast their lordship through building a major stone castle, demonstrated the effectiveness of their authority through the protection that extended from that building over the surrounding communities, and impressed on their peers, dependents, domestic and foreign rivals the reality of their domination of the region and its people. At the time of the next snapshot of land-use in Liddesdale in 1541, the records reveal a striking change; the value of the estate had collapsed to one third of its 1376 level and around 25 % of the farms were vacant. There had, however, been little overall decline in the number of component properties in 1541 (146) as opposed to 1376 (157)[27]. Most striking, however, was the disappearance of Hermitage itself as a significant economic feature.

Various factors delivered this new situation: environmental and demographic change reducing land values; changes in the nature of Anglo-Scottish conflict; and Liddesdale's marginalisation in the Angus estate. From c. 1475 Hermitage ceased to be a regular residence of the Earls, being placed in

---

26. Http://canmore.rcahms.gov.uk/en/site/67915/details/hermitage+castle/.

27. National Records of Scotland, GD246/59 – Rental of Liddisdaill, 1541; Dixon 1997, 36.

the keepership of the Scotts of Buccleuch, but its importance as a place of strength had grown. In 1481 as war again loomed, the Scottish parliament ordered the repair and garrisoning of key border castles, including Hermitage and in 1482 placed 100 men there[28]. Edward IV of England also recognised its importance and required that it with Liddesdale and neighbouring Eskdale, Ewesdale and Annandale be ceded to him as payment for supporting a rebellion against the Scottish king[29]. Suspicions of Angus's treasonable dealings with England led in 1491 to his forced exchange of Hermitage for Bothwell in Clydesdale, an important property but safely remote from the border[30]. The next year, Hermitage was given to the new strongman in the border region, Patrick Hepburn, Earl of Bothwell, Angus's greatest rival[31].

This transfer occurred against a backdrop of mounting local disorder in part attributable to the decline of Hermitage as a regular residence of its lords. Legislation from the 1480s onwards reveals a perception of Liddesdale as a den of lawlessness, a position compounded by the deaths in 1513 of many of the regional leadership in the carnage of Flodden and the long minorities of their heirs which followed. Bothwell was amongst the dead and with his heir an infant, it was 20 years before the next Hepburn earl asserted local lordship. In the interim, the crown assumed responsibility for maintaining Hermitage: James V saw it as vital not only for consolidating his authority in the region but also for strengthening Scotland's defences against England, in 1540 assigning £100 for "beting and mending of the Heremytage"[32]. When war resumed in 1542, James sent gunners to the newly-strengthened castle to prepare for its defence against English attack, payment being made for taking artillery there from Edinburgh[33]. Despite the main action of the war occurring nearby at Solway Moss, however, Hermitage escaped assault, an experience that remained the norm for the final 60 years of its existence as a frontier defence. Although maintained and garrisoned by the Scotts of Buccleuch, it functioned more as a local police post than the high-status residence or strategic fortress that it had been developed as in the 14th century. Following Anglo-Scottish union in 1603, it lost even that local significance, its decline accelerated by its remoteness from the new main routes connecting the component parts of the realm and its irrelevance as a residence in the market-oriented economy of the Scott estate.

The experience of Hermitage recoverable from the records presents a striking contrast to its traditional depiction as a grim border fortress. Conceived first as part of a stable economic system within an equally stable political frontier, the early castle was a "trophy" possession whose associated deer-trap signalled its owners' privileged tenurial status to external observers. The loss of political stability after 1296 brought new significance to Hermitage, first as a secure location for the *caput* of the lordship, then as the site for an expression of confidence in future stability with the building of a new manor-house. This, in turn, became the basis for a bold assertion of regional power in the new castle of the first Earl of Douglas, itself hugely enlarged by his son. Their castles projected their military might and social elevation, underscoring their political ambitions at home and status as defenders of the border. It was also a social expression of power, a leisure complex which reflected status, an economic jewel in the Douglases' crown. Shifts in emphasis within the family's portfolio and relegation to a secondary place amongst their possessions led to Hermitage's socio-economic decline, the loss of its social significance as a hunting-lodge, and consolidation of its once secondary function as a garrison-post. Finally, rendered redundant when the military significance of the border ceased in 1603, the castle was abandoned as a worthless relic of unhappier times.

---

28. BROWN *et al.* 2007-2013; RPS 1481/4/9; RPS 1482/3/44 (date accessed 4 February 2012).
29. MACDOUGALL 1982, 153.
30. THOMSON *et al.* 1882-1914, vol. 2 (1882), nos. 2072, 2073, 2074.
31. *Ibid.*, vol. 2 (1882), no. 2092; National Records of Scotland, GD224/918/24.
32. DICKSON & BALFOUR PAUL 1877-1916, vol. 7 (1907), 289.
33. *Ibid.*, vol. 8 (1908), 110-111.

Bibliography

Unpublished sources

National Records of Scotland: GD246/59 – Rental of Liddisdaill, 1541; RH4/23/178 OS Name Book Roxburghshire, Castleton Parish, Pt 2.

Published sources

ANON. (ed.) (1843), *Registrum Episcopatus Glasguensis*, vol. 1, Edinburgh, Bannatyne Club.

– (ed.) (1853), *Registrum Honoris de Morton*, vol. 1, Edinburgh, Bannatyne Club.

Bain J. (ed.) (1884), *Calendar of Documents Relating to Scotland*, vol. 2, Edinburgh, General Register House.

Barrow G. W. S. (ed.) (1999), *The Charters of King David I. The Written Acts of David I King of Scots, 1124-53 and of his Son Henry Earl of Northumberland, 1139-52*, Woodbridge, Boydell Press.

Dickson T. & Balfour Paul J. (eds.) (1877-1916), *Accounts of the Lord High Treasurer of Scotland*, Edinburgh, General Register House, 12 vols.

Dixon P. (1997), "Settlement in the Hunting Forests of Southern Scotland in the Medieval and Later Periods", *Medieval Europe Brugge*, 6, 345-354.

– (2009), "Hunting, Summer Grazing and Settlement: Competing Land Use in the Uplands of Scotland", *Ruralia*, 7, 27-46.

Gilbert J. (1979), *Hunting and Hunting Reserves in Medieval Scotland*, Edinburgh, Donald.

Luard H. R. (ed.) (1859), *Bartholomæi de Cotton, monachi norwicensis, Historia anglicana (A.D. 449-1298): necnon ejusdem Liber de archiepiscopis et episcopis Angliæ*, London, Longman.

– (ed.) (1877), *Matthæi Parisiensi Monachi Sancti Albani, Chronica Majora*, vol. 4, London, Longman.

Macdougall N. (1982), *James III, a Political Study*, Edinburgh, Donald.

McKean C. A. (2001), *The Scottish Château: the Country House of Renaissance Scotland*, Stroud, Sutton.

Royal Commission on the Ancient and Historical Monuments of Scotland (RCAHMS) (1956), *An Inventory of the Ancient and Historical Monuments of Roxburghshire*, vol. 1, Edinburgh, Her Majesty's Stationery Office.

Skene W. F. (ed.) (1872), *John of Fordun's Chronicle of the Scottish Nation*, vol. 2, Edinburgh, Edmonston and Douglas (The Historians of Scotland; 4).

Tabraham C. J. (1988), "The Scottish Medieval Towerhouse as Lordly Residence in the Light of Recent Excavation", *Proceedings of the Society of Antiquaries of Scotland*, 118, 267-276.

Thomson J. M. *et al.* (eds.) (1882-1914), *Registrum Magni Sigilli Regum Scotorum*, Edinburgh, Her Majesty's General Register House, 11 vols.

Websites

Brown K. M. *et al.* (eds.) (2007-2013), *The Records of the Parliaments of Scotland to 1707*, St Andrews: http://www.rps.ac.uk.

Http://canmore.rcahms.gov.uk/en/site/67913/details/hermitage+hill+white+dyke, Canmore NY49NE 3 [accessed 6 February 2012].

Grenzburgen des Deutschen Ordens im Südosten Livlands

◆

Ieva Ose*

Die Einwohner Alt-Livlands, die im Territorium des jetzigen Lettland und Estland wohnten, wurden seit dem Ende des 12. Jahrhunderts von norddeutschen Bischöfen zum katholischen Glauben bekehrt. Das Land wurde von dem 1202 auf Initiative des Bischofs Albert von Riga zur Missionierung gegründeten Schwertbrüderorden (*Fratres miliciae Christi de Livonia*) erobert. Nach dem Untergang dieses Ordens in der Schlacht bei Saule wurden seine Überbleibsel 1237 dem Deutschen Orden als sein livländischer Zweig angeschlossen. In den ersten Jahrzehnten des 13. Jahrhunderts eroberte der Orden die Länder der Liven und Lettgaller an den großen Flüssen – an der Düna (lettisch: *Daugava*) und an der Livländischen Aa (Gauja) – sowie Südestland. Der südöstliche Teil des von den Lettgallern bewohnten Landes kam nach 1264 in deutsche Hand, als Papst Urban IV. dem Orden die Schenkung bestätigte, mit der der Fürst von Polotsk auf die lettgallischen Länder verzichtet hatte[1]. Bis 1267 wurde der westliche Teil des Landes, Kurland, unterworfen, aber die Länder in Semgallen kamen 1290 unter die Macht des Ordens, nachdem ein Teil der Semgaller nach Litauen ausgewandert war. Damit endeten die Feldzüge des Ordens in Livland. Nach der Niederschlagung des großen Aufstands der Esten verkaufte der König von Dänemark 1346 dem Orden Nordestland. Danach blieben die Grenzen Livlands etwa zwei Jahrhunderte unverändert.

Livland – der in der ersten Hälfte des 13. Jahrhunderts entstandene Livländische Staatenbund – setzte sich aus fünf kleineren Staaten zusammen, die dem Orden, dem Erzbischof von Riga sowie den Bischöfen von Dorpat, Ösel und Kurland unterstanden. Livland grenzte im Norden und Westen an die Ostsee, im Süden an die litauischen und im Osten an die russischen Länder (Abb. 1). Im 14. Jahrhundert entstand ein

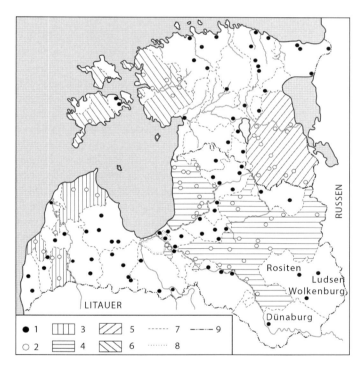

Abb. 1 – Livland im Mittelalter. 1) Ordensburgen; 2) bischöfliche Burgen; 3) Bistum von Kurland; 4) Erzbistum von Riga; 5) Bistum von Dorpat; 6) Bistum von Ösel-Wiek; 7) Grenzen der Komtureien und Vogteien; 8) Patrimonalgebiet der Stadt Riga; 9) ungefähre Grenze Livlands und heutige Grenzen Lettlands und Estlands. Zeichnung I. Ose.

gewisses Gleichgewicht zwischen Livland und seinen Nachbarn. Dem Streben des Ordens, neue Länder zu erobern, standen das wachsende Litauen im Süden und die mächtigen Republiken der reichen Kaufleute von Nowgorod und Pleskow sowie das Fürstentum Polotsk im Osten entgegen. Im

---

* Institut für die Geschichte Lettlands an der Universität Lettlands, Lettland.
1. Bunge 1853, Nr. 380.

Mittelalter gab es im südöstlichen Grenzgebiet Livlands viele natürliche Hindernisse – Flüsse und Seen, Wälder, Wildnisse und Sümpfe –; es fehlen in den Quellen aber Hinweise auf Kennzeichnungen der Grenze im Naturraum. Erst um 1400 begann das Präzisieren der äußeren Grenzen Livlands, als 1398 der Vertrag mit dem russischen Fürstentum Polotsk und 1426 mit Litauen geschlossen wurde[2]. Zuvor wurden in den Grenzgebieten sowohl vom Orden als auch von Litauern und Russen ständig gegenseitige Raubzüge und Plünderungen durchgeführt. Es waren Verheerungsfeldzüge, es wurde kein Land erobert. Ihr Ziel war vielmehr, im ausgewählten Nachbargebiet wehrfähige Männer zu erschlagen oder in Gefangenschaft zu nehmen, Burgen und Gesinde zu berauben, Haustiere und bewegliches Eigentum zu erbeuten. Wenn man das Beutegut nicht mitnehmen konnte, wurden Häuser und Vorräte verbrannt.

Aus der Chronik des Hermann von Wartberge kann man erfahren, dass im Laufe eines halben Jahrhunderts – in der Zeit von 1323 bis 1378 – der Orden 25 Raubzüge nach Russland und 40 Raubzüge nach Litauen durchführte. Russen fielen in derselben Zeit achtmal und die Litauer vierzehnmal in Livland ein[3]. Um die Grenzen gegen die Plünderer zu verteidigen und mögliche größere Einfälle zu verhindern, wurde vom Orden und dem Erzbischof von Riga längs der äußeren Grenze des Livländischen Staatenbundes eine Linie von 22 Grenzburgen gebildet. Diese Burgen waren gleichzeitig Verwaltungs- und Wirtschaftszentren der Herrschaftsgebiete, deshalb befanden sie sich in der Mitte jedes Gebietes oder an den Kreuzungen der Handelswege, aber nicht entlang der Grenze. Diese Lage abseits der Grenze war vorteilhaft, weil man ein Herrschaftsgebiet nur dann erobern konnte, wenn die Burg eingenommen wurde. Wenn die Burg von der Grenze entfernt gelegen war, wurde sie nicht immer in den Raubzügen der Feinde getroffen oder konnte noch rechtzeitig Verteidiger heranziehen. Grenzburgen wurden als Basis zum Sammeln des Ordensheeres vor den Plünderungen sowie als sichere Lagerstätte nach gelungenen Raubzügen verwendet.

In diesem Beitrag wird die Aufmerksamkeit dem südöstlichen Teil Livlands mit vier Ordensburgen – Wolkenburg (lettisch *Mākoņkalns*), Dünaburg (*Vecdaugavpils*), Rositen (*Rēzekne*) und Ludsen (*Ludza*) zugewandt. Dieses Territorium der Lettgaller hatte der Orden im zweiten Drittel des 13. Jahrhunderts etappenweise bekommen. Wann diese vier Burgen vom Orden gegründet wurden, ist unbekannt. Aufgrund der indirekten Geschichtsquellen wird vermutet, dass deutsche Stützpunkte anstelle dieser Burgen schon in den 60er bis 80er Jahren des 13. Jahrhunderts existiert haben könnten[4]. Nur eine Burg verlor ihre Bedeutung schon bald, während die anderen drei Burgen vom Orden nach und nach zu bedeutenden Steinbefestigungen umgebaut und bis zum Livländischen Krieg in der zweiten Hälfte des 16. Jahrhunderts aufrechterhalten wurden. Welche Bedeutung haben sie als Grenzburgen gehabt?

Im südöstlichen Teil Livlands baute der Orden seine Burgen an den Verkehrsstraßen, die in der vorigen Periode entstanden waren. Diese Straßen verbanden die größeren Siedlungen und wurden sowohl als Handels- als auch als Heerstraßen genutzt[5]. Die erste deutsche Burg in Lettgallen war die Komturei „Wolkenburg". Sie lag im Binnenland auf einer Erhöhung unweit der Kreuzung der Wege ein paar Kilometer vom großen Rāzna-See entfernt. Die Bauzeit der Burg ist nicht genau bekannt. Wolkenburg wurde 1263 zum ersten Mal in den Schriftquellen erwähnt, als ihr Komtur Theodorich (*Theodoricus commendator de Wolbenborch*) eine Urkunde ausstellte[6]. Zwar ist in der Literatur die Hypothese von der Existenz dieser Burg in der ersten Hälfte des 13. Jahrhunderts zu finden, doch gibt es dazu keine verlässlichen Daten. Deshalb hat der Historiker Friedrich Benninghoven darauf hingewiesen, dass es unbekannt sei, wann genau der Orden in der Zeit zwischen 1236 und 1260 das ostlettgallische Territorium erworben hat[7]. Die Wolkenburg verlor schon im letzten Viertel des 13. Jahrhunderts ihre Bedeutung, als in den 1270er Jahren das Zentrum der Komturei nach Dünaburg verlegt wurde. Deshalb wurden die Befestigungen von Wolkenburg im 14. Jahrhundert nicht mehr verbessert. Wann die Burg aufgelassen wurde, ist unbekannt.

Bis in unsere Tage hat sich die Burgruine Wolkenburg – eine 62,5 m lange, bis zu 7 m hohe und 3 m starke Schildmauer aus Feldstein und einzelnen Ziegeln – erhalten[8]. An beiden Enden der Mauer wurden in derselben Stärke rechtwinklig Vorsprünge, je knapp 10 m lang, angebaut (Abb. 2). Der Architekt Wilhelm Neumann führte 1888 an beiden Vorsprüngen Nachgrabungen durch und stellte fest, dass keine weiteren Fundamente vorhanden waren, dagegen befanden sich dort Kohlereste, die eine hölzerne Befestigung längs allen drei Seiten des Burgplateaus vermuten ließen[9]. Wilhelm Neumann vermutet, dass im Oberteil der Mauer ein 0,3 m breiter Absatz gewesen sei, wo sich ein Wehrgang befunden haben könnte. Folglich wurde die Schildmauer nur längs der nordwestlichen Seite der Kernburg errichtet, wo sich die einzige geneigte Böschung des Hügels befindet. Die anderen drei Seiten des Burgplateaus wurden mit niedrigen Erdwällen umgeben. Vielleicht wurde dort keine Mauer gebaut, weil der Hügel drei steile Abhänge hat. Vor der Schildmauer wurde ein trockener Graben gezogen und ein niedriger Erdwall gebildet. Auch innerhalb der Mauer wurde ein zur Mauer paralleler Graben gezogen. In der Mitte des Hofes war ein Brunnen, von dem sich eine etwa 4 m tiefe konische Vertiefung mit einem Durchmesser von circa 10 m erhalten hat. In den Urkunden gibt es keine Hinweise auf Überfälle der Wolkenburg.

2. Mugurēvičs 1999, 55.
3. Caune 2011, 53.
4. Caune & Ose 2004, 137ff.
5. Pāvulāns 1971, 118.
6. Bunge 1853, 482, Nr. 378.
7. Benninghoven 1965, 316.
8. Löwis of Menar 1926, 575.
9. Neumann 1890, 301.

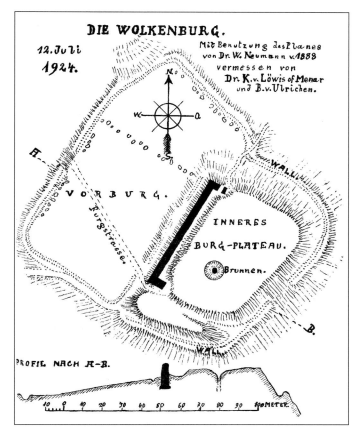

Abb. 2 – Grundriss von Wolkenburg (Löwis of Menar 1926).

Wie schon erwähnt, hat der Orden nach 1264 das ganze südlettgallische Gebiet erworben. Daraufhin wurde in den 1270er Jahren das Zentrum der Komturei nach Dünaburg verlegt. Der Grund dafür könnte die Lage der Wolkenburg tief im Binnenland sein, weil für Dünaburg die strategisch wichtige Lage an der Düna, der großen Wasserstraße unweit der Grenze des Ordenslandes mit Litauen und dem Fürstentum Polotsk ausgewählt wurde. Die Livländische Reimchronik berichtet, dass Dünaburg während der Regierungszeit des Landmeisters Ernst von Ratzeburg (Regierungszeit 1274-1279) erbaut wurde; Historiker vermuten den Bau der Burg zwischen 1274 und 1277[10]. Die 1982 bis 1987 durchgeführten Ausgrabungen von Ēvalds Mugurēvičs zeigten, dass vor der deutschen Burg an derselben Stelle vor dem 13. Jahrhundert eine Holzburg und Siedlung der Lettgaller vorhanden war[11]. Die im letzten Viertel des 13. Jahrhunderts von Deutschen neugebaute, hölzerne Dünaburg wurde 1305 von Litauern zerstört, aber vom Orden 1313 wieder aufgebaut. 1347 wurde die Burg vom Landmeister Goswin von Herreke zusätzlich um vier neue Türme erweitert sowie die Burgsiedlung befestigt[12].

Schon Ende des 19. Jahrhunderts gab es am Ort der Dünaburg kein aufgehendes Mauerwerk mehr zu sehen. Der Architekt Wilhelm Neumann hat den Grundriss der Burg entsprechend seinen 1888 durchgeführten Grabungen zeichnerisch rekonstruiert[13]. Dünaburg war auf einer erhöhten Landzunge zwischen zwei tiefen Schluchten situiert. Beide Vorburgen waren mit zwei Abschnittsgräben abgetrennt. Die Kernburg wurde von Wilhelm Neumann als eine 58 m lange und 14-26 m breite trapezförmige Befestigung mit zwei halbrunden Türmen an der Angriffsseite dargestellt[14]. Die Wohngebäude standen längs der westlichen und nördlichen Seite des Hofes. In den Ausgrabungen der 1980er Jahre wurden teils zwei Keller unter dem Westgebäude ausgegraben sowie das aus großen Feldsteinen gebildete Pflaster des Hofes stellenweise freigelegt. Man konnte feststellen, dass Wilhelm Neumann die Oberfläche der Mauern nur an einzelnen Stellen freigelegt hatte und einzelne Teile seines Grundrisses ohne empirische Belege ergänzt hatte. So wurde zum Beispiel im Jahr 2000 in den Ausgrabungen von Antonija Vilcāne festgestellt, dass sich in der südwestlichen Ecke der Kernburg, wo Wilhelm Neumann einen viereckigen Turm angenommen hatte, nur eine 2,4 m starke Außenmauer (Abb. 3), aber kein Turm befand[15]. Deshalb ist es auch nicht sicher, ob sich unter den Trümmern der Eingangsseite wirklich die von Wilhelm Neumann gezeichneten zwei runden Türme befunden haben.

In den Ausgrabungen der Burgruine hat man Artefakte des 14.-16. Jahrhunderts gefunden, darunter auch Pferdegeschirr, Teile der Rüstung, Pfeile und steinerne Kugeln der Feuerwaffen, die auf Feldzüge der Ordensbrüder hinweisen. Auf die Bedeutung von Dünaburg als Grenzfeste wird in den Chroniken hingewiesen. In der Livländischen Reimchronik wurde betont, dass man Dünaburg zur Betrübnis der Heiden und des litauischen Fürsten Thoreiden bauen ließ[16]. In der Chronik von Hermann von Wartberge wurden ausführlich mehrere vom Komtur von Dünaburg organisierte oder abgewehrte Raubzüge beschrieben. So kam zum Beispiel im März 1373 der Sohn des litauischen Königs mit 600 bewaffneten Männern an der Dünaburg an und brannte mehrere Häuser außerhalb der Burgsiedlung ab[17]. Im folgenden Jahr (1374) zog der Komtur von Dünaburg zur russischen „neuen Burg", tötete dort auf der Brücke drei Russen, nahm neun gefangen und erbeutete 70 Rinder. Die vor Ort von den Deutschen verzehrten und entführten Schafe waren dabei mitgezählt. Am 21. September desselben Jahres befand sich der Komtur von Dünaburg mit 100 Männern auf der Landstraße nach Russland, als die russischen Fürsten von Polotsk und Odrisk mit

---

10. Reimchronik 1998, 346.
11. Mugurēvičs 1985, 109.
12. Wartberge 2005, 65; 87.
13. Neumann 1890, Taf. 2,3.
14. *Ibid.*, 308.
15. Vilcāne 2002, 212.
16. Reimchronik 1998, 219.
17. Wartberge 2005, 129.

Abb. 3 – Archäologisch freigelegte Mauerreste der Dünaburg. Foto I. Ose (2003).

ihrem Heer zur Dünaburg kamen. Sie entwendeten Vieh des Komturs und der Bauern – Kühe, Schafe, Schweine und Pferde –, die sich außerhalb der Burg auf der Weide befanden. Von einem Gefangenen erfuhren die Russen, dass sich der Komtur auf einem Raubzug befände, woraufhin der Fürst Andei von Polotsk mit 250 Mann versuchte, die Deutschen einzuholen. Als die Kundschafter diese Nachricht dem Komtur überbrachten, änderte er seine Route und kehrte am nächsten Tag zur Dünaburg zurück. Die an der Burg gebliebene Mannschaft der Russen flüchtete[18]. Am 3. November des Folgejahres 1375 kam Fürst Andrei von Polotsk mit seinem Heer, Pferden und Schiffen zur Dünaburg, verbrannte die gesamten Heuvorräte des Komturs, entführte fünfzehn Personen und Pferde sowie alles Schlachtvieh, das der Komtur für ein ganzes Jahr besorgt hatte[19]. Am 12. August des folgenden Jahres 1376 versammelte der Komtur von Dünaburg die Ordensbrüder aus Rositen und Selburg sowie Männer des Erzbischofs von Riga, um die litauische „neue Burg" zu überfallen[20]. Dort wurden dreizehn Personen gefangengenommen und zwanzig Pferde getötet, außerdem Heu, Korn und die Brücke der Burg verbrannt. Die Beute wurde in 100 Booten mitgenommen.

Insgesamt zeigt sich somit, dass die Grenzburg Dünaburg als Ausgangspunkt und Heerlager für Raubzüge in die russischen und litauischen Länder diente. Gleichzeitig war die Burg das Verwaltungszentrum des vom Orden erworbenen Territoriums im südlichen Teil der lettgallischen Länder am rechten Ufer und der Selonen am linken Ufer der Düna. Die Dünaburg war der am weitesten nach Osten an der Düna gelegene Vorposten des Ordens, der diese wichtige Wasserstraße und das Grenzgebiet schützte und kontrollierte. Sie musste im 14. Jahrhundert Vorstöße der Litauer und Russen in das Ordensland abwehren. Die Dünaburg als Befestigung des Ordens bestand bis zum Livländischen Krieg in der zweiten Hälfte des 16. Jahrhunderts. 1582 wurde sie verlassen, als eine neue Befestigung von den neuen polnischen Landesherren mehrere Kilometer entfernt gebaut wurde.

Im 14. Jahrhundert kann man schon eine wichtige Landstraße im Süden der lettgallischen Länder belegen, die von Dünaburg nach Rositen und Ludsen und weiter nach Opotschka im Pleskower Land führte[21]. Neben dieser Straße wurde die Ordensburg „Rositen" als Zentrum einer Vogtei gebaut. Diese Vogtei war dem Komtur von Dünaburg unter-

18. Wartberge 2005, 133.
19. *Ibid.*, 141.
20. *Ibid.*, 143.
21. Pāvulāns 1971, Karte 4.

Abb. 4 – Burgruine Rositen. Foto I. Ose (2012).

stellt. Die 1980 bis 1982 von Ēvalds Mugurēvičs durchgeführten Ausgrabungen zeigten, dass an Stelle der Ordensburg im 13. Jahrhundert eine lettgallische Holzburg gestanden hatte[22]. Folglich nutzten die Deutschen nicht nur die schon in der vorchristlichen Periode entstandenen Straßen sondern auch die örtlichen Befestigungen sowohl in Dünaburg als auch in Rositen für ihre Stützpunkte. Vielleicht hielten sich die Deutschen dort schon in den 1280er Jahren auf, worauf hindeuten könnte, dass dieser Ortsname 1285 in den Urkunden aufkommt, als Ritter aus Rositen (*de Rositen*) die Männer von Pleskow überfallen hatten[23]. Als Ordensburg aber wurde Rositen erst 1324 erwähnt[24]. In der zweiten Hälfte des 14. Jahrhunderts wurde die Burg Rositen zur starken Befestigung ausgebaut. In der Chronik von Hermann von Wartberge wurden mehrere Raubzüge beschrieben, die mit der Burg Rositen verbunden waren. So plünderten Russen 1367 und 1373 einige Bauerndörfer des Vogtes von Rositen, während 1375 der Vogt von Rositen zusammen mit seinen und neugetauften Männern während des Raubzugs im Polotsker Land 100 Pferde und 86 Personen gefangen nahm[25]. Im folgenden Jahr, als am 12. August 1376 die Ordensbrüder aus Rositen unter der Leitung des Komturs von Dünaburg an den Raubzügen in Litauen teilnahmen, brannte der Fürst von Polotsk alles vor der Burg Rositen nieder (*cremavit omnia ante castrum*[26]). Der Meinung von Ēvalds Mugurēvičs zufolge, hat man darunter hölzerne Gebäude vor der Burg zu verstehen[27]. Im 15. Jahrhundert und in der ersten Hälfte des 16. Jahrhunderts ist Rositen eine der wichtigsten Befestigungen des Ordens an der südöstlichen Grenze Livlands gewesen. Der Vogt von Rositen musste den Vorgängen in den russischen Ländern – besonders um Pleskow – folgen, weil der Komtur von Dünaburg sich meistens auf die Ereignisse in Litauen konzentrierte.

Die Burg Rositen hat sich bis in unsere Tage als Ruine erhalten (Abb. 4). Die Burg ist am rechten Ufer des gleichnamigen Flusses gelegen und war von einem Altarm des Flusses anstelle eines künstlichen Grabens umgeben (Abb. 5). Die auf einem Hügel gelegene Befestigung bestand aus einer Kernburg, die im Grundriss ein unregelmäßiges Fünfeck bildet, und einer großen polygonalen Vorburg. Die Ausmaße der Kernburg sind 66 x 40 m. Längs von drei Seiten der Burgen standen die Wohngebäude. Die Vorburg nimmt eine Fläche von etwa 0,6 ha ein und war vermutlich nur mit Holzgebäuden bebaut. Wie die Ausgrabungen von Ēvalds Mugurēvičs zeigen, wurde anfänglich der alte Graben der lettgallischen Burg beibehalten, der die Kernburg der Ordensburg von der später gebildeten Vorburg abtrennte. Als eine Mauer um die Vorburg gebaut wurde, schüttete man den alten Graben zu. Bei den Ausgrabungen wurde festgestellt, dass der Eingang in die Kernburg nicht an der nordöstlichen Seite lag, wie von Wilhelm Neumann Ende des 19. Jahrhunderts vermutet. Vielmehr wurden an diesem Ort zwei beheizbare Gebäude und daneben der viereckige Turm – im Grundriss 3 x 3 m groß, mit 1,4 m starken Wänden und einem Eingang von der Seite der Kernburg – freigelegt. Der Turm wurde nicht früher als im 16. Jahrhundert gebaut. Er ist bis auf die Höhe des ersten Stockwerkes erhalten. Bei den Ausgrabungen wurden in den Schichten des 14.-16. Jahrhunderts Armbrustpfeile sowie steinerne Kugeln der Feuerwaffen gefunden[28]. Im Inventar der

22. Mugurēvičs 2011, 241.
23. *Ibid.*, 245.
24. Löwis of Menar 1922, 107.
25. Wartberge 2005, 107; 133; 137.
26. *Ibid.*, 144.
27. Mugurēvičs 2011, 247.
28. *Ibid.*, 260.

Abb. 5 – Situationsplan der Burgruine Rositen (Mugurēvičs 2011).

Burg von 1560, als Rositen von Polen übernommen wurde, sind elf verschiedene Geschütze (*steinbusse, serpentiner, schiven rohr, plumpkuilen, knipkernen*), 25 Hakenbüchsen (*haken, dubbelde haken*), zwei Tonnen Pulver und 1000 Kugeln erwähnt[29]. Es gibt aber keine sicheren Belege dafür, dass die Burg Rositen mit Kanonentürmen ausgestattet gewesen wäre. Die von Wilhelm Neumann vermuteten runden Türme[30] sind auf seinem Plan von 1888 als knapp aus der Mauer vorgeschoben eingezeichnet. Da jedoch weder aufgehendes Mauerwerk erhalten ist noch Ausgrabungen an den fraglichen Stellen stattgefunden haben, ist es nicht sicher, ob dort wirklich Türme standen und, falls ja, welche Form sie hatten.

30 km von Rositen entfernt wurde als Hilfsburg dieser Vogtei – fast an der Grenze zu den russischen Gebieten – die Ordensburg Ludsen erbaut. Ihre Bauzeit ist unbekannt. Schon 1286 befand sich in Ludsen vermutlich ein Stützpunkt der

---

29. Mugurēvičs 2011, 258.

30. Neumann 1890, Taf. 4.

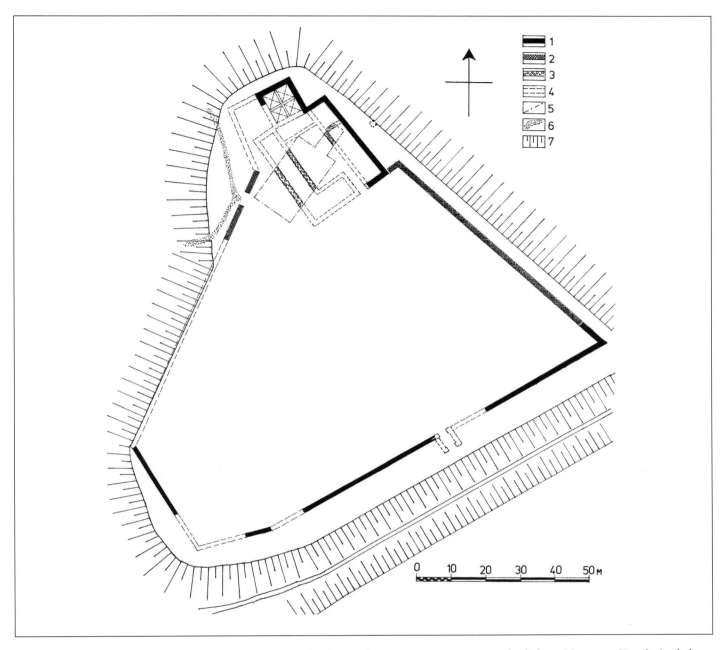

Abb. 6 – Grundriss der Burgruine Ludsen. Aufmessung und Rekonstruktion von CAUNE 2014, 103: 1) erhaltene Mauer aus Ziegel; 2) erhaltene Mauer aus Feldstein (Granit); 3) archäologisch freigelegte Fundamente; 4) vermutliche Mauer unter der Erde; 5) Platz der 1976 durchgeführten Ausgrabungen; 6) vermutlich ehemaliger Weg; 7) Abhang.

Deutschen. Darauf deutet hin, dass im Rigaer Schuldbuch der deutsche Kaufmann Heinrich von Ludsen (*Heinricus juvenis de Ludze; Heinricus de Ludzen*) genannt ist[31]. Urkundlich wurde die Ordensburg Ludsen erst 1433 erwähnt, und es ist zu vermuten, dass die Steinburg im 14. Jahrhundert gebaut wurde[32]. In den 1976 von Jolanta Daiga durchgeführten Ausgrabungen wurden im Hof der Kernburg auch Waffen und Pferdegeschirr gefunden[33], die auf das Leben der Ordensbrüder hinweisen. Funde, die nähere Aussagen zur Datierung der Bauzeit der Burg ermöglichen würden, liegen hingegen leider nicht vor.

Die Burg ist auf einer 18 m hohen Landzunge zwischen dem Großen und Kleinen Ludza-See situiert (Abb. 6). Auf dem Hügel mit natürlich steilen Abhängen an drei Seiten wurde an der Landseite ein Abschnittsgraben angelegt. Die geräumige

---

31. HILDEBRAND 1872, Nr. 1020ff.
32. OSE 2012, 170.
33. DAIGA 2011, 201.

Abb. 7 – Burgruine Ludsen. Foto I. Ose (2012).

Vorburg wurde mit einer Schutzmauer umgeben und war für das Sammeln von Heeresaufgeboten geeignet (Abb. 7).

Im Herrschaftsgebiet Ludsen gab es viele Wildnisse, undurchdringliche Sümpfe, Heiden, weit ausgedehnte Wälder und Seen, die natürliche Hindernisse bildeten. Deshalb waren nur einzelne Wegstrecken für den Verkehr geeignet[34]. Der Weg von der russischen Grenze zum Zentrum Livlands führte an der Burg Ludsen entlang, weshalb die Hauptaufgabe dieser Befestigung im Schutz des Ordenslandes – besonders der Vogtei Rositen – vor Überfällen aus den russischen Gebieten bestand. Bei Grenzkonflikten war Ludsen fast immer als erste Ordensburg betroffen. Als 1501 und 1503 das russische Heer in das Ordensland eindrang, wurde das Herrschaftsgebiet Ludsen geplündert[35]. Der Chronist Johann Renner berichtet, dass schon 1557 die Russen im Herrschaftsgebiet Rositen Güter und Dörfer verwüstet hätten, die in der Burg Ludsen gesammelten deutschen Heerschaften aber einen Gegenangriff gestartet hätten[36]. Als Ludsen 1560 von Polen übernommen wurde, gab es in ihrem Arsenal vier Kanonen und andere Waffen, anderthalb Tonnen Pulver und 1000 Kugeln[37]. Dennoch wurde Ludsen 1577 vom russischen Zaren Ivan IV. nach kurzem Beschuss eingenommen, da sich die Kernburg in derselben Höhe wie der danebenliegende Hügel befindet, sodass die Einnahme der Burg mit Feuerwaffen leicht zu bewerkstelligen war. Darauf wurde auch in der 1599 verfertigten Revision der Burg hingewiesen[38]. Danach begann die Burg allmählich zu verfallen; im 18. Jahrhundert wurde sie verlassen.

Diese Übersicht zeigt, dass Dünaburg, Rositen und Ludsen im 14. Jahrhundert bedeutende Befestigungen des Ordenslandes an der südöstlichen Grenze Livlands waren. Sie wurden sowohl als Schutz gegen die Einfälle der Russen und Litauer, als auch für die Lagerung von Nahrungsmitteln und Waffen für Raubzüge des Ordens in die Nachbarterritorien verwendet. Alle drei Burgen hatten große Vorburgen, wo man eine größere Heeresmenge versammeln konnte.

Im 15. Jahrhundert änderte sich die Bedeutung dieser Burgen. Nach der Schlacht bei Tannenberg im Jahr 1410 entstand der mächtige Staat Polen-Litauen, der die Fürstentümer Polotsk und Witebsk umschloss. Am 27. September 1422 schlossen die Herrscher Polens und Litauens mit dem Hochmeister von Preußen und Landmeister von Livland einen Friedensvertrag. Im Gefolge davon wurde 1426 die Grenze zwischen Litauen und Livland in der Natur markiert. Der letzte Versuch des Ordens im Jahr 1435, Litauer in der Schlacht bei Ukmerge an der Sventoja zu unterdrücken, endete mit einer Niederlage des Ordens und im selben Jahr wurde Frieden geschlossen. Damit endeten die gegenseitigen Raubzüge an der südlichen und südöstlichen Grenze Livlands und lange Jahre des Friedens begannen[39].

An der östlichen Grenze Livlands hingegen nahm im 15. Jahrhundert die Kriegsgefahr von der Seite des wachsenden Großfürstentums Moskau zu. In den 1460er Jahren begannen die Russen, ihre Grenzburgen zu befestigen. Anstelle der bisherigen kleinen Scharmützel begannen nun größere Auseinandersetzungen. 1480 belagerte das Heer Livlands das russische Pleskow, während 1481 ein großes Heer der Moskowiter in Livland eindrang. In Südestland gelang ein Vorstoß bis Fellin und im Zentrum Livlands bis Rujen und Kokenhu-

---

34. Stern 1926, 235.
35. Löwis of Menar 1922, 80.
36. Renner 1876, 173, 253.
37. *Ibid.*, 279.
38. Neumann 1890.
39. Šterns 1997, 404.

sen⁴⁰. Obwohl gleich danach der Orden Frieden mit Moskau schloss, wurden die militärischen Aktivitäten auf russischer Seite am Anfang des 16. Jahrhunderts erneut aufgenommen. Nachdem der Landmeister Wolter von Plettenberg 1502 in der Schlacht bei Smolin dem Heer des moskauischen Großfürsten eine Niederlage bereitet hatte, schloss man 1503 wieder einen Frieden, der bis zum Ausbruch des Livländischen Kriegs im Jahre 1558 mehrmals verlängert wurde.

Die steigende Aggressivität der Russen zwang die livländischen Herrscher, ihre Burgen an der östlichen Grenze – im Territorium des jetzigen Estland – zu befestigen. Solche Umbauten fanden besonders am Ende des 15. und Anfang des 16. Jahrhunderts von Narva bis Nordlettgallen statt. Es scheint aber, dass die Burgen an der südöstlichen Grenze, die in diesem Beitrag behandelt wurden, im 15.-16. Jahrhundert ohne große Modernisierung blieben, wie es besonders anschaulich im Fall von Ludsen zu sehen ist. Da an dieser Grenze mit Litauen fester Frieden geschlossen war, gab es im 15. Jahrhundert keine Raubzüge mehr. Eine weitere Befestigung dieser Burgen war daher vermutlich nicht notwendig und der Orden setzte seine Mittel für die Modernisierung der Burgen an der bedrohten Ostgrenze ein. Entsprechend zeigt der Bau von Befestigungen des Ordens an, in welcher Zeitperiode welcher Abschnitt der Grenze Livlands bedroht war.

40. *Ibid.*, 410.

Literatur

BENNINGHOVEN F. (1965), *Der Orden der Schwertbrüder. Fratres milicie Christi de Livonia*, Köln/Graz, Böhlau (Ostmitteleuropa in Vergangenheit und Gegenwart; 9).

BUNGE F. G. (1853) (hrsg.), *Liv-, Est- und Curländisches Urkundenbuch*, Bd. I, Reval, Kluge und Ströhm.

CAUNE A. (2011), "Livonijas robežpilis 13.-16. gadsimtā", in *Pētījumi un avoti par Livonijas ordeņpilīm*, I. OSE (hrsg.), Riga, Latvijas Vēstures Institūta Apgāds (Latvijas viduslaiku pilis; 7), 52-94.

– (2014), "Ludzas ordeņpils plāna rekonstrukcija", in *Pētījumi un avoti par ordeņa un bīskapu pilīm Latvijā*, I. OSE (hrsg.), Rīga, Latvijas vēstures institūta apgāds (Latvijas viduslaiku pilis; 8), 85-131.

CAUNE A. & OSE I. (2004), *Latvijas 12 gadsimta beigu – 17. gadsimta vācu piļu leksikons*, Riga, Latvijas Vēstures Institūta Apgāds (Latvijas viduslaiku pilis; 4).

DAIGA J. (2011), "Arheoloģiskie pētījumi Ludzas pils pagalmā 1976. gadā", in OSE 2011 (hrsg.), 194-215.

HILDEBRAND H. (1872) (hrsg.), *Das rigische Schuldbuch (1286-1352)*, Sankt Petersburg, Eggers.

LÖWIS OF MENAR K. (1922), *Burgenlexikon für Alt-Livland. Mit 24 Plänen und 56 Ansichten*, Riga, Verlag der Aktiengesellschaft Walters und Rapa.

– (1926), "Die Wolkenburg", *Mitteilungen aus der livländischen Geschichte*, 23, 575-577.

MUGURĒVIČS E. (1985), "Die archäologischen Ausgrabungen im Burgflecken bei der alten Dünaburg", in *Beiträge zur Geschichte der Kunst im Ostseeraum*, E. BÖCKLER (hrsg.), Bad Homburg, Martin-Carl-Adolf-Böckler-Stiftung (Homburger Gespräch; 6), 106-115.

– (1999), "Novadu veidošanās un to robežas Latvijas teritorijā (12. gs.-16. gs. vidus)", in *Latvijas zemju robežas 1000 gados*, A. CAUNE (hrsg.), Riga, Latvijas Vēstures Institūta Apgāds, 54-90.

– (2011), "Rēzeknes pils un novada vēsture 9.-17. gs. pēc rakstītiem avotiem un arheoloģisko izrakumu datiem", in OSE 2011 (hrsg.), 238-274.

NEUMANN W. (1890), "Die Ordensburgen im sog. polnischen Livland", *Mitteilungen aus der livländischen Geschichte*, 14, 299-323.

OSE I. (2012), "Ludsen – im 14. Jh. gebaute Grenzburg des Deutschen Ordens in Livland", in *Zwischen Kreuz und Zinne. Festschrift für Barbara Schock-Werner zum 65. Geburtstag*, T. BITTERLI-WALDVOGEL (hrsg.), Braubach, Deutsche Burgenvereinigung (Veröffentlichungen der Deutschen Burgenvereinigung. Reihe A; 15), 169-175.

PĀVULĀNS V. (1971), *Satiksmes ceļi Latvijā 13.-17. gs*, Riga, Zinātne.

REIMCHRONIK (1998), *Atskaņu hronika [Livländische Reimchronik]*, Riga, Zinātne.

RENNER J. (1876), *Livländische Historien*, Göttingen, Vandenhoeck und Ruprecht.

Stern C. (1926), „Livlands Ostgrenze im Mittelalter vom Peipus bis zur Düna", *Mitteilungen aus der livländischen Geschichte*, 23, 195-240.

Šterns I. (1997), *Latvijas vēsture 1290-1500*, Riga, Daugava.

Vilcāne A. (2002), „Arheoloģiskie pētījumi Dinaburgas pilī 2000. gadā", in *Arheologu pētījumi Latvijā 2000. un 2001. gadā*, Riga, Latvijas Vēstures Institūta Apgāds, 209-215.

Wartberge H. (von) (2005), *Vartberges Hermaņa Livonijas hronika* [*Hermanni de Wartberge Chronicon Livoniae*], Riga, Latvijas Vēstures Institūta Apgāds.

The Medieval Engineer and Castles at War

Peter Purton*

1. Introduction: unsolved questions

Famous Renaissance polymaths, such as Leonardo da Vinci, Leon Alberti or Francesco di Giorgio Martini, were experts in many fields, including designing castles and military engineering. There is also plentiful evidence that medieval engineers had multiple roles between the 12th century and the Renaissance.

The word "engineer" itself (and the similar terms in Romance languages; *Werkmeister* is the German equivalent, Greek *mechanarios*) only emerged in its modern meaning towards the end of this period, and even its origin remains subject to debate although most dictionaries opt for it deriving from the Latin *ingenium*. This is partly precisely because of the wide range of roles such a person might carry out, early uses of the word denoting an architect or a building-master, a mechanic, a maker of engines, a carpenter and a craftsman. In this paper, it is used as a shorthand term to cover a range of distinct functions.

There remain considerable gaps in our knowledge of medieval engineers, what they had to know to carry out their role, how their roles evolved over the years – and what might have influenced that development. The careers of the giants of the Renaissance were actually the exception: by the 15th century a clear specialist role of military engineer was emerging. This happened alongside the establishment of gunpowder artillery as a wall-breaking weapon. There was a link between the two processes, evident in the west with the emergence of high-ranking officials as masters of artillery (*Büchsenmeister, maître d'artillerie*) during the 15th century, but the arrival of this type of expert long preceded the arrival of the gun. The further back in time, however, the scantier the surviving evidence, and this itself is scattered across many different areas of study. Therefore, this paper advances some speculative hypotheses. They are based on the following propositions:

1. That a whole range of skills was required both to build a castle, and also to build or operate the military equipment with which to execute those of its functions that were defensive or offensive.

2. Many of these skills were basic to a particular craft, and were learned through apprenticeship or other forms of transmission. Others were more sophisticated. The construction, for example, of a battering ram or a stone-throwing engine must have been directed by someone with a higher level of knowledge than the ordinary artisan or craftsman.

3. By the 12th century, there is evidence that such experts were prized by rulers. An analogy would be the select group of experts who, for example, were responsible for designing cathedrals. It is suggested here that a similar situation applied in engineering for warlike purposes well before that time.

2. What skills were required?

What skills were required by the military engineer? If we take that humble instrument, the battering ram: figure 1 shows a replica at Malbork Castle (Poland) (fig. 1). This weapon was in continuous use from ancient times. It is briefly described in Vegetius' handbook *Epitoma de re militaris*[1]. But closer consideration shows that while the basic structure could be

---

* Independant scholar, London, United Kingdom.

1. Milner 1993, 120.

Fig. 1 – Battering ram reconstruction at Malbork Castle (Poland). Photo P. Purton.

built by any competent carpenter, the dimensions and proportions of the finished product would affect its mobility and would decide how many operatives could shelter beneath the roof, with space to swing the beam. The roof, too, needed to be made fireproof. Then, the dimensions of the beam had to be decided, and how to suspend it. The replica in the photo is probably not efficient – unless the beam was hung from v-shaped ropes or chains, it would wobble, therefore not hitting the same point each time.

How to calculate an efficient weapon? This is the equation to decide the optimum kinetic energy, devised by Rutherford Aris and Bernard Bachrach[2], using variables such as weight, back swing and velocity at impact: $K = (1/2)\{\xi^2 - 2\cos\theta.\xi\eta + \eta^2\}$. Vegetius offered no calculation. Furthermore, this weapon must have been constructed anew on the spot each time, using locally available materials. Therefore, someone with the besieging force must have possessed more than basic carpentry skills to design one that would achieve its purpose. Its unavoidable vulnerability, operating at the foot of the castle or city wall, put a premium on it achieving a breakthrough as fast as possible.

The wooden siege tower, also of ancient origin, was a much more substantial construction still. The chronicles tell of cases where the builder miscalculated, when the resulting tower built by carpenters, often at enormous cost, became (in some cases) stuck in the ground because it was too heavy, and was literally a sitting target for defenders to destroy by fire. The truth is that the siege tower, long used by the Byzantines, also became an implement of choice, particularly for West European armies, featuring prominently in the successes of the early Crusades. Most of the builders remain anonymous, but must have been experts. Many of the first specific chronicle

Fig. 2 – Reconstructed trebuchet at the Middelaldercentret, Denmark at rest. Photo P. Purton.

references to engineers are in the context of siege towers built to overcome a stubbornly resisting fortress.

3. The example of the trebuchet

If the skills needed for these devices were multiple, sophisticated stone-throwing artillery, such as the trebuchet, required more. This latter weapon became the heavy-siege artillery used throughout Europe, the Middle East and North Africa from the early 13th century onwards. Its origins are still, remarkably, uncertain. The design concept itself is simple: a lever with a heavy counterweight at the short end, propelling a shot from a sling attached to the longer end, the lever held in place in a strong frame. But creating one that works effectively is anything but simple.

Using the numerous contemporary illustrations and other information, many replicas have been constructed. One of the best is at the Middelaldercentret, at Nykøbing Falster in Denmark. Figures 2 and 3 are a side view of the engine at rest, then loaded and ready to shoot – the people alongside provide an idea of its great size (figs. 2 & 3). The issue here is that the efficiency of the weapon depended both on many different

2. Aris & Bachrach 1994, 1-14.

Fig. 3 – Ready to shoot. The human figures give an idea of its size. Photo P. Purton.

Fig. 4 – Trebuchet ammunition in the museum at Montségur (Ariège, France); two sizes, weighing 55 and 70 kg. Photo P. Purton.

characteristics, and on the relationship between them. To get it wrong might be catastrophic – the shot (often weighing between 50 and 100 kg) could fly backwards, while the consequences if the frame proved unable to bear the burden of a counterweight that might weigh 20 tons (over 20,000 kg) would be serious[3]. The best modern replicas have operated very effectively to demonstrate the range, the impact and the extraordinary accuracy of the machine, but have always used lighter counterweights and projectiles than the originals, for reasons of safety. This is itself telling testimony to the immense power of the real thing.

Even the subject of the ammunition is significant. A lot of trebuchet balls have survived in museums and at castle sites: those in figure 4 (from the museum at Montségur) are of two types and weigh either 55 or 70 kg (fig. 4). The engineer needed to give clear instructions to stone cutters about the size required. The weight (mass) of the stone used was a vital factor in the calculation of the dimensions and strength of the whole engine and would have a major impact on the range. This was not a calculation the engineer would want to get wrong, given the difficulty of re-siting a completed machine.

Modern physicists identify that there are 9 critical variables determining the effectiveness of the trebuchet: the mass of the counterweight and of the projectile; the lengths of the arm either side of the pivot; the starting angle; acceleration; speed; and the length and angle of the sling. An analysis of these characteristics on the Internet runs to 65 pages of mathematical calculations, deploying Newtonian physics, calculus and Lagrangian equations to arrive at conclusions about the most efficient set-up of the trebuchet. When seen in summary, the key principles of the optimum design are straightforward to state: that the initial angle of the beam should be 45°, that the long side of the beam is four times greater than the short, that the sling is as long as the long arm; and that the counterweight is 100 times the weight of the projectile[4].

The first person to build one, the first to operate one, and those who followed over the next century who were responsible for a considerable development of the capacities of the engine, did not have Newtonian physics to arrive at the right answers for their machines. But nor are the solutions obvious to the naked eye. Figure 5 shows the slider for the sling, and the release hook for it – the angle of the hook is also a critical variable – to demonstrate the complexity (fig. 5). Arriving at the correct combination of nine variables by experiment is possible, and once learnt, could be passed on. But it is also possible that the builders of trebuchets possessed some prior knowledge on the basis of which they could at least ask the right questions.

The skill of medieval carpenters is well known. The barn at Harmondsworth, Middlesex (fig. 6), was just a working building, but the knowledge needed to erect it is evident. It was put up by a team of carpenters working under the direction of master carpenters. A trebuchet needed a similar arrangement, and its own range of specialist skills. The degree of specialism is hinted at obliquely by the notice given of the first experts in this field – in England, Master Jordan, *trebuchettario nostro*, who made the king's trebuchet for Henry III and was well paid at 12 pence per day[5]. The same evidence indicates that these were prized weapons, stored in royal castles, disassembled for transport. But there might still be a need to build one *de novo*, as with the famous "War Wolf" built at Edward I's orders at the siege of Stirling Castle in 1304. It is recorded that this weapon, the subject of a reconstruction exercise televised in Britain in 2000, was built by 5 master carpenters, 50 carpenters and 4 pages. One of the masters, perhaps the man in overall control, was paid the very large sum of £40[6].

3. For a summary of research into the capacities of the trebuchet, see PURTON 2009, 382-387.
4. SIANO 2006; RADZINSKI 2006 (websites).
5. PUBLIC RECORD OFFICE 1916, 8, 26, 71, 121; RENN 2004, 25-32.
6. BAIN 1884-1887, vol. 2, 389, 395, 405; vol. 4, 477.

Fig. 5 – Slider and release hook on the replica trebuchet at the Middelaldercentret. Photo P. Purton.

Fig. 6 – Medieval carpentry skills demonstrated in the 15th-century Great Barn at Harmondsworth (Middlesex). Photo P. Purton.

The same situation applied with trebuchet makers in other European countries, and at the other end of the medieval world, Chinese records gave pride of place to "Ismail" and "Ala'uddin", the two men who introduced and built the weapon for Kubilai Khan[7]. These masters were an elite group, not just ordinary master carpenters.

4. Acquiring the knowledge

It is not known precisely what knowledge they possessed or where they acquired it, except to insist that it could not have been acquired through the standard master to apprentice route of transmission of knowledge for artisans and craftsmen – otherwise, there would have been many more people qualified for the work. What is known is the level of mathematical awareness known to teachers and students in the schools, where the standard *quadrivium* included geometry and arithmetic, derived from Classical writings, and at a much higher level after translations from the Arabic appeared after the 10th century. It was once believed that there was an un-bridged gulf between "pure" theoretical knowledge (*scientia*), acquired better to understand God's purpose and taught to those destined for ecclesiastical careers, and the "vulgar" mechanical arts: but modern scholarship suggests that the reality was more complex[8]. Outstanding, if still rare, examples are the bishops whose skill in vulgar arts such as estate management, or castle building was acknowledged in their *vitae* – such as Bernward of Hildesheim, at school from 1000 to 1007, Emperor Henry IV's Bishop Benno of Osnabrück

---

[7] Kubilai's builders may have been Ismail or Ala'uddin: from Chinese sources, see MOULE 1957, 72-76.

[8] In a substantial literature, the clearest summary was provided by WHITNEY 1990.

from 1068, and Gundulf, bishop of Rochester, from 1077[9]. This is not to claim that trebuchet makers were graduates of medieval universities but it is to propose that they had access to some of the scientific knowledge available to medieval society, whether in Christendom or in the Muslim world.

Scholars of medieval literacy have demonstrated that the ability to read spread much further than was once supposed, and included some master craftsmen. It is at least possible both that Master Jordan and his associates, and their forebears, were literate, and also that they were educated in some of the knowledge they would need to design and operate sophisticated machinery.

5. Instruction manuals?

As to the instructive material they might have studied, the 13th century was rich in new treatises describing siege weapons as well as defensive techniques. These texts were mainly written for the education of princes, but that does not mean they remained restricted to princes, while their authors demonstrably possessed real technical knowledge. The sketchbook of Villard de Honnecourt[10] (with its tantalising – because incomplete – drawing of the base of a trebuchet, with dimensions, which was used as a model for the reconstruction of the War Wolf mentioned above) may be the best known and most studied, but it was not alone.

This burst of new writing accompanied and was related to the development of new techniques of greater sophistication in both construction, and military technology, and it is associated with a strengthening and growing consolidation of royal governments in many countries. Governments in the Muslim world had operated with an educated civil service for centuries already, where treatises written for their education make clear that a degree of technical knowledge was expected, and this suggests that more organised and professional government included among its attributes better access to technical knowledge and the experts who could use it.

What happened under rulers in earlier periods? The 13th century treatises had antecedents. In the Eastern Roman Empire, the traditions of Antiquity, sustained by Maurice's *Strategikon* (*c.* 600), were reinforced with new treatises from the late 9th century (Leo VI's *Taktika*), while the 10th century was a golden age for the production of new writings offering strategic, tactical and technical advice. Constantine IX Porphyrogenitus insisted that military manuals were an essential part of a general's equipment, and Basil II, the "Bulgar-slayer", read books as part of his military training[11]. In the west, chronicles and other records confirm that it was the decision of Charlemagne to encourage and support scholars that represented a decisive turn. An element of the Carolingian Renaissance, the rediscovery of Vitruvius' *De Architectura* dates from his time, while new copies of Vegetius were made and there is evidence that they and other military manuals spread rapidly. Modern scholarship also demonstrates that this spread of education did not end with the Carolingians but was sustained, as has been shown now for the German kingdom under the Ottonian dynasty[12].

But all the evidence demonstrates that well before Charlemagne, Frankish armies and many of their enemies were using effectively both the siege equipment inherited from Rome, and the latest artillery in the form of the manually powered stone thrower that had arrived (from China) in the 7th century, to attack and defend the late Roman walled cities as well as more modern fortifications. Figure 7 shows a replica, and figure 8 a contemporary illustration showing one in use (figs. 7 & 8). If the Classical tradition had continued, all the while developing, in the Eastern Empire, and in the Islamic world, who was building or operating this machinery in the rest of Europe?

There are indications of the continuity of practical Classical knowledge that might contribute to an answer. The Roman Empire's infrastructure was based on measurement: the *agrimensores* measured land, surveyors plotted towns and cities, and a whole discipline was devoted to the skills needed to lay out and construct Roman legionary encampments. Numerous handbooks were produced, and used. Compilations of these handbooks survived and were copied into medieval times. The surveyor's skills required geometrical knowledge, and this was taught in the schools, albeit limited and basic before the 12th century[13]. The significance of the existence of this profession for castle building is obvious. Probably, medieval writers saw it as so elementary as to require no special comment, and the oft-cited account of the construction of the castle of Ardres in the chronicle of Lambert is unusual in its detail. The building of the castle began with the surveyor Simon the builder, "master of geometry", who measured out the site with his stick, in the process tearing up houses and gardens. This scenario, probably not popular with the locals, was no doubt commonplace[14].

Simon knew sufficient geometry and could use the available measuring equipment, and this knowledge was available from textbooks. To take another well-known example. Figure 9 is the plan of an ideal monastery preserved at St Gallen (Switzerland), and figure 10 is a reconstruction of what it might have looked like (figs. 9 & 10). Although the origins, purpose and significance of the plan are subjects of debate, its relevance here is that it exists at all, and that it is a scale drawing

---

9. Pertz 1846, 758; Pertz 1861, 58-64; Thomson 1977, 26; Allen Brown et al. 1963, 28-29, 31, 806-807.
10. Bowie 2006, 86-87.
11. Haldon 1990, 106-107; Sewter 1966, 46; Purton 2009, 116-119 for an analysis.
12. Bachrach 2012, 102-134.
13. Homann 1991, 3.
14. Shopkow 2001, 190-191. On post-Roman surveying and the transmission of manuscripts, see Homann 1991, 2-24; and on the transmission of texts, see Toneatto 1995, vol. 1 (1994), 13-47. See also Prouteau 2011, 60-71. More broadly, Bischoff 1971, part 1, 267-296.

Fig. 7 – Petrary (mangonel), the replica at Caerphilly Castle, Glamorgan (Wales). Photo P. Purton.

Fig. 8 – Petrary (mangonel), a contemporary 13th-century image of one from the church of St Nazaire, Carcassonne (Aude, France). Photo P. Purton.

based on Roman feet. Its very uniqueness leaves open many questions. But it confirms that high-level design and drawing skills were available in Reichenau around the year 820. It also, incidentally, confirms the central place of monasteries in the Carolingian state and economy, containing as it does workshops for the making of arms. The physical proximity of this manufacturing process to a place where higher education was undertaken raises other intriguing questions too[15].

The knowledge necessary for the construction of large buildings existed under the Carolingians, and similar levels of knowledge existed for military engineering from even earlier, although one can only guess at how this legacy of Antiquity was accessed or transmitted[16].

6. Princely experts, itinerant masters and royal retainers

Chroniclers have recorded the exceptional practical skills of some nobles and princes in carrying out siege warfare. In the 11th century, Roger Guiscard was lauded[17] for his hands-on abilities in his conquests in Sicily. It has been postulated that Roger II inherited a Muslim corps of siege engineers, and further north, Robert of Bellême's poliorcetic skills were well-known[18], but while they are not alone, it was unusual for medieval rulers to have had such a direct role in operations: they relied upon the skill of others whom they employed, who were generally anonymous. A mere handful of names have been transmitted for the period from late Antiquity to the 13th century, in contrast to more than three times as many in the records for the subsequent 300 years.

---

15. In an extensive literature, see primarily HORN & BORN 1979.
16. See the discussion by DOHR-VAN ROSSUM 2004, 291-307.
17. GAUFREDI MALATERRA 1724, passim, but especially 13, 48, 52-53.
18. CHIBNALL 1973, vol. 4, 288-291.

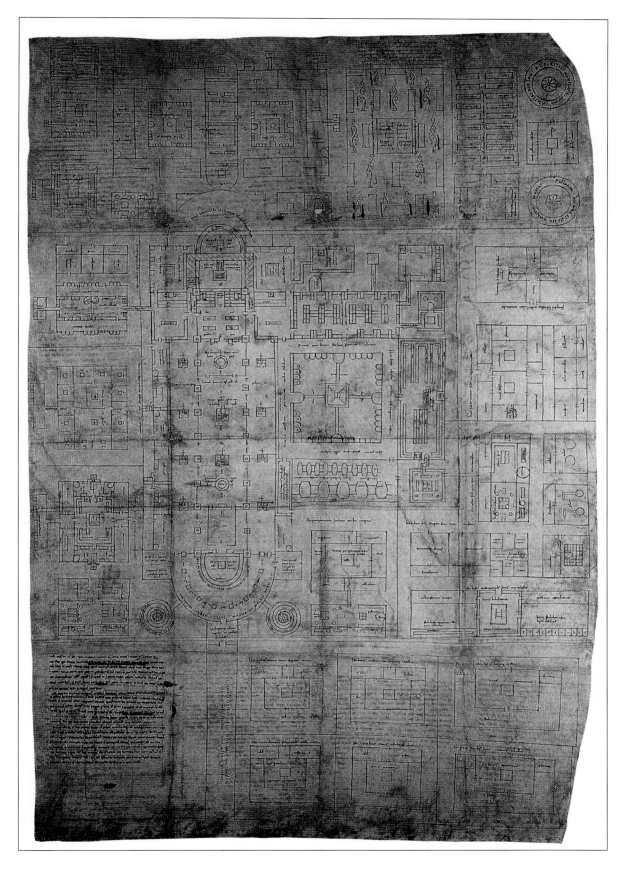

Fig. 9 – 9th-century plan of an ideal monastery preserved at St Gallen (Switzerland). With the permission of St Gallen Library.

Yet it is clear that skilled engineers were serving throughout this time. Some were itinerant: it is not unusual for a named creator of devilish machinery to be a foreigner, or sometimes a disgruntled former servant. This theme recurs quite frequently in chronicles. There are occasional references in medieval records. This provides one model.

What is not clear is to what extent another model applies: that is, specialists being retained by princes. For post-Conquest England, there is some evidence. After frustratingly brief references in the 1086 Domesday book to a land-holding *ingeniator*, there are the Exchequer accounts preserved in the Great Roll of the Pipe. This record, starting with the reign of Henry II and now published up to 1224, confirms a number of regular recipients of royal wages who are variously described as engineers, master carpenters, master masons and so on. Some appear year on year for decades. Others make single or occasional appearances, often in connection with some urgent military need – for example, Prince John's revolt against Richard I in 1194 entailing the need to organise a siege of Nottingham Castle[19]. Some were clearly architects or builders who carried on being architects or builders, others had a variety of roles including that of military engineer. They were well paid. They were not paid at other times, when they must have found employment elsewhere, or doing something else. But they must have been known to the government in order to have been hired when needed.

It is probably the case that a similar picture applies to earlier periods from which no government accounts survive. The 19 years of civil war that preceded Henry II's reign witnessed a great deal of castle warfare – contemporary chroniclers describe many sieges, the use of much siege equipment including stone-throwing artillery, the laying out and construction of numerous siege forts – without providing names for the engineers who must have been responsible for much of this work. Probably they saw such people as unworthy of mention. King Stephen (1135-1154) kept a core of professional soldiers about him during this long war, and it is a reasonable supposition that this group included one or more military engineers. It has been suggested that if one joins together the list of successive holders of the title *ingeniator* the result is evidence of a continuing post of royal military engineer in England from 1066. This conclusion cannot be sustained by the known evidence, but it is worth considering the possibility.

Fig. 10 – St Gallen (Switzerland), a model of how it might have looked if built. Photo P. Purton.

7. Some provisional conclusions

The range of tasks carried out by this anonymous group of experts over the whole period from late Antiquity through to the time when their contribution began to be recorded will have been substantial. If the routine elements of their work were handed on from father to son, master to apprentice, in the same way as happened with other crafts, then the more complex operations must have been undertaken by a small body of experts who may, or may not, have acquired a higher level of education, but had certainly acquired a high level of technical skill and know-how. These may have included the two men who built a siege tower for the ravaging Danes when they besieged Paris in 885. Their importance is confirmed by the fact that the work stopped when the defenders killed them with a ballista shot; while the engineers who constructed the stone-throwing engine, as Abbon recorded, "popularly called a manga", the projectiles from which crushed the Danish siege works and laid many of them low, also remained anonymous[20]. That they were unnamed should not obscure the fact of their presence here, and across the medieval world.

---

19. Keats-Rohan 1999, 446; Pipe Roll 1928, 68, 95, 175-176, 212, 251.

20. Waquet 1964, lines 211 (p. 32), 362-368 (p. 42).

Bibliography

Published sources

ALLEN BROWN R. et al. (1963), *The History of the King's Works*, vol. 1: *The Middle Ages*, London, Her Majesty's Stationery Office.

ARIS R. & BACHRACH B. (1994), "'De motu arietum' (on the Motion of Battering Rams)", in *Differential Equations, Dynamical Systems and Control Science. A Festschrift in Honor of Lawrence Markus*, K. D. ELWORTHY et al. (eds.), New York, Dekker (Lectures Notes in Pure and Applied Mathematics; 152), 1-14.

BACHRACH D. S. (2012), *Warfare in Tenth-Century Germany*, Woodbridge, Boydell Press (Warfare in History).

BAIN J. (ed.) (1884-1887), *Calendar of Documents Relating to Scotland*, Edinburgh, General Register House, 4 vols.

BISCHOFF B. (1971), "Die Überlieferung des technischen Literatur", in *Artigianato e tecnica nella società dell'alto Medioevo occidentale*, part 1, Spoleto, Centro italiano di studi sull'alto Medioevo (Settimane di studio del Centro italiano di studi sull'alto Medioevo; 18), 267-296.

BOWIE T. (ed.) (2006), *The Medieval Sketchbook of Villard de Honnecourt*, Mineola (NY), Dover.

CHIBNALL M. (ed.) (1973), *The Ecclesiastical History of Orderic Vitalis*, vol. 4, Oxford, Clarendon Press.

DOHR-VAN ROSSUM G. (2004), "Migration-Innovation-Städtenetze. Ingenieure und technische Experten", in *Le technicien dans la cité en Europe occidentale, 1250-1660*, M. ARNOUX & P. MONNET (eds.), Rome, École française de Rome (Collection de l'École française de Rome; 325), 291-307.

GAUFREDI MALATERRA (1724), *De rebus gestis Rogerii Calabriae et Siciliae comitis et Roberti Guiscardi Ducis fratris euis*, in *Rerum Italicarum Scriptores*, vol. 5, part 1, E. PONTIERI & L. A. MURATORI (eds.), edition of 1927-1928, G. CARDUCCI et al. (eds.), Bologna, Zanichelli.

HALDON J. F. (ed.) (1990), *Constantine Porphyrogenitus. Three Treatises on Imperial Military Expeditions*, Vienna, Verlag der österreichischen Akademie der Wissenschaften (Corpus fontium historiae Byzantinae. Series Vindobonensis; 28).

HOMANN F. A. (ed. and trans.) (1991), *Hugh of St Victor, Practical Geometry*, Milwaukee, Marquette University Press (Medieval Philosophical Texts in Translation; 29).

HORN W. W. & BORN E. (1979), *The Plan of St Gall. A Study of the Architecture and Economy of, and Life in a Paradigmatic Carolingian Monastery*, Berkeley/Los Angeles/London, University of California Press (California Studies in the History of Art; 19).

KEATS-ROHAN K. S. B. (1999), *Domesday People. A Prosopography of Persons Occurring in English Documents, 1066-1166. I, Domesday Book*, Woodbridge, Boydell Press.

MILNER N. P. (ed. and trans.) (1993), *Vegetius: Epitome of Military Science*, Liverpool, Liverpool University Press (Translated Texts for Historians; 16).

MOULE A. C. (1957), *Quinsai, with Other Notes on Marco Polo*, Cambridge (Eng.), University Press.

PERTZ G. (ed.) (1846), *Vita Bernwardi XIII Hildesheimensis Ecclesiae Episcopi*, in *Monumenta Germanica Historiae. Scriptores*, vol. 6, Hannover, Hahn.

– (ed.) (1861), *Vita Bennonis II, Episcopi Osnabrugensis*, in *Monumenta Germaniae Historica*, vol. 12 (XIV), Hannover, Hahn.

PIPE ROLL (1928), *The Great Roll of the Pipe for the Sixth Year of the Reign of King Richard the First*, London, The Pipe Roll Society (New Series; 5).

PROUTEAU N. (2011), "*Mensuratores castrorum*. Les arpenteurs militaires au Moyen Âge", in *Châteaux et mesures. Actes des 17ᵉ Journées de castellologie de Bourgogne, 23-24 octobre 2010, Château de Pierreclos*, H. MOUILLEBOUCHE (ed.), Chagny, Centre de castellologie de Bourgogne, 60-71.

PUBLIC RECORD OFFICE (1916), *Calendar of the Liberate Rolls Preserved in the Public Record Office. Henry III, Vol. I (1226-1240)*, W. H. STEVENSON (ed.), London, Hereford Times.

PURTON P. (2009), *A History of the Early Medieval Siege, c. 450-1200*, Woodbridge, Boydell Press.

RENN D. (2004), "Master Jordan who Made the King's Trebuchet", *Arms and Armour*, 1, 25-32.

SEWTER E. R. A. (ed. and trans.) (1966), *Fourteen Byzantine Rulers: the Chronographia of Michael Psellus*, revised ed., Harmondsworth, Penguin Books (Penguin Classics; 169).

SHOPKOW L. (ed. and trans.) (2001), *Lambert of Ardres. The History of the Counts of Guines and Lords of Ardres*, Philadelphia, University of Pennsylvania Press (Middle Ages Series).

THOMSON R. M. (ed.) (1977), *The Life of Gundulf, Bishop of Rochester*, Toronto, Pontifical Institute of Medieval Studies (Toronto Medieval Latin Texts; 7).

TONEATTO L. (1995), *Codices artis mensoriae. I manoscritti degli antichi opuscoli Latini d'agrimensura (V-XIX sec.)*, Spoleto, Centro italiano di studi sull'alto Medioevo (Testi, studi , strumenti; 5), 3 vols.

WAQUET L. (ed. and trans.) (1964), *Abbon. Le siège de Paris par les Normands. Poème du IXe siècle*, Paris, Les Belles Lettres (Les classiques de l'histoire de France au Moyen Âge; 20).

WHITNEY E. (1990), *Paradise Restored: the Mechanical Arts from Antiquity through the Thirteenth Century*, Philadelphia, American Philosophical Society (Transactions of the American Philosophical Society; 80).

Websites

RADZINKSI P. (2006), The trebuchet: http://www.geocities.com/siliconvalley/park/6461/1 (accessed 8 August 2012).

SIANO D. (2006), Trebuchet mechanics: http://www.real-world-physics-problems.com/trebuchet-physics.html (accessed 29 April 2014).

Landscapes of Conflict: Patterns of Welsh Resistance to the Anglo-Norman Conquest of North Wales, 1070-1250

An Overview of a New Study

Jacqueline Veninger*

1. Introduction

The sub-discipline of battlefield archaeology is concerned primarily with the identification and study of sites where armed conflict took place, and the archaeological signature of those events (fig. 1). Battlefield archaeology provides archaeologists with the methodological tools with which to reconstruct the development of a series of conflicts, identify patterns of conflict, assess the veracity of historical accounts and fill in gaps within the historical record. An integral part of this process is to place individual events and related sites into a broader cultural landscape. This method of approach to Welsh archaeology, during the period of the Anglo-Norman Conquest, has the unique ability to document the physical and cultural reactions to the Anglo-Norman incursion into Wales; without being subjected to the traditional biases that currently permeate this period of history. A long-term goal for this documentation includes working with the heritage community to develop a new set of criteria for defining, preserving and presenting landscapes of conflict within frontier zones. These criteria would move beyond the current post-medieval interpretations of battlefields, which do not take into account the somewhat more amorphous, yet culturally unique, landscapes of conflict endemic to frontier zones.

2. Problems with the existing research

Current challenges facing native Welsh archaeology during this period include a deficiency of native Welsh archaeological data, which is due in part to the Anglo-Norman centrism present in current and past academic dialogue. Compounding these issues are the tendencies of both historians and archaeologists towards the over-simplification of the Welsh experience. For instance, the effectiveness of Welsh military tactics and their ability to successfully adopt new technology introduced by the Normans, specifically castles, made them formidable military adversaries, is a fact often obscured by the favouritism of an Anglo-Norman dialogue[1]. The result is an incomplete archaeological record of native Wales during the period of conquest, leading to an inadequate landscape history and an absence of individual and group agency.

3. The role of conflict archaeology in researching the Anglo-Norman Conquest of Wales

The absence of battlefield archaeology, as a methodological tool, from archaeological endeavours relating to the Anglo-Norman conquest of Britain, and particularly of Wales, is unfortunate but not surprising. This absence is echoed throughout the medieval archaeology of the British Isles. There are some notable exceptions to this, namely the analysis of well documented large-scale and pivotal events of conflict like the Battle of Hastings (1066) and events or series of events dating to the later Middle Ages, such as the War of the Roses

---

* Ph.D. research student, University of Exeter, United Kingdom.
1. Davies 2004.

(1455-1487)[2]. This problem is compounded by the heritage communities' application of a post-medieval definition of "battle"[3] and does not give sufficient consideration to other types of armed engagements such as skirmishes or raids, unless these smaller actions were directly attached, temporally and spatially, to a larger battle event.

The heritage community currently defines a battle as "an action involving wholly or largely military forces, present on each side in numbers totalling c. 1 000 or more, and normally deployed in formal battle array"[4]. This constraining definition and intentional slight of so-called lesser actions stands to negatively impact our holistic comprehension of wider landscapes of conflict. Inherent to these constraints are the foreseeable difficulties in raising awareness for the preservation of these unique landscapes. The particularism that exists in this approach to battlefields is not conducive to the consideration and inclusion of other cultural aspects of conflict. Battlefield archaeology has provided the archaeologist with the necessary methodological tools to define and assess sites of armed conflict, but the theoretical elements of conflict archaeology are lacking.

These designations of battlefields further limit our understanding of conflict by placing the primary emphasis on the archaeological survey on military material culture. Material culture has an important role to play in the documentation and interpretation of discrete battlefield events. In fact military material culture documented *in situ* can lead to the temporal and spatial sequencing of discrete actions, producing a comprehensive order of battle that has been successful in documenting the actions of distinct individuals[5]. The ability of the battlefield archaeologist to document these events to this degree of detail is also dependent on the level of site preservation and the reliability and availability of accurate and multiple primary sources.

It is the potential for this degree of detail, possible with the archaeology of large-scale well preserved and documented battle events, which has understandably created a propensity for this type of battlefield survey while inadvertently diminishing the importance for the archaeological consideration of other types of armed conflict. Though lacking in notoriety, the events associated with small-scale warfare – the sieges, ambushes, raids and skirmishes that are endemic to the Anglo-Norman and Welsh conflicts[6] – have the potential to contribute to our understanding of past conflict particularly when examined *via* a landscape archaeology lens.

4. Research aims

Over the next two years a conflict landscape survey will be undertaken to demonstrate the Welsh reaction to the Anglo-Norman Conquest along the native Welsh and Anglo-Norman frontier

Fig. 1 – Sample of battles and sieges associated with the Anglo-Norman Conquest of Wales 1070-1250. Doc. J. Veninger.

regions of North Wales (including the coastal frontier), specifically within the medieval boundaries of Gwynedd, which encompassed the area west of the rivers Dee and Dyfi and included the Isle of Anglesey (fig. 2). This will be achieved through the analysis of the archaeological signature of discrete conflict events – for example, the battle and siege of Castel Aberlleiniog in 1094 by Gruffudd ap Cynan or the Battle of Crogen in 1165 – distributed across a broader landscape of conflict. The objective of this research is to demonstrate the complexity of the conflicts surrounding the Anglo-Norman incursion into Wales via a conflict landscape archaeology interpretation. The key aspect of this analysis is the reconstruction of the historic landscape and battlefield terrain to identify natural and cultural features present in the conflict landscape and determine how they were exploited by the combatants.

The castle is arguably the most durable testament to the culturally contested border zones that define the 11th-, 12th- and 13th-century Anglo-Norman Conquest of Wales[7]. A sample of the castles directly involved in armed conflict during this period can be seen below (fig. 3). The construction, location and control of castles were key determinates in the control of power and the resulting success of respective parties to dominate, preserve or expand native Welsh or Anglo-Norman territories. This is evident in the sheer quantity of castles con-

2. BROADMAN 1994.
3. ENGLISH HERITAGE, Battlefields designation selection guide.
4. FOARD & MORRIS 2012, 6.
5. SCOTT *et al.* 1989; MCBRIDE *et al.* 2011.
6. MORILLO 1994, 136.
7. LIEBERMAN 2010, 126.

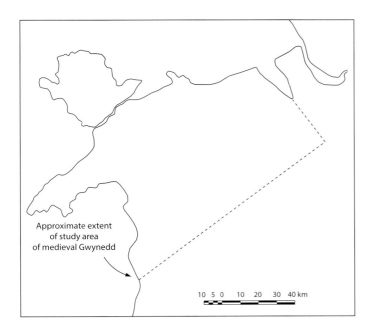

Fig. 2 – Study area of medieval Gwynedd. The reconstruction of these conflict landscapes will generate a comprehensive cultural and societal native Welsh context to the Anglo-Norman incursion into Wales. Doc. J. Veninger.

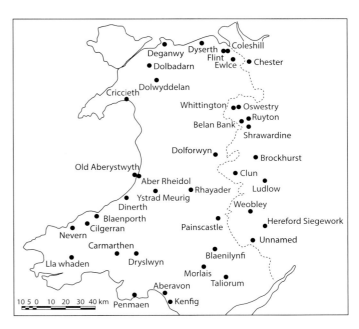

Fig. 3 – Distribution of castles known to be associated with sites of armed conflict in the period 1070-1250. Doc. J. Veninger.

structed, both by the Anglo-Normans and the Welsh, and the number of sieges or battles that were fought to gain control of those castles and the territory they commanded. As such, they need to be holistically interpreted and contextualized within a wider archaeological landscape of conflict. This can be done by conducting military terrain analysis for castle sites involved in armed conflict and placing them within the broader cultural landscape, including their relationship – spatially, temporally and culturally – to other sites of conflict, castle associated or otherwise. An element of this landscape of conflict survey includes documenting these relationships between sites of armed conflict and other important cultural and physical features on the landscape, including but not limited to: route-ways, monuments, native Welsh centres of power (prehistoric and medieval) and natural resources.

The phases of investigation involved in this conflict analysis are:

– 1) an analysis of primary sources, such as the *Brut y Tywysogyon* and *The Life of Gruffudd ap Cynan*, to construct a timeline of battlefield events with anticipated archaeological signatures;

– 2) an evaluation of the military significance of the terrain by conducting a military terrain analysis using KOCOA (defined below);

– 3) to conduct an archaeological landscape survey to locate, define and evaluate the integrity of conflict sites, part of this includes view-shed and line-of-site analysis;

– 4) the integration of conflict terrain, as well as historical and archaeological data (primarily built features) into GIS to reconstruct conflict events across time and space.

Military terrain analysis comprises the assessment of the military significance of the landscape by applying the military terrain device known as KOCOA[8]. These aspects include:

– key and decisive terrain;
– observation and fields of fire and assault;
– cover and concealment;
– obstacles;
– avenues of approach and retreat[9].

The historic environment must first be understood in order to apply KOCOA effectively to the medieval landscape and accurately reconstruct historical landscapes of conflict.

5. Concluding remarks

The ensuing research of a landscape of conflict approach to the Welsh resistance to the Anglo-Norman conquest of Wales and of medieval Gwynedd in particular, stands to contribute to the development of theoretical criteria for conflict archaeology concerned with the battlefields of medieval Britain. This edited approach to the traditional battlefield survey relies on landscape survey and utilizes the tools of military terrain analysis, alongside primary sources and any extant material culture data, to define and reconstruct these unique landscapes of conflict.

8. McBride *et al.* 2011.

9. American Battlefield Protection Program 2007.

Bibliography

American Battlefield Protection Program (2007), National Park Service Battlefield Survey Manual, Washington D.C.

Beeler J. (1966), *Warfare in England, 1066-1189*, Ithaca, Cornell University Press.

Broadman A. W. (1994), *The Battle of Towton*, Stroud, Sutton.

Brown I. (2004), *Discovering a Welsh Landscape. Archaeology in the Clwydian Range*, Bollington, Windgather (Landscapes of Britain).

Carman J. & Carman P. (2006), *Bloody Meadows. Investigating Landscapes of Battle*, Stroud, Sutton.

Davies R. R. (1987), *The Age of Conquest, Wales 1063-1415*, Oxford, Oxford University Press.

Davies S. (2004), *Welsh Military Institutions, 633-1283*, Cardiff, University of Wales Press (Studies in Welsh History; 21).

Davies W. (1990), *Patterns of Power in Early Wales. O'Donnell Lectures Delivered in the University of Oxford, 1983*, Oxford, Clarendon Press.

Edwards N. & Lane A. (1988), *Early Medieval Settlements in Wales, AD 400-1100. A Critical Reassessment and Gazetteer of the Archaeological Evidence for Secular Settlements in Wales*, Cardiff, University College Department of Archaeology.

English Heritage, Battlefields designation selection guide, online resource: http://www.english-heritage.org.uk/publications/dsg-battlefields/.

–, Registered battlefields, online resource: www.english-heritage.org.uk/caring/listing/battlefields.

–, National Monuments Record, online resource: www.pastscape.org.uk.

Foard G. & Morris M. (2012), *The Archaeology of English Battlefields. Conflict in the Pre-industrial landscape*, York, Council for British Archaeology (Research Report; 168).

Freeman P. W. M. & Pollard A. (2001), *Fields of Conflict: Progress and Prospect in Battlefield Archaeology*, Oxford, Archaeopress (BAR. International Series; 958).

Higham R. & Barker P. (2000), *Hen Domen Montgomery: a Timber Castle on the English-Welsh Border. A Final Report*, Exeter, University of Exeter Press in Association with the Royal Archaeological Institute.

Ithel J. W. (ed.) (1860), *Annales Cambriae*, London, Longman, Green, Longman and Roberts (Rerum Britannicarum medii aevi scriptores; 20).

Jones T. (ed.) (1952), *Brut Y Tywysogyon or The Chronicle of the Princes: Peniarth MS. 20 Version*, Cardiff, University of Wales Press (History and Law Series; 11).

Kenyon J. R. (1996), "Fluctuating Frontiers: Normanno-Welsh Castle Warfare c. 1075-1240", in *Château Gaillard 17*, Caen, Centre de recherches archéologiques médiévales, 119-126.

Kenyon J. R. & Avent R. (1987), *Castles in Wales and the Marches. Essays in Honour of D. J. Cathcart King*, Cardiff, University of Wales Press.

Lieberman M. (2010), *The Medieval March of Wales. The Creation and Perception of a Frontier, 1066-1283*, Cambridge/New York, Cambridge University Press (Cambridge Studies in Medieval Life and Thought. Fourth Series; 78).

Lloyd J. E. (1911), *A History of Wales from the Earliest Times to the Edwardian Conquest*, vol. 2, London, Longmans & Co.

McBride K et al. (2011), National Park Service American Battlefield Protection Program Technical Report: "Battle of Mystic Fort Documentation Plan" GA-2255-09-011.

Morillo S. (1994), *Warfare under the Anglo-Norman Kings. 1066-1135*, Woodbridge, Boydell Press.

Remfry P. M. (ed.) (2007), *Annales Cambriae*, Malvern, Castles Studies Research & Publishing.

Rowley T. (2001), *The Welsh Border. Archaeology, History and Landscape*, Stroud, Tempus.

Royal Commission of the Ancient and Historical Monuments of Wales (COFLEIN), online resource: www.coflein.gov.uk.

Russell P. (ed.) (2005), *Vita Griffini Filii Conani. The Medieval Latin Life of Gruffudd ap Cynan*, Cardiff, University of Wales Press.

Scott D. D. et al. (1989), *Archaeological Perspective on the Battle of the Little Bighorn*, Norman, University of Oklahoma Press.

– (2009), *Fields of Conflict. Battlefield Archaeology from the Roman Empire to the Korean War*, Washington D.C., Potomac Books.

Suppe F. C. (1994), *Military Institutions on the Welsh Marches: Shropshire 1066-1300*, Woodbridge, Boydell Press.

U.K. Battlefields Research Centre, online resource: http://www.battlefieldstrust.com/resource-centre/.

Das Problem der Barbakane an den Beispielen der Cité von Carcassonne (Okzident) und des Krak des Chevaliers (Orient)

Wehrtechnische Wechselwirkungen zwischen Frankreich und Outremer am Beispiel der Barbakane

◆

John Zimmer*

Einleitung

Die Barbakane gehört zum festen Bestandteil der mittelalterlichen Militärarchitektur und wird im Allgemeinen als vorgelagertes Verteidigungswerk bezeichnet. Aussehen und Architekturkonzept wurden zum ersten Mal in den Arbeiten von Eugène Viollet-le-Duc und Joseph Poux über die Cité von Carcassonne[1] ausführlich behandelt: Eugène Viollet-le-Duc definierte seinerzeit die Barbakane als „ein vorgeschobenes Befestigungswerk, das einen Durchgang, ein Tor oder eine Poterne schützte" und zugleich der Besatzung erlaubte, sich an einem vorspringenden, gedeckten Punkt zu sammeln, um auszurücken, einen Rückzug zu schützen oder Hilfstruppen heranzuführen[2]. Aufgrund seines damaligen Kenntnisstandes hat Eugène Viollet-le-Duc sie als halbrunde oder geschlossen runde, einem Torbereich vorgelagerte Befestigung rekonstruiert. In der Folge wurde diese Vorstellung einer Barbakane ein fester Begriff in der heutigen Burgenforschung. Vor allem der französische Sprachraum verwendet den Ausdruck, um eine bestimmte mittelalterliche Verteidigungsanlage zu beschreiben[3]. Ab der frühen Neuzeit wird diese Bezeichnung auch im englischen und deutschen Festungsbau verwendet.

Lange Zeit schienen Aussehen und Verwendung der Barbakane somit geklärt, so dass sich eine tiefer gehende Diskussion darüber erübrigte. Aber wie tragfähig ist dieses Bild der Barbakane heute noch, insbesondere für die Bauten des 13. Jahrhunderts? Denn in jüngster Zeit haben sich zwei Publikationen mit der Baugeschichte der Kreuzfahrerburg Krak des Chevaliers in Syrien[4] beschäftigt, wo eine Barbakane durch eine Bauinschrift nachgewiesen ist. Jedoch gibt es auf dem Krak überhaupt keinen Bau, der problemlos zu den bisher gängigen Vorstellungen einer Barbakane nach Eugène Viollet-le-Duc passen würde. Daher ist es in der Forschung umstritten, auf welchen Baukörper am Krak sich diese Bauinschrift eigentlich bezieht.

Es besteht somit Klärungsbedarf über das Architekturelement Barbakane. Eine der wichtigsten Fragen ist die nach der Terminologie, was also eigentlich mit dem Begriff der

---

* Luxemburg.
1. Viollet-le-Duc 1878; Poux 1927.
2. Viollet-le-Duc 1853, Bd. II, 111 : „Le terme ‚barbacane' désignait pendant le Moyen Âge un ouvrage de fortification avancé qui protégeait un passage, une porte ou poterne, et qui permettait à la garnison d'une forteresse de se réunir sur un point saillant à couvert, pour faire des sorties, pour protéger une retraite ou l'introduction d'un corps de secours."
3. Das schließt einen Gebrauch im englischen oder deutschen Sprachraum nicht grundsätzlich aus. Allerdings ist für den deutschen Sprachraum im Zusammenhang mit den Forschungsarbeiten für die drei Bände der Luxemburger Burgen bisher keine einzige Bezeichnung einer Barbakane für mittelalterliche Anlagen nachgewiesen worden: Zimmer 1996-2010.
4. Zimmer et al. 2011; Biller 2006.

Barbakane gemeint ist und was vor allem die zeitgenössischen Autoren darunter verstanden haben dürften[5]. Hier bietet es sich an, sich zunächst einmal kritisch mit einem wichtigen Ausgangspunkt der Definition von Eugène Viollet-le-Duc, nämlich den in historischen Quellen bezeugten Barbakanen der Cité von Carcassonne, auseinanderzusetzen und anhand des aktuellen Forschungstandes zu versuchen, das ursprüngliche Aussehen dieser dort – also in einer konkreten Befestigung im fränkischen Abendland – sicher als Barbakanen bezeichneten Bauteile zu klären. Denn die jüngere Forschung konnte nachweisen, dass die Arbeiten von Eugène Viollet-le-Duc zum Teil auf fehlerhaften Übersetzungen der Primärquellen beruhen[6]. Zudem sind die halbrunden bzw. kreisrunden Verteidigungsanlagen der Tore von Carcassonne, die die Vorstellungen von Eugène Viollet-le-Duc offenbar ganz wesentlich mit geprägt haben, erst nach den großen, monumentalen Bauarbeiten von 1280 entstanden[7].

Anschließend soll dann auf dieser neuen Grundlage versucht werden, die durch eine Bauinschrift belegte Barbakane auf dem Krak des Chevaliers zu identifizieren. Dabei wird auch auf die Etymologie des Wortes einzugehen sein. Zudem werden noch andere Beispiele der jüngeren Forschung im Vorderen Orient angesprochen, die für das bauliche Konzept der ersten Barbakanen, wie sie dort existiert haben, von Bedeutung sind.

Carcassonne „la Cité"

Die „Cité" von Carcassonne erhebt sich auf einem langgestreckten Felsrücken und überblickt in etwa 150 m ü. NN. weiträumig das Tal der Aude im „Languedoc-Roussillon" von Südfrankreich. Der Umstand, dass schon im 6. Jahrhundert v. Chr. ein gallisches Oppidum in dieser hügligen Landschaft entstand[8], ist zweifelsohne der äußerst günstigen Lage in der Passage von Carcassonne (Couloir de Carcassonne) zu verdanken, einer Öffnung zwischen den Pyrenäen im Süden und dem Massiv Central im Norden. Es ist diese Flusssenke der Aude, die eine Wegverbindung zwischen Atlantik und Mittelmeer ermöglichte. Dies waren die geopolitischen Voraussetzungen, die auf diesem Bergrücken eine Stadt entstehen ließen, welche eine Siedlungskontinuität vom 6. Jahrhundert v. Chr. bis in die frühe Neuzeit nachweisen kann[9]. Ohne auf die frühen Stadtphasen weiter einzugehen, sei hier nur erwähnt, dass der Verlauf der heute erhaltenen inneren Ringmauer noch in großen Abschnitten der spätantiken Befestigung entspricht (Abb. 1)[10].

Leider existieren bis zum heutigen Zeitpunkt keine bauhistorischen Untersuchungen, die zusammen mit gezielten archäologischen Sondierschnitten eine Bauchronologie der beiden äußeren Ringmauern erlauben würden. Die schon angesprochenen älteren Standardwerke[11], die nach den großen Restaurierungsarbeiten von Eugène Viollet-le-Duc entstanden, sind mittlerweile nicht mehr geeignet, eine tragfähige Definition der Barbakanen auszuarbeiten. Inwiefern in den noch immer aktuellen Planunterlagen der Cité falsche Ortsbezeichnungen durch fehlerhafte Übersetzungen[12] benutzt werden, kann hier nicht diskutiert werden. Erste bauhistorische und archäologische Untersuchungen erfolgten seit dem Jahr 2000 im Bereich der Grafenburg unter der Leitung von François Guyonnet und ergaben einige völlig neue baugeschichtliche Erkenntnisse in diesem Stadtbereich. Von 2008 bis 2010 sind in der Vorstadtsiedelung „Granholet" archäologische Sondierungen unter der Leitung von Marie-Élise Gardel unternommen worden, zu denen aber noch keine publizierten Resultate vorliegen[13]. Es sind hier also zunächst die genauen Lagen der Barbakanen zu klären, anschließend sind Überlegungen zu ihrem Aussehen anzustellen.

Wie bekannt, ist im Verlauf der Kreuzzüge gegen die Katharer in Beziers und Albi die Cité von Carcassonne am 15. August 1209 nach zweiwöchiger Belagerung eingenommen worden. Diese Kampfhandlungen beschreibt der Zisterziensermönch Pierre des Vaux-de-Cernay in einer Chronik[14] ziemlich genau, wobei Barbakanen noch nicht erwähnt werden. Außerdem gab es zu diesem Zeitpunkt noch keine äußere Ringmauer mit dem dazugehörigen Zwinger. Dass aber schon die südlich und nördlich gelegenen Unterstädte existiert haben, geht eindeutig aus den Quellen hervor (Abb. 1, A und B).

Vom 8. September bis zum 11. Oktober 1240 wurde die Stadt wiederum belagert, aber diesmal ohne Erfolg, weil angeblich kurz zuvor die zweite äußere Ringmauer fertiggestellt worden war. Auch diesmal wird gleich in zwei Quellen[15] das Kampfgeschehen detailgetreu festgehalten. Die Chronik von Guillaume de Puylaurens mit – im Anhang – dem Belagerungsbericht von Guillaume des Ormes, Seneschall von Carcassonne, ist von Louis Doüet d'Arcq 1846 erstmals

---

5. Bereits L. Doüet d'Arcq hat 1846 auf Ungenauigkeiten bei der Definition der Barbakane hingewiesen und auf eine ältere Definition verwiesen: „*portas et introitus spéciales quoedam sinuosoe barbacanoe intricant etobservant*". In: Doüet d'Arcq 1846, 369, Anm. 1.
6. Panouillé 2001, 65-68.
7. Ibid., 91-97.
8. Zu den Anfängen von Carcassonne im Allgemeinen: Guilaine et al. 1989.
9. Passelac 1999, 55-57.
10. Ibid., 46, Abb. 1.
11. Viollet-le-Duc 1878; Poux 1923.
12. Panouillé 2001, 67. J.-P. Panouillé hat nicht wie vermerkt die Übersetzung von Guillaume de Puylaurens übernommen, sondern die Übersetzung des Belagerungsberichtes von Guillaume des Ormes, Seneschall von Carcassonne. In: Doüet d'Arcq 1846, 365-379.
13. Diese Forschungsergebnisse sind von der verantwortlichen Grabungsleiterin M.-É. Gardel am 08.02.2012 in Carcassonne vorgetragen worden.
14. Panouillé 2001, 49-58 mit Quellenangabe.
15. Puylaurens 1976, sowie der Belagerungsbericht von Guillaume des Ormes, Seneschall von Carcassonne, in: Doüet d'Arcq 1846, 365-371.

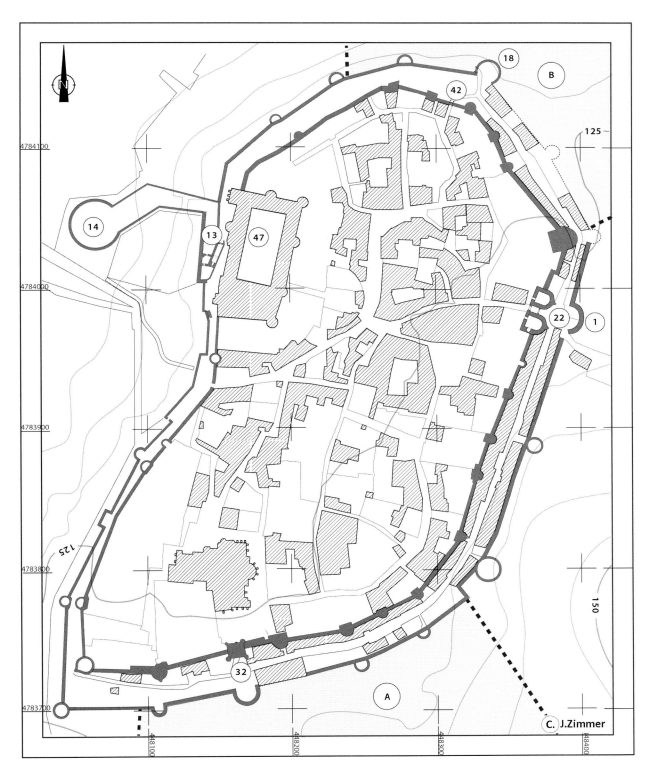

Abb. 1 – Carcassone, Grundriss der „Cité": A) Bourg „St. Michel"; B) Bourg „St. Vincent". Diese beiden Vorstädte werden kurz nach der Belagerung von 1240 aufgegeben und niedergelegt. Ob der Bourg „de Granoillant" zu diesem Zeitpunkt noch bestanden hat, konnte nicht eindeutig aus den Quellen ermittelt werden: 1) Barbakane vor dem Narbonner Tor, später Barbakane St. Louis genannt; 13) Burgbarbakane; 14) Aude-Barbakane; 18) Notre-Dame-Barbakane mit der Pforte „de Radez", auch Vorstadtpforte genannt (42); 22) Narbonner Tor; 32) Pforte de „St. Nazaire"; 47) Grafenburg. Aus praktischen Gründen ist die Nummerierung von den noch immer benutzten Plänen übernommen worden, die fast alle auf den Arbeiten von E. Viollet-le-Duc gründen. Es sei auch noch erwähnt, dass die hochmittelalterliche Straßenführung mit der dazugehörigen Bebauung großenteils bei der Erarbeitung der Urkatasterpläne noch bestanden hat. Auswertung vom Kataster 1809 mit Angaben aus den Quellen von 1244/1250. Dokument J. Zimmer.

publiziert worden. 1976 hat Jean Duvernoy in einer vollständigen Übersetzung die beiden Texte vorgelegt[16].

In der neuen, korrigierten Übersetzung des Berichtes von Guillaume des Ormes[17] sind die wichtigsten Ortsbezeichnungen zitiert, die es erlauben, die erwähnten Barbakanen zu identifizieren. Gleich zu Beginn der Kampfhandlungen wird dem Gegner der „*Bourg de Granoillant*" (heute Granholet), welcher der Toulouser Pforte vorgelagert ist, wieder abgenommen. „Die genannte Vorstadt erstreckt sich von der Barbakane der Cité bis zur (Süd-) Spitze der genannten Cité"[18]. Anhand dieser Beschreibung darf man diese Vorstadt zwischen der Aude und dem südwestlichen Abhang verorten, wie es anhand der rezenten Ausgrabungen von Marie-Elise Gardel bewiesen wurde.

Die Burgbarbakane zu lokalisieren, gestaltet sich etwas schwieriger. Sie wird in der Chronik an zwei verschiedenen Stellen erwähnt – wobei die Entfernung zur Grafenburg unterschiedlich angegeben ist. Die erste Erwähnung spricht – noch unpräzise – von Kampfhandlungen „…zwischen der Brücke [über die Aude] und der Burgbarbakane[19]…". Später heißt es präziser: „An beiden Orten [Brücke und Burgbarbakane] gab es so viel Armbrustschützen, dass keiner die Cité verlassen konnte, ohne verletzt zu werden"[20]. Hier wird deutlich, dass die Burgbarbakane sich gleich unterhalb der Burg befunden haben muss, weil der Abstand der heutigen Barbakane d'Aude von weit über 200 Metern zur Grafenburg es einem Armbrustschützen nicht erlaubt hätte, den Eingang der Grafenburg zu kontrollieren (also Abb. 1, Nr. 13 und nicht Nr. 14).

Im Zusammenhang mit dem Narbonner Tor (Abb. 1, Nr. 22) werden groß angelegte Pionierarbeiten der Belagerer beschrieben:

> Sie begannen, eine Mine gegen die Barbakane der Narbonner Pforte zu graben, aber gleich als wir die Geräusche der Pioniere hörten, minierten wir dagegen, und wir machten eine Trockenmauer groß und stark in einer Art und Weise, um die Hälfte der Barbakane gut zu behalten[21].

An dieser Stelle muss man sich Gedanken über die Grundrissform der genannten Barbakane machen, denn die heutige halbrunde Form mit offener Sehne wäre unmöglich anhand einer Trockenmauer in zwei Kompartimente zu unterteilen gewesen. Hier kommt eine rechteckige, vielleicht abgewinkelte Form deutlich eher in Frage.

In einem weiteren Passus werden Entfernungen und Richtungen der gegnerischen Pionierarbeiten angegeben:

> Sie unternahmen auch, die Barbakane der Rodez Pforte [Abb. 1, Nr. 42 und 18] zu unterminieren, und dort erreichten sie eine große Tiefe, weil sie bei unserer Mauer ankommen wollten [gemeint ist die Trockenmauer in der Narbonner Barbakane], sie machten da eine außerordentlich lange Strecke[22].

In einem letzten Abschnitt wird ein Großangriff auf die unter der Grafenburg gelegene Barbakane beschrieben, wobei die Verteidiger aber sehr schnell reagierten: „…wir stiegen bis zur Barbakane hinunter, wo wir sie mit so vielen Steinen und Armbrustbolzen überschütteten, dass sie sich mit einigen Toten und Verletzten zurückzogen"[23]. Zu dieser Erwähnung darf man bemerken, dass die über Tage andauernden Kampfhandlungen mit den großangelegten Pionierarbeiten sicherlich dazu geführt hätten, die im Westhang gelegene Barbakane d'Aude von der Grafenburg abzuschneiden (Abb. 1, Nr. 14 und 47).

In einem nächsten Arbeitsschritt wurden die drei in der Belagerungschronik erwähnten Barbakanen (Abb. 1, Nr. 13, 18, 1) in einen genauen Stadtgrundriss übertragen, der die Bebauung vor den großen Restaurierungsarbeiten von Eugène Viollet-le-Duc zeigt. Hierfür ist der Urkatasterplan von 1809/1810 (Abb. 2) mit Hilfe einer Entzerrungsmethode[24] an den heutigen Stadtplan angepasst worden. Die Nennungen in der Belagerungschronik wurden in den Stadtplan von 1810 eingetragen, um die damit verbundenen Ortsbezeichnungen mit bestmöglicher Genauigkeit zu identifizieren (Abb. 1). Schon in einem ersten Vergleich mit den Plänen von Eugène Viollet-le-Duc zeigen sich relevante Unterschiede.

Hervorzuheben ist zudem, dass gleich nach dem Ende der Belagerung die königlichen Baumeister mit großen Reparaturarbeiten und tiefgreifenden Neubauten begonnen haben[25], wobei hauptsächlich die Tore und Barbakanen von baulichen Veränderungen betroffen waren. So hat das Narbonner Tor sein noch heute monumentales Aussehen erst im Zuge dieser Arbeiten erhalten[26]. Dass im Verlauf dieser Um- und Neubauten die Barbakanen eventuell einem neuen Baukonzept angepasst wurden, ist gut möglich bis naheliegend[27].

Als gesichert kann man für Carcassonne abschließend festhalten, dass 1240 drei Barbakanen bekannt waren, die sich

---

16. Dieser Text von J. Duvernoy ist von J.-P. Panouillé übernommen worden. Panouillé 2001, 68-71 mit eigenem Kommentar. Leider hat der Autor nicht versucht, die Ortsbeschreibungen in einen genauen Stadtplan einzutragen.
17. Die wichtigsten Passagen im Zusammenhang mit einer Barbakane wurden wortgetreu vom Altfranzösischen in die deutsche Übersetzung übernommen und zitiert: Doüet d'Arcq 1846, 365-371.
18. *Ibid.*, 369; Panouillé 2001, 68.
19. Doüet d'Arcq 1846, 372 mit Anm. 4 zum Baudatum der Brücke 1185.
20. *Ibid.*, 371; Panouillé 2001, 70.
21. Doüet d'Arcq 1846, 377 mit Anm. 1; Panouillé 2001, 70.
22. *Ibid.*

23. *Ibid.*, 71.
24. Hierbei kam das speziell für die Archäologie entwickelte „ArchaeoCAD" zur Anwendung. Eine Software, bei der je nach Bedarf 3D-Vermessung (ArchaeoMAP), Geländemodelle (ArchaeoDGM), Fundkarteien mit Datenbanken (ArchaeoDATA) sowie ein Programm für Fotogrammetrie (Modul PhoToPlan von Kubit) in einer einzigen AutoCAD Applikation integriert sind.
25. Panouillé 2001, 91-93.
26. *Ibid.*
27. Man vergleiche nur hierzu die heute tiefgreifend restaurierte Barbakane des Narbonner Tores, die sich aus einem Rechteck und einem Halbkreis zusammensetzt.

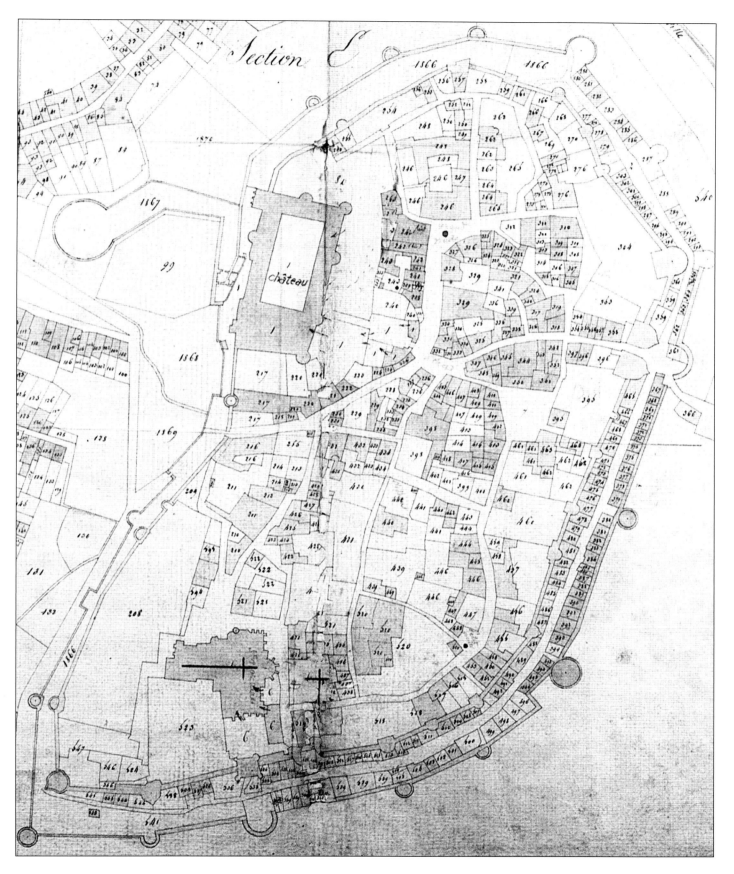

Abb. 2 – Urkataster von Carcassonne aus den Jahren 1809-1810. Dokument AD Aude.

im Grundrissplan lokalisieren ließen (Abb. 1, Nr. 13, 18, 1; die Barbakane d'Aude [Abb. 1, Nr. 14] hat 1240 offenbar noch nicht existiert). Die behandelten Beispiele zeigen zudem eindeutig, dass es sich bei den in der Chronik erwähnten Barbakanen um Verteidigungswerke handelte, die jeweils im Zusammenhang mit einem Tor standen („Barbakane der Narbonner Pforte"; „Barbakane der Rodez-Pforte"[28]).

Auch zu ihrer Form gibt es Hinweise: Denn in den Fundamenten unterhalb der Grafenburg sind noch heute die Reste eines doppelt abgewinkelten Zuganges mehrere Steinlagen hoch erhalten (Abb. 3, Pfeil), wobei es sich mit hoher Wahrscheinlichkeit um die 1240 genannte Barbakane handeln dürfte[29]. Auch die Überlieferung der Barbakane am Narbonner Tor, die durch eine provisorisch errichtete Trockenmauer geteilt werden konnte, spricht für eine solche Form.

Nach einer ersten Auswertung der 1240 in Carcassonne schriftlich und archäologisch fassbaren Barbakanen deutet sich somit an, dass es sich bei diesen um ein jeweils einem Tor vorgelagertes Verteidigungswerk handelte, bei dem der Zugang zum Eingangstor nur über einen doppelt abgewinkelten Weg möglich war, wie er am Eingang zur Grafenburg noch heute in einigen Steinlagen erhalten geblieben ist.

Um alle weiteren Fragen beantworten zu können, müssten die gesamten Befestigungsanlagen von Carcassonne in einer form- und steingerechten Bauaufnahme dokumentiert werden, die durch gezielte archäologische Sondierungen in den Fundamenten zu ergänzen wäre. Nur so könnte eine Bauchronologie für den Zeitraum des 13. Jahrhunderts erarbeitet werden, in der ebenfalls die bauliche Entwicklung der Barbakane – eventuell vom Rechteck zum Rundbau – mit eingeschlossen wäre. Leider ist fast ausnahmslos die von Eugène Viollet-le-Duc geprägte halbrunde sowie geschlossen runde Bauform[30] in die Fachliteratur eingeflossen und hat demzufolge zu manchen Fehlinterpretationen geführt.

Krak des Chevaliers in Syrien

Der Krak des Chevaliers gehört zu den bekanntesten und am besten erhaltenen Burgen aus der Zeit der Kreuzzüge in Syrien. Er erhebt sich auf einem felsigen Bergsporn auf knapp 700 m Höhe über dem Meer, ca. 45 km westlich von Homs und 55 km nordöstlich von Tripolis. Die Mittelmeerküste verläuft in etwa 30 km Entfernung westlich des Krak. Südlich erstreckt sich die Buqaia-Senke, die das Orontestal mit der Küstenregion verbindet. Die Festungsanlage bietet sich von allen Seiten als unregelmäßig gegliederter, aber sehr

Abb. 3 – Carcassone. Foto der Burgbarbakane unten. Dokument J. Zimmer.

kompakter Gebäudekomplex dar. Das nächstgelegene Umfeld wird durch moderne Straßen und Hausbauten gestört, das historische Mauerwerk ist aber größtenteils – abgesehen von restauratorischen Eingriffen und von der Abtragung der Zinnenbekrönung im 19. Jahrhundert – gut erhalten[31].

Über den Krak des Chevaliers liegt ein reiches, im 19. Jahrhundert einsetzendes Schrifttum vor. Dessen Aussagen stützen sich allerdings nicht auf Grabungsbefunde, sondern häufig auf oberflächliche sowie schlecht dokumentierte Beobachtungen. Als Grundlage für jede Auseinandersetzung mit dem Krak hat das Werk von Paul Deschamps 1934 – mit den Aufmaßen von François Anus – zu gelten[32].

Nun hat 2003 bis 2007 ein internationales Team mit Grabungen und umfassend dokumentierten Bauanalysen Resultate erzielt, die in wesentlichen Punkten das bisherige Bild über die Bau- und Siedlungsgeschichte des Krak korrigieren

---

28. Im Original Pforte „*Rodesie*": Doüet d'Arcq 1846, 373-374.
29. Dass es sich hier mit höchster Wahrscheinlichkeit um die erwähnte Burgbarbakane handelt, wird in einer von L. Doüet d'Arcq zitierten Quelle erwähnt: „Die Burg, welche in die beiden Ringmauern eingebunden ist... eine Seite (der Burg) ist mit der Stadt verbunden, die andere Seite über eine Barbakane mit dem offenen Land". In: Doüet d'Arcq 1846, 366. Ein herzlicher Dank gilt F. Guyonnet, welcher freundlicherweise seine neuesten Bauaufnahmen der Grafenburg für diesen Beitrag zur Verfügung gestellt

hat. Vgl. auch Guyonnet 2001, 271-289; Guyonnet 2010b, 144-179. Aus welchen Gründen E. Viollet-le-Duc an dieser wichtigen Stelle ein völlig verfälschtes Torkonzept errichtet hat, entzieht sich unserer Kenntnis.
30. Viollet-le-Duc 1853, Bd. II, 112-116.
31. Nicht einzugehen ist auf die jüngsten Zerstörungen durch den gegenwärtigen Bürgerkrieg.
32. Deschamps 1934.

bzw. ergänzen³³. Den Anfang der Arbeiten machte eine neue, nach modernen Methoden ausgeführte Grundvermessung in drei Dimensionen (Abb. 4). Dieser folgten archäologische Grabungen und eine umfassende, photogrammetrische Aufnahme des gesamten Mauerbestandes, welche die Grundlage für die baugeschichtliche Analyse der noch aufrecht Bauten bildete. Insgesamt konnten folgende Bauperioden und -phasen unterschieden werden (Tab. 1). Hier ist nur die fränkische Periode II relevant, in deren drei Phasen der noch heute bestehende Monumentalbau ausgeprägt wurde.

Die Bauinschrift von Nicolas Lorgne

Auf dem Krak des Chevaliers befindet sich die einzig bisher bekannte Bauinschrift, die eine Barbakane nennt. Eingemauert in der Innenwand der Nordkurtine der äußeren Ringmauer, nahe der sogenannten Nordpoterne bei Turm 33, berichtet sie, dass Nicolas Lorgne eine Barbakane errichtet habe (Abb. 5)³⁴. Nicolas Lorgne war ein Funktionsträger des Johanniterordens, seine Karriere bis hin zum Großmeister ab 1278 ist in groben Zügen bekannt. Von 1250 bis 1254 ist er als Kastellan der benachbarten Burg Margat belegt, ab 1269 war er zum Marschall aufgestiegen. Seine – nur zu erschließende – Kommandantentätigkeit auf dem Krak dürfte somit in die Jahre kurz vor 1250, eher aber in die Zeit zwischen 1254 und 1269 fallen³⁵. Aus dieser Zeit dürfte also die Inschrift und somit auch die Barbakane stammen.

Dass sich diese Inschrift heute nicht am ursprünglichen Ort befindet, sondern – nach Beschädigung der Ränder – an einer neuen Stelle angebracht worden ist, haben schon Max Van Berchem und Rey erkannt, 1812 hatte sie Burckhardt noch an einer anderen Stelle, nämlich am Eingang einer der später eingebauten Hütten im Burgbereich, dokumentiert³⁶. Die Inschrifttafel ist recht unsauber in den oberen Bereich eines Handquader-Mauerwerkes eingefügt³⁷. Es ist anzunehmen, dass die Mauerverblendung, in der sich die Inschrift heute befindet, erst in mamelukischer Zeit errichtet wurde³⁸. Damit stellt sich die Frage, auf welchen Baukörper sich der Text eigentlich bezieht.

In diesem Zusammenhang soll hier der unweit entfernt gelegene Nordturm ausführlicher behandelt werden, denn dort – das sei vorausgeschickt – könnte die Inschrift ursprünglich eingesetzt gewesen sein.

Der Befund des Nordturmes

Der Nordturm erhebt sich an der nordwestlichen Spitze der Oberburg (Abb. 4, Kreis). Die archäologischen Untersuchungen im Turminneren führten vor allem zur Freilegung und Reinigung von unter Schutt und Unrat begrabenen Mauerkronen und Wandflächen, die nun zu baugeschichtlichen Schlüssen zwingen, welche zum Teil erheblich von den bisherigen Deutungen und Datierungen abweichen. Die komplizierte Befundlage und die bauliche Entwicklung sind bereits an anderer Stelle detailliert beschrieben worden³⁹. Sie zeigen klar, dass der Nordturm einen Vorgängerbau in der ersten Bauperiode des heutigen Krak hatte. So erlauben es die archäologischen Untersuchungen nun, einen ersten, risalitartig aus der Flucht der Ringmauer vorspringenden Turmbau für Phase II/1 (ab 1170) nachzuweisen, der später bis auf einen wenige Lagen hohen Mauerblock (Abb. 6, Nr. 1) wieder abgetragen worden ist⁴⁰. Vom ehemals aufsteigenden Mauerwerk haben sich Quaderabdrücke an der Mörteloberfläche des noch stehenden Turmstumpfes erhalten. Der rechteckige Grundriss des Nordturmes wies die gleichen Außenmaße auf wie der des benachbarten Westturmes. Im Torbereich vom Nordturm hat sich noch ein kleines Fragment der westlichen Zwingermauer erhalten (Abb. 6, Nr. 2).

Die Errichtung des Westtalus in Phase II/2 (Anfang des 13. Jahrhunderts) war mit dem Bau zweier Türme verbunden, welche die bereits bestehenden Rechtecktürme aus Phase II/1 gerundet ummanteln sollten. Im Erdgeschoss des Nordturmes haben es die erwähnten Untersuchungen erlaubt, die Verbindung zwischen dem Talusgang und einem zweiten Gang, der zu einer nicht mehr erhaltenen Poterne führte, nachzuweisen⁴¹. Wie der neue Nordturm ausgesehen hat, lässt sich nicht sagen, da der heute noch stehende Nachfolgebau alle Teile dieses Baukörpers zerstört hat.

Phase II/3 (ca. 1250/1260) wird vor allem durch die Errichtung des neuen, rechteckigen Nordturmes geprägt. Seine beiden Langmauern sind in einem Quaderverband aus unregelmäßig verteilten Glatt- und Spiegelquadern errichtet worden, wobei die Spiegelquader der nordwestlichen Außenmauer deutliche Spuren einer Zweitverwendung zeigen (Abb. 7, über der Mauer 5). Im Turminneren belegen abgeschrägte Sockelsteine, dass sein damaliges Gehniveau gut 0,25 m höher lag als das heutige Quaderfundament des Vorgängerbaues (Abb. 6,

---

33. Zimmer et al. 2011.
34. Deutsche Übersetzung: „Zur Zeit von Bruder Nicolas Lorgne wurde diese Barbacane gemacht". Zur Person von Nicolas Lorgne mit weiterführender Literatur: Deschamps 1934, 165-166.
35. Zimmer et al. 2011, 280 mit Anm. 24; Biller 2006, 258.
36. Zimmer et al. 2011, 280 mit Anm. 24; Burckhardt 1822, 159; vgl. auch: Piana 2014, Anm. 114 (in Vorbereitung).
37. Zimmer et al. 2011, 281, Abb. 5.64. Sicher messbar ist noch die Höhe mit 75 cm, die erhaltene Breite beträgt 88 cm.
38. Ibid., 286-293. Leider war eine gründliche archäologische und bauhistorische Untersuchung der gesamten Mauerpartie aus zeitlichen und finanziellen Gründen nicht mehr möglich.
39. Ibid., 211-214 siehe Faltpläne 12 und 13.
40. Ibid., 259 mit Abb. 5.28.
41. Ibid., 267f. mit Abb. 5.41.

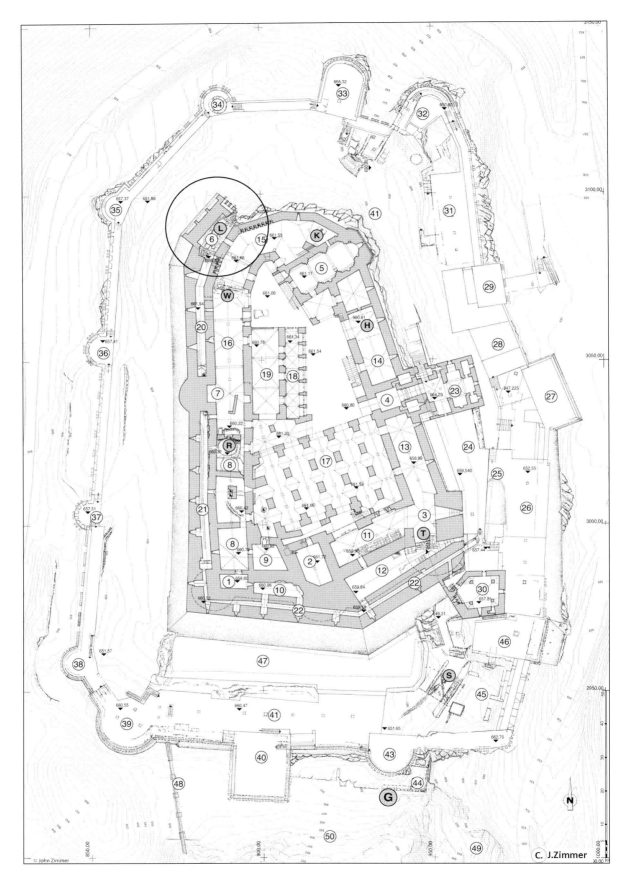

Abb. 4 – Krak des Chevaliers, Grundriss der Burganlage mit der Nummerierung der Baukomplexe (im Kreis der Nordturm). Dokument J. Zimmer.

Periode I	Phase I/1	um 980
	Phase I/2	ab ca. 1040/1050
	Phase I/3	1. Hälfte 12. Jahrhundert
Periode II	Phase II/1	ab 1170
	Phase II/2	beginn des 13. Jahrhunderts
	Phase II/3	ca. 1250/1260
Periode III	Phase III/1	ab 1271
	Phase III/2	um 1300

Tab. 1.

Abb. 5 – Krak des Chevaliers, die Inschrift von Nicolas Lorgne: links 2005 (extrahiert aus einem Foto von W. Meyer); rechts: Foto bei Deschamps 1934. Zur Zeit von Deschamps war die untere Kante noch nicht komplett freigelegt, was er in seinem Bericht festgehalten hat. Die Beschädigungen an allen Seiten zeigen deutlich, dass der ursprünglich sauber gearbeitete Inschriftenstein sekundär verwendet wurde.

Nr. 1). Zeitgleich mit der Errichtung des Nordturmes wurde der Talusgang durch einen sorgfältig gebauten Mauerwinkel verschlossen (Abb. 6, Nr. 3).

Vier vertikale Mauerschlitze am Innenmantel der Nordwestwand waren für die Aufnahme der Gurtbögen eines sekundär eingebauten Gewölbes bestimmt, wie Reste der abgeschlagenen Gurtsteine in den Schlitzen zeigen[42]. In der Mauer gegenüber sind die Pendants dieser Gewölbekonstruktion sichtbar (Abb. 7, über Mauer 5).

In der nordöstlichen Außenmauer sind drei Nischen mit Fallschächten eines Wehrerkers angebracht (Abb. 6, Nr. 8). Die bisherige Deutung als Latrinen wird weiter unten hinterfragt. Der Zugang zu den drei Nischen befand sich bereits im Außenbereich des Turmes, denn das sehr hohe Eingangstor lag bündig zur Innenflucht der nordöstlichen Turmmauer (Abb. 6, Nr. 9).

Die dem Talus zugewandte, südwestliche Schmalseite des Turmes wird im Oberbau von einem Entlastungsbogen getragen. Die ursprüngliche Bogenfüllung saß auf der Mauerecke (Abb. 6, Nr. 3) auf. Heute wird diese Füllung durch eine neuzeitliche Sicherung unterfangen. Die zunächst schwer verständliche Konstruktion findet ihre Erklärung im Vergleich mit der äußeren Nordwestwand, die ebenfalls einen Entlastungsbogen aufweist. Im Inneren des Talus endet dessen Mauer vor der nordwestlichen Turmwand mit einem durchbrochenen Mauergefüge und einer hälftig abgebauten Schießkammer (Abb. 7, Nr. 10), was somit eindeutig belegt, dass der Nordturm jünger ist als der Talus. In der Dokumentation von Paul Deschamps ist diese halbierte Öffnung als Scharte auch von außen gut erkennbar.

Konstruktion und Funktion des Nordturmes stehen zudem in engem Zusammenhang mit der bereits in Phase II/2 angelegten Birka[43]. Diese hatte neben der primären Rolle im Verteidigungskonzept die Aufgabe, die aus verschiedenen Kloaken und Abortschächten eingeleiteten Fäkalien nebst sonstigem Unrat aufzunehmen. Auch die Exkremente aus

---

42. Zimmer et al. 2011, 211ff., Abb. 4.57.

43. Weitere Informationen hierzu: *ibid.*, 240f. sowie 278-281.

den zwölf Latrinen für die Krankenstation im benachbarten Hallenringabschnitt sind ab Phase II/2 in die Birka entsorgt worden[44]. Nach der Errichtung des neuen Nordturmes mussten diese Latrinen stillgelegt werden, da nunmehr unterhalb der Mündung ihres Entsorgungskanals[45] die Zugangsrampe zum Turm vorbeiführte (Abb. 8). Stattdessen ist die bisherige Krankenstation in das obere Stockwerk des neuen Turmes verlegt worden, wo von 12 neuen Latrinenplätzen aus die Fäkalien hinter einer Blendmauer direkt in die Birka abgeleitet wurden (Abb. 7 oben).

Der Zugang zum Erker mit den drei Fallschächten (Abb. 6, Nr. 8) an der Schmalseite ist weitgehend zerstört. Bei diesen kann es sich aus den gleichen Gründen wie oben nicht um weitere Latrinen, sondern nur um Wehrerker zum Schutz der verschwundenen Zugangsrampe gehandelt haben. Man darf annehmen, dass eine schräge Rampe parallel zur nordöstlichen Turmwand unterhalb der Wurferker entlang geführt hat und dann eine Treppe zum großen Eingangstor mit dem hoch angesetzten Bogen rechtwinklig abbog. Ein solcher Zugang ließ sich von den oberen Plattformen des Turmes und der Ringmauer aus leicht verteidigen. Der eigentliche Burgzugang befand sich im Turminnern (Abb. 8). Eine – höchstwahrscheinlich mit Zinnen ausgestattete – Wehrmauer dürfte die Rampe an der Ostflanke geschützt haben (Abb. 8 C). Bei der Belagerung und Einnahme des Krak sind im Verlauf der Kampfhandlungen diese äußeren Verteidigungsanlagen (Rampe und Wehrmauer mit Wehrplattform) von den Pionieren Baibars offenbar tiefgreifend zerstört worden[46].

Der Nordturm bildete demnach ein vorspringendes Bauwerk, das den nördlichen Zugang zur Oberburg zu schützen hatte. Des Weiteren konnte man die Burgpforte nur durch einen doppelt gewinkelten Zugang erreichen (Abb. 8). Damit entspräche der Nordturm mit seinem indirekten Zugang einem ab 1200 in der orientalischen Militärarchitektur typischen Torkonzept, für das es in diesem Raum verschiedene Beispiele gibt[47]. Der Nordturm entspräche mit seinem indirekten, doppelt abgewinkelten Zugang aber auch einem Bauwerk, dass nach den oben angeführten Beispielen von Carcassonne Mitte des 13. Jahrhunderts im fränkischen Sprachraum offenbar als Barbakane bezeichnet wurde. Besonders die bauliche Parallele zu den abgewinkelten Mauerresten des ersten Zuganges zur Grafenburg ist evident.

Die Fotografie von Gertrude Bell

Die archäologischen und bauhistorischen Untersuchungen haben also gezeigt, dass der Nordturm ein für eine Barbakane typisches Torkonzept aufweist. Wenn es sich tatsächlich um eine Barbakane gehandelt hat, müsste sich die Bauinschrift von

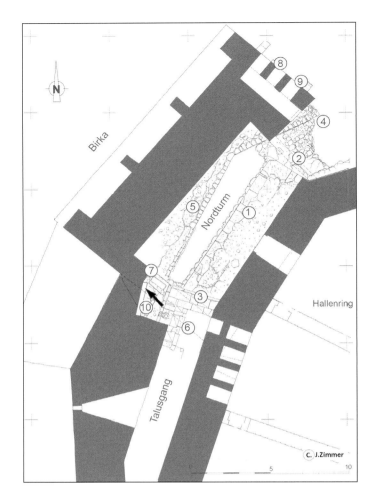

Abb. 6 – Krak des Chevaliers, Grundriss des Nordturmes mit den Befunden: 1) Quaderfundament (Periode II, Phase 1); 2) Die archäologisch untersuchte Zwingermauer (Periode II, Phase 1); 3) Mauerecke aus Periode II, Phase 3 (ca. 1250/1260); 4 und 5) Mauerfundamente aus Handquadern (Periode II, Phase 2, Beginn des 13. Jahrhunderts); 6) Latrinenabfluss; 7) Turmecke, welche die ältere Schießkammer 10 durchbricht; 8) Wurferker; 9) Konsole. Dokument J. Zimmer.

Lorgne auf diesen Turm beziehen. Leider ist der Zugangsbereich am Nordturm durch die Zerstörungen im Zusammenhang mit der Belagerung durch Baibars 1271 sowie spätere, unfachmännisch durchgeführte Restaurierungsarbeiten erheblich verunklart, so dass das Konzept der abgewinkelten Wegführung am heutigen Befund nur indirekt erschlossen werden kann. Hier bringt eine bis dato unbekannte Fotografie von Gertrude Bell aus dem Jahre 1905[48] neue, entscheidende Erkenntnisse: Sie zeigt nämlich deutlich, dass der Nordturm an dieser wichtigen Stelle – nahe der Toröffnung und unterhalb

---

44. Zimmer et al. 2011, 207-208 (Halle 15).
45. Ibid., 330, Abb. 5.140.
46. Ibid., 284-285, ebenfalls 359 mit weiterführender Literatur.
47. Yovitchitch 2008a, 110-117.

48. Die englische Archäologin und Historikerin G. Bell war Zeitgenossin von T. E. Lawrence und verweilte 1905 auf dem Krak, wo sie eine Fotodokumentation anfertigte, die heute im Archiv der Newcastle University in England aufbewahrt wird. Für die Genehmigung zur Veröffentlichung sind wir zu Dank verpflichtet.

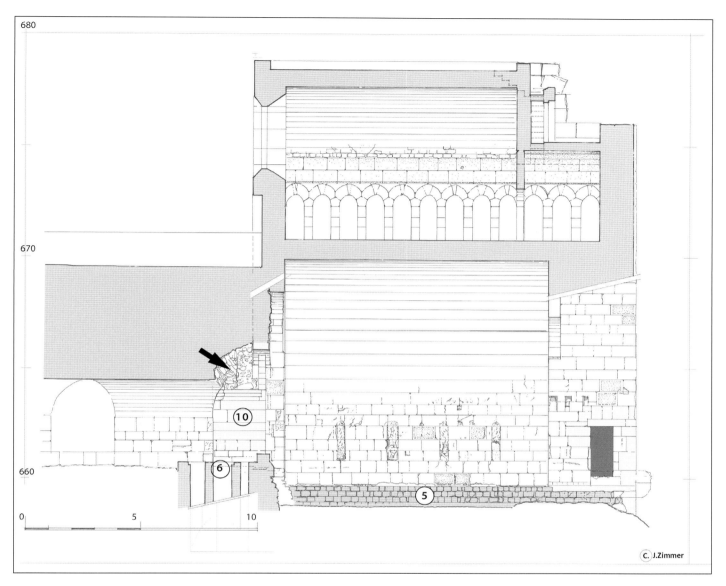

Abb. 7 – Schnitt mit Westansicht innen: 5) Mauerfundamente aus Handquadern (Periode II, Phase 2, Beginn des 13. Jahrhunderts); 6) Latrinenabfluss; 10) Schiesskammer, die vom neu errichteten Nordturm durchbrochen wird. Der Pfeil zeigt die deutliche Baufuge (hellgrau die Restaurierung). Dokument J. Zimmer.

des Wehrerkers – keine Ecke aufwies, sondern eine massive Mauerverlängerung (Abb. 9). Von der fehlenden ehemaligen Verblendung haben sich immerhin die Abdrücke der Steinquader erhalten[49]. Demnach bestand hier ursprünglich keine Ecke (wie sie später fälschlich restauriert worden ist), sondern tatsächlich eine mit dem Unterbau des Nordturmes verzahnte Mauerverlängerung, deren Außenseite mit Quadern verkleidet war. Damit gibt es einen bauhistorischen Beleg, dass sich hier tatsächlich eine weitere, quer zur Eingangsrichtung verlaufende Mauer befunden hat, es sich somit um einen doppelt abgewinkelten, indirekten Zugang zum Tor beim Turm gehandelt haben muss. Die Höhe der dortigen, anhand der Quaderabdrücke ermittelbaren Läuferschichten liegt zwischen 0,73 bis 0,75 cm und entspricht damit genau der Höhe des Inschriftsteins von 75 cm (Abb. 5). Auch die erhaltene Länge des Inschriftsteins (88 cm) passt zum Format der Quaderverkleidung des Nordturmes.

Die neu erstellte fotogrammetrische Auswertung des Originalbildes erlaubt es, die fehlenden Quader zeichnerisch zu ergänzen (Abb. 10 B und 11). Anhand dieser neuen und wichtigen Erkenntnisse befinden wir uns jetzt in der Lage, einen offenbar primären Standort der Inschrift vorzuschlagen: Es liegt die Vermutung nahe, dass die Lorgne-Inschrift an einer Partie dieser Mauerverlängerung am Unterbau des

---

49. In der leider an dieser Stelle unscharfen Fotografie von de Clercq aus dem Jahre 1859 scheinen die hellen Quader der unteren Verblendung noch umfangreicher erhalten gewesen zu sein: ZIMMER *et al.* 2011, 40, Abb. 2.16.

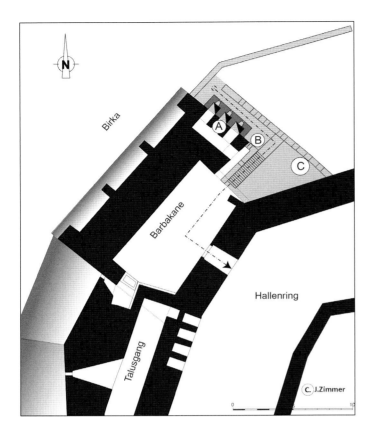

Abb. 8 – Krak des Chevaliers, Rekonstruktionsvorschlag der Barbakane Mitte des 13. Jahrhunderts: A) Wurferker; B) Turmecke mit Wehrplattform (im Verlauf der Belagerung von den Pionieren Baibars zerstört); C) Untere Wehrplattform mit Zinnenmauer (ebenfalls im Verlauf der Belagerung von den Pionieren Baibars zerstört). Dokument J. Zimmer.

Abb. 9 – Krak des Chevaliers, Foto des Nordturmes, von G. Bell (1905).

Nordturmes angebracht war (Abb. 12 B). Hier war sie für jeden gut sichtbar, der den Torbereich betrat. Gerade dieser Bereich wurde bei der Eroberung 1271 offenbar aber erheblich beschädigt. Erst im Zuge der Instandsetzungsarbeiten nach 1271 unter Baibars dürfte die Lorgne-Inschrift demnach an ihren jetzigen Standort gelangt sein[50].

Bevor wir uns mit dem Begriff der Barbakane im Vorderen Orient weiter beschäftigen, soll die Etymologie des Wortes kurz angesprochen werden[51].

Beim heutigen Forschungsstand über die Herkunft des Wortes zur Bezeichnung dieser Verteidigungsanlage ist ihr Ursprung im Vorderen Orient zu suchen. Im persischen Sprachraum gibt es die Wörter „bârbâk-khaneh" und „barbah-hané", die einen Erker oder eine gesicherte Passage bezeichnen[52]. Im arabischen Sprachraum werden diese Begriffe mit „Bashoura" übersetzt, um ein Befestigungswerk zu bezeichnen, welches einem Tor vorgelagert war[53], so wie es auch beim Krak seine Anwendung findet. Rein phonetisch liegen diese Wörter – persisch und arabisch – so eng zusammen, dass die Franken daraus den Begriff der „Barbakane" abgeleitet haben, der schließlich im französischen Wörterbuch aufgenommen wurde[54].

Ein weiteres Argument zur Identifikation der Barbakane ist der Chronik von Ibn Shaddâd über den Verlauf der Belagerung zu entnehmen. Nachdem schon zwei Barbakanen (= Bâshûra)[55] eingenommen waren, konnten die Pioniere ihre Anstrengungen auf die letzte konzentrieren, d. h. auf den Nordturm (nunmehr offenbar zu identifizieren mit der von

---

50. Deschamps 1934, 297-297. Eine mineralogische Untersuchung anhand eines Dünnschliffes in einem Vergleich der kristallinen Struktur vom Inschriftblock mit den noch erhaltenen Quadern der Ostfassade vom Nordturm würde vielleicht einen weiteren Beweis liefern.
51. Eine ausführlichere Abhandlung zu diesem komplexen Thema würde den Rahmen dieses Beitrages sprengen. Vgl. ebenfalls Biller 2006, 257f.
52. Gamillscheg 1969; CNRTL 2005.
53. Diese Angaben wurden dankenswerterweise dem Autor vom Direktor der Syrischen Antikenverwaltung Dr. M. Maqdisi bestätigt.
54. Dictionnaire de l'Académie française 1992.
55. Chronik von Ibn Shaddâd, nach: Deschamps 1934, 132, Anm. 3.

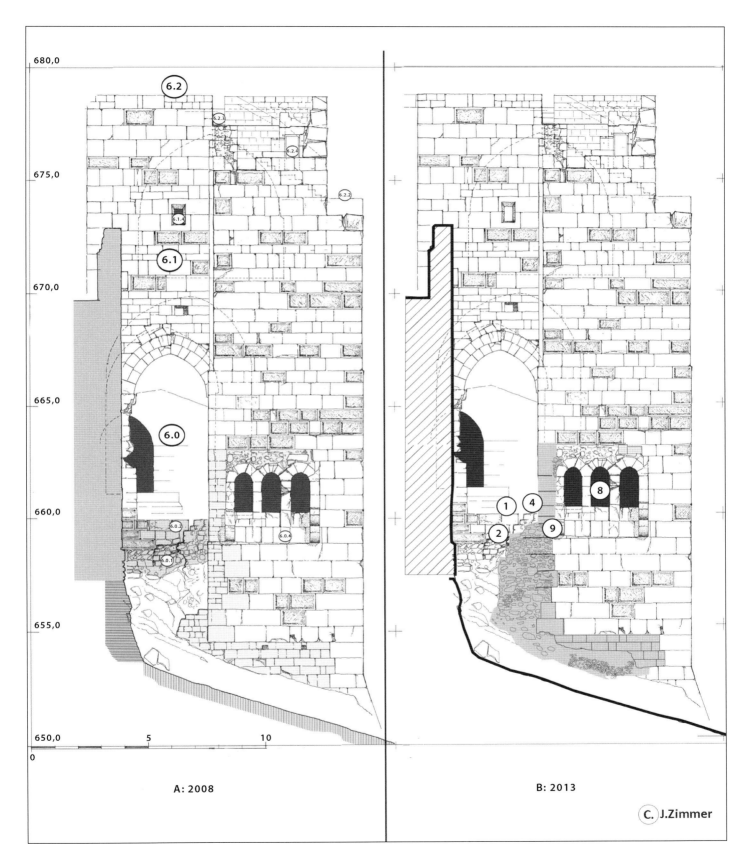

Abb. 10 – Krak des Chevaliers, fotogrammetrische Auswertungen der Ostansichten (A: 2008; B: 2013). Die neuen Erkenntnisse sind in der Zeichnung B: 2013 grau unterlegt. Die Nummerierung entspricht der von Abb. 5. Dokument J. Zimmer.

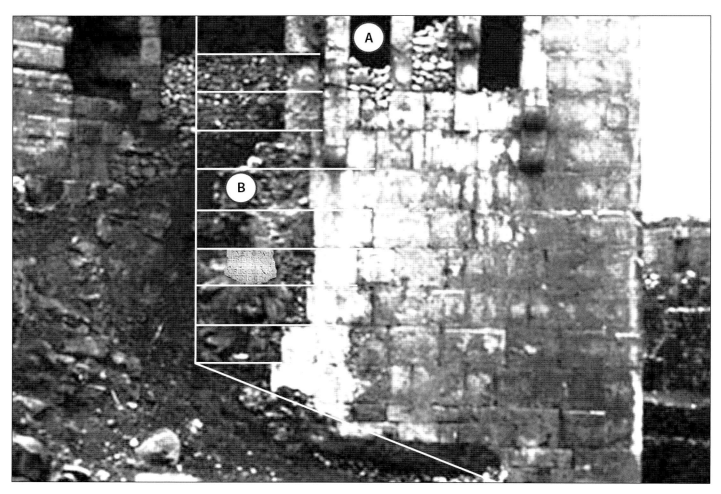

Abb. 11 – Krak des Chevaliers, Ausschnitt der Fotografie Bell mit der eingepassten Inschrift (dritte Lage von unten) und den nachgezeichneten Quaderlagen (Höhe 70-75 cm). In den vier unteren Lagen war die vertikale Ecke der Wehrplattform B um 1905 noch deutlich zu erkennen.

Lorgne errichteten Barbakane)[56]. Hier war der Wassergraben der Birka am leichtesten zu überschreiten. Wie die Beschädigungen am Mauerwerk in der Nordwand des Turmes sowie die darunterliegenden Felsausbrüche zeigen, konnten die Sturmtruppen den Bau einnehmen und von diesem aus durch einen schmalen Durchgang in den nördlichen Hallenring und den Innenhof vordringen.

Dass es im Orient noch andere Beispiele von Torbauten mit indirektem Zugang gibt, die man als Barbakane ansprechen könnte, steht außer Frage. Einige davon hat Cyril Yovitchitch in seinen Untersuchungen unlängst zusammengestellt (darunter z. B. Kairo, Tortum der Zitadelle von Aleppo, Harim, Bosra, Zitadelle von Damaskus)[57]. Auch am Krak ist dem Torbau 23 eine doppelt abgewinkelte Rampe 24 vorgeschaltet, und beim Torturm 43 ist der Zugang ebenfalls zweifach abgewinkelt[58].

Schließlich taucht in der urkundlichen Überlieferung der lateinischen Könige von Jerusalem – also im fränkischen Sprachraum Outremers – der Begriff „Barbakane" bereits in einem im August 1217 von der Kanzlei des Königs Johann von Brienne ausgestellten Diplom auf. Der König überlässt dem Deutschen Orden seine zwischen den beiden Stadtmauern von Akkon gelegene Barbakane unweit eines Baus, der sich in der Verfügungsgewalt des Seneschalls Gaufrid II. Le Tor befindet:

---

56. Eine unlängst erschienene Publikation von BILLER et al. 2013 ist in einer Diktion gehalten, die sich selbst kommentiert, bringt wissenschaftlich aber keine neuen Aspekte. Bezogen auf den hier wichtigen Nordturm muss allerdings angemerkt werden, dass, basierend auf BILLER 2006, 119-135, das Fehlen archäologischer Abklärung, unzulängliche bauhistorische Beobachtungen, die Vermischung von Befund und Interpretation sowie Nichtbeachtung bereits publizierter Befunde zu gravierenden Fehlinterpretationen geführt haben: Dass der Nordturm relativchronologisch jünger ist als der Talus, der seinerseits erst in Phase II/2 errichtet wurde, zeigt eindeutig die bei seiner Errichtung halbierte Talus-Schießkammer (Abb. 7, Nr. 10). Der Nordturm kann somit keinesfalls zur „Erstanlage" Phase II/1 (ab 1170) gehört haben, sondern er stellt eine letzte fränkische Bauphase II/3 dar.
57. YOVITCHITCH 2008a, 110-117.
58. ZIMMER et al. 2011, 221-223; 237f.

Abb. 12 – Krak des Chevaliers, Rekonstruktionsvorschlag der Barbakane Mitte des 13. Jahrhunderts, perspektivische Darstellung: A) Wurferker; B) Wehrplattform; C) Wehrmauer. Dokument J. Zimmer.

„[…] *meam barbacanam a muro prope domum swenescalci*" und „[…] *barbacanam infra duos muros civitatis*"[59]. Diese in den Schriftquellen genannte Barbakane, die zeitlich und räumlich nahe liegt, befindet sich eindeutig zwischen zwei Stadt- bzw. Ringmauern und ist somit nicht mit der äußeren Mauer identisch[60].

Zusammenfassung und Ausblick

Zusammenfassend ist hierzu festzuhalten, dass mit dem rapiden Aufkommen des Rammbocks um 1200 – was übrigens in den Chroniken ausgiebig beschrieben wird[61] – gleichzeitig fortifikatorische Gegenmaßnahmen zum Schutz der Toranlagen entwickelt wurden. Hieraus entstanden die indirekten oder abgewinkelten Zugänge[62]. Deren bauliches Konzept bestand darin, dass dem älteren Tor ein neuer Wehrbau vorgelagert wurde, bei dem sich der neue, zusätzliche Eingang seitlich befand. Auf den terminologischen Zusammenhang wurde oben hingewiesen. Ihre Gemeinsamkeit besteht darin, dass es keinen geradlinigen, direkten Zugang zum Burgtor mehr gab.

Anhand der Beispiele aus Outremer[63] konnte festgestellt werden, dass es sich dort bei der Barbakane üblicherweise um einen (recht)eckigen Baukörper handelt, der einem Eingangstor (Burg oder Stadt) vorgelagert wurde und somit einen doppelt abgewinkelten und leicht zu verteidigenden Zugang ermöglichte. Durch dieses Baukonzept wurde zudem der Einsatz des gefürchteten Rammbocks unmöglich gemacht, weshalb auf den arabischen respektive aiyubidischen Burgen die Barbakane (= Bâshûra) schon um 1200 bestanden hat. Auf dem Krak haben wir eine gesicherte Barbakane um 1250/1260 anhand einer Bauinschrift belegt. Die Frage, weshalb erst in dieser Zeit eine Rezeption dieses Baukonzepts auf dem Krak stattgefunden hat, bleibt noch offen.

In den fränkischen Stammländern ist die Barbakane anhand der Quellen um 1240 am Beispiel von Carcassonne belegt, wobei zu bemerken bleibt, dass die mit dem Begriff der Barbakane gemeinten Baukörper heute eine völlig andere Bauform darstellen. In diesem Zusammenhang müsste untersucht werden, aus welchen Gründen dort die frühen Formen mit offenbar doppelt abgewinkeltem Zugang (Grafenburg) durch eine halbrunde bzw. kreisrunde Befestigung ersetzt wurden. Weitere Fragen wären, wo und wann der Begriff der Barbakane auf anderen Befestigungen im damaligen Frankreich auftaucht, wobei auch der englische, italienische und deutsche Sprachraum einzubeziehen wären.

Jedenfalls wäre die bis jetzt gültige Definition der Barbakane von Eugène Viollet-le-Duc[64] im Lichte der neuen Erkenntnisse aus Outremer und Okzident neu zu überdenken. Beim Krak des Chevaliers gibt es jedenfalls gewichtige Argumente, die bauinschriftlich belegte Barbakane mit dem Nordturm zu identifizieren.

---

59. Vgl.: *Die Urkunden der lateinischen Könige von Jerusalem*, bearb. von H. E. Meyer, 3. Teil 8MGh Diplomata Regnum Latinorum Hieroselymitanorum Pars III9, Hannover, Hahnsche Buchhandlung, 2010, DD 633 (1217 Aug.). Freundlicher Hinweis von J. Friedhoff (Europäisches Burgeninstitut Schloss Philippsburg, Braubach).
60. Wie bei Biller 2006, 254-259 für die Barbakane am Krak angenommen, die dort mit dem die Kernburg umfassenden, äußeren Zwinger gleichgesetzt wird. Hingegen liegt die in Akkon genannte Barbakane möglicherweise unweit eines Torbaus, sofern man das vielleicht namengebende *domum* des Gaufrid Le Tor als solchen ansehen kann, was durchaus im Rahmen des Möglichen ist. Damit entspräche diese Situation einer Barbakane in Akkon exakt derjenigen am Krak.
61. Yovitchitch 2008a, 110.
62. *Ibid.* Die Diskussion zur Terminologie eines gewinkelten oder indirekten Zuganges, wie er auch in der französischen Übersetzung in der Fachwelt angewendet wird, ist hier ausgiebig geführt.
63. Yovitchitch 2008b, 118-125. Leider sagt der Autor nicht, ob der in Frage kommende Baukörper, der jedenfalls das Konzept einer Barbakane aufweist, in Quellen als Barbakane erwähnt wird.
64. Wie Anm. 2; Dictionnaire de l'Académie française 1992, Bd. I, s. v. „Barbacane".

Literatur

Biller T. (hrsg.) (2006), *Der Crac des Chevaliers. Die Baugeschichte einer Ordensburg der Kreuzfahrerzeit*, Regensburg, Schnell und Steiner.

Biller T. et al. (2013), „Nochmals zum Crac des Chevaliers – Anmerkungen zum Forschungsstand", in *Die Pfalz Wimpfen und der Burgenbau in Südwestdeutschland*, Wartburg-Gesellschaft zur Erforschung von Burgen und Schlössern e.V. (hrsg.), Petersberg, Imhof (Forschungen zu Burgen und Schlössern; 15), 239-250.

Burckhardt J. L. (1822), *Travels in Syria and the Holy Land*, London, Murray.

Centre national de ressources textuelles et lexicales (CNRTL) (2005), s. v. „Barbacane".

Deschamps P. (1932), „Les entrées des châteaux des croisés en Syrie et leurs défenses", *Syria*, 13/4.

– (1934), *Les châteaux des croisés en Terre sainte*, Bd. I: *Le Crac des chevaliers. Étude historique et archéologique* [Texte und Album], Paris, Geuthner (Bibliothèque archéologique et historique; 19).

DICTIONNAIRE DE L'ACADÉMIE FRANÇAISE (1992), 9 Aufl., Bd. I, Paris, Imprimerie nationale.

DOÜET D'ARCQ L. (1846), „Siège de Carcassonne. 1240", *Bibliothèque de l'École des chartes*, 7, 363-379.

DUSSAUD R. et al. (1931), *La Syrie antique et médiévale illustrée*, Paris, Geuthner (Bibliothèque archéologique et historique; 17), Brett 143, Abb. 4.

GAMILLSCHEG E. (1968), *Etymologisches Wörterbuch der französischen Sprache*, Heidelberg, Winter, 2 Aufl.

GUILAINE J. & FABRE D. (hrsg.) (1984), *Histoire de Carcassonne*, Toulouse, Privat (Pays et villes de France).

GUILAINE J. et al. (1989), *Carsac et les origines de Carcassonne*, Carcassonne, Musée des Beaux-Arts.

GUYONNET F. (2006), „Le château comtal de Carcassonne à la lumière des récentes recherches archéologiques", *Les dossiers de l'archéologie*, 314, 82-87.

– (2010a), „Le château comtal de Carcassonne. Nouvelle approche archéologique d'un grand monument méconnu", in *Trente ans d'archéologie médiévale en France. Un bilan pour un avenir*, J. CHAPELOT (hrsg.), Caen, Publications du CRAHM, 271-289.

– (2010b), „Du vicomte au sénéchal. Le château comtal de Carcassonne avant et après la croisade", in *Au temps de la croisade. Sociétés et pouvoirs en Languedoc au XIIIe siècle*, Carcassonne, Archives départementales de l'Aude, 144-179.

PANOUILLÉ J.-P. (1999), *Carcassonne. Histoire et architecture*, Rennes, Éd. Ouest-France.

– (2001), *Carcassonne. Le temps des sièges*, 2 Aufl., Paris, Caisse nationale des monuments historiques et des sites/CNRS Éditions (Patrimoine au présent).

PASSELAC M. (1999), „Carcassonne romaine. Observations sur l'organisation urbaine dans la Cité et ses abords", *Bulletin de la Société d'études scientifiques de l'Aude*, 99, 45-60.

PIANA M. (hrsg.) (2008), *Burgen und Städte der Kreuzzugszeit*, Petersberg, Imhof (Studien zur internationalen Architektur- und Kunstgeschichte; 65).

– (2014), „Wehrelemente an Befestigungen der Kreuzzugszeit und ihr potentieller Einfluss auf den europäischen Wehrbau", in *Wehrelemente an mittelalterlichen Burgen*, J. ZEUNE (hrsg.), Braubach, Deutschen Burgenvereinigung (Veröffentlichungen der Deutschen Burgenvereinigung e.V., Reihe B: Schriften, Bd. XIV), Anm. 114 (in Vorbereitung).

POUX J. (1923), *La Cité de Carcassonne. Précis historique, archéologique et descriptif*, Toulouse, Privat.

– (1927), *La Cité de Carcassone, histoire et description*, Toulouse, Privat.

PUYLAURENS G. (de) (1976), *Chronique*, J. DUVERNOY (hrsg.), Paris, Éd. du Centre national de la recherche scientifique (Sources d'histoire médiévale; 8).

VAN BERCHEM M. & SOBERNHEIM M. (1909), *Matériaux pour un „Corpus inscriptionum arabicarum"*, Teil II: *Syrie du Nord*, Kairo, Institut français d'archéologie orientale (Mémoires publiés par les membres de l'Institut français d'archéologie orientale du Caire; 25).

VIOLLET-LE-DUC E. (1853), *Dictionnaire raisonné de l'architecture française du XIe au XVe siècle*, Bd. II, Paris, Bance, 112-116.

– (1878), *La Cité de Carcassonne*, Paris, Morel.

YOVITCHITCH C. (2008a), „Die Befestigung der Tore aiyubidischer Burgen – Herausbildung eines Standards", in PIANA 2008 (hrsg.), 110-117.

– (2008b), „Die aiyubidische Burg Aglun", in PIANA 2008 (hrsg.), 118-125.

ZIMMER J. (1996-2010), *Die Burgen des Luxemburger Landes*, Luxemburg, Saint-Paul, 3 Bde.

ZIMMER J. et al. (2011), *Krak des Chevaliers in Syrien. Archäologie und Bauforschung 2003 bis 2007*, Braubach, Deutsche Burgenvereinigung (Veröffentlichungen der Deutschen Burgenvereinigung. Reihe A, Forschungen; 14).

Résumés

Bas Aarts, Taco Hermans

La construction de châteaux le long de la frontière entre le Brabant et la Hollande (*c.* 1290-*c.* 1400)

Au cours du xive siècle, il y avait quelques conflits au sujet de la véritable frontière entre la Hollande et le Brabant dans les Pays-Bas. À un moment donné, on a même dit que la frontière traversait le château de Strijen à Oosterhout. En ce qui concerne ce cas particulier, l'investigation historique apporte des précisions sur la « perception juridique ». Le riche Willem van Duvenvoorde, titulaire de hautes fonctions de chaque côté de la frontière, réussit à mettre fin au conflit et, en outre, modernisa considérablement le château de Strijen vers 1325. Une situation quasi semblable se produisit dans la seigneurie avoisinante de Loon op Zand. Vers 1385, Paulus van Haastrecht, également titulaire de hautes fonctions tant en Hollande qu'au Brabant, construisit une solide tour d'habitation pour renforcer sa position vis-à-vis de chaque côté de la frontière. Le dernier exemple cité dans cet article est celui de la tour d'habitation d'Onsenoort à Nieuwkuijk, construite après la destruction de la tour précédente par la Hollande en 1370-1372.

Les solides tours d'habitation de Loon op Zand et d'Onsenoort reflètent les moments turbulents dans cette région frontalière à la fin du xive siècle. Elles sont en contradiction avec la tendance plus générale à diminuer l'épaisseur des murs des nouvelles constructions de tours d'habitation constatées ailleurs dans les Pays-Bas.

Castle Building along the Border of Brabant and Holland (*c.* 1290-*c.* 1400)

During the 14th century there were some disputes about the exact boundary between Holland and Brabant in the Low Countries. At one point, it was even stated the border ran right through the castle of Strijen at Oosterhout. Historical investigation clarifies the "juridical perception" in this particular case. The wealthy Willem van Duvenvoorde, holding high offices on both sides of the border, succeeded in bringing the dispute here to an end and, furthermore, he greatly modernised Strijen Castle *c.* 1325. A somewhat comparable situation occurred in the nearby lordship of Loon op Zand. Paulus van Haastrecht, also with high offices in Holland as well as in Brabant, built a strong tower house *c.* 1385 to strengthen his position to both sides. The last example dealt with in the paper is the strong tower house of Onsenoort at Nieuwkuijk, built after the destruction of its predecessor by Holland in 1370-1372.

The strong tower houses at Loon op Zand and Onsenoort reflect the turbulent times in this border region by the end of the 14th century. Therefore, they contradict the more general tendency to diminish the wall thickness of newly built tower houses seen elsewhere in the Low Countries.

Der Burgenbau entlang der Grenze zwischen Brabant und Holland (um 1290 bis um 1400)

Im Verlauf des 14. Jahrhunderts gab es einige Konflikte hinsichtlich des richtigen Grenzverlaufs zwischen Holland und Brabant in den Niederlanden. Zu einem bestimmten Zeitpunkt hieß es gar, die Grenze verlaufe mitten durch die Burg Strijen in Oosterhout. In diesem besonderen Fall präzisiert die historische Untersuchung die „juristische Wahrnehmung". Es gelingt dem wohlhabenden Willem van Duvenvoorde, der auf beiden Seiten der Grenze hohe Ämter bekleidet, den Streit zu beenden, wobei er gleichzeitig die Burg Strijen um 1325 in beträchtlichem Umfang modernisiert. Zu einer ganz ähnlichen Situation kam es in der benachbarten Herrschaft von Loop op Zand. Um 1385 ließ Paulus van Haastrecht, seinerseits Inhaber hoher Ämter in Holland und Brabant, hier einen massiven Wohnturm errichten, um seine Position beiderseits der Grenze zu festigen. Das letzte im Aufsatz besprochene Beispiel ist das des Wohnturms von Onsenoort in Nieuwkuijk, der nach der Zerstörung des vorherigen Turms durch Holland 1370-1372 gebaut wurde.

Die massiven Wohntürme von Loon op Zand und Onsenoort sind Zeugen turbulenter Zeiten in dieser Grenzregion gegen Ende des 14. Jahrhunderts. Sie stehen deshalb im Widerspruch zur allgemein in den Niederlanden zu beobachtenden Tendenz, die Dicke der Mauern neuer Wohntürme zu verringern.

Susanne ARNOLD

Le château de Brauneck et sa prétendue « chapelle » – Études architecturales, archéologiques et géophysiques sur un château des Staufen à Creglingen dans le Bade-Wurtemberg

Le château de Brauneck, situé à l'extrême nord-est du Bade-Wurtemberg près de la frontière bavaroise, est l'un des châteaux forts les plus importants du Wurtemberg.

S'il est mentionné pour la première fois dans les documents en 1230 comme appartenant à Conrad von Hohenlohe, son mur d'enceinte et la courtine, avec ses deux tours de flanquement, renvoient cependant à une époque de construction située autour de 1200. Le *Palas*, qui n'existe plus, faisait également partie de l'aménagement initial du château. L'imposant donjon date d'environ 1230.

En raison de sa façade élaborée, le corps de bâtiment voisin de l'entrée du château a été appelé « chapelle » depuis le XIXe siècle. Des dommages structurels graves ont imposé ces dernières années des travaux qui se sont accompagnés d'examens archéologiques et historiques du bâtiment et de son architecture. Ceux-ci ont pu montrer que le bâtiment était probablement le logement des hommes d'armes du châtelain. De même que d'autres constructions du site, celui-ci subit de graves dommages causés par des incendies lors de la guerre des Paysans.

Brauneck Castle and its So-Called "Chapel" – Architectural, Archaeological and Geophysical Studies on a Castle Built in the Staufer Era near Creglingen in Baden-Württemberg

Brauneck Castle, in the extreme North-East of Baden-Württemberg, near the Bavarian border, is one of the most important castles in Württemberg.

It is first mentioned in a document in 1230 as belonging to Conrad von Hohenlohe, its surrounding wall and its curtain wall, with its two flanking towers, suggest, however, that it was probably built about 1200. The *Palas*, no longer existent, also formed part of the initial design of the castle. The impressive keep dates from about 1230.

Because of its decorated façade, the building near the castle entrance has been called a "chapel" since the 19th century. Serious structural damage has, in recent years, necessitated renovation work involving archaeological and historical studies on its construction and architecture. These have revealed that the building probably housed the lord of the castle's men-at-arms. Like other constructions on the site, this building was seriously damaged by fire during the Great Peasants' Revolt.

Die Burg Brauneck und ihr so genannter Kapellenbau – Baugeschichtliche, archäologische und geophysikalische Untersuchungen auf einer Staufischen Burg bei Creglingen in Baden-Württemberg

Die Burg Brauneck im äußersten Nordosten von Baden-Württemberg nahe der bayerischen Grenze zählt zu den bedeutendsten Burgen Württembergs.

Urkundlich erstmals 1230 mit Conrad von Hohenlohe als Besitzer überliefert, weisen jedoch die Umfassungs- und Schildmauer, letztere mit zwei flankierenden Türmen, in eine Entstehungszeit um 1200. Auch der abgegangene *Palas* gehörte zur Erstausstattung der Burg. Der mächtige Bergfried stammt aus der Zeit um 1230.

Aufgrund der aufwändigen Fassade wurde der Bau neben dem Burgtor ab dem 19. Jahrhundert „Kapellenbau" genannt. Gravierende Bauschäden machten in den letzten Jahren bauarchäologische und bauhistorische Untersuchungen im Zuge der Sanierung unumgänglich. Sie ergaben, dass es sich bei dem Gebäude wahrscheinlich um das Burgmannenhaus handelt. Auch dieses wurde, neben anderen Baulichkeiten auf dem Burggelände, im Bauernkrieg durch Brand sehr beschädigt.

Markus C. BLAICH, Tillman KOHNERT

Le château de Steuerwald au nord de Hildesheim – Histoire, recherche architecturale et archéologie

Dans le diocèse de Hildesheim se construisent au XIVe siècle, à côté de Steuerwald (1310-1313), deux autres châteaux forts entourés d'eau, relevant du même type de construction et remplissant une fonction semblable : Marienburg (1346-1349), à seulement 10 kilomètres, et Steinbrück dans la vallée de la Fuhse (1370-1380), à 20 kilomètres au sud de Hildesheim. L'ouvrage rectangulaire devient, aux XIVe et XVe siècles, le type de construction dominant dans la région de la Basse-Saxe d'aujourd'hui et, plus généralement, dans le nord de l'Allemagne. Les trois châteaux de Hildesheim se situent à la transition architecturale, importante pour l'Allemagne du Nord, de la « maison forte » à la demeure aristocratique du XVe-XVIe siècle. Outre leur date de construction précoce – qui suggère une sorte de rôle pionnier –, c'est leur bonne conservation qui leur vaut une attention particulière.

Le château de Steuerwald est, comme en témoigne la présentation du contexte historique, « la pièce majeure de la puissance épiscopale » de l'évêché de Hildesheim. Mais ce qui est particulièrement fascinant, c'est le fait que, bien que toutes marquées par les traces laissées par des changements d'utilisation, les constructions soient néanmoins totalement préservées dans leurs structures de base depuis près de 700 ans.

Steuerwald Castle to the North of Hildesheim – History, Construction and Archaeology

In the Diocese of Hildesheim, alongside Sterwald (1310-1313), were constructed in the 14th century two other castles surrounded by moats and similar in construction and performing a similar purpose: Marienburg (1346-1349), only 10 kilometres away, and Steinbrück in the vally of the Fuhse (1370-1380), 20 kilometres to the south of Hildesheim. The rectangular lay-out was in the 14th and 15th centuries the most common form for constructions in the region of what is today Lower-Saxony, and, more generally, in North Germany. Hildesheim's three castles can be situated in the architectural transition, important in North Germany, from the "fortress-home" to the aristocratic residence of the 15th-16th centuries. They merit our attention not only because of their early date – suggestive of their having had a sort of pionnier role – but also they are in a good state of preservation.

Steuerwald Castle was, as can be seen from the presentation of its historic context, "the major piece in Episcopal power" within the bishopric of Hildesheim. But what is especially interesting is the fact that, although all show the signs of changes in their utilisation, the constructions have nonetheless completely preserved their basic structures for close on 700 years.

Burg Steuerwald nördlich von Hildesheim – Historie, Bauforschung und Archäologie

Im Bistum Hildesheim entstehen im 14. Jahrhundert neben Steuerwald (1310-1313) noch zwei weitere Wasserburgen, die sich in Bautyp und Funktion ähneln: Marienburg (1346-1349), knapp 10 km entfernt, und Steinbrück im Fuhsetal (1370-1380), 20 km nordöstlich von Hildesheim. Das Prinzip der Rechtwinkelanlagen entwickelte sich zu einer bestimmenden Bauform des 14. und 15. Jahrhunderts im Bereich des heutigen Niedersachsens bzw. Norddeutschlands. Die drei Hildesheimer Burgen stehen an dem für Norddeutschland baugeschichtlich bedeutsamen Übergang vom befestigten „festen Haus" zum repräsentativen, adligen Wohnsitz des 15./16. Jahrhunderts. Neben ihrem frühen Baudatum – das auf eine Art Vorreiterrolle schließen lässt – verdient vor allem die gute Erhaltung Beachtung.

Burg Steuerwald ist, wie die Darstellung des historischen Hintergrundes zeigt, offensichtlich ein „Herzstück der bischöflichen Macht" im Hildesheimer Hochstift. Besonders faszinierend ist aber, dass die Gebäude zwar alle Spuren der sich beständig ändernden Nutzung zeigen, gleichwohl aber in ihrem Grundbestand seit beinahe 700 Jahren vollständig erhalten sind.

François BLARY

Châteaux et frontière occidentale du comté de Champagne (XIIe-XIVe siècle)

Entre la notion de réseau au sein d'une même entité comtale et les jeux d'alliance entre maison du domaine royal à l'ouest, cours de Bourgogne au sud et de Lorraine à l'est, il paraît intéressant de dresser un premier bilan de la recherche, reposant sur des travaux récents localisés à l'ouest du comté. Les analyses architecturales de quelques places remarquables permettent de faire émerger de véritables différences de traitement dans les modes constructifs tant dans le plan des châteaux que dans le recours systématique à certaines formes stéréotypées. L'examen archéologique s'est ainsi porté plus précisément sur les places fortes de Château-Thierry, Fère-en-Tardenois et Nesle-en-Dôle disposées à la frontière occidentale du domaine champenois. Le code architectural des châteaux de Champagne permet donc bien de définir une frontière lisible. Lors du rattachement au domaine royal, le programme de construction se consacre essentiellement aux ouvrages d'entrée et s'attache, au contraire, à estomper l'appartenance champenoise initiale.

Castles and Western Boundary of the County of Champagne (12th-14th Century)

Between the concept of a network within the same county and the interplay of alliances between the royal domain to the west, the court of Burgundy to the south and that of Lorraine to the east, it is interesting to make a preliminary research assessment based on recent projects in the west of the county. The architectural analysis of some of the outstanding sites reveals real differences of approach to the construction methods not only in the castle plans but also in the systematic recourse to certain stereotypical designs. The archaeological study was actually carried out therefore on the strongholds of Château-Thierry, Fère-en-Tardenois and Nesle-en-Dôle, along the western boundary of the Champagne domain. The architectural "code" of the Champagne castles enables us to define a visible boundary. At the time of its incorporation into the royal domain, the building program was essentially concerned with entry points and was linked, on the contrary, with playing down Champagne's initial ownership.

Burgen und Westgrenze der Grafschaft Champagne (12.-14. Jh.)

Im Netzwerk der Beziehungen innerhalb einer Grafschaft und den vielfältigen Verbindungen und Bündnisse zwischen Königshaus im Westen, Hof von Burgund im Süden und Lothringen im Osten ist es von Interesse, eine erste Forschungsbilanz zu ziehen, die sich auf jüngste, im Westen der Grafschaft verortete Arbeiten stützt. Architekturanalysen einiger bemerkenswerter Fundstätten offenbaren grundsätzliche Behandlungsunterschiede in der Bauweise, sowohl was den Plan der Burgen angeht, als auch in Bezug auf das systematische Aufgreifen bestimmter stereotyper Formen. Die archäologische Untersuchung hat sich daher insbesondere mit den Festungsanlagen von Château-Thierry, Fère-en-Tardenois und Nesle-en-Dôle befasst, die entlang der westlichen Grenze der Champagne gelegen sind. Der architektonische Code der Burgen in der Champagne ermöglicht in der Tat, eine klar erkennbare Grenze zu bestimmen. Beim Anschluss an die Krondomäne konzentriert sich das Bau-Programm in erster Linie auf den Eingangsbereich und man ist im Gegenzug bemüht, die Merkmale der Zugehörigkeit zur Champagne zu verwischen.

Maria-Letizia BOSCARDIN, Werner MEYER

« Clé et porte vers l'Italie » – La forteresse frontalière de Bellinzone

Sous les Visconti, qui prennent le pouvoir à Milan en 1300, la place de Bellinzone, fortifiée depuis le IVe siècle, devient forteresse frontalière contre la Confédération suisse qui, sous la conduite d'Uri, mène depuis environ 1400 une politique d'expansion vers le sud de plus en plus agressive. La place forte de Bellinzone, longtemps limitée à la colline rocheuse de Castel Grande, se transforme de plus en plus nettement depuis le XIIIe siècle en une chaîne de fortifications qui finira par occuper toute la largeur de la vallée. Les périodes de construction et de colonisation antérieures ne sont décelables dans le sol qu'archéologiquement. Les constructions fortifiées visibles aujourd'hui datent du XIIIe-XIVe et surtout du XVe siècle. Le concept de fortification avec ses remparts, tours de flanquement, meurtrières, merlons, mâchicoulis et embrasures est entièrement conçu pour répondre aux techniques de combat des Confédérés. Le vaste ouvrage de fortification sert aussi de garnison aux troupes mobiles. Avec la prise sans combat de Bellinzone par les Confédérés en 1500, la forteresse perd son importance militaire et n'évolue plus.

"The Key and the Gate to Italy" – The Border Fortress of Bellinzona

Under the Visconti, who came to power in Milan in 1300, the site at Bellinzona, which had been fortified since the 4th century, became a border fortress against the Swiss Confederation which, led by Uri, had developed from about 1400 onwards an ever more aggressive policy of expansion to the south. The stronghold of Bellinzona, for a long time limited to the rocky hill of Castel Grande, was transformed more and more clearly from the 13th century into a line of fortifications which ended up by stretching across the whole valley. The periods of construction and of former colonisation can only be detected in the ground through archaeological surveys of the terrain. The fortified buildings still visible today date from the 13th-14th centuries and especially from the 15th. The conception of the fortification, with its ramparts, flanking towers, arrow-slits, merlons, machicolation and embrasures, was entirely geared to providing a response to the military tactics of the Confederates. The vast fortification also served as a garrison for mobile troops. When, in 1500, the Confederates took Bellinzona without a fight, the fortress lost its military importance and did not subsequently evolve.

„Tor und Schlüssel zu Italien" – Die Grenzfestung Bellinzona

Unter den Visconti, welche um 1300 in Mailand die Macht übernehmen, wird der seit dem 4. Jahrhundert befestigte Platz von Bellinzona zur Grenzfestung, gerichtet gegen die schweizerische Eidgenossenschaft, die unter der Führung Uris seit ca. 1400 eine immer aggressivere Expansionspolitik gegen Süden betreibt. Die Wehranlage von Bellinzona, lange Zeit beschränkt auf den Felshügel des Castel Grande, entwickelt sich seit dem 13. Jahrhundert immer mehr zur linearen Sperrbefestigung, die sich schließlich quer über das ganze Tal erstreckt. Die älteren Bau- und Siedlungsperioden sind nur noch archäologisch im Boden fassbar. Die heute sichtbaren Wehrbauten entstammen dem 13./14. und vor allem dem 15. Jahrhundert. Das Befestigungskonzept mit seinen Sperrmauern, Flankierungstürmen, Zinnen, Maschikulis und Schießöffnungen ist ganz auf die Kampfweise der Eidgenossen ausgerichtet. Die weitläufige Befestigungsanlage dient auch als Garnisonsplatz für Mobiltruppen. Mit dem kampflosen Übergang Bellinzonas an die Eidgenossen im Jahre 1500 verliert die Festung ihre militärische Bedeutung und entwickelt sich nicht weiter.

Katherine Buchanan

Une ligne utile ? L'utilisation du paysage le long de la ligne de démarcation comtale dans l'architecture seigneuriale écossaise

Habituellement, on parle de châteaux et de limites territoriales dans des termes de contrôle, de conflit et de restriction d'accès aux terres que traverse une frontière internationale. Un autre aspect, cependant, peut-être plus répandu le long des limites internes à petite échelle, est celui de stimuler la mobilité et la communication. Cette étude concentrée sur le château de Baikie, une tour d'habitation dans la région frontalière du Forfarshire et du Perthshire à Strathmore en Écosse orientale, montre que le positionnement au sein du paysage détermine le degré de volonté exprimée dans l'architecture seigneuriale le long des frontières afin de faciliter plutôt que d'en limiter l'accès.

Drawing upon the Line? The Use of Landscape along Shire Borders in Scottish Noble Architecture

Castles and borders are usually discussed in terms of elements of control, conflict and restricting access to land across an international frontier. However, another aspect that is perhaps more common along small-scale internal borders is that of encouraging mobility and communication. This focussed study of Baikie Castle, a tower house in the Forfarshire/Perthshire border district in Strathmore in Eastern Scotland, demonstrates that landscape positioning determines the level to which noble architecture along borders opens itself to promoting rather than limiting access.

Genau auf der Linie? Die Verwendung der Landschaft entlang von Grafschaftsgrenzen in der schottischen herrschaftlichen Architektur

Burgen und Grenzen werden für gewöhnlich als Instrumente der Kontrolle, des Konflikts und der Zugangsbeschränkung in Territorien über internationale Grenzen hinweg diskutiert. Ein anderer Aspekt allerdings, der möglicherweise für innere Grenzen auf kleinräumlicher Ebene typischer ist, besteht in der Erleichterung von Mobilität und Kommunikation. Die Studie, die sich auf die Burg Baikie, einen Wohnturm in der Grenzregion zwischen Forfarshire und Perthshire bei Strathmore in Ostschottland konzentriert, zeigt, dass die Situierung in der Landschaft das Ausmaß bestimmt, in dem die herrschaftliche Architektur von Grenzen den Zugang eher fördert denn einschränkt.

Andrea Bulla, Hans-Werner Peine

Archéologie des châteaux d'une région frontalière – À propos de la construction de châteaux forts dans la région de la Diemel

Cet article traite des châteaux de la région de la Diemel, rivière qui formait la bande frontalière entre les Saxons et les Francs aux VIIe et VIIIe siècles. Après les guerres de conquête carolingiennes, qui s'accompagnèrent de la christianisation de la population et de l'intégration de la Westphalie dans l'organisation de l'Église et des comtés carolingiens, cette zone frontalière fut un point de contact entre les terres de mission des archevêchés de Cologne et de Mayence et de l'évêché de Würzburg, ainsi que, né de ce dernier, du diocèse de Paderborn, sur lesquels l'Empire carolingien, qui les englobait, faisait valoir ses droits.

Le « castro » sur le Gaulskopf, ouvrage de fortification datant des guerres saxonnes de Charlemagne, servit dans sa phase d'utilisation plus récente de demeure seigneuriale et de siège administratif représentatifs au très noble *Ekkika comes des Aslan*. Avec le château de Wartberg, nous avons affaire à un autre siège comtal de la région de la Diemel. Après la mort du comte Dodiko, partisan de la maison royale ottonienne-saxonne, le château, les terres et les privilèges échurent au diocèse de Paderborn sous l'évêque Meinwerk. Dans la période suivante, le château constitua le plus important bastion des évêques de Paderborn lors des luttes de pouvoir dans la zone frontalière westphalienne-hessoise. Avec la forteresse construite au sommet du Desenberg, nous avons affaire à un autre site de la haute noblesse, qui se trouva au centre des intérêts politiques de l'Empire aux XIe et XIIe siècles. Contrairement à ce château imposant qui domine sur les hauteurs, le château des nobles seigneurs de Holthusen, situé sur un terrain bas, témoigne, par son architecture impressionnante, de l'auto-mise en scène de ses propriétaires, qui en firent un symbole bien visible de leur statut social, ce qui valut à leur demeure un rayonnement qui s'étendait bien au-delà de l'horizon des châteaux westphaliens.

Presque en même temps que le château de Holsterburg, la famille d'Aslen fit construire dans la vallée de la Diemel sa demeure de ministériaux, en contrebas du Gaulskopf. Les recherches archéologiques ont pu prouver ici l'existence d'un établissement dont la construction s'étend du haut Moyen Âge au Moyen Âge tardif et qui fut recouvert en partie par une motte castrale construite au Moyen Âge central. Celle-ci a été remplacée par une « maison forte » au début du XIVe siècle.

Castle Archaeology in a Border Region – The Example of Castle Building near the River Diemel

This article is concerned with the castles around the Diemel, the river delimiting the border between the Saxons and the Franks in the 7th and 8th centuries. After the Carolingian wars of conquest, which led to the Christianisation of the population and the integration of Westphalia into the organisation of the Church and of the Carolingian "counties", this border zone was a point of contact between the mission territories of the archbishoprics of Cologne and Mainz and of the bishopric of Würzburg (including its subdivision, the diocese of Paderborn), over which the Carolingian empire, which included them, asserted its rights.

The "castro" on the Gaulskopf, a fortification dating from Charlemagne's wars against the Saxons, served subsequently as the headquarters of the administration and representatives of *Ekkika comes des Aslan*, a member of the upper aristocracy. Wartberg castle is another county seat in the Diemal area. Following the death of Count Dodiko, a supporter of the Ottonian-Saxon royal house, the castle, its lands and privileges passed to the diocese of Paderborn at the time of Bishop Meinwerk. In the following period, during the power struggles in the border area between Westphalia and Hesse, it became the most important stronghold of the bishops of Paderborn. At the top of the Desenburg, there is another site which belonged to the upper aristocracy, a fortress – at the centre of the political interests of the Empire in the 11th and 12th centuries. In contrast with this imposing castle, towering up above it, the castle of the lords of Holthausen, on a low-lying site, with its impressive architecture bears witness to the owners' wish to build it as a clearly visible symbol of their social status, which earned a reputation for their residence extending far beyond the scene of the Westphalian castles.

Almost at the same time as Holsterburg castle, the Aslen family had had built in the Diemel Valley, just below the Gaulskopf, a ministerial residence for its administrators. Archaeological findings have revealed here the existence of a construction built from the High to the Late Middle Ages and which was covered in part by a castle mound erected in the Central Middle Ages. This was replace by a "fortified house" at the beginning of the 14th century.

Burgenarchäologie in einer Grenzregion – Ein Beitrag zum Burgenbau im Diemelraum

Im vorliegenden Aufsatz werden Burgen des Diemelraumes vorgestellt, der im 7./8. Jahrhundert den Grenzstreifen zwischen Sachsen und Franken bildete. Seit den karolingischen Eroberungskriegen, die mit der Christianisierung der Bevölkerung und der Eingliederung Westfalens in die karolingische Kirchen- und Grafschaftsorganisation einhergingen, stießen in diesem Grenzbereich die Missionsgebiete der Erzbistümer Köln, Mainz sowie des Bistums Würzburg, aus dem das Bistum Paderborn hervorging, aneinander, überlagert von den räumlich übergreifenden Ansprüchen des karolingischen Königtums.

Die Wallburg auf dem Gaulskopf, eine Befestigungsanlage aus der Zeit der Sachsenkriege Karls des Großen, diente in ihrer jüngeren Nutzungsphase als repräsentativer Herren- und Verwaltungssitz des hochadligen *Ekkika comes des Aslan*. Mit der Burg Wartberg fassen wir einen weiteren Grafensitz im Diemelraum. Nach dem Tod des Grafen Dodiko, Parteigänger des ottonisch-sächsischen Königshauses, gingen Burg, Grundbesitz und Grafenrechte an das Bistum Paderborn unter Bischof Meinwerk über. In der Folgezeit stellte die Burg den wichtigsten Stützpunkt der Paderborner Bischöfe in den Auseinandersetzungen um die Landesherrschaft im westfälisch-hessischen Grenzraum dar. Mit der Gipfelburg auf dem Desenberg fassen wir eine Anlage des Hochadels, die im 11./12. Jahrhundert im Fokus machtpolitischer Interessen der Reichspolitik stand. Im Gegensatz zu dieser imposanten Höhenburg zeugt die Niederungsburg der Edelherren von Holthusen in ihrer beeindruckenden Architektur als weithin sichtbares Statussymbol von deren Selbstdarstellung und hebt ihren Wohnsitz nicht nur aus der westfälischen Burgenlandschaft hervor.

Annähernd zeitgleich mit der Holsterburg wird der Ministerialensitz der Familie de Aslen im Diemeltal unterhalb des Gaulskopfes errichtet. Die archäologischen Untersuchungen erbrachten hier eine früh- bis spätmittelalterliche Siedlung, die im Hochmittelalter in Teilen von einer Motte überbaut wurde. Diese wurde im beginnenden 14. Jahrhundert durch ein „festes Haus" abgelöst.

Frédéric CHANTINNE, Philippe MIGNOT

Le rôle des châteaux dans le contrôle de la vallée de la Meuse aux confins de la Lotharingie et du diocèse de Liège (IXe-XIe siècle)

Un long fleuve comme la Meuse a souvent été considéré comme repère de limites. Les châteaux qui jalonnent ses rives ont pu laisser croire à une ligne défensive. Pour la période envisagée (IXe-XIe siècle), les fortifications protègent des centres de pouvoir et surveillent des routes. Dans plusieurs cas, leur implantation s'inscrit dans la continuité du Bas-Empire. À cette époque déjà et au contraire du Rhin, la défense du territoire de l'espace mosan était établie en profondeur et non le long du fleuve.

Par ailleurs, il convient d'envisager les châteaux de cette période dans d'autres fonctions que celle uniquement défensive.

The Importance of the Castles in Controlling the Meuse Valley at the Border between Lotharingia and the Diocese of Liège

A long river like the river Meuse has often been considered as a landmark for boundary, as well as castles that line its banks could suggest a defensive line. During the considered period (9th-11th centuries), fortifications protect centres of power and stand guard on roads. In many cases, their position is a continuation of the Late Roman Empire. Already at that time and unlike what happened along the Rhine, the territorial defence of the Meuse area was established on the entire territory and not only along the river.

Moreover, one should consider that castles from this period could have served other purposes than an only defensive function.

Die Bedeutung der Burgen für die Kontrolle über das Maastal an der Grenze zwischen Lothringen und der Diözese Lüttich (9.-11. Jahrhundert)

Lange Flüsse wie die Maas wurden häufig als Grenzmarkierung betrachtet. Burgen und Schlösser, die das Ufer säumen, konnten eine Verteidigungslinie vermuten lassen. Für den Bezugszeitraum (9.-11. Jahrhundert), dienen die Befestigungsanlagen dem Schutz der Machtzentren und der Überwachung der Straßen. In vielen Fällen ist ihre Ansiedlung in einer Kontinuität zum spätrömischen Reich zu sehen. Bereits in dieser Zeit, und im Gegensatz zum Rhein, wurde im Maas-Raum eine gestaffelte Verteidigung praktiziert, keine lineare, entlang des Flusses.

Im Übrigen hat man die Burgen aus dieser Zeit in anderen als nur Verteidigungsfunktionen zu sehen.

Owain James CONNORS

L'influence des seigneuries anglo-normandes sur le paysage du Monmouthshire

Cet article constitue un bref résumé d'un projet de doctorat en cours qui s'interroge sur l'importance des modes de puissance politique et d'identité sociale anglo-normandes au pays de Galles dans la période post-conquête (vers 1066-1300), visibles dans le paysage historique, particulièrement dans le comté frontalier du Monmouthshire. En utilisant le SIG, cette thèse analyse les aspects de changement du paysage qui peuvent être attribués à la période post-conquête, tels que l'existence de systèmes de champs non enclos à grande échelle, de groupement d'habitations et du paysage « seigneurial », et les relie à la présence d'importants sites de seigneuries anglo-normandes, tels que châteaux et agglomérations. De cette façon, le projet établira si le changement dans le paysage était dû à un mouvement du « haut vers le bas » ou du « bas vers le haut » et dans quelle mesure les châteaux, en tant qu'importants centres seigneuriaux, ont joué un rôle de catalyseur du changement.

The Influence of Anglo-Norman Lordship upon the Landscape of Monmouthshire

This paper constitutes a brief summary of an ongoing Ph.D. research project which aims to investigate the extent to which patterns of Anglo-Norman political power and social identity in post-Conquest medieval Wales (*c.* 1066-1300 AD), specifically in the border county of Monmouthshire, are visible within the historic landscape. Using GIS, this thesis analyses features of landscape change attributable to the post-Conquest period, such as the presence of large-scale open-field systems, settlement nucleation and the "seigneurial" landscape, and relates them to the presence of major Anglo-Norman lordship sites, such as castles and boroughs. In doing this, the project will determine whether landscape change was a "top-down" or "bottom-up" process and the degree to which castles, as major lordship centres, acted as catalysts for this change.

Der Einfluss der anglonormannischen Grafschaften auf die Landschaft Monmouthshire

Dieser Beitrag bietet die kurze Zusammenfassung eines laufenden Dissertationsprojektes, in dem untersucht werden soll, in welchem Maße Strukturen anglonormannischer politischer Machtausübung und sozialer Identität im mittelalterlichen Wales nach dessen Eroberung (um 1066-1300) in der historischen Landschaft sichtbar werden, insbesondere in der grenznahen Grafschaft Monmouthshire. Unter Verwendung des GIS analysiert die Arbeit Veränderungen in der Landschaft, die sich der Epoche nach der Eroberung zuschreiben lassen, wie Gewannflursysteme großen Maßstabs, Siedlungsagglomerationen und „herrschaftliche" Landschaften, und setzt sie zu bestehenden wichtigen Einrichtungen der anglonormannischen Grafschaften wie Burgen und *boroughs* in Beziehung. Auf diese Weise wird die Studie klären, ob die Veränderung der Landschaft einer Bewegung „von oben nach unten" oder „von unten nach oben" folgte und in welchem Maße die Burgen als wichtige herrschaftliche Zentren als Katalysatoren dieser Veränderung gewirkt haben.

Oliver CREIGHTON

Château, burh et borough : le décodage d'un puissant paysage urbain à Wallingford, Oxfordshire

Le site de Wallingford, dans l'Oxfordshire, est bien connu parmi les spécialistes de l'archéologie médiévale britannique comme étant sans doute un exemple classique d'un *burh*, ou centre fortifié, anglo-saxon. La ville conserve aussi les remblais étendus d'un château royal fondé peu après la conquête normande et qui avait été transformé en une grande forteresse concentrique avant la fin du XIIIe siècle. Le projet de recherche « Wallingford : d'un *burh* à une agglomération » (*Wallingford Burh to Borough Research Project*) a étudié le château et son emplacement au sein d'un projet de plus vaste envergure, qui avait pour but la mise en place d'une biographie de la ville pour former la base d'une importante étude sur la transformation urbaine au cours de l'époque médiévale. Le projet a dressé le plan du château médiéval « perdu » au moyen d'une enquête géophysique et sur les remblais ; les fouilles, conduites à certains endroits de l'enceinte intérieure et des défenses du périmètre, ont permis la réinterprétation des anciennes fouilles effectuées dans les années 1960 et 1970, y compris celles des rares cuisines en pisé, et ont éclairé l'emplacement du site dans un paysage aquatique conçu autant pour exprimer son importance que pour sa défense. Le rapport entre château et agglomération était complexe et évoluait : si, d'une certaine manière, les institutions existaient en symbiose, d'une autre, l'enceinte du château constituait une sphère à part et il se peut que ce statut de haut standing ait finalement contribué au déclin éventuel de la ville médiévale.

Castle, Burh and Borough: Unravelling an Urban Landscape of Power at Wallingford, Oxfordshire

In British medieval archaeology the site of Wallingford, in Oxfordshire, is well known as a supposedly classic example of an Anglo-Saxon *burh*, or fortified centre. The town also preserves the extensive earthworks of a royal castle founded shortly after the Norman Conquest that was developed into a large concentric fortress by the end of the 13th century. The *Wallingford Burh to Borough Research Project* investigated the castle and its setting as part of wider project that sought to unravel the biography of the town to produce a major case study of urban transformation through the medieval period. The Project mapped the "lost" medieval castle through geophysical and earthwork survey; excavated areas of its inner bailey and perimeter defences; reinterpreted past excavations from the 1960s and 1970s, including on the castle's rare cob-built kitchens; and illuminated the site's location within a watery landscape designed for the display of status as well as for defence. The interrelationship between castle and borough was complex and evolving: while in some senses the two institutions were symbiotically linked, in other ways the precincts of the castle constituted a separate sphere and the high-status presence may ultimately have contributed to the town's later medieval decline.

Burg, burh und borough: Die Dekodierung einer städtischen Landschaft der Macht in Wallingford, Oxfordshire

In der britischen mediävistischen Archäologie ist der Fundort Wallingford in Oxfordshire wohlbekannt als vermutlich klassisches Beispiel eines angelsächsischen *burh*, d.h. eines befestigten Ortes. In der Stadt sind außerdem die ausgedehnten Erdwerke eines königlichen Schlosses erhalten, das kurz nach der normannischen Eroberung gegründet und zum Ende des 13. Jahrhunderts in eine große konzentrische Festung ausgebaut wurde. Im Forschungsprojekt „Wallingford: Vom *burh* zum *borough*" (*Wallingford Burh to Borough Research Project*) wurden das Schloss und seine Platzierung als Teil einer umfassenderen Untersuchung studiert, die die Biographie einer Stadt als Grundlage für eine große Fallstudie urbaner Transformation über das gesamte Mittelalter erarbeiten sollte. Das Projekt erstellte einen Plan des „verlorenen" mittelalterlichen Schlosses mithilfe einer geophysikalischen und Erdwerksuntersuchung; führte Ausgrabungen der inneren Vorburgen und der Festungsanlagen durch; leistete eine Neuinterpretation der früheren Ausgrabungen der 1960er und 1970er Jahre, einschließlich der seltenen in Lehmbauweise errichteten Schlossküchen; und wies die Situierung des Anlage in einer wasserreichen Landschaft nach, die sowohl ihren Status zeigen als auch zur Verteidigung dienen sollte. Die Beziehung zwischen dem Schloss und der Siedlung war komplex und veränderte sich über die Zeit: Während beide in gewisser Weise symbiotisch miteinander verbunden waren, bildete die Schlossfestung auf der anderen Seite eine eigenständige Sphäre, und diese hochgestellte Präsenz hat möglicherweise zum späteren Niedergang der mittelalterlichen Stadt beigetragen.

Koen DE GROOTE

Des fouilles conduites sur un château en briques (auparavant inconnu) de la fin du XIVe siècle à Aalter (Flandre, Belgique) – Une place forte bourguignonne se trouvant entre les villes flamandes insoumises de Gand et Bruges

En 2010, des fouilles à grande échelle ont été conduites à Aalter, au lieu-dit « Woestijne ». Le site, situé entre Bruges et Gand, révéla les fondations d'un château en briques qui remonte à la fin du XIVe ou au XVe siècle. Le château fut sans doute construit par la famille noble de Flandre, à savoir les seigneurs de Woestijne, apparentés au comte de Flandre. On ne connaît pour ainsi dire aucune source écrite qui le cite. Cet article est de nature préliminaire car ni les preuves archéologiques, ni les vestiges architecturaux du château, ni les sources historiques n'ont encore été pleinement étudiés.

A Previously Unknown Late 14th-Century Brick Castle Excavated at Aalter (Flanders, Belgium) – A Burgundian Stronghold that Lay between the Rebellious Flemish Towns of Ghent and Bruges

In 2010 a large-scale excavation took place at Aalter, at a locality called "Woestijne". The site, which is situated between Bruges and Ghent, revealed the foundations of a brick castle that dates from the late 14th or 15th century. The castle was probably built by a noble family of Flanders, the lords of Woestijne, who were related to the count of Flanders. Almost no written sources are known to refer to this castle. The study presented here is preliminary, as neither the archaeological evidence, nor the building characteristics of the castle remains, nor the historical sources, are fully studied yet.

Ausgrabungen einer bislang unbekannten Burg des 14. Jahrhunderts in Aalter (Flandern, Belgien) – Eine burgundische Festung, die zwischen den aufständischen Städten Ghet und Brügge gelegen war

Im Jahre 2010 wurden umfängliche Grabungen in Aalter, an einem Ort namens „Woestijne", durchgeführt. Die Fundstätte, die zwischen Brügge und Ghent liegt, enthüllte die Fundamente einer Burg in Ziegelbauweise, die auf das späte 14. oder das 15. Jahrhundert zurückgeht. Die Burg wurde vermutlich von einer flandrischen Adelsfamilie gebaut, den Herren von Woestijne, die mit dem Grafen von Flandern verwandt waren. Es gibt praktisch keine schriftliche Quelle, die diese Burg erwähnen würde. Der Beitrag ist vorläufiger Natur, da weder die archäologischen Befunde noch die baulichen Eigenheiten der Burgüberreste noch die historischen Quellen abschließend untersucht worden sind.

Gillian EADIE

Reflets d'un pays divisé ? Le rôle des tours d'habitation dans l'Irlande du bas Moyen Âge

Le but de cet article est de s'interroger de nouveau sur le rôle des tours d'habitation en Irlande en se concentrant sur une étude des signes de différence sociale au-delà des frontières aux multiples facettes de ce pays. Les tours d'habitation nous permettent d'établir une comparaison entre les priorités des divers groupes au sein de la société irlandaise au cours du bas Moyen Âge car elles furent construites tantôt par ceux d'origine anglo-saxonne et tantôt par ceux d'origine gaélique. Les résultats suggèrent que, tandis qu'il est possible de considérer l'adoption répandue de la tour d'habitation comme forme d'assimilation culturelle au cours des quelque 170 ans suivant la colonisation, les tours elles-mêmes témoignent de diverses fonctions et priorités. Bien que d'autres besoins aient pu également influencer ces priorités, la signification de la différence culturelle et la manifestation déterminée de cette différence peuvent indiquer une motivation non négligeable.

Reflections of a Divided Country? The Role of Tower Houses in Late-Medieval Ireland

This paper seeks to reassess the role of tower houses in Ireland with a focus on exploring manifestations of social difference across Ireland's multifaceted borders. Tower houses offer the opportunity to compare the priorities of different groups within late-medieval Irish society, as they were built by those of both Anglo-Norman and Gaelic descent. The results suggest that whilst the widespread adoption of the tower house can be viewed as a form of cultural assimilation c. 170 years post-colonisation, the towers themselves demonstrate differing functions and priorities. Whilst other needs could also influence these priorities, the significance of cultural difference, and the purposeful demonstration of that difference, cannot be overlooked as a motivating factor.

Spiegelungen eines geteilten Landes? Die Rolle der Wohntürme im spätmittelalterlichen Irland

Es ist das Ziel dieses Beitrags, die Rolle der Wohntürme in Irland neu zu untersuchen, wobei der Fokus auf Manifestationen sozialer Differenz über Irlands vielgestaltige Grenzen hinweg gelegt werden soll. Die Wohntürme ermöglichen es uns, einen Vergleich der Prioritäten der verschiedenen Gruppen innerhalb der irischen Gesellschaft während des Mittelalters anzustellen, da diese sowohl von Bauherren angelsächsischer als auch solchen gälischer Abstammung errichtet wurden. Die Ergebnisse lassen vermuten, dass es zwar möglich ist, die breite Übernahme des Wohnturms als Form kultureller Assimilation in den 170 Jahren nach der Kolonisierung anzusehen, dass aber die Türme selbst von unterschiedlichen Funktionen und Prioritäten zeugen. Obwohl auch andere Bedürfnisse diese Prioritäten beeinflusst haben mögen, darf doch die Bedeutung der kulturellen Differenz und die bewusste Zurschaustellung dieser Differenz als Motivation nicht unterschätzt werden.

Richard EALES

Châteaux et frontières en Angleterre après 1066

Si l'on considère de nos jours le terme « château » comme étant discutable et problématique, celui de « frontière » ne l'est pas moins pour l'époque médiévale. Cet article débute par l'examen des définitions des deux concepts utilisés par les historiens et les archéologues, afin de formuler des questions-clés à propos du rôle des châteaux dans les régions frontalières. Ensuite, on examinera une étude précise de la conquête normande de l'Angleterre, prétendant que l'implantation normande progressive, qui s'effectua durant la vingtaine d'années après l'invasion, avait créé toute une série d'aires frontalières à la fois fluides et temporaires à travers le pays. Ceci avait constitué un contexte fondamental et sous-estimé pour l'introduction de châteaux dans les années suivant la conquête et avait eu des conséquences à plus long terme.

Castles and Borders in England after 1066

If the term "castle" is now often treated as debatable and problematic, then "border" is no less so for the medieval period. This paper begins by reviewing some definitions of both concepts employed by historians and archaeologists, in order to formulate key questions about the role of castles in border regions. It then examines a case study of the Norman Conquest of England, arguing that the progressive Norman settlement which followed in the 20 years or so after the invasion of 1066 created a whole series of fluid and temporary borderlands across the country. This was a crucial and underrated context for the introduction of castles into post-conquest England, and also had longer-term consequences.

Burgen und Grenzen in England nach 1066

Wenn heute der Begriff „Burg" als strittig und problematisch angesehen wird, dann verhält es sich mit der „Grenze" für das Mittelalter nicht anders. Der Beitrag beginnt mit einer Betrachtung der Definitionen beider Begriffe, wie sie von Historikern und Archäologen verwendet werden, um dann Kernfragen in Bezug auf die Rolle von Burgen in Grenzregionen zu formulieren. Danach wird eine Fallstudie zur normannischen Eroberung Englands vorgestellt, in der die Auffassung vertreten wird, dass die fortschreitende normannische Ansiedlung in den etwa zwanzig Jahren nach der Invasion von 1066 eine Vielzahl von Grenzgebieten im ganzen Land geschaffen hat, die gleichzeitig fließend und temporär waren. Dies war der entscheidende und unterschätzte Kontext für die Einführung von Burgen in England nach der Eroberung und hatte auch langfristige Konsequenzen.

Peter ETTEL

Les « châteaux contre les Hongrois » dans le sud de l'Allemagne au xe siècle

L'interprétation des sites connus sous le nom de « *Ungarnburgen* » (« châteaux contre les Hongrois ») comme formant un système de châteaux forts dirigé contre les invasions hongroises doit être rejetée depuis qu'a eu lieu le débat autour des enceintes circulaires saxonnes. Il faut plutôt considérer les remparts de terre et les obstacles d'approche comme des éléments de fortification, répondant spécifiquement à la menace que faisait alors peser la Hongrie, réponse qui fut facile et rapide à mettre en œuvre sans beaucoup de connaissances préalables. Sur la cinquantaine de « châteaux contre les Hongrois » postulée, depuis longtemps pour certains d'entre eux, par la littérature, l'état de la recherche montre que seul un petit nombre est à interpréter comme munis de remparts de terre datant effectivement du temps des invasions hongroises, à la fin du IXe siècle et surtout pendant la première moitié du Xe siècle. Faute de recherches archéologiques, la datation et l'interprétation de la grande majorité d'entre eux restent incertaines. Certains sites sont sans aucun doute à supprimer de la liste. Il est sûrement trop simple, raisonnant par analogie avec la description historique de Saint-Gall, de dater tous les châteaux forts avec remparts de terre et obstacles d'approche de l'époque des invasions hongroises, et de les interpréter comme des refuges, en l'absence de fouilles archéologiques dans la zone des fortifications et à l'intérieur. L'existence des « châteaux contre les Hongrois » ne fait pas de doute, mais elle reste à vérifier et à établir au cas par cas au moyen de fouilles appropriées.

The "Castles against the Hungarians" in the South of Germany in the 10th Century

The interpretation of the sites known as "*Ungarnburgen*" ("castles against the Hungarians") forming a system of fortresses against attacks by Hungary has to be rejected in the light of the debate on circular Saxon enclosures. The earthen ramparts and the approach obstacles should rather be looked upon as elements of fortification, as a specific response to the threat that Hungary then presented, a response that was easily and quickly realisable without much previous knowledge. Out of the fifty or so "castles against the Hungarians" proposed in the literature (some of them for a long time), present research shows that only a small number of them can be said to have earthen ramparts dating in fact from the time of the Hungarian invasions, at the end of the 9th century and especially during the first half of the 10th century. Because of the lack of archaeological surveys, the dating and interpretation of the vast majority of them remain uncertain. There is no doubt that some of the sites should be removed from the list. It is obviously too simplistic, to argue by analogy with the historical description of Sankt Gallen, that all the castles with earthen ramparts and approach obstacles date from the period of the Hungarian invasions, and to interpret them as places to take refuge, in the absence of archaeological excavations in the zone of the fortifications and in the interior. The existence of "castles against the Hungarians" is not questioned but it needs to be verified and established case by case in the light of the appropriate excavations.

Ungarnburgen in Süddeutschland im 10. Jahrhundert

Die Interpretation der Anlagen als ein gegen die Ungarneinfälle errichtetes System von Burgen ist schon seit der Diskussion um die sächsischen Rundwälle abzulehnen. Eher wird man überlegen müssen, geschüttete Wälle und Annäherungshindernisse als befestigungstechnische Elemente, als zeitspezifische Reaktion auf die Ungarnbedrohung zu sehen, die leicht und schnell, ohne große Vorkenntnisse zu bewältigen war. Die neuere Forschung zeigt, dass von den etwa 50 in der Literatur teilweise seit langem postulierten Ungarnburgen nur einige tatsächlich als geschütteter Wall zu interpretieren sind und dazu auch in die Zeit der Ungarneinfälle, ausgehendes 9. Jahrhundert, v.a. 1. Hälfte 10. Jahrhundert datieren. Die große Mehrzahl muss infolge fehlender archäologischer Untersuchungen bislang in ihrer Deutung und Datierung unsicher bleiben, einige Fundplätze sind ganz sicher zu streichen. Im Analogieschluss zur historischen Schilderung von St. Gallen alle Burgen mit geschütteten Wällen und Annäherungshindernissen in die Ungarnzeit zu datieren und als Refugium zu interpretieren, ist sicherlich zu einfach, zumal wenn keine archäologischen Untersuchungen im Befestigungs- und Innenbereich vorliegen. Die Existenz von Ungarnburgen ist unzweifelhaft, sie ist aber im Einzelfall mit entsprechenden Grabungen zu prüfen und zu belegen.

István FELD

Les châteaux forts de la région frontalière austro-hongroise aux XIIe et XIIIe siècles

La zone frontalière entre le royaume médiéval de Hongrie et les régions orientales de l'Empire romain germanique est particulièrement riche en châteaux, souvent bien conservés, mais encore insuffisamment explorés archéologiquement. Leur date de construction, ainsi que la question de savoir dans quelle mesure ils sont à interpréter comme des « forteresses frontalières », sont encore fortement discutées dans la recherche autrichienne aussi bien que hongroise, et la réponse à y apporter reste ouverte. Les fortifications, pour la plupart petites (souvent en bois), qui ont été construites en très grand nombre de part et d'autre de la « frontière » à partir du XIIe siècle, sont à considérer plutôt comme « simples » demeures aristocratiques, le rôle d'un maître d'ouvrage royal ou seigneurial se laissant rarement démontrer. Mais en cherchant à exploiter les sources écrites et, plus rarement, archéologiques dont nous disposons sur la construction des châteaux de la zone frontalière austro-hongroise entre 1150 et 1250, nous arrivons à un constat surprenant. Selon les dernières recherches, il existe déjà vers 1150, dans le sud-est de la Basse-Autriche actuelle, près de 50 demeures aristocratiques, tandis que dans les zones du royaume de Hongrie immédiatement adjacentes à l'est, la construction de châteaux privés, nombreux là aussi, paraît peu probable avant 1200 – ceux-ci datant généralement au plus tôt du XIIIe siècle. La question de savoir si cette vision correspond à la réalité historique ou non ne pourra être tranchée que par de nouvelles recherches archéologiques.

The Castles along the Austro-Hungarian Border in the 12th and 13th Centuries

The border area between the medieval kingdom of Hungary and the eastern regions of the Roman Germanic Empire is particularly well-endowed with castles, often well preserved but not yet sufficiently explored by archaeologists. The date of their construction as well as the question of knowing to what extent they can be seen as "border fortresses" are contested by both Austrian and Hungarian researchers and the answers are still to be found. The fortified places, for the most part of modest proportions (often built of wood), constructed in large numbers on either side of the "border" from the 12th century, can be considered to be rather "ordinary" aristocratic residences, revealing rarely an architecture reflecting royal or noble influence. But when seeking to exploit the available written and less numerous archaeological sources concerning the construction of the castles in the Austro-Hungarian border area between 1150 and 1250, we were surprised by the outcome. According to the latest research, around 1150 there existed already close on 50 aristocratic residences in the south-east of what is now Lower Austria, whereas in the areas of the kingdom of Hungary immediately to the east; the construction of private castles, also in relatively large numbers, seems unlikely to have taken place before 1200 – the earliest of them dating generally from the 13th century. Only new archaeological surveys will allow us to ascertain whether this view corresponds to historical reality or not.

Burgen im österreichisch-ungarischen Grenzraum im 12. und 13. Jahrhundert

Der Grenzraum des mittelalterlichen Königreiches Ungarn und der östlichen Gebiete des Deutsch-Römischen Reiches ist besonders reich an oft gut erhaltenen, aber archäologisch noch ungenügend erforschten Burganlagen. Wann sie entstanden und inwieweit sie als „Grenzburgen" zu interpretieren sind, gehört zu den meist diskutierten, aber immer noch offenen Fragen sowohl der österreichischen als auch der ungarischen Burgenforschung. Die ab dem 12. Jahrhundert in sehr großer Zahl (oft mit Holzkonstruktion) errichteten, meist kleinen Befestigungen sind auf den beiden Seiten der „Grenze" eher als „normale" Adelsburgen zu bestimmen – ein königlicher bzw. landesherrlicher Bauherr ist selten nachzuweisen. Wenn wir aber den Burgenbau des österreichisch-ungarischen Grenzraumes in der zweiten Hälfte des 12. und in der ersten Hälfte des 13. Jahrhunderts anhand von schriftlichen und wenigen archäologischen Quellen analysieren möchten, kommen wir zu einem überraschenden Ergebnis: Im heutigen südöstlichen Niederösterreich existierten nach neuesten Forschungen schon um 1150 fast 50 Adelsburgen, dagegen rechnet man auf den östlich direkt benachbarten Gebieten des Königreiches Ungarn vor 1200 kaum mit einem privaten Burgenbau – die auch hier in großer Zahl vorhandenen Anlagen sind meist frühestens in das 13. Jahrhundert datiert. Ob dieses Bild der historischen Wirklichkeit entspricht, ist nur mit weiteren archäologischen Forschungen zu klären.

Thomas FINAN

Les sites entourés de douves dans le comté de Roscommon, Irlande : une approche statistique

De nos jours, nous savons que les sites entourés de douves en Irlande constituaient une partie importante du paysage irlandais au Moyen Âge. Dans le passé, ces places fortes ont été considérées comme exemple de l'implantation anglo-normande, mais des recherches récentes ont montré que les seigneurs gaéliques de haut rang avaient fait construire des sites entourés de douves comme fortifications élémentaires et centres seigneuriaux comparables à des « *crannogs* » (ces îles naturelles ou artificielles qui servaient d'habitation), occupant une grande partie des fonctions des châteaux contemporains. Cet article examine une méthode un peu différente pour étudier le rapport entre les sites entourés de douves dans le paysage en tenant compte des multiples variables relevant de l'importance du site et de sa proximité à d'autres traits du paysage médiéval grâce à une analyse fondée sur une classification hiérarchique ascendante (*Hierarchical Clustering analysis*). L'étude révèle que les sites entourés de douves qui sont d'origine gaélique dans le comté de Roscommon se trouvent dans un contexte paysagiste très différent de ceux de l'Irlande orientale, laissant supposer que ces sites étaient considérés plutôt comme des atouts stratégiques que comme des implantations agricoles de niveau intermédiaire.

Moated Sites in County Roscommon, Ireland: a Statistical Approach

Irish moated sites are now known to be a significant component of the medieval Irish landscape. In the past, these fortifications have been characterised as examples of Anglo-Norman settlement, but recent research has shown that high status Gaelic lords constructed moated sites as primary fortifications and lordly centres on a par with crannogs, with many of the functions of contemporary castles. This paper examines a slightly different method for examining the relationship between moated sites in the landscape by considering multiple variables related to the size of the sites and proximity to other medieval landscape features in a Hierarchical Clustering analysis. This study shows that the moated sites that are of Gaelic origin in County Roscommon display very different landscape contexts to ones in Eastern Ireland, which then suggests that perhaps these sites were viewed more along the lines of strategic assets than mid-level agricultural settlements.

Stätten mit Burggräben in der Grafschaft Roscommon, Irland: Eine statistische Untersuchung

Wir wissen heute, dass Bauwerke, die von Gräben umgeben waren, in Irland einen wesentlichen Bestandteil der irischen Landschaft des Mittelalters darstellten. Früher wurden diese befestigten Plätze als Zeichen der anglo-normannischen Invasion betrachtet; neuere Forschungen haben aber gezeigt, dass die hohen gälischen Adligen ihrerseits mit Gräben befestigte Plätze als elementare Befestigungen oder herrschaftliche Zentren wie die „crannogs" (jene natürlichen oder künstlichen Inseln, die als Wohnplätze dienten) gebaut haben, die die meisten Funktionen zeitgenössischer Burgen erfüllten. Der Beitrag zeigt eine neue Methode, um die Beziehungen zwischen den mit Gräben umgebenen Plätzen in der Landschaft zu untersuchen, bei der mehrere Variablen hinsichtlich der Bedeutung des Platzes und seiner Entfernung von anderen Landschaftsmerkmalen in einer hierarchischen Ballungsanalyse (*Hierarchical Clustering analysis*) berücksichtigt werden. Die Studie zeigt, dass von Gräben umgebene Stätten gälischen Ursprungs in der Grafschaft Roscommon sich in einem ganz anderen landschaftlichen Kontext finden als die im östlichen Irland, was darauf schließen lässt, dass diese Stätten eher als strategische Trümpfe verstanden wurden denn als bäuerliche Ansiedlungen mittlerer Ebene.

Anne-Marie Flambard Héricher

Les derniers acquis des recherches sur le Château Ganne

À la limite des départements du Calvados et de l'Orne, le Château Ganne, possession des seigneurs de La Pommeraye, est un site fossoyé bien conservé composé de trois enceintes successives dont la basse cour principale est fouillée depuis 2004. Les recherches ont permis de mettre au jour, dans ce périmètre protégé par un rempart de terre surmonté d'une courtine maçonnée, des bâtiments aux fonctions bien identifiées (chapelle, fournil, cuisine et deux résidences successives) et de préciser leur chronologie qui montre l'installation des premiers bâtiments dès le Xe siècle et un abandon du site au début du XIVe siècle.

La haute cour et la tour porche, aux dimensions et à la morphologie exceptionnelles, qui permet d'y pénétrer, restent à étudier dans le détail et à dater.

La contribution vise à faire le point sur l'avancement de l'étude du site et à s'interroger sur l'organisation vraisemblable de la haute cour.

Ganne Castle: the Latest Research Findings

On the border of Calvados and Orne, Ganne Castle, belonging to the La Pommeraye lordship, is a well-preserved ditch-work site comprising three successive enceintes of which the main bailey has been the object of excavations since 2004. These have revealed, in the perimeter protected by an earthwork rampart capped by a stone curtain wall, buildings with clearly identifiable functions (chapel, bakehouse, kitchen and two successive residences) and provided precisions about their chronology which points to the installation of the first buildings as early as the 10th century and to the abandonment of the site at the beginning of the 14th.

The upper bailey and the porch tower, which afford an entrance, are exceptional in both size and morphology and remain to be studied in detail and to be dated.

This article aims to provide an up-to-date account of the progress in the study of the site and to consider the likely organisation of the upper bailey.

Die neuesten Untersuchungsergebnisse zu Château Ganne

Auf der Grenze zwischen den Departements Calvados und Orne liegt Château Ganne, Besitztum der Herren von La Pommeraye, eine gut erhaltene, von einem Burggraben umgebene Anlage, bestehend aus drei gestaffelten Arealen. In der großen Vorburg finden seit 2004 Ausgrabungen statt. Die Forschungen konnten in dieser von einem geschütteten Wall mit aufgesetzter Schildmauer geschützten Zone Gebäude mit gut identifizierbaren Funktionen freilegen (Kapellenbau, Backstube, Küche und zwei hintereinander liegende Wohngebäude) und ihre Chronologie präzisieren, die die Einrichtung der ersten Gebäude bereits im 10. Jahrhundert zeigt und das Verlassen der Anlage im frühen 14. Jahrhundert.

Die Kernburg und der Torturm von außergewöhnlicher Form und Größe, über den der Zugang erfolgt, sind noch im Einzelnen zu untersuchen und zu datieren.

Der Beitrag möchte den aktuellen Stand der Untersuchungen an der Fundstätte darstellen und der Frage nach der mutmaßlichen Organisation der Kernburg nachgehen.

Christian Frey

L'organisation dite *burgward* dans les régions frontalières de l'est du royaume germanique – Mentalité et inculturation

Les régions frontalières de l'est du royaume germanique au Moyen Âge étaient des zones de conflit aussi bien que de coopération entre les cultures. Une forme d'organisation seigneuriale coloniale s'y trouvait, pour laquelle dans les sources écrites on n'utilise qu'un seul terme, *burgward*. Un *burgward* se composait d'un château et de 10 à 20 villages habités par des colons saxons et des fermiers slaves. Tandis que des études plus anciennes supposaient que les racines de l'organisation dite *burgward* se trouvaient dans des exemples d'infrastructure seigneuriale en France et en Angleterre, une nouvelle interprétation est proposée : à l'origine, *burgward* était le nom de la fonction d'un intendant, lequel, par la suite, était transféré à une forme de colonisation seigneuriale aux alentours d'un château. Puisque les terres non attribuées dans les régions frontalières pouvaient être exploitées par des colons et permettaient l'établissement de nouvelles seigneuries, des nobles de toute catégorie se dirigèrent vers les régions frontalières pour augmenter leur pouvoir. Les châteaux que construisirent ces colons nobles changèrent les points de repère des paysages environnants et furent les nœuds infrastructuraux les plus importants dans les aires frontalières. Ils devinrent des lieux d'inculturation occupant certaines fonctions auprès de tous les groupes culturels des environs.

The *Burgward* Organisation in the Eastern Marches of the German Realm – Frontier Mentality and Inculturation

The marches of the German East in the Middle Ages were zones of conflict, as well as of cooperation between cultures. Here a form of lordly colonial organisation can be found, that was named with the unique term *burgward* in the written sources. A *burgward* consisted of a castle and 10 to 20 villages inhabited by Saxon settlers and Slavic farmers. While the older research assumed the roots of the *burgward*-organisation lay in examples of lordly infrastructure in France and England, a new interpretation of the sources is presented: the origin of *burgward* is the name of the function of a steward which was transferred to a castle-centric form of colonising lordship. Since free land in the marches could be developed by settlements and presented an opportunity to establish new lordships, nobles of all kinds came to the border regions to widen their power. The castles that these noble settlers built rearranged their surrounding landscapes and were the most important infrastructural points in the marches. They became places of inculturation that served all cultural groups living around them with a number of functions.

Die *Burgward*-Organisation in den Ostmarken des germanischen Reichs – Mentalität und Inkulturation

Die Marken im Osten des Ostfränkischen Reiches waren gleichermaßen Zonen von Konflikt und Kooperation der hier ansässigen Kulturen. Aus den Quellen ist eine Organisationsform von Landesausbau und Herrschaft bekannt, die mit dem einzigartigen Begriff *burgward* benannt wird. Diese Burgwarde bestanden aus einer Befestigung und 10-20 Dörfern, die von sächsischen Siedlern und slawischen Bauern bewohnt waren. Nahm die ältere Forschung noch an, die Ursprünge der Burgwarde sei in Frankreich oder England zu suchen, wird hier eine neue Interpretation angeboten. Demnach ist der Ursprung im Amt eines Burgwardes, eines Wächters oder Beauftragten zu suchen; erst später erfolgte der Übertrag auf die burgenzentrische Herrschaftsform. In den Marken gab es viel freies Land zu erschließen, was Adelige aus dem ganzen Reich anzog. Die Burgen, die diese Adeligen bauten, formten die sie umgebenden Landschaften und wurden die wichtigsten Infrastrukturpunkte in den Marken. Sie wurden zu Orten der Inkulturation und dienten den umwohnenden Gruppen mit vielen Funktionen.

Reinhard Friedrich

Châteaux forts et frontières territoriales dans les électorats rhénans

Dans la vallée du Rhin moyen, importante voie de communication médiévale, plusieurs seigneurs territoriaux puissants, parmi eux les archevêchés de Mayence, de Trèves et de Cologne, mènent une politique castrale très active. La présente contribution se propose d'en donner une illustration en choisissant l'exemple des comtes palatins du Rhin, qui sécurisaient leurs propriétés sur la frontière, de part et d'autre du Rhin, par des châteaux forts. Sur la rive gauche du Rhin, le château de Stahleck, propriété du comte palatin éponyme, formait avec la ville de Bacharach le noyau d'un territoire sécurisé aux frontières, durant le XIIIe siècle, par les châteaux forts de Fürstenberg et Stahlberg.

La petite zone située sur la rive droite, avec l'importante douane de Kaub, jouait un rôle crucial pour le Palatinat électoral. Elle était directement sécurisée par la forteresse de Gutenfels (XIIIe siècle), ainsi que par le château fort de Pfalzgrafenstein, construit en 1327 sur une petite île du Rhin. Mais ce territoire du comté palatin était menacé également à ses frontières, d'autant plus que des seigneurs territoriaux voisins y avaient leurs propres châteaux frontaliers. C'est pour cette raison que, vers le milieu du XIVe siècle, les comtes palatins entreprirent la construction de deux châteaux de défense, dont seule la Sauerburg, située à la frontière avec le Kurmainz au sud-est, a été achevée, alors que le château de Herzogenstein est resté inachevé en raison de l'opposition de la ville voisine d'Oberwesel.

Castles and Border Areas in the Rhine Electorates

In the centre of the Rhine Valley, an important medieval nodal communication point, several powerful noble landowners, including the archbishops of Mainz, Trier and Cologne, followed a dynamic castle policy. The present paper aims to illustrate this with an example taken from the Counts Palatine of the Rhine, who protected their properties along either side of the border with castles. On the left bank of the Rhine, the castle of Stahleck, belonging to the Count Palatine of the same name, formed with the town of Bacharach, the heart of an area at the border protected during the 13th century by the castles of Fürstenberg and Stahlberg.

The small area situated on the right bank, containing the important customs post at Kaub, played a crucial role for the Electoral Palatinate. It was directly protected by the Gutenfels fortress (13th century) and by the castle of Pfalzgrafenstein, built in 1327 on a little island in the Rhine. But this area of the County Palatine was under threat at the borders, especially as the neighbouring noble landowners had their own border castles there. For this reason, towards the middle of the 14th century, the Counts Palatine built two defensive castles, of which only Sauerburg, situated on the border with Kurmainz to the south-east, was completed, whereas Herzogenstein Castle remained unfinished because of opposition from the neighbouring town of Oberwesel.

Burgen und Territorialgrenzen in den rheinischen Kurfürstentümern

Im Mittelrheintal, als bedeutendem mittelalterlichen Verkehrsweg, betreiben mehrere mächtige Territorialherren, darunter die Erzbischöfe von Mainz, Trier und Köln, eine rege Burgenpolitik. Im vorliegenden Fall wird dies am Beispiel der Pfalzgrafen bei Rhein dargestellt, die ihre links- und rechtsrheinischen Besitzungen an den Grenzen durch Burgen sicherten. Linksrheinisch bildete die frühe pfalzgräfliche Burg Stahleck mit Bacharach den Kern eines Territoriums, das im Laufe des 13. Jahrhunderts durch die Burgen Fürstenberg und Stahlberg an ihren Grenzen gesichert wurde.

Besonders wichtig war für die Kurpfalz das kleine rechtsrheinische Gebiet mit der bedeutenden Zollstelle in Kaub. Sie wurde unmittelbar durch die Burg Gutenfels (13. Jahrhundert) und die ab 1327 auf einer Rheininsel errichtete Wasserburg Pfalzgrafenstein gesichert. Aber auch an den Grenzen war das kleine rechtsrheinische Territorium der Pfalzgrafschaft gefährdet, zumal hier benachbarte Territorialherren eigene, grenznahe Burgen hatten. Daher begannen die Pfalzgrafen um die Mitte des 14. Jahrhunderts zwei Gegenburgen zu errichten, von denen aber nur die Sauerburg an der südöstlichen Grenze zu Kurmainz fertiggestellt wurde, während die Burg Herzogenstein zwar begonnen, aber wegen Widerspruchs des benachbarten Oberwesel nie vollendet wurde.

Martin HANSSON

Les paysages aristocratiques en Scandinavie au bas Moyen Âge

Au cours des deux dernières décennies, il devint évident que l'aristocratie créa des paysages d'élite autour de ses châteaux. Cet article a pour but l'examen de la présence de paysages aristocratiques en Scandinavie au bas Moyen Âge. L'étude porte principalement sur trois châteaux à l'époque médiévale, à savoir celui de Bergkvara en Suède et ceux de Glimmingehus et de Gurre au Danemark. Elle révèle que l'aristocratie scandinave utilisait le paysage autour de ses châteaux pour compléter le mode de vie aristocratique et il est possible de signaler des versions en Scandinavie de paysages d'élite repérées ailleurs en Europe. Il faut pourtant ajouter que celles-ci étaient ajustées pour s'intégrer au contexte local.

Later Medieval Aristocratic Landscapes in Scandinavia

During the last couple of decades it has become obvious that the aristocracy created elite landscapes around their castles. The purpose of this paper is to discuss the presence of late medieval elite aristocratic landscapes in Scandinavia. The castles of Bergkvara in medieval Sweden and Glimmingehus and Gurre in medieval Denmark are discussed. The results show that the Scandinavian aristocracy used the landscape around their castles for fulfilling the aristocratic lifestyle and that it is possible to find versions in Scandinavia of the elite landscapes we find elsewhere in Europe. It is important, however, to realise that they were adjusted to local circumstances.

Aristokratische Landschaften in Skandinavien im Spätmittelalter

In den letzten zwei Jahrzehnten ist deutlich geworden, dass der Adel um seine Burgen herum Elitelandschaften geschaffen hat. Der Beitrag will das Bestehen solcher aristokratischer Landschaften im spätmittelalterlichen Skandinavien diskutieren. Die Untersuchung nimmt in erster Linie drei mittelalterliche Burgen in den Blick, nämlich die von Bergkvara in Schweden sowie Glimmingehus und Gurre in Dänemark. Sie zeigt, dass der skandinavische Adel die Umgebung seiner Burgen dazu verwendete, seinen aristokratischen Lebensstil zu ermöglichen, und dass es möglich ist, in Skandinavien Spielarten solcher Elitelandschaften wiederzufinden, wie sie anderswo aufgefunden worden sind. Dabei ist zu betonen, dass diese an den lokalen Kontext angepasst waren.

Josef HLOŽEK

Les « forteresses frontalières » en Bohême et le problème de leurs basses cours

Les fortifications, construites le long de frontières aujourd'hui plus ou moins visibles, remplissaient au Moyen Âge des fonctions à bien des égards très similaires. Néanmoins, il est évident qu'une forteresse seigneuriale médiévale conçue comme base du pouvoir du seigneur ne répond pas aux mêmes exigences qu'une simple demeure aristocratique. On peut s'en rendre compte en particulier en étudiant les enceintes de basse cour et leur environnement économique spécifique, qui distinguaient ces châteaux des sites royaux et des châteaux fondés par des institutions ecclésiastiques. Ces derniers pouvaient prendre appui, surtout dans la période pré-hussite, sur les vastes structures économiques de l'Église. Ainsi, ces exigences diverses, appliquées différemment selon le contexte à l'organisation d'un château fort, se reflétaient nettement non seulement dans leur architecture et leur équipement, mais aussi dans les liens qui les unissaient aux réseaux d'urbanisation et de communication de l'époque, ainsi qu'à d'autres structures.

"Border Fortresses" in Bohemia and the Problem of their Baileys

The fortifications constructed along the borders, and which are still more or less visible today, fulfilled in the Middle Ages very similar functions. Nevertheless, it is obvious that a noble medieval fortress conceived as a power-base for the governing lord did not comply with the same criteria as those required for a simple aristocratic residence. This is especially clear when we study the lower-bailey enclosures and their specific economic environment which was a distinguishing feature between the castles on royal sites and castles founded by ecclesiastical institutions. The latter could rely, especially in the pre-Hussite period, on the support of the vast economic structures of the Church. And so these various criteria, applied differently, according to the specific circumstances, to the disposition of a castle, are to be seen not only in their architecture and their furnishings but also in the links which they developed with contemporary communication and urban networks as well as with other structures.

„Grenzburgen" in Böhmen und die Problematik ihrer Vorburgen

Burgareale, die entlang heute mehr oder weniger sichtbarer Grenzen erbaut wurden, erfüllten im Mittelalter in vielerlei Hinsicht sehr ähnliche Funktionen. Trotz dieser Tatsache ist offensichtlich, dass die Ansprüche an eine als landesherrlicher Machtstützpunkt erbaute mittelalterliche Burg von den Ansprüchen an eine Adelsburg abwichen. Dies kann man besonders an ihren Vorburgarealen und der Form ihres wirtschaftlichen Umfelds studieren, welches sich von königlichen Anlagen und von Burgen unterschied, die durch kirchliche Institutionen gegründet worden waren. Letztere konnten sich vor allem in der vorhussitischen Zeit auf die ausgedehnten kirchlichen Wirtschaftsstrukturen stützen. Die verschiedenen Ansprüche, die an den Burgorganismus in verschiedenen Umfeldern gestellt wurden, spiegelten sich daher nicht nur deutlich in ihrer Gestalt und Ausrüstung wider, sondern auch in ihren Verbindungen zu zeitgenössischen Siedlungs- und Kommunikationsnetzen und zu weiteren Strukturen.

Hans L. Janssen

Les châteaux frontaliers de l'évêché d'Utrecht (vers 1050-1528) – Transformation de places fortes militaires en sièges de pouvoir et d'autorité

Au cours du Moyen Âge, l'évêque d'Utrecht était également prince-évêque d'un État séculaire composé du *Nedersticht* à l'ouest et de l'*Oversticht* à l'est. La plupart des châteaux, construits par l'évêque en tant que souverain temporel, se trouvaient aux frontières. Avant le XIIe siècle, seules des places fortes militaires avaient été construites pour protéger des lieux sensibles spécifiques ou des passages de routes terrestres et commerciales. Autant que l'on sache, il s'agissait de mottes castrales. Des châteaux frontaliers permanents furent construits à partir du XIIe siècle. Bien que situés aux frontières, la plupart des châteaux avaient non seulement une fonction militaire mais aussi des fonctions résidentielle et administrative. Du point de vue architectural, il s'agissait de châteaux ayant une cour ronde ou ovale avec des bâtiments regroupés plus ou moins le long de la courtine.

À la suite d'un déclin important du pouvoir séculaire de l'évêque au cours du XIIIe et dans la première moitié du XIVe siècle, l'intégrité territoriale de l'État épiscopal fut restaurée avec l'aide des villes de l'évêché, de la cité d'Utrecht dans le *Nedersticht* et les villes hanséatiques de Zwolle, Kampen et Deventer dans l'*Oversticht*. Tout d'abord, l'évêque, la cité et les villes financèrent la construction d'une nouvelle ligne de défense le long des frontières avec un certain nombre de châteaux forts, généralement de forme carrée, qui protégeaient aussi les routes commerciales des villes. Ensuite, ils écrasèrent, vainquirent et reconstruisirent les châteaux des seigneurs frontaliers rebelles. Par la suite, ils remplacèrent les vassaux héréditaires en garnison dans les châteaux par des mercenaires, employés par le gouverneur du château. Enfin, les nouveaux châteaux frontaliers furent intégrés à la structure administrative de l'évêché en tant que sièges d'officiers « renvoyables » avec des zones d'activités nettement établies, des mandats fixes et – normalement – domiciliés dans un château épiscopal.

The Border Castles of the Bishopric of Utrecht *c.* 1050-1528 – From Military Strongholds to Seats of Power and Authority

During the Middle Ages the bishop of Utrecht was also prince-bishop of a secular state consisting of the *Nedersticht* in the west and the *Oversticht* in the east. Most castles built by the bishop as a temporal ruler, were situated at the borders. Before the 12th century only temporary military strongholds were built to protect specific trouble spots or crossings in land and trade routes. As far as is known, motte castles were used for this function. Permanent border castles appeared from the middle of the 12th century onwards. Although situated at the borders, most castles had not only a military function, but also residential and administrative ones. Architecturally it concerned round or oval court-yard castles with loosely grouped buildings along the curtain wall.

After a serious decline in the secular power of the bishop during the 13th and first half of the 14th century, the territorial integrity of the episcopal state was restored with the help of the towns of the bishopric, the city of Utrecht in the *Nedersticht* and the Hanseatic towns of Zwolle, Kampen and Deventer in the *Oversticht*. Firstly, the bishop, the city and the towns did so by financing the building of a new line of defence along the borders, with a number of strong castles on them, generally built on a square plan, which also protected the trade routes of the towns. Secondly, they crushed, conquered and rebuilt the castles of insurgent border lords. Thirdly, they changed the garrisoning of the castles from hereditary vassals to paid soldiers, who were employed by the castellan of the castle. Fourthly, the new border castles were incorporated into the administrative structure of the bishopric as seats of dischargeable officials with clearly defined districts, fixed terms of office and – generally – an episcopal castle as their residence.

Die Grenzburgen des Bistums Utrecht (um 1050-1528) – Die Umwandlung militärischer befestigter Plätze in Sitze der Macht und der Autorität

Im Laufe des Mittelalters war der Bischof von Utrecht gleichzeitig der Fürstbischof eines säkularen Staates, der aus *Nedersticht* im Westen und *Oversticht* im Osten bestand. Die meisten Burgen, die der Bischof als zeitweiliger Souverän errichten ließ, befanden sich an den Grenzen. Bis ins 12. Jahrhundert waren lediglich temporär militärische befestigte Plätze errichtet worden, um bestimmte Problembereiche oder Land- und Handelswege zu sichern. Soweit bekannt handelte es sich um Turmhügelburgen. Dauerhafte Grenzburgen wurden ab dem 12. Jahrhundert errichtet. Obwohl sie an den Grenzen lagen, hatten die meisten Burgen nicht bloß eine militärische Funktion, sondern fungierten auch als Residenzen und Verwaltungssitze. In architektonischer Hinsicht handelte es sich um Burgen mit rundem oder ovalem Hof, bei denen die Gebäude mehr oder weniger entlang der Kurtine angeordnet waren.

Nach einem massiven Niedergangs der säkularen Macht des Bischofs im Verlauf des 13. und in der ersten Hälfte des 14. Jahrhunderts wurde die territoriale Integrität des Bischofsstaates mithilfe der Städte des Bistums – der freien Stadt Utrecht im *Nedersticht* und den Hansestädten Zwolle, Kampen und Deventer im *Oversticht* – wieder hergestellt. Vor allem finanzierten der Bischof, die freie Stadt und die Hansestädte den Bau einer neuen Verteidigungslinie entlang der Grenzen mit einigen Festungen, meist mit viereckigem Grundriss, die auch die Handelswege der Städte sicherten. Zweitens besiegten und schliffen sie die Festungen der aufständischen Grenzherren und bauten sie neu auf. Drittens wurden die in den Burgen stationierten Erbvasallen durch Söldner ersetzt, die vom Kastellan der Burg angestellt wurden. Viertens wurden die neuen Grenzburgen in die Verwaltungsstruktur des Bistums als Sitze „abberufbarer" Beamter mit genau umgrenztem Territorium, definiertem Kompetenzbereich und – normalerweise – einem Wohnsitz in einer bischöflichen Burg integriert.

Michelle Joguin Regelin, Jean Terrier

Rouelbeau : un château en bois du XIVe siècle aux frontières du Faucigny (Suisse)

Dernier vestige d'un château médiéval conservé en élévation dans la campagne genevoise, le château de Rouelbeau fait l'objet d'un vaste projet d'étude et de restauration depuis 2001. Les ruines de cette forteresse, dont la mission était de protéger le territoire du Faucigny des Comtes de Genève, sont classées monument historique en 1921, puis sont laissées à l'abandon, à la merci d'une nature qui met en péril la conservation des maçonneries. Un programme de revitalisation des cours d'eau recréant une zone marécageuse, analogue à ce que devait être la nature autour de la bâtie au Moyen Âge, a encouragé à entreprendre l'étude de ce bâtiment, afin de le mettre en valeur.

Un texte ancien rédigé en 1339 fournit une description très précise d'un bâtiment en bois antérieur au château actuel. Riches de ces informations inédites, les fouilles ont pu être menées de façon à mettre au jour les différentes structures du château en bois.

Rouelbeau: a 14th-Century Wooden Castle on the Borders of Faucigny (Switzerland)

Last vestige of a medieval castle preserved in elevation in the Geneva countryside, Rouelbeau Castle has been the object of a vast project of study and restoration since 2001. The ruins of this fortress, whose mission was to protect the territory of Faucigny against the Counts of Geneva, are classified historic monument in 1921 and are abandoned. Then they are neglected, at the mercy of a nature which puts in danger the preservation of masonries. A program of revitalization of streams recreating a swampy zone, similar to the fact that had to be the nature around the built for the Middle Ages, has encouraged to undertake the study of this building.

An ancient text written in 1339 provides a very accurate description of a wooden building prior to the present castle. Rich in this new information, the excavations have been conducted to bring to light the various structures of the wooden castle.

Rouelbeau: Eine Holzburg aus dem 14. Jahrhundert an der Grenze des Faucigny (Schweiz)

Als letzter noch erhaltener Rest einer mittelalterlichen Burg ist das Schloss Rouelbeau in der Genfer Landschaft seit 2001 Gegenstand eines großangelegten Untersuchungs- und Restaurierungsprojekts. Die Ruinen dieser Festung, deren Aufgabe es war, die Region Faucigny gegen die Grafen von Genf zu sichern, werden zwar 1921 unter Denkmalschutz gestellt, dann aber ihrem Schicksal und einer Natur überlassen, die die Bausubstanz bedroht. Ein Programm zur Revitalisierung der Fließgewässer, mit dem ein Sumpfgebiet, wie es wohl im Mittelalter rund um den Komplex existiert hat, wiederhergestellt werden soll, hat den Impuls dazu gegeben, das Gebäude zu untersuchen, um ihm wieder Geltung zu verschaffen.

Ein alter, im Jahre 1339 verfasster Text gibt eine sehr genaue Beschreibung eines der heutigen Burg vorgängigen Holzbaus. Diese bisher unbekannten Informationen haben es ermöglicht, durch die Ausgrabungen die unterschiedlichen Strukturen der Holzburg freizulegen.

Thomas KÜHTREIBER, Markus JEITLER

Structures de pouvoir émergentes au début du Moyen Âge et construction de châteaux sur les franges de l'Autriche orientale actuelle – Études de cas comparées

Le rôle des châteaux comme centre du pouvoir dans le cadre du développement de ce qu'on appelle colonisation intérieure est depuis longtemps controversé dans la recherche autrichienne. Les approches méthodologiques utilisées par les historiens sont essentiellement la méthode, considérée comme obsolète, qui se fonde sur l'historique de la propriété, et celle qui, au contraire, se fonde sur le lien entre association de personnes et territorialisation. Pour la territorialisation et, en relation avec elle, la pénétration seigneuriale des régions frontalières, lesquelles jouent un rôle spécifique et particulièrement sensible, ces approches sont notamment bien représentées en raison de la recherche intensive de ces dernières années, en particulier pour la Haute et la Basse-Autriche. Les situations en question se rencontrent principalement, comme nous le savons notamment grâce aux recherches récentes, à la fin du Moyen Âge, mais de nombreux indices laissent supposer qu'elles peuvent se produire également plus tôt. Le « pays » et avec lui ses régions frontalières seraient ainsi à considérer comme une association complexe de personnes ayant coopéré en tant que communauté d'intérêts de dirigeants locaux avec les souverains, reconnus par eux comme autorité supérieure. À cette pratique seigneuriale s'opposait cependant une conception du « pays » existant depuis le XIe-XIIe siècle et reposant sur des principes seigneuriaux centralistes dans les pays voisins de Bohême, de Moravie et de Hongrie.

Nous nous proposons de présenter, comme exemples de ces processus et de ces opinions contradictoires, un choix de châteaux de la zone frontalière entre la Basse-Autriche, la Bohême et la Moravie, ainsi que de celle qui englobe la Basse-Autriche, la Styrie et l'ouest de la Hongrie (aujourd'hui Burgenland), et d'en discuter les conséquences possibles pour la « construction de châteaux frontaliers ».

Emergent Power-Structures in the Early Middle Ages and the Construction of Castles on the Borders of Present-Day Eastern Austria – Comparative Case Studies

The role of castles as power-centres within the framework of the development of what is known as "domestic colonisation" has long been a controversial subject amongst Austrian researchers. The methodological approaches used by the historians are essentially the method, now deemed obsolete, based on the history and details of the property and that based, on the contrary, on its links with people and the territory. As far as territorialisation is concerned and, connected with it, the manorial infiltration into the border areas, both of which played a specific and significant role, these approaches are especially well documented because of the intensive research over recent years, in particular for Upper and Lower Austria. The relevant situations were to be found mainly, as we know thanks to recent research, in the late Middle Ages but a great deal of evidence suggests that they may have also occurred earlier. The "country" and with it its border regions could thus be considered to have been a complex association of persons cooperating as a community of interests of local notables with their suzerains whom they recognised as their superior authority. In contrast with this aristocratic practice, there existed a conception of "country", based on centralist aristocratic principles, since the 11th-12th centuries in the neighbouring countries of Bohemia, Moravia and Hungary.

We discuss, as examples of these processes and contradictory views, a selection of castles from the border zone between Lower Austria, Bohemia and Moravia, as well as the one between Lower Austria, Styria and the west of Hungary (now known as Burgenland), and consider the possible implications for the construction of border castles.

Hochmittelalterliche Herrschaftsbildung und Burgenbau in Grenzsäumen des heutigen Ostösterreich – Fallstudien im Vergleich

Die Rolle der Burgen als Herrschaftsmittelpunkte im Zusammenhang mit dem sogenannten Landesausbau wird von der österreichischen Forschung seit langem durchaus kontroversiell diskutiert. Als methodische Ansätze dienen der Geschichtswissenschaft im Wesentlichen die als überholt geltende sogenannte „besitzgeschichtliche Methode" bzw. dem gegenüber die Verbindung zwischen Personenverband und Territorialisierung. Für die Landwerdung und damit auch die herrschaftliche Durchdringung von Grenzregionen, die eine spezifische und besonders sensible Rolle spielen, sind gerade diese Denkansätze vor allem für die Länder Oberösterreich und Niederösterreich aufgrund der intensiven Forschungen der vergangenen Jahre sehr gut nachweisbar. Die betreffenden Verhältnisse haben zwar in erster Linie wegen der verbesserten Quellenlage für das Spätmittelalter Gültigkeit, doch lassen sie sich mit Hilfe vieler Indizien auch auf das Hochmittelalter anwenden. Das „Land" und mit ihm seine Grenzregionen wären demnach als vielschichtiger Personenverband zu betrachten, der als Interessensgemeinschaft lokaler Machthaber mit der von ihnen als übergeordnet anerkannten Instanz des Landesherrn kooperierte. Dieser Herrschaftspraxis stand jedoch ein seit dem 11./12. Jahrhundert bestehendes und auf zentralistischen Herrschaftsprinzipien beruhendes Landesverständnis in den benachbarten Ländern Böhmen, Mähren und Ungarn gegenüber.

Als Beispiele dieser Vorgänge und gegensätzlichen Meinungen sollen ausgewählte Burganlagen aus dem niederösterreichisch-böhmisch-mährischen sowie dem niederösterreichisch-steirisch-westungarischen (heute burgenländischen) Grenzraum vorgestellt und deren mögliche Folgen für den „Burgenbau an der Grenze" diskutiert werden.

Heidi Maria Møller Nielsen

« Perdus et oubliés » : les châteaux d'Éric de Poméranie (roi du Danemark, 1396-1439) dans le duché de Schleswig

La construction de châteaux par le roi Éric de Poméranie (roi du Danemark, 1396-1439) dans le duché de Schleswig, la partie sud de la presqu'île de Jutland, n'a pas vraiment retenu l'attention des archéologues, ce qui est surtout dû au peu de connaissance de ces châteaux, qui ont quasiment totalement disparu. Le roi lança la construction d'au moins sept châteaux, d'au moins deux travaux de siège et il renforça ou en reconstruisit plusieurs autres. La province frontalière fut annexée par l'Allemagne en 1864 et c'est seulement la partie nord qui fut, par la suite, rattachée au Danemark. Ceci veut dire qu'il n'existe actuellement que très peu de châteaux du Schleswig du roi Éric au Danemark et traditionnellement la plupart des châteaux au sud de la frontière ne sont pas décrits dans la littérature sur la castellologie danoise. Ces sites sont ainsi « perdus et oubliés » dans les deux sens et il est donc très utile de s'y intéresser dans la mesure du possible.

"Lost and Forgotten": the Castles of Eric of Pomerania (King of Denmark, 1396-1439) in the Duchy of Schleswig

The castle building of King Eric of Pomerania (King of Denmark, 1396-1439) in the Duchy of Schleswig, the southern part of the Jutland Peninsula, has been rather unnoticed from an archaeological point of view, a fact which is first and foremost due to a very small amount of knowledge about these castles which have almost totally disappeared. The King initiated the building of at least seven castles, at a minimum two siege works and reinforcements or rebuilds of several other castles. The border province was lost to Germany in 1864 but only the northern part was later reunited with Denmark. This means that only a couple of King Eric's castles in Schleswig are situated within present Danish borders and traditionally most of the castles south of the border are not described in Danish castle literature at all. They are in a double sense "lost and forgotten" and it is indeed worthwhile to shed what little light is possible on these sites.

„Verloren und vergessen": Die Burgen Eriks von Pommern (König von Dänemark, 1396-1439) im Herzogtum Schleswig

Der Bau von Burgen durch den König Erik von Pommern (König von Dänemark, 1396-1439) im Herzogtum Schleswig, dem südlichen Teil der Halbinsel Jütland, hat bislang kaum das Interesse der Archäologen auf sich gezogen, was vor allem an dem geringen Wissen über diese Burgen liegt, die praktisch völlig verschwunden sind. Der König gab den Bau von mindestens sieben Burgen und mindestens zwei Belagerungsanlagen in Auftrag und baute einige weitere wieder auf oder verstärkte sie. Die Grenzprovinz ging 1864 an Deutschland verloren, und nur der nördliche Teil blieb in der Folgezeit bei Dänemark. Das bedeutet, dass es heute in Dänemark nur sehr wenige schleswigsche Burgen des Königs Erik gibt und die meisten Burgen südlich der Grenze in der dänischen burgenkundlichen Literatur traditionell nicht berücksichtigt werden. Diese Stätten sind auf diese Weise in doppeltem Sinne „verloren und vergessen", und es lohnt sich tatsächlich, sie im Rahmen des Möglichen zu betrachten.

Maxim Mordovin

Les fortifications post-médiévales en terre et en bois en Hongrie

Ce qui détermina le début de l'époque moderne en Hongrie fut la guerre continue contre l'Empire ottoman. L'occupation des régions centrales du pays créa une zone frontalière tout à fait nouvelle et obligea les deux partis en conflit à construire un nouveau réseau de places fortes. Le moyen le plus rapide et le plus économique pour faire de nouvelles fortifications dans un tel scénario fut d'avoir recours à une architecture traditionnelle en terre et en bois, apparemment passée de mode. Et pourtant, cette solution se répandit et fut même adoptée par de proéminents ingénieurs militaires italiens afin de fortifier d'immenses places fortes à cette époque. Les troupes royales et ottomanes se servirent de ce mode d'architecture pour défendre leurs territoires respectifs. De nombreux exemples de telles constructions ont déjà été étudiés. La petite ville frontalière de Szécsény fut, au cours des XVIe et XVIIe siècles, un centre militaire important et fut fortifiée de cette façon. Ses remparts en terre et en bois furent construits autour de 1562 et reconstruits plusieurs fois par la suite. Les fouilles à Szécsény ont permis la reconstruction visuelle de ce type de fortification.

The Post-Medieval Fortifications of Earth and Timber in Hungary

The early Modern period in Hungary was determined by persistent war against the Ottoman Empire. The occupation of the central parts of the country resulted in a completely new border zone and forced both sides in the conflict to construct a new network of strongholds. The cheapest and fastest way to make a new fortification in this scenario was to use a traditional, seemingly out-of-date, earth and timber architecture. This solution, however, became very widespread and was even used by prominent Italian military engineers to fortify huge strongholds at this time. Both the royal and Ottoman forces used this architecture for the defence of their respective territories. Many examples of these constructions have been investigated so far. The small border city of Szécsény was an important military centre during the 16th and 17th centuries and was fortified in this manner. Its ramparts of earth and timber were built *c.* 1562 and then were rebuilt several times. The excavations at Szécsény enabled a visual reconstruction of this type of fortification to be made.

Postmediävale Festungsanlagen aus Erdwerk und Holz in Ungarn

Die Frühe Neuzeit war in Ungarn bestimmt von permanentem Krieg gegen das Osmanische Reich. Die Besetzung der zentralen Teile des Landes führte zu einer völlig neuen Grenzzone und zwang beide Seiten in diesem Konflikt dazu, ein neues System von Befestigungen zu bauen. Der schnellste und billigste Weg, neue Festungen zu bauen, war in dieser Situation der Rückgriff auf eine traditionelle Architektur aus Erde und Holz, die aus der Mode geraten war. Gleichwohl wurde diese Lösung andernorts übernommen, und selbst bekannte italienische Militäringenieure setzen sie in dieser Zeit zum Bau riesiger befestigter Plätze ein. Sowohl die königlichen als auch die osmanischen Truppen nutzten diese Architektur, um ihre Territorien zu verteidigen. Zahlreiche Beispiele solcher Anlagen sind bereits untersucht worden. Der kleine Grenzort Szécsény war im 16. und 17. Jahrhundert ein wichtiges militärisches Zentrum und wurde auf diese Weise befestigt. Seine Schutzwälle aus Erde und Holz wurden um 1562 gebaut und in der Folgezeit mehrfach erneuert. Ausgrabungen in Szécsény ermöglichten eine visuelle Rekonstruktion dieser Art von Befestigungen.

Ben Murtagh

Le château d'Enniscorthy dans le comté de Wexford : un château élisabéthain à la frontière de l'Irlande gaélique

Jusqu'à récemment, beaucoup croyaient que l'actuel château dans la ville d'Enniscorthy était d'origine anglo-normande à cause de sa ressemblance avec plusieurs châteaux du XIIIe siècle des alentours. Nos récentes recherches ont cependant révélé que la partie la plus ancienne fut construite par sir Henry Wallop entre 1585 et 1595 pour remplacer un château médiéval. Entrepreneur et préposé de l'Angleterre, il s'était installé dans la ville située à la frontière entre la colonie anglaise et les Irlandais indigènes ou gaéliques du comté de Wexford, dans le sud-est de l'Irlande. Le nouveau château fut composé de deux parties : un enclos entouré de murs ou *bawn* et une maison fortifiée adjacente, encadrée de tourelles défendues par des canonnières. Il représentait une nouvelle forme de château colonial ou de plantations, avec des traits architecturaux reflétant ceux de l'Angleterre contemporaine.

Enniscorthy Castle, Co. Wexford: an Elizabethan Castle on the Borderland with Gaelic Ireland

Until recently, it was widely presumed that the present castle at the town of Enniscorthy was Anglo-Norman due to its resemblance to a local group of 13th-century castles. Recent investigations by the writer, however, have found that the earliest phase was built by Sir Henry Wallop in the period 1585-1595 to replace a medieval castle. He was an English official and entrepreneur, who had settled in the town, which was located on the borderland between the English colony and the native or Gaelic Irish in Co. Wexford in the south-east of Ireland. The new castle consisted of two parts: a walled enclosure or bawn and an adjoining fortified house, with flanking turrets defended by gun-loops. It represented a new form of colonial or plantation castle, which had architectural features that were derived from contemporary England.

Die Burg Enniscorthy in der Grafschaft Wexford: Eine elisabethanische Burg an der Grenze zum gälischen Irland

Bis vor kurzem glaubten viele, das heutige Kastell der Stadt Enniscorthy sei wegen seiner Ähnlichkeit mit weiteren Burgen des 13. Jahrhunderts anglonormannischen Ursprungs. Unsere jüngsten Nachforschungen haben jedoch gezeigt, das der älteste Teil von Sir Henry Wallop zwischen 1585 und 1595 gebaut wurde, um eine mittelalterliche Burg zu ersetzen. Er hatte sich als englischer Unternehmer und Beamter in der Stadt niedergelassen, die im Grenzland zwischen der englischen Kolonie und den eingeborenen oder gälischen Iren der Grafschaft Wexford im Südosten Irlands gelegen war. Die neue Burg bestand aus zwei Teilen: Einer ummauerten Einfriedung oder Bollwerk und einem anliegenden befestigten Haus mit Ecktürmen, die über Schießscharten zur Verteidigung verfügten. Sie repräsentierte eine neue Form eines kolonialen oder Plantationskastells mit architektonischen Merkmalen, die aus dem damaligen England stammten.

David NEWMAN JOHNSON

La forteresse sur la crête dans la région frontalière du Pale : le château de Dundrum dans le comté de Dublin

Le château de Dundrum fut un important château en pierre construit peu après 1187 par les Anglo-Normands à la limite sud de la ville de Dublin entre cette dernière et les montagnes de Wicklow sous le contrôle de tribus irlandaises hostiles envers les colons. Ainsi le château et les alentours furent-ils la cause de conflits pendant plus de 300 ans. Un résumé de leur histoire et la description de l'architecture des ruines nous aident à faire revivre et à mieux comprendre cette période tumultueuse.

The Fort on the Ridge in the Marches of the Pale: Dundrum Castle, Co. Dublin

Dundrum Castle was an important stone castle built shortly after 1187 by the Anglo-Normans on the southern border of the city of Dublin between it and the Wicklow Mountains which were controlled by Irish tribes hostile to the settlers. As such the castle and surrounding area were in the middle of strife for over 300 years. A brief history and architectural account of the ruins aids in bringing to life and promoting greater understanding of this tumultuous period.

Die Festung auf der Höhe in den Marschen des Pale: Die Burg Dundrum in der Grafschaft Dublin

Die Burg Dundrum war eine wichtige steinerne Burg, die kurz nach 1187 von den Anglonormannen an der Südgrenze der Stadt Dublin zwischen dieser und den Bergen von Wicklow errichtet wurde, die sich unter der Kontrolle irischer Stämme befanden, die den englischen Kolonisten feindlich gesinnt waren. Die Burg und ihre Umgebung standen daher für mehr als 300 Jahre im Zentrum von Konflikten. Eine Zusammenfassung ihrer Geschichte und eine architektonische Beschreibung der Ruinen helfen uns, diese turbulente Zeit wiederzuerwecken und besser zu verstehen.

Konstantin S. NOSSOV

Les forteresses médiévales russes à l'aune de nouvelles découvertes

La Russie médiévale pouvait se targuer de posséder plus de mille forteresses et de nombreuses lignes fortifiées atteignant parfois 1 000 kilomètres de long. Cet article étudie trois aspects discutables de l'histoire des fortifications russes qui ont été récemment radicalement révisés. La conception révolutionnaire de Yuri Yurievich Morgunov a mis fin au point de vue de longue date qui considérait des remparts en terre avec des structures en bois entre les remparts comme étant à la base des fortifications russes au Moyen Âge. Il s'est avéré que les remparts étaient des ruines de murs en bois remplis de terre. Une nouvelle interprétation des termes *byk* et *roskat* est proposée. Chacun avait trois significations : *byk* qualifiait des ouvrages de soutènement ou des défenses, en terre et en bois de renfort (des appentis sortis pour faire face à l'ennemi) et de solides structures en bois ressemblant à des tours ; *roskat* désignait un appentis, un bâtiment ressemblant à une tour et un bastion en terre. Une forte influence italienne sur les forteresses construites entre la fin du xve et le xviie siècle a été constatée.

Russian Medieval Fortresses in the Light of New Discoveries

Medieval Russia could boast more than a thousand fortresses and numerous fortified lines stretching up to 1,000 km in length. This paper examines three debatable aspects of Russian fortification history that have recently been dramatically revised. Yuri Yurievich Morgunov's revolutionary conception has destroyed a long-lived view of earthen ramparts with wooden intra-rampart structures as the basis of the medieval Russian fortification. The ramparts turned out to be ruins of wooden log walls filled with earth. New interpretation of the terms *byk* and *roskat* is offered. Each of them had three meanings: *byk* meant buttresses or strengthening lean-to, earth-wooden defences brought out to face the enemy and stout tower-like wooden structures, while *roskat* served to describe a lean-to, a tower-like building and an earthen bastion. A strong Italian influence on Russian fortresses dating from the late 15th to the 17th century has been established.

Die russischen mittelalterlichen Festungen im Lichte neuer Entdeckungen

Das mittelalterliche Russland konnte sich rühmen, mehr als eintausend Festungen und zahlreiche befestigte Linien mit einer Länge von bis zu 1.000 km zu besitzen. Der Beitrag untersucht drei strittige Aspekte der Geschichte der russischen Festungsanlagen, die in jüngster Zeit in radikaler Weise neubewertet wurden. Die revolutionäre Herangehensweise Yuri Yurievich Morgunovs hat die lange vertretene Auffassung widerlegt, Erdwerke mit Holzaufbau zwischen den Bollwerken seien die Basis der russischen Festungsanlagen des Mittelalters gewesen. Es hat sich herausgestellt, dass die Bollwerke die Überreste von hölzernen, mit Erde aufgefüllten Mauern waren. Eine neue Interpretation der Begriffe *byk* und *roskat* wird vorgestellt. Sie hatten jeweils drei Bedeutungen: *byk* waren Stützpfeiler oder stützende Anbauten, Wehre aus Holz und Erde, die nach außen wiesen, um dem Feind zu begegnen, sowie massive turmähnliche Bauten aus Holz, während *roskat* verwendet wurde, um einen Anbau, ein turmähnliches Gebäude oder eine Bastion aus Erdwerk zu bezeichnen. Es lässt sich ein starker italienischer Einfluss auf den Festungsbau vom Ende des 15. bis zum 17. Jahrhundert feststellen.

Kieran O'Conor, Paul Naessens, Rory Sherlock

Le château de Rindoon dans le comté de Roscommon – Un château à la frontière irlandaise

Le château de Rindoon contrôla et domina un des meilleurs ports le long du Shannon. On prétendait qu'aucun château fort pré-normand n'avait jamais existé sur le promontoire à Rindoon. Au contraire, on suggère que ces ouvrages en terre représentent les défenses sud-est d'une ville anglo-normande plus tardive. Il se peut que la forteresse pré-normande impliquée dans le toponyme *Rinn Duin* se trouve sous la maçonnerie du château anglo-normand plus tardif. Cette fortification antérieure aurait pu être construite comme place forte viking, « forteresse O'Conor » plus tardive, ou les deux. Le château anglo-normand en pierre fut commencé en 1227. Ce château royal révèle au moins cinq étapes architecturales dans sa construction. Celles-ci datent des premières années du xiiie siècle jusqu'aux dernières du xvie. Les preuves portent à croire que le château de Rindoon était beaucoup plus fort du point de vue de ses défenses que l'on a pensé dans le passé. Ceci est très plausible car les sources historiques laissent entendre qu'il était situé dans une aire frontalière relativement turbulente, à la frontière entre la partie gaélique et la partie dominée par les Anglo-Normands de l'Irlande médiévale. Enfin, l'emplacement des principaux bâtiments à l'intérieur du château suggère qu'il y eut une tentative délibérée de la part des constructeurs d'origine et des occupants successifs pour donner un aspect saisissant et dramatique à toute la façade nord et nord-ouest.

Rindoon Castle, Co. Roscommon – A Border Castle on the Irish Frontier

Rindoon Castle controlled and dominated one of the best harbours along the Shannon. It was argued that a pre-Norman promontory fort never existed at Rindoon. Instead, it is suggested that these earthworks represent the south-eastern defences of the later Anglo-Norman town. The pre-Norman fortress implied in the place-name *Rinn Duin* perhaps lies under the later Anglo-Norman masonry castle. This earlier fortification might have been built as a Viking stronghold, a later O'Conor fortress or both. The Anglo-Norman masonry castle was started in 1227. This royal castle has at least five identifiable architectural phases within it. These range in date from the early 13th century through to the very late 16th century. The evidence suggests that Rindoon Castle was far stronger in defensive terms than was once thought. This makes some sense as the historical sources suggest that it lay in a relatively turbulent border area, on the frontier between Gaelic and Anglo-Norman dominated parts of medieval Ireland. Lastly, the siting of major buildings within the castle suggests that there was a deliberate attempt by its original builders and later occupants to make its whole north-western and northern façades very dramatic looking.

Die Burg Rindoon in der Grafschaft Roscommon – Eine Burg an der irischen Grenze

Die Burg von Rindoon kontrollierte und beherrschte einen der besten Häfen am Shannon. Man hat argumentierte, dass niemals ein pränormannisches Fort auf der Landzunge Rindoon bestanden habe. Statt dessen wird erklärt, die vorhandenen Wallanlagen seien die südöstlichen Befestigungen einer späteren anglonormannischen Stadt. Es ist jedoch möglich, dass die im Namen des Ortes *Rinn Duin* angedeutete pränormannische Festung sich unter dem Ziegelbau des späteren anglonormannischen Kastells befindet. Diese frühere Befestigung hätte als befestigter Platz auf Wikingerart, als spätere „O'Conor-Festung" oder als beides ausgeführt sein können. Die anglonormannische steinerne Burg wurde 1227 begonnen. Das königliche Kastell zeigt in seinem Aufbau mindestens fünf architektonische Etappen. Diese datieren von den ersten Jahren des 13. bis zu den letzten des 16. Jahrhunderts. Die Funde weisen darauf hin, dass die Burg Rindoon hinsichtlich ihrer Verteidigungsanlagen weitaus stärker war als bislang angenommen. Dies ist auch sehr plausibel, da die Quellen uns mitteilen, dass sie in einer relativ unruhigen Grenzregion gelegen war, an der Grenze zwischen dem gälischen und dem von den Anglonormannen dominierten Teil Irlands. Schließlich suggeriert die Platzierung der wichtigsten Gebäude innerhalb der Burg, dass wir es mit dem bewussten Versuch der ursprünglichen Erbauer zu tun haben, der nördlichen und nordwestlichen Fassade einen möglichst machtvollen und dramatischen Ausdruck zu verleihen.

Richard ORAM

Loisirs, symbolisme et guerre: le château d'Hermitage à Liddesdale et la frontière anglo-écossaise

À l'origine pavillon de chasse du XIIIe siècle dans la seigneurie de Liddesdale, au fur et à mesure que les conflits anglo-écossais transformaient la région en zone frontalière contestée, Hermitage a remplacé l'ancien *caput* à Liddel. Sous les comtes de Douglas, Hermitage fut modifié pour être une projection symbolique de leur pouvoir et de leur raison sociale qui servait de logement spacieux et de forum cérémonial où ils pouvaient exercer leur pouvoir seigneurial, assurer la sécurité de leur famille et de ceux qui les servaient, défendre la région et être une base pour la gestion économique de Liddesdale. Initialement déclaration du pouvoir des Douglas, les guerres, le dépeuplement et les changements climatiques ont transformé cet élément central d'un domaine prospère en garnison et en poste frontalier dont l'importance n'a fait que diminuer. Lors de l'union de l'Écosse et de l'Angleterre en 1603, Hermitage fut abandonné.

Leisure, Symbolism and War: Hermitage Castle, Liddesdale and the Anglo-Scottish Border

Originating as a 13th-century hunting-lodge in the lordship of Liddesdale, as Anglo-Scottish warfare turned the area into a contested border zone, Hermitage replaced the old *caput* at Liddel. The Earls of Douglas developed Hermitage into a symbolic projection of their power and status that contained spacious accommodation and a ceremonial forum in which to exercise lordly authority, gave security for their household and the defence of the region, and a base for the economic management of Liddesdale. Originally a bold statement of Douglas power, warfare, depopulation and climate change converted it from the centrepiece of a prosperous estate into a garrisoned frontier-post of declining significance. When Scotland and England were united in 1603, Hermitage was abandoned.

Freizeit, Symbolismus und Krieg: Die Burg Hermitage in Liddesdale und die englisch-schottische Grenze

Ursprünglich eine Jagdhütte aus dem 13. Jahrhundert in der Grafschaft Liddesdale, ersetzt Hermitage allmählich in dem Maße, in dem die englisch-schottischen Konflikte die Region in ein umstrittenes Grenzgebiet verwandelten, den alten *caput* in Liddel. Unter den Grafen von Douglas wurde Hermitage umgestaltet zu einer symbolischen Darstellung ihrer Macht und ihrer sozialen Stellung, mit großzügigen Unterkünften und einem Forum für Zeremonien, wo die fürstliche Machtausübung stattfand, die Sicherheit der Familie und ihrer Bediensteten gewährleistet und die Region verteidigt werden konnte und die die Basis für die Bewirtschaftung Liddesdales war. Gedacht war es als kühne Demonstration der Macht der Douglas; Kriege, Entvölkerung und Klimawandel sorgten für die Transformation dieses zentralen Elements einer prosperierenden Herrschaft in eine Garnison und einen Grenzposten, dessen Bedeutung immer mehr abnahm. Anlässlich der Union Schottlands mit England im Jahre 1603 wurde Hermitage aufgegeben.

Ieva Ose

Châteaux frontaliers de l'Ordre teutonique au sud-est de la Livonie

La confédération de Livonie, formée au xiiie siècle, était bordée au nord et à l'ouest par la mer Baltique, au sud par la Lituanie et à l'est par les terres russes. Même s'il n'exista pas de menaces de guerre sérieuses avant la guerre de Livonie en 1558, les Lituaniens et les Russes faisaient régulièrement des incursions en Livonie. Les forteresses frontalières étaient des points d'appui importants pour la prévention des pillages et servaient de camps militaires. Au xiiie-xive siècle, l'Ordre des chevaliers teutoniques fit construire dans la zone frontalière sud quatre châteaux en pierre (Wolkenburg, Daugavpils, Rositen, Ludsen). La bataille de Tannenberg (1410) fut suivie par la constitution du puissant État de Pologne-Lituanie. Celui-ci soumit les principautés de Polotsk et Vitebsk et conclut la paix avec l'Ordre. C'est probablement pour cette raison que les châteaux à la frontière sud-est ne furent pas modernisés.

Border Castles of the Teutonic Order in South-Eastern Livonia

Created in the 13th century, the Confederation of Livonia was limited to the north and to the west by the Baltic Sea, to the south by Lithuania and to the east by Russian territories. Even if there were no serious threats of war before the Livonia War in 1558, the Lithuanians and the Russians made frequent raids into Livonia. The border strongholds were a major source of help in preventing pillaging and acted as military camps. In the 13th-14th centuries, the Order of the Teutonic Knights had built in the southern border zone four stone castles (Wolkenburg, Daugavpils, Rositen, Ludsen). The battle of Tannenberg (1410) was followed by the formation of the powerful Polish-Lithuanian Commonwealth, which subjugated the principalities of Polotsk and Vitebsk and made peace with the Order. It is probably for this reason that the castles on the south-eastern border were not upgraded.

Grenzburgen des Deutschen Ordens im Südosten Livlands

Der im 13. Jahrhundert entstandene Livländische Staatenbund grenzte im Norden und Westen an die Ostsee, im Süden an die litauischen und im Osten an die russischen Länder. Obwohl bis 1558, als der Livländische Krieg ausbrach, keine wesentlichen Kriege drohten, gab es regelmäßig Raubzüge von Litauern und Russen. Die Grenzburgen waren bedeutende Stützpunkte gegen die Plünderungen sowie Heerlager. Im südöstlichen Grenzgebiet wurden im 13.-14. Jh. vier Ordensburgen (Wolkenburg, Dünaburg, Rositen, Ludsen) als Steinbauten gebaut. Nach der Schlacht bei Tannenberg (1410) entstand der mächtige Staat Polen-Litauen, der die Fürstentümer Polotsk und Witebsk unterwarf und Frieden mit dem Orden schloss. Wahrscheinlich deshalb wurden die Burgen an der südöstlichen Grenze nicht aufgerüstet.

Peter Purton

Le génie militaire médiéval et les châteaux en temps de guerre

Le rôle spécialisé du génie militaire était apparu dès le xve siècle, mais on ne connaît pas encore très bien la nature de son évolution au cours des siècles précédents. On trouve dans les sources écrites des témoignages d'individus ayant des compétences techniques spécialisées et de l'expertise en conception qui, dès le xiie siècle, s'occupaient d'une vaste gamme de tâches dont la construction de châteaux et d'engins de siège. Il nous semble probable, étant donné le niveau de savoir nécessaire pour effectuer ces tâches, que ces ingénieurs avaient des compétences et un savoir supérieurs à ceux d'un simple artisan. Nous avons cherché des liens possibles avec des niveaux de formation dans les « arts mécaniques » que nous connaissons et étudié l'accessibilité de manuels et de modes de transmission du savoir. Finalement, nous démontrons que des personnes détentrices de telles compétences devaient exister depuis une époque bien antérieure, même si elles sont restées anonymes.

The Medieval Engineer and Castles at War

The specialist role of the military engineer had emerged by the 15th century but much remains unknown about how this process took place during previous centuries. Evidence appears in written records of individuals with specialist technical and design skills who were involved in a wide range of tasks including castle building, and in building siege equipment, from the 12th century. It is proposed, based on the level of knowledge necessary to carry out these tasks, that these engineers possessed more than the ordinary craftsman's skills and knowledge. Possible connections with known levels of education in the "mechanical arts", literacy and the availability of manuals, and modes of transmission of knowledge, are explored. Finally, it is shown that people possessing such skills and knowledge must have existed from much earlier times, although they remain anonymous.

Der Militäringenieur und die Burgen in Zeiten des Krieges

Der besondere Aufgabenbereich des Militäringenieurs hat sich bis zum 15. Jahrhundert herausgebildet; es ist aber bislang wenig darüber bekannt, wie dieser Prozess über die vorigen Jahrhunderte verlaufen war. Es gibt Hinweise in schriftlichen Zeugnissen von Einzelpersonen mit speziellen technischen und planerischen Kenntnissen, die sich seit dem 12. Jahrhundert mit einer großen Bandbreite an Aufgaben einschließlich des Baus von Burgen und Belagerungsmaschinen befassten. Es erscheint uns angesichts des für die Bewältigung solcher Aufgaben erforderlichen Wissensstandes als wahrscheinlich, dass die Kenntnisse und Fertigkeiten dieser Ingenieure über die eines einfachen Handwerkers hinausgingen. Wir suchen nach möglichen Verbindungen zum bekannten Ausbildungsniveau in den „mechanischen Künsten" und untersuchen die Zugänglichkeit von Handbüchern sowie die Wege des Wissenstransfers. Schließlich zeigen wir, dass es Personen, die über solche Kenntnisse und Fertigkeiten verfügten, bereits seit viel längerer Zeit gegeben haben muss, auch wenn sie uns unbekannt geblieben sind.

Jacqueline VENINGER

Des paysages de conflits : des profils de résistance galloise à la conquête anglo-normande du nord du pays de Galles (1070-1250) – Les grandes lignes d'une nouvelle étude

Cet article présente les grandes lignes d'une nouvelle étude sur l'importance et les avantages éventuels de l'application de méthodes et théories relevant de l'archéologie de champs de bataille et des conflits à une période historique turbulente. Les désignations post-médiévales actuelles de champs de batailles et l'archéologie des champs de bataille ont fait obstacle à l'élaboration de critères pour documenter et reconstruire les champs de bataille médiévaux et leur paysage plus large de conflits. Cet article maintient que de telles enquêtes sont possibles et établit une liste de critères de travail permettant la compréhension des paysages uniques endémiques aux zones frontalières de la Grande-Bretagne médiévale.

Landscapes of Conflict: Patterns of Welsh Resistance to the Anglo-Norman Conquest of North Wales, 1070-1250 – An Overview of a New Study

This paper is an overview of a new study that considers the importance and the benefits to be gained by the application of the methods and theories inherent to battlefield and conflict archaeology to a turbulent period in history. Current post-medieval designations of battlefields and battlefield archaeology have impeded the development of criteria for documenting and reconstructing medieval battlefields and their wider landscapes of conflict. This article argues that such surveys are possible and establishes a set of working criteria with which to understand the unique landscapes of conflict endemic to border zones in medieval Britain.

Landschaften des Konflikts: Strukturen des walisischen Widerstands gegen die anglonormannische Eroberung von Nordwales – Grundriss einer neuen Studie

Der Beitrag zeichnet die Grundlinien einer neuen Studie über die Bedeutung und möglichen Vorzüge der Anwendung von Methoden und Theorien aus der Archäologie der Schlachtfelder und Konflikte auf eine turbulente Epoche der Geschichte. Heutige nachmittelalterliche Auffassungen von Schlachtfeldern und Schlachtfeldarchäologie haben die Entwicklung von Kriterien zur Dokumentierung und Rekonstruktion mittelalterlicher Schlachtfelder und ihrer weiteren Konfliktlandschaften behindert. Der Beitrag zeigt, dass solche Untersuchungen möglich sind und erstellt eine Liste von Arbeitskriterien, die ein Verständnis der einzigartigen Konfliktlandschaften, wie sie in den Grenzzonen des mittelalterlichen Britanniens endemisch sind, gestatten.

John ZIMMER

Le problème de la barbacane selon l'exemple de la cité de Carcassonne (Occident) et du Krak des Chevaliers (Orient) – Interactions de techniques de défense entre France et Outremer : l'exemple de la barbacane

La barbacane fait partie intégrante de l'architecture militaire médiévale et est généralement considérée comme un ouvrage de fortification avancé défendant l'accès de la forteresse. Depuis les travaux d'Eugène Viollet-le-Duc et Joseph Poux sur la cité de Carcassonne, qui définissent la barbacane comme « un ouvrage de fortification avancé qui protégeait un passage, une porte ou poterne », on croyait savoir à peu près tout sur la barbacane. Conformément à l'état des connaissances de l'époque, elle fut reconstruite comme un ouvrage de fortification semi-circulaire ou circulaire avancé par rapport à l'entrée du château. Avec la publication de deux nouvelles recherches consacrées à l'histoire architecturale du château croisé du Krak des Chevaliers en Syrie, où l'existence d'une barbacane est prouvée par une inscription, une nouvelle discussion s'est ouverte dans le monde scientifique, témoignant de la persistance d'un besoin de clarification concernant le concept architectural et la terminologie de la barbacane. Prenant appui sur les exemples de barbacanes de la cité de Carcassonne ainsi que sur les dernières découvertes faites au Krak des Chevaliers (photographie G. Bell), nous avons tenté de répondre à un certain nombre d'interrogations ou au moins de remettre en question, grâce à des connaissances nouvelles, des idées reçues et solidement ancrées.

The Problem Posed by the Barbican as to be seen in the Town of Carcassonne (in the West) and Krak des Chevaliers (in the East) – Interaction of Defence Techniques between France and Overseas: the Example of the Barbican

The barbican is an integral part of medieval military architecture and is generally considered to be an "up-front" outwork of fortification protecting the access to the fortress. Since the studies made of the town of Carcassonne by Eugène Viollet-le-Duc and Joseph Poux, which defined the barbican as "a fortified outwork which protected a passage, a gate or a postern", it has been believed that this was virtually all one needed to know about the barbican. In keeping with the available knowledge on the period; it was reconstructed as a semi-circular or circular fortified outwork in relation to the castle entrance. With the publication of two new studies devoted to the architectural history of the Crusader castle of Krak des Chevaliers in Syria, where the existence of a barbican has been proved by an inscription, a new discussion has been created in the scientific world, indicating the continuing need for clarification concerning the architectural concept and the terminology of the barbican. Using the examples of the barbican of the town of Carcassonne and the recent discoveries made at Krak des Chevaliers (photography G. Bell), we have tried to reply to a certain number of questions or at least to question, in the light of the new discoveries, well and long established views.

Das Problem der Barbakane an den Beispielen der Cité von Carcassonne (Okzident) und des Krak des Chevaliers (Orient) – Wehrtechnische Wechselwirkungen zwischen Frankreich und Outremer am Beispiel der Barbakane

Die Barbakane gehört zum festen Bestandteil der mittelalterlichen Militärarchitektur und wird im Allgemeinen als vorgelagertes Verteidigungswerk bezeichnet. Seit den Arbeiten von Eugène Viollet-le-Duc und Joseph Poux über die Cité von Carcassonne in denen die Barbakane als „ein vorgeschobenes Befestigungswerk, das einen Durchgang, ein Tor oder eine Poterne schützte" definiert wurde glaubte man so ziemlich alles über die Barbakane zu wissen. Aufgrund des damaligen Kenntnisstandes wurde sie als halbrunde oder geschlossen runde, einem Torbereich vorgelagerte Befestigung rekonstruiert. Mit dem Erscheinen von zwei Publikationen die sich mit der Baugeschichte der Kreuzfahrerburg Krak des Chevaliers in Syrien beschäftigen, wo eine Barbakane durch eine Bauinschrift nachgewiesen ist wurde eine neue Diskussion in der Fachwelt ausgelöst die deutlich zeigt dass noch ein Klärungsbedarf über Architekturkonzept und Terminologie der Barbakane besteht. An den Beispielen der Barbakanen der Cité von Carcassonne, sowie den neuesten Entdeckungen auf dem Krak des Chevaliers (Fotografie G. Bell) wurde versucht eine Reihe von offenen Fragen zu beantworten oder wenigstens fest etablierte Vorstellungen anhand der neuen Erkenntnisse anzuzweifeln.

Table des matières

Niels-Knud LIEBGOTT: *Introduction* 7

Josef HLOŽEK: *Nachruf Tomáš Durdík* 9

Reinhard FRIEDRICH: *Château Gaillard trauert um Hans-Wilhelm Heine, verstorben am 2. August 2012* . . 11

Richard ORAM: *Charles McKean (1946-2013)* 13

Bas AARTS, Taco HERMANS: *Castle Building along the Border of Brabant and Holland (c. 1290-c. 1400)* . . 17

Susanne ARNOLD: *Die Burg Brauneck und ihr so genannter Kapellenbau – Baugeschichtliche, archäologische und geophysikalische Untersuchungen auf einer Staufischen Burg bei Creglingen in Baden-Württemberg* . . 27

Markus C. BLAICH, Tillman KOHNERT: *Burg Steuerwald nördlich von Hildesheim – Historie, Bauforschung und Archäologie* 39

François BLARY: *Châteaux et frontière occidentale du comté de Champagne (XIIe-XIVe siècle)* 57

Maria-Letizia BOSCARDIN, Werner MEYER: *„Tor und Schlüssel zu Italien" – Die Grenzfestung Bellinzona* . . 71

Katherine BUCHANAN: *Drawing upon the Line? The Use of Landscape along Shire Borders in Scottish Noble Architecture* 81

Andrea BULLA, Hans-Werner PEINE: *Burgenarchäologie in einer Grenzregion – Ein Beitrag zum Burgenbau im Diemelraum* 85

Frédéric CHANTINNE, Philippe MIGNOT: *Le rôle des châteaux dans le contrôle de la vallée de la Meuse aux confins de la Lotharingie et du diocèse de Liège (IXe-XIe siècle)* 101

Owain James CONNORS: *The Influence of Anglo-Norman Lordship upon the Landscape of Monmouthshire* . . 107

Oliver CREIGHTON: *Castle,* Burh *and Borough: Unravelling an Urban Landscape of Power at Wallingford, Oxfordshire* 113

Koen DE GROOTE: *A Previously Unknown Late 14th-Century Brick Castle Excavated at Aalter (Flanders, Belgium) – A Burgundian Stronghold that Lay between the Rebellious Flemish Towns of Ghent and Bruges* 125

Gillian EADIE: *Reflections of a Divided Country? The Role of Tower Houses in Late-Medieval Ireland* 135

Richard EALES: *Castles and Borders in England after 1066* 149

Peter ETTEL: *Ungarnburgen in Süddeutschland im 10. Jahrhundert* 159

István FELD: *Burgen im österreichisch-ungarischen Grenzraum im 12. und 13. Jahrhundert* 167

Thomas FINAN: *Moated Sites in County Roscommon, Ireland: a Statistical Approach* 177

Anne-Marie FLAMBARD HÉRICHER: *Les derniers acquis des recherches sur le Château Ganne* 181

Christian FREY: *The* Burgward *Organisation in the Eastern Marches of the German Realm – Frontier Mentality and Inculturation* 193

Reinhard FRIEDRICH: *Burgen und Territorialgrenzen in den rheinischen Kurfürstentümern* 199

Martin HANSSON: *Later Medieval Aristocratic Landscapes in Scandinavia* 207

Josef HLOŽEK: *„Grenzburgen" in Böhmen und die Problematik ihrer Vorburgen* 217

Hans L. JANSSEN: *The Border Castles of the Bishopric of Utrecht c. 1050-1528 – From Military Strongholds to Seats of Power and Authority* 225

Michelle JOGUIN REGELIN, Jean TERRIER: *Rouelbeau: un château en bois du XIVe siècle aux frontières du Faucigny (Suisse)* 243

Thomas KÜHTREIBER, Markus JEITLER: *Hochmittelalterliche Herrschaftsbildung und Burgenbau in Grenzsäumen des heutigen Ostösterreich – Fallstudien im Vergleich* 251

Heidi Maria MØLLER NIELSEN: *"Lost and Forgotten": the Castles of Eric of Pomerania (King of Denmark, 1396-1439) in the Duchy of Schleswig* 261

Maxim MORDOVIN: *The Post-Medieval Fortifications of Earth and Timber in Hungary* 273

Ben MURTAGH: *Enniscorthy Castle, Co. Wexford: an Elizabethan Castle on the Borderland with Gaelic Ireland* 283

David NEWMAN JOHNSON: *The Fort on the Ridge in the Marches of the Pale: Dundrum Castle, Co. Dublin* .. 295

Konstantin S. NOSSOV: *Russian Medieval Fortresses in the Light of New Discoveries* 305

Kieran O'CONOR, Paul NAESSENS, Rory SHERLOCK: *Rindoon Castle, Co. Roscommon – A Border Castle on the Irish Frontier* 313

Richard ORAM: *Leisure, Symbolism and War: Hermitage Castle, Liddesdale and the Anglo-Scottish Border* .. 325

Ieva OSE: *Grenzburgen des Deutschen Ordens im Südosten Livlands* 333

Peter PURTON: *The Medieval Engineer and Castles at War* 343

Jacqueline VENINGER: *Landscapes of Conflict: Patterns of Welsh Resistance to the Anglo-Norman Conquest of North Wales, 1070-1250 – An Overview of a New Study* 353

John ZIMMER: *Das Problem der Barbakane an den Beispielen der Cité von Carcassonne (Okzident) und des Krak des Chevaliers (Orient) – Wehrtechnische Wechselwirkungen zwischen Frankreich und Outremer am Beispiel der Barbakane* 357

Résumés 375

Achevé d'imprimer par Corlet, Imprimeur, S.A. - 14110 Condé-sur-Noireau
N° d'Imprimeur : 167782 - Dépôt légal : octobre 2014 - *Imprimé en France*